Second Edition

Strategic Compensation in Canada

Second Edition

Strategic

Compensation

in Canada

Richard J. Long
University of Saskatchewan

Series Editor: Monica Belcourt

NELSON

TM

THOMSON LEARNING

Australia • Canada • Mexico • Singapore • Spain • United Kingdom • United States

NELSON

THOMSON LEARNING ™

**Strategic Compensation in Canada,
Second Edition**

by Richard J. Long

Editorial Director and Publisher:
Evelyn Veitch

Acquisitions Editor:
Anthony Rezek

Developmental Editor:
Karina TenVeldhuis

Production Editor:
Natalia Denesiuk

Production Coordinator:
Hedy Sellers

Art Director:
Angela Cluer

Cover Design:
Anne Bradley

Interior Design:
Julie Greener

Copy Editor:
Jim Leahy

Compositor:
Carol Magee

Printer:
Transcontinental Printing Inc.

National Library of Canada Cataloguing in Publication Data

Long, Richard J. (Richard Joseph)
    Strategic compensation in Canada

(Nelson Canada series in human resources management)
First ed. published under title: Compensation in Canada.
Includes bibliographical references and index.

ISBN 0-17-616952-0

1. Compensation management—Canada. I. Title. II. Title: Compensation in Canada. III. Series.

HF5549.5.C67L56 2001
658.3'22'0971
C2001-903708-2

This book is dedicated to my family—Trisha, Jeffrey, Jeremy, and Michael—without whose support and forbearance it would never have been completed.

BRIEF CONTENTS

DETAILED CONTENTS

CHAPTER 3 A BEHAVIOURAL FRAMEWORK FOR COMPENSATION 61

PART II   COMPONENTS OF COMPENSATION

CHAPTER 4   BASE PAY   115

CHAPTER 5   INDIVIDUAL PERFORMANCE PAY   141

CHAPTER 6   GROUP AND ORGANIZATION PERFORMANCE PAY   173

CHAPTER 7   INDIRECT PAY   213

PART III   THE COMPENSATION STRATEGY

CHAPTER 8   FORMULATING THE REWARD AND COMPENSATION STRATEGY   255

PART IV   TECHNICAL PROCESSES FOR COMPENSATION

CHAPTER 9   EVALUATING JOBS   321

Chapter 10   Evaluating the Market   377

Chapter 11 Evaluating Individuals 401

Part V Implementing, Managing, Evaluating, and Adapting the Compensation System

Chapter 12 Managing the Compensation System 455

APPENDIX CASES FOR ANALYSIS   487

ABOUT THE SERIES

Human resources management (HRM) is a profession that is growing in importance and numbers. Human resources professionals do make a difference to employers and employees. Knowledgeable HR professionals can have a significant impact on their organization's ability to attract, train, reward, and retain motivated and productive employees. The specialized expertise of HR professionals is grounded in a growing body of knowledge.

The Nelson Series in Human Resources Management is dedicated to ensuring that HR professionals are well informed and current in their knowledge. In addition to this book, texts in the series include:

- *Management of Occupational Health and Safety (2nd edition)*
- *Managing Performance through Training and Development (2nd edition)*
- *Strategic Human Resources Planning*
- *Research, Measurement, and Evaluation of Human Resources*
- *An Introduction to the Canadian Labour Market*

The Nelson Series in Human Resources Management is important for many reasons. Each book in the series is Canadian in content and authorship. Human resources practitioners must work with Canadian laws, Canadian facts, Canadian policies, and Canadian values. This series serves these needs.

These texts, for the first time, also provide a standardized guide to the management of various HR functional areas. This standardization enables readers to locate material quickly, and to link and cross-reference information, thus providing an encyclopedia of knowledge about HRM. This one-stop resource will prove useful to anyone involved in the management of people.

Most important, the publication of these texts signals that the HR field has advanced to the stage where theory and applied research guide practice. Additionally, because HRM is an applied discipline, examples of best practices used by organizations that are leaders in HR are woven into the texts, thus allowing students to learn about emerging tools and methods.

Observers agree that this is the decade of human resources management. It is an incredibly exciting time to be learning about HRM and to be embarking on a career in this profession. I know that this text, and others in the series, will provide you with the very best preparation for practice in the field of human resources management.

Monica Belcourt, Ph.D., CHRP
Series Editor
Director, International Alliance for Human Resources Research
Professor, Human Resources Management, York University
June 2001

ABOUT THE AUTHOR

Richard J. Long is Professor of Human Resource Management at the College of Commerce of the University of Saskatchewan. He earned B.Com. and MBA degrees from the University of Alberta, and a Ph.D from Cornell University in New York. Dr. Long has been teaching, conducting research, and consulting in human resources management for more than 25 years, and has produced more than 80 publications based on his research and experience. He is currently on the editorial boards of *The International Journal of Human Resource Management* and *Relations industrielles/Industrial Relations*.

PREFACE

The premise of this book is that an organization's compensation system can have a major impact on the success of that organization, but that the most effective compensation system may be very different from one organization to the next, and may even differ over time for the same organization. However, if there is no single compensation system that fits all organizations, this makes life very complicated for those who manage organizations. The purpose of this book is to reduce that complexity by providing a systematic framework for identifying and designing the compensation system that will add the most value to the organization.

To do so requires a diagnostic approach. That is, to identify the most effective compensation system for a given organization, it is first necessary to understand that organization, its strategy, and its people. Part I of the book focuses on developing these understandings.

Beyond this, of course, it is equally necessary to understand the wide array of compensation options that are available, and to be able to predict their likely consequences when applied to a given organization. This is the focus of Part II. Armed with these understandings, along with an understanding of the constraints that define the parameters for the compensation system, a compensation strategy can then be formulated that has a high likelihood of success, as described in Part III.

However, the formulation of the compensation strategy does not mark the end of the compensation process. There are still many technical issues necessary to convert the compensation strategy into a compensation system, and Part IV provides detailed guidance on how to handle these. Finally, the compensation system needs to be implemented, managed, evaluated, and adapted, as Part V explains. If not handled effectively, these issues can jeopardize even the best compensation strategy.

This book was written for two main purposes: to help those wishing to learn how to create effective compensation systems, and to serve as a useful source of reference to compensation practitioners. In so doing, it attempts to fill a gap in the textual resources available in Canada. Previous Canadian books on compensation have lacked an integrated strategic framework, and have tended to focus on either the behavioural principles in compensation or the technical details. Both of these are important, but what is needed is a balanced, comprehensive, and integrated presentation of strategic, behavioural, and technical principles. That is what this book attempts to achieve.

The content of this book is based on a foundation of scientific research, informed by relevant theoretical principles, and verified by organizational experiences. Although there is still much to learn about the design of effective reward and compensation systems, our state of knowledge about compensation has advanced to the point where effective use of the available knowledge will significantly increase the likelihood of organizational success.

To maximize its value as an effective learning tool, this book incorporates a number of features. Although based on a solid scientific foundation, the informal and engaging writing style, augmented by a variety of learning devices, is intended to smooth the road to effective learning. Another key feature is the overall organizing framework for the book—which has been dubbed the "road map" to effective compensation. Getting to any destination is facilitated by a conceptual map of how to get there, and the entire book is organized around this conceptual road map.

Each chapter incorporates a variety of features to facilitate learning. Chapter goals orient readers to what they should bring away from each chapter. Extensive use of figures is made to provide visual representations of key concepts, and to provide examples of specific forms, templates, and other practical tools. Tables are used to augment and summarize textual material, and boxes provide specific experiences and practices from actual organizations. Margin definitions are provided to facilitate use of key concepts.

The summary and implications section highlights and reinforces the key compensation insights to be gleaned from the chapter, while the list of key terms provides a checklist for testing knowledge. The end-of-chapter exercises provide opportunities for discussion and application of the concepts. These are supplemented by a set of comprehensive cases at the back of the book, which can be used in conjunction with in-class exercises, as a basis for hand-in assignments or group projects, or for examination purposes. Also appearing at the end of each chapter is a list of suggested Web sites to help readers access resources available through the Internet or simply to provide interesting avenues for further exploration. WWW icons in the margin indicate text for which a Web site URL has been provided.

The book has been divided into 12 chapters, so it fits well with the standard 12- to 13-week university or college class. Some chapters will warrant more than a week of class time, and others less than a week, but averaging a chapter a week should not pose an unreasonable burden for most students. This book can stand alone as the principal resource for a course, but can also be effectively used in conjunction with the author's compensation simulation, also published by Nelson Thomson Learning. An instructor's manual is also available.

The objectives for this book are ambitious, and it is up to readers to judge how effectively they have been achieved. The author would welcome any suggestions, comments, or any other feedback from you, the reader. You can use e-mail (long@commerce.usask.ca), fax (306-966-2516), telephone (306-966-8398), or snail mail (College of Commerce, 25 Campus Drive, University of Saskatchewan, Saskatoon, S7N 5A7). I look forward to hearing from you!

ACKNOWLEDGMENTS

Many people have contributed to this book, in a variety of ways. A project such as this draws on the knowledge, experience, and insights of a large number of researchers, scholars, and practitioners, each of whom has played a role in developing the body of knowledge reflected in this book. I would especially like to express my appreciation to the many practitioners whom I spoke with during the course of this project and whose insights and experiences greatly enrich the book.

Many people at the College of Commerce deserve recognition. First and foremost, I would like to thank the hundreds of students I have had the opportunity to learn from over the years, many of whom are now themselves practitioners or scholars. It is truly a privilege to work with such a talented group of individuals, and they provide the inspiration for a project of this nature. I would particularly like to thank the students in my compensation courses, whose suggestions and feedback on earlier drafts of the book greatly improved it.

I would also like to express my gratitude to my colleagues and support staff at the College of Commerce. The College itself has provided a supportive environment for this project, while Lyla Sheppard and Eilene Sabat have provided invaluable secretarial assistance. My primary research assistants, Tanya Vetter and Marnie Polansky, were models of resourcefulness and efficiency. Special mention should be made of my colleague, Ron Edmonds, who was generous in sharing his knowledge, insights, and other resources with me.

A number of other people have played a significant role in this project. The series editor, Monica Belcourt, provided the impetus for this project, along with much encouragement and support along the way. Drafts of the manuscript benefited greatly from reviews by Naresh C. Agarwal, McMaster University; Nina Cole, Brock University; Paul Jones, Georgian College; Don Schepens, Grant MacEwan College; Kim Squires, Saint Mary's University; Andrew Templer, University of Windsor; and Diane White, Seneca College. Helpful comments were also received from Helen Lam. Carrie Gallant, Legal Counsel for the Ontario Pay Equity Commission, reviewed the section on pay equity procedures in Ontario. The team at Nelson—including Evelyn Veitch, Edward Ikeda, Karina TenVeldhuis, and others—exhibited a high degree of professionalism and dedication in support of this project.

Finally, I owe my greatest debt to my wife, Trisha, without whose support and affection this project could never have been completed, and to my three sons, Jeffrey, Jeremy, and Michael, who help to provide the quality of family life necessary to energize a project like this.

Richard J. Long
University of Saskatchewan

1

A ROAD MAP TO EFFECTIVE COMPENSATION

CHAPTER GOALS

By the end of this chapter, you should be able to:

1. Describe the purpose and role of a compensation system.
2. Explain why an effective compensation system is so important to most organizations.
3. Distinguish between extrinsic and intrinsic rewards.
4. Distinguish between a reward system and a compensation system.
5. Define "reward strategy."
6. Describe the two key aspects of a compensation strategy.
7. Explain why a compensation system must be viewed in the context of the total reward system.
8. Identify and explain the key criteria for evaluating a compensation system.
9. Describe the steps along the road to effective compensation, and understand how this book will facilitate that journey.

Introduction

Change or die! This refrain has been echoed by many management experts in recent years as they exhort organizations to make revolutionary changes to their traditional compensation systems or suffer dire consequences. Dump traditional job-based systems for determining pay in favour of person-based pay-for-knowledge systems! Eliminate hourly pay and put everyone on salary! Scrap individual incentives in favour of team-based pay! Replace seniority-based pay with performance-based compensation! Give everyone profit-sharing or stock options, or better yet, both!

But is this really good advice? Or more to the point, is it good advice for *your* organization? These experts cite many cases where their advice has led to favourable results and may have even helped save the company, and other cases where firms didn't change and have died (e.g., Lawler, 1990, 2000; Wilson, 1995; Zingheim and Schuster, 2000). And, as Box 1.1 shows, many successful firms consider these concepts to be key parts of their strategies for success.

However, there have also been many (less-publicized) cases where following this advice has not turned out to be such a hot idea, and firms quietly revert back to what they were doing before. For every compensation practice described in Box 1.1, cases can be found where the same practice failed to produce the desired results. And we all know of organizations where all of this earnest advice has been totally ignored, but somehow the organization is doing just fine. These firms haven't changed and they're not dead.

What on earth is going on here? Why do compensation practices that work in some firms fail in others? Why do some organizations that fail to change their traditional compensation practices do just fine, while others die? How can you determine just what is the best compensation system for your particular organization? Answering these questions is what this book is all about.

Your Compensation System: Asset or Liability?

Canadian firms typically spend from 40 to 70 percent of their operating budgets to compensate their employees. For most firms, compensation is their single largest operating expenditure. Last year, employers in Canada spent over $510 *billion* on wages and salaries alone, according to Statistics Canada, and another $65 billion on employee benefits. Are they getting their money's worth? Is this money being well spent?

In many cases, it is not. Some firms are spending too much. Others are spending too little. But the amount being spent, while important, is not the key issue. The real question is this: What is the organization receiving for its investment in wages, salaries, and benefits? Is the compensation system, and the money devoted to it, contributing to the achievement of organizational objectives in the fullest possible way? Does the firm have in place the compensation

BOX 1.1 Compensation Supports Strategy: From A to Z

Although many organizations regard their compensation systems as simply a source of cost, others believe that compensation can play a key role in the achievement of their goals and strategies. Here is a set of examples that span the alphabet:

- At Altamira Financial Services, a large mutual funds company, their on-line brokers and mutual funds specialists are paid salaries rather than the commissions that are the norm in this business. The company believes that this results in more objective customer advice.

- At Basell Canada's chemical plant in Sarnia, Ontario, pay is based not on the specific job an employee does, but on the number of jobs the worker is qualified to perform. The company believes that this radical departure from tradition results in a more flexible and efficient workforce.

- At Canadian Tire, management has always attributed a great deal of the firm's success to their employee profit-sharing plan, which they believe has led to a more committed and motivated workforce than is usual in the retail business.

- At Herman Miller, a large manufacturer of office furniture, the centrepiece of their compensation strategy is a gain-sharing plan, under which employees share in company productivity gains. This supports the company strategy of delegating a high amount of responsibility to employees.

- At the Royal Bank, an element of performance pay is being implemented for all employees in order to support the firm's increased focus on the customer and on performance. Traditionally, virtually all employees in the banking industry were paid fixed salaries.

- At Sears, measures of customer satisfaction are being factored into all employees' pay in an attempt to make the organization more flexible and customer-oriented. Executives are compensated on customer and employee satisfaction, in addition to financial indicators.

- At Starbucks, the coffee and dessert chain, all employees, including part-time clerks, are given stock options. This supports the company strategy of committed service from employees. In most organizations, stock options are limited to a few top executives.

- At Vanderpol's Eggs, in Surrey, British Columbia, management regards employee share ownership as a key means of supporting their managerial strategy, which is to create a partnership between owners and employees. They believe that employee owners will be more committed and productive.

- At Zenon Environmental, a developer of membrane filtering technologies for water treatment, employees are provided with a flexible benefits system under which they can transfer the value of benefits they don't need to those that they do. This freedom of choice supports the company's values of high employee input and involvement.

system that adds—after taking costs into account—the greatest possible value to the company?

The compensation system is potentially one of the most powerful tools available to an employer for shaping behaviour and influencing performance, yet many organizations waste this potential, viewing compensation as simply a cost to be minimized. Even worse, some firms not only waste this potential, but their compensation systems actually serve to promote unproductive or even counterproductive behaviour. As we will see in the following chapters, problems of low employee motivation, poor job performance, high turnover, irresponsible behaviour, and even employee dishonesty often have roots in the compensation system. Problems as varied as organizational rigidity, inability to adapt to change, lack of innovation, conflict between organizational units, and poor customer service may also stem, at least in part, from the reward system.

What complicates things further is that a compensation system that has worked well in the past can, without any obvious warning signs, become a serious liability when circumstances change. Failure to change reward systems accordingly has caused new strategies to falter, new structures to collapse, new technologies to malfunction, and entire companies to founder. However, because the reward system often affects behaviour in very subtle ways, an irony is that many firms never do pinpoint their reward system as a major contributor to these problems.

THE PREMISE OF THIS BOOK

The thesis of this book is that organizations that treat their reward system as a key strategic variable, and use it to support their corporate and managerial strategies, will receive more value from their compensation system than those that do not, resulting in superior company performance and better achievement of organizational objectives. The purpose of this book is to help the reader learn how to design and implement a reward and compensation strategy that best fits their particular circumstances—one that will add the greatest possible value to their organization. This chapter starts that process by clarifying some essential concepts and by presenting a "road map" of the steps along the path to effective compensation.

ROLE AND PURPOSE OF THE COMPENSATION SYSTEM

How do you get organization members to do what the organization wants and needs them to do? This is a central problem of organizations that has bedevilled those in charge of organizations ever since their invention. And it is a problem that has grown more complex than ever, especially for organizations whose products, services, and technologies have become increasingly complicated, whose environments have become more dynamic and competitive, who operate in democratic and relatively affluent societies, and who require complicated behaviours and high performance levels from their members. Compensation is normally a key part of the solution, although there are many

purpose of compensation system to help create a willingness among qualified persons to join the organization and to do the things needed by the organization

other important parts, all of which must fit together if the desired results are to be fully achieved.

At its most basic, the **purpose of a compensation system** is to help create a willingness among qualified persons to join the organization and to do the things needed by the organization. What this generally means is that employees must perceive that doing so will help them satisfy some important needs they have. These include economic needs for the basic necessities of life, as well as needs for security, for social interaction, for status, for achievement, for recognition, and for growth and development.

Extrinsic vs. Intrinsic Rewards

Anything provided by the organization that satisfies one or more of these needs can be considered a "reward." The types of rewards that are available in an organizational setting can be divided into two main categories: extrinsic and intrinsic. **Extrinsic rewards** satisfy our basic needs for survival and security, as well as our social needs and needs for recognition. They derive from factors surrounding the job—the job *context*—such as pay, supervisory behaviour, co-workers, and general working conditions. **Intrinsic rewards** satisfy higher-level needs for self-esteem, achievement, growth, and development. They derive from factors inherent in the work itself—the job *content*—such as the amount of challenge or interest the job provides, the degree of variety in the job, the extent to which it provides feedback and allows autonomy, as well as the meaning or significance attributed to the work.

Reward vs. Compensation Strategy

Both extrinsic and intrinsic rewards are important to people, and each, if utilized effectively, can produce important benefits for the organization. The mix of these rewards provided by an organization is termed its **reward system**. The **compensation system** deals only with the economic or monetary part of the reward system. But since behaviour is affected by the total spectrum of rewards provided by the organization, and not just compensation, the compensation system can never be regarded in isolation from the overall reward system.

Therefore, before development of the compensation system can be undertaken, the reward strategy needs to be established. The **reward strategy** is the plan for the mix of rewards, both extrinsic and intrinsic, that the organization intends to provide to its members—along with the means through which they will be provided—in order to elicit the behaviours necessary for organization success. The reward strategy is the blueprint for creating the reward system.

The compensation strategy is one part of the reward strategy, and is the plan for creating the compensation system. The compensation system has three main components: base pay, performance pay, and indirect pay. **Base pay** is the foundation pay component for most employees, and is generally based on some unit of time—an hour, a week, a month, a year. **Performance pay** relates employee monetary rewards to some measure of individual, group, or organizational performance. **Indirect pay**, sometimes known as "employee benefits," consists of noncash items or services that satisfy a variety of specific employee needs, such as for income security (e.g., disability and life insurance), for

extrinsic rewards factors that satisfy basic human needs for survival and security, as well as social needs and needs for recognition

intrinsic rewards factors that satisfy higher-order human needs for self-esteem, achievement, growth, and development

reward system the mix of intrinsic and extrinsic rewards provided to its members by an organization

compensation system the economic or monetary part of the reward system

reward strategy the plan for the mix of rewards to be provided to members, along with the means through which they will be provided

base pay the foundation pay component for most employees, usually based on some unit of time worked

performance pay relates employee monetary rewards to some measure of individual, group, or organizational performance

indirect pay noncash items or services that satisfy a variety of specific employee needs, sometimes known as "benefits"

health protection (e.g., medical and dental plans), or for retirement income (e.g., pension plans).

compensation strategy
the plan for the mix and total amount of base pay, performance pay, and indirect pay to be paid to various categories of employees

There are two key aspects to **compensation strategy**. One aspect is the mix across these three components, and whether and how this mix will vary for different employee groups. The other is the total amount of compensation to be provided to various individuals and groups. In short, "How should compensation be paid?" and "How much should be paid?" are the two key questions for compensation strategy. While simple to state, these questions are extremely complex to answer.

The optimal choice about these two aspects of compensation strategy ultimately depends on the organizational context, but the most immediate determinant is the reward strategy. At one extreme, the reward strategy may include no compensation components whatsoever; at the other extreme, compensation may be the only appreciable reward provided by an organization.

Therefore, the first step in formulating a compensation strategy is to determine the role that compensation will play in the reward system. Under the assumption that organizations will wish to minimize compensation costs whenever possible, it is useful to first identify what other rewards are being provided by the organization, and to ascertain whether these alone are sufficient to elicit the necessary behaviour from organization members.

For example, some voluntary organizations receive thousands of hours of labour from their members, for no pay whatsoever. The UNICEF store in Saskatoon is open during normal business hours six days a week, selling greeting cards, gift items, and even postage stamps. What does it pay its staff? Absolutely nothing. Intrinsic rewards alone are sufficient to motivate the needed behaviour. In this case, the intrinsic rewards do not flow from the nature of the tasks (e.g., ringing up sales, stocking shelves), but from the meaning assigned to these tasks. In their eyes, the volunteers are not simply "serving customers," they are "saving the lives of destitute children."

Of course, most work organizations cannot expect to get away with providing no compensation to their members, although some may try, such as the Screaming Tale Restaurant described in Box 1.2. (Of course, even at the Screaming Tale, servers are still receiving some compensation for their work; it simply flows directly from the customer to the server.) But the key point is that the amount of pay needed to attract and retain the appropriate workforce will vary with the other rewards that the organization can offer.

For example, some organizations, such as banks, have traditionally offered high job security. This has enabled them to pay less than other organizations that do not offer job security, and still attract the same calibre of employee. However, if job security ceases to be a reward provided by these organizations, it may be necessary to increase pay or other rewards if they wish to attract and retain the same calibre of employee. In fact, because bank jobs are no longer as secure as they once were, and because their needs for employee behaviour have changed, most Canadian banks have radically changed their compensation structures in recent years.

BOX 1.2 A Recipe for Low Labour Costs?

At the Screaming Tale Restaurants in Port Hope and Belleville, Ontario, management has cooked up a great recipe for cutting labour costs: don't pay your staff! They have eliminated payroll for serving staff by utilizing "volunteer" staff who work only for the tips they receive. Aside from the obvious advantage of saving the wages that would otherwise be paid to servers, this arrangement also eliminates the mandatory benefits and payroll taxes that would have to be paid to the government (which add nearly 20 percent to compensation costs), as well as the administrative work of calculating pay and preparing paycheques. Quite a competitive advantage!

However, after two "volunteers" complained, the Ontario Ministry of Labour launched an investigation to determine whether this arrangement is in violation of provincial employment standards legislation, which requires that a minimum wage be paid to all persons considered to be employees. Under the law, money received as tips does not count toward this minimum wage.

One of the restaurant chain's owners, Aldo Mauro, says the restaurants have come under attack because they have learned to operate more efficiently by reducing labour costs. In an interview with *The Globe and Mail*, Mauro said his company specializes in rescuing distressed restaurants and turning them into profitable ones and has used "volunteer" workers in the past throughout southeastern Ontario.

Brent Bowser, a manager of the chain's restaurant in Port Hope, said the restaurant provides a location where workers can act as service agents and do their business. The complaints, Bowser said, came from employees who didn't hustle. (*Human Resource Management in Canada*, 1996: 161.3)

Some organizations provide jobs that have high intrinsic rewards, which may allow them to attract employees more easily than those that do not. Similarly, firms that enjoy a high level of prestige and public esteem will often find it less necessary to offer as much pay as firms that do not enjoy such prestige. Firms that offer opportunities for learning and development may be able to offer less pay than those that do not.

Of course, firms that offer many noncompensation rewards may also choose to provide relatively high levels of compensation in order to attract high-calibre employees and elicit high commitment and performance. The key point here is that various combinations of intrinsic and extrinsic rewards need to be considered in developing the optimal reward strategy. It is only within this context that the most appropriate compensation strategy can be determined.

For example, if the firm is experiencing high turnover because employees find their jobs mind-numbingly dull, one solution might be to increase pay to make employees more reluctant to quit. But another approach might be to try to enrich the jobs to make them more interesting, thereby increasing intrinsic rewards. Of course, it may even be possible to dispense with these jobs, by automating them, which eliminates the reward issue entirely.

Which of these is the best choice depends on the relative costs and benefits of each approach. It may even be that the most cost-effective approach is to do nothing, if the cost of turnover is less than the cost of increasing extrinsic or intrinsic rewards or of automating the jobs. However, there may be other factors that should come into play in this decision-making process. For example, job enrichment may not only reduce turnover, it might also increase work quality. This may tip the scales toward job enrichment rather than increased pay. Or, some combination of job enrichment and increased pay may be optimal.

CRITERIA FOR SUCCESS: GOALS FOR THE COMPENSATION SYSTEM

What should an optimal reward and compensation system achieve? There are eight main criteria, as Table 1.1 shows. First and foremost, it must help promote the achievement of the organization's goals. Second, it must fit with and support the organization's strategy for achieving its goals and its structure for implementing its strategy. Third, it must attract and retain individuals who possess the attributes necessary to perform the required task behaviours. Fourth, it should promote the entire spectrum of desired task behaviour for every organization member. Fifth, it should be seen as equitable by all organization members. Sixth, it must comply with all relevant laws within the jurisdictions in which the firm operates. Seventh, it must achieve all this at a cost that is within the financial means of the organization. Eighth, it should achieve these objectives in the most cost-effective manner possible.

optimal reward system
the reward system that adds the most value to the organization, after considering all its costs

In general, the **optimal reward system** will be the one that adds the most value to the organization, after considering all its costs. It should be emphasized that this does not necessarily imply that the optimal compensation system will be the cheapest one possible. For example, for some firms, a high-wage compensation strategy may well be the one that maximizes overall company effectiveness. Of course, it should also be recognized that resource constraints may prevent the adoption of what would otherwise be the optimal reward strategy. But an effective reward system will maximize the value added relative to the resources devoted to the reward system.

The objective of this book is to help readers learn how to create a reward system that will accomplish all of the criteria outlined in Table 1.1. But wait a minute! Let's stop for a reality check. These goals sound very nice in theory, but, realistically, is it really necessary for a firm to achieve all of them? We all

TABLE 1.1   GOALS OF THE REWARD AND COMPENSATION SYSTEM

1. Promote achievement of the organization's goals.
2. Fit with and support the organization's strategy and structure.
3. Attract and retain qualified individuals.
4. Promote desired task behaviour.
5. Be seen as equitable.
6. Comply with the law.
7. Be within the financial means of the organization.
8. Achieve the above goals in the most cost-effective manner.

probably know of successful organizations that violate several of these criteria. For instance, there are some successful organizations where it would be difficult to find anyone who believes that their reward system is equitable. So does this mean that an equitable reward system may be desirable from a social and ethical viewpoint, but not from the viewpoint of organizational performance?

Not necessarily. As will be seen in Chapter 3, an inequitable reward system imposes various undesirable consequences on an employer, such as increased employee turnover and reduced work motivation. But the costs of these consequences vary dramatically for different employers. For some firms, these costs and consequences may be tolerable, while for others they may not. As will be discussed, there are a variety of factors that will determine how important an equitable reward system will be to a given employer.

However, this book will argue that the circumstances under which an organization can afford an inequitable reward system are diminishing in Canada, and that, for most organizations, an equitable reward system will actually be a competitive advantage, if not a business necessity. But the truth is that, overall, organizations vary greatly in terms of how important the reward and compensation system is to their performance, as Chapter 2 will discuss.

No matter how hard an organization tries, is it realistic that any reward system will fully achieve all eight of the effectiveness criteria? Probably not. But they do serve as goals to be pursued and criteria against which to measure progress. In today's rapidly changing environment, continual evaluation of the effectiveness of the reward and compensation system is crucial for most organizations. As firms struggle to find the right answers to the compensation puzzle, the whole area of compensation now attracts increasing interest in the business and popular media. Indeed, firms with comprehensive and attractive reward and compensation systems may even find themselves included among "Canada's 100 best places to work," a significant advantage when it comes to employee recruitment (Yerema, 2000).

A Road Map to Effective Compensation

All this may sound pretty complicated so far. So what are the steps to an effective compensation system? Figure 1.1 provides a "road map" of the path to follow, and links each step along the path to the section of the book that will provide the guidance for that step.

Step I: Understand Your Organization and Your People

The first step in creating an effective compensation system is to understand the organizational context within which it will operate. The reward system is just one part of the total organizational system, and each part must fit with and

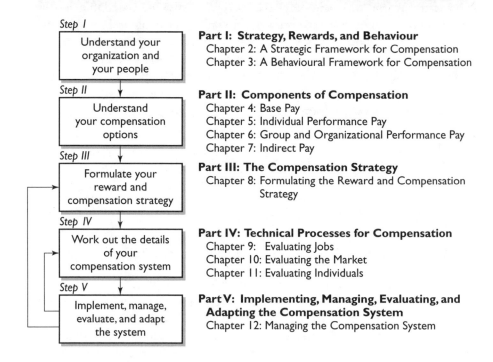

FIGURE 1.1   A ROAD MAP TO EFFECTIVE COMPENSATION

Step I
Understand your organization and your people

Part I: Strategy, Rewards, and Behaviour
Chapter 2: A Strategic Framework for Compensation
Chapter 3: A Behavioural Framework for Compensation

Step II
Understand your compensation options

Part II: Components of Compensation
Chapter 4: Base Pay
Chapter 5: Individual Performance Pay
Chapter 6: Group and Organizational Performance Pay
Chapter 7: Indirect Pay

Step III
Formulate your reward and compensation strategy

Part III: The Compensation Strategy
Chapter 8: Formulating the Reward and Compensation Strategy

Step IV
Work out the details of your compensation system

Part IV: Technical Processes for Compensation
Chapter 9:   Evaluating Jobs
Chapter 10: Evaluating the Market
Chapter 11: Evaluating Individuals

Step V
Implement, manage, evaluate, and adapt the system

Part V: Implementing, Managing, Evaluating, and Adapting the Compensation System
Chapter 12: Managing the Compensation System

support the other parts. There are several viable patterns into which these parts can be arranged, and each pattern constitutes one type of managerial strategy.

Each managerial strategy relies, for success, on a different reward and compensation strategy. The most appropriate managerial strategy is, in turn, determined by a number of key contextual factors, such as the nature of the firm's environment, its corporate strategy, its technology, its size, and, of course, its people. A key implication of all this is that whenever one of these factors changes, this may trigger a need for many other organizational changes, including change to the reward and compensation system. The purpose of Chapter 2 ("A Strategic Framework for Compensation") is to provide a conceptual tool for understanding the organizational context and identifying the compensation system that will best fit that context.

Another essential understanding is the linkage between reward systems and human behaviour. There are three main behaviours that may be desired by an organization—membership behaviour, task behaviour, and citizenship behaviour—but the importance of each of these can vary dramatically for different organizations. It is crucial to understand what specific attitudes and behaviours are needed by your organization, and the role that the reward system can play in eliciting these behaviours.

Besides understanding how reward systems can promote desired behaviours, it is also important to understand how reward systems can unintentionally generate *undesirable* attitudes and behaviours. As Chapter 3 will explain, this is a surprisingly common phenomenon. The purpose of Chapter 3 ("A Behavioural Framework for Compensation") is to provide a conceptual tool for understanding how compensation relates to employee behaviour.

STEP II: UNDERSTAND YOUR COMPENSATION OPTIONS

The next step toward an effective compensation system is to understand what compensation options are available to you, what are their advantages and disadvantages, and what consequences each can produce. There are three main compensation components—base pay, performance pay, and indirect pay—and Part II of this book (Chapters 4 to 7) has been devoted to examining these components, along with the many different elements and choices that are available within each component. The purpose of Part II is to provide an understanding of the available choices sufficient to allow readers to decide what mix of components and elements should be included in the reward strategy that best fits their organization. The technical details for designing and implementing these components will come later in the book.

STEP III: FORMULATE YOUR REWARD AND COMPENSATION STRATEGY

Based on these understandings, it should now be possible to identify the kinds of behaviour that your organization needs to elicit, and then to identify the most appropriate combination of rewards to elicit this behaviour (the reward strategy). The reward strategy will define the role that compensation will be expected to play in bringing about the desired behaviour. From this, specific compensation objectives can be developed.

A compensation strategy will then be formulated that defines the mix of compensation components to be used (along with the specific elements of these components) and the pay level strategy. In so doing, it is essential to understand the constraints on your organization that define the parameters within which choices can be made. These include legal constraints, labour market constraints, product/service market constraints, and constraints on the financial resources available to the organization. Chapter 8 ("Formulating the Reward and Compensation Strategy") is intended to guide you through this process.

STEP IV: WORK OUT THE TECHNICAL DETAILS

Once the compensation strategy has been formulated, many technical details will need to be put in place to create an operating compensation system. Part IV of the book provides a detailed description of the key technical processes necessary to do that. Of course, not all of these technical processes may be relevant to a particular compensation strategy.

For compensation strategies in which job evaluation plays a role in determining base pay, Chapter 9 ("Evaluating Jobs") provides a description of the key steps and procedures in that process. For firms that wish to systematically calibrate their pay system to the "going market rates," Chapter 10 ("Evaluating the Market") will describe how to gather and analyze wage survey and labour market data, and how to apply it to a given compensation system. For compensation strategies that include pay-for-knowledge systems, or that utilize performance appraisals in allocating pay, Chapter 11 ("Evaluating Individuals") provides the necessary background.

STEP V: IMPLEMENT, MANAGE, EVALUATE, AND ADAPT THE COMPENSATION SYSTEM

Once developed, the compensation system needs to be implemented and then managed on an ongoing basis. Key issues here include the procedures for implementing the system, for communicating the system, for dealing with compensation problems, and for budgeting and controlling compensation costs.

Once implemented, the compensation system needs to be continually evaluated to see whether it is accomplishing the objectives that have been set out for it, and whether it is doing so in the most cost-effective manner possible. If it is not doing so, changes may be needed in some of the technical processes, or there may need to be a rethinking of the compensation and rewards strategy as a whole, as the feedback loops in Figure 1.1 illustrate.

Furthermore, if the circumstances facing the organization change, or if any of the key contextual variables change, or if any of the other aspects of organization structure change, there may well be a need to change the compensation strategy or system. In addition, the organization must have a way of detecting unintended negative consequences that the compensation system may be generating. The final chapter in this book, Chapter 12 ("Managing the Compensation System"), provides guidance on how to deal with all of these issues.

And now, good luck on your journey to effective compensation!

KEY TERMS

base pay, p. 5

compensation strategy, p. 6

compensation system, p. 5

extrinsic rewards, p. 5

indirect pay, p. 5

intrinsic rewards, p. 5

optimal reward system, p. 8

performance pay, p. 5

purpose of compensation system, p. 4

reward strategy, p. 5

reward system, p. 5

EXERCISES

1. In a small group, describe to each other the compensation system at your most recent job, in terms of base pay, performance pay, and indirect pay. Then, discuss your reactions to this system. Do you believe it was equitable? What impact did it have on your motivation and commitment to the organization? How could it have been improved? Of the compensation systems described by your group members, which appeared to be the most effective, and why?

2. Consider the pay system in use for servers at the Screaming Tale Restaurant, described in Box 1.2. Do you believe that it meets the criteria for effectiveness identified in Table 1.1? Do you think it will be an effective system for this restaurant? Is it fair to servers? Can you think of any possible disadvantages or negative consequences that this system could cause for the employer?

SUGGESTED WEB SITES

Page 2: For the latest information on labour income in Canada, go to Statistics Canada's Web site at <www.statcan.ca>

Page 9: To get a flavour of compensation issues making the news, go to <www.hrreporter.ca> and click on "compensation" or "benefits."

REFERENCES

Human Resource Management in Canada. 1996. "'Volunteer' Staff: One Way to Cut Costs." Report Bulletin No. 161: 161.3.

Lawler, Edward E. 1990. *Strategic Pay: Aligning Organizational Strategies and Pay Systems.* San Francisco: Jossey-Bass.

Lawler, Edward E. 2000. *Rewarding Excellence: Pay Strategies for the New Economy.* San Francisco: Jossey-Bass.

Wilson, Thomas B. 1995. *Innovative Reward Systems for the Changing Workplace.* New York: McGraw-Hill.

Yerema, Richard. 2000. *Canada's Top 100 Employers, 2001 Edition.* Toronto: Mediacorp.

Zingheim, Patricia A., and Jay R. Schuster. 2000. *Pay People Right: Breakthrough Reward Strategies to Create Great Companies.* San Francisco: Jossey-Bass.

Part I

Strategy, Rewards, and Behaviour

2

....

A STRATEGIC FRAMEWORK FOR COMPENSATION

CHAPTER GOALS

By the end of this chapter, you should be able to:

1. Explain why the same compensation system may be a success in one firm but a failure in another.
2. Describe an organizational system.
3. Explain how the strategic framework for compensation can be used as a tool for designing effective reward and compensation systems.
4. Describe the three main sets of elements in the strategic compensation framework, and explain how they relate to one another.
5. Describe the three main managerial strategies that organizations can adopt, and explain the implications for the most effective reward and compensation system.
6. Describe the five main determinants of managerial strategy, and explain how they can be used to select the most appropriate managerial strategy.
7. Analyze any organization to determine the most appropriate managerial strategy.

8. Discuss how conditions in North America changed during the twentieth century, and explain how this has affected today's managerial and compensation strategies.

INTRODUCTION

Let's start this chapter with a little contest. The reward for winning? Strictly intrinsic. Below are two firms with completely different compensation systems. Your skill-testing question: Which compensation system is the most effective? Note that this question does not ask you to pick the one that you like the most, but the one that best fits our definition of an effective compensation system. As we discussed in Chapter 1, the most effective compensation system for a given firm is the one that adds the most value to the organization, after considering all its costs.

L-S Electrogalvanizing (LSE) produces corrosion-resistant sheet steel for the automotive industry. The firm receives large coils of sheet steel from steel mills, unrolls and cleans them, and then applies a coating of zinc to precise specifications. Although the process is highly automated, many things can go wrong, and mistakes are very costly.

Rather than hourly pay geared to the specific task that a worker does (such as packaging or process control), which is the norm in this industry, plant workers are paid salaries, with their salary level based on the number of different plant jobs that they are qualified to perform. (This is known as a "pay-for-knowledge" system.) To maintain their skills, workers rotate through the various plant jobs, which means that someone working at one of the traditionally lower-paying jobs, such as packaging, may be earning twice what a worker would receive at a competitor for doing this same job. As if this weren't enough, employees receive an excellent benefits package, as well as gain-sharing bonuses based on plant productivity and profit-sharing bonuses based on company performance. Taking all this into account, LSE ends up paying its workers far more than its competitors. Are you surprised to learn that hardly anyone ever quits?

B.C. Rogers Processors operates a plant that converts live chickens into packages of chicken parts. All work is centred around "the chain" on which the chickens are hung, which rattles along at 90 birds per minute. Workers are posted along the chain, performing various operations on the chickens as they pass by, such as reaching in and yanking out their innards. Unlike LSE, B.C. Rogers hasn't implemented any pay innovations and simply pays workers an hourly wage that doesn't go much above the legal minimum. Employee benefits are virtually nonexistent. Are you surprised to learn that employee turnover often exceeds 100 percent a year?

So back to our question. Which of these compensation systems do you think is the most effective? LSE sounds like a workers' paradise, but how can the company stay competitive when it pays its workers so much more than its competitors pay theirs? And while B.C. Rogers is certainly no workers' paradise, and can't be accused of overpaying its workers, wouldn't that turnover rate cause serious problems?

Aha, you think, maybe this is a trick question, and neither system is effective. In fact, despite being so different, *both* compensation systems are effective. How can this be? The answer is that they each fit the organization in which they are implemented and its strategy. But if these firms were to trade compensation systems, they would both soon be as dead as the B.C. Rogers chickens.

Why is it that a compensation system that is a great success in one organization is a miserable flop in another? And how do you know, in advance, whether a particular type of compensation system will be successful for your organization? These are puzzles that must be solved if a compensation system is to be successfully designed or redesigned.

The Concept of Fit

The solution to these puzzles is *fit* (Lawler, 1990; Gomez-Mejia and Balkin, 1992). Ultimately, the success or failure of any reward system depends on how well it fits the organizational context and total organizational system in which it is implemented. Therefore, in successfully designing, managing, and modifying any reward system, the key is to understand this context and how it links to the reward system.

But what are the key aspects of the organizational context, and exactly how do they relate to reward strategy? It is the purpose of this chapter to address that question. It does so by developing a framework that first identifies the key aspects of the organizational context, and then illustrates how each of them affects the reward system.

This framework will identify three managerial strategies that an organization can adopt, and show how each of these strategies has different implications for the way in which an organization is structured, and for the type of reward system that best fits that structure. Next, the determinants of managerial strategy will then be identified, since these will ultimately determine the most appropriate reward strategy. Finally, there will be a discussion of trends in managerial strategies and in compensation systems. But first, we need to get through some basic organizational concepts.

Organizations as Systems

As Figure 2.1 illustrates, **organizations** are systems that apply procedures to a set of resources in order to transform input materials into outputs that somebody values. Automakers transform thousands of component parts into automobiles. Hospitals transform sick people into well people. An accounting firm transforms a shoebox full of receipts, invoices, and bank records into a set of financial statements. Prisons transform homicidal maniacs who are a threat to

organizations systems that apply procedures to a set of resources to transform inputs into valued outputs

FIGURE 2.1   AN ORGANIZATIONAL SYSTEM

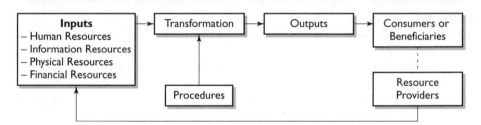

technology   the proce-
dures and resources used
by an organization to
transform inputs into
outputs

society into captive homicidal maniacs. The procedures and resources used to
carry out these transformation processes constitute the **technology** of the organization.

If the output of the system is not valued sufficiently that somebody or
some group is willing to provide the resources necessary for the transformation process to continue, the organization will cease to operate. In a business
organization, it is normally the consumer of the output who provides the
resources (usually money) that can be used to acquire the other necessary
resources.

However, in other types of organizations, such as hospitals or public
schools, the direct consumer of the output (i.e., patients or students) may provide few or none of the resources necessary for the organization to continue.
But the point is that someone or some group, somewhere, must value the outputs of the organization sufficiently (even if they themselves do not consume
the output) that they will provide the resources necessary for continuation. Of
course, in the case of hospitals and public schools, this group is taxpayers.

corporate strategy   an
organization's plan for
how it will achieve its
goals

organization structure
the means through which
an organization generates
the behaviours necessary
to execute its corporate
strategy

contingency approach to
organization design   key
contingencies or contex-
tual variables associated
with a given organization
must first be considered
in order to identify the
most appropriate
structure for that
organization

Organizations typically utilize four types of resources in the transformation process—human, information, physical, and financial. It is the role of
management to acquire these resources, and to combine and deploy them in
such a way that organizational goals will be achieved and that the transformation process will be carried out as efficiently as possible. Doing so requires that
some type of strategy for achievement of organizational goals be developed.
The **corporate strategy** (sometimes known as the competitive or business
strategy) is the organization's plan for how it will achieve its goals. The **organization structure** is the vehicle for the execution of this strategy. The purpose
of the organization structure is to generate the behaviours necessary to carry
out the organization's strategy.

For the organizational system to be effective, the corporate strategy and
organization structure must fit with certain other key variables, including the
type of environment in which the organization operates, the type of technology
it utilizes, the size of the organization, and the nature of the people the organization employs. This is known as the **contingency approach** to organization
design (Daft, 2001) and is the foundation for the strategic framework presented
in this chapter.

A Strategic Framework for Compensation

Pay is a "red phone." When it rings, employees want to find out who is on the other end and what is being said. The goal is to wire the red phone to company strategy. (Turnasella, 1994: 65)

Sounds good. So how, exactly, do you do that? Unfortunately, properly wiring "the red phone" is more complex than it sounds. Fortunately, this chapter develops a tool to do just that. But be prepared! Initially, this tool will only seem to make things more complicated! But once you invest the effort necessary to understand it, you should find it an indispensable part of your conceptual tool kit for building effective compensation systems.

Figure 2.2 presents the strategic framework. Two main sets of variables are depicted—contextual and structural—linked by managerial strategy. As can be seen, the reward system is one of the variables that makes up the organization's structure. To be effective, the reward system must fit with the other structural variables, as well as the managerial strategy, which must, in turn, fit with the contextual variables. What are all the double-sided arrows trying to convey? Simply that all of the structural variables are interrelated and must fit with each other if the organization is to be effective. The same thing is true for the contextual variables.

The first step in understanding how to use this framework is to understand each of its components.

Structural Variables

To generate the behaviours necessary to execute the corporate strategy, an organization structure needs to do two main things. It first needs to *divide* the total task that needs to be done into manageable subtasks (a process sometimes known as "differentiation"), and it then needs to *coordinate* the completion of these subtasks in such a way that they fit together to accomplish the total task of the organization (a process sometimes known as "integration").

An effective organization structure serves to reduce internal and external uncertainty for the organization. It reduces internal uncertainty by structuring and directing employee behaviour. It reduces external uncertainty through the creation of specialized units to interpret and deal with key aspects of the firm's environment, and to bring appropriate information to organizational decision makers. For example, a firm may create a marketing department to understand and deal with its customers, a purchasing department to understand and deal with its suppliers, and an economic forecasting unit to help it understand economic trends and how they may affect the organization.

The organization structure consists of a number of separate variables or dimensions. These variables are the *levers* that are used to try to produce the

FIGURE 2.2   A STRATEGIC FRAMEWORK FOR COMPENSATION

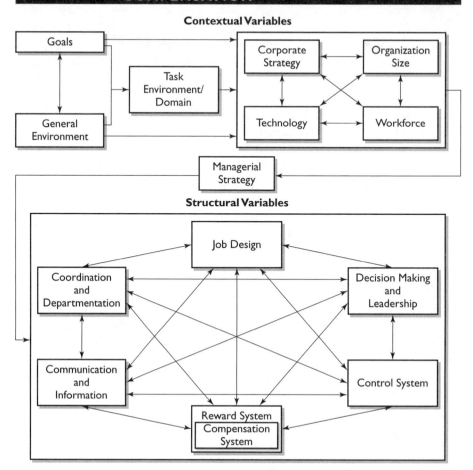

Contextual Variables

Structural Variables

job design a dimension of organization structure that describes the manner in which the total task of an organization is divided into separate jobs

coordination and departmentation a dimension of organization structure that describes the methods used to coordinate the work of individual employees and subunits in an organization

decision-making and leadership structure a dimension of organization structure that describes the nature of the decision-making and leadership processes used in an organization

communication and information structure a dimension of organization structure that describes the nature of and methods for communication in an organization

control structure a dimension of organization structure that describes the nature of the processes used to control employee behaviour in an organization

behaviour desired by the organization. Besides the reward system, there are five other structural variables. **Job design** describes the manner in which the total amount of work to be done is divided into subtasks that can be handled by individual workers. **Coordination and departmentation** mechanisms are the methods used to ensure that the work of individual employees will fit together such that the overall task will be accomplished.

The **decision-making and leadership structure** comprises the mechanisms through which the organization's decisions are made and the type of leadership role played by those in managerial positions. The **communication and information structure** describes the methods used to communicate information throughout the organization and the amount and kinds of information to be transmitted. The **control structure** is the means used to ensure that organization members are actually doing what they are intended to do.

MANAGERIAL STRATEGY

The structural variables described above can be arranged in a virtually limitless number of ways. However, over time, three main patterns, or managerial strategies, have emerged. Each of these managerial strategies represents a particular combination of these structural variables that has proved to be successful when applied in the right circumstances. The particular **managerial strategy** used by a given firm is the most important single determinant of what will or will not be a successful reward system for that firm. The specific linkages between managerial strategies and the structural variables, including reward systems, will be discussed in more detail a little later in the chapter.

managerial strategy the combination of structural variables adopted by an organization

CONTEXTUAL VARIABLES

So what determines the most appropriate managerial strategy? The five main **contextual variables** are shown in Figure 2.2—the organization's environment, corporate strategy, technology, size, and workforce. Each of these will be discussed in more detail later in the chapter, along with their linkages to managerial strategy.

But if they differ for different organizations, how are the contextual variables themselves determined? As Figure 2.2 has shown, it all starts with organizational goals. But where do organizational goals come from?

When they create an organization, the founders have certain goals that they hope the organization will accomplish. In a business enterprise, the goals may include making money and/or providing employment for the owner. In a governmental organization, the goal may be to satisfy some collective need, such as the need for fire or police protection, or for education. In a not-for-profit enterprise, the goal may be to address some need that the founders believe is important but is not currently being met. For example, the Canadian Cancer Society was created to serve the needs of those who have cancer, and to find a way to cure or prevent cancer. UNICEF was created to help serve the needs of children in poverty-stricken areas.

From the interaction between the goals of the founders and the general environment in which they are located, the organization's *domain* emerges. The **domain** defines the specific products or services to be offered by the organization. The domain also defines the **task environment**, which is the specific slice of the general environment that is of particular relevance to the organization. Key elements of the task environment include the customers or clients of the organization, competitors, suppliers, and regulatory agencies.

Once goals are established and the domain is defined, some plan for achieving the organization's goals (the corporate strategy) needs to be formulated. Decisions can then be made about the most appropriate type of technology to be used to produce the product or service, the most appropriate size

contextual variables factors in the firm's context that indicate the most appropriate managerial strategy and organizational structure

domain describes the specific products or services offered by a given organization

task environment the portion of the general environment that has direct relevance to a given organization

for the organization, and the nature of the workforce that will be needed. These decisions need to be seen as interrelated, since changes in one will affect each of the others. For example, a change in the technology may well necessitate changes to the corporate strategy and the nature of the workforce, as well as to the size of the organization.

The key thing about all this is that a change in any of these factors may trigger a need for a change in the reward system. Thus, a company that changes its corporate strategy, that implements a new technology, that grows in size, or whose workforce changes may need a new reward strategy. A company attempting to introduce work teams or flexible production will almost always need to change its reward system. A firm striving to change its managerial strategy will usually need to change its reward system. As discussed earlier, failure to make the right changes to the reward system in the light of these other changes may have dire consequences. Because organizations are systems, change in one aspect of the organization almost inevitably has implications for other parts of the organization.

Managerial Strategies and Reward Systems

As organizations have evolved, three main patterns of management, or managerial strategies, have emerged (Miles, 1975). Each of these strategies reflects different assumptions about employees and how they should be managed. Adherents of the **classical managerial strategy** believe that people are inherently lazy, dislike work, and would prefer to get as much as they possibly can from a work relationship, while giving as little as possible. According to this perspective, the only way to get people to work is by creating circumstances under which satisfaction of their economic needs will be threatened if they do not behave as the organization wants them to. Essentially, this school of thought tends to view employees as potentially dishonest shirkers, who need to be tightly controlled if the organization is going to be sure of getting any work out of them.

Adherents of the **human relations managerial strategy** agree with the classical managers that people inherently dislike work, but they differ in that they believe that people can be motivated by appealing to their social needs. They have observed that the classical school of thought frequently creates an adversarial and unpleasant relationship between management and workers that is rife with conflict, and that peer groups of workers often form within the firm in order to satisfy human needs unmet or threatened by the formal organization.

These peer groups often have more influence over their members than does management, and often work against management. But by treating employees fairly and with consideration, and by supporting and encouraging peer groups of workers (rather than trying to break them up, which would be the classical approach), human relations managers believe that positive

classical managerial strategy   an approach to management that assumes most employees inherently dislike work but can be induced to work in order to satisfy their economic needs

human relations managerial strategy   an approach to management that assumes most employees inherently dislike work but can be induced to work in order to satisfy their social needs

employee norms will develop. Employees will work loyally for the firm to comply with these norms and in gratitude for the satisfying social environment it provides. The human relations view of employees tends toward paternalism—the organization is like a family, in which employees are like children who need to be treated kindly but firmly by a benevolent employer who knows what is best for them and the organization.

The **high-involvement managerial strategy** (Lawler, 1992) differs from the previous two schools in its belief that if jobs are structured correctly, people can actually enjoy their work and be motivated intrinsically by it. Adherents believe that people are motivated by needs for interesting work, challenge, autonomy, growth, and development, and that people can exercise self-control if the organization provides these conditions, while treating employees fairly and equitably. As a note in passing, readers should be aware that the high-involvement managerial strategy is sometimes labelled somewhat differently by various authors. The "mutual gains enterprise" (Kochan and Osterman, 1994), the "high-performance work system" (Betcherman, McMullen, Leckie, and Caron, 1994; Appelbaum, Bailey, Berg, and Kalleberg, 2000), "open book management" (Case, 1995), and "high commitment management" (Wood, 1996) are all very similar to the "high-involvement" managerial strategy described here.

Given the disparate assumptions that each perspective holds about employees, it is not surprising that organizations will be structured very differently, depending on the managerial strategy held by the organization. Table 2.1 compares each of the three managerial strategies in terms of the six main dimensions of organization structure.

> **high-involvement managerial strategy** an approach to management that assumes that work can be intrinsically motivating if the organization is structured properly

CLASSICAL MANAGERIAL STRATEGY

Under the classical managerial strategy, there is a complete separation of the thinking and the doing. Jobs are designed narrowly, with only a few basic elements, so they can be supervised closely, and so that employees can be replaced easily if they quit or are dismissed. The specific duties and work methods for each job are planned and defined in detail by management, since employees cannot be trusted to do so effectively and responsibly on their own. Jobs are arranged in strict, hierarchical, pyramidal fashion because of the overriding need for accountability. Coordination is always handled vertically, by a common superior. Employees are organized by function; for example, all engineers are put into one department, all marketers in one department, and all production staff in one department.

The major role of the supervisor is to control and evaluate subordinates, who, it is assumed, will try to shirk and goof off if given the opportunity. Decisions are made at a relatively high level in the organization, and the main leadership role is autocratic with a high emphasis on the task. Essentially, senior management makes the decisions, middle management transmits them, and first-line management (supervisors) enforces them.

STRUCTURAL VARIABLE	CLASSICAL STRATEGY	HUMAN RELATIONS STRATEGY	HIGH-INVOLVEMENT STRATEGY
TABLE 2.1 COMPARISON OF THE THREE MANAGERIAL STRATEGIES AND THEIR STRUCTURAL IMPLICATIONS			
Job Design	Separate thinking from doing; narrow, fragmented jobs.	Similar to classical, but design may allow more social contact.	Joint planning and goal setting; broader, more meaningful jobs.
Coordination and Departmentation	Strict, formalized pyramidal hierarchy emphasizing accountability; vertical coordination (by superiors); departmentation by function.	Similar to classical; possibly use of some work teams.	Horizontal coordination (by employees) in addition to vertical coordination; use of work teams; departmentation by product, customer, project, or matrix.
Control	External—through supervision, rules, punishments, and some extrinsic rewards.	External—through use of social or peer pressure, rules, some extrinsic rewards.	Internal—through intrinsic rewards from the work itself, self-control through internalized commitment.
Communication	Formal and vertical; restricted.	Use of formal and informal (grapevine) communication; some restriction.	High amount of vertical and horizontal communication; less formal; climate of open communication.
Decision Making and Leadership	Autocratic decision making; task-oriented; controlling role.	Autocratic decision-making with minor consultation; employee-oriented; controlling role.	Participative or democratic decision style; both task- and employee-oriented; facilitator role.
Reward Systems	Extrinsic economic rewards related to individual output (e.g., piece rates, commissions) or to time worked (e.g., hourly pay).	Extrinsic economic rewards, unrelated to performance; liberal fringe benefits and loyalty rewards; social rewards.	Intrinsic rewards from job itself; pay for knowledge; extrinsic rewards focusing on group/ organization performance (e.g., gain sharing, profit sharing, stock ownership.)

Control is exercised through close supervision and the threat of punitive action should the employee deviate from organizational policies. There is often a large body of formal rules and procedures, which are strictly enforced. Frequently, control is also embedded in the technology or the work process itself, as in the case of assembly lines, which do not allow deviation from the standard procedures.

Communication is quite low, with an emphasis on a downward vertical flow, and tends to be formal. Informal communication (i.e., the "grapevine") will be discouraged, although, ironically, the grapevine will usually flourish as employees attempt to fill in all the information gaps that surround them. Generally, management will disseminate as little information as possible, in the belief that information is power. Communication upwards from employees will not generally be sought, and when sought, will likely be minimal and distorted, due to the adversarial relations.

Since management's key task is to minimize variations in employee behaviour from the specified behaviour, the reward system will be quite simple—an extrinsic (economic) reward. If feasible, a system that ties pay directly to output—such as piece rates or sales commissions—will be used. Where this is not feasible, pay will be tied directly to hours of work. In both cases, pay will be no higher than absolutely necessary to attract a sufficient flow of job applicants. Little indirect pay will be used, because it is not tied to individual performance, and management will not see much value in incurring large benefit costs in order to promote loyalty and reduce turnover. This is because classical organizations are structured to minimize the cost of turnover—with their narrow jobs, workers are easy to replace, train, and supervise.

Box 2.1 illustrates how one firm, Electronic Banking System Inc., has taken the classical strategy about as far as anyone could take it.

One exception to the general rule about poor compensation in classical organizations may occur in unionized classical firms. Because of the low consideration for worker needs in most classical firms and their adversarial worker–management relations, workers in these organizations often become unionized in an attempt to protect their interests. These unions are often able to win substantially higher compensation packages than management would wish to provide, often including extensive benefits packages. This often causes non-union classical firms to provide more compensation than they would wish, in order to attract employees, and as a union-avoidance tactic. An irony is that these classical firms may end up paying very well indeed, which is precisely the opposite of the compensation strategy they would prefer!

HUMAN RELATIONS MANAGERIAL STRATEGY

The human relations approach is similar to the classical approach in terms of job design, although an attempt may be made to arrange jobs in such a way as to allow social interaction among employees. It is also similar to the classical school in how it coordinates employees. But the supervisor's role is much more

BOX 2.1 Control Is an Art Form at EBS

Because they don't believe that employees can be trusted to put in an honest day's work on their own volition, classical organizations often go to great lengths to structure themselves to constrain workers from doing anything except the desired behaviour. Ron Edens, president of Electronic Banking System Inc. (EBS) of Hagerstown, Maryland, has refined "control" to an art form.

EBS offers a type of financial service known as "lockbox processing." Other firms contract with EBS to process, record, and deposit incoming payments and donations. For example, EBS processes donations for organizations such as Mothers Against Drunk Driving, Greenpeace, and the National Association for Women.

Inside the plain brick building that houses the company, long lines of women sit at spartan desks, each performing a small fragment of the total work process. Some women open envelopes and sort their contents, others compute figures, and still others key information into the computer. Strict quotas are maintained. Workers who open envelopes must process three envelopes a minute, and data entry workers must key at least 8500 strokes an hour.

The work is deliberately structured to avoid the use of any high-level skills. "We don't ask these people to think—the machines think for them," Mr. Edens says. "They don't have to make any decisions." At the end of each day the computer produces a printout of the productivity and error rate for every woman, which management uses to weed out workers who don't meet quota.

The work floor itself resembles an enormous classroom in the throes of exam period. Desks point toward the front, where a manager keeps watch from a raised platform that workers call "the pedestal" or "the birdhouse." Other supervisors are positioned toward the back of the room. "If you want to watch someone," Mr. Edens explains, "it's easier from behind because they don't know you're watching." The room is silent. Talking is forbidden. The windows are covered. "I'm not paying people to chat. I'm paying them to open envelopes," he says. Of the blocked windows, Mr. Edens adds: "I don't want them looking out—it's distracting. They'll make mistakes."

In his office upstairs, Mr. Edens sits before a TV monitor that flashes images from eight cameras posted through the plant. "There's a little bit of Sneaky Pete to it," he says, using a remote control to zoom in on a document atop a worker's desk. "I can basically read that and figure out how someone's day is going." At EBS, workers handle thousands of dollars in cheques and cash, and Mr. Edens says cameras help deter would-be thieves (Horwitz, 1994: A8).

The company does not believe in fancy pay innovations. Pay for clerical staff is based on an hourly rate starting at the minimum wage and ranging no more than a couple of dollars above it. Minimal benefits are provided. Turnover is high. But that is not a major problem since it takes little time to recruit and train a new worker. EBS runs smoothly, like a well-oiled machine, and business is booming. All in all, Mr. Edens has reason to be pleased with how his organization works.

---

complicated than in the classical school. Leadership is still autocratic in the sense that senior management makes all the important decisions, but there is a much greater attempt to "sell" the decisions, which the classical manager does not bother with.

Human relations managers understand that people like to feel they have some control over their work lives, and so attempt to provide a *feeling* that employees have some influence over company decisions (although employees typically have little *real* influence). Therefore, employees are sometimes asked for their opinions on decisions, or are permitted to make a number of minor, inconsequential decisions. In addition to attempting to sell decisions, the supervisor also has the added task of exhibiting a high concern for people and fostering a pleasant atmosphere. Overall, the role of the leader is controlling, but employee-oriented.

Under the human relations school of thought, control is still external but is preferably exercised mainly through the work group. The human relations organization devotes a considerable effort toward developing loyal employees who are dedicated to the norms of the organization. It is expected that pressure from the work group will cause individual members to conform to the expectations of the organization. If this fails, the supervisor is then expected to step in. However, punishments will not be extensively used, for fear they will disrupt the social harmony that management is trying to create.

Communication within informal work groups is encouraged, and management will likely recognize and attempt to utilize the grapevine. A considerable effort will be made to facilitate social communication (such as when an employee marries or has a baby). However, work-related communication flows downward and upward will not be high, and management will still try to restrict what it considers to be important information. Use may be made of suggestion systems and newsletters.

Under the human relations strategy, rewards are mainly extrinsic and focus on rewarding loyalty to the organization. Salaries (rather than hourly pay) are often used to foster a feeling of permanence on the part of employees. Seniority increases will likely be provided, to encourage workforce stability. Liberal employee benefits may be provided, again to develop employee loyalty. A number of noneconomic rewards may also be provided, such as five-year pins and employee-of-the-month citations, to show the interest of the organization in its employees. Management will expect employees to find the positive social environment in these firms rewarding.

One firm that is famous for its use of the human relations strategy is Kodak, as described in Box 2.2, although the firm has in recent years been attempting to move to a more high-involvement strategy.

HIGH-INVOLVEMENT MANAGERIAL STRATEGY

Job design under the high-involvement model is very different from the previous two management schools. Here, a major effort is made to design jobs that are both interesting and challenging and that provide workers with considerable autonomy over the planning and execution of the work activity as well as job-based feedback on how well they are performing. Therefore, jobs are broader, involve more elements, and attempt to include a meaningful cycle of work activity. Joint employee–management planning and goal setting are often utilized. In contrast to the classical approach, a conscious effort is made to *combine* the thinking and the doing.

Coordination is horizontal as well as vertical. In fact, horizontal coordination, where workers coordinate directly with one another in task completion, is preferred to vertical coordination. Jobs are often arranged in clusters, in

BOX 2.2 Does Human Relations Still Work for Kodak?

Eastman Kodak, the huge photographic products firm, is renowned for the fierce loyalty it generates among its employees. This didn't happen by accident. Historically, Kodak's management practices have included rigid adherence to a "promote-from-within" policy, an excellent compensation package, with large profit-sharing bonuses, and a "no layoff" policy to maintain employment security (Jacoby, 1997). Its benefits package is truly remarkable, including everything from an excellent pension plan, to generous sick leave entitlements (employees receive full pay for the first 52 weeks of sick leave), and even free noon-time movies. As a result, Kodak has attracted top-notch employees.

Although most companies in its industry are unionized, there has never been any interest in unionization among Kodak employees, and the company is non-union to this day. The company has many long-term employees who are committed to the traditional "Kodak way" of doing things, which has proved to be successful for so many years. "One classic illustration of this love of tradition was the case of a supervisor who had recently retired. He had kept employment records from the 1930s in his office drawer 'because they had always been there' " (Robbins, 1990: 514).

Management style at Kodak could best be described as patient and paternalistic, with an extensive system of written rules, policies, and procedures. Decisions percolated to the top for even minor issues. The head of photographic and information products, for instance, could be called on to make a decision on any one of 50 000 products (Robbins, 1990: 514–15).

Although the company had many years of success with this human relations managerial strategy, coming to dominate the world market for many photographic products, it started to encounter problems in the 1980s, resulting in financial difficulties by the end of the decade. Profit-sharing bonuses shrank to nothing, and the company was forced to sell divisions, close plants, and lay off thousands of employees, the first such layoffs in the company's history. What happened?

Several things. New competitors, such as Fuji, entered the film market, long a high-margin market dominated by Kodak. Technological change in the photographic business increased dramatically, and Kodak couldn't seem to keep up, despite spending billions on research and development. Kodak did not believe that 35 mm cameras or video cameras would amount to much, and delayed entry into these fields until they were dominated by others. When Kodak did introduce new products, such as the disc camera and a CD system to view snapshots on a television screen, they flopped.

In late 1993, Kodak brought in a new CEO, George Fisher, who had previously been head of Motorola (a highly innovative and effective producer of communications technology), to try to get the company back on track. Shortly after his arrival, he attempted to move toward a high-involvement managerial strategy in those areas of the business that depend on innovation (Maremont, 1995). However, Kodak's problems continued, resulting in layoffs in 1998 that reduced the company's workforce from 100 000 to about 84 000 employees; continuing reductions decreased total employment to 80 000 by mid-2000. While this did improve the company's bottom line, it didn't seem to make the firm any more flexible or innovative. This has prompted some commentators to argue that Kodak should give up on innovation entirely, and hive off the innovative portions of its business—such as digital imaging—into a separate business not under the control of Kodak management (Coy, 2000).

which a group of employees has the responsibility for coordinating the completion of a set of tasks among themselves. These clusters, or teams, often consist of people from various specialties mingled together. Departmentation is based on the product, customer, or project, not functional groupings.

Under high involvement, the role of the supervisor is very different from that in the other two schools. Rather than being seen primarily as a controller and evaluator, the supervisor is seen as a facilitator. It is his or her job to remove barriers to effective performance and to provide adequate resources and other assistance to enable subordinates to perform effectively. Since employees are assumed to be able to exercise self-control and to be self-motivated, the supervisor does not need to perform a control function. Because employees are assumed to be self-motivated and competent, decisions can be made at the lowest possible level in the organization. The overall leadership style will be participative or democratic in nature.

Control is internal (within the individual). Employees are expected to exercise self-control, because of their identification with the goals of the organization and the intrinsic rewards flowing from the work itself, and because they have sufficient training and knowledge to behave responsibly. Because of this internalized commitment, little supervision is necessary, and formalized rules and regulations can be kept to a minimum.

Full disclosure of information is essential, since decisions are being made at all levels throughout the organization. Without adequate information, poor decisions will be made. The firm recognizes this, so communication is a major focus of management attention. Great effort is made for communication to flow vertically (both up and down the organization), horizontally, and diagonally.

Under high involvement, a wide variety of both intrinsic and extrinsic rewards will be utilized. Employees will be expected to receive substantial intrinsic rewards directly from performing their jobs and from their involvement in decision making within the organization. Extrinsic rewards are geared toward fostering good performance, rather than control of substandard output, and tend to focus on the work unit, not the individual, since tasks are usually complex and require teamwork to accomplish them.

Base pay tends to be salary, augmented by profit- and gain-sharing plans of various types, as well as employee stock ownership. Pay will often be person-based (i.e., pay for knowledge) rather than job-based, in order to promote skills acquisition and flexibility within the organization. Because of the complex behaviour and high performance levels required in high-involvement organizations, their reward and compensation systems are usually more complex than those in firms utilizing the other two managerial strategies.

Box 2.3 illustrates how one high-involvement firm, Gennum Corporation, puts all these dimensions together.

INTERRELATIONSHIPS AMONG STRUCTURAL VARIABLES

It should now be apparent that there are strong interrelationships among the structural variables. Some elements are *complementary* and must occur together for any of them to be effective. For example, pushing decision making down to lower-level employees in the organization is dangerous without providing them with adequate information on which to make informed decisions, a knowledge base to understand this information, and a reward system that

BOX 2.3 High Involvement at Gennum Corporation

Based in Burlington, Ontario, Gennum Corporation designs and produces miniature integrated circuits used in a variety of special applications. For example, a large proportion of the hearing aids produced worldwide incorporate Gennum circuits. The firm has about 450 employees, a large proportion of them professionals and highly skilled technicians. Because of rapidly evolving technologies, the company is continually working at the frontiers of knowledge.

When established in 1973, the firm's founders believed that three characteristics would be key to their success: an atmosphere of innovation and challenge, a commitment to egalitarianism, and the participation of all employees in the company's financial success. Their managerial philosophy is illustrated by this quote from founder Doug Barber:

> The company really is its people ... It is clear that we need not just the hands and bodies, but the minds and ideas of everyone. We believe in teamwork and interdependence. It is important that everyone feels they are playing a significant role, and that they personally have opportunities to develop. We like to challenge people to take on new responsibility to develop them to their fullest potential. (Innes, Lyon, and Harris, 1991: 58–59)

Sounds good, but how does the company actually achieve all this? Essentially, by applying virtually every element of the high-involvement model. Jobs are broad. The company has few supervisors, and their role is employee support, not control. Employees are expected to speak up if they believe they have a better way of doing something than management. In the words of one employee: "In some places they say 'Do it this way,' even if you don't believe it's going to work. Here, you have a free hand." As Barber put it during a 1997 interview: "When you have a lot of skilled people in the company, to think that one or two or three people should tell them what to do is crazy."

At many firms, employees are told that they can exercise initiative and try new things, but woe to them if they fail! So most employees just play it safe. But not at Gennum. As one employee puts it, if employees think they see a better way to do something, "you suggest it. Fine. It's your idea. Do it. If it doesn't work, that's fine. If you try something and it doesn't work, it's not held against you."

According to John Griffiths, former manager of human resources, "We try to cloud over the lines of authority. We don't want people to be inhibited about speaking up because they're low on the totem pole." Employee knowledge about the total business and communication is crucial. According to president Barber: "We deliberately try to keep employees mixing. We encourage interdisciplinary team problem solving. We also have a fairly active social committee."

So what kind of reward and compensation system do you think would best fit this organization? In fact, consistent with theory, the firm utilizes a complex mix of intrinsic and extrinsic rewards. Intrinsic rewards stem from the broad nature of the tasks and the freedom employees are given in performing them, as well as the high degree of learning and development the company fosters.

Extrinsic rewards include a policy of job security for all employees who are competent performers, and opportunities for social interaction and career development.

All three components of compensation are used. All employees, including production workers, are on salary, rather than hourly pay. The company uses market surveys to set base pay at the midpoint of competitive salaries each year.

There are four elements of performance pay. All employees, regardless of job category, are eligible. First, everyone with at least six months' seniority is eligible for the profit-sharing plan, which pays 6 percent of pre-tax profits into a deferred profit-sharing trust. This trust invests in one of three types of investment funds, at the option of the employee. The total profit-sharing funds available are allocated 60 percent according to salary, and 40 percent equally to all employees. (This is in contrast to

BOX 2.3 Continued

many profit-sharing plans, where all of the profit-sharing bonus is allocated by salary level.)

A second element of performance pay is the firm's incentive compensation plan. If return on net assets exceeds 5 percent, then an additional amount is allocated to every employee for each percentage point above that level. (In recent years, return on net assets has been exceeding 20 percent.) This money is allocated according to salary. Those employees earning above the median salary in the company are required to take a portion of this bonus in company stock, which is vested to them over a four- to five-year period. This incentive is intended to reward the efficient use of company assets, and to maintain a four- to five-year perspective on company performance.

The third element is an employee stock plan. Employees are permitted to utilize up to 5 percent of their earnings to purchase company stock (traded on the Toronto Stock Exchange); the company provides another share of stock for every two that the employee purchases. Most employees take full advantage of this offer, and virtually all employees own company stock.

Fourth, there is a merit pay plan under which top performers can receive annual salary increases that exceed market increases.

For indirect pay, the company provides a benefits package that matches its competitors (with the exception of a pension plan), on a cost-shared basis, in which the employees pick up half the costs of each benefit. Every employee (including top management) receives equal benefits. Because it has no pension plan, the company relies on the deferred profit-sharing plan to help employees generate retirement savings. Payments from the incentive compensation plan can also be placed directly into a registered retirement savings plan. To help employees plan their retirement funds, the company brings in financial advisers every year, at no cost to employees.

---

creates a strong sense of identity with the company. Creating knowledgeable, well-informed employees, with a financial stake in the firm's performance, and then not allowing them input in decision making is a recipe for producing frustrated employees.

Research has also shown that some structural elements can serve as *substitutes* for others. For example, a Canadian study (Long, 1994) has shown that profit-sharing and gain-sharing systems can serve as a substitute for managerial control. This study found that firms that had profit- or gain-sharing systems (or preferably both) were able to operate with 31 percent fewer managers and supervisors, and significantly fewer rules and regulations than firms without these systems. These firms are apparently substituting internal (self-) control for external control, as Gennum Corporation has apparently done. On the other hand, Electronic Banking System, which makes no attempt whatsoever to generate self-control, must depend heavily on external management control.

All of this suggests that organizations that consistently adopt a single managerial strategy, no matter what that managerial strategy is, will usually be more effective than those that have an inconsistent mix of structural elements. MacDuffie (1995) refers to these internally consistent practices as "human resource bundles" and presents evidence that firms that utilize these "bundles" perform better than those that do not.

Indeed, it should be noted that even within a given managerial strategy, there are different combinations of human resource policies that are possible. For example, a firm may choose to hire only experienced workers, or it may hire inexperienced workers and train them. Hiring experienced workers will usually cost more in compensation, but hiring inexperienced workers will cost more in training costs, and there is the risk of losing them once they are trained.

But different managerial perspectives will have different preferences. Because of the high turnover that typifies classical organizations, they would prefer not to incur high training costs. So their tendency is to hire experienced, trained workers, where jobs require this. (Their preferred course of action, of course, is to fragment tasks into small pieces, so little training is necessary.)

Other human resource policies will also tend to fit with the managerial strategy. Because they need workers with high potential for growth and who are capable of self-control and motivated by higher-order needs, high-involvement organizations will have the most comprehensive selection processes. In contrast, because their demands are simple task performance, classical organizations will have the least sophisticated procedures. Human relations organizations will fall in between because they want to screen out people who would disrupt the social environment of the firm.

Before we leave organization structure, there is one other concept that is relevant—organizational culture. "**Organizational culture** is the set of values, guiding beliefs, understandings, and ways of thinking that are shared by members of an organization" (Daft, 2001: 314). Organizational culture can be thought of as the informal structure of the organization; a strong culture can play a major role in shaping and directing behaviour within the organization.

Culture can supplement the formal structure of the organization, or it can substitute for it. For example, because of their need to stay flexible, high-involvement organizations like to use as little formal structure as possible, so a strong organizational culture is important to them. Classical firms, on the other hand, prefer to depend on the formal structure, so they focus very little on organizational culture. Human relations firms will use both formal structure and culture to shape behaviour.

A given culture may be beneficial to one organization, but detrimental to another, depending on whether it fits with the managerial strategy. A culture can also be just plain detrimental. For example, many classical organizations develop a strong anti-management culture, which may include norms such as "never cooperate with management," "never go beyond your minimum work requirements," and "ignore the rules when the supervisor is gone." In human relations firms, a culture of avoiding conflict, never criticizing the company or a fellow employee, valuing tradition, and doing things the way they have always been done tends to develop. Remember the Kodak employee who kept 50-year-old employment records in his desk drawer because they "had always

organizational culture
the set of core values and understandings shared by members of an organization

been there"? Key cultural values in high-involvement organizations include honesty, trustworthiness, open communication, and acceptance of risk taking, as Gennum tries to foster.

How does an organization shape culture? By its actions. For example, a firm that says it values initiative and risk-taking, but punishes every initiative that fails, is teaching employees not to exercise any initiative. The reward system is critical in shaping culture. A firm that says it values cooperation and teamwork but then promotes a group member who can't get along with anybody is signalling a very different message. If a company's top management is fond of talking about how "we are all partners in this enterprise," but lays off employees at the first sign of trouble and doesn't share the gains when the firm is successful, employees may not feel much like "partners."

Both human relations and high-involvement organizations typically spend considerable effort developing their cultures, but culture is the most important to high-involvement organizations because they depend on it to substitute for the formal structure. It is no accident that organizational culture, as a concept, came into prominence with the rise of high-involvement organizations.

DETERMINANTS OF THE MOST APPROPRIATE MANAGERIAL STRATEGY

If the most appropriate reward system is determined by the managerial strategy, then it is important to understand the factors that determine the most appropriate managerial strategy, since these factors will ultimately decide the type of reward system the organization should implement. Of course, the answer to this lies in the five key contextual variables that were identified in Figure 2.2—the environment, corporate strategy, technology, size of the organization, and nature of the workforce. But simply knowing the names of these variables is not very useful if we do not know how each relates to managerial strategy.

The purpose of this section is first to show how each of these contextual variables can be categorized into types, and then to show how each type relates to managerial strategy. By the end of this section, a template will be provided that readers can use as a tool to identify the most appropriate managerial strategy (and hence, reward strategy) for any given organization. Of course, just because the contextual variables point to a particular managerial strategy for a given organization doesn't necessarily mean that the organization has actually adopted that managerial strategy. Indeed, some firms really have no distinct managerial strategy (Hodson, 2001). But if they don't, company performance will be lower than it should be, and company survival could even be threatened, if their competitors have adopted the most appropriate managerial strategy. Of course, at any point in time, organizations may be in transition from one managerial strategy to another, which could be very appropriate if this change is driven by the need to respond to changes in the contextual variables.

ENVIRONMENT

Of the five contextual variables, the most important is the environment that faces a given firm. Is it stable or dynamic? Is it simple or complex? A dynamic environment exists where product or service life cycles are short, where product or service demand is volatile, where customer needs change quickly and unpredictably, where technologies are changing rapidly, where new competitors frequently enter the field, and where the regulatory environment is unpredictable. Firms generally have little control over the degree of *stability* in the task environment. Because of their rigidity, classical and human relations firms have great difficulty operating successfully in dynamic, unstable environments.

Firms do, however, have some degree of control over the complexity of their task environments. For example, a firm that chooses to operate in a number of unrelated product/service domains creates a more complex environment for itself than a firm that operates in only one product/service domain. Thus, the complexity of a firm's environment depends in part on how broadly it defines its domain(s). But certain domains (e.g., designing microcircuits) are inherently more complex than others (e.g., processing chickens).

However, even if a task environment is complex, as long as it is stable, a classical or human relations approach can be effective. If the complexity is due to operating in many domains, either a classical or human relations approach should work, but if the complexity is due to the domain itself, then a human relations approach may work best. This is because complex domains often require a high level of expertise on the part of employees, and the high turnover that typifies a classical organization will be very costly in these circumstances.

But when its task environments are dynamic, then complexity compounds the uncertainty facing the organization. Under these circumstances, where quick adaptation to environmental changes is crucial, neither classical nor human relations organizations are able to cope effectively, as Kodak seems to have found. In general, the high-involvement approach will be needed whenever environments are highly unstable or dynamic, and will be even more essential when the environment is also complex.

CORPORATE STRATEGY

Although there are a number of ways to classify the type of corporate strategy that may be adopted by a firm, one useful categorization was developed by

Miles and Snow (1978). They suggest that company strategies can be divided into three main types (defender, prospector, or analyzer), with a residual type (the reactor) to cover firms that do not practise any distinct overall strategy.

The **defender strategy** entails taking a fairly narrow product or service segment and excelling in it, based on a combination of product quality and price. A defender firm may not always be the low-cost leader, but it will always try to provide the best possible quality/price tradeoff, so that its products offer the best value to customers. The byword for this strategy is *consistency*. The key need is to identify the most efficient process for providing the product or service and then to lock it in. For defenders, the classical or human relations approaches are most suitable. In general, classical works well for manufacturing, and human relations for service enterprises, where there is extensive contact with customers.

The **prospector strategy** is the complete opposite of the defender, and focuses on identifying new product and market opportunities and being the first to exploit them. However, prospectors will tend to move on to other new products or services as competitors enter the market. These competitors can copy the product and mass produce it at a lower cost than the prospector can because the competitors do not have to include development costs or costs of failed products in their pricing structures. The byword for the prospector strategy is *speed*. The key need is to have a process for identifying new opportunities quickly and an organization flexible and dynamic enough to get them to market before anybody else. Clearly, a high-involvement approach is essential.

The **analyzer strategy** is the most complex of the three corporate strategies, because it attempts to combine both the prospector and defender strategies. This strategy entails being able to both identify and exploit new product or service opportunities at a relatively early stage—not long after the prospectors—while also maintaining a firm base of traditional products or services. The byword for the analyzer strategy is *balance*. The key need is to be able to balance stability and flexibility. This often requires a hybrid or dual organization structure: one that promotes speed and flexibility for new product development and one that promotes stability and consistency for the established products. Typically, analyzer firms are not first with new products or services, but they do enter these markets early, after the prospectors have identified them. They are also likely not as efficient in production as a defender, but will have their products on the market long before the defenders in the industry get around to doing so.

Analyzers will likely operate best with something close to a high-involvement approach for new product development and a classical approach for the traditional products. But it is very difficult to practise two so divergent managerial strategies in the same firm, so analyzers often seem to end up practising a compromise human relations strategy across the board. This can be successful as long as the environment is not too dynamic.

defender corporate strategy focuses on domination within a narrow product or service market segment

prospector corporate strategy focuses on identifying and exploiting new opportunities quickly

analyzer corporate strategy attempts to exploit new opportunities at an early stage while maintaining a base of traditional products or services

TECHNOLOGY

The organization's technology can be classified in a variety of ways. One way of doing so is according to the type of production process. Thompson (1967) suggests three main types: long-linked, mediating, and intensive. A **long-linked technology** divides the total task into many tiny steps performed in a sequential fashion, with each step performed by a different employee, such as an automobile assembly line. This is the technology used at Electronic Banking System and the B.C. Rogers chicken-processing plant.

A **mediating technology** uses standardized transactions to connect two parties who wish to have some kind of mutually beneficial relationship. Banks connect people who want to lend money with people who want to borrow it. Transportation companies connect people who have an item with people who want that item. Retailers connect manufacturers of a product with people who wish to purchase the product. Real estate agents connect people who want to sell houses with people who want to buy houses.

An **intensive technology** requires that each item or case be dealt with individually. Examples of organizations with intensive technologies would include general hospitals, custom home builders, tailors who produce made-to-order suits, auto repair shops, legal firms specializing in criminal law, and consulting firms.

Clearly, an intensive technology requires a high-involvement structure, while a long-linked technology would suit a classical structure. Because most mediating technologies involve considerable contact with people (in contrast to manufacturing, where the main interaction is with objects, such as dishwashers or vacuum cleaners), the human relations strategy is usually the most appropriate for them.

Another approach to classifying technology concerns the degree to which it is routine or nonroutine (Perrow, 1967). There are two aspects in determining this: how many exceptions or different types of problems are involved in a particular task, and whether there is a standardized process for dealing with these exceptions. A **routine technology** is defined as a technology in which there are relatively few exceptions to the standard work processes, and when these exceptions do occur, a standardized process for solving these problems is in place. Examples would include a plant that manufactures washing machines, or an electrical utility.

A **nonroutine technology**, on the other hand, has many exceptions inherent in the work, and there is no standardized way to deal with these exceptions. Examples would be consulting firms, aerospace engineering firms, and pharmaceutical firms attempting to discover new drugs. In these firms, the key need is the production not so much of goods or services but of new ideas. Gennum Corporation would be classified as using a nonroutine technology since its lifeblood is the production of new ideas and innovations in micro-circuitry.

Between routine and nonroutine are two other types, the craft technology and the engineering technology. The **craft technology** has relatively few excep-

---

long-linked technology divides the total task of producing a product or service into a series of small sequential steps performed by different employees

mediating technology uses standardized transactions to connect parties wishing a mutually beneficial relationship

intensive technology requires that each item or case be dealt with individually, depending on the specific nature of each case

routine technology few exceptions occur during the production process, and those exceptions that do occur can be dealt with in a standardized way

nonroutine technology many exceptions inherent in the production process and no standardized way to deal with these exceptions

craft technology few exceptions in the production process, but no standardized way to deal with them

tions, but there is no standardized way to solve these exceptions when they occur—solutions depend on the judgment and intuition of the worker. Specialty glass-blowing is one example. Comedians, such as Jerry Seinfeld, would be another example. You can buy one of his books, with all of his joke material in it, but would anybody be willing to pay you over $30 000 000 a year to tell them?

The **engineering technology** has many exceptions, but there is a standardized way for dealing with them. Examples would include an accounting firm, in which every client is different but there are standardized ways to generate the necessary financial reports (e.g., GAAP—generally accepted accounting principles), or an engineering firm that designs bridges, each of which is different but there is a standardized way for designing them.

Clearly, a firm that utilizes a nonroutine technology requires a high-involvement managerial strategy, while a firm that uses a routine technology can use a classical or human relations approach. Firms with craft or engineering technologies generally depend on the judgment of relatively skilled employees, who would prefer autonomy in performing their job duties. It may not be essential to have a full high-involvement structure for the engineering technology, but a strict classical structure would tend to alienate these employees. For the craft technology, something close to a high-involvement approach is probably necessary, since the organization depends on the intuitive judgment of its employees.

Finally, one other typology can provide some useful insights. Woodward (1965) suggests that manufacturing technologies can be divided into three main types: unit/small batch, mass/large batch, and process. A **unit/small batch technology** produces one-of-a-kind items, or small batches of them, and is analogous to the intensive technology. A **mass/large batch technology** produces large amounts of a single item in a standardized way, and is analogous to the long-linked technology. The **process technology** produces the product in a continuous flow, such as an oil refinery, chemical plant, or electrical power plant, and has no equivalent in the typologies already discussed. It is different from the long-linked technology because of the continuous product flow, which usually makes these firms highly capital-intensive, and workers are focused on monitoring and maintaining this flow. The key task of these workers is to either prevent or respond effectively to problem situations when they arise. Therefore it is important that these employees be both highly knowledgeable and highly diligent and committed in their work, which requires at least a human relations structure, and possibly a high-involvement structure, as in the case of L-S Electrogalvanizing.

ORGANIZATION SIZE

Because of the need to coordinate and control large numbers of people, large organizations generally tend to utilize classical or human relations strategies, although these strategies can be found in organizations of all sizes. In general, it is easier to implement high involvement in a small- to medium-sized organization because the larger the organization, the greater the need for some formal structure. However, some large organizations have resolved this problem by segmenting their organization into a series of relatively small units, and practising high involvement in these. Hewlett-Packard, the computer products firm, utilizes this approach.

Size also affects structure in at least one other way. As organizations get larger, the impact of technology on their structure lessens. Indeed, some large organizations may utilize a number of different technologies. This may call for different managerial strategies in different parts of the organization, which can be a very difficult thing to manage, since top management will tend to prefer one particular managerial strategy (the one consistent with their assumptions about people).

THE NATURE OF THE WORKFORCE

The nature of the people employed by the organization—their skills, educational characteristics, and expectations—will also have a major impact on the managerial strategy that should be adopted. In general, highly skilled, well-educated, or professional employees will be more suited to the high-involvement school. Indeed, a high-involvement strategy requires these characteristics because of the broad jobs and decision-making responsibility expected of employees.

On the other hand, classical organizations are specifically designed to utilize employees with relatively low skills and, because of their motivation and control approach, are most suited to workers who badly need the money the job provides. Their motivational approaches work best in poor economic circumstances and in areas with a high level of unemployment and a low standard of living. (This helps to explain why many classical firms move their production operations to third world countries, where living conditions make their managerial strategy effective.) Because of their structure, human relations organizations can tolerate relatively low-skill workers but do not need to depend on poor economic circumstances for their motivational policies, since they offer both economic and social rewards.

TYING IT ALL TOGETHER

From the discussion in this section, it can be seen that the contextual variables must align not only with managerial strategy but with each other as well. For example, using a long-linked technology or a defender strategy in an unstable environment is courting disaster, because the organization may not be able to respond to change quickly enough. Compatible combinations would be those that are consistent with a given managerial strategy. Thus, a defender strategy, stable environment, long-linked technology, relatively low-skilled workforce, and large organization would be a good combination and well suited for the classical managerial strategy. Table 2.2 has been developed to help understand these combinations and to provide a template for selecting the most appropriate managerial strategy for a given organization to adopt. (Where the contextual variables are out of alignment with each other, it means that there will be no ideal managerial strategy and no ideal reward strategy.)

Table 2.2 helps solve the mystery of why some firms do quite nicely without adopting fancy new pay innovations, and why compensation systems that work well for some firms would be totally inadequate in others. Let's use this template to revisit some of the organizations we met earlier in the chapter. Let's start with B.C. Rogers chicken processors. But before doing so, you need a little more background on chicken processing, which Box 2.4 provides.

After reading Box 2.4, you probably know more about chicken processing than you really wanted to know! Let's compare B.C. Rogers Processors with the characteristics in the template. Rogers has a stable, simple environment, uses a defender strategy (where low-cost production is crucial), a long-linked technology, requires low-skilled employees, and is located in a region where economic conditions are generally poor. Perfect for a classical structure!

TABLE 2.2 TEMPLATE FOR SELECTING THE MOST APPROPRIATE MANAGERIAL STRATEGY FOR AN ORGANIZATION TO ADOPT

CONTEXTUAL VARIABLE	CLASSICAL	HUMAN RELATIONS	HIGH-INVOLVEMENT
Environment			
• Stability	Stable	Stable	Unstable
• Complexity	Simple	Simple or Complex	Complex
Corporate Strategy			
• Competitive Strategy	Defender	Analyzer	Prospector
Technology			
• Thompson's Typology	Long-linked	Mediating	Intensive
• Perrow's Typology	Routine	Routine or Engineering	Craft or Nonroutine
• Woodward's Typology	Mass	Process	Process or Unit
• Product Transformed	Things	People	Ideas
Size			
• Number of Employees	Any Size	Any Size	Small/Medium
Workforce			
• Skills/Education	Low	Moderate	High
• Economic Circumstances	Poor	Moderate	Good

BOX 2.4 Anyone for Chicken Fingers?

If chickens don't have fingers, then where do chicken fingers come from? One story is that a marketer was trying to come up with a name for the company's new chicken product when there was an accident on the processing line. An employee had two fingers lopped off, which fell into the boxes of chicken parts. As workers shouted "get the fingers from the chicken," inspiration struck the marketer! But whether or not this story is really true, safety on a chicken-processing line is no joking matter, and accident rates are high in this line of work.

The demand for poultry has been growing by leaps and bounds in North America. Because turnover is high—often exceeding 100 percent a year—poultry companies are hiring constantly, and they don't waste time being choosy about whom they hire. Writing an article on the poultry industry, Tony Horwitz, a reporter with the *Wall Street Journal*, decided to see for himself what work was like in a chicken-processing plant.

At a B.C. Rogers Processors Inc. plant in Morton, Miss., the first this reporter visited in search of work, the plant manager, Jerry Duty, barely glanced at an application that listed my university education and Dow Jones & Co. (publisher of this newspaper) as my employer. "It's tough work and will make you sore as hell," he said, offering a job starting the next day at $5.10 an hour. "But it won't kill you—only the chickens."

On the factory floor—a noisy, wet expanse of chutes and belts loosely linked by the ubiquitous chain—a supervisor pointed me to a space along a conveyor belt where workers frantically weighed chicken parts and crammed them into cardboard boxes. "Show him the ropes," he shouted at no one in particular, and no one ever did.

Each job carries its own hazards and hardships. By common acclaim, the toughest is held by "live hangers," who hitch incoming birds to shackles at a rate of 25 or more a minute. So strenuous that only a few can do it, live-hanging exposes workers to struggling birds that scratch, peck and defecate all over them. Some hangers spend breaks in the bathroom, coughing up feathers and dust.

After the birds have been stunned with electric current, slaughtered and plucked—largely by machine—they are re-hung, dangling headless and upside-down for their journey through the plant. At one station, a worker who calls herself a "butthole cutter" slits open the bird so a "gut-puller" can reach in and yank out the animal's innards. Others lop off limbs, pull skin or separate organs.

Packed tightly and working quickly with knives and scissors, workers often cut themselves and others. At break times I would find fat globules and blood speckling my glasses, bits of chicken caught in my collar, water and slime soaking my feet and ankles and nicks covering my wrists.

While foremen circulate, joining in the work or urging employees to speed up, the labour is effectively self-supervising. As in many factories, the conveyor belt sets the pace and anyone who flags creates more work for those farther down the line. So workers tend to vent their fatigue and frustration on each other, shouting at colleagues to do a better job. "Someone's putting thighs in the leg boxes!" rang the refrain of a self-appointed coxswain near me. "And I'm going to kick some butt if people don't close those boxes tight!" (Horwitz, 1994: A8)

Although turnover is high, *it doesn't matter*, because employees are so easy to replace and train. Employee commitment is not needed because control is easy, with the technology itself ("the chain") providing most of the necessary control. Given this, the sole purpose of the compensation system is to assure a sufficient flow of applicants that the chain is always staffed and to do this at the lowest possible cost.

Let's take a closer look at L-S Electrogalvanizing, which pays top wages to its employees. Because of overcapacity in their industry and stagnant demand for their products, the environment can be considered quite unstable, although relatively simple, since LSE specializes in a narrow range of products. The firm uses a defender strategy, with a focus on high-quality products. Process technology is in use. The plant is relatively small, with only about a hundred production workers. Because of the complexity of the production process, the skill levels required by workers are high. The cost of errors is potentially high, as is the cost of downtime due to equipment failures and other problems. Economic conditions in Cleveland, where the plant is located, are moderately good, supported by the presence of many high-paying industrial jobs.

As can be seen, this case is not as clear-cut as the chicken plant, with various contextual variables pointing toward different managerial strategies. Indeed, examples of each of the three managerial strategies can be found in this industry, although the classical approach predominates. LSE has obviously chosen a high-involvement strategy. Worker tasks and responsibilities are broad. There are few supervisors in the plant, and each shift crew operates as a team to handle whatever needs to be done to maintain production and quality. Each team is delegated a lot of decision-making power in how to run the plant. To do this, employees need to be knowledgeable, informed, and committed to the goals of the organization. They must be flexible enough to work together to prevent and cope with production problems. This means they must have broad knowledge of the entire production process, rather than just a tiny part of it.

Clearly, the pay-for-knowledge system, gain and profit sharing, and high indirect pay amount to a compensation strategy that supports the high-involvement managerial strategy. But how can LSE get a payback from this very expensive compensation strategy? In several ways. First, because of employee flexibility, the plant has eliminated the specialized maintenance personnel that most plants need to have on hand in case of a breakdown.

Second, because of delegation of decision making and self-control, fewer supervisors are needed. In addition, LSE operates its plant with fewer workers than comparable plants using conventional management practices. Third, turnover is low, which reduces recruiting and training costs. Fourth, and probably most important, the presence of multiskilled personnel reduces plant downtime and improves product quality. When the system does go down, everybody can play a role in getting the plant up and running again in a minimum period of time. In this business, plant downtime is the single biggest driver of cost, followed by production of an unusable coil, each of which may be valued at $25 000 or more.

Once all of this is factored in, guess what happens? You guessed it! The LSE plant actually turns out to be *more* profitable than its lower-paying competitors.

Remember Mr. Edens and his firm, Electronic Banking System, from Box 2.1? Let's use the strategic template to classify EBS. We have a firm that uses low-skill labour and a routine, even long-linked, technology. The firm deals with things, not people, and certainly not ideas. The environment is simple and, because of increasing demand, relatively stable. The firm uses a defender strategy to compete on the basis of low-cost production.

From this information, we would predict that Mr. Edens could use a classical managerial strategy very successfully, which, of course, he does. Given this, his pay system is a perfect fit with the circumstances his firm faces. We may not like Mr. Edens, and we can predict that his employees probably don't either, *but it doesn't matter!* Whether by accident or design, he has created an organizational system that matches the conditions facing his firm, with a simple reward system that matches his organization's needs.

What we see at Kodak is an illustration of what can happen when circumstances change, and what was once a highly effective management strategy no longer fits these circumstances. Conditions had fit the human relations strategy well. Kodak has always had a complex environment, as evidenced by the vast array of products it makes, but the dominance of the firm resulted in a relatively stable environment. In the 1970s and 1980s it tended to practise a defender strategy for some products and an analyzer strategy for others. Technology was routine for most products. Except in the research and development areas, moderate employee skills and education were required.

But as competitors entered the field and product innovations occurred, Kodak could not change rapidly enough to adjust to these changes. It was too slow moving, and its overloaded hierarchical decision-making systems did not have the capacity to perceive its environment accurately. This problem was compounded by the firm's acquisition of unrelated companies, such as Sterling Drug in 1988.

Kodak's organizational culture of stability, which had been an asset, became a liability when the firm tried to move toward a prospector strategy. The company has done several things to try to deal with these problems, by reducing environmental complexity (through sale of noncore divisions) and moving toward a high-involvement strategy in areas of the business that depend on innovation. But as Box 2.2 suggests, these changes have not necessarily borne fruit. Moving from a human relations organization to a high-involvement organization is a very difficult and long-term process, especially for large organizations with well-entrenched cultures.

Finally, let's consider Gennum Corporation. It is an excellent example of fit. Look at how its high-involvement managerial style fits the company's context: unstable, complex environment, prospector strategy, intensive technology (many of Gennum's products are made to order for specific customers), relatively small size, highly educated workforce, operating in a relatively prosperous region. Instead of formal structure, the organization cultivates a culture of commitment, egalitarianism, teamwork, and risk-taking. And look at how the reward system fits with and supports the company's strategy!

Therefore, according to our strategic framework, Gennum should be very successful. So let's do a reality check, and look at the actual results. In the past eight years, sales have quadrupled, from $27 million to $106 million. During this period, total profits also quadrupled. Since 1993, the firm has never provided an annual return on average equity of less than 24 percent per annum. Shareholders (many of whom are employees) also have another reason to be happy with the firm—company shares are worth more than nine times their value in 1993! Incredibly, reality matches theory!

So, shareholders are happy. But what about employees? They seemed to be happy in 1991, when the company was listed among the "100 Best Companies to Work for in Canada" (Innes, Lyon, and Harris, 1991). And ten years later, in the 2001 edition, Gennum was one of the few companies from that original 100 still on the list (Yerema, 2000)!

Trends in Managerial and Compensation Strategies

All three managerial strategies can be effective, if used in the right context. But how are circumstances changing in North America, and how will these changes affect the optimal choice of managerial strategy? This is an important question for those designing reward systems, since the most appropriate reward system depends on the managerial strategy that is utilized. To get a handle on this question, it is helpful to understand how conditions and managerial strategies have evolved over time. As will be discussed at the end of this section, these changes also help to explain some of the recent trends in compensation practices.

The Evolution of Managerial Strategies

Initial Dominance of the Classical Approach

Historically, there is no question that the classical managerial strategy, when fully implemented, has been an extremely successful approach. Of the most successful firms in the first half of the twentieth century, virtually all were classical. The largest and most successful company in the world in 1950 was General Motors, and it is no coincidence that GM had the most fully developed classical system anywhere. Although Henry Ford had pioneered the modern classical organization, with its strict division of labour into tiny fragments, Alfred P. Sloan of General Motors had taken the concept and applied it more fully, adding the other structural elements. By 1960, this approach to management allowed the big three automakers (GM, Ford, Chrysler) in the United States to virtually control the North American automobile industry.

Why were these firms so successful? It is no mystery. Look at their contextual variables: long-linked technology, stable environment, defender strategy, large size, and a large pool of unskilled labour. Perfect for the classical managerial strategy.

But while classical organizations have great advantages flowing from their high division of labour and strict control, they also have numerous disadvantages. One of these is a very high cost of coordination and control, especially as the firm gets larger. (Even at a relatively small firm, such as EBS [see Box 2.1], look at the costs of all those supervisors and all that surveillance equipment!) Another disadvantage is that people do not enjoy fractionated work under tight control. They tend to develop negative work norms, and the negative assumptions that this school holds about workers tend to be self-fulfilling. In order to exert more control over their working lives and to protect their own interests, workers in classical organizations are very likely to form strong adversarial unions.

Classical managers are strongly opposed to unionization because they know that unionization weakens their basis for control of employees (i.e., power) in a variety of ways, most notably by making it harder to dismiss workers. With this threat diminished, management must resort to more inspectors and supervisors, rules, and procedures to control employee behaviour. Unionization increases labour costs in three ways: first, there are the costs of the additional inspectors and controls; second, more workers are needed, because the union imposes controls on the amount of work that can be extracted from workers and on the ways they can be deployed; and, third, because of the strong anti-management solidarity of the workers, the union is usually able to win higher wages and benefits than it would otherwise.

Not surprisingly, the result is lower profitability, as research has shown (Addison and Hirsch, 1989). Research has also shown that unionized Canadian companies experience lower employment growth than non-union firms (Long, 1993a), probably due to their lower profitability.

RISE OF THE HUMAN RELATIONS APPROACH

The disadvantages of the classical approach were apparent to perceptive employers as far back as the 1920s, as they asked themselves if there was some way to maintain the advantages of the classical system, especially its high division of labour and well-developed hierarchy for coordination and control, while avoiding the bitter and adversarial labour–management relationship normally found in classical organizations.

Their solution was the human relations school of management, in which employees would be treated with high consideration by management. Pay and benefits would be relatively good, job security would be high, other security needs would be addressed, and the company would play a role in satisfying social needs (Jacoby, 1997). This would create positive group norms that would augment and support the formal structure. Since the company would make every effort to satisfy employee needs, workers would see no need for a union. Indeed, companies that used the human relations model seldom became unionized, and employees often felt a fierce loyalty toward the company. Turnover was low, with the result that these firms had low recruiting and training costs, and a highly knowledgeable and experienced workforce.

By the 1960s, companies practising the human relations model had begun to supplant classical firms as the model for a well-managed firm. Companies like Kodak and Sears began to dominate their industries, along with IBM, often considered in the 1960s and 1970s to be the best-managed company in the world. IBM practised all the key elements of the human relations school, with a few aspects of the high-involvement approach tacked on. These companies truly seemed to have overcome the disadvantages of the classical school, while still capturing its advantages, and were rewarded with great success.

However, as long as environmental conditions are favourable, it is possible for firms that practise the classical and the human relations strategies to coexist in the same industry. If practised well, there may be room for both. But when conditions become adverse, the firms with the approaches least suited to the conditions, or least well executed, will be the first to suffer.

Changing Conditions

However, the most serious shortcoming of the classical system did not turn out to be its poor employee–management relationship, but its rigidity. Classical organizations spend huge sums to discover the "one best way" of doing something, to develop specialized technology and job structures, and then to lock the behaviour in. Obviously, "innovation" on the part of employees is to be discouraged; if we already have the best system, then any deviation is, by definition, inefficient. Human relations firms differ little from classical organizations in this regard.

This rigidity at the workplace level is compounded by a decision-making structure that requires all major decisions go to the top of the organization for resolution. This causes three problems. First, decision making is slow. Second, it takes a long time for decisions to be implemented, since change is resisted in classical organizations. Third, decision makers at the top of the organization can be seriously out of touch with the problems they are trying to solve, and make poor decisions. This is partly due to the poor communication that usually exists in these firms.

Of course, rigidity is not a problem when there is no need to change. In fact, if the organization has truly discovered the "one best way" of doing things, rigidity is an asset. But when the nature of the market, the environment, or technology does start to change quickly, and that "best way" is no longer the best, what had been the key advantage of the classical organization becomes a huge liability.

By the 1980s, the environment in many industries was becoming much more dynamic. For the auto industry, it started with the oil crisis of the 1970s, coupled with the emergence of foreign competition (especially from the Japanese). In computers, it started with the invention of the microchip. For established retailers, it started with the recession of 1981–82 and the emergence of large-scale discount stores. For cameras and photo supplies, it started with the invention of new camera technology (the easy-to-use 35 mm camera and the video camera) coupled with foreign competition, again, especially from the Japanese.

By the 1980s, the Japanese had become the exemplars for good management, and many North American firms looked to the Japanese for inspiration. Many tried to copy certain obvious Japanese management practices, such as "quality circles"—groups of employees and managers that meet once a week to try to solve organizational problems and improve productivity. However, "quality circles" at most North American firms fizzled out and were quietly dropped. What these North American firms didn't realize was that these practices only work within the context of the total organizational system used by a firm. It turned out that the Japanese had taken the human relations management system, which fit in very well with their culture, refined it, and had added some elements of the high-involvement approach.

Two key aspects of the Japanese system are employment security and a compensation system in which a significant amount of an employee's pay is in the form of an annual bonus based on company performance. Japanese firms also make extensive use of employee stock ownership (Kato, 2001). Most North American observers failed to recognize the key role that these compensation elements played in the success of the Japanese management system.

By 1990, the same North American companies that had once been so admired had become the subject of ridicule and scorn, even being labelled "dinosaurs" (Looney, 1993). GM watched as its market share plummeted from 50 to 30 percent and continued to drop. In a radical departure from its no-layoff policy, IBM cut 140 000 jobs in the early 1990s. Sears was forced to sell its landmark headquarters in Chicago (the Sears Tower), close dozens of stores, and lay off thousands of employees.

What are the options available to human relations firms to get them back on track? Before we go on to discuss this question, it should be noted that many fundamental socioeconomic changes have also taken place in Canada that have created conditions more suitable for high-involvement organizations and less suitable for classical and human relations organizations. Since the first half of the twentieth century, when both of these managerial strategies were first developed, educational levels have increased, economic and social security has improved, and social values have become more democratic and egalitarian. At the same time, products and services have become more complex, along with the technologies used to produce them, which generally calls for greater skill, initiative, and motivation from employees. Rapid discovery of new knowledge causes old knowledge to become obsolete at a rapid rate, and it is not uncommon for new employees in many firms to understand far more about the firm's technology than their bosses. All of these conditions militate against classical and human relations organizations.

Finally, one other development warrants a special note. The emergence of sophisticated information technology (IT) has the potential to have a major impact on organizations. Some observers fear that the technology will be used as a mechanism of employee control, facilitating use of the classical management system. Look, for example, at what Mr. Edens has done at EBS. Others argue that IT will be used to facilitate the use of high-involvement management by serving as a vehicle to disseminate the information necessary for the decentralization of decision making.

So how will IT affect managerial strategy? No one knows for sure, but one plausible scenario is that organizations will attempt to use IT to reinforce their existing managerial philosophy, whatever that is. For example, classical organizations will use IT to facilitate control, while high-involvement organizations will use IT to decentralize decision making (Long, 1987).

Two large-scale studies done in Canada shed some light on the effect of IT on managerial strategy. One study examined 114 major Canadian companies in a wide cross-section of industries. These firms employed over 882 000 workers, about 10 percent of all private-sector employment. The overall finding was that the higher the use of information technology, the greater the degree of employee involvement practised by the firm (Long, 1993b). Analysis of a sample of individual computer users in these firms, who had been computerized in the previous five years, showed that 70 percent had experienced a net gain in the intrinsic characteristics of their jobs, while most of the remainder reported no significant change, and a few reported declines (Long, 1993c).

In the other study, Lowe (1992) examined the responses of 9000 users of new technology who were among the respondents to the General Social Survey conducted by Statistics Canada. He found that 61 percent of the respondents said that introduction of computers or new technology to their jobs had made their work more interesting, while only 4 percent said the opposite. A review of more recent evidence indicates that computerization continues to upskill more jobs than it downskills (Lowe, 2000). Taken together, these studies seem to suggest that, in Canada, IT is being used more often to support the high-involvement model than the classical approach.

THE REACTION OF HUMAN RELATIONS FIRMS

Human relations companies were forced to react to the changes described above in one of three ways. First, they could try to become more classical, eliminating job security, cutting wages and benefits, and cutting staff—in other words, undoing the very things that had made them so successful. However, while this "lean and mean" approach may prolong their survival, it does nothing to deal with their fundamental problem: their inability to cope with change. Paradoxically, there is considerable evidence that such actions actually make the organization more resistant to and/or incapable of change. Feeling betrayed, the best employees seek jobs elsewhere, while the remainder try to keep their heads down. High stress levels are also antithetical to effective change. Interestingly, there is evidence, based on samples of Canadian firms, that downsizing, on average, does not increase future profitability (Mentzer, 1996), and actually decreases worker efficiency (Wagar, 1998).

A second option is to retain their human relations school of thought but attempt to shift to markets that are less dynamic. In other words, if your environment no longer fits your management style, find one that does. This course of action frequently requires major surgery, with entire divisions being sold or closed down. However, for those parts of the organization that remain, there are no major changes to managerial strategy or to the reward system. Some organizations have used this approach, known as *downscoping*, very successfully. Sometimes simply reducing the number of disparate markets served is an effective strategy for reducing environmental complexity. Both Sears and Kodak have used downscoping as a part of their turnaround strategies, with Sears now focusing only on retailing and Kodak only on photographic products and imaging technology.

The final option for coping with environmental change is to retain the current domain but attempt to become flexible and innovative—that is, to become a high-involvement organization. Converting to the high-involvement approach is in many ways the toughest road, but it is probably the only one that will lead to long-term success if the firm chooses to stay in a dynamic environment. (Indeed, environments that are not dynamic are becoming increasingly scarce.) This approach has major implications for all aspects of the organizational system. As Figure 2.2 showed, virtually every structural variable—including the reward system—must undergo dramatic change to make this conversion.

Box 2.5 shows how Sears is trying to move away from its human relations approach toward a high-involvement approach.

THE REACTION OF CLASSICAL FIRMS

Classical organizations that find themselves facing a dynamic environment are in an even worse position than human relations organizations. Since they are already "lean and mean," there is not much fat that can be easily trimmed, and tough unions may prevent them from being as mean as they would like to be. Seeing unions as a threat to their power, some firms have attempted to destroy their unions or at least weaken them as much as possible. They then have a freer hand to cut costs by cutting pay and benefits, reducing staffing levels, and increasing workloads. Or, they may attempt to circumvent the union by contracting out as much work as possible to non-union firms or to firms that have weak unions. Another tactic is to shift production to regions or countries where unions are not strong or economic conditions are poor. Sometimes simply threatening to do so may be sufficient to get the union to agree to various concessions.

However, some classical firms have chosen the opposite approach—to work with the union to develop a more cooperative problem-solving atmosphere. Box 2.6 tells the story of how two firms in the same industry chose opposite approaches in dealing with their unions. Of course, the lean and mean approach does not always lead to such tragic results as it did at Westray Mining, but recent Canadian research suggests that, on average, the cooperative approach is more effective in improving company performance than the lean and mean approach (Wagar, 1997).

Some firms have gone so far as to include labour as partners in management, moving to a high-involvement approach in the process. The most promi-

BOX 2.5 Can the Circus Help Sears?

It is 9:00 a.m. on a Friday morning in November 1995, and 900 employees are packed into the auditorium at Sears' head office in Chicago. None of them knows exactly what to expect.

Suddenly, a spotlight stabs through the semi-darkness, "revealing a ringmaster. 'Welcome to the Sears PSE Circus,' he says. 'It's eye-popping. Death defying. Larger than life. Well, not death defying.' Next comes Jim La the clown, in orange hat, turquoise-and-pink jacket and plaid pants. He tells a few corny jokes. Then he breaks into a rap song, ending with 'we work real hard; now it's time to play. Hey, hey, what do you say?'" (Dobrzynski, 1996: B16).

In the early 1990s, Sears was in big trouble. Low customer satisfaction, a fierce, competitive environment, declining sales, and high costs added up to huge losses. So, under new CEO Arthur Martinez, the company launched an ambitious program to move away from their famous human relations strategy—which Martinez believes no longer fits their environment—toward a high-involvement model. But Martinez is not pinning all his hopes to change the rigid Sears culture (which included a 29 000-page manual of rules, policies, and procedures) on Jim La the clown and his musical comedy act.

The first thing to go was the policy manual, replaced by a 35-page folder entitled "Freedoms and Obligations." The many changes to the managerial system included decentralizing decision making, starting at head office and going all the way to the sales staff. But for that to be effective, employees needed a common frame of reference and a solid understanding of the business and its goals.

So Sears launched a multifaceted training program, including sessions like the PSE circus. (Once Mr. La finished, by about 9:20 a.m., the session transformed into a more serious learning environment, in which "PSE" was translated to mean "Pure Selling Environment.") Other training mechanisms included a "learning map" that all Sears employees journeyed around in 1995 and 1996, and a management training institute dubbed "Sears University."

In a reversal of the traditional policy of high job security, the 100 top managers were told to "change or leave," and many managers who couldn't or wouldn't grasp the new concepts were replaced.

A key part of these changes include changes to the compensation system, starting right at the top, where the top 200 senior executives are no longer compensated only on financial measures. Revenue growth, return on assets, and operating margins will determine half of their annual bonus, while the other half will depend equally on customer satisfaction and employee ratings of Sears as an employer. The firm believes (as it always has) that disgruntled employees will not give good customer service. So the challenge is to create a work system that is both motivating and satisfying.

All employees are expected to boost their performance, and every employee's compensation now includes a measure of customer satisfaction. This augments the profit-sharing program that Sears has always had, which seemed to boost employee loyalty, but not employee performance.

---

nent example of this is the Saturn Division of General Motors, which was designed from the ground up as a high-involvement organization (Rubenstein, 2000).

Classical firms that have chosen to move to a high-involvement management approach have an even tougher task than human relations organizations, because they are starting off with very poor and adversarial employee–management relationships, and the key ingredient for movement to a high-involvement school of thought—trust—is sorely lacking. Furthermore, their structural characteristics are the exact opposite of what is needed. It often takes

BOX 2.6 Do You Have to Be Mean to Be Lean?

This is the story of two firms in the same industry, facing similar problems: an oversupply of their product, and the need for low-cost, efficient, and reliable production in order to survive. Both firms had a tradition of classical management and strong adversarial unions. But the two firms took different routes to try to solve their problems, and the results were dramatically different.

Cardinal River Coals has been mining coal in the foothills of the Rocky Mountains of Alberta since 1969. Despite poor union–management relationships, it had been quite successful until the early 1980s, when the bottom dropped out of its market. This, coupled with chronic union–management conflict, put the whole operation in danger of closure. In 1982, both management and the union came to the conclusion that cooperation offered a better way out than continuation of their warfare. So, instead, they developed a new process of open communication and information sharing, and a willingness to look at the situation from the perspective of the other party (HRDC, 1994).

The result? No work stoppages in over 18 years, grievances reduced to virtually nil, and improved production as the parties focused on keeping the mine running, not on fighting each other.

Westray Mining produced coal on Cape Breton Island. From its inception, the mine used a classical management approach, but as it became more and more difficult to keep the mine cost-competitive due to problems with the coal formation, the firm intensified its lean and mean approach. A variety of methods were used to maintain productivity and keep costs down, some of which involved skimping on safety procedures. Although a few miners complained to the Nova Scotia Department of Labour, little was done, possibly because the company was so important to the economy of the area. Since the company kept threatening to close the mine, the union and most miners felt they had little option but to go along. It didn't help their bargaining power that there were few alternative jobs available in this high-unemployment region. Employee morale and motivation were rock-bottom.

The result? On May 9, 1992, the mine blew up, with the loss of 26 lives. It never reopened.

a major crisis, coupled with visionary leadership, in order to successfully make the transition.

A key part of making the transition to high involvement, and some would say the most crucial part (Lawler, 1992; Schuster and Zingheim, 1996; Wilson, 1995), is changing the reward and compensation system. The compensation system can be a powerful tool for change or a powerful inhibitor of change, as will be seen in Chapter 3. There is considerable evidence that business firms that attempt to move to high-involvement management will find their success in doing so short-lived if their reward and compensation system is not supportive of the new managerial strategy (Lawler, 1992). Even if employees value high-involvement management for its intrinsic rewards, if none of the extrinsic rewards generated by the new management system flow to employees, this can create a sense of inequity that destroys the foundation of trust and goodwill that is necessary for high involvement to be successful.

An exception to this last point can occur in nonbusiness organizations. Where the organization generates no financial surpluses that can be shared, employees may be willing to accept high-involvement management (and even welcome it) on its intrinsic rewards alone. But even here, it is unlikely that high involvement can survive long unless organization members perceive that whatever extrinsic rewards are available are being distributed in an equitable manner. Overall, reward equity, to the extent that it is within the organization's control, is a critical underpinning of the high-involvement approach, as will be discussed further in Chapter 3.

CURRENT INCIDENCE OF HIGH INVOLVEMENT

To what extent have Canadian companies actually adopted the high-involvement model? In the early 1990s, Betcherman and his colleagues studied this very question (Betcherman, McMullen, Leckie, and Caron, 1994). Although they used slightly different labels for the three schools of thought (industrial, salaried, and high performance), they parallel the three labels used here (classical, human relations, and high involvement).

They found that about 40 percent of Canadian firms had adopted some key elements of the high-involvement model, which represented a dramatic increase from earlier years (Long, 1989). It appears that the recession of the early 1980s may have been the catalyst that many organizations needed to recognize the increasing inadequacy of traditional management models and to start looking for new alternatives (Long and Warner, 1987). However, it was not clear how many of the firms in the Betcherman study were planning to adopt the whole model. At the time of that study, relatively few Canadian firms had adopted all elements of high-involvement management.

More recently, Long (2002) conducted a study of 240 medium to large Canadian companies in a wide variety of business sectors. (For convenience, this survey will be referred to throughout the book as the **Compensation Practices Survey.**) All told, these firms employed more than 459 000 Canadians at the time of the study (mid-2000). The author found that about 18 percent of these firms had adopted most of the elements of high involvement, but that only about 2 percent had adopted the full model. However, given the changes that continue to take place in the Canadian business context, it is probable that these numbers have increased since then.

Compensation Practices Survey a survey of the compensation practices of 240 medium to large Canadian companies carried out by the author in 2000

TRENDS IN COMPENSATION STRATEGIES

The strategic framework presented in this chapter helps to explain some of the trends currently taking place in Canadian compensation systems. These trends include a major increase in the adoption of pay-for-performance systems—especially those aimed at organizational performance, such as profit-sharing and employee stock plans (Chaykowski and Lewis, 1995; Long, 2001). There has also been an increase in group or team-based incentive systems, and more firms are also experimenting with pay-for-knowledge systems, in place of traditional job-based pay systems. Flexible benefit plans are increasing in popularity, and there continues to be gradual movement away from hourly pay to the use of salary.

The interest in these types of plans comes both from organizations that are adopting the high-involvement model and from those firms that are not adopting that model but are simply hoping that adoption of these pay innovations alone will solve the problems they are facing. But without making the other necessary changes to their structures, it is unlikely that traditionally managed firms will find these pay innovations very effective.

The 1980s and 1990s saw wage freezes and rollbacks and the increased use of two-tier wage systems (under which new employees do not receive the same pay structure as existing employees), although use of these practices declined as economic conditions improved in the late 1990s. Some firms were attempting to deal with their problems by simply cutting the amount of compensation they provide to employees. These tended to be classical organizations and some human relations organizations that were attempting to survive by simply growing meaner.

Some observers even talked about a "new system of employment relations," based on a low employer commitment to employees (providing little job security, little training, and few prospects for career advancement), with employers shuffling employees in and out of their organizations as their needs changed (Cappelli, 1999). However, while this may be viable for firms in which employee commitment and organizational citizenship are unnecessary, and when labour markets are loose, there are real costs to such an approach, and in recent years many firms have had to reverse this "new" employment relationship in order to attract and retain employees.

However, even during the 1990s, most high-involvement firms did not embrace this lean and mean approach, and employee earnings in these firms held steady or even increased, especially when organizational performance pay is included. So the real picture is that employee earnings were going down in some organizations, but up in others, with the net overall result of stagnant worker earnings during the last two decades of the twentieth century. (There was one striking exception to the overall picture of stagnant wages: since 1980, earnings of top corporate executives have increased dramatically.)

Another change that has direct implications for compensation was the increased use of part-time, temporary, and contract workers (often known as "contingent workers") that occurred during the 1980s and 1990s (although this trend appears to have levelled off in recent years). While there were a number of reasons for this trend, as will be discussed in Chapter 8, a major advantage of these workers is that they are often much cheaper to employ than regular full-time employees, because of lower wages and employee benefits.

Organizations can also dismiss contingent workers without demonstrating cause or providing severance pay, which not only provides flexibility, but fits well with the classical management philosophy. Another reason that classical organizations like these workers is that they are easier to manage because of their economic insecurity. As conditions have become more difficult for classical organizations, many have looked to contingent workers as one way of helping their classical system continue to work.

However, it should be noted that some high-involvement organizations have also increased their use of contingent workers, although for different reasons. A prime reason is to help provide employment security for their core workforce, by using contingent workers as a buffer to deal with demand fluctuations. In many of these firms, contingent workers are compensated on the same basis as permanent employees, because the motivation for using them is not cost cutting.

Of course, factors other than changing managerial strategies are also driving changes in compensation systems, and all of these factors will be discussed later in the book. But it is clear that there is a strong connection between the changes that are currently taking place in managerial strategies and the changes taking place in reward and compensation strategies. For example, the Compensation Practices Survey revealed that Canadian high-involvement firms were much more likely to have a whole range of pay innovations, including group/team performance pay, organizational performance pay, pay for knowledge, and flexible benefits, than more traditional firms.

SUMMARY AND IMPLICATIONS

The purpose of this chapter has been to develop a strategic framework that will serve as a tool in identifying the reward and compensation system that best fits the organization's strategy and structure. It was noted that the key to the success of any compensation system is the concept of fit, and that the compensation system must be developed in the context of the total reward system, which in turn must be developed in the context of the organizational structure and the managerial strategy used by the organization.

Three managerial strategies—classical, human relations, and high involvement—were identified, each of which requires a different reward and compensation system. Since the most appropriate managerial strategy (and therefore the most appropriate reward and compensation system) depends on certain key factors in the organization's context, it is important to understand what these factors are and how they relate to managerial strategy. Five main contextual factors were identified: the organization's environment, its corporate strategy, its technology, its size, and the nature of its workforce. A strategic template was developed as a tool to help in the selection of the managerial strategy that best fits these contextual factors.

It was noted that conditions have generally become much less favourable for the human relations and classical managerial strategies in recent years, and the shift to high involvement is creating a change in the nature of reward systems. Although it was also noted that there are still circumstances under which a classical or human relations strategy will still be viable, these circumstances are likely to become increasingly scarce. Organizations with a suboptimal managerial strategy can often continue to survive for a period of time, but only as long as market conditions are favourable, or as long as none of their competitors is managed any better than they are. (Of course, if they have no competitors at all, as in the case of a monopoly, they may be able to survive for an indefinite period of time even with an inappropriate managerial strategy.)

Finally, it should be noted that not all organizations have a conscious managerial strategy. In fact, for most organizations, their managerial strategy is implicit, rather than explicit, but it still serves to govern managerial behaviour in their organizations. Of course, the degree of development and refinement of managerial strategies varies enormously across firms. However, for some firms, there is no consistent managerial strategy at all. What this means is that there is no ideal reward and compensation system for these firms. When there is no coherent managerial strategy, how can you design a compensation system to support that strategy? In these cases, the design of an optimal reward and compensation system cannot really be undertaken until these underlying organizational problems are sorted out.

But enough about strategy and compensation for now! The next milestone on our journey to effective compensation will be the development of a conceptual framework to help understand how reward systems are linked to human behaviour. Accomplishing that is the central focus of Chapter 3.

KEY TERMS

analyzer corporate strategy, p. 37

classical managerial strategy, p. 24

communication and information structure, p. 22

Compensation Practices Survey, p. 53

contextual variables, p. 23

contingency approach to organization design, p. 20

control structure, p. 22

coordination and departmentation, p. 22

corporate strategy, p. 20

craft technology, p. 38

decision-making and leadership structure, p. 22

defender corporate strategy, p. 37

domain, p. 23

engineering technology, p. 39

high-involvement managerial strategy, p. 25

human relations managerial strategy, p. 24

intensive technology, p. 38

job design, p. 22

long-linked technology, p. 38

managerial strategy, p. 23

mass/large batch technology, p. 39

mediating technology, p. 38

nonroutine technology, p. 38

organizational culture, p. 34

organizations, p. 19

organization structure, p. 20

process technology, p. 39

prospector corporate strategy, p. 37

routine technology, p. 38

task environment, p. 23

technology, p. 20

unit/small batch technology, p. 39

EXERCISES

1. Take an organization that you know well, such as a current or former employer, and apply the strategic template in Table 2.2 to determine the most appropriate managerial strategy for that firm. Does this match the managerial strategy actually in use? If not, why not? Do you agree with what the template indicates as the best managerial strategy? Would you consider this an effective organization? Does the organization's reward system match its managerial strategy?

2. In a group of five or six people, share the results of your analysis from the first exercise. Compare the organizations that were considered to be effective with those that were not. Did the firms in which their strategy matched their contextual variables perform better than those that did not? Discuss why or why not. If you find some organizations that seem effective despite a poor fit between contextual variables and managerial strategy, discuss why this might be.

3. Box 2.5 discussed how Sears is trying to move toward a high-involvement strategy. Using the strategic template, analyze whether this is the right move for the company to make. Based on your analysis, what advice would you give to Sears' top management? Discuss your conclusions with your group. In the process, ask any group members who have been employed in retailing to discuss their experiences and the managerial strategies these firms seem to use.

4. Read "The Fit Stop" (in the Appendix) and determine which managerial strategy would be most effective for this firm. Given what you know about Susan Superfit, which managerial strategy do you think she would prefer to use? Does this match your choice?

5. Read "Multi-Products Corporation" (in the Appendix) and determine the managerial strategy that would be most effective for this firm. What reward and compensation strategy would fit this managerial strategy? What problems might you encounter in using this managerial strategy?

SUGGESTED WEB SITES

Page 44: To track the success of Kodak's efforts to reinvent itself, visit the company Web site at <www.kodak.com>

Page 45: To follow Gennum's ongoing performance, visit the company Web site at <www.gennum.com>

Page 54: For the latest trends in compensation, click on <www.worldatwork.org>

REFERENCES

Addison, John T., and Barry T. Hirsch. 1989. "Union Effects on Productivity: Has the Long Run Arrived?" *Journal of Labor Economics*, 7(1): 72–105.

Appelbaum, Eileen, Thomas Bailey, Peter Berg, and Arne L. Kalleberg. 2000. *Manufacturing Advantage: Why High-Performance Work Systems Pay Off*. Ithaca, NY: Cornell University Press.

Betcherman, Gordon, Kathryn McMullen, Norm Leckie, and Christina Caron. 1994. *The Canadian Workplace in Transition*. Kingston: IRC Press.

Cappelli, Peter. 1999. *The New Deal at Work*. Boston: Harvard Business School.

Case, John. 1995. *Open Book Management: The Coming Business Revolution*. New York: Harper Business Publications.

Chaykowski, Richard, and Brian Lewis. 1995. *Compensation Practices and Outcomes in Canada and the United States*. Kingston: IRC Press.

Coy, Peter. 2000. "The Myth of Corporate Reinvention." *Business Week*, October 30: 80–82.

Daft, Richard. 2001. *Organization Theory and Design*. Cincinnati: South Western College Publishing.

Dobrzynski, Judith H. 1996. "Sears Goes to the Circus to Motivate Employees." *The Globe and Mail*, January 10: B16.

Gomez-Mejia, Luis, and David Balkin. 1992. *Compensation, Organizational Strategy, and Firm Performance*. Cincinnati: South-Western Publishing.

Hodson, Randy. 2001. "Disorganized, Unilateral, and Participative Organizations: New Insights from the Ethnographic Literature." *Industrial Relations*, 40(2): 204–30.

Horwitz, Tony. 1994. "9 to Nowhere: These Six Growth Jobs Are Dull, Dead-End, Sometimes Dangerous." *The Wall Street Journal*, December 1: A1–A8.

HRDC. 1994. "The Cardinal River RBO Story: A Union–Management Relationship with a Dark History but a Bright Future." *Labour–Management Innovation in Canada*. Ottawa: Human Resources Development Canada, 100–104.

Innes, Eva, Jim Lyon, and Jim Harris. 1991. *The Financial Post 100 Best Companies to Work for in Canada*. Toronto: HarperCollins.

Jacoby, Sanford M. 1997. *Modern Manors: Welfare Capitalism since the New Deal*. Princeton, NJ: Princeton University Press.

Kato, Takao. 2001. "Financial Participation and Pay for Performance in Japan." In Michelle Brown and John S. Heywood, eds., *Paying for Performance: An International Comparison*. Armonk, NY: M.E. Sharpe.

Kochan, Thomas A., and Paul Osterman. 1994. *The Mutual Gains Enterprise*. Boston: Harvard Business School Press.

Lawler, Edward E. 1990. Strategic Pay: Aligning Organizational Strategies and Pay Systems. San Francisco: Jossey Bass.

Lawler, Edward E. 1992. *The Ultimate Advantage: Creating the High Involvement Organization*. San Francisco: Jossey Bass.

Long, Richard J. 1987. *New Office Information Technology: Human and Managerial Implications*. London: Routledge Publishers.

Long, Richard J. 1989. "Patterns of Workplace Innovation in Canada." *Relations industrielles/Industrial Relations*, 44(4): 805–26.

Long, Richard J. 1993a. "The Impact of Unionization on Employment Growth of Canadian Companies." *Industrial and Labor Relations Review*, 46(4): 691–703.

Long, Richard J. 1993b. "New Information Technology and Employee Involvement." *Proceedings of the Administrative Sciences Association of Canada, Organizational Behaviour Division*, 14(5): 161–70.

Long, Richard J. 1993c. "The Impact of New Office Information Technology on Job Quality of Female and Male Employees." *Human Relations*, 46(8): 939–61.

Long, Richard J. 1994. "Gain Sharing, Hierarchy, and Managers: Are They Substitutes?" *Proceedings of the Annual Conference of the Administrative Sciences of Canada, Organization Theory Division*, 15(12): 51–60.

Long, Richard J. 2001. "High Involvement Management and Performance Pay in Canada: An Empirical Study." *Proceedings of the Annual Conference of the Administrative Sciences of Canada, Human Resources Division*, 22(9): 77–86.

Long, Richard J. 2002. "Performance Pay in Canada." In Michelle Brown and John S. Heywood, eds., *Paying for Performance: An International Comparison*. Armonk, NY: M.E. Sharpe.

Long, Richard J., and Malcolm Warner. 1987. "Organizations, Participation, and Recession: An Analysis of Recent Evidence." *Relations industrielles/ Industrial Relations*, 42(1): 65–90.

Looney, Carol J. 1993. "Dinosaurs?" *Fortune*, May 3: 36–42.

Lowe, Graham S. 1992. *Human Resource Challenges of Education, Computers, and Retirement*. Ottawa: Statistics Canada.

Lowe, Graham S. 2000. *The Quality of Work*. Don Mills, ON: Oxford University Press.

MacDuffie, John Paul. 1995. "Human Resource Bundles and Manufacturing Performance: Organizational Logic and Flexible Production Systems in the World Automobile Industry." *Industrial and Labor Relations Review*, 48(2): 197–221.

Maremont, Mark. 1995. "Kodak's New Focus." *Business Week*, January 30: 62–68.

Mentzer, Marc S. 1996. "Corporate Downsizing and Profitability in Canada." *Canadian Journal of Administrative Sciences*, 13(3): 237–50.

Miles, Raymond E. 1975. *Theories of Management: Implications for Organizational Behaviour and Development*. New York: McGraw-Hill.

Miles, Raymond E., and Charles Snow. 1978. *Organizational Strategy, Structure, and Process*, New York: McGraw-Hill.

Perrow, Charles. 1967. "A Framework for Comparative Analysis of Organizations." *American Sociological Review*, 32: 194–208.

Robbins, Stephen P. 1990. *Organization Theory: Structure, Design, and Applications*. Englewood Cliffs, NJ: Prentice-Hall.

Rubenstein, Saul. 2000. "The Impact of Co-Management on Quality Performance: The Case of the Saturn Corporation." *Industrial and Labor Relations Review*, 53(2): 197–218.

Schermerhorn, John R., Andrew J. Templer, R. Julian Cattaneo, James G. Hunt, and Richard N. Osborn. 1992.

Managing Organizational Behaviour.
Toronto: John Wiley.

Schuster, Jay R., and Patricia K.
Zingheim. 1996. *The New Pay: Linking
Employee and Organizational
Performance.* San Francisco: Jossey-
Bass.

Thompson, James D. 1967. *Organizations
in Action.* New York: McGraw-Hill.

Turnasella, Ted. 1994. "Aligning Pay
with Business Strategies and Cultural
Values." *Compensation & Benefits
Review,* 26(5): 65–72.

Wagar, Terry H. 1997. "The
Labour–Management Relationship
and Organization Outcomes: Some
Initial Findings." *Relations indus-
trielles/Industrial Relations,* 52(2):
430–47.

Wagar, Terry H. 1998. "Exploring the
Consequences of Workforce
Reduction." *Canadian Journal of
Administrative Sciences,* 15(4): 300–9.

Wilson, Thomas B. 1995. *Innovative
Reward Systems for the Changing
Workplace.* New York: McGraw-Hill.

Wood, Stephen. 1996. "High
Commitment Management and
Payment Systems." *Journal of
Management Studies,* 33(1): 53–77.

Woodward, Joan. 1965. *Industrial
Organization: Theory and Practice.*
London: Oxford University Press.

Yerema, Richard. 2000. *Canada's Top 100
Employers, 2001 Edition.* Toronto:
Mediacorp.

3

A BEHAVIOURAL FRAMEWORK FOR COMPENSATION

CHAPTER GOALS

By the end of this chapter, you should be able to:

1. Identify the three main types of reward problems that can afflict organizations.
2. Define the three key employee behaviours desired by employers.
3. Identify three key job attitudes, and explain their role in determining employee behaviour.
4. Describe the causes and consequences of reward dissatisfaction.
5. Explain how to generate membership behaviour.
6. Outline the process through which task behaviour is motivated.
7. Explain how to generate organizational citizenship behaviour.
8. Understand the integrated model for human behaviour and explain the implications for the design of effective reward systems.
9. Discuss the role that managerial strategy plays in determining the type of employee attitudes and behaviour needed by an organization.

INTRODUCTION

What would you think of a reward system that rewarded irresponsible and dishonest employees while causing responsible and conscientious employees to quit? Probably not much. But this is precisely the effect produced by the reward system (described in Box 3.1) used by a multibillion-dollar soft drink producer for its summer employees at the Canadian National Exhibition.

The results described in Box 3.1 are certainly not what the soft drink company had in mind. But are such examples of dysfunctional reward systems so unusual? As the following list of examples shows, the answer is no.

- Green Giant wished to improve the quality of its canned vegetables, so it decided to give a bonus for the number of insect parts plucked from the processing line. The plan seemed to be enormously successful—hundreds and hundreds of insect parts were turned in, and large bonuses were paid. The only problem was that most of the additional insect parts came from the workers' backyards, where they were much easier to find, rather than from the canning line.

BOX 3.1 Fun and Games at the Exhibition

A major soft drink maker has a prominent booth at the Canadian National Exhibition in Toronto each summer. The company employs students at minimum wage to serve soft drinks to customers. There are no benefits, and the only opportunity for advancement is to become a shift supervisor, which pays only slightly more money. Shift supervisors are also temporary employees. The jobs are numbingly dull and repetitive—simply serving soft drinks all day. A manager, with an enclosed office at the back of the booth, is in charge, but is frequently not around, due to the fact that the booth operates 12 hours a day every day. Turnover is very high on this job, with few employees lasting the whole summer.

Management does not trust these employees, and makes this clear in many ways. For example, to discourage employees from "pocketing" any of the receipts, they have sewn shut all the pockets in the uniforms that the employees wear. As further insurance against employee misconduct, a count is kept of all the paper cups used in a day, and this is balanced against actual cash on hand.

Although employees are supposed to be friendly and courteous to customers, this frequently does not happen.

Furthermore, when the manager is not around, horseplay is common. Supervisors, who are usually the same age as the servers, either tolerate or join in the horseplay. In some cases, it gets so bad that customers are discouraged from approaching the booth.

Many employees have also found a way to augment the meagre extrinsic rewards flowing from the job by simply retrieving used cups from the trash and reusing them. Thus, employees can augment their income and the official count of cups and the receipts will still balance.

Not all employees participate in the horseplay or the cup scam, because this behaviour would violate their values—such as a strong work ethic or a strong sense of honesty—or simply because they are afraid of getting caught. Denying themselves access to the extrinsic rewards received by the other employees, these employees often quit, leaving only dishonest and/or irresponsible employees. These are the only employees for whom the ratio of rewards to contributions is balanced. Thus, the effect of the pay system used by this company is to create a workforce of dishonest, irresponsible employees.

- In order to encourage efficient work from its computer programmers, IBM rewarded them on the number of lines of computer code they produced. It took the company years to notice that IBM computer programs tended to be much longer and more inefficiently written that those of other companies.

- Sears wanted to increase sales in its service department, and so started to pay a commission to its mechanics on the amount of service work done. This did increase sales dramatically, but many customers found that much of the work done was unnecessary. When word of this hit the newspapers, it caused serious damage to the firm's reputation.

- In order to boost book sales in its college division, a major Canadian publisher introduced a plan that would pay bonuses to its sales reps if annual sales exceeded a target set by the regional sales manager. The plan seemed to have no effect on sales whatsoever and was eliminated within a year.

- A Saskatchewan chemical company redesigned the jobs of operators so that they contained more intrinsic rewards. This greatly boosted the job effort and performance of some operators but did not change the performance of other operators at all.

- A manufacturer of consumer products had the following system for rewarding its three main units: marketing was evaluated on volume of sales; production was evaluated on production costs; and research and development was evaluated on number of patents registered. Not only did this system cause enormous conflict between the three units, but the company found it almost impossible to bring new products to the market on a timely basis. Those that did reach the market either did not achieve customer acceptance or were not profitable.

- For years, purchasing officers at Canadian National Railways were evaluated on the basis of reducing item costs in comparison to the previous year. For example, one key part of a boxcar is the axle, a round bar of steel on which the wheels are mounted. Since thousands of axles are used in a year, a purchasing officer who could reduce the cost of each axle by even 2 or 3 percent was regarded as a hero. But it turns out that by spending slightly more on each axle, and ordering them slightly thicker, they would last much longer. However, under the previous reward system, any purchasing officer who acted on this would have been penalized.

- A Canadian retailer wished to create a more cooperative "team" atmosphere among its sales staff by having experienced sales personnel take more responsibility for training new sales staff. Compensation for sales staff was straight commission on volume sold. Management couldn't understand why, despite their exhortations, senior sales personnel showed little interest in training new sales staff.

- Bausch and Lomb, the huge optical company, instituted a reward system for its sales managers that rewarded them highly if they met their monthly and quarterly sales targets, but penalized them severely if they did not. In order to achieve their targets, sales managers resorted to tactics such as using month-end discounting, offering excessively easy payment terms, threatening to cut off distributors if they did not purchase enough product, and shipping product to customers even though they had not ordered it. These tactics caused serious problems for the company, as Box 3.2 indicates.

These examples serve to illustrate that reward systems may have a powerful effect on behaviour, but that the behaviour we get is not always the behaviour we want. Why do people behave as they do? Why do they often not behave as we want them to? How can we get them to behave as the organization needs them to behave? What role can reward systems play in influencing their behaviour?

As any manager will know, the answers to these questions are not obvious. But finding these answers is crucial for designing an effective reward system. The purpose of this chapter is to develop a conceptual framework that can be used to find these answers.

We will start with a more systematic look at the problems that an ineffective reward system can cause by identifying three main categories of reward problems: failure to produce desired behaviour; production of desired behaviour and undesirable consequences; and production of reward dissatisfaction. After that, we will look at three types of desired employee behaviour: membership behaviour, task behaviour, and organizational citizenship behaviour. Since reward systems can generate these behaviours only through their impact

BOX 3.2 Cloudy Vision at Bausch and Lomb

Bausch and Lomb is a major producer of contact lenses, sunglasses, and other optical products. In order to promote product sales, the company instituted large bonuses for sales managers who met their monthly and quarterly targets, but severe penalties for those who did not. Managers lived in fear of "red ball" days, named for the red dots marking the end of fiscal quarters on B&L calendars. Red ball days also fell at the end of each month.

Managers resorted to various tactics for meeting their "red ball" targets. If they were coming up short, they offered large discounts in the two or three days preceding red ball days. Customers learned to wait for these periods and seldom booked orders unless they could receive a hefty discount. In other cases, managers threatened to cut off distributors unless they took far more of the product than they wanted. Managers also offered deferred payment plans to their distributors, since a product was counted as being sold when it was shipped, not when payment was received. In some cases, sales managers simply shipped product that had not been ordered at all.

Among the problems created by this system were major cost inefficiencies. As a *Business Week* investigative report found:

> The lumping of orders into a few frantic days each month also made B&L's distribution operations woefully inefficient. Its sunglass distribution center in San Antonio, Texas stayed open around the clock the last few days of every month in recent years. That meant hiring up to 35 temporary workers, while staffers racked up huge overtime. "We'd ship 70 percent of the month's goods in the last three days," says a former operations manager. "The hourly workers must have thought we were nuts." (Maremont, 1995: 82)

on employee attitudes, the job attitudes that generally lead to these behaviours will be identified. From there, we will move on to the issue of reward dissatisfaction, examining the possible causes and consequences of this potentially damaging phenomenon.

After that, we will examine each of the three desired employee behaviours in depth, and consider how the reward system can help to generate these behaviours. The culmination of all this will be an integrated model of behaviour that can be used as a tool to design reward systems that will generate the employee behaviour the organization needs and wants.

TYPES OF REWARD PROBLEMS

As you saw at the beginning of this chapter, a multitude of different reward problems can occur. To get a better handle on these problems, it is useful to boil them down to several basic types. The first type of problem occurs when the reward system fails to produce the desired behaviour. The second type of problem occurs when the reward system does produce the desired behaviour but also produces undesirable consequences. The third problem occurs when the reward system produces a state of reward dissatisfaction among employees.

FAILURE TO PRODUCE DESIRED BEHAVIOUR

One type of reward problem occurs when the reward system simply has no impact on behaviour, as in the case of the publisher. Or, it may produce the desired behaviour, but only for some employees, as in the case of the Saskatchewan chemical plant. Obviously, if the behaviour the organization needs isn't occurring, or is only occurring for some employees, this can be a serious problem.

However, there can be an even nastier variation of this problem. In some cases, the reward system not only fails to produce the desired behaviour, but also produces undesirable behaviour, or behaviour that leads to negative consequences. The Green Giant reward system did not produce significantly cleaner product but it did produce higher costs. The IBM reward system made the computer programming process less, not more, efficient.

PRODUCTION OF DESIRED BEHAVIOUR AND UNDESIRABLE CONSEQUENCES

Another type of problem occurs when the reward system does indeed generate the desired behaviour, but there are also unanticipated negative consequences. The new reward system for Sears service technicians did cause them to generate increased sales, as the company wanted. But Sears didn't want them to do it by cheating their customers. The Bausch and Lomb system did produce higher sales, but also lower profits, dissatisfied customers, and higher shipping costs. The reward system used at CN Rail did reduce per item purchasing costs, but it also discouraged examination of other, potentially more valuable, approaches to cost savings.

The reward system at the consumer goods company did motivate marketing to increase sales, production to minimize costs, and research and development (R&D) to develop new products. However, while the R&D department did secure many patents, most of these products either had no market or were difficult to manufacture. Production did minimize costs, but they did so by using poor-quality materials and oversimplifying the product. Marketing did try to sell these products, but found that the only way to do so was by making outlandish promises or by cutting prices, which put even more pressure on the production department to reduce costs.

As you might imagine, another result was low cooperation and high conflict between departments. Marketing blamed the R&D department for developing "useless" products and production for producing poor-quality products. R&D blamed production for destroying "good product designs" and marketing for not knowing how to sell. Production accused both R&D and marketing of incompetence.

In short, the more that each department tried to meet its own reward goals, the less successful the company was. By rewarding mutually incompatible goals in a situation where interdependence was high and cooperation essential, the company was guaranteeing failure. Thus, a reward system that may look reasonable when viewed in a narrow (departmental) context may in fact be very damaging when the total picture is taken into account.

A slightly different variation of reward problem occurs when the reward system does generate the rewarded behaviours, with no obvious negative consequences, but also serves to suppress other desirable behaviours that are not measured and rewarded. The case of the retailer illustrates this problem. If the sales staff are paid only on the basis of their individual sales, why would they want to spend time training possible competitors? When an organization rewards only one aspect of a job, is it really surprising that the other aspects are neglected?

So why do companies do this? As Kerr (1975) noted many years ago, and as more recent studies (*Academy of Management Executive*, 1995; Kerr, 1995) have confirmed, companies tend to reward job aspects that are easy to measure—aspects that are highly visible and for which objective data are available—while hoping that employees will also perform job tasks that are not measured or rewarded. Some employees may indeed perform all of the desired job aspects, but if they do, it is in spite of the reward system, not because of it.

PRODUCTION OF REWARD DISSATISFACTION

A final type of problem is not specifically related to any single aspect of the reward system but is potentially very serious. When employees believe that the rewards they receive are not consistent with the contributions they are making to the organization, or that the reward system is unfair, they will experience reward dissatisfaction. Reward dissatisfaction can result in a variety of negative consequences, such as poor work performance, high turnover, poor customer service, and even employee dishonesty, as illustrated by the soft drink company in Box 3.1. Because reward dissatisfaction can be such a serious problem, its causes and consequences will be examined in depth later in the chapter. But before doing so, we need to focus briefly on the other side of the coin—what outcomes *should* the reward system produce?

DESIRED REWARD OUTCOMES

THREE KEY EMPLOYEE BEHAVIOURS

An effective reward system should not only avoid causing undesirable behaviour, it should also promote desired behaviour. There are three general sets of behaviours that most organizations find desirable. **Membership behaviour** occurs when employees decide to join and remain with a firm. **Task behaviour** occurs when employees perform the specific tasks that have been assigned to them. **Organizational citizenship behaviour** occurs when employees voluntarily undertake special behaviours beneficial to the organization that go beyond simple membership and task behaviour, such as extra effort, high cooperation with others, high initiative, high innovativeness, extra customer service, and a general willingness to make sacrifices for the good of the organization. Organizational citizenship behaviour is sometimes known as "contextual performance" (Van Scotter, Motowidlo, and Cross, 2000; Gellatly and Irving, 2001) in contrast to "task performance."

membership behaviour occurs when employees decide to join and remain with a firm

task behaviour occurs when employees perform the tasks that have been assigned to them

organizational citizenship behaviour occurs when employees voluntarily undertake special behaviours beneficial to the organization

THREE KEY EMPLOYEE ATTITUDES

So how do you create a reward system that will generate these behaviours? This question is complicated by the fact that reward systems do not affect human behaviour directly. They first affect employee perceptions and attitudes, which then drive behaviour. So, this brings us to another question. What are the key employee attitudes that need to be created in order to generate the employee behaviour we desire?

The three key attitudes are: job satisfaction, work motivation, and organizational identification. **Job satisfaction** can be defined as the attitude one holds toward one's job and workplace, either positive or negative. **Work motivation** can be defined as the attitude one holds toward good job performance, either positive or negative. Essentially, it is the strength of an employee's desire to perform his or her job duties well. **Organizational identification** consists of three interrelated elements: a sense of shared goals and values with the organization, a sense of membership or belongingness, and an intention to remain a member of the organization. This third element is sometimes known as "organizational commitment."

job satisfaction the attitude one holds toward one's job and workplace

work motivation the attitude one holds toward good job performance

organizational identification a sense of shared goals, belongingness, and desire to remain a member of the organization

Each of these attitudes can lead to behaviour that is beneficial to the organization in different ways. Job satisfaction leads to membership behaviour, work motivation leads to task behaviour, and organizational identification leads to citizenship behaviour, although it also contributes to the other two behaviours. Figure 3.1 illustrates these relationships.

You will notice that Figure 3.1 has arrows leading from organizational identification to both job satisfaction and motivation. That is because organizational identification can have a positive impact on each of these elements. For example, a sense of membership and belongingness can help to satisfy social needs, which then enhances job satisfaction. A sense of shared goals, and the positive group norms that develop, can increase employee motivation.

But wait a minute! Isn't there an arrow missing? Shouldn't job satisfaction also increase motivation and task behaviour? In the past, many people believed that job satisfaction was virtually synonymous with work motivation. But we now know that this is not true. (Of course, classical managers, such as Mr. Edens of EBS [Box 2.1], have always known that it is possible to get a lot of work out of employees without providing much job satisfaction!)

Satisfied, happy workers are not necessarily more productive workers. But they are less likely to quit, to be absent, or to submit grievances, and more likely to be pleasant with other employees and customers. Satisfied employees also suffer less work stress, which then reduces errors and accidents and produces fewer health problems that would cause absenteeism.

Because of low turnover rates, organizations with high job satisfaction have lower recruiting and training costs and more knowledgeable employees, who often develop cordial relationships with customers, than firms with low job satisfaction. So although high job satisfaction does not automatically bring high productivity, it certainly can bring a number of real benefits. As with the other two key employee attitudes, the reward system can have a major impact on job satisfaction.

Figure 3.2 summarizes some of the specific consequences of each job attitude. As just discussed, the consequences of job satisfaction include decreased turnover, absenteeism, and grievances, reduced stress, and positive group norms. Work motivation leads to job effort, which should in turn lead to task performance. Organizational identification leads to positive group norms, cooperative behaviour, innovative behaviour, and increased job effort, along with decreased turnover, absenteeism, and grievances.

FIGURE 3.1   HOW REWARDS AFFECT EMPLOYEE BEHAVIOUR

Clearly, all three of these attitudes are desirable. But exactly how important they are to a given firm will vary enormously. Consider the example of B.C. Rogers chicken processors, described in Box 2.4. From the point of view of its top management, employee job satisfaction and organizational identification would probably be nice to have, but they are certainly not essential. The firm doesn't need innovative or cooperative behaviour from its employees, nor does management care if turnover is high, since employee replacement costs are so low. It doesn't even need particularly high motivation, since the "chain" dictates productivity. What the firm needs is simply enough physical job effort from each employee to keep up with the chain. No more, no less. In return for this minimal expectation, the firm provides minimal rewards. All that the reward system needs to accomplish is a flow of new employees sufficient to replace those who quit. Under current conditions, the company's reward system, while very simple and exclusively extrinsic, appears to be appropriate. It fits the firm's classical managerial strategy, which in turn fits the firm's contextual variables.

Of course, for many firms, such minimal employee contributions will be wholly inadequate, and their reward systems will need to be much more sophisticated to promote the full range of desired behaviours. As a general rule, the more complex the desired behaviour—and the higher the performance level required—the more complex the reward system will have to be, as we have already seen at Gennum Corporation (Box 2.3).

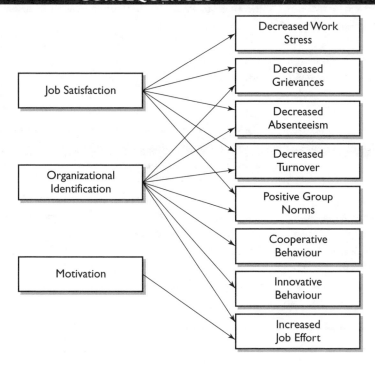

FIGURE 3.2 KEY EMPLOYEE ATTITUDES AND THEIR CONSEQUENCES

Box 3.3 illustrates this point further by describing the multifaceted reward system at Toyota Motors. For Toyota, all three job attitudes are important. High job satisfaction is important because the firm wants to develop a

BOX 3.3 Rewards Support Strategy at Toyota

At its Kentucky assembly plant, Toyota uses a carefully conceived reward system to support its managerial strategy, which focuses on three central concepts: employee loyalty and commitment to the firm, teamwork, and high performance. So how do you create the attitudes necessary to generate these behaviours?

The reward system includes all three compensation components. Base pay is reasonable, but not high for the industry. But to create a feeling of cohesion among production workers, all receive the same pay once they have completed 18 months' service. Annual bonuses, based on company performance, make up a big chunk of earnings for all employees. Although Toyota provides an extensive array of benefits to employees, including child care and on-site recreational facilities, they are not out of line for the auto industry, which is famous for the benefits its unions have won.

What is unusual is that benefits are structured identically for everyone, from assembly workers to the plant manager. There are no executive dining rooms, preferred parking, or private offices for executives. The company believes that egalitarianism is necessary to avoid the division between workers and managers that is so common in this highly unionized industry. (Toyota employees have never voted to unionize.)

Special award money is distributed to groups or teams that have made suggestions that result in safety, cost, or quality improvements. This money is distributed equally among group members, and usually consists of gift certificates that can be used at local retailers. The purpose of this is to make sure that this money simply doesn't get lost in the paycheque, to create family involvement, and to make the reward more tangible. For example, every time the employee looks at her new VCR, purchased with these certificates, she will be reminded of why she received it. In addition, PT (personal touch) money is made available to team leaders to support team social activities such as a summer picnic, monthly team lunches, or trips to ball games.

As a part of its reward strategy, the company offers numerous rewards beyond compensation, one being job security. "Of all the rewards an organization can offer, the one which was seen as most important by nearly all my informants was the job security offered them by Toyota. Every American interviewee mentioned job security in one form or another as either the reason they took a job with Toyota and/or the reason they would remain, even if offered a better paying job" (Besser, 1995: 391).

Another key pillar of the reward system is training and promotion opportunities. The company has a promote-from-within policy, and invests heavily in training for its employees. Toyota focuses on bringing in top-calibre employees with the potential to grow and develop. However, to keep them interested in what is essentially routine and repetitive work is a challenge. Toyota deals with this challenge by providing job enrichment, team-based decision making, job rotation, and the possibility of advancement to other jobs.

Finally, there are a number of recognition rewards, such as plaques for a perfect safety record. These rewards are valued by employees for the symbolic meaning behind them rather than for any economic value. But they must be seen in the context of the total reward system. As Besser (1995: 395) notes: "Certainly, these tokens alone would be insufficient, perhaps even insulting to employees. However, in conjunction with the other rewards already discussed, they encourage employees to believe that they will not be 'fools for busting their butts for the company.'"

The result of all this? A tightly knit, team-oriented workplace, with very low turnover, high productivity, and high quality.

stable and loyal workforce, with cohesive work teams. Employee motivation is important because Toyota expects very high employee job performance. Organizational identification is important because the firm depends on employee initiative for constantly improving the production process, and on employee self-control to reduce the need for costly inspection and supervision. Positive group norms are also important to motivate and direct employee behaviour. As the box shows, it takes a complex combination of extrinsic and intrinsic rewards to produce the kinds of attitudes and behaviour Toyota needs for its high-involvement managerial strategy to work.

By now, it should be apparent that different managerial strategies will require different behaviours and different attitudes. Classical organizations need only provide sufficient rewards to create some degree of membership behaviour. Little attempt will be made to create job satisfaction. Work motivation can be achieved through rewards tied directly to the needed behaviours, or through the use of control systems, with the underlying threat of dismissal providing the basic motivation. These organizations will pay a price for not having job and reward satisfaction, or organizational identification, but this price may well be tolerable in the total context of these organizations.

In contrast, human relations organizations rely on job satisfaction and positive work norms and must ensure that they have equitable reward systems that generate job satisfaction and a substantial degree of commitment. Organizational identification, while desirable, is not essential.

Because they typically require the most complex behaviour from their employees and the highest level of performance, high-involvement organizations will generally require the most complex reward systems. They need to generate all three job attitudes and behaviours. The key job attitude for them is organizational identification, which is needed to generate the organizational citizenship behaviour that is so important to these firms, and which also plays a major role in generating membership and task behaviour. Work motivation needs to be high. And job satisfaction must also be high enough to help generate the high membership behaviour that the firm needs. Clearly, a key element in maintaining these attitudes is employee satisfaction with the reward system.

CAUSES AND CONSEQUENCES OF REWARD DISSATISFACTION

Reward dissatisfaction can cause a wide variety of undesirable consequences for organizations. But what causes reward dissatisfaction? And what exactly are the consequences that can flow from reward dissatisfaction? It is the purpose of this section to develop a framework that can provide answers to these questions.

CAUSES OF REWARD DISSATISFACTION

There are four main factors that can play a role in causing reward dissatisfaction, as Figure 3.3 illustrates. These are violation of the psychological contract, perceived inequity, relative deprivation, and lack of organizational justice.

VIOLATION OF THE PSYCHOLOGICAL CONTRACT

When people decide whether to join a firm, they do so based on their expectations about the rewards they will receive and the contributions they will have to make. This is known as their **psychological contract** (Schein, 1965; Rousseau, 1995; Rousseau and Ho, 2000). Similarly, an organization hires someone based on the expectation that the individual will make certain contributions to the organization, in return for certain rewards. In some cases, these psychological contracts will also include legal contracts, enforceable under law, spelling out the rewards to be provided and the contributions to be made. In most cases, they will not.

When an employee accepts an offer and joins a firm, problems with the psychological contract can occur for several reasons: first, if there has not been accurate communication about the nature of the rewards provided and/or contributions required, and these turn out to be different from (and less favourable than) what the employee expected; and second, if the employer unilaterally changes the "contract" to the perceived detriment of the employee.

Morrison and Robinson (1997) label these two possibilities "incongruence" of expectations and "reneging" and argue that either can lead to a perceived violation of the psychological contract. They cite evidence showing that perceived violation can cause employees to have less trust in their employer, decreased job satisfaction, reduced citizenship behaviour, and decreased work performance, as well as increased turnover, theft, and even sabotage.

psychological contract expectations about the rewards offered by a given job and the contributions necessary to perform the job

FIGURE 3.3   CAUSES OF REWARD DISSATISFACTION

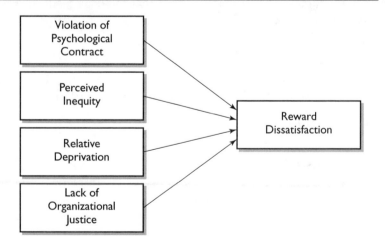

There are at least two other ways in which a psychological contract may relate to reward dissatisfaction. One is when employee perceptions of the fairness of the "contract" change. Employees may come to see the original contract (even though it is being honoured) as being unfair, in the light of new information they receive. The other is when employees feel compelled to accept a "contract" even though they believe it to be unfair right from the outset. In all four of these cases, reward dissatisfaction will likely occur.

In the 1980s and early 1990s, economic conditions caused many firms to make reductions to their reward structures that were in violation of long-standing psychological contracts. For example, Lucero and Allen (1994) note that reductions in employee benefits had a negative impact on the psychological contract. But the impact of these violations depends on the nature of the firm. For human relations firms, the costs of contract violations can be especially high, since employee satisfaction and trust of management form the glue that holds these organizations together. These problems will be particularly severe if the cuts appear to be unnecessary—if, for example, cuts are made even in the face of acceptable company profitability, a previously rare practice that became more common in the 1990s.

Box 3.4 illustrates the consequences that can arise when an organization makes promises for a fundamentally new type of psychological contract, but is perceived as violating these promises, as management at the CAMI auto plant in Ontario found out.

PERCEIVED INEQUITY

Individuals use at least two screens in deciding whether the rewards/contributions balance is fair. The first is an internal calculus, based on their own valuations of the rewards received and contributions made. The second is a comparison with the rewards/contributions ratio of relevant others, a process explained by **equity theory** (Adams, 1965).

Equity theory helps to explain a number of mysteries, such as why a person making over $5 million a year doing a job he has coveted all his life may bitterly proclaim that he is under-rewarded, and even threaten to quit, while another person earning $40 000 a year at a job she never particularly wanted is quite satisfied with her rewards. Sound far-fetched? Not if the first person is a baseball player with the highest batting average in the National League, and the second is an accounting clerk with a high school education, employed by a firm that provides high job security. The accounting clerk may look around and see that most people with performance, education, and job security similar to what she has are earning less than she is; the baseball player may look around and see six players with lower batting averages earning more.

Equity theory also helps to explain why, for two employees working side by side at the same job, each making $50 000 per year, one may believe this arrangement to be equitable, while the other regards it as highly unfair. Why? The dissatisfied employee believes that his or her contribution is much greater

equity theory
employees base perceptions of equity (fairness) on a comparison of their contributions/rewards ratio to the ratios of others perceived as similar

BOX 3.4 Violating the Psychological Contract at CAMI

Perceived violation of the psychological contract helped to derail an attempt to create a collaborative union–management relationship at CAMI Inc., a joint GM–Suzuki venture that was established to manufacture small cars in Ingersoll, Ontario, in 1988. Before the new plant came on stream, it agreed to a voluntary recognition of the union (the Canadian Auto Workers). The union agreed to accept somewhat lower wages and benefits than were offered by the big three automakers in return for a non-classical approach from management, in which workers would be treated with respect and dignity and their ideas and inputs would be valued (Rinehart, Huxley, and Robertson, 1997).

To reinforce this image of equality, time clocks, executive parking spaces, and executive cafeterias were eliminated, and production was organized into teams. Hourly employees were known as production associates, team leaders, and maintenance associates. However, relatively few changes were made to the nature of the work itself. And, perhaps most significantly, no changes were made to the usual reward system for hourly employees, and no rewards were provided for productivity or performance. Part of the reason for this may have been that the Canadian Auto Workers is philosophically opposed to performance pay, although it is not clear that the company pushed for these compensation changes.

Consequently, despite all the symbolic changes, workers soon came to believe that the promise of a fundamentally different relationship was an empty one, and that all the changes were simply superficial changes oriented toward manipulating workers to higher productivity. Workers pointed to extremely lean staffing levels, which put great pressure for production on the employees.

As a result of this perceived violation of the psychological contract, and the nonappearance of the intrinsic rewards the employees were expecting, union–management relationships became bitter, culminating in 1992 in the first and only strike at any Japanese "transplant" in North America. Prominent among the strike issues were reducing workloads and narrowing the wage/benefit gap between CAMI and other big three plants, concessions that were made by the company.

Following the strike, a psychological contract more in line with the North American auto industry appears to have emerged, in which workers believe that the firm is "just another car factory" and do not really expect treatment different from the industry norm. Since then, there have been no new major strikes, and in 1998 CAMI was selected as lead plant for the production of two new sport utility vehicles. However, this decision was likely prompted more by the plant's relatively new production technology than by any special union–management relationships. An example of the continuing tense relationships occurred on May 30, 1999, when workers refused to report to work in protest over the firing of a union steward involved in an altercation with a supervisor. In response, the company replaced the termination with a suspension, and work resumed.

than the contribution of the other employee, yet both are receiving the same rewards.

Thus, the essence of equity theory is simple: people make comparisons between the ratio of contributions they make and the rewards they receive, and the ratios of relevant others, often co-workers. They are often more concerned about the perceived fairness of this comparison than the absolute level of the rewards received. For example, research (Clark and Oswald, 1996) has found that employee satisfaction is determined more strongly by their relative pay than by the absolute amount of pay they receive (much to the astonishment of economists).

A key issue in equity theory is the selection of the comparison other (Miceli and Lane, 1991). For example, management of a veterinary hospital at a Canadian university were astonished when they discovered that their veterinary hospital technicians considered themselves underpaid, even though their pay and working conditions were considerably better than those enjoyed by technicians employed by private veterinary hospitals. It turns out that rather than comparing themselves with their private-sector colleagues, veterinary technicians at the university were comparing their pay and working conditions with those of the professors and research scientists with whom they were working.

As another example, in recent years the gap between the earnings of rank and file employees and top executives has been widening dramatically. For example, between 1980 and 1995 executive pay in the United States increased from 42 times the average worker's pay to 141 times (Pratt, 1996). By 1999, executive compensation (including share options) in the 500 largest publicly traded U.S. companies amounted to 475 times an average manufacturing worker's pay (*Economist*, 2000). Although workers may recognize that the job of a top executive is not similar to theirs, they may still believe that it is inequitable for their CEO to be receiving 475 times as much as they receive. This is particularly true in cases where workers are being asked to make sacrifices in their rewards, while executives are receiving increases.

RELATIVE DEPRIVATION

Crosby (1976) suggests that employee dissatisfaction with pay level will occur under six conditions: (a) there is a discrepancy between the outcome they want and what they actually receive; (b) they see that a comparison other receives more than they do; (c) past experience has led them to expect more than they now receive; (d) future expectancies for achieving better outcomes are low; (e) they feel a sense that they are entitled to more; and (f) they absolve themselves of personal responsibility for the lack of better outcomes.

To check on the validity of this theory, Sweeney, McFarlin, and Inderrieden (1990) utilized four separate employee samples. They found strong support for this theory. They found that while actual pay level did predict pay satisfaction (the higher the pay, the higher the satisfaction), in every sample the conditions cited above were at least three times as important in predicting pay satisfaction. Three conditions were of particular importance: social comparisons (condition b), the discrepancy between desired and actual pay (condition a), and sense of entitlement (condition e). Of course, it will be noted that condition (b) subsumes equity theory.

LACK OF ORGANIZATIONAL JUSTICE

The concept of organizational justice (Greenberg, 1990b) is also useful in understanding how people judge the fairness of their rewards. Organizational justice has two main components. **Distributive justice** is the perception that overall reward *outcomes* are fair, which is what equity theory is all about.

distributive justice the perception that overall reward outcomes are fair

Procedural justice is the perception that the *process* through which rewards are determined is fair. Unless people believe that both of these are fair, they will not feel that the reward system is fair (Tremblay, Sire, and Balkin, 2000).

For example, let us suppose that an individual has no faith in the process through which rewards are determined, regarding it as arbitrary or even capricious. Even if the actual outcome turns out be fair in a given instance (distributive justice), the employee may still feel dissatisfied with the reward system, because there is no assurance that the outcome will turn out to be fair the next time rewards are determined. On the other hand, even if the reward outcome is less than the employee believes to be warranted, but procedural justice has been done, reward dissatisfaction will be reduced.

As an example, let us suppose that a firm is facing extreme financial pressure, and the total salary bill must be cut by 10 percent. At the moment, employees are fairly compensated, when compared with industry standards. If the process by which it is determined that a 10 percent cut is necessary is viewed as reasonable, and if the cut is distributed in a fair way, it is much less likely to cause reward dissatisfaction.

A research study on the impact of distributive and procedural justice was conducted by Scarpello and Jones (1996). They found that although both distributive and procedural justice had an impact on employee satisfaction with the pay system (including pay level), distributive justice had by far the stronger effect.

Interestingly, these findings were reversed when employee satisfaction with the supervisor was examined—apparently employees strongly blame their supervisor for unfair pay procedures but only mildly blame them for perceived lack of fairness in the total amount of pay they receive (distributive justice). When organizational commitment—the degree of attachment to the firm expressed by employees—was examined, only procedural justice had an impact. An earlier study (Folger and Konovsky, 1989) also found that procedural justice had the greatest impact on trust of the supervisor and organizational commitment, while distributive justice had the greatest impact on pay satisfaction. Tremblay and Roussel (2001) found in a sample of Canadian managers that while both distributive and procedural justice influenced both pay satisfaction and job satisfaction, distributive justice had a greater impact on pay satisfaction, and procedural justice had a greater impact on job satisfaction.

In practical terms, Theriault (1992: 131–32) argues that the procedural justice will be achieved if the pay system meets the following conditions. The pay system must be:

- consistent—procedures are applied uniformly to different jobs and time periods;
- bias free—personal interests do not enter into application of the procedures;
- flexible—there must be procedures for appealing pay system decisions;
- accurate—application of procedures must be based on factual information;

- ethical—accepted moral principles must guide application of the procedures;
- representative—all affected employees must have an opportunity to express their concerns, which will be given serious consideration by the organization.

In general, when an organization is faced with a need to make changes (unfavourable to employees) in the psychological contract, the negative impact of these changes will be reduced to the extent that the firm practises principles of both distributive and procedural justice.

CONSEQUENCES OF REWARD DISSATISFACTION

What happens if employees experience reward dissatisfaction—if they perceive that the balance between rewards and contributions is unfair? Figure 3.4 provides a schematic illustration of some of the possible consequences. As can

FIGURE 3.4 CONSEQUENCES OF REWARD DISSATISFACTION

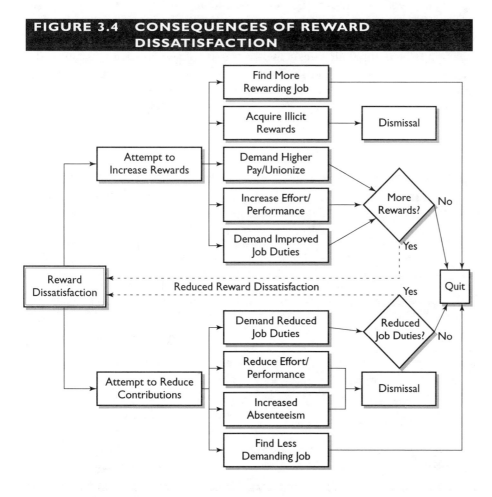

be seen, employees have two main options to redress the imbalance: to increase the rewards they receive or to reduce the contributions they make.

ATTEMPT TO INCREASE REWARDS

If employees choose to try to increase their rewards, they have a number of options. One option is to quit the organization and take a more rewarding job. Of course, this is only an option if a more rewarding job is available to the employee.

Another alternative is to simply demand higher extrinsic rewards, either individually (i.e., ask for a raise) or collectively through a union (i.e., demand wage increases during the next round of collective bargaining). If no union exists, employees may attempt to form one, if enough of them perceive an unfair rewards/contributions balance. If this approach succeeds, then reward dissatisfaction is reduced, as Figure 3.4 illustrates. But if this fails, employees may simply quit, or they may attempt to even the balance in another way.

Some employees may resort to illicit means to increase their rewards, such as padding their expense accounts or stealing the firm's property or money. As you will recall, this was how some employees at the Canadian National Exhibition reacted to their reward dissatisfaction. Such behaviour may be rationalized by employees on the basis that since the company is short-changing them (in their eyes), they are perfectly justified in "evening the score." In some sectors where rewards are low, and many illicit reward opportunities exist (such as in retailing), this can be a serious problem, as Box 3.5 illustrates.

BOX 3.5 The Devil Made Me Do It! (Or Was It Reward Dissatisfaction?)

"The devil made me do it!" This was a trademark line used by an old-time comedian to explain any malfeasance he committed. But it is not a very scientific explanation. In the grocery industry, theft by employees can be a serious problem. For instance, in one U.S. study, supermarket employees admitted stealing an average of $168 of merchandise a year.

Rather than the devil, one explanation for this situation may come from a sense of reward dissatisfaction or inequity. As one survey respondent noted: "During the last couple of years, the company has kept raising the standards and cutting back on the hours allotted for keeping those standards up. If you don't work *off the clock* the job won't get done. Some people steal as a way to get even." (From a study by

London House/Food Marketing Institute, *Third Annual Report on Theft in the Supermarket Industry* [Rosemont, IL: London House, 1992], cited in Johns, 1996: 176.)

The relationship between reward dissatisfaction and employee theft has been supported by a more scientific study in manufacturing plants (Greenberg, 1990a). Employee theft was measured before, during, and after a temporary ten-week pay cut caused by lack of orders. Greenberg found that theft increased dramatically during the rollback, but returned to normal levels once the normal pay level was restored. Interestingly, the increase in theft was less pronounced in a plant where management explained the need for pay cuts in a candid way, and where they expressed concern for the well-being of employees.

In some instances, employees may actually increase their work performance in response to reward dissatisfaction, but only if they are quite certain this will lead to significantly increased rewards. For example, if a promotion will provide a job in which their rewards and contributions will be balanced, and increased performance has a high probability of leading to this promotion, then the employee may attempt to improve performance, even though, in the short run, this will be worsening the rewards/contributions imbalance. But this is not the most likely response to reward dissatisfaction.

Finally, some employees may seek to even the balance by increasing their intrinsic rewards. For example, they may seek improvements to their job duties such that their work becomes more intrinsically satisfying. Their reasoning may go like this: "I may not be getting the pay I deserve, but at least I will now have a job I enjoy doing."

ATTEMPT TO REDUCE CONTRIBUTIONS

If rewards cannot be increased in some way that is significant to the employee, the employee may remain with the firm but redress the imbalance by reducing their contributions. This may be done formally or informally. For example, employees may formally request that their job duties be reduced. They may ask to be relieved of duties that require them to spend weekends away from home or that cause them to put in unpaid overtime.

This reduced contribution may take the form of reduced effort or care applied to their usual work activities, or longer coffee breaks. It may involve reducing the quality of customer service they provide. It could entail reducing or eliminating any activities that they had been performing on a voluntary basis. Organizational citizenship behaviour is one of the first things to go if employees seek to reduce their contributions. This is a major reason why reward dissatisfaction can be particularly damaging to high-involvement organizations.

Reduced contribution may take the form of increased absenteeism. Some employees may even resort to various types of negative behaviour, such as sabotage, as a means of evening the balance. Of course, these behaviours, if carried too far, can result in dismissal from the organization. This may not, however, be seen as much of a loss from the employee's point of view.

If the perceived imbalance cannot be evened out somehow, then an individual may seek a less demanding job in a different firm, even if it pays no more than his or her current job. If able to find such a job, the employee will quit. But even if there are no other employment opportunities available, some employees may still quit, preferring unemployment, if the imbalance is perceived as being intolerable or if the stress caused by the imbalance results in physical or mental health problems.

PREDICTING EMPLOYEE REACTIONS

But exactly how will each employee respond? This is difficult to predict, because it depends on the personal characteristics and circumstances of the employee as well as the specific characteristics of the situation. Are alternative jobs readily available? Can the employee afford to be unemployed? Does the employee have strong values about honesty, or a strong work ethic, which would preclude that person from using illicit rewards or reducing work performance?

In some instances, certain options are simply not available to employees, because organizations deliberately structure themselves to prevent them. For example, at Electronic Banking System (Box 2.1), employees handle a lot of cash. But with the cameras and other surveillance procedures, augmenting your income with some of this cash is pretty well impossible. And how would you really reduce work performance at the chicken-processing plant? About the only way is by not showing up for work. But if you don't show up, you simply don't get paid, so absenteeism doesn't get you very far.

So, at these classical firms, there is not much you can do to increase rewards or decrease contributions, other than threaten to quit. But that would be unlikely to be effective either, because turnover is not costly at these firms. Clearly, classical organizations are much more able to tolerate reward dissatisfaction than are human relations or high-involvement firms.

Of course, the response taken by the employer when the employee raises concerns will have a strong influence on what further actions are taken by the employee. Employee reactions will also depend on their tolerance for stress and perceived inequity. For example, some employees are high in **equity sensitivity**, which is a focus on maximization of personal rewards and a predisposition toward perceiving inequity, whether imagined or real (Huseman, Hatfield, and Miles, 1985). These employees are more likely to resort to drastic action to reduce their perceived reward imbalance.

One determinant of employee reactions may be the nature of the factor that caused the imbalance. For example, have additional job duties been added, have wages been cut, or has job security been reduced? Additional job duties may trigger demands for more pay in recognition of this greater contribution. A wage cut may lead to increased illicit rewards, reduced work contributions, or withdrawal from the organization, depending on the personal values of the employee. Reduction in job security may cause employees to seek employment where greater job security exists, or to seek higher pay to compensate them for the increased risk of job loss.

equity sensitivity a personality trait that entails a high predisposition toward perceiving personal inequity

UNDERSTANDING MEMBERSHIP BEHAVIOUR

Why would anyone choose to pull chickens apart for a living? In fact, why would a person choose to engage in paid employment at all? Not everyone does. Of the potential Canadian labour force (defined as persons ranging from 15 to 64 years of age), just under 71 percent are currently engaged in paid employment or self-employment, according to Statistics Canada. Approximately 5 percent of the potential labour force are not employed, but are seeking employment. That leaves about 24 percent who are choosing not to seek paid employment at this time.

The majority of those not currently seeking employment consist of married people, where one spouse engages in paid employment while the other handles the family responsibilities; students pursuing their educations; early retirees; and single parents. Interestingly, the proportion not choosing employment has been declining steadily over the past 50 years. For example, in 1951 about 40 percent of the potential labour force chose not to seek paid employment, nearly double the proportion today. Thus, more people are choosing to engage in paid employment than in the past.

So back to our question. Why do people work? Basically, people will accept employment with a given organization (1) if they have unsatisfied needs, (2) if employment by that organization is seen as being the best vehicle to satisfy these needs, and (3) if they are able and willing to do the things that this employment will require. Put another way, people will accept a job if the inducements or rewards associated with that job exceed the cost of the contributions they will have to make to secure and retain that job. If there are several job opportunities available that fit the above criteria, they will tend to choose the one in which the value of the rewards exceeds the cost of the contributions to the greatest extent.

That part is simple. The complicated part is that every individual will put a somewhat different valuation on the rewards provided, and on the value or costs of their contributions, depending on their personal characteristics and personal circumstances. Thus, when three people are each presented with the same two job offers, one person may choose the first offer, another may choose the second offer, and a third person may reject both. The integrated model of behaviour, to be presented later in the chapter, will shed more light on the process that goes into making these decisions.

CAUSES OF MEMBERSHIP BEHAVIOUR

Let's assume that an individual has selected a given employer. What factors determine whether she will choose to continue her employment with that employer? Although many factors can play a role, two job attitudes—job satisfaction and organizational identification—play a pivotal role, as has been discussed earlier in the chapter.

In general, job satisfaction occurs when one's important needs are satisfied through the job. One well-known model (Smith, Kendall, and Hulin, 1969) suggests that there are five main "facets" to job satisfaction: satisfaction with pay, promotion, supervisors, co-workers, and the job itself. Although the weighting of each of these facets will vary across individuals, each will likely play some role in overall job satisfaction.

Satisfaction with pay is the extent to which economic rewards meet employee needs and are seen as fair. Satisfaction with promotion is the extent to which advancement opportunities are available. Satisfaction with supervisors is the extent to which supervisors are seen as supportive, helpful, and fair in the treatment of employees. Satisfaction with co-workers is the extent to which co-workers are viewed as friendly, sociable, helpful, cooperative, and supportive. Satisfaction with the job itself is the extent to which the job contains various intrinsic rewards.

It should be noted that the above list of facets is not necessarily complete. For example, one important omission is job security. It is safe to say that for most employees, the degree of job or employment security provided by the organization plays a major role in their level of job satisfaction, as Ashford, Lee, and Bobko (1989) have found. Other important employee needs will be identified in conjunction with work motivation, which will be discussed shortly.

While job satisfaction is a positive contributor to ongoing membership behaviour, it is not the only important factor. The strength of an individual's attachment to an organization is known as his or her level of **organizational commitment**. However, there are two main types of commitment: affective commitment and continuance commitment. In **affective commitment,** an individual remains with the organization because of a sense of belongingness and loyalty to the organization, as well as an identification with the goals of the organization.

In **continuance commitment**, individuals stay with an organization because they would lose too much by quitting—they cannot find another job that would be comparable in terms of the ratio of rewards to contributions. Continuance commitment implies nothing about an employee's level of emotional attachment to the employer or that employee's level of job satisfaction; instead, it is simply a hard-headed calculation that "I have no better opportunities available to me." Indeed, it is quite conceivable that an individual might have high continuance commitment, but extremely low levels of job satisfaction and affective commitment. In fact, studies have shown no relationship between continuance commitment and affective commitment (Gellatly, 1995) and between continuance commitment and job satisfaction (Cramer, 1996). However, affective commitment and job satisfaction *are* related, and an analysis of 155 studies found that affective commitment and job satisfaction are each of about equal importance in influencing turnover (Tett and Meyer, 1993). Other studies have shown that continuance commitment also has an additional, separate effect on turnover (Jaros, Jermier, Koehler, and Sincich, 1993).

REWARDS, SATISFACTION, AND COMMITMENT

So the key question now is this: what role can the reward system play in generating job satisfaction and organizational commitment? Since a reward is anything provided by the organization that satisfies a person's needs, it is clear that rewards have a direct impact on job satisfaction. Of the five facets of job satisfaction discussed earlier, four are extrinsic and one (the job itself) intrinsic. Two of the facets are compensation-related: pay satisfaction and promotion satisfaction. We have already discussed the factors that affect reward satisfaction at considerable length.

As far as organizational commitment is concerned, the key issue is not so much what individuals receive from their jobs, but the relationship between

organizational commitment the strength of the individual's attachment to his or her organization

affective commitment attachment to an organization based on positive feelings toward the organization

continuance commitment attachment to an organization based on perceived lack of better opportunities

members and the organization as a whole. Therefore, it is likely that the concepts of the psychological contract, trust, and organizational justice, especially procedural justice, will play a major role. For example, Masterson and her colleagues (2000) found a strong relationship between procedural justice and affective commitment. Finegan (2000) found that organizations perceived to be concerned about employee welfare had higher affective commitment than other organizations. Employee benefits can help to create this perception, and rewards geared to organizational performance, such as profit sharing and employee stock plans, should help to create a feeling of belongingness and shared goals, leading to organizational identification and affective commitment.

Job security has also been found to relate to both job satisfaction and affective commitment. However, the impact of job security may vary, depending on its source. For example, some unionized employees have a high level of job security built into their contracts. This should enhance job satisfaction. But it may not enhance affective commitment if the employer is seen as granting the job security grudgingly. For job security to have a positive impact on affective commitment, it needs to be seen as something granted willingly by the employer. Employees need to feel "I am a valued and loyal employee and the firm is recognizing this by giving me job security," not "They'd love to fire me, but they can't."

For continuance commitment, several types of compensation strategies can be used. Seniority-based rewards will be a cornerstone, including seniority increases in pay, and benefit packages that increase with continued employment (especially if they are not entirely portable). Of course, simply having higher pay levels than competitors will increase the costs of quitting (thus increasing continuance commitment), and reduce employee turnover (Delery et al., 2000).

But if high pay levels are the only strategy a firm adopts to decrease turnover, it may be a very costly one. For example, based on an empirical study, Powell, Montgomery, and Cosgrove (1994: 245) found that higher pay levels did decrease quit rates somewhat, but concluded: "raising wages to reduce turnover would be profitable only if turnover costs were enormous." This finding is not surprising, since we have seen that pay level is only one factor of many that affect turnover.

A recent study by Miceli and Mulvey (2000) looked at the consequences of employee satisfaction with pay level (distributive justice) and with the pay system (procedural justice). They found that satisfaction with pay level had absolutely no impact on affective commitment, while satisfaction with the pay system had a significant impact.

IS LOW TURNOVER ALWAYS GOOD?

You have no doubt noticed that most of the foregoing discussion assumes that employee turnover is a bad thing. But is a very low turnover rate always a good thing? For example, low turnover may not be a sign of organizational health if it is due only to continuance commitment. If the firm focuses on continuance commitment but neglects job satisfaction and affective commitment, it risks ending up with a workforce of dissatisfied, uncommitted employees *who will never quit.*

Excessively low turnover can also cause stagnation in an organization, especially when the organization is not expanding. Some firms have launched early-retirement programs specifically to provide opportunities to younger employees. Finally, it should be noted that turnover rate by itself does not always tell the whole story. Two firms may have identical turnover rates, but this does not mean they have equally good reward and compensation systems. The key is *who is quitting*? Are they employees for whom there is not really a good fit between their characteristics and the needs of the organization, or are they valuable employees whom the firm sorely needs? Recall the soft drink company described in Box 3.1, whose reward system served to retain only dishonest, irresponsible employees, while causing honest, conscientious employees to quit.

UNDERSTANDING TASK BEHAVIOUR

Have you ever watched somebody do something, and then wondered, "now why did they do that?" To understand this, we need to understand *motivation*. Fortunately, some useful concepts have been developed to help us do that. Over the years, two main sets of motivation theory have emerged: content theories and process theories.

content theories of motivation focus on understanding motivation by identifying underlying human needs

Content theories of motivation focus on identifying and understanding our underlying needs, based on the commonsense notion that people perform behaviours they think will help them satisfy their key needs. For example, a basic need is the need for survival—for food and shelter. In our society, this really means a need for money. But content theories cannot predict the precise behaviours that human beings will undertake to try to satisfy a given need, in this case to attain money. For example, some of us will seek paid employment. Some of us will buy lottery tickets or go to the racetrack. Some of us will seek a rich spouse. Some of us will rob banks.

process theories of motivation focus on understanding motivation by determining the process humans use to make choices about the specific actions they will take

If we all have the same need, but can pursue many different paths to satisfy that need, what determines how we will go about satisfying it? **Process theories of motivation** help us to understand the process we go through to determine the specific actions we will take to satisfy a given need. We will first discuss content theories of motivation and then examine process theories.

CONTENT THEORIES OF MOTIVATION

What are the important needs that human beings seek to satisfy? Using a variety of classification systems, psychologists have identified literally dozens of specific needs that may drive behaviour. For example, Murray (1938) listed over 40 categories of needs. However, for our purposes, it is useful to group these needs.

MASLOW'S HIERARCHY OF NEEDS

Maslow (1954) suggested that people have five sets of needs, arranged in a hierarchy of prominence, as shown in Figure 3.5. There are two key aspects to his theory. First, so-called lower-order needs must be satisfied before higher-order needs come into play. Second, a satisfied need no longer motivates.

Thus, only when a person's physiological (survival) needs for the basic necessities of life—food and shelter—are satisfied will that person become concerned about the next-higher need. Once a person's immediate survival needs are addressed, that person then becomes concerned about how to satisfy these needs tomorrow and the next day and the day after that (safety and security needs). People like to have the security of knowing that their basic needs will be satisfied in the future.

Once they have this assurance, people become concerned about satisfying their needs for companionship and positive social regard by others, a need to be with and be accepted by other humans. Once these social or belongingness needs are met, people then become concerned with ego or esteem needs—for accomplishment, achievement, and mastery or competence. Finally, if these needs are satisfied, the final set of needs is activated—the need for self-actualization. This is the need to maximize one's human potential, the need for continued learning, growth, and development. Maslow argues that self-actualization is the ultimate motivator, because, unlike the other needs, it can never be satisfied.

But is Maslow correct? Does human motivation really work the way he suggests? So far, research has not been able to confirm the theory precisely as outlined by Maslow. Some researchers (Alderfer, 1972) have collapsed Maslow's five categories into three: existence (corresponding to Maslow's

Maslow's hierarchy of needs content theory of motivation that states that human needs are grouped into five main levels and that humans seek to satisfy the lowest-order needs before satisfying higher-order needs

FIGURE 3.5   MASLOW'S HIERARCHY OF NEEDS

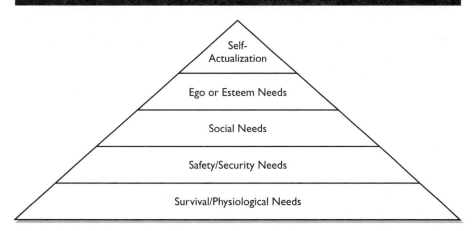

lower two need levels), relatedness (corresponding to Maslow's middle or social need level), and growth (corresponding to Maslow's upper two levels). Other studies have shown that lower-order needs do not have to be completely satisfied before the others are activated, and that people can be motivated simultaneously by all of the needs.

To illustrate the possible variation in needs, consider the most basic need—the need for survival. Most of us will agree that the need for survival is the most important need. But even here people vary. If the basic need for survival dominates all else, how do you explain the electrical crew of the *Titanic*, faced with certain death from drowning if they did not leave, but staying at their stations deep in the bowels of the ship and keeping the vital electrical system operating even as the ship slid beneath the waves? Of course, it is possible that they believed that the ship really was unsinkable, and this is why they stayed at their stations. But what about secret service agents, who willingly accept the duty to shield their heads of state from an assassin's bullet with their own bodies? And what about those cases where people intentionally take their own lives?

The reality is that people differ greatly in the strength of their various needs. And the same individual may vary over time in the strength of her or his different needs. For example, a single person may have relatively low economic needs but relatively high social needs. Therefore, that person will turn down opportunities to earn overtime in order to socialize with friends. But suppose that person gets married, buys a house, and has children. Economic needs may increase, reducing the importance of social needs. That person will then be more likely to be motivated to work overtime.

Although it is unable to predict any given individual's motive pattern, Maslow's theory is useful because it does appear to describe behaviour at a group level. For example, as the income of a group or society increases, there tends to be a greater concern for satisfying higher-order needs. Thus, in a relatively wealthy society, such as Sweden, where the social welfare system ensures that lower-order needs are met, it is difficult to entice people to work at jobs that do not satisfy their higher-order needs.

In Canada, in the 1960s and 1970s, when jobs were plentiful and income was steadily rising, people also became more concerned with the intrinsic qualities of their jobs. A "good job" was one that allowed autonomy, self-expression, and personal growth. As jobs became more scarce in the 1980s and 1990s, and income stagnated, lower-order needs became more predominant. Although economic conditions improved in the late 1990s, in the eyes of many people today, a "good job" is a job that has good pay and benefits and provides job security.

THE TWO-FACTOR THEORY OF MOTIVATION

two-factor theory of motivation argues that intrinsic factors influence work motivation, while extrinsic factors influence job satisfaction

In an attempt to determine the most important factors causing job satisfaction or dissatisfaction, Frederick Herzberg asked a sample of employees to write a list of things that made them feel good about their jobs, and a list of things that made them feel bad about their jobs (Herzberg, Mausner, and Snyderman,

1959). He was surprised to find that the two lists were completely different. He had expected many of the same items on both lists, just reversed. For example, he expected high pay to make people feel good about their job, and low pay to make people feel unhappy about their jobs.

Instead, while he found that low pay did indeed make people dissatisfied, high pay did not make them enthusiastic about their work. Things that made them feel good about their work had to do with their job content—mastering a difficult task, learning a new skill, or completing a major job accomplishment. Things that made them dissatisfied were things like pay, a poor relationship with their supervisor or co-workers, and working conditions.

Subsequently, Herzberg (1966) realized that he was really dealing with two different concepts—job satisfaction and work motivation. The factors that caused job dissatisfaction he called "hygienes" and the factors that made people feel good about their work he labelled "motivators." From this, he concluded that job satisfaction was caused by extrinsic factors and motivation by intrinsic factors. He suggested that to have both satisfied and motivated employees, an organization must provide both extrinsic (hygiene factors) and intrinsic (motivators) rewards. This fits well with Maslow's theory, since the hygienes correspond to the lower-order needs and the motivators to the higher-order needs.

JOB CHARACTERISTICS THEORY

Richard Hackman and Greg Oldham (1980) extended Herzberg's work by attempting to identify the specific job characteristics that cause intrinsic motivation and by developing a method to calculate the amount of intrinsic motivation in a particular job. They identified what they call five *core job dimensions*—task identity, task significance, skill variety, autonomy, and feedback—and suggest that jobs high in these dimensions will be intrinsically motivating: people will enjoy doing these jobs for the satisfaction they derive from performing them, rather than the extrinsic rewards flowing from them.

Task identity is defined as the extent to which a worker is able to perform a complete cycle of activities, from start to finish, rather than only one small part of the job cycle. **Task significance** is the perceived importance of the job in the general scheme of things. For example, the job of heart surgeon would carry more task significance than that of a hot dog vendor.

Skill variety is the extent to which a substantial number of skills are required for task completion. **Job autonomy** is the extent to which workers are able to decide for themselves how to perform their jobs. **Job feedback** is the extent to which an individual receives feedback, from the job itself, on work quantity and quality. For example, a typist using a spellcheck program gets feedback on the quality of work from the job itself. A bomb disposal expert does not need outside feedback to know if he or she has been successful in a job!

Although Hackman and Oldham originally hypothesized that jobs high in these characteristics would be motivating only for persons with a high growth need, subsequent research has shown that most people respond favourably to jobs with these characteristics. For example, Fried (1991) analyzed 79 studies

task identity the extent to which a worker performs a complete cycle of job activities

task significance the perceived importance or social value of a given task

skill variety the variety of skills required for task completion

job autonomy the degree of freedom workers have in deciding how to perform their jobs

job feedback the extent to which the job itself provides feedback on worker performance

job enrichment the process of redesigning jobs to incorporate more of the five core dimensions of intrinsically satisfying work

and found that the core job dimensions were significantly related to higher work performance and even more strongly related to employee satisfaction.

A conscious effort by organizations to redesign their jobs to include higher amounts of the five core dimensions is known as **job enrichment**, and many organizations, especially those wishing to use the high-involvement strategy, have job enrichment programs. It is probable that as long as employees are capable of performing the enriched jobs, and don't perceive the enriched jobs as simply an attempt to load more work on them, they will respond favourably to job enrichment. However, some organizations may forget that if employees are performing at a higher level, the compensation system should recognize this, or perceived inequity may ensue, along with reward dissatisfaction. This could undo the favourable effects of job enrichment.

Although it is a separate theory, job characteristics theory fits well with the other content theories of motivation. As Figure 3.6 illustrates, the intrinsic job characteristics identified by Hackman and Oldham correspond to the motivators identified by Herzberg and address the higher-order needs specified by Maslow. The figure also shows how these content theories relate to the three managerial strategies.

MONEY AS A MOTIVATOR

According to Herzberg and many other experts (Kohn, 1993), money is not a motivator. Is this really true? Before settling this, one must realize that money itself is not technically a need, but a generalizable resource that can be used to acquire other things that will satisfy a wide array of needs. But money also has a symbolic value and may represent status and accomplishment.

FIGURE 3.6 CONTENT THEORIES OF MOTIVATION AND THEIR RELATIONSHIP TO MANAGERIAL STRATEGY

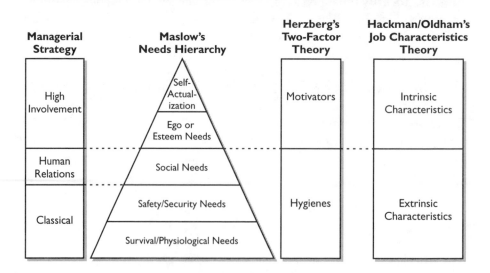

In organizations, the amount and manner in which one is paid sends important signals about how one is regarded by the employer. For example, if a person receives a slightly smaller raise than a co-worker receives, even if the raise itself is a generous one, that person may infer that the co-worker is more highly regarded and has the inside track on the next promotion. And we have already seen how perceptions of relative inequity can have a greater impact than the absolute value of compensation received.

The multifaceted nature of money as a motivator adds complexity to the compensation process, as does the fact that people vary in their "money ethic"—the inherent value they place on money (Tang, Kim, and Tang, 2000). But one thing is clear: for many people, money is an important motivator. However, the type of motivation produced by an extrinsic reward like money is different from the type of motivation produced by intrinsic rewards, as we will see when discussing attribution theory.

SALIENCE OF NEEDS

Before leaving our discussion of human needs, we need to consider the issue of **need salience**. The salience of a particular need for a given individual determines the extent to which that individual will be impelled to attempt to satisfy that need. If a reward is to be motivating, it must address a salient need. Clearly, for some people certain needs are salient, while for others different needs are salient. As Figure 3.7 shows, two sets of factors—personal characteristics and personal circumstances—interact with basic human needs to determine need salience.

need salience the degree of urgency attached by an individual to satisfying a particular need

How does this process work? Two key factors determine the salience of a need for a given person at a given point in time: the *amount of need deprivation* and *the importance of the need*. Need deprivation is the difference between how much a person currently has of something and how much he or she requires to satisfy a particular need.

Need deprivation is strongly influenced by personal circumstances. For example, if a person needs several close friendships to satisfy social needs, but currently lives in an isolated area and has no friends at all (personal circumstances), there is high need deprivation. As another example, if a family

FIGURE 3.7 HOW NEED SALIENCE IS DETERMINED

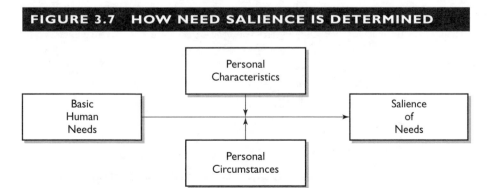

requires about $50 000 a year to maintain what they consider a suitable standard of living, but actual family income is $25 000, there is considerable need deprivation. Clearly, personal circumstances, such as the size of your family, your financial obligations, and your current financial condition (e.g., no savings), affect the degree of need deprivation for money.

Need salience is also determined by the importance placed on the need by an individual. For example, someone may have a high deprivation of a certain need, but if that person does not consider it an important need, it may be less salient than a more important need for which there is less deprivation. Personal characteristics tend to determine the relative importance of a given need. For example, some individuals value self-actualization more highly than any other need and must pursue this need regardless of whether their other needs are satisfied. We have the classic example of the "starving artist" who must pursue artistic and creative endeavours despite high deprivation of other needs. On the other hand, some people are high in "money ethic" and have a much higher tendency to change jobs if they perceive that so doing will increase their financial rewards (Tang, Kim, and Tang, 2000).

So a combination of high importance and high deprivation adds up to high need salience. The higher the need salience, the higher the value that will be placed on things that will satisfy that need. Box 3.6 illustrates the role that personal circumstances can play in this process.

PROCESS THEORIES OF MOTIVATION

If two individuals are seeking to satisfy exactly the same need, they can choose many different paths or behaviours to satisfy that need. Process theories of motivation attempt to explain the process by which individuals make the decision to pursue one path or another to reach their goal of satisfying a particular need.

BOX 3.6 Need Salience in the Klondike

The rush to the Klondike in 1896–98 was the greatest gold rush in Canada's history. Almost overnight, Dawson City went from an unpopulated, mosquito-infested mud flat in the middle of Yukon Territory to the largest city west of Winnipeg and north of Seattle. Those who struck gold found themselves in a odd position: there was nothing to buy, not even labour. At this time in the rest of North America, top wages for a working man were $1.50 a day. In Dawson, it was difficult to find someone who would work for ten times that much.

But as economic needs became less salient, other needs became more so. Because of the isolation, things that would have had little or no value elsewhere commanded exorbitant prices. For example, "when one man drifted in with an ancient newspaper soaked in bacon grease, he was able to sell it for fifteen dollars" (Berton, 1972: 373)—equivalent to about $1000 today. With their economic needs satisfied, the needs of grizzled miners changed dramatically. Because of their isolation, a need that became highly salient was for news of the outside world.

REINFORCEMENT THEORY

The simplest process theory is **reinforcement theory** (Skinner, 1953), sometimes called behaviourism, operant conditioning, or behaviour modification. The underlying premise of this theory is that an individual will repeat behaviours that have led to need satisfaction in the past, and will discontinue behaviours that do not contribute to need satisfaction. This theory is based on learning theory. As young children, we all experiment with a variety of behaviours. We repeat behaviours that have positive consequences, and discontinue behaviours that have negative consequences.

For reinforcement theory to work, the individual must perceive a link between the behaviour and the consequence. If, for example, children grow up in a household in which rewards and punishments are provided in a capricious or arbitrary manner, then they may "learn" that there is little connection between their behaviour and what happens to them. They will tend to develop a personality trait known as an "external locus of control." Persons with an external locus of control tend to believe that they have very little control over outcomes. In the work setting, these individuals tend to believe that the degree of job effort they exert will have very little influence on the degree of performance they achieve or on the rewards they receive.

The key to understanding how a person will behave in the future, according to reinforcement theory, is to understand how that person and others around them were reinforced for various types of behaviour in the past. As an example, if someone grows up in an environment where most people are unemployed, and those who are employed never earn more than minimum wage, that person may come to regard employment as a very unlikely way to satisfy the need for money. If the same person sees local drug dealers driving around in fancy cars and wearing fancy clothes, that person may perceive drug dealing as a much more viable way to satisfy the need for money.

Reinforcers can be of two types: positive and negative. Positive reinforcement takes place when a reward follows a valued behaviour; negative reinforcement takes place when an undesirable consequence occurs whenever the valued behaviour does not occur. This undesirable consequence can be either the removal of something valued (such as docking a day's pay for an unauthorized absence) or the imposition of something not wanted (such as assigning an employee to the least desirable job in the plant on the day following an absence).

For those who are designing a reward system, the guidelines offered by reinforcement theory are quite clear. Desired behaviours for each employee need to be clearly specified. Then, each time that behaviour occurs, it is followed by a reward that is of significant value to the recipient. The closer the reward is to the behaviour, the better. Behaviour modification theory also says that unrewarded behaviours eventually will disappear, so this can be a way of dealing with undesirable behaviours. It is very important that undesirable behaviours not be inadvertently rewarded, as was the case at Bausch and Lomb (Box 3.2).

reinforcement theory
a behaviour will be repeated if valued outcomes flow from that behaviour, or if performing the behaviour reduces undesirable outcomes

There are numerous problems in the practical application of this theory. One problem is that it assumes that all desired behaviours are measurable, and that it is practical to identify and respond to every instance of the behaviour. As we have seen, rewarding only a portion of the range of behaviours desired from an employee can cause serious problems.

The second problem is that reinforcement theory considers only rewards the organization can control. For example, an autoworker who welds pop bottles into car rocker panels is not receiving any kind of company-based reward for doing so, but may be receiving psychological rewards for "outsmarting" the company. Behaviourism is an extrinsically based theory that does not recognize differences between individuals in how they value rewards, or how they evaluate the costs of different behaviours open to them. It does not recognize the concept of intrinsic rewards flowing from a given activity, or the possibility of altruism. Third, there is the issue of what happens when rewards stop—will the desired behaviour cease? Reinforcement theory predicts it eventually would, so behaviour needs to be continually rewarded under this system.

Some critics argue that behaviourism takes away employee responsibility for their actions, making them incapable of self-control (Kohn, 1993), and removes intrinsic motivation (Deci, 1975; Deci and Ryan, 1985), as will be discussed shortly. It can make many employees feel manipulated, like powerless pawns, and can cause resentment toward the punisher, and even the rewarder in some cases. However, there is no doubt that application of reinforcement principles can change human behaviour (O'Hara, Johnson, and Beehr, 1985). Reinforcement theory appears to work best for simple behaviours and short-term behavioural change.

EXPECTANCY THEORY

Although reinforcement theory is important, it does not help us understand the thought process that takes place when individuals choose a particular behaviour from the virtually infinite possibilities. The main theory to explain this process is known as the *expectancy theory of motivation* (Vroom, 1964; Lawler, 1973). **Expectancy theory** suggests that the likelihood of performing one behaviour or another is dependent on three things: (1) the net value (valence) of the consequences that may flow from that behaviour, (2) the perceived likelihood that the behaviour will lead to those consequences (instrumentality), and (3) the perceived likelihood of actually being able to perform those behaviours (expectancy). As Figure 3.8 indicates, valence, instrumentality, and expectancy must all be positive before effort will be exerted to perform a given behaviour.

In essence, individuals ask themselves three questions before attempting to exert effort to perform a particular behaviour. Is the thing worth doing—do the rewards exceed the costs (valence)? Will I actually receive the rewards if I do the thing (instrumentality)? Am I actually able to do the thing (expectancy)? Only when the answers to all three questions are positive will the behaviour be attempted. Box 3.7 provides an illustration of this process.

expectancy theory individuals are more likely to attempt to perform a particular behaviour if that behaviour is perceived to lead to valued consequences and if the perceived probability of actually being able to perform that behaviour is high

FIGURE 3.8   EXPECTANCY THEORY OF MOTIVATION

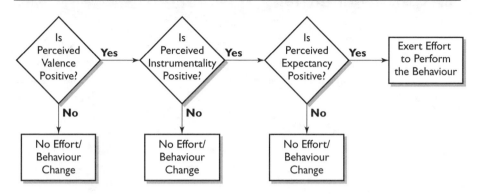

The implications of this theory for reward systems are quite clear. First, make sure that the net valence for performing the behaviour will be positive, *in the eyes of the person expected to perform the behaviour*. This involves maximizing the person's rewards while minimizing their costs of performing the behaviour. To do so, you need to understand the needs and personal values of those you are attempting to motivate. This is made much more complicated if they all vary in their needs and values. This is one reason why firms have an implicit preference for a homogeneous workforce, and tend to hire "clones"— employees who are very similar to those they have now.

Second, make sure that instrumentality is strong. It must be clear to employees that performance of the desired behaviours will in fact lead to the specified rewards. Trust and credibility may be an important issue here. Have you promised rewards in the past that failed to materialize? And third, make sure that employees have confidence in their ability to actually perform the desired behaviours. This may involve providing the physical and mental tools necessary to get the job done, and providing a context in which task performance is facilitated.

ATTRIBUTION THEORY

Expectancy theory does not distinguish between extrinsic and intrinsic rewards in determining the valence for performing a particular behaviour. It assumes that they simply add up: there is a greater likelihood of performing a behaviour that has both intrinsic and extrinsic rewards, other things being equal. However, there is one line of theory that argues that provision of extrinsic rewards may actually destroy intrinsic rewards for performing a particular behaviour.

This theory is known as **attribution theory** (Deci, 1975; Deci and Ryan, 1985). The premise of this theory is that human beings are active creatures, continually engaging in a variety of activities, without necessarily having a conscious understanding of their motives before performing these activities. But after performing any activity, we often feel compelled to try to understand

attribution theory
theory of motivation arguing that humans often act without understanding their motives for their behaviour and afterwards attempt to attribute motives for their actions

BOX 3.7 The $50 000 Hamburger

Picture this. It is a beautiful summer day. You are sitting on a park bench, eating your lunch. Suddenly, your reverie is interrupted by an elderly stranger sitting next to you, who offers you $10 if you will run to the hamburger stand two kilometres away and bring him back a "Big Mike" sandwich. But there's a catch. He will only pay you the $10 if you can bring it back within ten minutes, because he has to leave then. Would you do it? Let's use expectancy theory to predict your reaction.

First, you would likely consider whether the net value (valence) of the outcome is positive, once the costs are subtracted from the rewards. For example, getting the hamburger will make you late for work, and your boss has warned you that one more late appearance could cost you your job. You are pretty sure that you would not be fired for getting back a few minutes late, but you are not positive about that. The boss would certainly be angry, and who needs that? Given the small size of the reward, the net valence of the outcome is probably negative, and you will probably not go any further in considering whether to perform the desired behaviour.

But suppose that the stranger bumps the reward up to $50 000. You might then conclude that the size of that reward outweighs the risk of job loss, and the valence is now positive. So would you now get the hamburger? Probably not. Why not? You are likely not convinced that the behaviour (getting the hamburger) would actually lead to the reward (would the stranger really give you $50 000?). In other words, you perceive a low instrumentality.

But let's suppose that the stranger reveals himself to be an eccentric billionaire well known for such bizarre acts as paying $50 000 for a hamburger, and shows you that he has more than $50 000 in his billfold. You now believe that it is very probable you would receive the $50 000 if you brought back the hamburger (instrumentality is high). Now would you go get the hamburger? Of course! You'd be crazy not to!

Well, that depends on your expectancy that you could actually perform the behaviour—that is, bring the hamburger back within ten minutes. You are at the centre of the park, the sidewalks are crowded, and you would probably have to stand in line for at least five minutes. In high school your best time for running the 1000 metres was three minutes, and that was quite a few doughnuts ago! If you believe that there is no chance of bringing back the hamburger within the ten minutes (zero expectancy), you will still not be motivated to attempt to perform the behaviour.

How could the stranger attempt to motivate you at this point? What if he made the reward $1 million? This would have no impact on your behaviour. When either instrumentality or expectancy is zero, the size of the reward is irrelevant. So the only thing he could do would be to somehow change the expectancy, by, say, loaning you a bicycle or increasing the time allowed for task completion.

why we performed that activity—"Now why did I do that?" In other words, we seek to attribute some motive to that activity. If there is an "obvious" reason for so doing, we will attribute our activity to that motive. The following story may help to illustrate this:

> An elderly man who lived next to a vacant lot had enjoyed his peace and quiet until the neighbourhood children selected the site for various noisy games every day after school. After vainly trying a number of approaches, such as admonishing them to be quiet or trying to convince them to play elsewhere, he tried a new approach. He gathered the children around one day and

announced that he had come to enjoy the sound of their play so much that he wanted to reward them. He told them that he would give each of them 50 cents for each day they would come and play at the vacant lot.

The children thought this was great, and the noise actually increased! However, after several days the old man regretfully announced that since he was not a wealthy man, he would have to reduce their payment to 25 cents a day. Although the children grumbled, they accepted this. He subsequently lowered their pay to 10 cents and then 5 cents, at which point the children announced that they would not be coming back to play anymore. It was simply not worth it for a nickel a day!

This story indicates how intrinsic motivation was apparently replaced by extrinsic motivation, which was then extinguished when the extrinsic rewards were removed. Research studies in laboratory settings, involving intrinsically interesting activities such as doing a puzzle, have confirmed this result. Subjects usually are children, and half of them are told that they will be paid for the number of puzzles that they complete in, say, 30 minutes. The other half are simply told to complete as many as they can in 30 minutes, with no mention of money. At the end of the 30 minutes, both groups are told that they now have some free time, and can do whatever they want. Almost invariably, the nonpaid group continues to do more puzzles, while the group that had been paid stops doing them. This is taken as evidence that the extrinsic reward has destroyed the intrinsic motivation for the paid group.

Wiersma (1992) analyzed 20 studies and found that when actual work behaviour is simulated and extrinsic rewards are not removed, extrinsic rewards add to intrinsic rewards to create greater task behaviour. However, it should be noted that most of these studies are simulated in a laboratory and are short-term in nature. Perhaps intrinsic motivation would disappear over time, as Deci (1975) argues.

So what are the implications of attribution theory for reward systems? Deci (1975) argues that pay should not be related to output, and that intrinsic rewards should be used to motivate performance. Of course, this may be fine if there is intrinsic motivation in the first place. If there is not, either intrinsic motivation must be generated by enriching jobs or extrinsic means must be used.

So does this mean that you should never provide extrinsic rewards for good individual performance if it is already intrinsically motivated? Not necessarily. Some researchers argue that providing extrinsic rewards as recognition for accomplishment can actually increase feelings of equity and satisfaction, without damaging intrinsic motivation, but only if rewards are not seen as driving or controlling behaviour, or evaluating behaviour (Harackiewicz and Larson, 1986).

To illustrate, consider the UNICEF gift shop volunteers discussed in Chapter 1. Suppose UNICEF decides it would like to recognize their services, by providing one dollar an hour as a token of appreciation. They would fill in time cards, which would be verified by a supervisor. Would this increase motivation? Likely not. We can predict that the volunteers will be insulted by the implication that they are involved with the organization to serve their own self-interest, by the implication that their time is worth just one dollar an hour, and by the implication that they cannot be trusted. But, on the other hand, if dedicated service is recognized by paying the expenses to a valued national convention, this would not likely decrease intrinsic motivation, and may enhance overall commitment.

ECONOMIC THEORY

Finally, one theory of work motivation is based on economic theory. Although it can be a useful predictor of behaviour of some employees, it represents a much narrower version of motivation theory. Essentially, economic theory assumes that people are motivated only by extrinsic (economic) rewards, and will always seek to maximize these rewards while minimizing their contributions to the organization. This theory sees all work as being inherently distasteful, and assumes that whenever given the opportunity, people will seek to do as little of it as possible.

agency theory agents (employees) will pursue their own self-interests rather than the interests of their principals (owners) unless they are closely monitored or their interests are aligned with the interests of their principals

One of the most prominent economic theories is known as **agency theory** (Jensen and Meckling, 1976; Eisenhardt, 1989). This theory makes a key distinction between principals (those who own the enterprise) and agents (those who work on their behalf within the organization). Agency theory assumes that the interests of principals and agents will be divergent, and that faced with a choice between advancing the principal's interests or their own, agents will always seek to further their own interests. This creates a need for the principals to put procedures in place for the monitoring of agent behaviour to minimize the extent to which they pursue their own interests at the expense of the principal. However, this monitoring is expensive, and principals will seek to reduce the costs of this whenever possible. Therefore, principals will favour, whenever possible, reward systems that closely tie individual rewards to specific behaviours desired by the principals.

Economic theory represents a simplified view of employee behaviour. It assumes that all people are fixated at the lowest level of Maslow's needs hierarchy, that personal values such as honesty and strong work ethics do not exist, and that intrinsic rewards have little or no relevance to behaviour. Of course these are all classical beliefs, and classical organizations tend to favour economic theory as the underpinning for their managerial systems. Economic theory is only useful if the employees of the organization actually match these assumptions. When they do, it can be a useful model of behaviour in designing reward systems. When they do not, it can result in the development of reward systems that are suboptimal, ineffective, or even counterproductive.

Understanding Organizational Citizenship Behaviour

Organizational citizenship behaviour is a relatively new concept that has developed to describe voluntary or discretionary behaviours that go beyond task and membership behaviour. At a broad level, it is a "willingness to cooperate" in the pursuit of organizational goals. It is no coincidence that this concept has emerged simultaneously with the emergence of high-involvement organizations. Because of the nature of this managerial strategy, and the conditions of high uncertainty and dynamism in which these firms operate, organizational citizenship behaviour is of key importance, in contrast to human relations firms and especially classical firms.

Although this concept is continuing to evolve from its original formulation (Bateman and Organ, 1983), current thought suggests five main dimensions (Organ, 1990). *Altruism* is the extent of willingness to offer help to a co-worker, supervisor, or client without any expectation of personal reward for so doing, and without any negative repercussions if the help had been withheld. *General compliance* is the extent to which conscientiousness—in terms of attendance, use of work time, and adherence to policies—goes beyond the minimum necessary standards. *Courtesy* is the extent of "touching base" with people before taking actions that could affect their work. *Sportsmanship* is the ability to tolerate, with good grace, the minor nuisances and impositions that are a normal part of work life. *Civic virtue* is the extent to which individuals take an interest and participate in the broader governance and operation of the organization.

Causes of Citizenship Behaviour

The prime source of citizenship behaviour is organizational identification. There are two aspects of organizational identification that are relevant. One aspect has to do with shared organizational goals, and there are two varieties of goal identification. One type is where the interests of the individual and the interests of the organization are congruent: "If the organization is successful, I will share in the rewards." Argyris (1964) refers to this as organizational integration. An example would be a firm in which employees are also significant shareholders.

The other variety of goal identification occurs when the goals of the organization match important values of the individual. This is similar to what some researchers refer to as "moral" or "normative" commitment. An example of "moral" identification might be people who join UNICEF because they wish to help fight child poverty. Another example might be a person who chooses to work in a hospital because of a desire to help heal the sick.

The second relevant aspect of organizational identification is a feeling of membership or belongingness. If people feel that they are valued, respected, and important members of their organization, they are much more likely to engage in citizenship behaviour. This is also tied in with justice, fair treatment, and reciprocity: "The organization does whatever it can to look after my interests, and I will therefore do the same for the organization."

Employees with high organizational identification will seek to further organizational goals in any way possible, ranging from increasing job effort to making innovative suggestions. Employees will also promote a spirit of cooperation within the organization, since this will further organizational goals. Another result of organizational identification should be decreased turnover, absenteeism, grievances, and other negative behaviours.

A key value of organizational identification is as a counterweight to narrow self-interest. In the Green Giant case discussed at the beginning of the chapter, employees pursued their own self-interest at the expense of the interests of the company by "cheating" on the payment system. But if organizational identification had been high, this result would have been much less likely.

CREATING CITIZENSHIP BEHAVIOUR

So how can organizational identification be created, and what role can the reward system play in this process? Before we answer these questions, there appear to be several preconditions without which citizenship behaviour will not develop. One of these is employment security. It is unreasonable to expect employees to be loyal to an organization that exhibits no loyalty toward them. Research also shows that an organization that shows genuine concern for the needs of its employees—for example, through the use of benefits to help employees successfully mesh their work and family lives—provides more fertile ground for organizational citizenship (Lambert, 2000).

Another precondition is a sense of both distributive and procedural justice, and the sense that the organization is attempting—within the means available to it—to provide as fair a psychological contract and reward structure as possible. Moorman (1991) found that procedural justice was a key determinant of organizational citizenship, while Konovsky and Organ (1996) cited supervisory fairness as a key determinant. Janssen (2000) found that worker innovation was reduced by perceived unfairness in the reward system. Trust is another key precondition—if employees do not trust management, little citizenship behaviour will take place.

One way of creating identification is by developing reward systems in which both employees and the organization benefit when organizational goals are met. These may include gain sharing, goal sharing, profit sharing, or employee stock plans. Another way the reward system can foster shared goals and values is by attracting and retaining employees who already possess compatible values. The needs of people who share organizational goals and values need to be identified, and the reward system can then be geared to their needs.

Participation in decision making has also been shown to foster organizational identification, especially participation in goal setting. People who play a role in setting goals are much more likely to be committed to those goals. Employee participation in development of the reward system will likely produce reward systems that are consistent with employee needs and result in more trust in the system itself. But all types of participation in decision making have been shown to create greater commitment to the decisions that are made, as well as providing the sense that employees are true "citizens" in the organization, and that their views are valued and respected.

An example of how the creation of organizational identification can occur, and its results, can be seen at a trucking company located in western Canada that was purchased from its corporate owner by its employees (Long, 1995). In addition to the change in ownership, management style became more open, with information sharing and participative management. In short, the firm moved from a classical to a high-involvement managerial style. Subsequent to employee purchase, a whole variety of employee attitudes and behaviours changed, almost overnight. Group norms, which had been somewhat poor under corporate ownership, improved dramatically. Losses resulting from "shrinkage" (employee theft) declined dramatically, as did customer damage claims, and employee turnover. Grievances disappeared. A whole new attitude of commitment and cooperation permeated the company. Truck drivers would go above and beyond the call of duty to try to satisfy customers, and everyone, whatever their position, was always on the lookout for potential customers. The result? A dramatic increase in profitability, which had been absent in the years prior to employee purchase.

An Integrated Model of Behaviour

Now that we've looked at the individual pieces of the human behaviour puzzle, it's time to put them together. The rather intimidating-looking Figure 3.9 does just that.

As can be seen, all behaviour starts with human needs. But individuals will vary in their need salience (which is the important thing for reward systems), depending on their personal circumstances and their personal characteristics. Personal characteristics, in combination with salient needs, will strongly influence employee perceptions of the valence, instrumentality, and expectancy for a particular behaviour.

If these are all positive, people will attempt to perform the behaviour in question. But whether they are actually able to perform the behaviour depends on their individual attributes and the organizational context, including the organizational support provided. If the behaviour is successfully carried out, and the expected rewards follow, the behaviour is reinforced, and will continue. If the expected rewards do not materialize, the behaviour will cease.

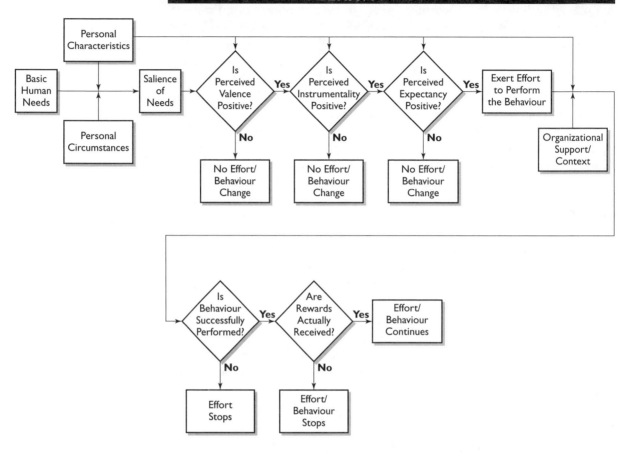

FIGURE 3.9 AN INTEGRATED MODEL OF MOTIVATION AND BEHAVIOUR

That's the model in a nutshell. It is actually not as intimidating as it may appear at first glance. But to really understand it and its implications for reward systems, we need to work our way through it, focusing on parts that have not received much attention so far.

PERSONAL CHARACTERISTICS

Personal characteristics are one part of the equation that has received little attention so far. **Personal characteristics** include the beliefs, values, competencies, personality, demographic characteristics, and perceptual frame of reference that belong to a given individual. The nature of these personal characteristics is a result of the experiences and learning that an individual has acquired, in combination with inherent individual differences.

Personal beliefs reflect people's understanding of how the world around them works, based on their own experiences and what they have learned

personal characteristics a person's beliefs, values, competencies, personality, demographic characteristics, and perceptual frame of reference

personal beliefs a person's understanding of how the world around them works through both their formal and informal learning processes. Major sources of beliefs are parents, teachers, and the peer group. These beliefs are subject to change depending on further experiences and encounters with new people. **Personal values** are core beliefs about what is appropriate and inappropriate behaviour that are formed early in life and endure over time. Examples of personal values would include the importance of honesty, altruism, loyalty, friendship, and the work ethic.

Personal competencies comprise the particular abilities and skills—physical, verbal, and mental—that an individual possesses. **Personality characteristics** are the particular behavioural and emotional tendencies (traits) exhibited by a person. Personality traits include pessimism vs. optimism, extroversion vs. introversion, passivity vs. aggressiveness, risk tolerance vs. risk aversion, cynicism vs. trust, and internal vs. external locus of control. **Demographic characteristics** include such items as age, gender, ethnicity, education, and marital status.

The **personal frame of reference** is the set of perceptual filters that people use in interpreting and understanding the world around them. The world is a complicated place with many more perceptual cues than we are able to assimilate and interpret. Instead, every human being practises *selective perception*—a largely unconscious process of selecting only certain perceptual cues for interpretation. An individual's personal frame of reference determines which cues will be selected and how they will be interpreted. As a general rule, people tend to select cues that reinforce their preexisting beliefs. The frame of reference results from the person's previous experiences, beliefs, values, personality type, and demographic characteristics.

How are personal characteristics relevant to reward systems? We will get into this question a little later, but here are a few examples now. A person high in cynicism will regard promises of future rewards with skepticism, causing that person to have a low perception of the instrumentality of a particular behaviour (and thus low motivation). A young person may not even "hear" the presentation about pension benefits during the employment interview, so an employer trying to attract young employees with a generous pension plan may be barking up the wrong tree. And, of course, personal values and personality type will play a major role in determining which needs are salient for a given employee, and therefore what rewards will likely motivate him or her.

personal values a person's core beliefs about appropriate and inappropriate behaviour

personal competencies a person's physical, verbal, and mental skills

personality characteristics a person's behavioural and emotional tendencies

demographic characteristics a person's age, gender, ethnicity, education, marital status, and similar characteristics

personal frame of reference the perceptual filters that people use in interpreting and understanding the world around them

PERSONAL CIRCUMSTANCES

Personal circumstances influence the amount of need deprivation that currently exists, which, of course, then affects need salience. For example, someone who has a million dollars in the bank likely has less financial deprivation than a person whose total financial assets amount to ten dollars. Of course, need deprivation is not only a function of how much is currently possessed, but also how much is needed. A person with three young children to support will have a higher financial need than a childless person, all other things being equal.

People living in jurisdictions where health care is free will have lower financial needs than those living in jurisdictions where it is not.

Other personal circumstances are also relevant. Does a person have high student loans to pay off? Does that person have skills that are in high demand? What are the alternatives for a person with a given set of skills and competencies?

The judgment about how much of a need is "enough" is not entirely objective. Personal experience may also affect the desired level. People accustomed to a high standard of living will likely set higher threshold levels than those accustomed to a lower standard of living. People who grew up in poverty during the Great Depression, and who experienced great uncertainty about their very survival, set a very high threshold for security needs. In many cases, it is almost impossible for then to fully satisfy this need, and many have remained fixated on this need throughout their lives.

EVALUATING VALENCE

Need salience plus personal characteristics determine how a person will calculate the valence of a particular behaviour. Need salience is particularly important in evaluating the rewards flowing from a behaviour. Will performing this behaviour help to satisfy salient needs? In considering this question, an individual will take into account both the short- and long-term extrinsic and intrinsic rewards that will flow from this behaviour. For example, the current extrinsic rewards for an aspiring actor to perform in a television show may be low. But the future value of this performance may be high if it leads to additional roles in other shows.

Personal values and competencies play a key role in determining how the costs of the behaviour will be evaluated. There are three main types of "costs" that flow from performing any behaviour: physical or tangible costs, psychological costs, and opportunity costs. For example, let's assume that the behaviour is accepting a job rather than continuing to remain unemployed. There are some obvious tangible costs, such as transportation and child care costs. There are also physical costs, such as fatigue or possibly risks to health, especially if the work is hazardous.

Psychological costs may include factors such as stress and frustration, or the need to violate one's personal values in order to perform the job. Some people may find the loss of autonomy and freedom inherent in accepting a job to be a high cost. A person strongly opposed to smoking may consider a job in a tobacco factory much more problematic than someone who does not oppose smoking.

Finally, there are opportunity costs. Performing any behaviour at a point in time means that the opportunity to perform other behaviours is lost. For example, accepting a job may mean less time available to spend with children or other family members. Certainly, accepting a job will mean less time for leisure or social activities.

Personal values and personal competencies will determine how costs are valued. For example, personal values will determine what costs one will assign to physical activity (are you an active person who likes physical activity or not? how highly do you value your health?). Personal competencies also play a role—if the job requires competencies that you do not have in abundance (e.g., physical strength, manual dexterity, good communication skills), you will likely find the job more draining than someone else might.

Personal values also affect psychological costs. For example, you are offered a well-paying job selling fur coats, but you believe that trapping animals to produce fur coats is inhumane. Or, you are offered a good job in a distillery, but you strongly oppose the consumption of alcohol. Or, you are offered a highly paid job working on an assembly line, but you value your autonomy very highly. These kinds of mismatches will cause frustration and stress, increasing the costs of accepting these types of jobs (and increasing the rewards necessary to induce you to accept them).

Finally, consider opportunity costs. Again, personal values may play a key role in evaluating these. Accepting a job will take you away from your preschool-aged children. Some people may consider this a very severe cost, while others may not consider it a cost at all, but in fact a reward! Or, you may have to give up some volunteer work that you find fulfilling. Or, you may have less time for socializing with friends. What value do you place on these items? Of course, opportunity costs are a function of personal circumstances—what other alternatives are available?

Evaluating Instrumentality

If the balance of perceived costs and benefits nets out to a positive valence, the next question individuals will ask is, "What is the likelihood that the promised rewards will actually materialize?" If you perform the behaviour (accept and perform the job), will you really receive all the promised rewards? For example, a firm may promise pay of $10 an hour, with a raise to $12 after six months, and to $14 after a year, subject to satisfactory performance. It may also promise lucrative opportunities for overtime pay, as well as profit-sharing bonuses, if company performance is good.

But a major issue here is one of credibility: can the employer be trusted to carry through with the rewards that have been promised? Has the firm been in financial difficulty? Does it have a history of laying off employees on some pretext just as they are about to receive an increase in pay? Your perception of the likelihood of promised rewards materializing will be conditioned by your past experiences and your personality. Have you been associated with a previous employer whose promises never materialized? Are you high or low in the personality trait of cynicism? A person high in cynicism may have a predisposition not to trust promises of future rewards.

EVALUATING EXPECTANCY

If you do believe that the promised rewards will materialize, what is your likelihood of being able to successfully perform the necessary behaviour? Your sense of personal competencies, along with your personality and your past experiences, will affect perceived expectancy. For example, if you have been able to perform the behaviour successfully in the past, your expectancy of being able to do it again will be increased; if you believe that you have the skills and competencies necessary to perform the job, this increases your expectancy. If you are high in the personality trait of optimism, your expectancy will increase.

Two main factors determine whether effort will actually lead to successful performance of the behaviour in question: individual attributes, and organizational context and support. Individual attributes comprise the abilities, knowledge, and skills necessary to successfully perform the job. Organizational context means the circumstances in which the behaviour will take place. For example, if the behaviour is selling sporting equipment, the quality and price of the products will have a great deal to do with success.

Organization support consists of the resources, training, tools, and other factors that the organization needs to provide in order for successful job performance to occur. Before attempting to perform the job, an individual must perceive that there is sufficient organizational support such that there is a high likelihood of being able to successfully perform the necessary behaviour and achieve the required results. This perception will directly affect perceived expectancy.

ACHIEVING THE DESIRED BEHAVIOUR

Of course, actual performance is a function not only of effort, but also of personal characteristics and organizational context, and these will determine whether effort actually leads to the desired behaviour. If the expected behaviour does not take place, rewards will not follow, and effort will cease. If the behaviour takes place, but the expected rewards are not perceived to follow, effort will again cease.

As you may have noticed, we've reached the last element in our model for predicting human behaviour. So what are the implications of this model for reward systems? The following are the steps for designing a reward system that should produce the behaviour the organization wants and needs:

- Define the behaviour that is really needed.

- Determine the employee attributes and qualifications needed to perform these behaviours.

- Identify the needs that individuals possessing these qualifications are likely to find salient.

- Develop rewards that will address these salient needs.

- Ensure a positive valence for needed behaviours.

- Make it clear that performance of the behaviour will lead to the rewards.

- Be sure that employees perceive that effort on their part will very likely lead to the expected behaviour.

- Provide conditions that make it likely that effort will in fact lead to performance.

- Make sure that the promised rewards are actually provided as promised.

SUMMARY AND IMPLICATIONS

The purpose of this chapter has been to provide a framework for understanding how reward systems can affect behaviour in organizations. The chapter started by illustrating how reward systems may not only fail to produce the desired employee behaviour, but may actually cause a variety of undesirable consequences, some of which could even threaten the survival of the organization. The potentially high costs of reward dissatisfaction were examined, and it was noted that these costs can range from low motivation and low employee satisfaction to high turnover and even employee theft. Possible causes of reward dissatisfaction were examined, including violation of the psychological contract, perceived reward inequity, discrepancy between desired and actual reward levels, and a perceived lack of distributive and procedural justice.

Next, the chapter focused on three main sets of desired employee behaviours—membership behaviour, task behaviour, and citizenship behaviour—and presented a number of conceptual tools to help in understanding these behaviours. It was noted that these behaviours can be produced only by first influencing several key job attitudes—job satisfaction, work motivation, and organizational identification—and we examined how reward systems can play a role in promoting these job attitudes.

However, it was also noted that the importance of these job attitudes and behaviours varies for different organizations. Firms practising high-involvement management will find all three attitudes/behaviours of great importance; firms practising human relations management will find the first two attitudes/behaviours of particular importance; and classical firms will be primarily concerned with work motivation/task behaviour.

Finally, the chapter developed an integrated model for predicting and understanding human behaviour, from which a number of reward implications flow. Nine steps in designing an effective reward system were enumerated.

A number of other factors also affect reward system success. Caution must be exercised when using extrinsic rewards (especially individual rewards) to motivate specific behaviours, since unrewarded behaviours will likely be neglected, and various negative consequences may be generated (such as lack of concern for the performance of other employees or of the organization as a whole). As the following chapters will discuss, individual extrinsic incentives can be used in only a limited number of circumstances. Whenever possible, intrinsic rewards are to be preferred. But extrinsic rewards tied to group and organizational performance avoid the problems of individual incentives and will also be beneficial for many organizations.

Tying in the findings from this chapter with those of Chapter 2, we can see that the three managerial strategies will each require their own reward systems to generate different behaviours. Classical organizations need only provide sufficient rewards as to create a tolerable psychological contract that will result in some degree of membership behaviour. Work motivation can be achieved through rewards tied directly to the needed behaviours, or through the use of control systems, with the underlying threat of dismissal providing the basic motivation. These organizations will pay a price for not having job and reward satisfaction, or organizational identification, but this price may well be tolerable in the total context of these organizations.

In contrast, human relations organizations rely on job satisfaction and positive work norms. They must ensure that their reward systems are equitable and that they generate job satisfaction and a substantial degree of commitment. Organizational identification, while desirable, is not essential.

And finally, because they typically require the most complex behaviour from their employees and the highest level of performance, high-involvement organizations will generally require the most complex reward systems, those that produce all three of the key job attitudes. These reward systems need to be seen as equitable and as adhering to principles of organizational justice. Of the three managerial strategies, reward dissatisfaction will be most damaging to high-involvement firms, because this undermines the foundation of trust needed for successful utilization of this strategy.

Having developed an understanding of how strategy links to rewards and how rewards link to behaviour, you have now finished the first two steps along your road to effective compensation. The next step is to understand the compensation options that are available to you, to enable you to choose those that will best fit your strategy and be most likely to produce the behaviours you want. That is the challenge for Part II.

KEY TERMS

affective commitment, p. 82

agency theory, p. 96

attribution theory, p. 93

content theories of motivation, p. 84

continuance commitment, p. 82

demographic characteristics, p. 101

EXERCISES

1. In a group of four to six people, think about situations in which you know that employees experienced reward dissatisfaction. What caused it? How did people react to it? What were the consequences for the organization? Were they serious? Why or why not?

2. This chapter contained two examples of auto companies—Toyota (Box 3.3) and CAMI (Box 3.4)—that apparently wanted to move away from the classical system. This was not successful at CAMI, but very successful at Toyota. Are there any concepts from this chapter or previous chapters that could help explain this result? Assuming that management at CAMI really wanted to move away from the classical school, what should they have done differently?

3. Think of an important decision that you recently made. Then, utilize the integrated model for behaviour to analyze your decision-making process. Is the decision that you actually made consistent with what the model predicted you would make? If not, why not? Get together in a small group and share your results and conclusions.

4. Analyze Henderson Printing (in the Appendix). Why do you think there is such a high turnover of new employees? What concepts may help to explain employee reactions to the compensation system? Do you think that the compensation system is fair? Is it effective? What principles for effective reward systems does it violate? What changes should be made?

5. Machine operators at Plastco Packaging (in the Appendix) appear to be suffering from poor worker job satisfaction and motivation. Develop a plan for solving these problems by redesigning these jobs to add more intrinsic rewards to them. Besides these changes to job design, are there any other changes to the various dimensions of organization structure (including the reward structure) that you would also recommend?

6. Analyze Duplox Copiers (in the Appendix). What do you think is the cause of the problems the company is encountering? Are there any concepts from this chapter that can help in explaining this? Are there any concepts from previous chapters that are also relevant? What does Duplox need to do now to solve its problems?

SUGGESTED WEB SITES

Page 79: To examine the costs of employee turnover, click on <www.business.com/directory/human_resources/workforce_management/turnover>

Page 82: To look at a variety of ways to stimulate membership behaviour, click on <www.Sasknetwork.gov.sk.ca/pages/tw/k13.htm>

REFERENCES

Academy of Management Executive. 1995. "More on the Folly." 9(1): 15–16.

Adams, J. Stacy. 1965. "Inequity in Social Exchange." In L. Berkovitz, ed., *Advances in Experimental Social Psychology*, vol. 2. New York: Academic Press.

Alderfer, C. 1972. *Existence, Relatedness, and Growth*. New York: The Free Press.

Argyris, Chris. 1964. *Integrating the Individual and the Organization*. New York: Wiley.

Ashford, Susan J., Cynthia Lee, and Philip Bobko. 1989. "Content, Causes, and Consequences of Job Insecurity: A Theory-Based Measure and Substantive Test." *Academy of Management Journal*, 32(4): 803–29.

Bateman, T. S., and D.W. Organ. 1983. "Job Satisfaction and the Good Soldier: The Relationship between Affect and Employee Citizenship." *Academy of Management Journal*, 26: 587–95.

Berton, Pierre. 1972. *Klondike: The Last Great Gold Rush 1896–1899*. Toronto: Penguin Books.

Besser, Terry L. 1995. "Rewards and Organizational Goal Achievement: A Case Study of Toyota Motor Manufacturing in Kentucky." *Journal of Management Studies*, 32(3): 383–99.

Clark, Andrew E., and Andrew J. Oswald. 1996. "Satisfaction and Comparison Income." *Journal of Public Economics*, 61: 359–81.

Cramer, Duncan. 1996. "Job Satisfaction and Organizational Continuance Commitment: A Two Wave Panel Study." *Journal of Organizational Behaviour*, 17: 389–400.

Crosby, F. 1976. "A Model of Egoistical Relative Deprivation." *Psychological Review*, 83: 95–113.

Deci, E.L. 1975. *Intrinsic Motivation*. New York: Plenum Press.

Deci, E.L., and R.M. Ryan. 1985. *Intrinsic Motivation and Self-Determination in Human Behavior*. New York: Plenum Press.

Delery, John E., N. Gupta, Jason D. Shaw, G. Douglas Jenkins, and Margot L. Ganster. 2000. "Unionization, Compensation, and Voice Effects on Quits and Retention." *Industrial Relations*, 39(4): 625-45.

Economist. 2000. "Chief Executives' Pay." September 30: 110.

Eisenhardt, Kathleen. 1989. "Agency Theory: An Assessment and Review." *Academy of Management Review*, 14(1): 57–74.

Finegan, Joan E. 2000. "The Impact of Personal and Organizational Values on Organizational Commitment." *Journal of Occupational and Organizational Psychology*, 73: 149–69.

Folger, Robert, and Mary A. Konovsky. 1989. "Effects of Procedural and Distributive Justice on Reactions to Pay Raise Decisions." *Academy of Management Journal*, 32(1): 115–30.

Fried, Yitzhak. 1991. "Meta-Analytic Comparison of the Job Diagnostic Survey and Job Characteristics Inventory as Correlates of Work Satisfaction and Performance." *Journal of Applied Psychology*, 76(5): 690–97.

Gellatly, Ian R. 1995. "Individual and Group Determinants of Employee Absenteeism: Test of a Causal Model." *Journal of Organizational Behavior*, 16: 469–85.

Gellatly, Ian R., and P. Gregory Irving. 2001. "Personality, Autonomy, and Contextual Performance of Managers." *Human Performance*, 14(3): 229–43.

Greenberg, Jerald. 1990a. "Employee Theft as a Reaction to Underpayment Inequity: The Hidden Cost of Pay Cuts." *Journal of Applied Psychology*, 75: 561–68.

Greenberg, Jerald. 1990b. "Organizational Justice: Yesterday, Today, and Tomorrow." *Journal of Management*, 16(2): 399–432.

Hackman, J. Richard, and Greg Oldham. 1980. *Work Redesign*. Reading, MA: Addison-Wesley.

Harackiewicz, J.M., and J.R. Larson. 1986. "Managing Motivation: The Impact of Supervisor Feedback on Subordinate Task Interest." *Journal of Personality and Social Psychology*, 51: 547–56.

Herzberg, Frederick. 1966. *Work and the Nature of Man*. Cleveland, OH: World Publishing.

Herzberg, Frederick, B. Mausner, and B.B. Snyderman. 1959. *The Motivation to Work*. New York: John Wiley.

Huseman, R.C., J.D. Hatfield, and E.W. Miles. 1985. "Test for Individual Perceptions of Job Equity: Some Preliminary Findings." *Perceptual and Motor Skills*, 61: 1055–64.

Janssen, Onne. 2000. "Job Demands, Perceptions of Effort-Reward Fairness, and Innovative Work Behaviour." *Journal of Occupational and Organizational Psychology*, 73: 287–302.

Jaros, Stephen J., John M. Jermier, Jerry W. Koehler, and Terry Sincich. 1993. "Effects of Continuance, Affective, and Moral Commitment on the Withdrawal Process: An Evaluation of Eight Structural Equation Models." *Academy of Management Journal*, 36(5): 951–95.

Jensen, M., and W. Meckling. 1976. "Theory of the Firm: Managerial Behavior, Agency Costs, and Ownership Structure." *Journal of Financial Economics*, 3: 305–60.

Johns, Gary. 1996. *Organizational Behaviour: Understanding and Managing Life at Work.* New York: HarperCollins.

Kerr, Steven. 1975. "On the Folly of Rewarding A, While Hoping for B." *Academy of Management Journal*, 18(4): 769–83.

Kerr, Steven. 1995. "On the Folly of Rewarding A, While Hoping for B." *Academy of Management Executive*, 9(1): 7–14.

Kohn, Alfie. 1993. *Punished by Rewards: The Trouble with Gold Stars, A's, Praise, and Other Bribes.* Boston: Houghton-Mifflin.

Konovsky, Mary A., and Dennis W. Organ. 1996. "Dispositional and Contextual Determinants of Organizational Citizenship Behaviour." *Journal of Organizational Behavior*, 17: 253–66.

Lambert, Susan J. 2000. "Added Benefits: The Link between Work-Life Benefits and Organizational Citizenship Behaviour." *The Academy of Management Journal*, 43(5): 801–15.

Lawler, Edward E. 1973. *Motivation in Work Organizations.* Monterey, CA: Brooks/Cole.

Long, Richard J. 1995. "Employee Buyouts: The Canadian Experience." *Canadian Business Economics*, 3(4): 28–41.

Lucero, Margaret A., and Robert E. Allen. 1994. "Employee Benefits: A Growing Source of Psychological Contract Violations." *Human Resource Management*, 33(3): 425–46.

Maremont, Mark. 1995. "Blind Ambition: How the Pursuit of Results Got out of Hand at Bausch and Lomb." *Business Week*, October 23: 78–92.

Maslow, A.H. 1954. *Motivation and Personality.* New York: Harper and Row.

Masterson, Suzanne S., Kyle Lewis, Barry M. Goldman, and M. Susan Taylor. 2000. "Integrating Justice and Social Exchange: The Differing Effects of Fair Procedures and Treatment on Work Relationships." *Academy of Management Journal*, 43(4): 738–39.

Miceli, Marcia P., and Matthew C. Lane. 1991. "Antecedents of Pay Satisfaction: A Review and Extension." *Research in Human Resources Management*, 9: 235–309.

Miceli, Marcia P., and Paul W. Mulvey. 2000. "Consequences of Satisfaction with Pay Systems: Two Field Studies." *Industrial Relations*, 39(1): 62–87.

Moorman, Robert H. 1991. "Relationship between Organizational Justice and Organizational Citizenship Behaviors: Do Fairness Perceptions Influence Employee Citizenship?" *Journal of Applied Psychology*, 76(6): 845–55.

Morrison, Elizabeth W., and Sandra L. Robinson. 1997. "When Employees Feel Betrayed: A Model of How Psychological Contract Violation Occurs." *Academy of Management Review*, 22(1): 228–56.

Murray, H. 1938. *Explorations in Personality.* New York: Oxford University Press.

O'Hara, K., C.M. Johnson, and T.A. Beehr. 1985. "Organizational Behavior Management in the Private Sector: A Review of Empirical Research and Recommendations for Further Investigation." *Academy of Management Review*, 10: 848–64.

Organ, Dennis W. 1990. "The Motivational Basis of Organizational Citizenship Behavior." *Research in Organizational Behavior*, 12: 43–72.

Powell, Irene, Mark Montgomery, and James Cosgrove. 1994. "Compensation Structure and Establishment Quit and Fire Rates." *Industrial Relations*, 33(2): 229–48.

Pratt, Nancy C. 1996. "CEOs Reap Unprecedented Riches While Employees' Pay Stagnates." *Compensation and Benefits Review*, 28(5): 20–24.

Rinehart, James, Christopher Huxley, and David Robertson. 1997. *Just Another Car Factory?* Ithaca, NY: ILR Press.

Rousseau, Denise M. 1995. *Psychological Contracts in Organizations: Understanding Written and Unwritten Agreements*. Thousand Oaks, CA: Sage.

Rousseau, Denise M., and Violet T. Ho. 2000. "Psychological Contract Issues in Compensation." In Sara L. Rynes and Barry Gerhart, eds., *Compensation in Organizations: Current Research and Practice*. San Francisco: Jossey Bass.

Scarpello, Vida, and Foard F. Jones. 1996. "Why Justice Matters in Compensation Decision Making." *Journal of Organizational Behavior*, 17: 285–99.

Schein, Edgar. 1965. *Organizational Psychology*. Englewood Cliffs, NJ: Prentice–Hall.

Skinner, B.F. 1953. *Science and Human Behavior*. New York: Macmillan.

Smith, P.C., L. Kendall, and C. Hulin. 1969. *The Measurement of Satisfaction in Work and Retirement*. Chicago: Rand McNally.

Sweeney, Paul D., Dean B. McFarlin, and Edward J. Inderrieden. 1990. "Using Relative Deprivation Theory to Explain Satisfaction with Income and Pay Level: A Multistudy Examination." *Academy of Management Journal*, 33(2): 423–36.

Tang, Thomas L., Jwa K. Kim, and David S. Tang. 2000. "Does Attitude toward Money Moderate the Relationship between Intrinsic Job Satisfaction and Voluntary Turnover?" *Human Relations*, 53(2): 213–45.

Tett, Robert P., and John P. Meyer. 1993. "Job Satisfaction, Organizational Commitment, Turnover Intention, and Turnover: Path Analyses Based on Meta-Analytic Findings." *Personnel Psychology*, 46(2): 259–93.

Theriault, Roland. 1992. *Mercer Compensation Manual*. Boucherville, PQ: G. Morin Publisher.

Tremblay, Michel, and Patrice Roussel. 2001. "Modelling the Role of Organizational Justice: Effects on Satisfaction and Unionization Propensity of Canadian Managers." *International Journal of Human Resource Management*, 12(5): 717–37.

Tremblay, Michel, Bruno Sire, and David Balkin. 2000. "The Role of Organizational Justice in Pay and Employee Benefit Satisfaction and Its Effects on Work Attitudes." *Group and Organization Management*, 25(3): 269–90.

Van Dyne, Linn, Jill W. Graham, and Richard M. Dienesch. 1994. "Organizational Citizenship Behavior: Construct Redefinition, Measurement, and Validation."

Academy of Management Journal, 37(4): 765–802.

Van Scotter, James R., Stephan J. Motowidlo, and Thomas C. Cross. 2000. "Effects of Task Performance and Contextual Performance on Systemic Rewards." *Journal of Applied Psychology*, 85(4): 526–35.

Vroom, Victor V. 1964. *Work and Motivation*. New York: Wiley.

Wiersma, Uco J. 1992. "The Effects of Extrinsic Rewards in Intrinsic Motivation: A Meta-Analysis." *Journal of Occupational and Organizational Psychology*, 65: 101–14.

Part II

Components of Compensation

4

BASE PAY

CHAPTER GOALS

By the end of this chapter, you should be able to:

1. Define base pay and discuss why it is used and the circumstances in which it is most appropriate.

2. Identify and differentiate between the three main methods for establishing base pay.

3. Define market pricing and discuss its advantages and disadvantages.

4. Define job evaluation and discuss its advantages and disadvantages.

5. Define pay for knowledge and discuss its advantages and disadvantages.

6. Identify and discuss some of the other issues in using base pay.

INTRODUCTION

Why does the person who cuts your hair get paid per head, while the person who pumps your gas gets paid per hour? In fact, why use time-based pay at all? Some compensation systems do not. For example, realtors get paid only when they sell a house, auto salespeople are paid only when they sell a car, and stockbrokers are paid only when they make a trade. Carpet installers are paid for each square metre of carpet laid, long-haul truck drivers are paid per kilometre driven, and dentists are paid for each tooth drilled. Why not pay everybody this way?

That's a good question, and one that will be addressed in this chapter. In designing any compensation system, we must address two key questions. First, what role should each of the three compensation components (base pay, performance pay, indirect pay) play in the compensation mix? Second, what is the total level of compensation that should be provided?

The purpose of Part II (Chapters 4, 5, 6, and 7) is to provide a foundation for answering the first question, by examining in depth the advantages and disadvantages of each of these three pay components—and of their key elements—along with the circumstances in which each is most appropriate. This chapter will focus on base pay—why it is used, its pros and cons, and the methods for determining it. Three specific methods for establishing base pay—market pricing, job evaluation, and pay for knowledge—will be examined in depth. The chapter concludes with a discussion of some of the other issues and choices associated with base pay.

WHAT IS BASE PAY?

base pay the portion of an individual's compensation that is based on a unit of time worked

Base pay is the portion of an individual's compensation that is based on time worked, not on output produced or results achieved. For the great majority of employees in Canada, it serves as the largest component of their compensation package. According to the Compensation Practices Survey (CPS) of 240 medium to large Canadian firms conducted for this book by the author in 2000, base pay accounted for 79 percent of total compensation for the typical employee, performance pay about 9 percent, and indirect pay (benefits) about 13 percent.

Base pay is "guaranteed" by the employer—if you work for a certain amount of time, you will be paid a prespecified amount of money. In some cases, it is calculated on an hourly basis (e.g., $10 per hour); in others, daily (e.g., $200 per day); in others, weekly (e.g., $1000 per week); in others, monthly (e.g., $4000 per month); and in still others, annually (e.g., $50 000 per year). When calculated on an hourly basis, it is known as a *wage*; when calculated on a weekly, monthly, or annual basis, it is known as a *salary*.

WHY USE BASE PAY?

Why use base pay at all? Wouldn't it be more efficient just to use output-related pay? Why not simply eliminate base pay, as the Screaming Tale Restaurant, described in Chapter 1 (Box 1.2), has done? We will first examine why output-related pay cannot always be used, thus forcing the use of base pay, and then explain why base pay may be preferred to output-related pay, even where output-related pay could be used.

WHY NOT USE OUTPUT-RELATED PAY?

In some cases it is simply not practical to use output-related pay. Substitution of output-related pay for time-based pay is only possible under certain circumstances. Jobs that are amenable to output-related pay are those in which the output is: (1) easily measurable, (2) easily priced in terms of its value to the employer, (3) easily attributable to individual employees, (4) within the control of the individual employee, and (5) not highly unstable. Obviously, most jobs do not meet all these criteria. Attempts to utilize output-related pay in situations where these criteria are not met can cause serious problems, as Chapter 5 will discuss.

In some cases it may be possible to use output-related pay but it is not desirable to do so because of the unintended consequences that may arise. For example, some mines do not use output-related compensation because of a concern that this might lead to a high concern for production at the expense of safety. In the retail sector, salespeople may become too aggressive or may resort to unethical sales practices in order to maximize their commission income. Jobs that combine some measurable outputs with nonmeasurable outputs are also not good candidates for a pay system based only on output, since employees will tend to focus on the measured behaviours and neglect other behaviours. Chapter 3 has discussed problems that can be caused by compensation systems that only reward specific behaviours or outputs, and Chapter 5 will examine these problems in more depth.

In still other cases it may be both practical and desirable, from the employer's point of view, to rely on output-related pay, but it is unacceptable from an employee's point of view. In general, people prefer certainty in their rewards, and thus prefer a large component of base pay in their compensation package. Trade unions have worked for many years to make wages more certain and have generally pushed for base pay as the primary pay component.

Indeed, because of the general preference among employees for base pay, it may be necessary to offer higher total pay in order to induce employees to accept jobs in which all pay is performance-contingent. This may actually result in higher total compensation costs, as employees demand a premium for the additional risk that these jobs pose (Mitchell, Lewin, and Lawler, 1990). If the performance-contingent pay plan does not boost output sufficiently to cover the additional pay costs, then a firm would be better off with a time-based pay system.

REASONS FOR USING BASE PAY

So far, base pay has been portrayed as something to be used simply because no other alternative is viable, and this is indeed the major motivation in many instances. But base pay can also be used for more positive reasons. One reason is flexibility. With time-based pay, the employer is essentially buying time from the employee. Within certain limits, this time may be directed in a variety of ways, and redirected as the need arises. Base pay doesn't confine employee attention to only one or two behaviours, as output-based pay tends to do.

A second reason is that base pay allows for recognition of various job aspects that an employer may regard as important, such as skill development. Third, base pay can signal the relative importance of various jobs within the organization. Fourth, base pay demonstrates a commitment on the part of the employer to the employee, creating a greater likelihood of employee commitment to the employer. Finally, an important reason for the use of base pay is simplicity—it is usually much simpler to implement and administer than an output-related system.

DISADVANTAGES OF BASE PAY

What are the disadvantages of base pay? First, base pay represents more of a fixed commitment than performance-contingent pay, especially if salaries are used. Base pay does not relate to variability in an employer's ability to pay, the way performance-contingent pay does. Second, while base pay does contribute to membership behaviour, it does not directly motivate task behaviour, nor does it signal key task behaviours. Third, since it does not relate organizational success directly to individual success (as a performance-contingent plan such as profit sharing would do), it does not directly contribute to citizenship behaviour. Fourth, it is not self-correcting. Under an output-related system, employees who do not perform up to standard will likely voluntarily remove themselves from the organization because they are unable to earn enough money. Time-based pay provides no such mechanism.

Of course, it should be noted that time-based pay and output/ performance-related pay are not mutually exclusive, and can be combined. In this way, it may be possible to capture the advantages of both, while minimizing their disadvantages. Indeed, there has been a trend in recent years away from compensation systems that rely solely on either one of these. Many firms that have traditionally relied only on base pay are starting to add some performance-contingent elements to their pay systems, such as those in the banking industry (Box 4.1), while others that have relied only on performance pay (such as stock brokerage firms) are starting to add base pay to their compensation systems, as at Altamira Financial Services (Box 1.1).

BOX 4.1 Pay Systems Are Changing in Banking

In banking, the traditional practice has been to utilize base pay with virtually no output-related pay. However, in recent years, many banks have added a performance-contingent component to virtually every job, and some jobs are even paid entirely on commission. For example, at the Royal Bank, customer service representatives (tellers) are now included in profit sharing, as well as employee stock plans.

Some personnel in mobile banking and registered retirement funds now have the option of selecting straight commission as their primary compensation. The bank hopes that these changes will focus employee attention on performance and create a greater understanding of the link between employee performance and organizational performance.

METHODS FOR ESTABLISHING BASE PAY

Like most employers, you have decided to include base pay in your compensation system. But how do you determine the value of each job to the organization so that it can be compensated accordingly? There are three main methods. The first method—**market pricing**—is to simply offer the lowest possible wage that will attract a qualified person to join the firm. The second method—**job evaluation**—is to systematically develop a ranking of all jobs in the organization in terms of their value to the employer, and then calibrate this system to the labour market. The third method is to develop a system based on the total value of the skills and competencies that each employee has acquired, known as a **pay-for-knowledge system** (PKS).

Each of these three methods is very different from the others, and each has its own advantages and disadvantages, as will be discussed shortly. However, in order to maintain focus on understanding the key features of each method and the circumstances under which they are most appropriate, discussion of the technical details involved in utilizing each method will be deferred until Part IV, where an entire chapter will be devoted to each method.

MARKET PRICING

Market pricing is the simplest of the three methods, and is the most common one used in small firms. The method is straightforward. If you need a secretary, or a machinist, you observe what other firms are paying for these jobs and then make similar offers. If you need exceptional performance from your employees, and you can afford it, you may pay somewhat above the "going rate," in order to attract the most qualified individuals. If you don't need exceptional performance, and are prepared to put up with higher turnover, you may decide to pay somewhat less than the going rate.

market pricing establishing base pay by determining the minimum amount of pay necessary to attract qualified individuals from the labour market

job evaluation establishing base pay by ranking all jobs in the firm according to their value to that firm

pay-for-knowledge system (PKS) establishing base pay according to the total value of the skills and competencies an employee has acquired

As the labour market changes over time, the employer simply adjusts the pay levels of current employees and the starting pay levels for new employees in accordance with these changes. To simplify the process of determining the "market rates" for each job, there are numerous compensation consulting firms that specialize in collecting these data and making them available to clients on a commercial basis. Data are also available through governmental agencies, such as Statistics Canada, through industry associations, and through organizations such as the Conference Board of Canada.

ADVANTAGES OF MARKET PRICING

There are two key advantages to market pricing. The first is simplicity. The other methods for determining base pay are much more complicated, and ultimately, some market pricing still must be done in order to calibrate their systems. For example, job evaluation is a complex process that depends on the use of formalized and comprehensive job descriptions. Many firms do not have such job descriptions and do not wish to develop them. Job descriptions are not needed for pay-for-knowledge systems, but these systems are also complex to develop and administer and they do not necessarily fit all jobs and all organizations. As a result, market pricing can be a much cheaper system than either of the alternatives. One expert (Sibson, 1990) claims that this method can be used for one-tenth of the cost of a job evaluation system.

The second advantage of market pricing is that it keeps all jobs in the organization aligned with market conditions. This helps to avoid the problem of turnover caused by noncompetitive wages, and makes recruiting easier.

DISADVANTAGES OF MARKET PRICING

Market pricing has a number of drawbacks. The first problem is that it is not as simple as it sounds. There are numerous difficulties in carrying out market pricing. One such difficulty is that identifying one specific "going rate" for a given job can be very elusive. Different wage surveys turn up different results, because they make different judgments about whom to survey and how to define different labour markets. Labour markets can be defined in terms of industry type, occupational group, and geographic areas, as well as firm size.

Another difficulty is job definitions. Different employers will define jobs in different ways. For example, the responsibilities of a "secretary" can range from serving mainly as a typist or receptionist all the way to functioning as an office manager and executive assistant. Thus, one firm may report that it is paying its "secretaries" $20 000 per annum, while another pays $40 000 per annum, but the "secretaries" in each firm are in reality doing different jobs. In these circumstances, a wage survey that indicates an "average" pay of $30 000 for secretaries may be misleading.

Thus, while it is important for wage surveys to compare jobs that are consistently defined in the same way by different employers, this is very difficult to achieve. This problem is compounded if the user of wage surveys has job definitions that are inconsistent with standard definitions or has many jobs that are unique and do not fit into standard occupational categories.

Finally, aside from measurement difficulties, there is strong evidence that there is no such thing as a standard "market wage" for a given job (Rynes and Milkovich, 1986). Gomez-Mejia and Balkin (1992: 16) note that even in the same geographical area, wage rates for the same job titles may vary dramatically. For many job titles, some employers paid two to three times what other employers did. Of course, as has been discussed, some of this discrepancy may be due to inconsistencies in defining the jobs, or possibly to differences between industries. However, other research (e.g., Foster, 1985) shows that there may be wide discrepancies between firms in the same industry and the same geographic area in what they pay for jobs that are actually identical. In that study, even "after controlling for job content, company size, and company performance, differences between 35 to 54 percent for identical jobs within the same industry are not uncommon" (cited in Gomez-Mejia and Balkin, 1992: 15).

Although this result is often mystifying to economists, it should not be to us. We know that membership behaviour is motivated by the total mix of rewards that flow from a given job, and it is very likely that these "identical" jobs vary considerably in the total package of rewards that they offer. Market surveys often do not adequately account for performance pay, such as profit sharing, and usually do not take indirect pay into account at all. They take absolutely no account of the other extrinsic and intrinsic rewards that may be offered by a given firm, such as job security, and the type of work environment, atmosphere, or the managerial strategy practised by a firm.

Does the firm provide training and are there opportunities for advancement? Does the job provide intrinsic rewards, such as autonomy and job feedback? Compensation surveys take none of this into account, yet these characteristics vary dramatically across firms. Given these variations across firms, it would be extraordinary if there were *not* wide divergencies in wages across firms. The lack of such divergencies would suggest that monetary wages are the only rewards valued by employees, and we know that this is not true.

Compensation surveys may therefore not provide as much useful guidance as they would appear to. As discussed in Chapter 1, employers need to assess their total reward packages and then adjust their wages and salaries in light of that. For example, if a firm offers no benefits, it may find itself unable to attract qualified applicants, even if it pays at the market average. Similarly, if a firm offers poor working conditions, or no job security, it may be unable to retain employees even if paying at the market average is sufficient to attract employees to the firm.

The second major problem of market pricing is that it does not address internal equity. Under market pricing, there is little or no attempt to relate jobs to each other in terms of value to the firm. Thus, some jobs that are more important to the organization may pay less than jobs of lesser importance, simply because of characteristics of the labour market. Furthermore, if a firm is geographically dispersed, market conditions may vary for a given job in different parts of the country, causing the same job to be paid differently in various parts of the company.

A related problem is lack of control. In essence, when using only market pricing, the firm is allowing competitors to set its compensation policy. It is not able to tailor compensation to suit the particular strategy and needs of the firm, and the firm is losing compensation as a possible source of competitive advantage.

Finally, critics of market-based pay argue that the market does not necessarily produce pay systems that are equitable from a societal point of view. They point to a "pay gap" between jobs that have been traditionally performed by women and those that have been performed by men. Their argument is that the market has systematically undervalued work performed by women, and that when a firm adopts market-based pay, it may simply be perpetuating these inequities.

This argument has been accepted by a number of Canadian governments, most notably the province of Ontario, which in 1987 enacted "pay equity" legislation, covering all organizations that employ ten or more persons. (Numerous other provinces also have some form of this legislation, although it often applies only to jobs in the public sector.) This legislation requires that jobs of "equal value" be compensated equally, regardless of what the market conditions may indicate. (This issue will be addressed in more depth in Chapter 8, and also in Chapters 9 and 10.)

JOB EVALUATION

Job evaluation involves analyzing the descriptions for every job in the organization, and then relating each job to the others in some systematic way. The most common approach is to identify a number of key factors (compensable factors) and then evaluate each job according to how much of each factor is present. This creates a ranking of all jobs, known as a "hierarchy of jobs." Exact pay levels for each job are determined by relating certain "key jobs" or "benchmark jobs" to the external market, and then interpolating the rest.

Job evaluation first gained popularity in the 1920s and 1930s as large classical organizations began to dominate industry. For them, job evaluation provided a method for centralizing and controlling compensation costs. Before this time, compensation was handled in a haphazard, often chaotic manner, with individual supervisors and managers given the authority to pay employees as they saw fit. For example, before the use of job evaluation, American Steel and Wire had more than 100 000 pay rates (Milkovich and Newman, 1996: 146). According to Theriault (1992), the first book on job evaluation was published in the mid-1920s (Lott, 1926).

Lacking control over such a key element of cost was a major frustration to top management in classical firms, and job evaluation was seen as a way of both gaining control and ensuring that compensation costs would be no higher than they had to be. Job evaluation also fit perfectly with the narrowly structured jobs that these types of organizations like to create. The best classical firms of the time had already developed careful definitions and formal descriptions of jobs in their organizations. Thus, the raw materials for job evaluation—comprehensive job descriptions—already existed in many major firms.

This system was perfectly compatible with the strategy utilized by unions at that time—job control unionism—which is facilitated by tight and narrow job descriptions that the union can use for restricting arbitrary treatment of employees by management. For employers, job evaluation served as a systematic basis for negotiating pay levels with the union. World War II increased the popularity of job evaluation because it could be used to circumvent wage controls that were in place at that time, and firms were having difficulty retaining their employees due to a war-induced labour shortage.

Job evaluation was enthusiastically received by the human relations firms that were gaining ascendancy in the 1940s and 1950s. They regarded it as an important tool to foster a sense of reward equity and fairness among employees, to keep employees loyal and satisfied, and to forestall unionization. While it was used as a vehicle for cost control, its ability to serve as a vehicle to foster equity was probably seen by human relations firms as its most important virtue. As in the case of classical firms, job evaluation also fit well with the narrow jobs and centralized policies preferred by human relations firms.

The system also fit well with the bureaucratic nature of government organizations, with their need for a systematic and equitable approach to compensate thousands of employees, so it is not surprising that the U.S. federal government was one of the earliest adopters of job evaluation, beginning more than a hundred years ago (Gupta and Jenkins, 1991). Many state governments followed suit, and the system also spread to the federal and provincial governments in Canada.

Advantages of Job Evaluation

Job evaluation presents several major advantages, especially when seen in the context of the managerial practices prevailing at the time the method was first developed. First, it provides the ability for centralized control of compensation costs to ensure that compensation costs are minimized. Second, by linking pay level to the importance or value of the job to the organization, job evaluation provides a way of signalling the importance of jobs to employees, and provides an incentive to motivate people to seek these jobs.

Third, it provides a systematic way to promote equitable pay within the organization, diminishing the role of factors such as favouritism and nepotism. When used effectively, job evaluation should also eliminate gender-based pay inequities. Fourth, the system of standardized jobs makes market pricing easier, which still needs to be done for a portion of the jobs to calibrate the job evaluation system. Fifth, job evaluation provides a systematic way to evaluate new jobs. Sixth, over time, a number of consulting firms that specialize in job evaluation have emerged, with well-established technologies for conducting job evaluation. Finally, it fits with and even reinforces two of the most widely prevailing managerial strategies (classical and human relations).

DISADVANTAGES OF JOB EVALUATION

Job evaluation has numerous disadvantages, some related to the process itself, and others related to the rigidity that this type of system reinforces. Ed Lawler (2000), one of the most vocal critics of job evaluation, believes that it should rarely be used because it retards the transformation of classical and human relations organizations to high-involvement organizations. He advocates the use of pay for knowledge whenever possible. Another prominent expert (Sibson, 1990: 115) argues that market pricing systems "are far better than traditional job evaluation and can be installed and administered at a far lower cost."

One set of problems centres around the need for comprehensive job descriptions. The underlying assumption of a job description is that it is desirable to carefully and precisely specify an employee's job duties. When accurate and up-to-date, job descriptions do provide guidance to employees regarding their roles in the organization and to those who are recruiting employees. They provide some assurance that nothing is "falling between the cracks"—that all important tasks are being done. They also allow for tight control of employees.

But job descriptions also have many drawbacks. First, they are expensive. They take a considerable effort to develop and to update. Job descriptions, by their nature, also tend to create a "not my job" syndrome, as employees use their job descriptions to avoid taking on any duties that are not specified in their job descriptions. Finally, job descriptions can inhibit change. When circumstances change, and job duties need to change, job descriptions can slow this adaptation, as people are unwilling to change until their current job description is changed.

Because of all this, many firms, especially those with a need for frequent reorganization, don't bother with job descriptions at all. In fact, some highly successful high-involvement firms, such as W.L. Gore (makers of Gore-Tex), don't even have job *titles*, let alone job descriptions! (Strictly speaking, information can be gathered for job evaluation even in the absence of job descriptions, through job analysis and job questionnaires, but the process is made much more onerous without job descriptions.)

Another problem is that job evaluation may not be suitable for certain employee groups, especially those where behaviour is complex or difficult to describe, as in the case of managers and many professionals. For example, one study found highly negative consequences when applying job evaluation to research and development employees (Gomez-Mejia, Balkin, and Milkovich, 1990). As Gomez-Mejia and Balkin (1992: 13) put it:

> *By establishing an elaborate hierarchy of grade levels for scientists and engineers and making rewards contingent on fine distinctions in the nature of the task being accomplished, many high tech firms foster competition, artificial barriers among people, fragmentation, and an individualistic climate in the work force. The behaviors and culture fostered by traditional job evaluation procedures in this situation run counter to what it takes to succeed in a R & D envi-*

ronment, namely intense team effort, integration of activities among many individuals, fluid tasks, exchange of knowledge, and minimal status barriers to facilitate interactions among S & Es [scientists and engineers] working on common problems.

Evaluating jobs can also become an adversarial process, eroding honesty and trust, since it is in the best interests of the employee to inflate the difficulty of the job whenever possible. If successful, this not only inflates costs of the pay system, but causes real inequity with other jobs that are not inflated. Although job evaluation is presented as a fair and scientific way of achieving equitable pay, most employees will realize that there is still substantial subjectivity in the process.

Furthermore, some frequently used factors can encourage inefficiency. For example, many job evaluation systems have a factor covering "number of persons supervised." Thus, it is in the best interests of managers to increase the number of staff under their supervision (so that their job can get a higher evaluation), regardless of whether this is in the best interests of the organization.

Job evaluation systems are also costly to develop and maintain, involving continual updating of job descriptions and reevaluations as jobs change. This is obviously a particular problem for those organizations that operate in dynamic environments. And, of course, job evaluation does not eliminate the need for market pricing, which still must be done for key benchmark jobs in order to align the system with the market.

In some cases, job evaluation is not as fair and objective as it would appear at first glance. Indeed, job evaluation systems, along with market pricing systems, have often been accused of perpetuating gender-based pay inequity, rather than combating it (Weiner, 1991). However, this does not seem to be a problem inherent in job evaluation, but rather in the way that job evaluation has traditionally been applied, as will be discussed further in Chapter 9.

But perhaps the most important drawback of job evaluation systems is that they can inhibit change, flexibility, and skill development (Gupta and Jenkins, 1991). Employees will be unwilling to move to needed areas if the jobs there pay less. As has been discussed, job descriptions in themselves inhibit change. If employees must accept new job duties, they will want to have their job reevaluated before accepting these duties. Or if jobs do change, but new job descriptions are not developed and reevaluations are not conducted promptly, the system becomes inequitable.

There is also no incentive for employees to learn jobs that are not in the direct line of advancement. If advancement to better jobs is not possible, there is no incentive at all to learn additional skills. Job evaluation also gives the impression that the only worthwhile movement is vertical, up the hierarchy, because this is the only way to increase your rewards.

A relevant trend is the move by many firms toward "broadbanding"—the practice of reducing the dozens of job grades produced by job evaluation to as few as six large job "bands" at large firms such as General Electric (Ledford, 1995). Supporters of job evaluation argue that this can be a solution to the rigidity problems caused by job evaluation (Milkovich and Newman, 1991). But others point out that it is illogical to go to the trouble of using job evaluation to make fine distinctions between jobs and then to throw jobs together into large bands (Ledford, 1995). Instead, some firms that adopt broadbanding simply eliminate job evaluation.

In Canada, the great majority of medium to large firms (73 percent) use job evaluation, according to the CPS. This high usage is at least in part due to legislated pay equity standards, which require the use of a systematic method to compare job value within organizations. Among firms that utilize job evaluation, two-thirds included all of their employees in the job evaluation system. About 29 percent of Canadian firms utilized broadbanding, and most (81 percent) of these firms also used job evaluation.

In closing our discussion on job evaluation, we should note that many of the problems cited here have to do with change. Clearly, job evaluation poses more problems when the organization is faced with rapid change, or when the organization wishes to use a high-involvement managerial strategy (McNabb and Whitfield, 2001). For those organizations where classical or human relations managerial strategies are still appropriate, it is possible that the advantages of job evaluation will outweigh its disadvantages. For example, job evaluation will likely continue to be well suited to public-sector organizations.

Pay for Knowledge

The third method for determining base pay is radically different from job evaluation. It involves basing pay on the capabilities of individuals rather than on the characteristics of jobs. It is often known as *person-based pay,* in contrast to job-based pay. There are various labels for this method, including pay for knowledge, competency-based pay, and skill-based pay, and they are generally used interchangeably. The underlying premise is that employees are paid according to the package of skills, knowledge, and competencies that each possesses, regardless of the particular job that they happen to be doing at any given time.

Advantages of Pay for Knowledge

Two of the most important advantages of pay-for-knowledge systems (PKS) relate to skills development and flexibility. PKS provides a major incentive for employees to learn a variety of skills, which then makes it easier to shift employees from one job to another as the need arises. And PKS avoids the disincentive to movement caused by traditional job evaluation systems, which result in strictly defined jobs that are "owned" by the people currently doing them. Thus, under traditional pay systems, if a nut on a machine needs tightening, it is often necessary to call a mechanic, because maintenance is not part of the machine operator's job description. However, under PKS, an operator will simply grab a wrench and tighten the nut.

Flexibility is especially beneficial for organizations in which various parts of the production or service process peak and ebb at different times. For example, a big customer order may need expediting, or there may be parts shortages in certain production processes, requiring employees to move from an idle function to one in which there is high activity. Of course, PKS also makes it easier to cover for employee absences and vacations. PKS makes the use of job rotation essential, and job rotation itself has been shown to be beneficial for some organizations (Cheraskin and Campion, 1996).

The following example illustrates how PKS can facilitate flexibility and change, while traditional job evaluation can inhibit change (Lawler, 1990: 161):

> *As a result of the Tylenol poisoning tragedy, Johnson & Johnson decided to completely redo its packaging of Tylenol to add greater safety. The skill-based plant quickly installed the new technology needed and got back into production. Not so with its sister plant, which was a traditional job-based seniority driven plant. Seniority rights and traditional pay grades got in the way of people's flexibility in adapting to the new technology. In addition, the traditional plant, unlike the skill-based plant, did not have a history of providing training, valuing personal growth, and encouraging employees to do new things. Thus, the transition to new packaging equipment was a major challenge for it.*

A major advantage of PKS is that it does not require job descriptions as a foundation, in contrast to job evaluation, thus avoiding many of the problems of job descriptions discussed earlier. This is a major advantage for organizations in which change is rapid. Jobs are also broader and provide more intrinsic rewards.

Knowledgeable employees performing broader jobs may also be highly beneficial for customer service. As Schuster and Zingheim (1992: 108) put it: "Skill-based pay prepares employees to handle a wider range of customer issues without switching the customer from place to place. This is more efficient for the organization and for the customer."

Although the earliest adopters of pay for knowledge tended to apply PKS to production employees (especially in firms with process technologies, such as chemical plants), firms have also applied PKS to their service employees. As Box 4.2 illustrates, Nortel Networks was one of the pioneers in application of PKS to service employees.

Because of the more efficient use of the workforce, a firm using PKS should be able to operate with a smaller labour force. Part of this reduction will come from a reduction in managerial, supervisory, and inspection positions, as

BOX 4.2 Pay for Knowledge Boosts Service at Nortel

Nortel Networks produces and sells a wide variety of telecommunications products, and a key aspect of their business is the proper installation and servicing of this equipment at the customer's premises. In the late 1980s, the company had serious concerns about the quality of customer service, a higher than desirable rate of turnover among service technicians, and perceived inequity in their traditional pay system for these positions (LeBlanc, 1991). In an attempt to provide high-quality service, the company had always provided extensive training to these technicians, but many technicians quit shortly after they had been fully trained. They cited a lack of advancement opportunities and the higher pay being offered by other firms for fully trained technicians.

To deal with these problems, Nortel implemented a pay-for-knowledge system for their service technicians in 1988. Various "skill blocks" were created, and as a technician acquired competency in each skill block, pay increased. But in addition to this skill-based pay, the company also introduced performance pay that related to customer service quality.

Interestingly, the company also altered the pay system for service managers. A significant part of the manager's

bonus is now awarded on the basis of successful employee training results. Each manager is responsible for ensuring a specified amount of training time for technicians every year.

Two years after these changes in the pay system were implemented, customer satisfaction was up and voluntary turnover among technicians had been cut in half. But the system has not been without problems. Technicians have complained about insufficient training opportunities and the difficulty of acquiring certain skills because they are given little opportunity to work on certain types of equipment or installations. Others believe that some of the required skill levels for a given block are unrealistic in the context of the actual work requirements. Other perceived problems include too few skill blocks, and excessive difficulty in qualifying for these blocks.

To resolve these problems, which may have resulted from insufficient involvement of technicians during the initial design process, the company involved the technicians in determining the necessary modifications to the system. This is in keeping with the high-involvement and employee-oriented managerial philosophy that earned the company a position among "Canada's Top 100 Employers" in 2000 (Yerema, 2000).

well as some specialty positions, such as maintenance mechanics or electricians.

A key advantage of PKS is that it supports the behaviour needed by a firm attempting to practise high-involvement management. The knowledge that the system imparts allows for employees to be more effectively involved in decision making, and to be able to exercise judgment and take quick action when the situation requires it. It allows individuals and teams to be more self-managing. When Shell Canada wanted to build a new chemical plant that would practise high-involvement management, the company saw that this would be difficult, if not impossible, using traditional pay methods, and made pay for knowledge a central part of this process, as Box 4.3 describes.

Not only does PKS fit with a high-involvement management strategy, it can help to promote movement to this style of management. As Ledford (1991: 205–6) puts it:

[Pay for knowledge] can be a powerful force in helping an organization live up to a commitment to become a high-involvement organization. This is because employees, acting in their own self-interest, begin to exert pressure for greater training, information, and control over job rotation and other key decisions. In short, they begin to demand that the organization behave more like a high-involvement organization.

BOX 4.3 Pay for Knowledge Finds Good Chemistry at Basell Canada

One of the first organizations anywhere to implement pay for knowledge was the Shell Chemical plant in Sarnia, Ontario (now known as Basell Canada Ltd.), which opened in 1978. The plant produces polypropylene and isopropyl alcohol in a 24-hour continuous process operation. About 75 grades of state-of-the-art plastics are formed into pea-sized pellets. These versatile polymers are then sold worldwide for use in such products as compact discs, car-door panels, carpets, toys, and pop bottles (HRDC, 1994). Consistent, high product quality is essential, but the production process is very complicated and many things can go wrong during the various stages of production.

Quick and accurate reactions to production problems are essential, but traditional plant design made that difficult, since the production process was often divided into four or more separate departments, within which each person had a narrowly specified job. Few employees understood the entire production process and the complex interrelations between the various production phases.

Shell had noticed numerous problems in their traditional plants, including slow responses to production problems, underutilization of employees, and high boredom, dissatisfaction, and turnover among employees (Halpern, 1984). To avoid these problems, they decided to base their new plant on the high-involvement model. In so doing, the company also wished to develop a collaborative relationship with the union (the Communications, Energy, and Paper Workers Union) by involving it in the plant design process as well as in the continuing operation of the plant.

The new design eliminated the separate departments and created 20-person "shift teams" to operate the plant during each shift. These shift teams were supported by a craft team of electricians, pipefitters, and other specialized personnel, who were present only during the day shift, or when called in for emergency situations. Each member of the shift team was expected to eventually be able to perform all necessary tasks in the production process.

The company recognized at the outset that the traditional approach to compensating operators, which defined jobs narrowly and had a different pay grade for each job, would not be compatible with the new system. Therefore, job categories on each shift team were reduced to one: shift team member. To foster employee multiskilling and flexibility, a pay-for-knowledge system was developed.

When they start at the plant, each operator receives the training needed to perform a basic set of shift functions and is paid a base rate. To increase his or her pay rate, a worker needs to demonstrate competence in one additional job knowledge cluster, and in four modules of a "specialty skill." (For the purposes of training and compensation, the "operations" area of the complex was divided into ten job knowledge clusters.) Each specialty skill (e.g., instrumentation, electrical, pipefitting) was divided into 40 skill modules, and every worker is expected to select one specialty skill. Thus, there are ten levels in the pay progression system, and workers will make the top pay when they have mastered all ten job knowledge clusters and all 40 modules of their specialty skill. On average, it takes about six years for this to happen (HRDC, 1994).

How well does the system work? When interviewed in 2001, company officials indicated that the original pay-for-knowledge system, implemented more than 20 years ago, has shown such success that it has been carried forward with very few changes since then.

DISADVANTAGES OF PAY FOR KNOWLEDGE

A major disadvantage of pay for knowledge is that it may give rise to situations where employees are "overpaid" relative to what competitors are paying for the specific job currently being performed. In fact, this is quite likely, especially if PKS has been in place for some time, resulting in most employees achieving the top pay grade ("topping out"). In general, employees operating under PKS earn considerably more than employees not working under this system.

Another issue has to do with topping out. Once an individual is at the top grade, what is the incentive to continue learning and updating skills? There must be some system that requires reskilling as certain skills become out of date. Furthermore, there is the issue of lack of use. If employees are not rotated through jobs regularly, then skills may atrophy. But senior employees may resent having to spend some of their time doing the less-advanced jobs in order for less-senior employees to perform the more advanced jobs. As Milkovich and Newman (1996: 193) put it, a bit whimsically:

> At some point, having all chefs and no dishwashers (and having to pay chef wages to those who are assigned to scrub pots and pans) is uncompetitive. And probably dissatisfying to certified chefs with dishpan hands.

In addition, pay-for-knowledge systems lead to increased training costs, both in terms of the cost of training and the need to take employees off the job while training takes place. For example, at LS Electrogalvanizing (LSE) in Cleveland, a "fifth shift" had to be created, even though the plant could run with four shifts, in order to provide the necessary time off the job for training. At LSE, training costs run at about 12 percent of payroll, compared with less than 1 percent in conventional firms in the same industry.

Pay for knowledge is more complex to administer than job-based pay, due to the necessity to identify and administer certification procedures (through which it is determined whether an employee actually possesses a given skill and is entitled to be paid for it). Adjusting the system to the market may also be more difficult than for job evaluation if there are no other firms with skill-based pay systems to use as a comparison. PKS is also more complex for employees to understand. Moreover, not all employees may have the ability or desire to learn multiple jobs. Unions may resist PKS because wages are based on skill levels, not seniority.

Pay-for-knowledge systems may also appear to violate some pay equity laws, which generally stipulate that employees should be paid for what they actually do rather than for their capabilities (Barrett, 1991). Thus, a woman performing a bagging operation in a dog food plant who receives lower pay than a man doing the same job may appear to be unfairly treated. However, most pay equity laws do make exemptions for factors such as skill levels and relevant experience, as long as these are applied consistently to both male and female employees.

Finally, it may not be feasible to apply PKS to all jobs in a given firm, creating a need to maintain both skill- and job-based systems.

EXPERIENCE WITH PAY FOR KNOWLEDGE

Pay-for-knowledge systems appear to have grown rapidly in popularity during the past few years. In 1991, a survey of 224 mostly small to medium-sized Canadian firms (Betcherman, Leckie, and Verma, 1994) indicated that only 9 percent had any employees on pay-for-knowledge systems, although usage was considerably higher among larger firms. Consistent with this, a study of 114 mostly large Canadian firms conducted in 1990–91 (Long, 1993) indicated that 17 percent had pay-for-knowledge systems. Most of these PKS firms covered only a small number of their employees. However, by 2000, the CPS indicated that 25 percent of medium to large Canadian firms had pay-for-knowledge systems, and that these systems covered nearly half (47 percent) of all their employees, on average. Sixteen (27 percent) of these PKS firms indicated that PKS covered *all* of their employees.

As one would expect, use of PKS was significantly higher in firms utilizing a high-involvement managerial strategy. As Wallace (1991: 155) concluded from a study of 15 U.S. firms that had implemented pay-for-knowledge systems:

> *It is important to note that skill-based pay is not so much a compensation system as it is a radical departure from traditional organizational design. It works best in work systems where there is a high level of employee involvement, where work has been organized in self-managed teams ... and where there is a commitment to high levels of investment in human capital.*

As has been discussed, classical and human relations organizations are not likely to be attracted to PKS because it does not fit well with their managerial philosophies. Moreover, in situations that are truly suited to classical or human relations managerial strategies, PKS is not likely to pay off. Flexibility will only pay off if the environment and technology are such that flexibility is essential. Extra knowledge will pay off only if the organization is structured in such a way as to utilize this knowledge. Clearly, classical and human relations organizations will not likely receive much value from a pay-for-knowledge system. But even traditional unionized organizations can benefit from PKS, if both management and the union are willing to adopt new, collaborative roles, as Mericle and Kim (1999) have found.

There has not been a great deal of systematic evidence on the effects of PKS on organizational performance. Wallace (1991) reported that all the companies in his sample who used PKS found it beneficial and planned to stay with it. Parent and Weber (1994) compared a Ford auto parts plant in Ontario that had skill-based pay with another Ontario Ford plant that did not have it, and found inconclusive results. Long (1989) found a 25 percent discontinuation rate of PKS plans in Canadian firms during 1980 to 1985, although he noted that many of these firms may not have been suitable candidates for PKS in the first place. In another study, Long (1993) found that Canadian firms with PKS experienced significantly greater increases in employee productivity during the period 1985–90 than did firms without such systems.

The most comprehensive study of skill-based pay systems was conducted by Jenkins and his colleagues (Jenkins, Ledford, Gupta, and Doty, 1993). Through a mail survey, they examined 97 different skill-based plans in 70 U.S. companies. They found skill-based plans most common in manufacturing firms—especially those using continuous process technologies—but also found growing usage in the service sector. As expected, skill-based plans were much more likely to be found in firms with high-involvement workplace practices than in other firms.

Overall, 42 percent of the respondents judged skill-based pay to be "highly successful," while almost all of the others reported it as "quite successful." Virtually all respondents cited increased workforce flexibility and increased employee satisfaction as key benefits. Over 90 percent believed that PKS had increased effectiveness of work teams, enhanced employee growth and development, led to better use of work technology, enhanced employee motivation, and increased output per labour hour. More than 75 percent believed it had increased their ability to recruit employees, reduced turnover, lowered absenteeism, and decreased labour costs. At the same time, however, more than two-thirds indicated that pay rates had increased as a result of skill-based pay.

This latter finding is not a contradiction. Most employers believed that skill-based pay was a win-win innovation for the company and employees. Individual employees earned more than they otherwise would have, but the productivity gains caused by skill-based pay outweighed these increases in pay rates. Murray and Gerhart (1998) replicated this result in their study of the implementation of skill-based pay at a U.S. manufacturing plant, where they found that labour costs per unit dropped, even though average hourly wages increased. According to Jenkins and his associates, key factors for success of PKS plans were an emphasis on employee training, growth and development, local management's commitment to the plan, and a managerial philosophy (i.e., high involvement) that fit with these plans.

The researchers also attempted to uncover cases in which skill-based plans had been introduced but then abandoned, but were able to find only a few. Reasons for failure seemed to be unique to each case. Some of these were inadequate management commitment to the plan, unwillingness to endure short-term implementation problems with the plan, poor plan design that increased labour costs without providing offsetting benefits, conflicts between employees covered by skill-based plans and those not covered, inadequate training opportunities, and failure to ensure skill competence before granting pay increases.

In concluding our discussion of the three main systems for establishing base pay, we should note that there are many firms, especially smaller firms, that do not use any systematic approach for determining base pay, while others have developed their own unique systems, as Box 4.4 describes.

OTHER ASPECTS OF BASE PAY

Aside from choosing a method for determining base pay, a number of other issues need to be dealt with when establishing base pay. These include whether to utilize wages or salaries, whether to adjust pay for the cost of living or seniority, and other miscellaneous issues.

WAGE VS. SALARY

Which is preferable: a **wage** based on an hourly period, or a **salary** based on a weekly or monthly period? Employees prefer salaries because they provide predictability, allowing for easier financial planning and an increased sense of

wage pay based on an hourly time period

salary pay based on a weekly or monthly time period

BOX 4.4 How Much to Pay Employees? Let Them Decide!

Semco is a Brazilian manufacturer of marine pumps, digital scanners, commercial dishwashers, truck filters, and mixing equipment for various food products. In 1980, when Ricardo Semler took over management from his father, this family-owned business teetered on the brink of insolvency. Semler promptly instituted many high-involvement practices, including completely open company books, extensive employee participation in decision making, and flexible work hours. Employees are allowed to define their own jobs and to invent their own job titles.

Semler's unconventional approach extends to pay setting (Semler, 1989: 83):

At Semco, we eliminated Frederick Winslow Taylor's segmentation and specialization of work.... We did away with hourly pay and now give everyone a monthly salary. We set the salaries like this:

A lot of our people belong to unions, and they negotiate their salaries collectively. Everyone else's salary involves an element of self-determination.

Once or twice a year we order salary market surveys and pass them out. We say to people "Figure out where you

stand on this thing. You know what you do; you know what everyone else in the company makes; you know what your friends in other companies make; you know what you need; you know what's fair. Come back on Monday, and tell us what to pay you."

When people ask for too little, we give it to them. By and by, they figure it out and ask for more. When they ask for too much, we give that to them too—at least for the first year. Then, if we don't feel they are worth the money, we sit down with them and say, "Look, you make x amount of money, and we don't think you're making x amount of contribution. So either we find something else for you to do, or we don't have a job for you anymore." But with half a dozen exceptions, our people have always named salaries we could live with.

The results of all this? Over 900 percent growth during the past ten years, and by 2000 the company had become the largest marine and food processing machinery company in Brazil. It has also frequently been named as the best company to work for in Brazil.

---

financial security. But from an employer standpoint, it is not obvious which is preferable.

Traditionally, hourly pay has been used for blue-collar workers and in certain service industries. Salaries have been used for white-collar, professional, and managerial employees. Hourly pay has the advantage of tying pay directly to hours worked. If an employee is absent, there is no pay for that period. If an employer has a limited amount of work, employees are paid only when the employer needs them. In other words, risks due to variability in product or service demand are shifted from the employer to the employee.

On the other hand, compensating some employees with hourly pay and others with salary conveys the impression that some classes of workers are more valuable than others. Hourly pay also implies a lack of commitment to the employees on the part of the employer, and this may be reflected in a lack of commitment to the employer. Hourly paid workers must also be paid overtime when their daily or weekly hours exceed the statutory maximums, while no such obligation generally exists for salaried employees.

A major concern in switching from wages to salaries is possible abuse by employees, such as an increase in absenteeism. However, a study of large U.S. firms (Lawler, Mohrman, and Ledford, 1995) showed that 76 percent of firms with all-salaried systems deemed them successful, while just 8 percent deemed them unsuccessful.

In general, it seems likely that the impact of changing to salaries will depend on the current level of commitment by employees and the quality of employee–management relationships. For classical firms, if all they do is to switch from hourly pay to salary, the outcome will likely be detrimental, since the firm is dismantling one type of control mechanism without having anything else to replace it. On the other hand, salaries fit well with human relations firms, since they wish to create a sense of loyalty among employees and a sense of togetherness within the firm, which can best be created with a salary system for all organization members. For high-involvement firms, salaries are an important and tangible symbol of commitment by the firm to its employees, and hourly wages are incompatible with the type of commitment that is desired. Indeed, when firms convert to high-involvement management, one of the first changes they make is putting everyone on salary.

ADJUSTING BASE PAY

Once base pay is established, it must be adjusted over time. The firm must decide how it will respond to changes in external conditions, such as the cost of living, and whether to recognize seniority through adjustments to base pay.

ADJUSTING TO EXTERNAL CONDITIONS
Of course, even after base pay is established, there must be some method for adjusting it to changing circumstances, such as inflation. When inflation was high, many employers developed policies to adjust base pay according to

changes in the cost of living. **Cost of living adjustment (COLA) clauses** were included in many collective agreements in order to deal with rapid changes in the cost of living.

Without these clauses, unions were reluctant to sign collective agreements that exceeded a year in length. As inflation abated, most of these clauses and policies were removed. The advantage of COLA systems is that they allow orderly adjustment to economic circumstances; the disadvantage is that they reduce the firm's control over labour costs and take no account of the employer's ability to pay. But even in periods of low inflation, a firm needs some systematic way of adjusting base pay to changing market conditions. This will be discussed further in Chapter 10.

cost of living adjustment (COLA) clause a clause in a collective agreement that automatically adjusts compensation levels on the basis of increases in the cost of living

ADJUSTING FOR SENIORITY

A key question is whether to adjust base pay in accordance with seniority. Organizations that value employee stability highly will be most likely to do so, as will organizations in which years of service are highly related to performance and those for which the cost of turnover is high. Cost of turnover is especially high for firms that invest heavily in employee training, that have high recruitment and selection costs, where personalized employee–customer relationships are important, or where teamwork and close cooperation are needed among employees.

However, it is not always necessary to use base pay to create employee stability. For many organizations, indirect pay is the major vehicle used to encourage continued organizational membership. Organizations using pay-for-knowledge systems also have no need to use seniority to recognize and retain skilled employees since PKS does this directly.

It can be seen that firms from each of the three managerial strategies will value seniority differently. Human relations organizations will value it the most, because the cornerstone of their managerial strategy is a stable, contented workforce. It is very difficult to develop positive social norms and close personal bonds between employees and management and among employees if there is high turnover. Since a pay-for-knowledge system will not likely pay off for human relations organizations, they are left to fall back on seniority and indirect pay.

High-involvement organizations will also value employee stability, since they regard their workforce as a key asset, and they will wish to protect their investment in this asset. Costs of recruitment and selection are typically high in these firms, as are training costs. But they may not need to use seniority pay to retain their workforce. Pay for knowledge can be used to recognize increased employee value, and internalization of goals can be used to maintain commitment, along with features such as job security and intrinsic rewards flowing from the work itself.

Finally, classical firms might like to have employee stability, but not if it costs them much. Classical organizations are designed to minimize the costs of turnover. Therefore, these firms will not wish to invest much in creating employee stability, and will seek to minimize both seniority-based pay and indirect pay.

OTHER ELEMENTS OF BASE PAY

Finally, there are a number of miscellaneous features that can attach to base pay. For example, a shift differential (increment to base pay) may be provided for employees when they are working an undesirable shift or during weekends or holidays. Overtime may be provided when work exceeds the standard workweek or workday. Although there are statutory requirements to pay overtime for hourly paid employees, a firm may choose to pay in excess of this under certain circumstances. Overtime may also be provided to salaried employees, or possibly just time off in lieu of extra pay. These illustrate just some of the variations that base pay can include.

SUMMARY AND IMPLICATIONS

The purpose of this chapter was to begin our examination of the three main compensation components by focusing on base pay. The possible role of base pay within a compensation system was discussed, along with motives for its use and its advantages and disadvantages. It was noted that although base pay remains the largest component in most pay systems, it is increasingly being supplemented by performance pay. At the same time, some firms that traditionally have not utilized base pay are adding it to their compensation mix.

Three main methods for establishing base pay (market pricing, job evaluation, pay for knowledge) were identified, and the advantages and disadvantages of each were discussed. It was noted that the different methods are compatible with different managerial strategies, with job evaluation fitting well with classical and human relations strategies, and pay for knowledge fitting with the high-involvement strategy. Finally, several other aspects of base pay were examined, including wages vs. salaries, and adjustments for inflation and seniority.

The next chapter will continue our examination of the three components of pay by focusing on individual performance pay.

KEY TERMS

base pay, p. 116

cost of living adjustment (COLA)
  clause, p. 135

job evaluation, p. 119

market pricing, p. 119

pay-for-knowledge system (PKS),
  p. 119

salary, p. 133

wage, p. 133

EXERCISES

1. Analyze the Fit Stop Ltd. case (in the Appendix) and determine whether base pay should be an important component of compensation. If so, identify the most appropriate method for determining base pay. What factors did you consider in making these decisions?

2. Analyze the Multi-Products Corporation case (in the Appendix) and determine what would be the most appropriate method for determining base pay. What factors led you to the choice you made?

3. Pay for knowledge appears to work very well at Basell Canada, as discussed in Box 4.3. Why does it work so well there?

4. Box 4.4 describes an unconventional method for determining base pay. What are the pros and cons of this system? Why does the system apparently work so well? Could it be applied successfully to other organizations?

SUGGESTED WEB SITE

Page 120: If you would like to know what employers are paying for particular jobs in your area, try checking <www.salaryexpert.com>

REFERENCES

Barrett, Gerald. 1991. "Comparison of Skill-Based Pay with Traditional Job Evaluation Techniques." *Human Resource Management Review*, 1(2): 97–105.

Betcherman, Gordon, Norm Leckie, and Anil Verma. 1994. "HRM Innovations in Canada: Evidence from Establishment Surveys." Working Paper QPIR 1994-3. Kingston, ON: Industrial Relations Centre, Queen's University.

Cheraskin, Lisa, and Michael A. Campion. 1996. "Study Clarifies Job-Rotation Benefits." *Personnel Journal*, 75(11): 31–38.

Foster, K.E. 1985. "An Anatomy of Company Pay Policies." *Personnel*, September, 66–72.

Gomez-Mejia, Luis, and David Balkin. 1992. *Compensation, Organizational Strategy, and Firm Performance*. Cincinnati, OH: South-Western.

Gomez-Mejia, Luis, David Balkin, and George Milkovich. 1990. "Rethinking Your Rewards for Technical Employees." *Organizational Dynamics*, 18(4): 62–75.

Gupta, Nina, and G. Douglas Jenkins. 1991. "Practical Problems in Using Job Evaluation Systems to Determine Compensation." *Human Resource Management Review*, 1(2): 133–44.

Halpern, Norm. 1984. "Sociotechnical Systems Design: The Shell Sarnia Experience." In J.B. Cunningham and T.H. White, eds., *Quality of Working*

Life: Contemporary Cases. Ottawa: Labour Canada, 31–75.

HRDC. 1994. "Moving Parts and Moving People: Sociotechnical Design of a New Plant." In *Labour Management Innovations in Canada*. Ottawa: Human Resources Development Canada, 72–76.

Jenkins, G. Douglas, Gerald E. Ledford, Nina Gupta, and D. Harold Doty. 1993. *Skill-Based Pay: Practices, Payoffs, Pitfalls and Prescriptions*. Scottsdale, AZ: American Compensation Association.

Lawler, Edward E. 1990. *Strategic Pay: Aligning Organizational Strategies and Pay Systems*. San Francisco: Jossey-Bass.

Lawler, Edward E. 2000. *Rewarding Excellence: Pay Strategies for the New Economy*. San Francisco: Jossey Bass.

Lawler, Edward E., Susan A. Mohrman, and Gerald E. Ledford. 1995. *Creating High Performance Organizations*. San Francisco: Jossey-Bass.

LeBlanc, Peter V. 1991. "Skill Based Pay Case Number 2: Northern Telecom." *Compensation and Benefits Review*, 23(2): 39–56.

Ledford, Gerald. 1991. "The Design of Skill Based Pay Plans." In Milton L. Rock and Lance A. Berger, *The Compensation Handbook*. New York: McGraw-Hill, 199–217.

Ledford, Gerald E. 1995. "Designing Nimble Reward Systems." *Compensation and Benefits Review*, 27(4): 46–54.

Long, Richard J. 1989. "Patterns of Workplace Innovation in Canada." *Relations industrielles/Industrial Relations*, 44(4): 805–26.

Long, Richard J. 1993. "The Relative Effects of New Information Technology and Employee Involvement on Productivity in Canadian Companies." *Proceedings of the Administrative Sciences Association of Canada (Organizational Theory Division)*.

Lott, M.R. 1926. *Wage Scales and Job Evaluation*. New York: Ronald Press.

McNabb, Robert, and Keith Whitfield. 2001. "Job Evaluation and High Performance Work Practices: Compatible or Conflictual?" *Journal of Management Studies*, 38(2): 293–312.

Mericle, Kenneth, and Dong-One Kim. 1999. "From Job-Based Pay to Skill-Based Pay in Unionized Establishments: A Three Plant Comparative Analysis." *Relations industrielles/Industrial Relations*, 54(3): 549–80.

Milkovich, George T., and Jerry N. Newman. 1996. *Compensation*. Chicago: Richard D. Irwin.

Mitchell, Daniel J.B., David Lewin, and Edward E. Lawler. 1990. "Alternative Pay Systems, Firm Performance, and Productivity." In Alan S. Blinder, ed., *Paying for Productivity: A Look at the Evidence*. Washington, DC: The Brookings Institution, 15–87.

Murray, Brian, and Barry Gerhart. 1998. "An Empirical Analysis of a Skill-Based Pay Program and Plant Performance Outcomes." *The Academy of Management Journal*, 41(1): 68–78.

Parent, Kevin J., and Caroline L. Weber. 1994. "Does Paying for Knowledge Pay Off?" *Compensation and Benefits Review*, 26(5): 44–50.

Rynes, Sara L., and George T. Milkovich. 1986. "Wage Surveys: Dispelling Some Myths about the Market Wage." *Personnel Psychology*, 39(1): 71–90.

Schuster, Jay R., and Patricia K. Zingheim. 1992. *The New Pay: Linking Employee and Organizational*

Performance. New York: Lexington Books.

Semler, Ricardo. 1989. "Managing without Managers." *Harvard Business Review*, 67(5): 76–84.

Sibson, Robert E. 1990. *Compensation*. New York: American Management Association.

Theriault, Roland. 1992. *Mercer Compensation Manual: Theory and Practice*. Boucherville, PQ: Morin.

Wallace, Marc J. 1991. "Sustaining Success with Alternative Rewards." In Milton L. Rock and Lance A. Berger, *The Compensation Handbook*. New York: McGraw-Hill, 147–57.

Weiner, Nan J. 1991. "Job Evaluation Systems: A Critique." *Human Resource Management Review*, 1(2): 119–32.

Yerema, Richard. 2000. *Canada's Top 100 Employers: 2001 Edition*. Toronto: Mediacorp.

5

....

INDIVIDUAL
PERFORMANCE PAY

CHAPTER GOALS

By the end of this chapter, you should be able to:

1. Identify and distinguish among the three main types of performance pay.
2. Discuss the advantages and disadvantages of individual performance pay, and the circumstances in which it would be appropriate.
3. Discuss the advantages and disadvantages of piece rates, and the circumstances in which they would be appropriate.
4. Discuss the advantages and disadvantages of commissions, and the circumstances in which they would be appropriate.
5. Identify and explain the three main types of merit pay.
6. Discuss the advantages and disadvantages of each type of merit pay, and the circumstances in which each type would be appropriate.
7. Identify two important types of special-purpose incentives, and discuss their advantages and disadvantages.
8. Discuss the role that nonmonetary rewards may play in motivating individual performance.

....

INTRODUCTION

Paying employees only when the desired performance takes place sounds like a wonderful idea, if you are an employer. Yet, many employers choose not to use performance pay at all, and among those who do use it, it generally constitutes a relatively small proportion of total compensation.

As we have seen from the previous chapter, there are many reasons why base pay is the largest component of compensation for most firms. But performance pay is rapidly gaining popularity and is playing a larger role in the total compensation package for many employees. The purpose of this chapter and the next is to examine the role of performance pay in the compensation strategy, to identify the various types of performance pay that can be used, to explore the pros and cons of each, and to identify conditions for its successful use.

This chapter will focus on plans that relate pay to individual employee performance, while Chapter 6 will focus on pay plans that are related to group or organizational performance. The overall objective for these two chapters is to help readers decide which type of performance plan, if any, is most suitable for their organizations.

WHAT IS PERFORMANCE PAY?

performance pay any type of financial reward that is provided only when certain specified performance results occur. These results may be based on the performance of individual employees, the performance of a group or team, or the performance of an entire organization

Performance pay can be defined as any type of financial reward that is provided only when certain specified performance results occur. It is sometimes known as "performance-contingent pay," "variable pay," or "at-risk pay." Pay-for-performance plans can be classified into three main categories, depending on whether the performance relates to the individual employee, to the group or work team, or to the entire organization. *Individual performance plans* include piece rates, commissions, merit pay, and targeted incentives. *Group performance plans* include group/team bonus plans and productivity gain-sharing plans. *Organizational performance plans* include profit sharing and employee stock plans.

WHY USE PERFORMANCE PAY?

There are numerous advantages of performance pay plans. Properly designed, they signal key behaviours and motivate action toward achieving them. They reduce the need for other types of mechanisms for controlling employee behaviour. They create an interest among employees about performance and provide information about current performance levels. They can be used to support a specific managerial strategy and thereby promote achievement of the organization's goals.

They also make pay more variable, and therefore help to relate compensation levels to the firm's ability to pay. This allows organizations to have more stability in their employment levels, as Gerhart and Trevor (1996) have found, lessening the need to lay off employees in difficult times only to rehire them when times improve. This employment stability has advantages for both employers and employees, since employers risk losing employees whenever they are forced to lay them off, and employees prefer stable employment to layoffs.

Disadvantages of Performance Pay

It is difficult to generalize about the disadvantages of performance pay plans because the types of plans differ so radically, and each has its own specific advantages, disadvantages, and limitations. But a general drawback is that employees generally prefer predictable and certain rewards to unpredictable and uncertain rewards. Of course, employees usually do not object to performance pay if it is clearly an add-on, to top off base pay and indirect pay. But employees will generally resist *substitution* of performance pay for base pay or indirect pay.

In order to induce employees to accept this substitution, it may be necessary to offer higher total compensation than would otherwise be necessary. Some organizations that rely heavily on performance pay appear to pay a very steep price for so doing. For example, *The Globe and Mail* reported that some stock traders received as much as $800 000 in gross pay in recent years. Is it really necessary or efficient to pay this much? Research in the United States (Mitchell, Lewin, and Lawler, 1990) indicates that workers on incentive systems average about 20 percent more earnings than comparable workers on time-based pay systems.

As has been discussed in previous chapters, performance pay may cause employees to focus only on aspects of behaviour that are being measured, ignoring other unmeasured but still important behaviours. If poorly designed, performance pay can have unanticipated negative consequences. Getting performance pay to work right is usually not an easy matter, and base pay is frequently much simpler and more flexible.

But to generalize beyond this would not be useful, since pay-for-performance plans vary so dramatically. The remainder of this chapter will examine individual performance pay plans. There are four main types, two of which may substitute for time-based pay, and two of which are always used in conjunction with base pay.

Rather than being paid by the amount of time worked, an employee may be paid according to the amount of output produced. There are two main methods for output-related pay: piece rates and commissions. Of course, piece rates and commissions need not supplant base pay entirely, but they can also be used in combination with base pay, which is probably the most common arrangement. The other two types of individual incentives—merit pay and targeted or special-purpose incentives—are always used in conjunction with base pay. Each of these four individual performance plans will be discussed in depth; the chapter will also discuss the role that nonmonetary performance rewards may play within the organization.

USE OF PERFORMANCE PAY IN CANADA

To what extent have Canadian firms adopted performance pay? To answer this question, we will use data from the Compensation Practices Survey (Long, 2002).

Overall, the great majority of Canadian firms (94 percent) reported that they used some type of performance pay for at least some of their employees in 2000. Individual performance pay was most common (used by 88 percent of firms), followed by pay based on organizational performance (52 percent of firms). About 36 percent of firms used group-based performance pay. In firms that used some form of performance pay, individual performance pay averaged 13.9 percent of total compensation for a typical employee, group performance pay averaged 6.2 percent, and organizational performance pay averaged 5.2 percent of total compensation.

As Table 5.1 shows, the most common form of individual performance pay was the merit raise, used by 72 percent of firms, followed by merit bonuses, used by 37 percent of firms. Special incentives were used by 29 percent of firms, sales commissions by 27 percent, and piece rates by 11 percent. Among firms using each individual pay plan, mean percentage of employees covered by the plan ranged from 73 percent for merit raises to 20 percent for sales commissions.

TABLE 5.1 USE OF PERFORMANCE PAY BY CANADIAN FIRMS		
TYPE OF PERFORMANCE PAY	MEAN INCIDENCE (%)	MEAN EMPLOYEE COVERAGE (AMONG USERS) (%)
Individual Performance Pay		
Piece rates	11	43
Sales commissions	27	20
Merit raises	72	73
Merit bonuses	37	51
Special incentives	29	57
Group/Team Performance Pay		
Gain sharing	14	56
Goal sharing	18	61
Other group/team plans	16	50
Organizational Performance Pay		
Profit sharing	32	78
Stock bonus plans	4	80
Stock purchase plans	21	92
Stock option plans	10	68
Other organizational plans	5	88

Piece Rates

Under **piece rates**, an employee receives a fixed sum for each unit of output produced. The objective of piece rates is to maximize individual productivity by creating a clear linkage between behaviour and reward. Piece rates are commonly associated with the manufacturing sector, but they are also used in the service sector. Barbers are paid per head, tree planters are paid per tree, freelance journalists are paid per column inch, and physicians are paid for each procedure they perform. In the service sector, market pricing is generally used to set the piece rate, although for medical doctors it is a negotiation process between each provincial government and each provincial college of physicians and surgeons. But in manufacturing, where the concept of piece rates was developed and popularized by Frederick Winslow Taylor in the beginning of the twentieth century, the process is more complicated.

piece rates a pay system under which individuals receive a fixed sum for each unit of output they produce

Setting Piece Rates

In manufacturing, piece rates are established in the following way. First, a job analyst or methods engineer notes how long a particular task or job typically takes to perform, allowing for factors such as operator fatigue, rest breaks, ability of the worker, and unavoidable delays. The result of this is a production standard; that is, the number of units that could be produced in an hour by a typical worker.

Independent of this, the employer establishes the amount of money a worker with the skills and abilities to perform these tasks should earn hourly, on average. This may be a function of a variety of factors, such as the prevailing wage in the industry for this type of employee. Then, this hourly amount is divided by the production standard. The result is the *piece rate* or dollar payment per piece produced. This type of piece rate is the simplest, and is known as a **straight piece rate**. A more complicated type of piece rate is the **differential piece rate**, in which an employee receives a lower rate for each piece if the production standard is not met.

straight piece rate the same fixed sum is paid for each piece produced, regardless of how many pieces are produced

differential piece rate a lower sum per piece is paid if employee production does not meet the production standard

Problems with Piece Rates

The first problem with piece rates is that they can be applied in only a limited number of circumstances. Jobs with a high degree of interdependence are not good candidates for piece rates, since an individual cannot control the rate of production, nor can responsibility for productivity be attributed to a specific individual. In jobs where there is diversity of activities and tasks, it will be very difficult to keep track of all of these. Jobs where quality cannot be monitored are also not good candidates, nor are jobs in which only some tasks can be measured.

Jobs in which tasks are continually changing, or where tools, materials, and technologies are rapidly changing, are also not amenable to piece rates. Jobs normally need to be retimed each time a major change occurs in them, and this is an onerous task. But the largest problem with change is that each change provides an opportunity for friction between employees and management. For example, if a better machine is purchased, and a worker can now produce twice as much, it makes sense to cut the piece rate in half. Although workers may understand the rationale for this, they still cannot be expected to be pleased with having their piece rate cut. Moreover, where there is little trust between management and workers, workers may suspect that management is simply using new technology as an excuse to cut the piece rate.

Indeed, setting the piece rate is not nearly as "scientific" a process as it would seem to be. When a job is first being timed, a typical worker being studied would not wish to do the work in the shortest possible time, for fear that it only helps to establish a high or "tight" standard. This problem has been going on for a long time, as the next two examples illustrate. The following comment was made by a worker whose job had just been timed (Whyte, 1955: 18):

> *When the time study man came around, I set the speed at 180. I knew damn well he would ask me to push it up, so I started low enough. He finally pushed me up to 445, and I ran the job later at 610. If I'd started out at 445, they'd have timed it at 610. Then I got him on the reaming, too. I ran the reamer at 130 speed and .025 feed. He asked me if I couldn't run the reamer any faster than that, and I told him I had to run the reamer slow to keep the hole size. I showed him two pieces with oversize holes that the day man ran. I picked them out for the occasion!*

In another example, a group of workers worked together to establish a "loose" piece rate for one job (Gardner, 1945: 164–65):

> *In one case, a group, who worked together in assembling a complicated and large sized steel framework, worked out a system to be used only when the rate-setter was present. They found that by tightening certain bolts first, the frame would be slightly sprung and all the other bolts would bind and be very difficult to tighten. When the rate-setter was not present, they followed a different sequence, and the work went much faster.*

However, the experienced industrial engineer, well aware of these tendencies, tries to compensate by guessing the extent to which this is occurring. Thus, the "scientific process" has already deteriorated into a guessing game— one that pits workers against management. In addition, the allowances made for factors such as faulty materials and machine breakdowns are often arbitrary at best. Thus, standards may only be very rough estimates, with some jobs having very "tight" rates and others having very "loose" rates.

Piece rates frequently do not motivate maximum effort because of social forces within the work group. Since production is an important part of the activity of the work group, it is likely that group norms defining an acceptable amount of production will develop. The quality of the worker–management relationship largely determines whether norms will be positive or negative. Unfortunately, the very type of organization most likely to look favourably on piece rates—the classical organization—is most likely to have poor labour–management relationships.

If management has eliminated workers whenever productivity has increased, work groups will not look favourably on high production. Except in rare instances, the amount of work to be done is finite, so if workers increase production, fewer workers will be needed. Few workers want to work themselves out of a job. Moreover, while a few members of the work group may be able to produce far above standard, most will not, and they will exert pressure on the high producers ("rate busters") to moderate their production levels. (High producers are known as "rate busters" because it is feared that management will observe their high performance, and then cut the piece rate, using the argument that it must have been too loose in the first place.) Of course, if management has had a history of cutting piece rates, workers will not be motivated to increase productivity.

Even when the system does serve to promote productivity, it can create other problems. One has to do with product quality. Since the emphasis is on quantity produced, workers may be tempted to cut corners on the quality of the output, frequently necessitating increased inspection. Even with inspection, quality is not likely to be much above the minimum acceptable levels. And of course, there is the cost of inspection and record keeping, which can be considerable.

In some cases, the system creates conflict and lack of cooperation among workers. Workers may all vie for the "loose" jobs and attempt to avoid the "tight" ones. There is also little incentive to advise or help new workers, or to do any job that does not relate directly to production, such as maintaining equipment or keeping the work area clean.

There may also be problems in terms of equipment and material usage. For example, workers might find that they can make the production standard on a drilling job more easily if they replace their drill bits more frequently or run their machines at high speed. But drill bits may be expensive, and machines may burn out more quickly at higher speed. Unless these costs are somehow incorporated into the pay system, the worker is unlikely to be concerned about these problems. But to incorporate them increases the complexity of the system, creating a need to keep more records.

Finally, piece rates have been blamed for encouraging accidents and safety violations. For example, many mines do not use piece rates for fear that miners may sacrifice safety for productivity. In another example, on-time delivery incentives for pizza delivery drivers were found to be related to reckless driving.

As a practical matter, to get piece work to be successful in a manufacturing setting requires a sense of trust between management and workers (in order to facilitate rate setting and rate changes, and to assure workers that management will not attempt to arbitrarily cut rates) and a sense of job security among workers (so that they can be sure that increased productivity will not put them out of a job). The irony is that the firms most likely to want to use piece rates—classical firms—are the firms least likely to provide these conditions. It should not be surprising, then, that most manufacturing firms have abandoned piece rates over the years (Peck, 1993). Box 5.1 provides an interesting exception to this trend, and illustrates how one unique company gets piece rates to work.

APPLICABILITY OF PIECE RATES

In sum, when would piece rates be a viable option? Suitable jobs are those where each worker controls her or his own production, where there is low interdependence between workers, where the unit of production can be easily measured and priced, where individuals perform a limited number of tasks (all of which can be compensated with piece rates), where tasks do not change frequently, where there is sufficient work that increased productivity will not cause layoffs, and where it is easy to monitor whether production meets quality standards.

SALES COMMISSIONS

sales commissions pay that is geared to the number of units sold or the dollar volume of sales

Sales commissions are used to compensate sales personnel in many industries, ranging from automobiles to real estate to stock brokerage. Typically, salespersons receive a certain percentage of their gross sales, although the commission rate may vary according to the different types of products sold by a given salesperson. In contrast to piece rates, commissions have remained a popular payment system, although they are more popular as a complement to base pay rather than as a complete substitute.

ADVANTAGES OF COMMISSIONS

There are several reasons for the popularity of commissions. First, commission rates are relatively easy to set and to measure. Second, there is usually less interdependence among sales employees than there is among production workers. Third, there is, in theory, an almost unlimited number of sales that can be made without creating a need to reduce the salesforce.

BOX 5.1 Piece Rates Spark Productivity at Lincoln Electric

Lincoln Electric, based near Cleveland, Ohio, is the world's largest producer of arc welders. While it is an acknowledged industry leader in its field, the company often attracts more attention for its reward system. The company provides no base pay to its production workers—all are paid on an intricate piece rate system—and very little indirect pay. The firm offers no paid sick days and only the minimum paid holidays allowed by law. Lincoln employees have to pay their own health insurance, and have no choice about accepting overtime work and unexpected job assignments. If older workers decrease in productivity, they earn less. Management does not take seniority into account for promotions. The firm has no union to protect the interests of the company's 3400 employees.

This sounds like a classical manager's dream. But what worker would want a job at a sweatshop like this if he or she could find something better? Think of the employee turnover there must be! Imagine all the problems that there must be with conflict over piece rates and adversarial relations between workers and management.

But in fact, productivity is very high at this company, and hardly anyone ever quits. Workers and management have an excellent relationship. Whenever jobs become available, there are hundreds of applicants. Over the past 50 years, the company has never lost money. What is going on here? Doesn't this example contradict everything we have just said about the problems with piece rates?

This case actually reinforces the points we have been making about piece rates. In reality, this is not a classical organization, nor is it a human relations organization. Look at some of the other policies of the firm. First, job security. The company makes it a policy never to lay off employees. According to a company spokesperson: "We don't lay off anyone unless he steals, lies, fights, or has a record of very low productivity" (*The Globe and Mail*, October 21, 1996). The firm guarantees workers at least 30 hours of work a week, even in lean times. So workers don't have to worry about working themselves out of a job.

Employees also don't have to worry about cuts to the piece rate either. If workers think up a way to improve productivity, the company never cuts piece rates. But doesn't this system cause employees to think only about themselves, rather than the best interests of the firm? To avoid this, the firm also provides profit sharing to all employees, which is distributed according to employee merit. In some years, this bonus can approach 100 percent of regular earnings (Chilton, 1994). Another feature is an employee stock purchase plan under which employees own a large chunk of the company's shares. Profit sharing and employee stock ownership balance the individual perspective caused by the piece rates and encourage citizenship behaviour, with job security as the foundation. Extrinsically, the result is production workers who are among the most highly paid in the United States. Intrinsically, the result is employees who are highly committed to their employer. Because of the self-control these features generate, the company has very few supervisors.

A bedrock of this system is trust between management and employees, accompanied by a system of open communication. As part of this, the company has an elected advisory board of employees that meets with top management twice a month. (There is no union, although this is normally a unionized industry.) Mutual trust also allows adjustments to the piece rates to be made in a nonadversarial way without the conflict that normally accompanies this process.

One reason for the good employee–management relationship lies in the pay system for managers. Managers are not treated much differently from workers. They too depend heavily on profit sharing for their income. They receive no executive "perks"—no cars, no executive dining room, no club memberships, and no reserved parking. When new MBAs join the firm, they must spend eight weeks on the welding line so that they truly come to understand and appreciate Lincoln's unique shopfloor culture (Johns, 1996: 295). Selection for both managers and workers is a lengthy process, with a key criterion being their "fit" with the high-involvement managerial strategy that is in place.

Fourth, the use of commissions reduces the need for other types of control mechanisms, such as supervision or internalized commitment. In many cases, where selling takes place off the business premises, it is difficult to exert direct control and supervision, so output-based control may be the only viable option if the salesforce does not have internalized commitment to the company. Fifth, commissions can serve as a source of feedback and as a self-correcting mechanism—sales personnel can easily see whether their performance is adequate and will tend to leave the organization if they are unsuccessful.

Finally, and most important, use of sales commissions does increase sales. From a motivational perspective, it is easy to see why. The necessary behaviour (making sales) is clearly defined. The valence of successful behaviour (earning money) is very positive compared with the valence of unsuccessful behaviour (no money). Instrumentality is high (successful behaviour leads to rewards). Commissions also fit with reinforcement theory. Box 5.2 provides an example of how one retailer increased sales (and profits) by adding commissions to its pay system.

BOX 5.2 Paying More Increases Profits in Retailing

At an upscale retail chain in the United States, management wanted to increase both sales and customer satisfaction. To achieve this, they introduced a customer focus/satisfaction training program, as well as adding commissions to the pay system for sales consultants. Sales employees had been compensated with hourly pay. This base pay was left unchanged, but a sales quota was set for each sales consultant. When quarterly sales reached the quota level, a sales consultant would receive a commission on all sales above this level. If the quota was not reached, the sales consultant simply received base pay, although sales staff were warned that failure to meet quota in two consecutive quarters could result in termination.

Of the 34 stores in the chain, 15 stores implemented the new pay system during the period 1987 to 1990. From the employee's point of view, the plan was quite successful: on average, the commissions added 23.5 percent to their total compensation by the end of 1991.

But what about the effect on store sales and profits? According to the researchers who studied the system (Banker, Lee, Potter, and Srinivasan, 1996), sales per square foot in the stores with the new pay system increased by about 28 percent between 1987 and 1991, while those stores that carried on with the old system increased by about 11 percent. But recall that the new system also increased sales pay. So, did the new system add to profitability, after including the increased sales compensation costs? The researchers found that the stores on the new system showed significantly higher increases in profitability than the conventional stores. They also showed significantly higher increases in customer satisfaction. Aside from the increased sales, another reason for the increased profitability is that the stores on the new system were able to cut down on the number of supervisors they employed.

The researchers made one other interesting finding. The new pay system was not equally successful for all stores. In fact, for some stores, the new system did not increase sales (after an initial uptick) and actually reduced profitability. It turns out that the new system improved results primarily for stores in highly competitive upscale markets. The researchers hypothesize that the customer focus program will produce the most benefits when customers have substantial choice about where to shop, and when consumers are more service- than cost-oriented.

PROBLEMS WITH COMMISSIONS

Nonetheless, we should recognize some problems associated with using commissions. First, income to the salesperson may be highly variable, making personal financial planning difficult. As noted previously, most people prefer more predictable pay, so it may be difficult to attract high-calibre applicants. Sole reliance on commissions may also cause high turnover. Some of these problems are illustrated by the following quote from a sales representative who works on straight commission for a firm that sells consumer telecommunications equipment (Harrison, Virick, and William, 1996: 332):

> *If I go on vacation, I lose money. If I'm sick, I lose money. If I am not willing to drop everything on a moment's notice to close with a customer, I lose money. I can't see how anyone could stay in this job for long. It's like a trapeze act and I'm working without a net!*

In this sales job, half of all sales reps quit within six months of joining the company. However, because costs of recruitment and training are quite low, the company is willing to accept this turnover level, especially since those who quit tend to be low performers. But to attract and retain top performers, firms using individual commissions often end up being forced to provide a higher total pay than would be necessary if a different compensation mix were used. Other drawbacks to commission sales include:

- Under poor economic conditions, commission income may drop precipitously, through no fault of the sales worker. This may cause good salespeople to leave the firm due to financial necessity.

- During the period when they are learning the business and developing customer contacts, new sales workers receive little income.

- A salesperson may resist doing work that does not directly contribute to new sales, such as training new salespeople, keeping up records, or servicing clients.

- Straight commission may encourage salespeople to be overly aggressive, to make misleading claims about the product to encourage sales, and to attempt to sell more units or more expensive units than the customer really needs.

- Such a system often produces intense competition among salespeople, resulting in a lack of cooperation.

- Apportioning responsibility for making sales can be a major problem. A customer may be "sold" by one salesperson, but after taking time to "think it over," may place the order with the salesperson who happens to be available when the customer makes the purchase. This can create perceptions of inequity and cause conflict among the sales workers. To avoid this problem, it is often necessary to devise some system for apportioning customers, or for establishing sales territories. Establishing sales territories may be difficult to do fairly, and use of fixed territories also creates rigidity if conditions change and territories need to be altered.

Using straight commissions may also cause some subtle shifts in behaviour on the part of the employer. For example, since the sales rep—not the firm—is absorbing the risk of poor performance, the employer may be less careful in recruitment and selection. When certain salespeople are not performing well, rather than attempting to assist them to improve, possibly through training and coaching, it may be tempting for management to just let them "sink or swim" and simply hire other salespeople to replace them.

But these practices may have hidden costs. First, although the firm is not paying the sales rep when he or she makes no sales, the firm is also not receiving any sales revenue. Second, these practices may encourage high turnover, such that recruiting and training new salespeople may represent a significant cost. Third, customers may be disconcerted by a continuing turnover of salespeople, and they may tire of always having to deal with someone new.

Fine-tuning the commission system to create the desired behaviour may be a difficult process. Employers should not be surprised when salespeople work the system to maximize their income rather than company welfare. Under straight commission the employer is showing very little commitment to the salesperson and is implicitly saying that there is only a financial attachment between the firm and the salesperson. Salespeople will also be resistant to changes in the system, since they then need to learn all over again how to maximize their income from it.

Furthermore, when the system needs to be changed, sales workers may be suspicious of management motives and may see the changes as simply a disguised attempt to reduce their earnings. The following incident illustrates what a touchy matter this can be (Keenan, 1994: xv):

> In one case ... the vice president of sales for a multi-media communications company hired a professional wrestler to pose as a salesperson at the company's annual sales meeting. When the sales VP announced the change in the compensation plan and started to go through the details, the wrestler-cum-salesperson charged the front of the room, lifted the sales VP off the ground, held him over his head, and threatened to toss him to the back of the room if he didn't leave the compensation plan well enough alone. At this point, the company's regional sales managers rushed up to the front of the room to calm the "angry" salesperson by explaining the virtues of the new plan.

Keenan goes on to reveal that although this ruse did forestall questions and angry debate from the sales reps, it did not eliminate the grumbling about the new plan.

Finally, another problem is that commissions on sales volume focus attention on gross revenue generation, not profitability of sales. Sales personnel may be tempted to focus on selling low-margin, fast-moving items, or to cut prices excessively. Recall all the problems caused by a bonus system based on gross sales at Bausch and Lomb, discussed in Chapter 3 (Box 3.2). So some companies are switching to different indicators. For example, IBM has shifted from a system whereby the variable portion of sales pay (they also use base pay) is no longer based on sales revenues (Sagar, 1994), but is based on profitability of sales (60 percent) and customer satisfaction (40 percent). For this to work, IBM recognizes that they now need to provide information on profit margins to each sales rep, information that traditionally has been a closely guarded secret.

Some of the other problems can also be overcome. One method to deal with fluctuating income is to use a system that provides a basic salary but also uses commissions. This also serves to "pay" the individual for work not directly related to sales. A variation of this is a "draw" system, in which regular advances are made against future commissions. Commission rates can also be varied to reflect the profitability or the selling ease of particular products. Excessive competition among sales personnel can be reduced by apportioning potential customers on some systematic basis, such as by geographic district or customer type. Of course, the most important way of avoiding problems is not to use commissions in circumstances where they are not suited, as will be discussed next.

APPLICABILITY OF COMMISSIONS

What are the circumstances under which commissions are appropriate? To help answer this question, Coletti and Chicelli (1991) have suggested three key dimensions: degree of independence, degree of persuasive skills required, and length of the sales cycle (the time between meeting a new customer and closing the deal). The more that each salesperson works independently of others, the higher the degree of persuasive skills required, and the shorter the length of the sales cycle, the greater should be the amount of commission relative to base pay.

Coletti and Chicelli also distinguish four types of selling, based on whether the product is new or established, and whether the customer is a new or an existing one. **Maintenance selling** is selling an established product to existing customers; **conversion selling** is selling established products to new customers; **leverage selling** is selling new products to existing customers; and **new market selling** is selling new products to new customers. Coletti and Chicelli suggest that because new market selling requires the most initiative on the part of the sales rep, it should have a high incentive opportunity (high ratio of commission to base pay), while conversion selling and leverage selling should have a moderate incentive opportunity, and maintenance selling should have a low incentive opportunity.

maintenance selling
selling established products to existing customers

conversion selling
selling established products to new customers

leverage selling selling new products to existing customers

new market selling
selling new products to new customers

Another way of looking at this is to examine the managerial strategy of the firm. For example, in high-involvement firms, the self-control that these firms generate may make extrinsic output-based control unnecessary. In contrast, classical firms will need to use output-based control where direct control is not feasible, and will tend to use straight commissions. Human relations firms will value employee loyalty by providing base pay, but will also provide some commissions to supplement social control in circumstances where there is no cohesive group, as in cases where sales reps are alone out in the field.

A Canadian study (Tremblay, Cote, and Balkin, 1997) surveyed 325 Quebec firms to determine what factors affect the mix between base pay (salary) and performance pay (commissions) for sales employees. The researchers found a lower proportion of commissions for sales jobs that were highly programmable (for which behaviours could be easily observed but where individual outcomes could not be easily measured), that involved working inside the office, that included nonselling tasks, that required cooperation in closing sales, and in larger organizations. They also found that organizations which used a higher proportion of base pay had lower employee turnover than those which relied more heavily on commissions.

MERIT PAY

The objective of merit pay is to recognize and encourage continuing good performance by individual employees. Types of merit pay include merit raises, merit bonuses, and promotions. These incentives are always used in combination with base pay.

MERIT RAISES

merit raise an increase to an employee's base pay in recognition of good job performance

Merit raises represent a permanent increase to base pay for a given employee, and thus are extremely expensive to the employer, especially when applied to young employees, who may benefit from the same raise for 30 years or more. This expense is increased even more if indirect pay—such as pension benefits—is geared to base pay levels, which is the usual practice. Merit raises are normally based on employee performance during the previous year, but in order to justify the continuing increase, there must be some expectation that the performance level evidenced during the appraisal period will be permanent—that it will be maintained over the long term. This is, of course, difficult to predict, and most organizations will simply grant the increase and hope for the best.

Merit raises are one way for individuals to advance within the pay range associated with their particular job. Of course, there are other options as well, such as seniority or skill-based pay. Surveys have shown that people in North America believe that the notion of being paid according to merit is a good idea, as long as performance standards are fair and objective, and as long as performance appraisals help to improve job performance (Heneman, 1990). While most organizations claim to use merit pay, research indicates a high degree of skepticism among both managers and nonmanagers about the extent to which pay is truly related to meritorious performance (Kerr, 1995). However, despite this perception, a review of 42 studies by Heneman (1992) actually did show a positive relationship between merit increases and previous performance.

But the practice is fraught with many difficulties. The first problem deals with performance measurement. As we will see in Chapter 11, performance appraisal is far from an exact science. Studies have shown that managers as well as nonmanagers frequently have little confidence in the results of performance appraisal (Lawler, 2000). This may help to explain why many managers are reluctant to differentiate among employees in terms of pay—they have doubts about the validity of the data on which these differentiations are to be based. Of course, they may also be concerned about antagonizing subordinates, on whom they depend.

The second problem is to ensure that there is a noticeable difference in pay treatment between good and average performers. Research has shown that in many companies professing to use merit pay, the pay levels of above-average performers are not very different from those of average performers. To be motivating, the difference in pay increase between a person performing at a high level and a person performing at an average level must be perceived as significant.

What is the difference needed to be perceived as significant? This amount is known in research jargon as a **just noticeable difference** (JND). Unfortunately, there is scant evidence on what size a JND is, probably for the good reason that it will vary depending on the individual, the job, and the circumstances. For example, in times of high inflation, when everyone is getting a 10 percent increase, giving top performers 14 percent may not qualify as a JND. But in times of low inflation, where most employees are receiving 2 percent, an increase of 6 percent for top performers may be perceived as a significant difference.

just noticeable difference (JND) the amount of pay increase necessary to be considered significant by employees receiving the increase

Cook (1991) argues that it is "conventional wisdom" that a merit increase should be no less than 4 percent, although he provides no supporting evidence for this number. Based on a laboratory study, Mitra, Gupta, and Jenkins (1995) concluded that the "critical threshold" for a pay raise to be motivating is about 6–7 percent of base pay. They found that merit raises below this amount actually seemed to be demotivating; subjects receiving less than this amount tended to perceive that the merit system did not actually reward performance (even though raises were still based on performance). On the other hand, researchers did not find that merit raises that were much above the 6–7 percent threshold added much to motivation, although they did increase satisfaction with pay.

Another problem with merit raises is that once an individual rises to the top of his or her pay range, there will be no more merit raises. No organization can afford to continue to provide merit pay raises indefinitely for a given job. There is only so much an organization can afford to pay a bookkeeper or a junior supervisor, no matter how meritorious the individual. At that point, what motivation is there for the employee to continue to improve performance, or to even maintain the high performance level that has earned the merit raises?

Traditionally, the answer is the carrot and the stick—the carrot of promotion up the hierarchy to a job that carries a higher pay range, and the stick of dismissal. However, it is legally difficult to dismiss someone who is performing at an acceptable level, even if they are being paid to perform at a superior level. Even if possible, such action would tend to destroy the motivational value of the system if receipt of merit raises is seen as increasing vulnerability to future dismissal.

As for promotions, as organizations become flatter, and as many firms experience slow or even negative growth, promotion opportunities have become increasingly rare. But even for those organizations that do have promotional opportunities, it is not clear that rewarding outstanding performance in a lower-level position through promotion to the next higher position is necessarily a wise policy, as will be discussed shortly.

As a result, if merit raises are the only element of performance pay an organization uses, there is no longer any element of performance pay for employees once they reach the top of their pay range. It may be possible to rely on intrinsic motivation and organizational identification to maintain performance (in a high-involvement organization), or possibly social norms (in a human relations organization), but classical organizations will not be able to depend on these. One solution may be the use of merit bonuses, which will be discussed in the following section.

There are several other problems with merit raises. Because they are usually based on a judgment by a superior, they may cause antagonism between the superior and those who do not receive merit raises. They can also cause divisiveness within the work group itself, and resentment against those employees receiving a merit raise from those not receiving one.

Rewarding only one or two employees when effective performance is really dependent on effective cooperation among all employees can exacerbate divisiveness and lead to reduced cooperation. This problem is especially severe if the amount of money for merit raises is fixed for a given department or if the supervisor is allowed to provide merit raises to only a fixed proportion of the subordinates. What this creates is a zero-sum game—if you get more, I get less or none at all. This is certainly not a system to encourage cohesiveness and cooperation among employees, if this is what the organization needs! Of course, if an organization does not need cooperation among its employees, this is not a big problem.

In sum, although the idea of rewarding individuals through merit raises is an appealing one, the practice of doing so is fraught with so many difficulties that the disadvantages may outweigh the advantages for many firms.

Indeed, for some firms where close collaboration between employees is necessary and separating out individual performance is not possible, even the idea may not be a good one (Pearce, 1987), as Toyota concluded for its production workers (see Box 3.3). Fortunately, there are many other means for motivating and rewarding good performance.

MERIT BONUSES

As has been discussed, merit raises have numerous problems, including the topping-out problem and the risk of providing a long-term future reward for short-term past performance. A **merit bonus** will avoid these problems since it is granted only for the period in which good performance occurs, and good performance must be repeated each year in order for the employee to continue to receive the bonus. Merit bonuses can also be used in conjunction with a merit raise system. For example, for those employees no longer eligible for further merit raises, an opportunity to obtain an annual merit bonus may keep them focused on performance.

merit bonus a bonus provided to recognize good employee performance that does not increase base pay

Beyond these advantages, merit bonuses also have the advantage of not being a fixed amount, and thus can be varied from year to year depending on the financial circumstances of the employer. They can also be paid out in lump sums, either quarterly or annually, and they may have more visibility as a result. Many firms like to prepare completely separate cheques to reinforce this visibility.

One variation of a merit bonus system is a special award program. For example, Theriault (1992) describes a program at IBM that has three levels of bonuses. At the work unit level, there is the informal award plan, where decisions about awards are made by immediate supervisors. The second level rewards employees who have had an impact on the performance of their entire division, and the third level rewards employees who have had an impact on the total corporation.

Merit bonuses still have many of the disadvantages of merit raises. They still depend on reliable and accepted performance measures, which may not exist. Managers and nonmanagers alike may have little faith in the available measures. They can cause poor relations between supervisors and their subordinates, and among subordinates, especially if the bonus pool is limited. Merit bonuses are not suited for work that depends on collaboration and cooperation. Since they apply only for one year, they may be seen as less valuable than merit raises, and may need to be much higher to attract an equivalent amount of attention from employees.

One key issue is how to set the amount of the total available bonus pool. If it is simply an arbitrary decision by top management, then this in itself may cause dissatisfaction, especially if it causes bonuses to be low or allows few people to receive them. In some cases, firms are now tying the bonus pool to some measure of organizational performance, such as profit sharing, and then allocating this amount to employees based on individual merit. This combines the benefits of individual and organizational incentive plans, as will be discussed in Chapter 6.

A major issue in the use of merit bonuses is defining the behaviours that will be rewarded. Merit bonuses can be based on the overall performance of the individual, or they can be based on specific behaviours or indicators. Frequently, they are based on meeting some quota or goal. Research has shown that employees who work to challenging but attainable goals—especially when they have had a role in formulating these goals—outperform those without specific work goals (Bartol and Locke, 2000).

These goals can range widely. In some cases, they are geared to productivity: produce a certain number of units or serve a certain number of clients and receive a bonus. Some organizations are starting to give bonuses to employees who score high in customer service ratings. A bonus may also be provided for minimizing errors or for low scrap rates. As seen in Chapter 3, bonuses can be provided for finding insects during vegetable processing. Book sales reps can be given a bonus for finding new authors. Baseball players can be given a bonus if they score a specified number of home runs. Bonuses can be given for making creative suggestions, or even for just showing up at work consistently, as will be discussed later in this chapter.

The possibilities are endless. This flexibility is one of the most attractive features of bonuses. But whenever bonuses focus on only a subset of the total behaviour expected from an individual, extreme caution must be exercised to ensure that the other, unbonused, aspects of the job are not neglected. Of course, care must also be taken that the behaviours being rewarded are actually the behaviours that are wanted, as has been discussed in Chapter 3.

Promotions as Incentives

Since they usually bring extra pay, many organizations rely on promotions as their major reward for superior performance. They expect a "promotion from within" policy to be a key factor in motivating good employee performance. However, there are some significant problems in using promotions for these purposes. First, heavy reliance on promotions in lieu of other rewards can result in a meaningless reward system if the organization has few upper-level vacancies.

This is particularly a problem in firms that are expanding slowly or not at all, or that are deliberately reducing their hierarchy in order to cut costs or to move toward a high-involvement managerial strategy. Even in expanding firms, it is the rare firm that has sufficient upper-level vacancies to reward all deserving candidates. And for some organizations (i.e., high-involvement firms), rewarding people only for moving up the hierarchy is inconsistent with their managerial philosophy even if the firm does have many promotion opportunities.

Where promotions are an important part of the reward strategy, the psychological consequences for those not promoted can be detrimental to future motivation. To illustrate, suppose that there is one vacancy and three deserving candidates. No matter how good they are, two will be turned down. What is the message that the rejected individuals perceive? Probably that the firm does not value their contributions as highly as they thought. It may also shake their confidence in the fairness of the reward system. As discussed in Chapter 3, these perceptions may cause them to find continued good performance difficult to sustain.

From the organization's point of view, promoting outstanding performers to higher-level (usually managerial) positions can lead to serious problems if the attributes needed to be successful in the higher-level position are different from those of the lower positions. For example, most of us have probably heard the story of the outstanding salesperson who becomes a poor sales manager.

This result may be no coincidence. The very skills and abilities that make for a successful salesperson, such as independence, competitiveness, and aggressiveness, may be undesirable in a sales manager, who must work through the recruiting, training, coordinating, and motivating of others. In addition, the sales manager loses the satisfaction of dealing directly with customers and personally closing sales. In circumstances such as these, promotions based on outstanding performance in a qualitatively different job can result in negative consequences for both the employer and the employee. As an employee progresses up the hierarchy, the jobs become systematically more different from those below them.

Lawrence J. Peter has summarized the results of a strict promote-from-within policy in what he has named the "Peter principle" (Peter and Hull, 1969): "In a hierarchy every employee tends to rise to his level of incompetence." What he means by this is that individuals will be promoted only if they are performing competently in their present job. If they are not performing well, they will stay where they are. If the promoted individual is competent at the next-higher job, that person will continue to be promoted until reaching a position in which she or he cannot perform well. There that person will stay. Thus, "in time, every post tends to be occupied by an employee who is incompetent to carry out his or her duties." Although exaggerated, the Peter principle does contain an element of truth.

For all of these reasons, it seems clear that promotions should not be used as the sole component of the system for compensating superior performance. It may well be preferable to base the awarding of promotions on factors other than current performance, assuming that the candidate is at least competent in her or his current duties. However, this can create other difficulties, such as the perception that the organization does not care about outstanding performance.

Clearly, outstanding performers must be considered for promotions, if they wish to be. It may be possible to prepare such individuals for promotion through the use of effective training and development programs. Failing this, an in-depth explanation of why the candidate is unsuitable for the promotion must be provided. Ideally, unsuitable candidates will, through effective discussion, reach this conclusion on their own.

In some instances, it may be desirable to place an individual in the higher position on a trial basis. If so, that person should be given every possible opportunity to succeed in order to prevent perceptions of injustice. Under this approach, it is crucial that a graceful way to return to the former job be made available.

In order to avoid the problem of forcing employees to move up the managerial hierarchy simply to advance their pay levels, some companies are now creating dual-track programs for advancement, with a technical track (sometimes known as a "technical ladder") and a managerial track. Pay-for-knowledge systems also provide an avenue for advancing pay levels without requiring promotion to management.

SPECIAL-PURPOSE (TARGETED) INCENTIVES

targeted incentive an incentive designed to motivate a specific type of employee behaviour

In order to foster certain behaviours that are of special importance to an organization, or to counteract some behaviours that are causing problems for the organization, some firms have developed **targeted incentive** programs. An example would be the Green Giant insect bonus plan. Although targeted incentives could be used for a wide variety of purposes, perhaps the most common are suggestion programs (to encourage creativity) and attendance programs (to discourage absenteeism). Each of these will be examined briefly.

INCENTIVES FOR ATTENDANCE

Because of a concern with absenteeism in recent years, some organizations have started providing incentives for regular attendance (Booth, 1993). For example, the latest collective agreement between La-Z-Boy Canada (makers of the famous recliners) and its union, signed in March 2001, included a new clause providing for an attendance bonus. Employees who do not have absences in a calendar year will have eight hours of their base rate deposited into their RRSP account.

While these plans vary, one approach is to provide a bonus or prize to employees who have a perfect attendance record in a given time period. One interesting system was used by a manufacturing plant (Lawler, 1977). Each day an employee comes to work on time, he or she is allowed to draw one card from a deck of playing cards. At the end of the week, the employee with the best five-card poker hand in each department receives a $20 prize. This plan was found to reduce absenteeism by about 18 percent, but since the period under study was quite short, it is not clear whether this result would hold up over the longer run. As another example, Box 5.3 describes an attendance incentive scheme for school teachers.

There is very little research on the long-term effects of attendance incentives, so it is not clear whether short-term benefits would hold up over time, and in what circumstances these plans would be likely to work best. Indeed, one interesting question centres around what would happen if a firm implemented and then discontinued its attendance incentive. According to attribution theory, attendance might actually end up *lower* than before the program was instituted, since any intrinsic motivation to attend would have been eliminated by the economic attendance incentive, as in the case of the elderly man and the boisterous children (discussed in Chapter 3).

Or is it more likely that attendance levels would simply return to what they had been initially? There is no evidence on this, but attribution theory would predict that the greater the intrinsic motivation prior to the attendance program, the greater the impact of its discontinuation. Therefore, attendance programs are less risky for organizations in which intrinsic motivation is low in the first place.

Aside from this, there are some obvious drawbacks to such plans. First, of course, is the cost of the bonus. Second is the possibility of extra paperwork. Third, once an individual becomes ineligible for the bonus, by exceeding the number of allowable absences, there is no longer any incentive to curtail

---

BOX 5.3 What Do You Do about Teachers Who Play Hooky?

In 1986, the State of New York provided special funding to school districts to improve teacher salaries. One school district opted to allocate a portion of its funds to help improve teacher attendance. Absenteeism (from all causes) among the district's 318 teachers had averaged seven days in the previous school year. The total amount of incentive available was $72 809. Teachers were informed at the beginning of the school year that if they were absent less than seven days in the school year, they would receive one share of this pool for every day less than seven. Thus, a teacher with no absences would receive seven shares in the bonus pool. The amount to be received for each day's reduction in absenteeism would not be known until the end of the year.

Conceivably, if only one teacher had absences fewer than seven, he or she would receive the entire pool. But in fact, 1274 shares were awarded, making each share worth $57.16. The maximum received by any teacher was $400.12, awarded to teachers with no absences. This amount represented an increase in earnings of slightly over 1 percent.

But did the plan decrease absenteeism? To determine this, absenteeism in the bonus year was compared with absenteeism in the previous year (Jacobson, 1989). The findings indicated a significant reduction, from 7.21 to 5.34 days. The proportion of teachers with less than seven absences increased from 58 to 71 percent, and the proportion of teachers with perfect attendance increased from 8 percent to 34 percent.

Overall, the net gain was 595 days. Since teachers earned, on average, about $200 a day for the 187 school days in the school year, the theoretical value of the reduced absenteeism was about $119 000—significantly more than the bonus pool. However, since substitute teachers were paid much less than the regular teachers—$43 per day—the actual dollar savings from the plan amounted to about $25 000. Not included in this cost/benefit analysis is any estimate of the value added to the educational process by decreased absenteeism by the regular classroom teachers.

Because the study covered only one year, there is no way of knowing whether these results would continue over time. Perhaps these results were partly driven by expectations that the payout would be much larger. Indeed, if absenteeism had not been reduced from the previous year, the payouts to teachers with good attendance would have been substantially higher.

absences during the review period. Fourth is the issue of whether "legitimate" absences should detract from the record, and if so, how they should be defined and verified. Fifth, many employers will have a philosophical objection to paying extra for something (attendance) that should be taken as a given.

But perhaps the greatest drawback is that the incentive plan may only treat symptoms without getting at the true source of the problem. If absenteeism really is a problem, a first step is to try to understand the cause. The assumption underlying attendance incentive programs is that absenteeism is caused by a lack of will to attend on the part of the employee. That may be partly true, but are there other reasons for absenteeism, and are there more appropriate solutions?

For example, we know that reward and job dissatisfaction affect absenteeism, and high absenteeism may just be the tip of the iceberg in terms of the underlying and more serious problems facing the organization (Goodman and Atkin, 1984). One possibility is that the workplace itself may be responsible for an excessive number of accidents or injuries, or may provide conditions that promote illness. The work may cause absenteeism if it is highly stressful and employees find it difficult to face another day doing work they find boring, tedious, or repetitive.

It has been established that jobs that place high demands on employees but allow them little or no control over how to respond to these demands produce high stress. It has also been documented that jobs with low intrinsic rewards (i.e., low skill variety, task identity, task significance, feedback, and worker autonomy) are less attractive to most employees and generate higher absenteeism. The work environment may be unpleasant, the boss unreasonable or oppressive, customers surly or abusive, and relations among co-workers poor. As has been seen in Chapter 3, dissatisfaction with the compensation system may cause attendance problems. All of these factors may also lead to negative group norms about attendance, which Gellatly and Luchak (1998) found to have strong negative effects on individual attendance behaviour. Addressing the root causes of attendance problems is likely to be more successful than simply dealing with the symptoms.

Absences can be classified into four main categories. First, there is absence due to sickness or injury. Second, an individual may be experiencing personal problems, such as depression or alcohol or drug abuse. Third, absences may be due to a need to deal with family matters, such as a sick child. As the number of dual-income families has increased, this has become a major problem for many families. Fourth are absences for discretionary reasons, better known as "goofing off."

In some cases, sick leave policies themselves may be at fault, and may actually work to encourage absences. For example, employees may be docked pay if they arrive late, but receive no penalty if they call in sick for the whole day. In a study conducted by Booth (1993: 8), she cited the example of one firm in which "many people make a point of using up their full sickness benefit of ten days per year, even when they are obviously not sick." Aside from the costs of unnecessary absenteeism, a major concern is that of equity. Employees who are consistently present may actually be penalized for their good attendance by having to do the work of the absentees.

An Ontario company improved its attendance by 30 percent by lengthening the period necessary to qualify for sick pay and by providing an attendance bonus of $100 per quarter for absences of 12 hours or less during that quarter (Booth, 1993). Another firm improved absenteeism simply by requiring employees to speak directly to their supervisor for a brief interview if time is to be missed (Booth, 1993).

One potential solution to some types of absenteeism is flextime. There are various systems under which employees can adjust their workday to allow them to take care of matters such as medical appointments. Flextime systems have been shown to reduce absenteeism, and often have the side benefit of improving productivity (Zeytinoglu, 1999). Another possible solution is the development of employee assistance programs. Some employers, noting a correlation between fitness, health, and absenteeism, have established employee health and fitness programs of various types. For example, after Alberta Blue Cross instituted a wellness program, average annual days lost dropped from 5.5 to 4.1 (Booth, 1993).

Of course, an alternative way of dealing with absenteeism is to simply dismiss employees who have an excessive number of absences. This has the downside of losing some employees who might be valuable employees if their absenteeism problem could be corrected. In some cases, it may be difficult to establish that the absences were not due to legitimate reasons. In many unionized workplaces, it is difficult to fire employees unless it can be shown that the absences are not justified.

Another approach to controlling absenteeism is by tying absenteeism into bonus pay. (Employees on hourly pay, or piece rates, are automatically docked for absenteeism, which is seen as a major advantage of these systems.) For example, Belcher (1996) describes a gain-sharing plan in which individuals lose a portion of their group gain-sharing bonus if their attendance falls below allowable limits. In one case, at an automotive plant, one day's absence (for any reason) during a six-month payout period reduces the individual's bonus allotment by 25 percent, two days by 50 percent, and three days of absence wipes it out.

While such a system may provide an incentive for attendance, it does have several problems. First, if the gain-sharing system produces no bonuses in a given time period, the penalty for absence disappears. Second, for those who miss more than two days, there is no incentive not to miss more. Third, it may be seen as unfair for dedicated workers to lose all of their bonus because of real illness. Fourth, gain sharing may have no meaning for any employee who misses more than two days in a six-month period. Adding the attendance rider to the gain-sharing plan decreases the perceived probability of a linkage between performance and reward, and motivation theory predicts that this will result in reduced motivation.

In short, a plan like this may end up effectively destroying the value of gain sharing without providing significant improvements in attendance. For reasons like these, it is probably best to keep absenteeism control programs separate from other types of performance pay programs.

Attendance incentives are likely to suit some organizations more than others, depending on the causes of attendance problems. Of course, in some instances, attendance should not be an issue—what counts is getting the work done, and whether or not an employee physically appears at the workplace may be irrelevant. For some organizations, especially those within the high-involvement school, where self-control is exercised, there will be very little voluntary absenteeism. If there are problems with attendance, they are not likely due to a simple lack of will to attend. Thus, attendance programs are likely to do more harm than good for these organizations by implying that employees are shirking their duties and by reducing intrinsic motivation.

In any case, when examining this issue, the first step is to determine whether absenteeism is in fact a problem. Norms for absenteeism vary dramatically across industries. In Canada, the average absenteeism rate (for all reasons, including sickness and accidents) in 1995 was 5.8 days a year, virtually unchanged from the previous few years (Isaac, 1995). Assuming a 230-day work year, this would represent an absenteeism rate of about 2.5 percent. However, over the period 1977 to 1991, Statistics Canada data showed steadily increasing absences, part of which were attributed to dual-income families and an aging population (Booth, 1993).

Incentives for Creativity

suggestion system an incentive plan through which employees receive cash bonuses for submitting money-saving suggestions

Suggestion systems are intended to promote and reward innovative thinking by employees. In general, if an employee has a suggestion that may improve organizational effectiveness, she or he submits it through the suggestion system. It is then evaluated by a committee, and if it is implemented the employee will receive a percentage (usually between 10 to 20 percent) of the projected cost savings during the first year. When the savings from the suggestion are difficult to compute, a standard lump sum is awarded.

Many Canadian firms use such plans. A survey by Booth (1990) of about 100 "progressive" Canadian firms indicated that about 42 percent of them had formal suggestion systems, with large firms much more likely to have these programs than small firms. However, there can be a number of problems with such plans. First, it is important that the reasons for rejecting a suggestion be explained fully to the author of the suggestion, or else there may be considerable resentment and a reluctance to contribute further suggestions. Second, employees may feel that the amount of the award is not equitable. Indeed, it is often difficult to arrive at a fair reward for a given suggestion. Third, supervisors or staff specialists may resent employees who make suggestions, feeling that this reflects negatively on their own performance.

Fourth, co-workers may resent the individual making the suggestion if it appears to create more work for them or if it disrupts former work practices.

Fifth, there is the issue of who receives the credit for the idea, since it may have been developed by several individuals. In some cases, employees (including supervisors) have been accused by other employees of "stealing" their ideas. As a result of these latter problems, some organizations are installing group-based suggestion and incentive schemes, as will be discussed in Chapter 6.

Suggestion systems need to provide three things: a system through which suggestions are channelled, a systematic process for evaluating them, and an incentive for submitting usable ideas. Of course, an underlying assumption for developing such systems is that people have useful suggestions but are currently not motivated to submit them without the carrot of the incentive. This assumption is most likely to apply to classical and, to some extent, to human relations organizations. Ironically, the problems with these systems, such as managerial or employee resentment and conflict, are most likely to occur in classical organizations, which may help to explain why many classical organizations do not bother with these incentives, and do not find them useful when they do adopt them.

In a high-involvement organization, because of the internalized commitment of members and because of participation in gain sharing, profit sharing, and employee stock plans, employees can be expected to want to submit useful suggestions regardless of whether there are special bonuses; indeed, special bonuses may cause more trouble than they are worth. So it may well be that a suggestion bonus system will be most useful to human relations organizations.

There has been little research evaluating the effectiveness of employee suggestion plans. Theriault (1992: 374) states that in-depth studies "have not proved the effectiveness of suggestion programs," but does not cite the studies to back up this assertion. However, as will be discussed in Chapter 6, there is positive evidence for plans in which suggestions are generated in conjunction with gain-sharing programs.

McAdams (1995) compared traditional suggestion plans with team-based suggestion plans that rewarded an entire team for suggestions made by team members with nonmonetary rewards, such as merchandise and travel awards. He found that team-based suggestion plans resulted in a much higher employee participation rate (the percentage of employees submitting suggestions) than the traditional plans, and a much higher value of each adopted suggestion. Although many of the team plans were short-term and experienced a drop in participation rates over time, they continued to produce many more suggestions than traditional systems.

NONMONETARY PERFORMANCE REWARDS

"Dump the cash, load on the praise!" This is the advice of a well-known consultant who has come up with "1001 Ways to Reward Employees," most of which do not involve money (Nelson, 1994, 1996). Other consultants offer similar advice (Spitzer, 1996). These authors argue that what employees really want is recognition for their achievements and affirmation as a valuable member of their organization. This recognition can take a variety of forms, ranging from simple praise to formal awards to substantial prizes, such as an all-expenses-paid holiday.

Although some of these rewards may have monetary value, the key is the symbolic value. An example of this is the "golden banana award" (Spitzer, 1996: 48–49):

> *When a senior manager in one organization was trying to figure out a way to recognize an employee who had just done a great job, he spontaneously picked up a banana [which had been packed in his lunch], and handed it to the astonished employee with hearty congratulations. Now, one of the highest honours in that company has been dubbed the "Golden Banana Award."*

Certainly, many employers will find this attractive advice, since not spending money is usually a popular thing with employers. And, as we have seen, there are many problems and difficulties with individually based economic incentive plans. However, there are some important caveats on the use of nonmonetary rewards. Such rewards do not provide a substitute for a fair and equitable pay system. Indeed, without an adequate pay system and a collaborative and trusting relationship between workers and management, employees will not likely attach much value to nonmonetary rewards. They will likely see such rewards as an attempt to manipulate them into working harder while withholding "real" (financial) rewards. And they will not value praise or recognition from managers whom they don't respect or trust.

But where there is equitable pay and employee–management trust, nonmonetary rewards can be effective, as the Toyota case (Box 3.3) illustrated. Overall, the arguments by proponents of these reward systems are consistent with Maslow's theory: once lower-order needs are satisfied, then the needs for achievement and recognition for this achievement can come to the fore. But to be effective, praise must be grounded in actual achievement, it must follow accomplishment closely, and it must come from a credible and respected source. Critics of individually based extrinsic rewards (e.g., Kohn, 1993) contend that even praise can be counterproductive if it is seen as an attempt to control behaviour rather than to simply recognize achievement.

Given all this, nonmonetary rewards seem most suited to high-involvement organizations, although they may also have utility in human relations organizations. But because the base conditions do not exist in classical organizations, nonmonetary rewards will likely be of relatively little value there. In fact, in the CPS data set, classical management was negatively related to use of nonmonetary rewards, and high involvement positively related.

Summary and Implications

The purpose of this chapter was to begin our examination of the role that performance pay can play in a compensation strategy and to provide a basis for evaluating the suitability of the various performance pay options for a given organization. Three main types of performance pay were identified, depending upon whether pay was contingent on individual performance, group/team performance, or organizational performance.

This chapter focused on individual performance pay, which includes four main types: piece rates, sales commissions, merit pay, and targeted incentives. The main purpose of these individual incentives is to foster task behaviour, although they can also serve a variety of other purposes, including controlling employee behaviour and adding flexibility to compensation costs.

Individual incentives can be effective, but only if carefully designed and utilized in the right circumstances. These circumstances include low interdependence and low need for cooperation among employees; the availability of valid measures of the behaviours being rewarded; jobs that are narrowly defined; employees for whom money carries a high salience; employees who will be willing to accept the risk inherent in most individual incentive plans; and a relatively stable business environment in which the required behaviours do not change rapidly.

Necessary features of these plans include high visibility, high employee understanding of the linkages between behaviour and rewards, and high confidence that rewards will actually be provided when the behaviour takes place. Employees must also perceive that the behavioural requirements are realistic and that they have a reasonable chance of being able to attain them.

A key aspect for success of these plans is to ensure that they do not result in negative consequences for employees (e.g., where productivity gains result in layoffs) or unintended negative consequences for the employer. If employees are being dealt with strictly on an economic basis, employers should not be surprised if employees will attempt to "work the system" to maximize their own personal returns, even if this works to the detriment of the employer.

Because many types of individual incentives tend to contribute to an adversarial relationship between the employees and the employer, steps frequently need to be taken to anticipate and close loopholes to the plan. But this frequently requires increased inspections, monitoring, record keeping, and the like, the costs of which may outweigh any positive benefits of the incentive. It is not surprising then that many firms have moved away from individual incentives and choose to regulate behaviour directly, through supervision and controls (classical firms), indirectly through group norms (human relations firms), or attempt to develop circumstances where self-control will occur (high-involvement firms).

By combining individual incentives with other elements of compensation, it may be possible to cancel out or at least moderate their negative aspects while maintaining their benefits. For example, concomitant use of group and organizational performance plans may reduce the tendency for conflict that some individual incentives generate. Some individual incentives may even be used to foster cooperation and teamwork—for example, by basing a merit bonus partly on the extent of teamwork evidenced by the individual.

But although some firms have been adding individual performance pay to their compensation packages, the major focus in recent years has been on group and organization performance pay. Chapter 6 will complete our discussion of performance pay by examining these two types of plans and then drawing some overall conclusions about the use of performance pay.

KEY TERMS

conversion selling, p. 153

differential piece rate, p. 145

just noticeable difference (JND), p. 155

leverage selling, p. 153

maintenance selling, p. 153

merit bonus, p. 157

merit raise, p. 154

new market selling, p. 153

performance pay, p. 142

piece rates, p. 145

sales commissions, p. 148

straight piece rate, p. 145

suggestion system, p. 164

targeted incentive, p. 160

EXERCISES

1. Analyze the pay system at Alliston Instruments (in the Appendix). Why is the new pay system apparently not working? Do you think that the individual production bonus system could be made to work if some changes were made to it? What changes? Is individual performance pay suitable at all? If management insists on staying with some type of individual performance pay system, what type would you recommend?

2. Form into small groups of four to six people. Each group member should contact one local retailer and ask what its pay system is for sales staff. Compare the systems, and discuss whether these systems relate to the type of product sold and the type of sales activity that is necessary. Do they fit with the advice offered in this chapter for the type of sales compensation system to use? Do they fit with the firm's managerial strategy, as far as you can determine what that strategy is? Get together with other groups and share your conclusions.

3. Box 5.3 describes an incentive system intended to improve teacher attendance. What do you think will happen in the long run if this system is kept in use? What are the pros and cons of this system? Think back to your high school days. Do you think a similar system would have been beneficial at your high school? Why or why not? Would you recommend such a system to your local school board? What changes would you make to the system described in Box 5.3?

SUGGESTED WEB SITES

Page 165: For more information on employee suggestion systems, contact the Employee Involvement Association at <www.eianet.org>

Page 166: For creative and practical ideas about recognition programs, click on <www.changedynamics.com/samples/reinfor.htm>

Page 166: For software to develop and manage employee recognition programs, go to <www.hrpress-software.com/incentiv.html>

REFERENCES

Banker, Rajiv D., Seok-Young Lee, Gordon Potter, and Dhinu Srinivasan. 1996. "Contextual Analysis of Performance Impacts of Outcome-Based Incentive Compensation." *Academy of Management Journal*, 39(4): 920–48.

Bartol, Kathryn M., and Edwin A. Locke. 2000. "Incentives and Motivation." In Sara L. Rynes and Barry Gerhart, eds., *Compensation in Organizations: Current Research and Practice*. San Francisco: Jossey-Bass, 104–50.

Belcher, John G. 1996. *How to Design and Implement a Results Oriented Variable Pay System*. New York: American Management Association.

Booth, Patricia L. 1990. *Strategic Rewards Management: The Variable Approach to Pay*. Ottawa: Conference Board of Canada.

Booth, Patricia L. 1993. *Employee Absenteeism: Strategies for Promoting an Attendance Oriented Corporate Culture*. Ottawa: Conference Board of Canada.

Chilton, Kenneth W. 1994. "Lincoln Electric's Incentive System: A Reservoir of Trust." *Compensation and Benefits Review*, 26(6): 29–34.

Coletti, Jerome A., and David J. Chicelli. 1991. "Increasing Sales Force Effectiveness through the Compensation Plan." In Milton L. Rock and Lance A. Berger, eds., *The Compensation Handbook*. New York: McGraw-Hill, 290–306.

Cook, Frederic W. 1991. "Merit Pay and Performance Appraisal." In Milton

Rock and Lance A. Berger, eds., *The Compensation Handbook*. New York: McGraw-Hill, 542–68.

Gardner, B.B. 1945. *Human Relations in Industry*. Chicago: Irwin.

Gellatly, Ian R., and Andrew A. Luchak. 1998. "Personal and Organizational Determinants of Perceived Absence Norms." *Human Relations*, 51(8): 1085–1102.

Gerhart, Barry, and Charlie O. Trevor. 1996. "Employment Variability under Different Managerial Compensation Systems." *Academy of Management Journal*, 39(6): 1692–1712.

Goodman, Paul S., and Robert S. Atkin. 1984. *Absenteeism: New Approaches to Understanding, Measuring, and Managing Employee Absence*. San Francisco: Jossey Bass.

Harrison, David A., Meghna Virick, and Sonja William. 1996. "Working without a Net: Time, Performance, and Turnover under Maximally Contingent Rewards." *Journal of Applied Psychology*, 81(4): 331–45.

Heneman, Robert L. 1990. "Merit Pay Research." *Research in Personnel and Human Resources Management*, 8: 203–63.

Heneman, Robert L. 1992. *Merit Pay: Linking Pay Increases to Performance Ratings*. Reading, MA: Addison-Wesley.

Isaac, Kerry. 1995. *Compensation Planning Outlook 1996*. Ottawa: Conference Board of Canada.

Jacobson, Stephen L. 1989. "The Effects of Pay Incentives on Teacher Absenteeism." *The Journal of Human Resources*, 24(2): 280–86.

Johns, Gary. 1996. *Organizational Behaviour: Understanding and Managing Life at Work*. New York: HarperCollins.

Keenan, William. 1994. "Beyond the Basics." In William Keenan,

Commissions, Bonuses, and Beyond. Chicago: Irwin, xv–xviii.

Kerr, Steven. 1995. "On the Folly of Rewarding A, While Hoping for B." *Academy of Management Executive*, 9(1): 7–14.

Kohn, Alfie. 1993. *Punished by Rewards: The Trouble with Gold Stars, A's, Praise, and Other Bribes*. Boston: Houghton-Mifflin.

Lawler, Edward E. 1977. "Reward Systems." In J. Richard Hackman and J. Lloyd Suttle, eds., *Improving Life at Work: Behavioral Sciences Approaches to Organizational Change*. Santa Monica, CA: Goodyear Publishing.

Lawler, Edward E. 2000. *Rewarding Excellence: Pay Strategies for the New Economy*. San Francisco: Jossey-Bass.

Long, Richard J. 2002. "Performance Pay in Canada." In Michelle Brown and John S. Heywood, eds., *Paying for Performance: An International Comparison*. Armonk, NY: M.E. Sharpe.

McAdams, Jerry L. 1995. "Employee Involvement and Performance Reward Plans." *Compensation and Benefits Review*, 27(2): 45–55.

Mitchell, Daniel J.B., David Lewin, and Edward E. Lawler. 1990. "Alternative Pay Systems, Firm Performance, and Productivity." In Alan S. Blinder, ed., *Paying for Productivity: A Look at the Evidence*. Washington, DC: The Brookings Institution, 15–87.

Mitra, Atul, Nina Gupta, and G. Douglas Jenkins. 1995. "The Case of the Invisible Merit Raise: How People See Their Pay Raises." *Compensation and Benefits Review*, 27(3): 71–76.

Nelson, Bob. 1994. *1001 Ways to Reward Employees*. New York: Workman Publishing.

Nelson, Bob. 1996. "Dump the Cash, Load on the Praise." *Personnel Journal*, 75(7): 65–70.

Pearce, Jone L. 1987. "Why Merit Pay Doesn't Work: Implications from Organization Theory." In David B. Balkin and Luis R. Gomez-Mejia, eds., *New Perspectives in Compensation*. Englewood Cliffs, NJ: Prentice-Hall, 169–78.

Peck, Charles. 1993. *Variable Pay: Nontraditional Programs for Motivation and Reward*. New York: The Conference Board.

Peter, Lawrence J., and Raymond Hull. 1969. *The Peter Principle*. New York: William Morrow and Company.

Sagar, Ira. 1994. "IBM Leans on Its Sales Force." *Business Week*, February 7: 110.

Spitzer, Dean R. 1996. "Power Rewards: Rewards That Really Motivate." *Management Review*, 85(5): 45–50.

Theriault, Roland. 1992. *Mercer Compensation Manual: Theory and Practice*. Boucherville, PQ: Morin.

Tremblay, Michel, Jerome Cote, and David Balkin. 1997. "Explaining Sales Compensation Strategy Using Agency, Transaction Cost Analysis and Institutional Theories." Paper presented at the Academy of Management Annual Meetings, Boston.

Whyte, William F. 1955. *Money and Motivation: An Analysis of Incentives in Industry*. New York: Harper.

Zeytinoglu, Isik U. 1999. "Flexible Work Arrangements: An Overview of Developments in Canada." In Isik U. Zeytinoglu, ed., *Changing Work Relationships in Industrialized Countries*. Amsterdam/Philadelphia: John Benjamins Publishing, 41–58.

6

GROUP AND
ORGANIZATION
PERFORMANCE PAY

CHAPTER GOALS

By the end of this chapter, you should be able to:

1. Identify the main types of group performance pay plans and describe the purposes they serve.

2. Discuss the advantages and disadvantages of gain-sharing plans, and identify the circumstances under which they are or are not appropriate.

3. Discuss the advantages and disadvantages of goal-sharing plans, and identify the circumstances under which they are or are not appropriate.

4. Identify the main types of organization performance pay plans and describe the purposes they serve.

5. Discuss the advantages and disadvantages of profit-sharing plans, and identify the circumstances under which they are or are not appropriate.

6. Discuss the advantages and disadvantages of employee stock plans, and identify the circumstances under which they are or are not appropriate.

7. Discuss how different managerial strategies affect the appropriateness and effectiveness of different types of performance pay.

Introduction

Chapter 5 began our discussion of performance pay by focusing on individual performance pay. However, although some firms have been adding individual performance pay to their compensation packages, a more general trend is toward less emphasis on individual incentives and more on group- and organization-based performance rewards. There are several reasons for this.

In many organizations, the work flow is so interdependent that one individual, alone and unaided, is unlikely to be able to have much impact on productivity. In most situations, the cooperation of others is essential. However, by their very nature, individual incentives can be divisive. As has been seen in earlier chapters, the work group may exert a stronger influence on employee behaviour than individual incentives in any case. So it is important to have a reward system that brings the work group together, and on side with the organization.

As work, products, services, and technology have become more complex, and as firms face an increasingly demanding and complex competitive environment, work teams are increasingly being used. But to be effective, work teams must be supported with an appropriate reward system (Booth, 1994). Finally, group and organizational performance pay help to create an integration of employee and company goals, something especially important in the high-involvement organizations that are becoming more numerous across the Canadian landscape.

This chapter completes our discussion of performance pay systems by focusing on group and organizational performance pay plans. As Figure 6.1 shows, there are two main types of group performance plans—gain sharing and goal sharing—and two main types of organization performance plans—profit sharing and stock plans—along with a number of other group or organization performance plans. The overall objective of this chapter is to provide enough knowledge of these plans to allow you to decide which of these, if any, should be incorporated into your compensation strategy.

Group Performance Plans

In this section, the oldest and best-known group performance plans—productivity gain-sharing plans—will be examined first, followed by discussion of a much newer variation, goal-sharing plans. This section will conclude with some examples of other types of group or team payment plans. In so doing, we will describe the nature of these plans, identify their advantages and disadvantages, summarize the experience of various companies with the plans, and discuss their applicability.

FIGURE 6.1   TYPES OF PERFORMANCE PAY PLANS

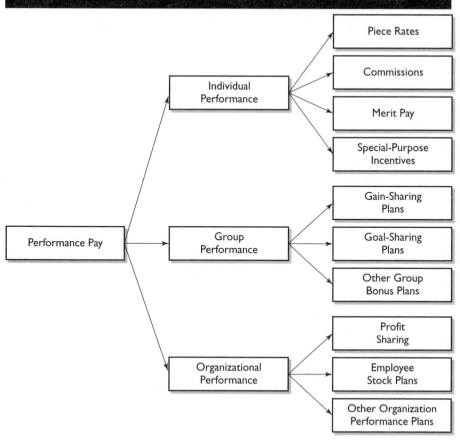

GAIN-SHARING PLANS

In **gain-sharing plans**, whenever employees in a particular work group are able to reduce costs, these gains are shared among all the employees in the work unit in a systematic way. These cost savings can be brought about in a variety of ways, ranging from increased productivity, improved quality, and decreased waste to improved methods of working.

TYPES OF GAIN-SHARING PLANS

There are three main types of gain-sharing plans—the Scanlon plan, the Rucker plan, and IMPROSHARE—and countless permutations of these.

The **Scanlon plan** was developed by Joseph Scanlon, a United Steelworkers local president, at a financially troubled steel mill during the Great Depression. First, a "normal" labour cost is computed, based on past experience. Labour costs are expressed as a percentage of the sales value of production. For example, labour costs may be 50 percent of the sales value of

gain-sharing plan   a group performance pay plan that shares cost savings or productivity gains generated by a work group or team with all members of that group

Scanlon plan   a gain-sharing plan that creates mechanisms for employee participation in developing productivity improvements and shares the financial benefits of those improvements with the employee group that generated them

production. If workers lower this to, say, 47 percent, they will split this productivity gain (3 percent of sales value) with management along a prearranged formula. Traditionally, the split has been 25 percent for management, and 75 percent for employees, based on the notion that the workers are primarily responsible for the productivity gain, but many gain-sharing plans use a different split, often 50-50.

But the Scanlon plan is much more than simply a financial incentive plan. The key to its success lies in the development of a cooperative relationship between workers, the union, and management, and the establishment of a process through which workers can contribute to problem solving. Within each unit, gain-sharing committees are established, composed of both management and worker representatives. These committees solicit and examine suggestions for improvements made by employees, and recommend either approval or disapproval. If the proposal is outside the jurisdiction of the department or involves large expenditures to implement, it is passed on to a plant-wide committee, where it is discussed by top management and union officials. The savings from any resulting improvements are typically shared by all members of the gain-sharing plan.

The Scanlon plan has been modified over time. A major modification has been the inclusion of additional costs beyond labour (Belcher, 1991). There are two reasons for this change. First, many possible cost savings do not show up in labour costs, such as a reduction in the wastage of raw materials. Second, it is usually possible to decrease labour costs at the expense of other costs. For example, a worker may simply scrap slightly defective raw material rather than trying to work with it, since using the poorer-quality raw material would delay production and increase labour costs. As another example, a worker may discard tools that become somewhat dull, even though replacements may be expensive. With this "multi-cost" approach, the split for employees is usually lower, perhaps 50 percent, because potential savings are much higher with a broader cost base.

Another type of gain-sharing plan was developed in the 1930s by Alan **Rucker**, who modified the Scanlon plan in a small but very significant way by expressing labour costs as a percentage of value added (sales value of production minus purchased inputs), rather than the sales value of production. The effect of this is that employees will benefit from reductions in materials or any other purchased input, and will be therefore motivated to find ways to reduce these costs. This plan typically includes a worker participation component.

A third type of gain-sharing plan, known as **IMPROSHARE**, was developed by industrial engineer Mitchell Fein in the 1970s (Fein, 1981). This plan does not use dollar values of production but simply labour hours per unit of output, as derived from some historical period, usually the previous year. The plan also takes into account indirect labour hours and includes them in the base productivity factor. When productivity exceeds the base productivity factor, a bonus will be paid, usually 50 percent of the labour savings.

Rucker plan a gain-sharing plan that is similar to the Scanlon plan but that expresses labour costs as a percentage of value added

IMPROSHARE a gain-sharing plan that focuses on labour hours per unit of output, and that does not usually include worker participation

A disadvantage of IMPROSHARE is that it does not take other cost savings into account. It does not make employee involvement an integral part of the system (which might in fact be regarded as an advantage by classical firms). However, the general belief among most experts is that the participation element is fundamental to the success of gain sharing.

Many gain-sharing plans have been modified in such a way as to be considerably different from any of these plans, primarily by widening the variety of indicators that are used for calculating the bonus. According to Belcher (1991: 83), the "family of measures category describes any gain sharing formula that uses *multiple, independent measures*. A gain (or loss) is calculated for each measure separately, and then aggregated to determine the size of the bonus pool." The key attractions of this method are flexibility and focus. Flexibility comes from the ability to include performance measures that are particularly important to the success of that business. Focus comes from the ability to specify the types of performance that will lead to bonus payouts.

For example, the performance measures could include not only labour and materials efficiency, but also measures of production schedule attainment, quality levels, customer satisfaction measures, and even accident rates. Some of these are based on historical records, while others are based on achievement of targets or goals set by management. Some measures (known as "modifiers") may not add to the bonus but simply subtract from it. For example, some firms will subtract from labour savings if there are excessive accident levels. The logic of this is that increased labour productivity should not come at the expense of unsafe work practices. Box 6.1 provides an example of a family of measures approach utilized at a service enterprise.

The **family of measures plan** has some disadvantages compared with the other types of plans. A major disadvantage is that some of the payouts are not based on calculated cost savings but on achievement of certain goals. The payout for achieving these goals may bear little resemblance to actual cost savings, since these cost savings are often hard to quantify. Related to this, employees may see the payouts as arbitrary (since there is no firm basis for them) and the goals as unrealistic. Where goals are seen as unrealistic, little effort will be made to attain them.

family of measures plan
a gain-sharing plan that utilizes a variety of measures to determine the extent to which a bonus payout is justified

Aside from the issue of the base for the bonus pool, there are many other issues that must be decided when setting up a gain-sharing plan. These include the group to be included, the share between the employees and employer, the split among employees, the frequency of payout, and how to make modifications to the baseline. Each of these, if not resolved appropriately, could cause the gain-sharing plan to founder.

For example, how should the bonus pool be allocated across employees? Should everyone receive an equal share? Sounds fair, but is it? What about employees who have been employed by the firm only a few days during the bonus period? What about employees who are only part-time? What about employees who have performed exceptionally well during the bonus period?

BOX 6.1 Gain Sharing at Control Data Corporation

At Control Data Corporation, management of the Business Management Services Division—which provides computerized human resource, payroll, and related services to external clients through 40 branch offices—wanted to establish a new business strategy with more focus on the customer. They believed that a gain-sharing plan might help support this new strategy (Belcher, 1991).

To develop the gain-sharing plan, management selected one branch office (one of their highest-performing ones), and set up an employee team to design the plan. The design team was aware they were breaking new ground, since no existing examples of gain sharing could be found in this industry.

The plan, which was launched in 1990, had five performance measures and two modifiers. The performance measures were the cost for processing each customer order, controllable expenses as a percentage of revenues, the number of customer credits issued, retention of customers, and number of suggestions submitted. The first two items are standard cost measures, and a historical baseline was established for each. The third item—number of credits issued—was taken as an indicator of quality of customer service, using the reasoning that each credit represented some type of error committed by the office. An analysis showed that each credit cost $80 to process, so for each credit less than the baseline, $80 was added to the bonus pool.

Customer retention was a measure of the proportion of customers lost to competitors, and the gains from increasing retention rate were added to the bonus pool. Finally, for each plausible suggestion made by the team at each office, $100 would be added to the bonus pool, along with another $100 if the suggestion was accepted.

Two modifiers were also used. The total bonus pool would be adjusted depending on the level of gross profits realized at the office and the results of customer satisfaction surveys. The first modifier acknowledges that without profit, there is no money to fund the bonus plan; the second modifier signifies that customer satisfaction is the way through which profitability will be achieved. This modifier is important in preventing the office from cutting costs at the expense of customer satisfaction. For example, one way of reducing customer credits is by refusing to issue them in all but the most extreme cases. This might be tempting, if not for the customer satisfaction modifier.

What about senior employees? Do they deserve more of the pool? In some cases, performance, seniority, and salary level are used as a basis for allocation. What are the consequences of the different methods?

The answers to these questions depend on the organization's goals for the gain-sharing plan. However, the bonus allocation method that is most in keeping with the underlying philosophy of gain sharing is equal allocation across employees, after adjusting for time worked during the bonus period. Gain sharing is intended to create cooperation and teamwork, and equality is an underlying condition for that. If it is desirable to single out individuals for special treatment, there are other elements of the compensation system that can do that.

Advantages of Gain-Sharing Plans

From an employer's point of view, undoubtedly the most attractive feature of gain-sharing plans is that, properly designed, they are self-funding. That is, the plans themselves produce the funds from which the gain-sharing bonus will be paid. Proponents argue that gain sharing will result in improved productivity and efficiency, greater labour–management cooperation, and increased employee acceptance of change (Graham-Moore and Ross, 1995). Improved productivity is hypothesized to stem from several sources. One source, perhaps the least important, is direct incentive—people may work more productively because of the expectation that they will receive a share of the financial benefit from so doing. However, as critics point out, this source of motivation is limited at best, since the extent to which an individual's increased effort will be reflected in their overall income is small.

A more important source of productivity flows from the social dynamics of gain sharing, inasmuch as gain sharing can contribute to the creation of social norms favourable to productivity. Positive social norms can enhance productivity in many ways, including stimulation of work effort, greater cooperation among employees and with management, and a lessened need for hierarchical and supervisory control. This comes about because gain sharing can promote internalization of company objectives and therefore self-control. For those employees not capable of self-control, they can still be controlled by social norms (under behavioural theory) or mutual monitoring (under agency theory). Since external controls are costly, their reduction should produce significant savings for the firm.

But do firms that practise gain sharing really have lower levels of supervisory and hierarchical control? While evidence is scanty, one study has been done. In a study of 44 large Canadian manufacturing firms, Long (1994) found that firms with either gain sharing or profit sharing had significantly less formal hierarchy, and had about 31 percent fewer managers than firms without these programs. Thus, even if gain sharing produced no direct gain in employee productivity, it could still be highly beneficial by diminishing the costs of hierarchy and management.

Another advantage of gain sharing is increased employee commitment, which reduces costs due to turnover and absenteeism. In addition, there is the value of the cost-saving suggestions and innovations that may be generated by the system, as well as more general benefits, such as increased employee knowledge about and understanding of the business, and improved communication between management and employees, which is an essential part of most gain-sharing plans. Finally, one advantage gain sharing has over other types of group programs, such as profit sharing or employee stock ownership, is that gain sharing can be applied to not-for-profit and government organizations.

DISADVANTAGES OF GAIN-SHARING PLANS

What are the potential disadvantages of gain sharing? First, there are some obvious ones, such as the costs of establishing and administering the program. There are also the costs of the managerial and employee time devoted to the program, including time consumed in meetings, in preparation for meetings, in evaluating suggestions, and in communicating about the program. In many cases, to make gain sharing work well, additional employee training is necessary.

But the biggest potential drawback is that the expected results may simply not emerge. In terms of labour–management relations, gain sharing may simply exacerbate conflict, since it can provide a whole agenda of things to disagree and argue about. Improperly implemented, or implemented into inappropriate circumstances, gain sharing may be a dissatisfier and a demotivator rather than a motivator. Even in firms where there is a reservoir of trust between management and workers, this can be sorely tested by all of the adjustments and changes necessary to get just about any gain-sharing system working right. Few gain-sharing systems are wholly successful on the first try.

Critics claim that group-based payment systems can actually be detrimental to motivation and productivity. Under collective reward systems, any additional effort expended by an individual employee will have a negligible effect on the reward she or he receives. But the employee will share in the benefits of the cumulative effects of other employees. Therefore, an individual will tend to "shirk" and become a "free rider" (Olson, 1971; Jensen and Meckling, 1973). If everyone does this, collective reward systems will actually serve to reduce productivity, especially if heightened hierarchical controls are needed to prevent shirking.

EXPERIENCE WITH GAIN-SHARING PLANS

Gain-sharing plans appear to be increasing in popularity in Canada, although they are still used only by a relatively small proportion of firms. According to the Compensation Practices Survey, approximately 14 percent of medium to large Canadian firms had gain sharing in 2000. This compares with about 11 percent in 1995 (Isaac, 1995), and 8 percent in 1990–91 (Betcherman, Leckie, and Verma, 1994).

However, like any pay innovation, not every gain-sharing plan achieves success. The only available Canadian data on gain sharing's success rate (Long, 1989) indicated that in the five-year period 1980–85, approximately 17 percent of firms that had gain sharing in 1980 no longer had it in 1985. This is quite close to a discontinuation rate of 20.4 percent found by Kim (1999) in a 1992 sample of North American firms, and a 15.1 percent discontinuation rate found in another U.S. study (Markham, Scott, and Little, 1992).

In general, the evidence suggests that gain-sharing plans usually bring positive results. For example, a study by the United States General Accounting Office (GAO, 1981) revealed that firms that had gain sharing in place for at least five years averaged an annual savings of 29 percent in labour costs. Other studies have shown improved labour costs, higher productivity, and improved product quality (Schuster, 1984, 1985; Wallace, 1990). Although most studies have been conducted in manufacturing firms, positive results have also been found in other settings. For example, Bowie-McCoy, Wendt, and Chope (1993) found gain sharing reduced labour costs by 11–12 percent in accounting firms.

There has also been considerable research on conditions that lead to success (Cooper, Dyck, and Frohlich, 1992; Welbourne, Balkin, and Gomez-Mejia, 1995; Welbourne and Cable, 1995; Kim, 1996). It is crucial that the gain-sharing system be seen by employees as fair and equitable, both in terms of procedural and distributive justice. Employee participation in the development of the gain-sharing system is one way of helping to achieve this goal.

Effective employee participation in the ongoing management of the plan is also important, along with effective participation mechanisms for eliciting employee suggestions and ideas for improvement. Of course, effective communication of the plan, so that it is understood by all employees, is fundamental. Because of the need to make adjustments to these plans over time, a certain level of trust between management and employees is needed. As with piece rates, there must be some assurance that employees will not "work themselves out of a job."

In unionized firms, union support for the plan will likely play a pivotal role, according to Kim (1996), who found that gain sharing is generally less successful in unionized settings, a finding also reported by Cooke (1994). In fact, Cooke found that while non-union firms benefited significantly from gain sharing, unionized firms showed no benefit whatsoever. Kim's explanation for this finding is that unionized employees may be more reluctant to engage in mutual monitoring than non-union employees. But another explanation is that unionized firms tend to be more classically managed, and gain sharing is not well suited to that managerial strategy.

APPLICABILITY OF GAIN SHARING

Like many other pay elements, gain sharing fits far better with some managerial strategies than others. Classical firms will not look favourably on gain sharing because it doesn't allow individual accountability, and they will be concerned about free riding. Furthermore, they will be reluctant to encourage employee participation in decision making. Employees will likely be reluctant to participate, due to the adversarial relationship that often prevails in classical organizations and due to concerns about job security if productivity increases.

Because of the fragmented job structure, low training, and low information dissemination often prevailing in classical organizations, productive employee participation will be unlikely in any case, even if both management and employees did want it. In general, organizations with classical managerial strategies are right to avoid gain sharing—the odds of positive consequences are low, and the worries of economists about free riding may well turn out to be true in this type of organization.

Human relations organizations may find gain sharing attractive because it fits in with their concept of group cooperation. Some of the foundations for effective gain sharing will likely be in place, such as trust between managers and employees. Strong and favourable social norms may be able to prevent free riding, and the practice of job security will allay fears of layoff. However, though it may not be a failure, gain sharing will likely not realize its full potential in human relations organizations. This is because these firms will not have a true participative culture. Like classical organizations, employees will not be accustomed to participating in decision making, and because of the fragmented jobs that prevail in human relations organizations, and relatively low information flows, along with managerial roles that do not encourage worker participation, effective employee participation will be difficult.

It is in high-involvement organizations that the payoff for gain sharing will be greatest, since virtually all the conditions for success will already be in place, including a participative culture, trust, communications, training, broad-based jobs, and reasonable job security. These organizations will also likely be favourably disposed toward these plans, since they fit the managerial philosophy so well, encouraging teamwork and participation as well as innovative solutions to problem solving. The main problem with gain sharing for high-involvement firms is that things may change so quickly that development of valid performance baselines may be difficult, and the package of performance measures may need to continually change to meet changing conditions.

GOAL-SHARING PLANS

goal-sharing plan a group performance pay plan in which a work group or team receives a bonus when prespecified performance goals are met

Goal sharing is another group pay plan that has been gaining popularity in recent years. The essence of goal sharing is that work groups or teams receive a bonus when certain prespecified performance goals are met (Belcher, 1996).

Goal-sharing plans differ from gain-sharing plans in several fundamental ways. Under gain sharing, cost savings are quantified and then shared between the company and the group. There are no set goals with gain sharing other than to simply improve as much as possible relative to the historical baseline. There is an expectation of continuity—the gain-sharing system will not be arbitrarily changed. Finally, in gain-sharing plans there is usually an explicit expectation of employee involvement in suggesting ideas for productivity gains.

In contrast, under goal sharing, goals on one or more performance indicators are set for each group or team, to be met within a specified time period, and a bonus is paid to all team members if the goal is achieved. Employee involvement is not necessarily a component, although it can be.

ADVANTAGES OF GOAL SHARING

Goal-sharing plans have several advantages over gain-sharing plans. They can be much simpler to develop and are much more flexible. They can therefore be applied in a much broader set of circumstances. They can also be tied to specific objectives that support company strategy. Another advantage is that meaningful performance increases must take place before any bonus will be paid out. In essence, the company retains 100 percent of any gains below the targeted level.

When they work, goal-sharing plans can produce many of the same advantages as gain-sharing plans. Group norms may develop that value high productivity (as long as negative consequences, such as layoffs or reduction in valued overtime, do not result from this increased productivity). These favourable group norms will lead the group to police itself by encouraging lower-producing workers to improve their performance. Group members will also be motivated to help new employees learn their jobs quickly and effectively. A collaborative attitude may prevail, and workers who develop better ways of performing their jobs will be more likely to share their knowledge.

Disadvantages of Goal Sharing

But the flip side of their flexibility is that goal-sharing plans can be much more arbitrary than gain-sharing plans. Goal-sharing systems can be arbitrary in terms of the goal level necessary to qualify for a bonus and in terms of the amount of bonus that will be paid if the goal is achieved; in addition, they may be modified or dropped at virtually any time.

None of these characteristics is particularly desirable for enhancing motivation. For example, if goals are perceived as being unrealistic (low expectancy), no extra effort will be expended to meet them. If the bonus is not perceived as sufficiently attractive relative to the effort required (low valence), no extra effort will be expended. If the program may be modified or ended at any time, there may be skepticism about whether the promised rewards will actually be forthcoming or will continue once goals are met (low instrumentality). If management modifies the goal-sharing system frequently, it may be considered as a "flavour of the month" to be simply ignored.

There is also the issue of equity. Goal-sharing systems often have no established basis for judging the value of meeting a particular goal, and no fixed, mutually agreed-upon basis to apportion gains between the company and employees. Employees may feel that the company is trying to "rip them off" by providing token rewards for major gains in productivity. For all these reasons, we would expect goal-sharing programs to be less motivational than gain-sharing programs, other things being equal.

There may also be other problems. A group may become discouraged and frustrated if prevented from attaining their output goals by one or two workers who are unwilling or unable to perform at the necessary levels. If the group believes the productivity goal is set unrealistically high, little effort will be made to attain it. If the goal is reached, there is no incentive to surpass it.

Employee dissatisfaction may occur if, despite major effort, the goal is not quite attained, and no reward is allocated. It is tempting to redress this by lowering the goal and providing the reward, but this teaches that goal attainment is unnecessary for reward attainment.

There are many situational factors that may affect goal achievement, and using the identical goals for different work teams may be highly unfair. But attempts to correct this by having "easier" goals for some work teams may simply make work teams with "harder" goals believe they are being treated unfairly.

Many of these problems are surmountable. Extensive employee participation in the development of these plans can help to create realistic goals, and research has shown that this significantly increases employee motivation for goal achievement. Multi-tiered goals can be used to recognize different goal achievement levels. Management can try to find some way to quantify the value of reaching the specified goals in order to give some assurance of equity in determining reward size.

APPLICABILITY

To work well, goal-sharing plans should be designed with input from employees, should clearly communicate factors affecting goal achievement and how employees can affect these factors, and should communicate progress toward meeting goals on an ongoing basis. A key underlying factor is a high level of trust between management and employees. All of this suggests that goal sharing will be most effective in high-involvement organizations, somewhat effective in human relations organizations, and ineffective in classical organizations.

One indication of the rapid acceptance of goal-sharing plans is that despite their relative newness, they have already outstripped gain-sharing plans in usage. While 14 percent of Canadian firms used gain sharing in 2000, a larger proportion (18 percent) used goal sharing.

As with gain sharing, there are numerous issues to be decided prior to implementation. For example, a key issue is allocation of the bonus across employees. It can be allocated to each member of the work group equally or on the basis of relative pay levels. The first approach emphasizes the importance of each group member in accomplishing the unit objective, while the second approach recognizes differential contributions to the performance of the unit (assuming wage differentials are, in fact, related to performance differentials).

OTHER TYPES OF GROUP BONUS PLANS

competitive bonus plan
a group pay plan in which groups of employees compete with other groups to win bonuses

Besides gain or goal sharing, there are numerous other types of group bonus plans that can be used, and about 16 percent of Canadian firms utilize one or more of these. One such type is a **competitive bonus plan.** For example, many real estate firms with multi-office operations encourage competition between sales offices by providing a bonus to all sales personnel in the highest-producing office each month. In retail chains, all employees in a particular store may receive a bonus if the store has the highest customer satisfaction ratings in the chain within a given time period.

Welbourne and Gomez-Mejia (1991) describe a plan in which engineering teams in a Boston-area high-technology firm are eligible for up to a 25 percent bonus if they can show, in a written report, that they have made a significant contribution to company performance. These reports are judged, on a competitive basis, by a management committee that decides whether to grant a bonus and the amount of the bonus.

The researchers do not report the results of this plan, but there are many dangers of such a plan. One obvious danger is that teams will attempt to inflate the value of their work. The second is that this system may inhibit cooperation and even cause conflict between teams if other teams are seen as rivals for scarce funds. There is also potential for conflict with the management committee over its choices. From a motivational point of view, this plan is deficient in that rewards are uncertain, as are the performance levels needed to achieve these rewards. The plan may be seen as inequitable if there are numerous instances of major achievements, but some cannot be recognized just because of the structure of the system.

In general, competitive bonus systems that pit one group against another should be used only if the groups are truly independent and never need to cooperate with one another. They do not fit well with the philosophy of human relations organizations or high-involvement firms.

Another type of team-based system might be dubbed **"pooled performance pay."** For example, the variable pay for a group of sales reps might be based on the total sales the group generates, with each member receiving an equal share. Or, a group piece rate system could be used, in which group members get paid based on the number of completed products or components produced by the group. The value of these plans is that it is in the interests of each group member for the other group members to succeed, and each may share tips, techniques, and pointers. In other words, this type of plan encourages teamwork. The danger with these plans is that they may encourage "free riding" or "social loafing." However, this may not be a problem if the groups are kept relatively small and if members understand the linkages between their behaviour and group rewards.

pooled performance pay a pay plan where the performance results of a group or team are pooled, and group members share equally in the performance bonus

Finally, another way of encouraging teamwork while discouraging social loafing is through the use of **team-based merit pay** (Heneman and Von Hippel, 1995). Team-based merit pay provides rewards to individuals based on their contributions to the team. For example, at Johnsonville Foods, team leaders and members rate each member's contribution to team goals, their communication with other team members, their willingness to work with other team members, and their attendance and timeliness at group meetings (Stayer, 1990).

team-based merit pay a performance pay plan that rewards individuals on the basis of their contribution to a group or team

ORGANIZATION PERFORMANCE PLANS

Both profit-sharing and employee stock plans have experienced growing popularity in Canada, and in many other countries as well. This section will discuss each in detail. In addition, we will look at other organization performance plans, most notably long-term incentives (LTIs).

PROFIT SHARING

In general terms, profit sharing can be defined as "any arrangement whereby an employer shares with a designated group of employees a portion of the profits derived from the business" (Nightingale and Long, 1984: 7). However, to be recognized as a "true" employee profit-sharing plan, there are a number of additional criteria.

First, a plan that applies only to management is not generally considered to qualify as an employee profit-sharing plan. Second, a plan for which there is no fixed relationship between profitability and the size of the profit-sharing bonus pool also does not qualify. To qualify as having an **employee profit-sharing plan**, a firm must have a formal program in which payments are made to a wide cross-section of employees (although not necessarily to all employees, or every employee group) on at least an annual basis, based on a formula relating the size of the bonus pool to the profitability of the business.

TYPES OF PROFIT-SHARING PLANS

Profit-sharing plans may take one of three forms: (1) the current distribution plan, (2) the deferred profit-sharing plan, and (3) the combination plan. The **current distribution plan** (also called a "cash plan") pays a share of company profits to employees in cash or occasionally in company stock. (When stock is used, it is also a type of employee ownership plan.) In most firms the distribution is made annually, but it can be made more frequently, depending on the availability of profit data.

Under a **deferred profit-sharing plan (DPSP),** an employee's share of the profit bonus pool is placed in a trust fund to be distributed at a future date, usually on the employee's retirement or termination of employment. This type of plan is often used as a type of retirement savings plan. A **combination plan** provides both cash (or stock) and a deferred payout. The objective here is usually to take advantage of the provisions for tax deferral in federal tax legislation to help build some retirement income, while also providing a more visible incentive to employees through the cash portion. Cash-based plans are usually thought to provide a better incentive to employees, since the connection between company performance and employee rewards is more obvious.

Profit-sharing plans can vary significantly in structure. Important structural variables include the process for bonus determination (fixed proportion of profits, discretionary), bonus eligibility (all employees, specified groups only), bonus form (e.g., cash, stock, deferred), and bonus allocation across employees (according to salary, seniority, employee performance, or equally). How these plans are structured may have a significant impact on their consequences.

In Canada, there are two kinds of government-sanctioned profit-sharing plans: the *deferred profit-sharing plan* (DPSP) and the *employee profit-sharing plan* (EPSP). The DPSP is a tax-deferred plan. Both the employer contributions and the annual earnings of the trust are exempt from taxation until the employee

---

employee profit-sharing plan a formal pay program under which a firm provides bonus payments to employees based on the profitability of the firm

current distribution plan a profit-sharing plan that distributes the profit-sharing bonus to employees in the form of cash or shares, at least annually

deferred profit-sharing plan (DPSP) a profit-sharing plan in which the profit-sharing bonuses are allocated to employee accounts but not actually paid out until a later date, usually on termination or retirement

combination plan a plan that combines the current distribution and deferred profit-sharing plans by paying some of the profit-sharing bonus on a current (cash) basis and deferring the remainder

---

actually receives the benefit. Because of this feature, DPSPs were often used as a form of pension plan, especially in many small to medium-sized companies where no other pension plan exists. However, the attractiveness of the DPSP was reduced in 1983 when the federal government tied the maximum tax deduction to the unused portion of the employee's registered retirement savings plan (RRSP) contribution. Another amendment made that year eliminated tax protection for "top hat" plans (those in which only senior management is eligible) by excluding "significant shareholders" from participating and by requiring wide employee eligibility.

Additional changes to DPSP legislation occurred in 1990 (Income Tax Act, Section 147). Although a number of changes were made, including a slight reduction in contribution limits, a key feature was one that made it more attractive for the DPSP to invest in shares of the employer by providing certain income tax advantages to the employee on withdrawal from the plan (whether at retirement or not). Instead of being taxed on the full market value of the shares at the time of withdrawal, the employee is taxed only on the original value of the shares when they were placed in the plan. When the shares are sold, the difference between the original value and the selling price is considered a capital gain rather than employment income. However, it should be noted that only publicly traded shares are eligible for purchase by a DPSP (Tyson, 1996).

The EPSP is not a tax-deferred plan. However, both employer and employee contributions to the trust can be made without limits. These plans are really a type of unsheltered company-supported savings/investment plan, and their main purpose is to provide a vehicle to accumulate savings after the tax-deferred approaches have been exhausted. They are rarely used.

To provide some idea of the diversity of profit-sharing plans, Box 6.2 gives examples of these plans at three different Canadian companies.

ADVANTAGES OF PROFIT-SHARING PLANS

As part of a study on profit sharing, a business owner was questioned about whether his firm had employee profit sharing (Long, 1992). In response, he exclaimed, "Give away my profits? Why would I want to do *that*?" Why, indeed, would employers want to share their profits with their employees?

Advocates of profit sharing argue that there are many sound business reasons to do so, other than philanthropy (Tyson, 1996). When the interests of employees and the employer are aligned, employees may be more motivated to help improve productivity. Profit sharing may also contribute to the development of favourable group norms, improved cooperation among employees and between employees and management, improved labour–management relations, and greater organizational identification, which may lead to more organizational citizenship behaviour. These improved norms may reduce the need for supervision, thus reducing costs. Profit sharing also fits with and supports a move to high-involvement management, if the firm desires to move in that direction.

BOX 6.2 Profit Sharing at Three Canadian Companies

A company with one of the longest histories of profit sharing in Canada is Dofasco Steel of Hamilton, Ontario. A non-union firm in a unionized industry, Dofasco has always seen profit sharing as a major part of its renowned human relations managerial philosophy. The plan was started in 1938 as a pension plan, and continues as a DPSP and group registered retirement savings plan (Tyson, 1996). Any amounts that exceed the government limits on these plans may be received in cash. The bonus pool is 14 percent of pre-tax profits from operations, and it is allocated equally to eligible employees in its 7000-person workforce. All employees with at least two years of service are included in the plan. In 2000, the company made headlines when it split a bonus pool of $53.3 million—the highest payout ever—among employees, who each received $7906 (Kilpatrick and Walton, 2000).

Another company with a long-standing commitment to profit sharing is Canadian Tire. The founder of the chain, A.J. Billes, always believed in profit sharing in both a philosophical and a practical way. He believed that it was morally just that employees receive a portion of the profits that they help to generate, and also that this would create employee commitment to the firm. The company has always had a profit-sharing plan that applies to the employees of the parent firm, and strongly encourages profit sharing at its independently owned associate stores.

At the Canadian Tire Associate Store in Barrie, Ontario, which has 73 full-time and 94 part-time employees, the profit-sharing bonus is allocated based on salary level (40 percent), merit rating (40 percent), and seniority (20 percent). The plan is a DPSP that invests in Canadian Tire class A shares, so it is also a stock plan as well as a profit-sharing plan. Amounts that exceed the allowable government limits on DPSPs are placed in an EPSP, which pays interest at the prime rate.

Valley City Manufacturing is a maker of architectural woodwork and cabinetry located in Dundas, Ontario. Unionized by Local 1057 of the Carpenters and Joiners, the firm has about 105 full-time employees, all of whom participate in profit sharing after one year of service. The plan is a generous one, paying 27 percent of pre-tax profits. The profit-sharing bonus is allocated according to employee earnings, and the employee has the choice of whether to take it in cash or to place it in a DPSP. Established in 1964, the purpose of the plan is "to promote a harmonious working environment and reward success" according to Robert Crockford, the company president (Tyson, 1996).

Other advantages stem from the fact that profit sharing is a reward that is related to ability to pay. By providing profit sharing, an employer is able to offer a more attractive compensation package but does not have to continue payments when business conditions are unfavourable. For some organizations, it is the only way they can afford to offer a retirement plan. Profit sharing may also reduce the need for layoffs in poor economic circumstances, since labour costs are automatically adjusted downward.

Indeed, at the societal level, some commentators (Weitzman, 1984) have called for widespread profit sharing as a way to increase employment levels and stability, while others have seen it as a way of reducing labour–management conflict, and still others have seen it as a way of increasing the competitiveness of businesses in the global marketplace. From an employee point of view, profit sharing may improve job security by making layoffs less necessary and by improving company performance. Employees may also gain greater job satisfaction working in an environment where there is more harmony.

Finally, compared with plans such as gain sharing, profit sharing is far simpler to set up and administer. Profit measures are readily available. There is no need to compute baselines or to try to quantify the value of cost savings. Administration is relatively simple, and the plan and results are relatively easy to communicate to employees.

DISADVANTAGES OF PROFIT SHARING

The most important potential disadvantage of profit sharing is that it may not pay off for the employer—costs of the profit-sharing bonus and of administering the profit-sharing system may exceed the gains from profit sharing. Some critics even argue that as a collective reward system, profit sharing may actually reduce employee performance by causing "free riding." These arguments have already been discussed in connection with gain sharing, and are really no different for profit sharing.

In fact, because the connection between individual performance and the expected reward for that performance is more tenuous, profit sharing actually has a weaker "line of sight" between performance and reward than gain sharing and so should have little direct impact on employee performance. There are so many factors that intercede between worker performance and company profitability that worker performance could improve dramatically while profits could actually go down or even disappear due to market conditions or poor management decisions.

The arguments about general employee aversion to uncertain rewards also apply. In fact, one of the factors causing the separation of the Canadian Auto Workers from the United Auto Workers Union was the refusal by the Canadian union to accept profit sharing (Katz and Meltz, 1991). With only one exception (Long, 1997), studies in Canada have shown a negative link between unionization and the presence of profit sharing (Long, 1989; Jones and Pliskin, 1991; McMullen, Leckie, and Caron, 1993; Betcherman, McMullen, Leckie, and Caron, 1994; Wagar and Long, 1995; Long, 2002). Part of the union concern is that by increasing worker commitment to the company, profit sharing might weaken worker allegiance to the union, although the evidence is not clear on this.

The apparent antipathy of unions toward profit sharing in Canada is borne out by examination of collective agreements. Although the proportion of collective agreements containing profit-sharing provisions doubled between 1987 and 1993 (Chaykowski and Lewis, 1995), only about 2 percent of collective agreements had these provisions in 1993. Of course, it is not absolutely clear whether this low incidence is entirely due to resistance by unions to profit sharing or also to a lack of desire on the part of unionized employers to adopt profit sharing.

Another drawback of profit sharing, in the eyes of some employers, is that it requires them to share financial information about the company. Of course, profit sharing also requires some effort and expertise to establish, and some effort for ongoing administration.

EXPERIENCE WITH PROFIT SHARING

Profit sharing is growing rapidly in popularity in Canada. In 1989–90, Long (1992) found that about 17.3 percent of Canadian firms had employee profit sharing, while a 1991 survey by the Economic Council of Canada showed 18 percent, and a 1993 survey (Betcherman et al., 1994) showed 21.6 percent. By 2000, nearly a third (32 percent) of medium to large Canadian firms had broad-based employee profit sharing, according to the CPS.

Why are companies increasingly implementing profit sharing? What are their motives? To address these questions, Long (1997) conducted telephone interviews with chief executive officers (CEOs) at 108 Canadian companies. CEOs stated a wide variety of objectives for profit sharing. The most frequently cited motive was "improving employee motivation," followed by "rewarding loyal employees" and "improving company performance." Other frequently cited motives were "retaining employees," "helping employees understand the business," "promoting teamwork/cooperation," "improving the compensation package," and "building employee commitment."

Looking at these motives, we can see that, by and large, chief executive officers do not see profit sharing in the same way as economists do. Not one CEO cited the concept of "making pay more variable" as a reason for implementing profit sharing, nor did any see profit sharing as a way of weakening the union. Profit sharing was seen either as a way to increase company performance (through "improving employee motivation," "promoting teamwork," and "helping employees understand the business") or as a way to provide better rewards to employees, thus increasing their loyalty and commitment to the firm. Overall, most CEOs reported that profit sharing had "largely" or "completely" achieved the objectives they had set out for it.

Chief executive officers were also asked to rate the impact of employee profit sharing on a variety of possible consequences, using a scale ranging from "–5" (very negative impact) to "zero" (no impact) to "+5" (very positive impact). Overall, very few reported any negative consequences. Virtually every CEO indicated that profit sharing had a positive impact on the company overall, and over 90 percent believed that profit sharing had a positive impact on employee interest in company performance, employee motivation and effort, employee loyalty, and job satisfaction. Substantial majorities also believed that profit sharing had a positive impact on employee turnover, company profitability, cooperation within the firm, ability to recruit employees, and industrial relations.

CEOs were also asked to cite the disadvantages of profit sharing. Many, 38 percent, could not think of any disadvantages at all. Of those who could, the most commonly cited were employee discontent if profits go down (cited by 17 percent) and a concern that employees might come to take the profit-sharing bonus for granted (12 percent). Eleven percent thought it was difficult to set up profit sharing in such a way as to obtain the potential benefits, and 5 percent indicated that profit sharing does not "take" for every employee.

What kinds of firms implement profit sharing? Three Canadian studies have addressed this question (Wagar and Long, 1995; Long, 1997; Long, 2002), and the one factor common to all three studies was the presence of high-involvement management. Two of the three studies also found unionized firms less likely to have profit sharing. Beyond these two factors, there were no other commonalities, suggesting that profit sharing is applicable to firms in a wide variety of circumstances, as long as they have a high-involvement managerial strategy.

What are the structural characteristics of Canadian profit-sharing plans? Long (1997) found that the majority (75 percent) were cash-based plans, and another 15 percent were deferred profit-sharing plans, while six firms (5.6 percent) had combination plans. Two firms paid the profit-sharing bonus in a combination of cash and company stock, and one paid out the bonus only in company stock. More than half of the firms (55 percent) used a fixed percentage of annual profits—ranging from 1 percent to 33 percent of profits—to determine the amount of the profit-sharing bonus. The median percentage of profits was 10 percent.

The most common bases for allocating the profit-sharing bonus across employees were salary level or individual performance (each used in about 30 percent of firms). Seniority was used in 13 percent of firms, while 17 percent used a combination of salary and seniority. Five firms (4.6 percent) allocated the bonus equally to all employees. In the majority of cases (73 percent), all full-time employees were included in the plan, while 7.5 percent of the firms excluded unionized employees, and 16 percent restricted profit sharing to designated employees only. In 39 percent of profit-sharing firms, part-time employees were also included.

Extensive analysis of the data revealed three main factors that significantly affected the success of profit sharing, as perceived by chief executive officers (Long, 2000). CEOs reported better results in firms that utilized high-involvement management, that had extensive profit-sharing communication, and that allocated the bonus according to measures of individual performance. Rather surprisingly, none of the other company characteristics or plan characteristics were very important in influencing the results of profit sharing, suggesting that profit-sharing plans can be implemented into a variety of different companies and have a range of different design characteristics and still be effective. One interesting caveat to this finding, however, is that while there was no major difference in results between firms that used a fixed percentage for bonus determination and those that did not (except industrial relations were more favourable in firms with a fixed percentage), for those with fixed percentage plans success increased with the size of the bonus percentage. Performance of the plan appears to improve when the bonus percentage exceeds 10 percent of profits.

What about the impact of profit sharing on the financial success of the firm? Only one Canadian study directly addressed this question. Magnan, St-Onge, and Lalande (1997) studied the impact of profit sharing in 294 Quebec caisses populaires (credit unions), some of which had adopted profit sharing and some of which had not. Of the eight financial performance indicators examined, three increased significantly after adoption of profit sharing, while no indicator showed a decline.

While there are few Canadian data on this question, there is considerable evidence from other countries. From a review of more than 20 econometric studies, Weitzman and Kruse (1990) concluded that profit-sharing firms were significantly more productive (a median of 4.4 percent) than firms without profit sharing. From a large-scale longitudinal study he conducted in the United States, where most profit-sharing plans are of the deferred nature and are viewed primarily as pension plans, Kruse (1993) concluded that adoption of profit sharing is associated with productivity increases averaging 4.3 percent (although 25 percent to 33 percent of firms showed no productivity increase whatsoever); a subsequent meta-analysis of empirical studies (Doucouliagos, 1995) revealed a similar result. Bhargava (1994) found a significant positive relationship between profit sharing and company profitability in his longitudinal study of British firms. In his sample of U.S. firms, Kim (1998) also found that profit sharing had significant positive effects on profitability, but only in firms that also had employee involvement programs.

An interesting study was recently conducted by two U.S. researchers (see Box 6.3). They found that companies that made extensive use of organization-based performance rewards, such as profit sharing and employee stock plans, showed a much higher five-year survival rate than firms that did not utilize organization-based performance pay.

Finally, there is also evidence that profit sharing improves employment stability. In a recent study of managerial pay, Gerhart and Trevor (1996) found that U.S. organizations in which managerial staff had a larger variable pay component to their earnings experienced significantly less variation in employment levels over a four-year period. Chelius and Smith (1990) also found that firms with profit-sharing systems had less employment variability than those without, although their results were not as strong as those of Gerhart and Trevor.

APPLICABILITY OF PROFIT SHARING

Profit sharing is particularly important in companies where a high level of cooperation across company units, between management and employees, and among employees is needed. These characteristics describe high-involvement organizations, and profit sharing fits best with this type of management philosophy. It is an important way of promoting internalization of company goals, as well as providing a mechanism for keeping employees informed about the financial state of the business. To maximize the benefits of profit sharing, there need to be well-developed communication channels up and down the organization. Employees will want to be informed about what is going on in the company, and to contribute ideas and suggestions for improvement.

Profit sharing may be useful in human relations organizations to the extent that it serves as an additional means to cement loyalty to the firm, and

BOX 6.3 How Many Stock Market Analysts Does It Take to Change a Light Bulb?

How many stock market analysts does it take to change a light bulb? The answer: None. If the bulb really needed changing, the market would have already changed it. The humour in this joke is based on the belief of many stock market analysts in the "infallibility of the market"—the notion that the stock market takes account of all information about a company and accurately incorporates it into the valuation of the company's stock. Indeed, through the individual actions of stock traders, the market continually passes collective judgment on the decisions of company management, and reflects that through changes in the firm's stock price.

The measure of many management decisions in publicly traded corporations then becomes whether they "add value" to a company—whether they cause a company's share price to go up or down. So researchers have started to examine the quality of various management decisions in terms of the market's reaction to them. But is the market always right?

An interesting study that bears on this question was undertaken by Theresa Welbourne and Alice Andrews. As a part of their study, they examined the five-year survival rate of firms that were first listed on a stock exchange in 1988, and related this to the extent to which these firms had organizationally based performance rewards, such as profit sharing and employee stock plans. Their results were impressive. They found that the use of organizationally based performance rewards significantly increased the likelihood of company survival.

This is an interesting finding in its own right, but the researchers also made another interesting discovery. They wished to see whether the stock market, at the time of the initial public offering, had valued the shares of companies with organizational rewards more highly than those firms without organizational rewards. It should have, since these firms had a higher survival rate.

In fact, they did find a significant difference in stock price, but opposite to the expected direction. Firms with organizational rewards were valued significantly *lower* than firms without these rewards. The researchers conclude that "investors seem to respond negatively to a factor that actually has a positive impact on survival chances" (Welbourne and Andrews, 1996: 913). They also found that the top executives of survivor companies, while believing that organizational rewards had played some role in their company's success, substantially undervalued the role that organizational rewards had actually played in company survival.

---

to the extent that it can help foster positive work norms. However, the impact of profit sharing is not likely to be dramatic, since the participative culture necessary to maximize the contribution of profit sharing is not generally in place at human relations firms.

For classical firms, profit sharing may yield few benefits, in line with economic thought. Profit sharing is not philosophically compatible with the classical managerial philosophy, in which workers and management are seen as adversaries, and where control requires that individuals be accountable for their own performance. In a situation of low trust, profit sharing may simply become another source of conflict, as employees believe that management will somehow attempt to cheat them out of their rightful share of the profits or will try to use profit sharing to reduce other compensation or to weaken union allegiance. Reluctance of management to release financial information will foster mistrust and also make it difficult for employees to understand how they could contribute to profitability. In addition, a major potential benefit of profit sharing—the ability to operate with less hierarchy and fewer supervisors—will not likely be viable in classical firms.

What are the desirable conditions for the establishment of profit sharing? First, there must be some expectation of profits in at least the first one or two years of the plan. And the profitability level should be sufficient to afford an annual payout that amounts to at least 3 to 5 percent of base pay for each employee (Tyson, 1996). Firms with highly unstable profits and/or in which employee performance has very little impact on profitability may not be ideal candidates. There should be reasonably good relationships between management and employees, and management must be willing to share financial information and to value employee input.

Although economists would argue that profit sharing will have more impact if it substitutes for base pay, consultants and practitioners are virtually universal in opposing this (Tyson, 1996). Instead, they argue that competitive base pay and an equitable compensation system are preconditions to successful use of profit sharing. In fact, research indicates that profit sharing is usually used as an "add-on," rather than as a substitute for base pay, and that employees in profit-sharing firms earn more than in comparable firms without profit sharing (Kruse, 1993).

EMPLOYEE STOCK PLANS

employee stock plan
any type of plan through which employees acquire shares in the firm that employs them

An **employee stock plan** is any type of plan through which employees acquire shares in the firm that employs them. In some plans employees will receive shares at no cost to them, while in other plans employees are given the opportunity to purchase them, sometimes on very favourable terms. Related types of plans that tie employee rewards to company stock performance but do not actually provide employees with the opportunity to acquire shares—share appreciation rights and phantom stock plans—will also be briefly discussed.

TYPES OF EMPLOYEE STOCK PLANS

employee stock bonus plan a plan through which employees receive shares in their employer at no cost to the employee

There are three main types of employee stock plans: stock bonus plans, stock purchase plans, and stock option plans. An **employee stock bonus plan** is very simple in concept—an employer provides company shares to employees at no cost to the employee. This can be done through simply granting these shares to employees, or it can be done in conjunction with some other type of performance plan, such as profit sharing, as we have seen earlier.

employee stock purchase plan a plan through which employees may purchase shares in their employing firm

Under an **employee stock purchase plan,** employees provide some kind of direct payment in return for company shares. However, they often do not have to pay full market price for these shares, and there are many incentives that firms may offer to promote employee share purchases. These may include some type of subsidized or discounted price, or a matching program in which the firm provides an additional share for each share purchased by an employee. In some cases the company pays the brokerage fees, while in others they provide low- or no-interest loans for stock purchase. In many cases, the convenience of payroll deduction is offered. Box 6.4 describes two fairly typical stock purchase plans, one in a public corporation and one in a private corporation.

Under an **employee stock option plan**, employees are provided with options to purchase company stock at some future time at a fixed price. For example, if company stock is now trading at $10 a share, then 1000 options with an exercise price of $12 a share might be issued to each employee. Half of the options might be exercisable in a year, and the other half in two years, with an exercise deadline (option expiry) of three years. What this means is that, one year from now, the employee has the option of purchasing up to 500 shares of company stock at a price of $12 each. Obviously, if the stock is trading at that time at, say, $9 a share, there would be no reason to exercise the options. If employees wanted the stock, they could just purchase it through a stockbroker for $9 a share.

But if the stock is trading at, say, $13 a share, employees have a decision to make. They can exercise their options and purchase 500 shares at $12. But if they do purchase the shares, there is the possibility that these shares will go down in price. Of course, they might also go up in price. It's a gamble. But employees who don't want to gamble, or don't have the money with which to

employee stock option plan a plan through which employees are provided with options to purchase shares in their employer at a fixed price within a limited time period

---

BOX 6.4 Ownership Eggs on These Employees

At Vanderpol's Eggs in Abbotsford, British Columbia, most employees are shareholders in this privately held firm. A typical employee may hold $75 000 worth of company shares, and many own much more than that. Most of this ownership results from employees choosing to invest their allocations from the company profit-sharing plan in company stock. (Because the company wishes to preserve working capital, their other alternative for the profit-sharing payout is to loan it back to the company, which pays interest of prime plus 1 percent on these funds.) Although the company provides no discount on the shares that are purchased with profit-sharing money, the British Columbia government does provide a 20 percent tax credit on funds so invested. Employees are allowed to remove their funds at retirement or termination. The company finds that stock ownership creates a keen interest among employees in company performance.

The Royal Bank of Canada, a publicly traded firm, has for many years had an employee savings program under which employees may purchase bank stock. All employees with at least six months' service have the option of placing up to 10 percent of their annual income in a savings plan that may be invested in a deposit account, mutual funds, or bank stock. The bank will provide a 50 percent match in company shares, up to a limit of 3 percent. That is, if an employee invests 6 percent of his or her income in any of the three options listed above, that person will receive bank shares amounting to 3 percent of his or her gross income at no extra cost. If the employee's annual RRSP allowance is not used up, these shares will be placed in a deferred profit-sharing plan, and there will be no income tax liability until redemption. If the RRSP allowance is used up, the shares will be placed in an employee profit-sharing plan, and income taxes will not be deferred.

---

purchase the shares, can simply cash out by turning around and selling the shares immediately at $13, thus realizing a gain of $500 minus brokerage costs.

But they need not exercise their options at this time either. They could just continue to hold their options (for up to another two years, since that is the expiry date) in the expectation that stock prices will go up over the next two years. But if the stock price sinks below the exercise price of $12 (when the stock price is below the exercise price, the stock options are said to be "under water") and never again rises above that price (during the next two years), employees will not realize any value from their options. On the other hand, they are not out of pocket any money either, as they would be if they had purchased and held the shares as they dropped below the $12 mark.

A variation that merges the stock bonus plan with the stock option concept is **share appreciation rights.** Employees are first "allocated" a number of shares of company stock, although they do not actually receive any shares. If these "shares" appreciate over time within a fixed time period, employees will receive, as a bonus, the number of actual company shares that this appreciation will purchase. As an example, suppose an employee is "allocated" 1000 company shares, and the share price is $20 at the outset. Then, suppose the shares rise to the value of $25 each by the end of the specified period. The employee would then receive 200 actual company shares (the $5000 appreciation will buy 200 shares at $25 each) as a bonus, at no cost to the employee.

A **phantom stock plan** ties an employee's bonus to the performance of company stock, but that person never actually receives any stock. The employee is granted a certain number of "units," each corresponding to a share of stock. The employee is entitled to the same dividends that accrue to the actual stock, and also the appreciation in share value, which are both paid in cash at periodic intervals.

One new and interesting variation on a phantom stock plan is a **phantom equity plan** (Morrison and Adams, 2001). This plan has been developed by professional service firms—including firms such as management consulting giants McKinsey and Company, Arthur Andersen, and Accenture—to help them retain staff who might otherwise be drawn to high-tech companies that are able to offer stock options or equity shares (which professional services firms generally cannot do, since they usually do not have a corporate ownership structure). The plan is not in fact an employee stock plan, since the shares in question are not those of the employer, but a plan in which employees are granted participation units in a pool of equities of client firms. The value of the units varies with the value of the fund, and employees are allowed to cash out only at certain intervals and only while they are still employed with the firm.

Compared with the situation in the United States, direct federal support for employee ownership in Canada is minimal, consisting primarily of legislation surrounding deferred profit-sharing plans. One of the allowable investments for the DPSP trust fund is shares of the employer. If the company opts to invest these funds in its own shares, the normal provision requiring diversification of pension trust funds is waived. As discussed earlier, the federal gov-

share appreciation rights a plan through which employees are awarded company shares at no cost if the price of company shares rises during a specified period

phantom stock plan a plan through which employees participate in the appreciation of company shares and any associated dividends, without ever owning any company stock

phantom equity plan a plan that helps retain key employees by providing rewards based on the stock performance of a portfolio of promising new high-tech firms

ernment made income tax changes in 1990 that serve to encourage DPSPs to invest in employer shares.

The only other possible avenue of federal support for employee ownership is through labour-sponsored investment funds (LSIFs), in which any bona fide labour or employee group may establish a fund that can invest in qualified Canadian businesses. Employees investing through this vehicle are entitled to a deduction from their federal personal income taxes of 15 percent of the value of shares purchased (some provinces match this), to a specified maximum value (currently $700). An LSIF can be structured to allow members of the fund to invest in shares of their employer, if their employer qualifies. As with DPSPs, however, these vehicles have rarely been used for employee ownership.

Although the federal government provides minimal support, several provinces have legislation specifically designed to encourage employee stock ownership. The province of British Columbia, under its Employee Investment Act of 1989, provides a 20 percent provincial tax credit for employees purchasing shares in companies registered under the act, and also has provisions for setting up a type of labour-sponsored investment fund that would invest in shares of a specific employer, which provides a 20 percent provincial tax credit and a 15 percent federal tax credit. In Manitoba, a special labour-sponsored investment fund has been established as a vehicle through which employees can purchase shares in Manitoba firms at no out-of-pocket cost.

The first province to provide a legislative framework that can be used to support employee ownership was Quebec, first through the Quebec Stock Savings Program launched in the late 1970s, through the Fonds de solidarité set up by the Quebec Federation of Labour through the Régime d'épargne du Québec (REAQ) created in the early 1980s, and the Société de placements dans l'entreprise québécoise (SPEQ) created in the mid-1980s. Although none of these programs was designed specifically to encourage employee ownership, they can be used as vehicles for employee ownership.

ADVANTAGES OF EMPLOYEE STOCK PLANS

The general objective of most stock ownership plans is to get employees "to think like owners"—that is, to merge the goals of employees with those of the owners. This may encourage internalization of company goals and lead to enhanced citizenship behaviour and membership behaviours. Large-scale employee ownership plans, in which employees acquire a significant portion of the ownership, can serve as a catalyst toward a shift to a more flexible and entrepreneurial high-involvement type of organization.

Stock ownership may encourage decision makers within the firm to look at ways of maximizing share value. It may also serve as a spur toward improved management, as employee owners will hold managers to a higher performance standard than they might otherwise. These plans are also intended to promote cooperation among employees and between employees and management, and to create a stronger understanding of and concern for overall company performance. In some cases, these plans serve as a way of improving the compensation package, making it easier to attract and retain employees. They can also serve as a means for accumulating retirement funds. Some companies also adopt them for philosophical reasons, on the grounds that employees should benefit financially from the success of the firm, since they have helped to create that success.

This philosophical position may also have a practical slant. In recent years, many top executives have watched their earnings soar, relative to the earnings of other employees, mainly due to stock options. By 2000, U.S. chief executive pay had reached 475 times the pay of an average worker (*The Economist*, 2000), up from 209 times in 1996 (Reingold, 1997), and 42 times in 1960 (Byrne, 1995). In contrast, for many employees, real wages in the United States and Canada have hardly budged in the last 20 years. For some companies, the creation of stock plans, especially stock options, can help to redress this apparent inequity.

Stock plans also have some practical advantages. One is that the company often does not actually have to lay out any cash. Thus, for companies that are cash-poor and cannot afford pay raises, shares may be one means to reward employees. In a very limited number of cases, shares have been used to help compensate for pay reductions. For publicly traded companies, another practical advantage is that mechanisms are already in place for the pricing and trading of shares, and the company is geared toward providing information to shareholders in any case, so including employees is not a big issue.

For employees, there are five main types of possible benefits. First are financial gains. For example, literally thousands of Microsoft employees are millionaires, due to the employee stock plans at that firm. Second, employee stock plans can provide a vehicle for retirement savings. Third, if employee ownership enhances company performance, this can result in greater job security. At Spruce Falls Pulp and Paper, in Kapuskasing, Ontario, conversion to employee ownership literally saved the company, along with the jobs of those employed there. Fourth, stock ownership, particularly if accompanied by employee participation, can provide employees with a say in the enterprise and a sense of control over their own destiny. Fifth, stock ownership can foster a sense of pride and membership among employees.

DISADVANTAGES OF EMPLOYEE STOCK PLANS

Employee stock plans have some general and some specific disadvantages pertaining to each type of plan. For plans in which employees do not purchase their shares at full value, there is some dilution in the equity held by other owners. There is the cost of establishing and administering these plans. There may be employee dissatisfaction if share prices decline, especially if this is due to poor management decisions. There may be a backlash if employees become interested in participating in decisions to improve company performance but if this participation is not encouraged and supported by management. Finally, there is also the risk that the expected advantages of employee ownership will not materialize.

Employee stock plans are much more difficult for privately held corporations, in comparison with publicly traded corporations, because many of the necessary mechanisms are not in place and have to be created. Procedures for issuing, pricing, selling, and trading shares will need to be developed, as well as procedures for shareholder voting and communicating financial information. However, these problems are not insurmountable, and although stock plans are most common in publicly traded corporations, many privately held corporations do adopt them.

For employees, the main disadvantages of stock plans are that gains are very uncertain, and that by investing in one's employer, employees are at risk for losing not only their jobs but also their investment in company shares. Of course, an obvious disadvantage for share purchase plans is that the employee must come up with the necessary funds to make the purchase, even if shares are sold on a discounted or subsidized basis. The risks of investment may also be greater when the employer is a private corporation, because there is no established market through which to price and liquidate holdings. In private corporations where employees hold less than 50 percent of the voting shares, employees may have little real say in the operation of the enterprise, and coupled with the inability to easily liquidate their shares, this situation can make them very vulnerable to adverse decisions that may be taken by the majority owner.

EXPERIENCE WITH EMPLOYEE STOCK PLANS

Employee stock plans have enjoyed a surge in popularity in many industrialized countries during the last two decades (Long, 2001b). This has been most notable in the United States, where a major impetus for their popularity is a body of very favourable tax legislation that dates back to 1974. But although Canada has no strong tax incentives for employee stock plans, it has nonetheless experienced a major increase in these plans, particularly in publicly traded companies.

For example, a 1986 study of its members conducted by the Toronto Stock Exchange (1987) found that 23 percent had some type of broad-based employee stock plan. By 1989–90, Long (1992) found that 37 percent of the publicly traded firms in his sample had broad-based stock bonus or purchase programs, and in 1995 the Conference Board of Canada (Isaac, 1995) found that 43 percent of publicly traded firms had broad-based stock purchase plans. However, in 2000, Long (2002) found that the exact same proportion (43 percent) of publicly traded firms had stock bonus or purchase plans (8 percent had stock bonus plans and 39 percent had stock purchase plans), suggesting that growth in these plans may have levelled off in recent years after a rapid expansion during 1987 to 1995.

However, this picture changes when stock options are included. Although stock options are not a new concept, prior to 1990 they were restricted almost exclusively to top executives. What is radically new is the idea of extending stock options throughout the organization. This trend was started by soft drink maker PepsiCo Inc. in 1989, when it granted every employee bonus stock options worth 10 percent of their salary. By 1996 an estimated 2000 U.S. companies had adopted broad-based employee stock option programs (Capell, 1996) and by the year 2000, it was estimated that at least 7 million U.S. workers had received stock options, up from less than one million in 1992 (NCEO, 2000).

Despite less favourable tax legislation for options (until recently), Canada has also experienced a dramatic increase in the use of broad-based employee stock options. In 1995, about 4.4 percent of medium to large Canadian companies provided stock options to nonmanagerial employees (Isaac, 1995). However, by 2000, the number doing so had more than doubled to 10 percent (Long, 2002), with an even higher percentage (17 percent) reported by publicly traded companies. (The proportion of all firms with stock option programs increases to 36 percent when plans that cover only managerial employees are taken into account.)

On average, firms with broad-based plans provided options to about 68 percent of company employees, and the majority of companies (57 percent) using these plans covered *all* employees. As an example, in 2001 the Canadian telecommunications firm Telus Corporation granted 100 stock options to every employee not covered by existing option programs—more than 20 000 workers—and plans to do so in each of the next two years (Stueck, 2001). Many workers will be eligible for more than the basic 100 options, depending on their skills and marketability.

In 2000, in recognition of the increasing importance of employee stock option plans in competing for and retaining employees, the Canadian federal government amended income tax legislation to make capital gains on options taxable at the time company shares are sold, not at the time the options are exercised. The same legislation allowed 50 percent of the capital gain to be excluded entirely from taxation. These changes brought Canadian tax treatment of options in line with U.S. treatment and make options much more attractive to employees as a form of compensation and much more valuable to companies as a compensation instrument. At the same time, the federal government also made the overall tax treatment of capital gains more favourable, which also increases the relative attractiveness of stock plans as a compensation instrument.

Not surprisingly, employee stock plans of all types are much less common in privately held corporations. In his study, Long (1992) found that about 4 percent of privately held corporations had broad-based employee stock plans. By 2000, this proportion had increased marginally, to 4.8 percent, if only employee stock bonus or purchase plans are considered, but to 7.3 percent when broad-based stock option plans are taken into account.

Why do firms implement employee stock plans? To answer this question, Long (1991) questioned chief executive officers at 47 Canadian companies that had introduced employee share purchase plans. The most important motives were to "build employee commitment" and to "improve employee motivation." "Improving the compensation package," "promoting teamwork/cooperation," "increasing employee participation in decision making," "rewarding loyal employees," and "helping employees understand the business" were also important motives. When asked about how successful employee ownership had been in achieving these objectives, most CEOs indicated that these objectives had been either partially or completely accomplished.

CEOs were also asked to identify disadvantages of employee stock plans. Many, 39 percent, could not think of any. Of those who could, the main disadvantage, cited by 26 percent of respondents, was a concern about the impact on employee morale and motivation if share prices go down.

Chief executive officers were also asked to rate the impact of employee stock ownership on a variety of possible consequences, using a scale ranging from "–5" (very negative impact) to "zero" (no impact) to "+5" (very positive impact). One striking finding was that employee stock ownership virtually never had any negative impact on any of the 13 factors that were examined. A majority of respondents reported that employee ownership had had a positive impact on employee interest in company performance, employee loyalty, the company overall, employee motivation and job effort, employee job satisfaction, cooperation within the firm, ability to recruit new employees, employee turnover, and company profitability.

These positive CEO perceptions are supported by evidence on actual employee performance recently collected by Renaud, St-Onge, and Magnan (2000). They found that participation in a stock purchase plan significantly improved worker performance at a major Canadian financial institution.

In the Long (1991) study, several factors differentiated successful employee stock plans from less successful ones. The perceived impact of employee ownership increased with the proportion of the employees who held shares, the proportion of the firm owned by employees, and the degree of employee consultation in the development of the share plan. As will be seen, a participative company culture also appears to be a key factor in success.

Beyond CEO perceptions, is there hard evidence that employee stock plans affect the performance of the firm overall? Although no large-scale studies of this subject have been conducted in Canada, numerous studies have been conducted in the United States. In general, the results range from moderately positive to neutral (but rarely negative), when employee ownership is considered on its own (Doucouliagos, 1995; Blasi, Conte, and Kruse, 1996). For example, publicly traded firms with at least 10 percent employee ownership outperformed the market (by about 18 percent) in share price appreciation during the period 1992 to 1998 (Hollod, 1998), although not every firm with significant employee ownership did so.

However, when combined with employee participation, the results of employee ownership become dramatic. For example, a study by Rosen and Quarrey (1987) that compared the performance of a set of firms before and after they introduced employee share ownership with a matched sample of conventional firms revealed no significant differences between the two sets of firms. But when they compared firms that introduced employee ownership and practised employee participation in decision making, they found that the employee-ownership firms grew 11 to 17 percent faster than their competitors. Other studies have found similar results (Logue and Rogers, 1989; Kardas, Gale, Marens, Sommers, and Winther, 1994). Perhaps reflecting this better performance, firms that combine ownership with employee participation were also found to provide a significantly greater financial return (including both employment earnings and stock earnings) to their employees than comparable conventional firms (Kardas, Scharf, and Keogh, 1998).

What are the results of introducing stock options? Some dramatic results have been reported. For example, at the hamburger chain Wendy's International, annual turnover of assistant crew managers has dropped from 60 to 38 percent since the assistant managers were granted stock options (Capell, 1996). The company believes that the reduced turnover among assistant managers has also been responsible for significantly reduced turnover among crew members.

A major study, using a matched sample longitudinal design, has recently been conducted by researchers from Rutgers University (Blasi, Kruse, Sesil, and Kroumova, 2000). They found that firms that adopted broad-based stock option programs were more productive—by about 6.3 percent—than comparable firms even before they adopted their programs. However, in the period subsequent to adoption, stock option companies more than doubled their productivity advantage (to 14 percent) over their competitors.

However, some market analysts have argued that extensive use of stock options can dilute the returns enjoyed by other stockholders, if the options are exercised (if not exercised, they have no impact, of course). The Rutgers team also addressed this question, and found that returns to shareholders were not reduced, and some of the analyses indicated that returns on assets were greater than in other firms. (Interestingly, these positive results may not hold true for executive stock option plans, as will be discussed in Chapter 8.)

One further issue is the impact of stock option plans on employee earnings. Many stories circulate about how new dot-com companies attract employees by providing stock options in lieu of competitive salaries. To what extent do broad-based stock options substitute for conventional employee earnings? The Rutgers team found that employees in stock option companies actually earned *more* than those in comparable companies (about 8 percent more) before adoption of stock options, and that this difference was unchanged after adoption of stock options. Thus, employees were not giving up any conventional earnings in return for the stock options. Since there was no net substitution effect, employee gains from their stock options would serve to increase the difference in total employee earnings between stock option firms and other firms.

APPLICABILITY OF EMPLOYEE STOCK PLANS

As with profit sharing, employee stock plans fit best with high-involvement organizations. In fact, the idea of ownership fits even better with high-involvement organizations than profit sharing does, because it connotes a greater degree of unity of purpose between employees and the other owners. It also carries expectations about information and control rights. Of the four elements Lawler (1992) deems essential for a high-involvement organization, employee ownership has the potential to deliver three of them to employees: power, information, and rewards (Lawler's other key element is knowledge).

Employee stock plans may hold some benefits for human relations organizations, especially if they are regarded by employees as an attractive part of the compensation system. They may help to retain employees and foster positive group norms. But because these organizations will not likely provide the opportunities for participation, nor the information and training to make this participation effective, the positive consequences are likely to be limited. There is also the risk of damage to morale if stock prices drop.

Given the adversarial nature of employee–management relations usually prevailing in classical organizations, employee stock ownership is not likely to be offered by classical managers, nor would it be greeted with much enthusiasm by employees, especially if they are required to give up something to acquire the shares. Unless the stock plan is very generous, there is not likely to be much uptake among employees. If stock bonuses or options are granted outright, employees in a classical firm will likely sell their shares at the first possible opportunity.

Employees in classical firms who do retain their shares and who attempt to improve company performance are likely to experience hostility from their peers, since co-workers will likely be concerned that productivity increases may lead to negative consequences such as layoffs. Attempts to increase employee involvement in decision making will likely be met by indifference or resistance from classical managers, since these managers are unlikely to believe that the workers are capable of making useful suggestions or participating responsibly in the decision-making process. These attitudes will likely lead to frustration on the part of employee-owners.

OTHER ORGANIZATION PERFORMANCE PLANS

In recent years, many companies have been experimenting with other reward plans based on organization performance. One new type of plan is known as **long-term incentives (LTIs)**. They are generally limited to top management, on the assumption that "only high level executives are in a position to significantly impact the long-term financial performance of the corporation" (Peck, 1995: 6). In essence, these plans are set up so that a payout is contingent on the achievement of three- to five-year performance goals.

Long-term compensation traditionally has typically involved stock options and stock grants. But LTIs may also utilize performance units rather than shares. A **performance unit plan** grants an organizational member (usually an executive) a number of performance units, each of which carries a monetary value that will be realized if certain performance targets are met. There are two ways to establish a value for these units. One way is to issue units where the value of each unit is constant, but the number of units actually

long-term incentives (LTIs) a type of performance pay in which the incentives are tied to an organizational performance horizon that ranges beyond one year, often three to five years

performance unit plan a long-term incentive in which the bonus amounts are expressed in units for which the monetary value will fluctuate, depending on degree of goal accomplishment

performance share plan
a long-term incentive in
which the bonus amounts
are expressed in company
shares

payable depends on the degree of attainment of targeted goals. The second way is to vary the value of each unit based on the degree of goal attainment.

A **performance share plan** uses company shares instead of units. Depending on the degree of goal attainment, the individual will receive a certain number of company shares at the end of the performance period. This plan has a double-barrelled incentive: to meet targeted goals and to increase company share value.

The main reasons for developing LTIs stem from the perceived inadequacy of the traditional long-term performance bonus, stock options. During the 1970s, company earnings continued to increase, but stock prices remained static or declined. Therefore, executives might perform well but not receive any incentive award for this performance. Conversely, in a "bull" market, executive pay could escalate dramatically, regardless of actual firm or executive performance.

This problem resulted in the development of the performance unit plan. Types of goals used can vary. For example, some firms use profit and growth goals. One manufacturing firm uses return on assets and earnings per share relative to industry averages (Peck, 1995). Some companies use nonfinancial measures, including technology adoption, customer service, and workforce talent.

As with stock options, LTIs were originally granted only to the three or four top executives (Peck, 1995). But in 1996 a major departure from this practice occcurred when apparel giant Levi Strauss announced a six-year long-term incentive plan that included *all* employees (*Star-Phoenix*, 1996). If, by the year 2001, the company had achieved a cash flow target of $7.6 billion, all employees would receive an extra year's pay. If the company had achieved a cash flow of $5 billion, a partial payout would be made. (A cash flow target differs from net income [profitability] because it is not affected by complicated accounting procedures, such as provisions for amortization of capital and provisions for taxes.)

So, will this program be motivational and produce results? Let's use our behavioural principles to examine this question. To be motivated, employees will need to see the potential reward as significant. No problem there! They will also have to see the goal as realistic. That depends on communication and whether the goal is in fact a realistic one. Employees will also have to believe that they will actually receive the reward if the goal is achieved. Much can happen in six years—some people will quit, others may be terminated, and some will retire before the six years are up. For these people, there may not be much direct motivation because they do not expect to be there to receive the reward. Finally, for the incentive to add value, employees will need to be able to identify and effectively perform new behaviours that will contribute to achievement of the goal. Clearly, there are a lot of "ifs" in an LTI program.

So, what actually happened at Levi Strauss? Due to a variety of factors, including low-cost foreign competition and management difficulties at the top of the firm, company performance actually declined steadily from 1996, and by 1999 the company was so far from meeting its LTI goals that the bonus program was cancelled (Schoenberger, 2000). This illustrates one of the problems of long-term incentives—it is very hard to predict what will be a reasonable goal three to four years in the future. If the goal is too ambitious, and becomes seen as unrealistic, no extra effort will be made to meet it; if the goal is too easy, it will no longer motivate and could still cost a lot of money in bonuses.

Nonetheless, it appears that, like the PepsiCo example with broad-based stock options, the Levi Strauss LTI example may have caused some firms to follow suit. According to the CPS, about 5 percent of Canadian firms had adopted broad-based LTIs by 2000. (On average, these programs covered 88 percent of the employees in user companies.) A much larger number of firms (14 percent) had LTI plans restricted to management, but not just top management. (On average, these restricted programs covered 52 percent of managerial employees in user companies.)

Summary and Implications

Taken together, this chapter and the previous chapter have sought to examine the role that performance pay can play in a compensation strategy, to identify the choices of plans that are available, and to provide a basis on which the reader can evaluate the suitability of the various pay plans for application to a given organization. Three main types of performance pay were identified, according to whether pay was contingent on performance of the individual, the work group, or the organization as a whole.

Each type of plan has distinct advantages and disadvantages, tends to serve different objectives, and produces different consequences. Individual performance pay—which includes piece rates, sales commissions, merit pay, and targeted incentives—focuses on promoting task behaviour. Group performance pay—which includes gain sharing, goal sharing, competitive bonus plans, and pooled performance plans—promotes task behaviour, as well as positive social behaviour within groups/teams, and favourable group norms. Organization performance pay—which includes profit sharing and employee stock plans—tends to promote organizational citizenship behaviour and membership behaviour, as well as positive group norms. But it should be noted that within each of the three main types of performance pay, there are many variations, and each variation may produce somewhat different results and be appropriate in somewhat different circumstances.

Various factors influence the appropriateness of each type of performance pay. One key factor for individual performance pay is whether individuals have exclusive control over the desired performance behaviours or whether performance is dependent on collaboration with others in the organization. Another factor is the ability to separate out, measure, and price individual performance behaviours.

Group performance rewards are appropriate where good individual performance is not really possible without effective cooperation from other members of the work group or team, and where it is difficult or not practical to measure the performance of individuals. Organization-based performance pay plans are most appropriate when there is a need for cooperation between various segments of the organization. They are intended to foster a holistic perspective among organization members, and focus attention on the good of the organization as a whole.

In general, individual performance pay fits best with the classical managerial strategy, although it can cause a variety of unintended negative consequences for these organizations. Because many types of individual incentives tend to foster an adversarial employee–employer relationship, management needs to be constantly on the lookout for loopholes in the plan and for ways to close them. But this frequently requires increased inspections, monitoring, record keeping and the like, the costs of which may outweigh any positive benefits of the incentive. Given these problems, it is not surprising that many classical firms have moved away from individual incentives and output-based control systems, and choose to regulate behaviour directly, through rules and supervision.

However, by combining other elements of compensation with individual incentives, it may be possible to cancel out or moderate their negative aspects while maintaining their benefits. Some individual incentives may even be used to promote cooperation and teamwork—for example, by basing a merit bonus partly on the extent of teamwork evidenced by the individual.

It was argued that classical organizations will tend to benefit very little from group- and organization-based performance rewards because these firms do not provide the context in which employees will be willing and able to significantly affect organizational performance. Although human relations firms may realize some benefits from group- and organization-based performance pay, it was argued that high-involvement firms will benefit the most from these pay systems, since these organizations provide conditions that will allow the increased employee interest in performance that is generated by these systems to translate into increased organizational performance. These conditions include well-trained, knowledgeable employees who have ready access to the information they need to allow them to identify various actions beneficial to the organization and who are empowered to take these actions.

Now that base pay and performance pay have been covered, only one compensation component—indirect pay—remains to be examined. That task forms the focus of the next chapter.

KEY TERMS

combination plan, p. 186

competitive bonus plan, p. 184

current distribution plan, p. 186

deferred profit-sharing plan (DPSP), p. 186

employee profit-sharing plan, p. 186

EXERCISES

1. The current individual performance pay system at Alliston Instruments (in the Appendix) does not seem to be working, so management has decided to scrap it. However, they have not decided what, if anything, will replace it and have called you in to advise them. They want you to examine the various group and organization performance plans that are available and recommend the one that fits best with Alliston and the problems they are facing. In preparing your report, be sure to include the pros and cons of each approach, and why your recommended approach is the best.

2. Top management at Alliston have accepted your recommendation. Impressed with your work so far, they have authorized you to go ahead and design your recommended pay plan. In so doing, they expect you to produce a plan specific enough that it could be implemented with little or no further development. They also expect an implementation plan.

3. Examine the three profit-sharing plans described in Box 6.2. Evaluate the possible impact of each. Which do you think will be most effective and why? What additional information would be useful for you to have in order to draw firm conclusions?

4. Do you think that the Fit Stop (in the Appendix) would be a suitable organization in which to implement an organization performance plan? Explain why or why not. If the Fit Stop is suitable, what type of organization performance plan would be most appropriate? Describe the key elements of this plan, as applied to the Fit Stop.

SUGGESTED WEB SITES

Page 194: For more information on profit sharing, check the Web site of the Profit Sharing Council of America, based in Chicago: <www.psca.org>

Page 202: For a full report of the Rutgers study, and links to other information on stock plans, go to <www.nceo.org/library/optionreport.html>

Page 203: For the best source of information on all types of employee ownership plans, go to the National Center for Employee Ownership Web site (based in San Francisco): <www.nceo.org>

In Canada, there are two associations that promote and provide information about employee ownership plans: the Employee Ownership and Incentives Association, based in Vancouver <www.esopcanada.org> and the ESOP Association of Canada, based in Toronto <www.esop-canada.com>

REFERENCES

Belcher, John G. 1991. *Gain Sharing*. Houston, TX: Gulf Publishing.

Belcher, John G. 1996. *How to Design and Implement a Results Oriented Variable Pay System*. New York: American Management Association.

Betcherman, Gordon, and Kathryn McMullen. 1986. *Working with Technology: A Survey of Automation in Canada*. Ottawa: Canadian Government Publishing Centre.

Betcherman, Gordon, Norm Leckie, and Anil Verma. 1994. "HRM Innovations in Canada: Evidence from Establishment Surveys." Working Paper Series QPIR 1994-3. Kingston: Industrial Relations Centre, Queen's University.

Betcherman, Gordon, Kathryn McMullen, Norm Leckie, and Christina Caron. 1994. *The Canadian Workplace in Transition*. Kingston: IRC Press.

Bhargava, S. 1994. "Profit Sharing and the Financial Performance of Companies: Evidence from U.K. Panel Data." *The Economic Journal*, 104: 1044–56.

Blasi, Joseph, Michael Conte, and Douglas Kruse. 1996. "Employee Stock Ownership and Corporate Performance among Public Companies." *Industrial and Labor Relations Review*, 50(1): 60–79.

Blasi, Joseph, Douglas Kruse, James Sesil, and Maya Kroumova. 2000. "Broad Based Stock Options and Company Performance." *The Journal of Employee Ownership Law and Finance*, 12(3): 69–102.

Booth, Patricia L. 1994. *Challenge and Change: Embracing the Team Concept*. Ottawa: Conference Board of Canada.

Bowie-McCoy, Susan W., Ann C. Wendt, and Roger Chope. 1993. "Gain Sharing in Public Accounting: Working Smarter and Harder." *Industrial Relations*, 32(3): 432–45.

Byrne, John A. 1995. "Why Executive Compensation Continues to Increase." In Thomas Hall, ed., *Compensation: Present Practices and Future Concerns*. New York: The Conference Board, 19–20.

Capell, Kerry. 1996. "Options for Everyone." *Business Week*, July 22: 80–84.

Chaykowski, Richard, and Brian Lewis. 1995. *Compensation Practices and Outcomes in Canada and the United States*. Kingston: IRC Press.

Chelius, James, and Robert S. Smith. 1990. "Profit Sharing and

Employment Stability," *Industrial and Labor Relations Review*, 43(3): 256–74.

Cooke, William N. 1994. "Employee Participation Programs, Group-Based Incentives, and Company Performance: A Union-Nonunion Comparison." *Industrial and Labor Relations Review*, 47(3): 594–609.

Cooper, Christine, Bruno Dyck, and Norman Frohlich. 1992. "Improving the Effectiveness of Gainsharing: The Role of Fairness and Participation." *Administrative Science Quarterly*, 37(3): 471–90.

Doucouliagos, C. 1995. "Worker Participation and Productivity in Labour-Managed and Participatory Capitalist Firms: A Meta-Analysis." *Industrial and Labor Relations Review*, 49(1): 58–77.

Economist, The. 2000. "Chief Executives' Pay." September 30: 110.

Fein, Mitchell. 1981. *IMPROSHARE: An Alternative to Traditional Managing*. Hillsdale, NJ: Mitchell Fein Inc.

GAO. 1981. *Productivity Sharing Programs: Can They Contribute to Productivity Improvement?* Washington, DC: United States General Accounting Office.

Gerhart, Barry, and Charlie O. Trevor. 1996. "Employment Variability under Different Managerial Compensation Systems." *Academy of Management Journal*, 39(6): 1692–1712.

Graham-Moore, Brian, and Timothy L. Ross. 1995. *Gainsharing and Employee Involvement*. Washington, DC: BNA Books.

Heneman, Robert L., and Courtney von Hippel. 1995. "Balancing Group and Individual Rewards: Rewarding Individual Contributions to the Team." *Compensation and Benefits Review*, 27(4): 63–68.

Hollod, Lisa M. 1998. "The ACS Employee Ownership Index Update."

The Journal of Employee Ownership Law and Finance, 10(4): 105–10.

Isaac, Kerry. 1995. *Compensation Planning Outlook 1996*. Ottawa: Conference Board of Canada.

Jensen, M., and W. Meckling. 1973. "Theory of the Firm: Managerial Behavior, Agency Costs and Ownership Structure." *Financial Economics*, 3: 305–60.

Jones, Derek C., and Jeffrey Pliskin. 1991. "Unionization and the Incidence of Performance-Based Compensation: Evidence from Canada." Working Paper No. 89/4, Department of Economics, Hamilton College.

Kardas, P.A., K. Gale, R. Marens, P. Sommers, and G. Winther. 1994. "Employment and Sales Growth in Washington State Employee Owner-ship Companies: A Comparative Analysis." *The Journal of Employee Ownership Law and Finance*, 6(2): 83–131.

Kardas, P.A., A.L. Scharf, and J. Keogh. 1998. "Wealth and Income Conse-quences of Employee Ownership: A Comparative Study from Washington State." *The Journal of Employee Ownership Law and Finance*, 10(4): 3–52.

Katz, Harry C., and Noah M. Meltz. 1991. "Profit Sharing and Auto Workers' Earnings: The United States vs. Canada." *Relations industrielles/Industrial Relations*, 46(3): 515–30.

Kilpatrick, Ken, and Dawn Walton. 2000. "What a Joy to Work for Dofasco." *The Globe and Mail*, February 12: B1.

Kim, Dong-One. 1996. "Factors Influ-encing Organizational Performance in Gainsharing Programs." *Industrial Relations*, 35(2): 227–44.

Kim, Dong-One. 1999. "Determinants of the Survival of Gainsharing Programs." *Industrial and Labor Relations Review*, 53(1): 21–42.

Kim, Seongsu. 1998. "Does Profit Sharing Increase Firms' Profits?" *Journal of Labor Research*, 19(2): 351–70.

Kruse, Douglas L. 1993. *Profit Sharing: Does It Make a Difference?* Kalamazoo, MI: W.E. Upjohn Institute.

Lawler, Edward E. 1992. *The Ultimate Advantage: Creating the High Involvement Organization.* San Francisco: Jossey-Bass.

Lawler, Edward E., Susan Albers Mohrman, and Gerald E. Ledford. 1995. *Creating High Performance Organizations.* San Francisco: Jossey-Bass.

Logue, John, and Cassandra Rogers. 1989. *Employee Stock Ownership Plans in Ohio: Impact on Company Performance and Employment.* Kent, OH: Northeast Ohio Employee Ownership Center.

Long, Richard J. 1989. "Patterns of Workplace Innovation in Canada." *Relations industrielles/Industrial Relations*, 44(4): 805–26.

Long, Richard J. 1991. *Employee Profit Sharing and Share Ownership in Canada: Results of a Survey of Chief Executive Officers.* Toronto: Profit Sharing Council of Canada.

Long, Richard J. 1992. "The Incidence and Nature of Employee Profit Sharing and Share Ownership in Canada." *Relations industrielles/Industrial Relations*, 47(3): 463–88.

Long, Richard J. 1993. "The Relative Effects of New Information Technology and Employee Involvement on Productivity in Canadian Companies." *Proceedings of the Administrative Sciences Association of Canada (Organization Theory Division)*, June.

Long, Richard J. 1994. "Gain Sharing, Hierarchy, and Managers: Are They Substitutes?" *Proceedings of the Administrative Sciences Association of Canada (Organization Theory Division)*, 15(12): 51–60.

Long, Richard J. 1997. "Motives for Profit Sharing: A Study of Canadian Chief Executive Officers," *Relations industrielles/Industrial Relations*, 52(4): 712–33.

Long, Richard J. 2000. "Employee Profit Sharing: Consequences and Moderators," *Relations industrielles/Industrial Relations*, 55(3): 477–504.

Long, Richard J. 2001a. "High Involvement Management and Performance Pay in Canada: An Empirical Study." *Proceedings of the Administrative Sciences Association of Canada, Human Resources Division*, 22(9): 77–86.

Long, Richard J. 2001b. "Profit Sharing and Employee Shareholding Schemes." In Malcolm Warner, ed., *The International Encyclopedia of Business and Management.* London: Thomson Business Press.

Long, Richard J. 2002. "Performance Pay in Canada." In Michelle Brown and John S. Heywood, eds., *Paying for Performance: An International Comparison.* Armonk, NY: M.E. Sharpe.

Magnan, Michel, Sylvie St-Onge, and Marie-Pierre Lalande. 1997. "The Impact of Profit Sharing Plans on Firm Performance: An Empirical Investigation." *Proceedings of the Administrative Sciences Association of Canada (Human Resources Division)*, 18(9): 106–17.

Markham, Steven E., K. Dow Scott, and Beverly L. Little. 1992. "National Gain Sharing Study: The Importance of Industry Differences." *Compensation and Benefits Review* (August): 36–40.

McMullen, Kathryn, Norm Leckie, and C. Caron. 1993. *Innovation at Work: The Working with Technology Survey,*

1980–91. HRM Project Series. Kingston: IRC Press.

Morrison, Helen H., and Joseph S. Adams. 2001. "New Type of Phantom Equity Plan Used to Combat Employee Defections." *The Journal of Employee Ownership Law and Finance*, 13(1): 109–26.

NCEO. 2000. "Seven to Ten Million Employees Now Eligible for Stock Options." *Employee Ownership Report*, 20(3):1.

Nightingale, Donald V., and Richard J. Long. 1984. *Quality of Working Life: Gain and Equity Sharing*. Ottawa: Labour Canada.

Olson, M. 1971. *The Logic of Collective Action*. Cambridge, MA: Harvard University Press.

Peck, Charles. 1995. *Long-Term Unit/ Share Programs*. New York: The Conference Board.

Reingold, Jennifer. 1997. "Executive Pay: Special Report." *Business Week*, April 21.

Renaud, Stephane, Sylvie St-Onge, and Michel Magnan. 2000. "The Impact of Stock Purchase Plan on Employees' Individual Job Performance: The Case of a Financial Institution." *Proceedings of the Administrative Sciences Association of Canada (Human Resources Division)*, 21(9): 78–93.

Rosen, Corey, and Michael Quarrey. 1987. "How Well Is Employee Ownership Working?" *Harvard Business Review*, 65: 126–30.

Schoenberger, Karl. 2000. "Levi Strauss Stitches Together Turnaround Plan." *The Globe and Mail*, July 4: B11.

Schuster, Michael. 1984. "The Scanlon Plan: A Longitudinal Analysis." *Journal of Applied Behavioural Science*, 20(1): 23–38.

Schuster, Michael. 1985. "Models of Cooperation and Change in Union Settings." *Industrial Relations*, 24: 382–94.

Star-Phoenix. 1996. "Keep Your Pants On! Levi Offers Huge Employee Bonus." Saskatoon, June 13: C11.

Stayer, Ralph. 1990. "How I Learned to Let My Workers Lead." *Harvard Business Review*, 68(6): 65–72.

Stueck, Wendy. 2001. "Telus Options Passed Down Food Chain." *The Globe and Mail*, March 2: B1.

Toronto Stock Exchange. 1987. *Employee Share Ownership at Canada's Public Corporations*. Toronto: Toronto Stock Exchange.

Tyson, David E. 1996. *Profit Sharing in Canada: The Complete Guide to Designing and Implementing Plans That Really Work*. Toronto: John Wiley and Sons.

Wagar, Terry H., and Richard J. Long. 1995. "Profit Sharing in Canada: Incidence and Predictors." *Proceedings of the Administrative Sciences Association of Canada (Human Resources Division)*, 16(9): 97–105.

Wallace, M. 1990. *Rewards and Renewal: America's Search for Competitive Advantage through Alternative Pay Strategies*. Scottsdale, AZ: American Compensation Association.

Weitzman, Martin L. 1984. *The Share Economy*. Cambridge, MA: Harvard University Press.

Weitzman, Martin L., and Douglas L. Kruse. 1990. "Profit Sharing and Productivity." In Alan S. Blinder, ed., *Paying for Productivity: A Look at the Evidence*. Washington, DC: Brookings Institution, 95–142.

Welbourne, Theresa M., and Alice N. Andrews. 1996. "Predicting the Performance of Initial Public Offerings: Should Human Resource Management Be in the Equation?" *Academy of Management Journal*, 39(4): 891–919.

Welbourne, Theresa M., David B. Balkin, and Luis Gomez-Mejia. 1995. "Gain Sharing and Mutual Monitoring: A Combined Agency-Organizational Justice Interpretation." *Academy of Management Journal*, 38(3): 881–99.

Welbourne, Theresa M., and Daniel M. Cable. 1995. "Group Incentives and Pay Satisfaction: Understanding the Relationship through an Identity Theory Perspective." *Human Relations*, 48(6): 711–26.

Welbourne, Theresa M., and Luis R. Gomez-Mejia. 1991. "Team Incentives in the Workplace." In Milton L. Rock and Lance A. Berger, eds., *The Compensation Handbook*. New York: McGraw-Hill, 236–47.

7

INDIRECT PAY

CHAPTER GOALS

By the end of this chapter, you should be able to:

1. Define indirect pay, and describe the possible motives for using it.
2. Discuss the advantages and disadvantages of indirect pay.
3. Identify the six major categories of employee benefits, and the specific types of benefits included in each category.
4. Discuss the advantages and disadvantages of fixed vs. flexible benefits, and the circumstances in which each would be most appropriate.
5. Describe the issues that must be addressed in the process of designing a benefit system.
6. Discuss how your managerial strategy may affect the type of indirect pay that you might choose.

Introduction

Picture this. It is mid-morning, and you are at the Vancouver head office of a major Canadian computer software company. Some employees are in a nearby kitchen area helping themselves to a late breakfast of bagels and cheese, cereal, or other breakfast items—all provided free to employees at a cost to the company of more than $20 000 per month. That's a lot of corn flakes! Also nearby, another employee is taking a ten-minute time-out on one of several large couches provided for the purpose, while other employees are working out in a fully equipped gym. In an employee lounge, an enormous log cabin is under construction, destined to become an in-house movie theatre. This is the scene at Radical Entertainment, a designer of video games for companies like Sony and Microsoft, where the CEO, Ian Wilkinson, makes no apology for these expenditures—"If creating a good place to work means that people who work here will be inspired and that they will stay with us, then it's worth the cost" (Chisholm, 2001: 35).

The perks are a little more conventional at Calgary-based Imperial Oil, where employees receive, at no cost to them, a pension plan, life and accident insurance, disability benefits, three to six weeks' annual vacation, free tuition on any work-related course they may wish to take, payment of tuition fees for dependent children, and a savings plan in which the company matches employee contributions. The company also offers, on a shared-cost basis, supplemental medical coverage, dental coverage, additional life insurance, long-term income protection, and 75 percent payment of any approved physical fitness programs taken by an employee. These features cost Imperial a lot of money. So why provide them? Many companies don't. Why not keep things simple and just use direct pay?

In Canada, indirect pay (often known as "employee benefits") constitutes a major expense for many firms. According to the Compensation Practices Survey, indirect pay averaged 16 percent of total compensation in private-sector firms, although this ranged from 19 percent in the resource industry down to 9 percent in the accommodation/food industry, where only 50 percent of employers provided any benefits beyond the statutory minimum. In her sample of somewhat larger Canadian organizations, Baarda (2000) found benefits constituted an average of 19.7 percent of total compensation. Besides a larger firm size, her sample included public-sector organizations, which traditionally have provided more benefits, on average, than private-sector firms.

So, what do employers hope to gain from these expenditures? Why do some employers invest heavily in indirect pay while others provide only the minimum required by law? In fact, why bother to use indirect pay at all? Is indirect pay really just a costly frill, or can it play a significant role in furthering key compensation objectives? If so, how?

These are important questions, and it is the purpose of this chapter to address them. To start this process, we will first define indirect pay, next examine why firms might or might not want to utilize it, and then briefly discuss what we know about the impact and effects of indirect pay. Next, the chapter will identify six major categories of indirect pay and describe the specific employee benefits that are included in each category. Following that, the issue of whether to use flexible or fixed benefit systems will be discussed, and the chapter will conclude with an outline of the issues that need to be dealt with when setting up an employee benefit system.

WHAT IS INDIRECT PAY?

What kinds of items are classified as indirect pay? Basically, **indirect pay** can be anything that costs the employer money, addresses some type of employee need (thus conferring some type of "benefit" on the employee), and is not included as part of base or performance pay. There are six main types or categories of indirect pay:

> **indirect pay** any type of employer-provided reward (or "benefit") that serves an employee need but is not part of base or performance pay

1. benefits that are mandated by law, including employer contributions to the Canada/Quebec Pension Plan, Employment Insurance, and Workers' Compensation Benefits;

2. deferred income plans, more commonly known as retirement or pension plans;

3. health and life insurance;

4. pay for time not worked, such as paid holidays and leaves;

5. various employee services, ranging from psychological counselling to food services;

6. a variety of miscellaneous benefits, which may range from provision of company cars to purchase discounts on company products or services.

Beyond the specific items to be included, an indirect pay system may vary in several other ways. One key aspect is whether employees have some choice about what benefits they will receive (a flexible benefit system) or whether they do not (a fixed benefit system). Another issue is whether a benefit is fully paid by the employer (a noncontributory benefit), or whether employees are required to share in the cost of that benefit (a contributory benefit). Yet another important aspect is whether coverage will vary for different employee groups. This chapter addresses all of these issues.

WHY USE INDIRECT PAY?

Why do firms provide indirect pay? There are seven main motives. One is competitive pressure. If competitors are offering benefits that are important to the people the firm wants to hire, then it may be necessary to offer similar benefits to attract these employees. For example, some employees would never dream of working for an employer who does not provide an adequate pension plan.

Second, in order to satisfy the security needs of their members, unions have always bargained strongly for comprehensive employee benefits, and unionized firms have had to respond to these pressures. Non-union firms may match the packages won by unions at other firms in order to remove one possible incentive for unionization, but they certainly do not always do so. On average, employees in unionized firms receive about 45 percent higher benefits than comparable non-union Canadian employees (Renaud, 1998).

Third, certain types of indirect pay receive more favourable income tax treatment than direct pay. In these cases, a firm may use indirect pay to provide a higher total amount of after-tax compensation to employees than if the firm had paid out the same number of dollars in the form of direct pay.

Fourth, many benefit items—such as medical or dental coverage—can be purchased more cheaply by the employer than the employee, due to economies of scale in purchasing these items. (Indeed, in some cases, certain employees, such as those with serious health problems, might not even be able to acquire such insurance on their own.) Again, this provides a higher level of reward to employees for the same amount of company money.

Fifth, benefits can provide a way of protecting the financial security and peace of mind of employees, which may help to maintain employee performance. When employees have concerns about their ability to deal with health expenses they are facing, or are concerned about what would happen should they become disabled, or are experiencing a variety of personal problems, it may be difficult to focus their attention on good job performance.

Sixth, many employers feel a genuine sense of responsibility for the welfare of their employees, and want to help protect them from various types of adversity. Others may not have the same genuine concern about the welfare of their employees, but still do not want to appear hard-hearted when employees encounter financial or health problems. The benefit system can provide a systematic way for dealing with these types of problems if and when they arise.

Seventh, benefits can reinforce a particular managerial strategy. For example, the human relations strategy relies on a stable workforce. Since benefits for a given employee usually increase as their tenure increases, they can encourage membership behaviour. They can also create a sense of gratitude and obligation by employees toward their employer—a key feature of the human relations strategy. It is no coincidence that the boom in benefit plans started during the 1950s and 1960s, when human relations firms were becoming preeminent. (Indeed, employee benefits were commonly known as "employee welfare plans" in the 1950s.) Of course, there were also other favourable circumstances at the time, including good economic conditions, low unemployment, and the efforts of unions, which were beginning to turn some of their attention toward benefits rather than focusing only on direct pay.

Let's take another example of how indirect pay might be used to reinforce managerial strategy. Because of their focus on employee learning and development, firms practising a high-involvement managerial strategy will likely want to provide generous tuition reimbursement and educational leave plans.

This helps to provide the intrinsic rewards on which these organizations rely for employee retention and motivation.

Specific benefits can be used to promote various specific consequences that are beneficial to the organization. Subsidizing fitness classes or providing supplemental medical coverage may create healthier employees who miss less work due to sickness. Employee assistance programs may help employees resolve personal problems that could have a negative impact on work performance. Provision of company cars may reinforce a particular image for the salesforce. Purchase discounts on company products may avoid the potential embarrassment that could be generated if company employees purchase products from a competitor, and also help to give employees direct knowledge of the company's products. As Box 7.1 indicates, these perks can range from pork to Prozac, from vehicles to Viagra!

DISADVANTAGES OF INDIRECT PAY

So if indirect pay can provide these advantages, why doesn't every firm use it? There are numerous disadvantages of indirect pay. First and foremost, of course, is the issue of cost, which can be very substantial. Second is rigidity. Indirect pay is generally a fixed cost. Once it commits itself to providing certain benefits, a firm is liable for the costs of maintaining these benefits, even if the firm is not performing well. Once provided, it becomes very difficult (and sometimes may even be illegal) to eliminate a particular benefit. Even if the benefit is not highly valued by employees, simply eliminating it (without replacing it with something else) is likely to cause negative employee reaction. Where benefits are part of the terms and conditions of employment, it may be illegal to unilaterally discontinue them, which is the case for unionized employees.

Third, it is often difficult to develop a benefits package that is successful in meeting the true needs of employees and that does not waste money providing

---

BOX 7.1 Pick Your Perk: Pork or Prozac?

Would you rather have free pork or free Prozac? Too tranquil? How about free Viagra? As part of their indirect pay packages, employees at Big Sky Farms of Saskatchewan receive two sides of pork every year, while employees at Eli Lilly Corporation receive free Prozac (and any other drug the company manufactures). Employees at Pfizer Corporation receive free Viagra (which retails at $20 a pill!) along with other drugs it manufactures, and employees of auto manufacturers receive purchase discounts on new vehicles. In the travel business, employees are eligible for low-cost flights and package tours, as long as they select them from unsold inventory. Besides providing a valued benefit to employees, and helping employees become familiar with company products, most of these indirect benefits carry no tax liability to the employee, since companies are generally allowed to provide their own products to employees without having to declare them as taxable benefits.

---

benefits that are not valued highly by employees. Fourth, administration and communication of a benefits program can be much more costly than simply providing higher direct pay. This is particularly relevant for smaller firms, which do not have economies of scale in purchasing the benefits and administering them.

A fifth disadvantage is the generally weak link between indirect pay and specific employee task behaviour. Since most or all employees in a firm are typically covered by benefits, regardless of employee performance, and the amount of the benefits received does not vary with performance, indirect pay is the opposite of performance pay and is not a good motivator for task behaviour.

Sixth, a benefit program may succeed too well at creating employee stability, causing unhappy employees to remain with the firm simply because they do not want to forgo the generous benefits package. Seventh, certain specific benefits or the way they are administered may actually promote various types of undesirable behaviour. For example, an excessively generous or poorly designed sick leave policy may actually encourage absences by increasing the attractiveness of not coming to work, and may serve to penalize those who do come to work by requiring them to do the work of the absentees.

EXPERIENCE WITH INDIRECT PAY

Despite the large amount of money expended on benefits, there has not been a lot of research about the impact of indirect pay on employee and company performance. More than a decade ago, two prominent experts complained that "the state of knowledge about the influence of benefits on employee attitudes and behaviors is dismal" (Gerhart and Milkovich, 1992: 541), and things have not improved dramatically since then.

But we do know that satisfaction with benefits is an important component of overall pay satisfaction (Judge, 1993), and that reward dissatisfaction has very negative consequences, as we have seen in Chapter 3. Research is also quite clear about what contributes to satisfaction with the level of benefits received: employee input in system design, effective benefits communication, a sense of equity in regard to the benefits received by the self and by others, and a high employer share of benefits costs (Williams, 1995).

However, there has been virtually no evidence on whether simply eliminating the benefit system and adding the equivalent amount to salaries would actually make a greater contribution to reward satisfaction. In theory, a properly designed benefit system that provides valued benefits to employees *should* deliver more reward satisfaction than simply adding extra pay, due to tax advantages relating to benefit plans and to economies of scale in purchasing benefits. However, this proposition has never been effectively tested.

But even if true, there must be some point beyond which the value of additional indirect pay declines below the value of additional direct pay. Many employers apparently believe that this point has now been reached. After a steady upward trend since the 1960s (McKay, 1996), benefits costs appear to have peaked in 1995 at 21.4 percent of total compensation (Carlyle, 1996), and have been gradually edging down every year since then (Baarda, 2000), reaching 19.7 percent of total compensation in 2000 in large firms, and lower than that in smaller firms.

After mandatory benefits, the single largest component of indirect pay is usually pensions. There has been some research directed at examining the impact of pensions on company performance and employee job attitudes. Based on a comprehensive review of the evidence, Allen and Clark (1987) found that, on average, firms with pension plans were neither more nor less profitable than firms without pension plans, after controlling for variables such as company size.

Interestingly, these researchers also found that total compensation was higher in firms with pension plans, and therefore concluded that firms with pension plans must be more productive than firms without them, since these greater compensation costs apparently did not reduce profitability. However, when they examined productivity, they discovered no overall difference between those firms that had pension plans and those that did not. They did discover that pensions apparently had a positive effect on productivity in industries that were not highly unionized and that had high wages, younger workers, and a stable workforce.

Several effects of pensions are well established. Firms with pensions have lower turnover and their employees retire earlier than those at firms without pension plans (Allen and Clark, 1987). This can be beneficial to two types of firms—those for whom turnover is expensive and those for whom employee productivity drops off (relative to their earnings) as employees near retirement. But it should be recalled from Chapter 3 that turnover can be low due to either affective or continuance commitment. The impact of continuance commitment is for employees to exert only enough effort to meet the minimum standards necessary to avoid being fired, whereas affective commitment can lead to positive job attitudes and behaviour.

This may help to explain the earlier findings suggesting a negative impact of pensions in unionized firms—if continuance commitment is the only type of commitment generated by the firm, then high job security may allow employees to perform at the minimum standards necessary for job retention. For example, in a study of a large Canadian hospital, Luchak and Gellatly (2001) found that the pension plan generated continuance rather than affective commitment. In fact, as the amount of pension that employees would lose by quitting went up, affective commitment actually went down. What this suggests is that many employees who would prefer to quit are continuing their employment because they do not want to lose pension benefits.

This argument helps to explain why classical firms implement benefits, such as pensions, only with great reluctance, especially in unionized firms. First of all, the cost of turnover is often not high for them. Second, the job security provided by the union may make it difficult to terminate employees unless they are clearly below the minimum performance standards, and may cause performance of most employees to gravitate toward minimum levels. In contrast, it is easy to see why pensions are an asset to human relations organizations, which depend on employee stability and on a sense of gratitude and obligation on the part of employees. For them, positive social norms are sufficient to maintain employee productivity at acceptable levels. Since these firms are often not unionized, a generous benefits package can also help to forestall future unionization, which they regard as a threat to the close relationships between management and employees that they like to cultivate.

TYPES OF EMPLOYEE BENEFITS AND SERVICES

What are the specific benefits that can be included in the indirect pay component of the compensation system? This section will address that question, using the six categories of benefits identified earlier. First to be covered will be mandatory benefits, followed by pension plans, health and life insurance, pay for time not worked, employee services, and miscellaneous benefits.

MANDATORY BENEFITS

mandatory benefits
government-provided employee benefits, such as pension and employment insurance, to which employers must contribute on behalf of their employees

The federal and provincial governments require employers to contribute toward a number of government-provided employee benefits. Employers have no option but to participate in these programs, including the Canada/Quebec Pension Plan, Employment Insurance, and workers' compensation benefits (under which payments are made to cover treatment expenses and other costs for workers who are injured on the job). Employers must also provide minimum levels of statutory vacation, holiday, and rest breaks, and, in some provinces, are liable for health care taxes. These items are based on total cash compensation received by an employee. CPP/QPP, Employment Insurance, and workers' compensation premiums alone can amount to up to 10 percent of total compensation for lower-income employees. However, because of caps on the premiums, these programs amount to a much smaller percentage of compensation of more highly paid employees.

RETIREMENT INCOME AND PENSION PLANS

One of the greatest concerns for many employees is securing a stream of income for the period after they retire. Therefore, many firms offer pension plans that go beyond the basic pension plans provided by the government. All citizens are currently entitled to Old Age Security, which pays a small fixed pension; low-income pensioners also receive a Guaranteed Income Supplement; and all employees qualify for the Canada Pension Plan, with the amount of their pension dependent on their credited contributions. After mandatory benefits, company pension and retirement plans are the biggest item in most company benefits packages. There are two main types of private pension plans: defined benefit plans and defined contribution plans.

DEFINED BENEFIT PLANS

Defined benefit plans undertake to provide a specified stream of income from the time of retirement until death. The amount is usually geared to some proportion of an employee's annual earnings, modified by the number of years the employee has been covered by the plan. For example, at Imperial Oil, employees receive 1.6 percent of the average of their best three years' earnings for each year of service. Therefore, if an employee retired after 40 years of service, and had averaged $50 000 per year during his or her three best years, that person would receive an annual pension of $32 000 from Imperial, in addition to other payments from the Canada Pension Plan and Old Age Security.

defined benefit plans pension plans that provide retirement income based on a proportion of the employee's pay at the time of retirement

DEFINED CONTRIBUTION PLANS

With **defined contribution plans** (sometimes called "money purchase plans"), the employer commits to put a certain amount of money in an investment trust on behalf of each employee, and at the time of retirement the amount of annual pension that will be paid is based on whatever amount of money is in that trust. Thus, there is no guarantee about what amount the annual pension at retirement will actually be. Contributions can be defined in two ways: either as a fixed sum of money, with the amount established each year, or as a fixed proportion of company profits. In the latter case, the plan is known as a deferred profit-sharing plan (DPSP), which has been discussed in Chapter 6.

defined contribution plans pension plans that provide retirement income based on the accrued value of employer and employee contributions to the plan

Both defined benefit or defined contribution pension plans can be contributory, with employees required to make an annual contribution to the plan, or noncontributory, where employees make no contribution to the plan. (The exception is deferred profit-sharing plans, which can only be noncontributory.)

Although defined benefit plans are still the most common pension plan in Canada (Babcock and Pitcher, 2000), there has been a gradual trend away from defined benefits plans toward defined contribution plans. There are several reasons for this. A major reason has to do with inflation, which was very high in the 1970s and 1980s. As a result of inflation, the best three years of earnings would end up being far higher than the company had anticipated. As a result, money set aside over the years to fund the pension plan became insufficient to meet the obligations of the plan, and firms were forced to make large contributions to enable their pension plans to meet their obligations. There is no such problem with a defined contribution plan, as the employer's liability is limited to the amount placed into the plan.

Another source of unexpected cost for defined benefit plans occurs as life expectancies increase. This may pose a particular problem in fields in which an increasing proportion of the workforce are female, since the life expectancy of females (81.4 years at birth) is currently more than five years longer than that of males (75.8 years at birth) according to the most recent statistics (Mofina, 2001). For persons who reach age 65, the typical man can expect to live another

15 years, and the typical woman another 20 years (Ho and Robinson, 1996). This can make a big difference in the amount of money needed to fund these pensions. Moreover, if life span continues to increase, then pension liability in defined benefits plans will also increase. Box 7.2 illustrates some interesting actuarial estimates for life expectancies, and how they may relate to needs for retirement income.

Of course, the actuarial projections illustrated in Box 7.2 will vary for specific employee groups. Accountants will have a better chance of surviving to a ripe old age than coal miners. Making accurate actuarial predictions for a particular employee group and then incorporating them into the pension plan is a complex process, one that is not necessary for defined contribution plans. From an employer's point of view, defined contribution plans are much simpler than defined benefit plans.

Finally, some defined benefit plans, especially for individuals with relatively high earnings, are running into difficulty with Income Tax Act regulations in regard to the maximum payouts that are permissible under the terms of a registered pension plan. Thus, many highly paid employees with long ser-

---

BOX 7.2 Would You Take This Bet?

Picture this. You are just celebrating your 90th birthday. An obnoxious relative (how did *he* get invited to my party, you wonder) who always lords it over you because he is four years younger than you, has the poor taste to comment that he is glad to see you enjoying your birthday party so much, because it will probably be your last!

Hotly, you tell him that you plan to be around for a few more birthdays yet. He replies that if you are so sure about that, why don't you make some money from it? He offers to pay you $1000 if you make it to your 91st birthday, but you have to pay him $1000 if you don't (the money to be collected immediately and held by a third party until your demise or your 91st birthday, whichever comes first—he may be obnoxious, but he is no idiot!).

You stop to think. You are in normal health for a person of your age, but just how likely is it that you will see your next birthday? Should you take that bet?

You should! In fact, you should try to up it! According to actuarial statistics, your chances of making it to your 91st birthday are greater than 80 percent (Ho and Robinson, 1996). In fact, you could be 105 and still have a better-than-even chance of making it to your next birthday!

Next to the Japanese, Canadians have the longest life expectancy in the world. This is good news from a health perspective, but bad news from a retirement income perspective. Recent statistics indicate that only a minority of Canadians are putting away enough money to maintain their standard of living in retirement (Scott, 1997). Less than half of Canadian employees are covered by company pension plans, and many of those who are covered will not receive pensions adequate to maintain their standard of living over the 15 to 20 years, or more, of retirement they will enjoy.

But people vary in how much they value retirement income plans. Many young employees are especially prone to not worry about retirement. Some say, why worry—I'll never even make it to retirement! But just what are the odds for a 25-year-old making it to age 65? In fact, better than 80 percent for males, and nearly 90 percent for females. And if you are in normal health at age 25, and not in a hazardous occupation, the odds are much better than that! As this realization sinks in, it is likely that companies that offer pension plans will be increasingly favoured by potential employees.

---

vice in the pension plan are at risk of receiving much less than the total that their own and company contributions would normally entitle them to. Switching to a defined contribution plan (or a hybrid plan) would avoid these difficulties.

However, there are some drawbacks to defined contribution plans as well. Coward (1991) indicates that such plans are most beneficial to employees who enter these plans at a young age and have a long period of contributions. But, as he also notes, defined contribution "pensions tend to be seriously inadequate for employees who join late in life" (15). If long-term employment with single employers becomes less common, many employees may be subject to this problem. Furthermore, "the employee is saddled with the investment risk and the risk that annuity prices will be high at retirement." In essence, defined contribution plans transfer the risk of retirement income accumulation from the employer to the employee.

Hybrid Plans

Hybrid pension plans combine elements of both the defined benefit and the defined contribution pension plans. For example, some firms have a defined benefit plan, but they also allow employees to contribute to a contributory defined contribution pension plan. In some cases, firms will match employee contributions, to a certain maximum level. Often, these contributory plans are set up as group registered retirement plans. Employees are allowed to deduct their contributions from their taxable income, and the earnings of the plan will accumulate on a tax-deferred basis. Employer and employee contributions to either defined benefit plans or defined contribution plans (both of which must be registered with the government and are known as registered pension plans) are deducted from the amounts that may be contributed to a group RRSP, which have contribution limits established by the federal government. Overall, a recent survey indicated that about half of defined contribution plans are in fact implemented in conjunction with defined benefit plans (Babcock and Pitcher, 2000).

hybrid pension plans
pension plans that combine features of the defined benefit pension plan and the defined contribution pension plan

Health and Life Insurance

One of the most common and highly valued benefits is coverage in the event of health problems, including death and disability. These benefits are usually provided through some type of insurance program, and may include supplemental health insurance, dental insurance, disability insurance, life and accident insurance, and health care expense accounts.

Supplemental Health Insurance

Canadians enjoy a large number of government-sponsored medical benefits under the system generally known as "medicare." In the United States, where government-sponsored universal medical coverage does not exist, employers are expected to bear the cost of medical insurance. This cost can be staggering.

However, because of medicare, the cost to Canadian employers of providing health coverage to their employees is much lower, resulting in much lower benefits costs. Nonetheless, there are many medical services that are not covered by medicare, including optical/vision care, chiropractic treatments, and prescription drugs. In recent years, the cost of providing health insurance to employees has been increasing at 14 to 17 percent per annum, mainly due to the prescription drug component (Mozill, 2001).

DENTAL INSURANCE

Dental care insurance has expanded rapidly in the past few years. It has become popular because dental coverage is not provided under medicare, and can be a major expense (especially when it comes to orthodontic services for dependent children). It is also a highly tax-favoured benefit.

DISABILITY INSURANCE

Many employers purchase long-term disability insurance for their employees, which covers disabilities arising from nonwork-related causes. (Work-related disabilities are covered under workers' compensation benefits.) This coverage typically provides for 60 to 70 percent of normal pay, and carries on until the employee is able to return to work, reaches retirement age, or dies (in which case, there are usually benefits provided to the surviving spouse and/or dependent children).

LIFE AND ACCIDENT INSURANCE

One item included in virtually all benefit plans is term life and accident insurance. The coverage is usually expressed in terms of a multiple of annual salary (e.g., two times annual salary). Frequently, employees are given the option of increasing their coverage, either at their own expense or on a cost-shared basis. In some cases, insurance coverage is also available for family members, if the employee opts to pay the premiums for this coverage.

TAX STATUS OF INSURANCE AND PENSION BENEFITS

At this point, it is useful to summarize the tax status of the various insurance and pension benefits, and Table 7.1 does this. As can be seen, there are six aspects that may have tax implications. First, how are employer contributions treated? Are they deductible from corporate taxes, and are they considered as a taxable benefit to employees, on which income tax must be paid? If employees make contributions to the benefit, are their contributions tax-deductible? Is the item subject to a premium or sales tax that may be levied by a provincial government? In the case of pension funds, are the earnings of the fund taxable as they are accumulating? Finally, when the benefit pays out to employees, must they include it as income and pay tax on it?

As can be seen, pension plans receive favourable tax treatment, up to the limits that are imposed by the Canada Customs and Revenue Agency. Employees ultimately have to pay taxes on the payouts from these plans, but

	EMPLOYER CONTRIBUTIONS		EMPLOYEE CONTRIBUTIONS			
TABLE 7.1 THE TAX STATUS OF PENSION AND INSURANCE BENEFITS	Deductible by Employer?	Taxable for Employee?	Deductible by Employee?	Purchase of Benefit Subject to Premium or Sales Taxes?	Fund Income Is Taxable?	Benefit Payouts Taxable for Employees?
Registered Pension Plans	Yes	No	Yes	No	No	Yes
Group Registered Retirement Savings Plans	N/A	N/A	Yes	No	No	Yes
Deferred Profit-Sharing Plans	Yes	No	N/A	No	No	Yes
Health and Dental Insurance	Yes	No[1]	No	Yes[2]	N/A	No
Short-Term Disability (Self-Insured)	Yes	No	N/A	N/A	N/A	Yes
Long-Term Disability Insurance	Yes	No	No	Yes[3]	N/A	Yes/No[4]
Group Life Insurance	Yes	Yes	No	Yes[4]	N/A	No
Group Accidental Death and Dismemberment	Yes	No	No	No[5]	N/A	No

[1] Except in Quebec for provincial income tax.

[2] Applies to both insured and uninsured plans in Ontario and Quebec; only uninsured plans elsewhere.

[3] Provincial premium tax applies in all provinces; provincial sales tax in Ontario and Quebec.

[4] Yes, if premiums are paid by employer; no, if premiums are paid by employee; partially, if premiums are shared.

[5] Not subject to provincial premium tax, but subject to provincial sales taxes in Ontario and Quebec.

not until retirement, when they are likely to be in a much lower tax bracket. At retirement, employees can use the funds to purchase annuities, so that income tax is spread over a number of years rather than being payable in the year of retirement. However, it should be noted that because of RRSP legislation, individual employees can now create retirement plans that have tax benefits similar to those of company-provided plans. In the past, this was not the case, and company-provided pension plans had dramatic tax advantages over individual retirement plans.

Looking to the various types of insurance plans, we can see that they enjoy favourable tax treatment as well, especially health and dental insurance and accidental death and dismemberment insurance. In both cases, employees do not pay tax either on the employer contributions for these plans or on the benefits that are paid out. Since employee contributions to these plans are not tax-deductible, but employer contributions are, it makes sense for the company to provide these plans.

Look at it this way. Suppose that an employer currently pays $800 per employee to support a dental plan. If the employer decided to instead give the $800 directly to each employee to purchase dental coverage, the employee would lose as much as $400 of this to federal and provincial income taxes, leaving only $400 to purchase the dental coverage. On top of this, the employee would have to pay a higher price for the coverage itself, since individual plans typically cost much more than company plans. In fact, most employees would not purchase dental coverage at all, leaving them liable to major dental bills that may arise. Indeed, if an employer is not willing to provide the coverage, employees would be much better off to have their pay reduced and have their employer pay this money toward health or dental coverage.

In contrast, employer-provided long-term disability insurance may seem tax-neutral, in the sense that employees are not liable for taxes on employer contributions to these plans but are liable for tax on any benefits received. (On the other hand, if the employees pay for these plans, employee contributions are not tax-deductible, but any benefits received are not taxable.) They are certainly not as beneficial as company-provided health and dental plans. However, since disability payments are typically only some portion of normal salary, then an employee who is unfortunate enough to receive these benefits will pay less tax on them than on the premiums paid by the company. Furthermore, company-provided plans amount to a type of tax deferral, which is always advantageous to employees. Finally, the great majority of employees will be lucky enough never to receive these payments, and it is far better for them to have the employer purchase the coverage with pre-tax money than for the employee to have to purchase the coverage with after-tax money.

Group life insurance has become less tax-favoured as the tax rules have changed. It is the only one of these benefits in which employer contributions must be considered as a taxable benefit and fully included as income for tax purposes. (However, the benefits paid out are not taxable.) There is therefore no tax advantage in the employer purchasing the coverage. However, because employers receive much more favourable rates on purchase of this insurance, a company-provided plan (whether or not the employer or employees pay the premiums) will still be beneficial to employees.

HEALTH CARE EXPENSE ACCOUNTS

health care expense account a tax-favoured employee benefit that allows employees to utilize employer-provided health care credits to purchase a wide array of health care services

Due to quirks of the tax system just discussed, an option that has become popular in recent years is known as a **health care expense account** (McKay, 1996).

Under this concept, employers place a certain amount of money (health care expense credits) in a separate account for each employee. Employees may then draw on their individual accounts to cover a wide variety of health care expenses not covered by their other plans, including nonprescription drugs, services that are only partly reimbursed under other plans, cosmetic surgery, and even the deductible amounts from other insurance plans. The key advantage of this benefit is that while employer contributions are still fully deductible for the employer, the funds paid to each employee are not taxable at any point—not when they are placed in the health care account, and not when they are received by employees (except in Quebec, where reimbursements to employees are subject to provincial income tax). This is a very significant tax benefit.

Health care expense accounts have shown a dramatic surge in popularity in recent years (Mozill, 2001). Aside from the tax advantages, employers like the idea of having a fixed amount that they set for health coverage. In conventional health insurance plans, as costs increase, the employer must either pay them, pass them along to employees, or reduce coverage—all unpopular options. With the health care expense account, the employer has the option of not adjusting the health care credits, or doing so at a lower rate. Of course, the result of this may be employee discontent if the plan is no longer able to cover their needs.

PAY FOR TIME NOT WORKED

This awkward-sounding but descriptive term is used to cover a variety of circumstances in which employees receive pay even though they are not actually working. As discussed earlier, some of this is mandatory, including basic vacations, statutory holidays, and some rest breaks. But many firms go beyond these mandatory levels and provide pay for additional holidays, for sickness and personal leave, for educational and other types of leave, and for severance pay.

pay for time not worked an employee benefit that covers a wide array of different types of employee absences from work

VACATIONS, HOLIDAYS, AND REST BREAKS

Most major employers go beyond the two or three weeks' vacation mandated by law (depending on the jurisdiction), and the nine statutory holidays. Most employers give 11 to 13 paid holidays on fixed dates and up to three paid "floater" holidays that can be moved around from year to year. Most workplaces also give two paid rest breaks of 15–20 minutes (besides an unpaid lunch break) during a seven- or eight-hour day.

One new twist on vacations is the concept of "vacation buying or selling." Some firms allow employees to "buy" additional vacation days by forgoing the pay for these days. On the other side of this is the concept of vacation "selling," where employees "sell" vacation days that they don't intend to use back to the employer. Essentially, vacation buying or selling simply provides some additional flexibility to employees.

Sickness, Compassionate, and Personal Absences

Most firms provide pay continuation for short-term absences from work due to illness, or for other specified reasons, such as the death of a family member. Some firms have formal plans that allot a certain number of allowable sick days in a given period, and absences beyond these limits may not be paid. In some cases sick days can accumulate beyond a year; in most cases they cannot. In other cases, employers do not formally provide sick leave, but do not dock absences if the missing time is made up at some future time. In still other cases, absences may be counted against the annual vacation allotment.

One issue here is whether the only allowable paid absences are for personal sickness, or whether other reasons (such as sickness of a child) are allowable reasons for absence under the plan. In some cases, firms are relabelling their "sick leave" days to "personal leave" days to avoid forcing employees to claim personal illness when the actual reason is an illness or personal emergency involving a family member. In other cases, employers are simply rolling all leave days together, including vacation and sick leave, and providing these as the total allowable number of paid absences. In a few cases, employers are willing to "buy back" unused leave days, so that employees who do not use all their allotted days are not penalized relative to employees who do use all of their leave days. However, it may not be wise to buy back all of these days at full rates if this creates too strong an incentive for employees to come to work even when they are seriously ill.

Many firms also offer compassionate or bereavement leaves to permit employees to attend the funerals of close family members. Most major firms also provide paid leaves for jury duty. Short-term absences to give birth or attend the birth of a child are also included here. (Longer-term maternity/paternity leaves will be discussed shortly.)

Supplemental Unemployment Benefits

supplemental unemployment benefits (SUBs) an employer-provided benefit that extends government-provided unemployment benefits

When an employee is temporarily laid off, and goes on Employment Insurance, many firms offer **supplemental unemployment benefits (SUBs)**, designed to "top up" the EI benefits to some proportion of the employee's normal pay. The usual process is for the employer to set up a fund, to which they contribute regular amounts based on the number of hours worked by employees. This fund is then used to provide the supplemental unemployment benefits to eligible employees, and may also include employees on maternity or paternity leave. The firm's liability is limited to the amount in the fund. These plans have to be approved and registered with the Employment Insurance Commission.

Parental Leaves

Some firms may also offer some period of paid maternity or paternity leave, usually in conjunction with Employment Insurance, which provides coverage for up to 50 weeks of maternity or paternity leave (but not both to the same couple at the same time). Firms may treat maternity or paternity leave in the same way as a temporary layoff, and utilize funds from their supplemental unemployment fund to top up the EI benefits to a certain proportion of normal income. Or, if the firm does not have an SUB fund, they may simply have a policy for topping up EI in the case of maternity or paternity leaves.

EDUCATIONAL AND SABBATICAL LEAVES

Some organizations have paid educational leave plans, in which employees are compensated while undertaking a full-time educational program. In some cases, full pay is provided, while in others some portion of normal pay is provided. There is normally an expectation that the employee will return to the employer after completing the educational program, and employees who don't return are usually expected to reimburse the employer for the cost of the leave. Because of their high cost, these plans are usually restricted to key individuals within the organization, and/or there may be some competitive process that awards a restricted number of paid leaves each year.

In some cases, firms will offer unpaid sabbaticals. To facilitate these, the Income Tax Act has created some opportunities for employees to defer income taxes while putting aside money for the sabbatical. Once an employer has registered a sabbatical leave plan with Canada Customs and Revenue Agency, employees may put aside a portion of their earnings each year, for a period of three to five years prior to the sabbatical. For example, school teachers in Toronto may set aside a fifth of their annual income for four years, and then receive this money in the fifth (sabbatical) year. There are two tax advantages to this plan. First, the earnings from the deferred salary fund can accumulate tax-free until the funds are withdrawn. Second, the total amount of tax paid is reduced, because income is being "smoothed." Instead of being taxed for four years at a higher marginal rate (and then having zero income in the sabbatical year), income is spread evenly over the five-year period.

SEVERANCE PAY

The ultimate form of pay for time not worked is severance pay. The federal and provincial governments have statutory requirements either for notice to be provided when terminating employees without cause or for pay in lieu of this notice, but these requirements can be quite minimal. For example, for employers covered by the federal jurisdiction, the only requirement is for two weeks' notice, as long as an employee has been employed for at least three months. In Ontario, the requirement is generally a week's notice (or pay in lieu) for each year of service up to eight years, to a maximum of eight weeks. Unionized firms typically have a formula that goes beyond these minimums for providing a lump-sum payment to employees who receive permanent terminations. At the executive level, extensive severance packages (often referred to as "golden parachutes") are often negotiated on an individual basis at the time of employment.

Technically, if an employee has been dismissed for cause, no notice or severance pay is required (England and Wood, 2001). However, unless cause can be proven, an employer may end up with a wrongful-dismissal suit against them and be required to pay a substantial severance award if they lose the suit. There are no hard-and-fast rules that specify the minimum notice for a given employee. The following would seem to be the minimal amounts for fair severance in cases of termination without cause: hourly paid workers, one week per year of service, two-week minimum; administrative support staff, two weeks per year of service, one-month minimum; technical, professional, supervisory, and middle management, three weeks per year of service, three-month minimum; senior management, four weeks per year of service. For all groups the maximum is 24 months.

However, these guidelines can be modified by many factors. In deciding a reasonable notice period, the courts take four main factors into account: (1) the employee's age, (2) the length of service, (3) the character of the employment, and (4) the availability of similar employment. Essentially, the more difficult it will be for an employee to find similar employment, the longer the notice period. Another factor is enticement. Recently, Ontario courts have awarded a month per year even to clerical employees (Litherland, 2000). If an employer entices an employee away from secure employment in a different region of the country, the notice period goes up dramatically, even for new employees or those who have not yet started their employment.

EMPLOYEE SERVICES

Employee services are often not included in traditional surveys of employee benefits but are frequently of considerable value to employees and may produce some favourable spinoffs for the organization. A major advantage of these services is that most are tax-deductible to the employer, but are not subject to income tax for employees. This section will discuss several of the most common and important employee services.

EMPLOYEE ASSISTANCE PROGRAMS

employee assistance programs (EAPs) employer-provided programs to help employees deal with a variety of personal problems

Many firms have established **employee assistance programs (EAPs)** to help employees deal with personal problems that have the potential to affect their work performance. About 85 percent of major Canadian firms had EAPs in 2000, up from 58 percent in 1990 (Baarda, 2000). A prominent example of the problems covered by EAPs is abuse of alcohol, drugs, and other substances. In these cases, the firm may contract the services of professional counsellors or other specialists, who help employees to diagnose their problems and chart a course of action for dealing with them. This course of action may include paid leave to attend alcohol or drug treatment centres, and coverage of the costs of these programs. EAPs may also deal with other problems as well, such as stress, workplace conflict, and marital, family, or financial problems, either through the use of in-house counsellors or through referrals to outside specialists. Some organizations maintain 24-hour counselling hotlines.

There are obvious advantages to the employer if the EAP can help to solve these problems, since many of them have the potential to severely affect work performance or cause safety problems. Unresolved, these problems may also cause valued employees to quit the firm. In some cases, EAPs provide an alternative to simply firing troubled employees, an act which may be seen as hard-hearted and may be damaging to employee morale. Indeed, in order to effectively dismiss a problem employee, and to avoid or win an unjust dismissal suit, it may be necessary to show that the firm did all it could to solve the problem, and employee assistance programs can be used as evidence that the firm attempted to do so.

RECREATIONAL SERVICES

Some organizations purchase memberships in recreational clubs or sports facilities that can be used by employees and their families. Some organizations also sponsor company sports teams, or may help support other types of recreational programs. Some firms provide an on-site fitness centre or exercise room. In general, these are nontaxable benefits for employees.

FOOD SERVICES

Many organizations offer various types of subsidized food services at company facilities. This may be necessary in areas where other types of food services are not readily available. An advantage of on-site food services is that employees do not need to consume scarce break time by leaving the company premises. Subsidized food services constitute a taxable benefit for employees only if prices are set "unreasonably low."

CHILD CARE/ELDERCARE SERVICES

A key issue for many employees with young children is obtaining suitable child care. Over half (54 percent) of major Canadian employers have some type of program to support child care. The most common program is information and referral services, but 11 percent provide financial assistance, 11 percent provide emergency child care, and 14 percent provide either on-site or off-site child care (Baarda, 2000). Subsidies are sometimes provided to the child care centre to reduce the costs to employees. These subsidies are not considered a taxable benefit. At Ford Motors in Oakville, Ontario, the company offers an on-site daycare centre, and provides a $2000-per-child subsidy for children enrolled in it (Galt, 2001).

At the other end of the spectrum, some employees have the responsibility for care of aged parents or other elderly relatives. Nearly half (48 percent) of firms now provide some type of eldercare program, although most programs simply provide information and referral services (Baarda, 2000). About 8 percent are providing some type of financial assistance, including provision of subsidized services. Given the demographic trends in Canada, the issue of eldercare will be of growing importance to many employees in the near future, and if not dealt with effectively, has the potential to lead to a variety of problems for both employee and employer.

Financial or Legal Services

As retirement and financial planning becomes more and more complex, some firms are providing access to financial planners in order to help employees make good decisions. This service is most likely to be found in firms offering flexible benefits in order to help employees understand the ramifications of the different choices they may have.

In a few companies, prepaid legal services are provided. There are two main types of plans. Access plans provide free telephone or office consultation, document review, and discounts on fees for more complex matters. Comprehensive plans cover matters such as real estate transactions, divorce cases, and civil and criminal cases.

Outplacement Services

Finally, some firms provide assistance to employees who are being terminated, beyond simply awarding severance pay. This assistance may include advice on how to secure new employment and how to manage financial affairs until new employment is found, and counselling to ease the shock of termination. Although these services will, by definition, not be utilized by continuing employees, employees will note whether terminated employees are being treated fairly, and this will condition their attitudes toward the employer; thus, provision of these services has a positive impact beyond the direct recipients.

Other Benefits

A wide array of other benefits can be provided, and these are often geared to the type of work a given employee does, or the type of industry in which the firm operates. For example, sales personnel who must travel extensively by automobile are frequently provided with a vehicle, which can also serve personal uses. Retailers may provide discounts on their products. Banks may provide subsidized loans. There are endless possibilities, and this section will briefly highlight just a few of the most common.

Use of Company Vehicle

In the past, a company-provided automobile that could be utilized for personal as well as business use was a major benefit. However, recent changes in income tax legislation have made this benefit less attractive, since employees are now required to declare the personal-use portion of the automobile as a taxable benefit. Nonetheless, since companies that lease a large number of vehicles for their employees may be able to negotiate favourable lease terms, it may still be advantageous for employees to utilize a company-provided vehicle for personal use. In addition, transportation to and from the job site may not be considered personal use, so even if an employee is permitted to use the vehicle only for transportation from home to the job site, and during the workday, this may still be a significant benefit—and a nontaxed one.

PRODUCT OR SERVICE DISCOUNTS

Many organizations offer their products or services to employees at a discount. As discussed earlier (see Box 7.1), this may be a significant financial benefit to employees, and may also serve organizational objectives.

HOUSING OR MORTGAGE SUBSIDIES

Employers who require employees to relocate to remote areas frequently provide housing at a nominal rate. Some provide mortgage subsidies or low-interest loans. Unless the employer is a financial institution, the mortgage or loan subsidies are considered as a taxable benefit for the employee.

PROVISION OF WORK CLOTHING OR EQUIPMENT

Firms that require their employees to wear uniforms may provide these uniforms to employees as a nontaxable benefit. Similarly, equipment or tools that are used in the course of performing job duties are also deemed nontaxable benefits. One particular piece of equipment that might be highly valued is a home computer, and a number of major firms have implemented programs to provide them. For example, in February 2000, Ford Motor Company announced a program to offer all its 350 000 workers, including 17 000 in Canada, a home computer, colour printer, and Internet access, for an employee cost of approximately $5 per month (*Maclean's*, 2000). Besides serving as an attractive benefit, Ford is hoping that the program will encourage more computer-literate employees, and that this will eventually benefit the company.

EMPLOYEE SAVINGS PLANS

In order to promote the financial stability of their employees, many firms offer some type of employee savings plan, such as the Royal Bank plan described in Chapter 6. As another example, Imperial Oil offers a plan whereby employees may place up to 30 percent of their annual earnings in a savings plans. The company also provides some matching contributions, depending on length of service. After one year, the company matches 1 percent, after two years, 2 percent, and then up to 5 percent after five years. That is, for a five-year employee who contributes 5 percent of her or his pay to the savings plan, the company will contribute 5 percent. However, unless the savings plan involves a registered retirement savings plan, and the employee has not exceeded the allowable contribution limit, the company contribution is subject to income tax.

TUITION REIMBURSEMENTS

In an era of constant change, one benefit of particular value to many employees is tuition reimbursement. Some firms will reimburse full tuition and book expenses for any work-related course undertaken by employees. Employers vary in how broadly they define "work-related," with some employers reimbursing virtually any course undertaken by an employee, and others reimbursing only a very narrow set of courses that are directly related to the employee's job. As long as the employer is deemed to benefit more than the employee from the training, the training subsidies are not considered a taxable benefit.

With the increased costs of education, one benefit that employees may find attractive is educational assistance for dependent children. Some firms offer a fixed number of scholarships that are awarded on a competitive basis. Others undertake to provide tuition assistance to all dependent children who meet their eligibility requirements. A major advantage of these plans is that the awards are made directly to the student, rather than the parent, and are therefore taxable for the student, not the parent/employee. Since the student will typically have much lower income than the parent/employee, this reduces the taxes dramatically.

EMPLOYEE EXPENSE ACCOUNTS

employee expense account an employer-provided benefit that provides a fund from which individual employees can draw to cover work-related expenses

Employee expense accounts are similar to health care expense accounts, but they are used to reimburse employees for expenses they incur in the course of their employment. For example, some universities have established nontaxable professional allowance accounts under which faculty can be reimbursed for various expenses they incur in their work. Care needs to be taken to ensure that the system is set up to comply with tax laws. For example, if a faculty member purchases a computer and is reimbursed for it, this reimbursement is taxable if the faculty member holds title (ownership) to the computer. But if the university holds title to the computer, the reimbursement is not taxable.

FIXED VS. FLEXIBLE BENEFIT SYSTEMS

How would you like to be able to pick and choose among the benefits your firm offers, selecting more of the benefits that are of greater value to you and less or none of benefits that are of little value to you, or possibly even forgoing some benefits and receiving the equivalent in cash? Some Canadian employers are now giving employees this flexibility, including such well-known firms as IBM Canada, Chrysler, Du Pont, Husky Oil, and the Potash Corporation of Saskatchewan. The purpose of this section is to provide an understanding of the factors involved in deciding whether to utilize a fixed or flexible benefit system. After briefly defining the main types of benefit systems, we will examine the forces for and against these plans, along with the results of flexible benefit systems when they have been implemented.

TYPES OF BENEFIT SYSTEMS

FIXED BENEFIT SYSTEMS

Under fixed benefit plans, which have been the norm in the past, all employees are covered by a standard package of benefits. The advantages of this approach are many, including simplicity, economies of scale in purchasing the benefits, relatively low administrative costs, and ease in communicating the plan to employees. The key disadvantage of this approach is that it does not recognize differences among employees in how they will value different benefits. Also, fixed benefit plans have a tendency to grow and grow, as existing benefits escalate in cost, or as new benefits are brought on stream to meet the diverse needs of the workforce. Existing benefits are seldom dropped to make way for the new benefits.

fixed benefit system an employee benefit plan that provides a standard set of benefits to all those covered by the plan

SEMI-FLEXIBLE BENEFIT SYSTEMS

Most benefit systems are not entirely fixed. There are a variety of ways of making fixed systems somewhat more flexible. These approaches involve a "core" set of benefits, to which employees may be allowed to "add on" additional levels of coverage, or even additional benefit options, at their own expense. Another approach is the "modular plan," in which employees are given the choice between two or more different fixed benefits packages, each of which is designed to be of similar cost to the company.

FLEXIBLE BENEFIT SYSTEMS

The distinguishing feature of a flexible benefit plan is that employees not only have control over the disposition of funds that they themselves provide, but they are also able to direct the use of the employer's contributions. Under a fully flexible approach, there is no core or standardized benefits package. Instead, employees are given a set of "flexible credits" they can use to "purchase" the combination of benefits that best suits them. An example of this approach is the "Beneflex" system at telecommunications giant Telus Corporation, under which an employee can select several different levels of coverage (including none) for each of numerous options. Employees can also use real money to purchase higher levels of benefits in certain areas, after their "flexible credits" run out, or they can receive cash for any unused flexible credits.

flexible benefit system an employee benefit plan that allows employees to allocate employer-provided credits to purchase the benefits of most value to them

In 1984, Cominco, a Vancouver-based mining company, introduced "Flex-Com," Canada's first flexible benefit plan (McKay, 1996). The plan applies to the firm's 2000 non-union employees and was offered as part of a program to help satisfy the benefits needs of these employees, who had suffered wage cutbacks in previous years due to the company's financial difficulties.

The plan was developed by a management team and then "test-marketed" on a subsample of employees, resulting in some modification to the plan. Essentially, the existing fixed benefit plan was divided into two components—a core section and an options section. The resulting savings were given back to the employees in the form of flexible credits, which could be used to purchase any combination of options they desired. (Employees are also allowed the option of taking any unused credits in cash, although they must then pay income tax on this money.) Sufficient credits were provided that employees could buy back their existing benefits package if they wished.

About 25 percent chose to do so, and 75 percent ended up with a benefits package different from what they initially had. Employees are allowed to re-adjust their program annually.

Overall, the company has been happy with the flexible benefit plan and believes that employees have also been happy with it (McKay, 1996). Over time, Cominco has added several new elements to the plan, including a health care expense account. In order to assess whether the flexible plan is costing more than the previous plan, every two or three years the company determines what the previous fixed plan would now be costing the company. They have found that the flex plan is always within 5 percent of this amount, suggesting that the flex plan has served to limit cost increases.

FORCES FOR AND AGAINST FLEXIBLE BENEFIT SYSTEMS

During the early 1990s, flexible benefit plans were the fastest-growing pay innovation in Canada, as the number of major Canadian firms with flex plans increased from 10 percent in 1990 to 27 percent in 1996 (Carlyle, 1996). Since then, growth has occurred much more slowly, and by 2000, just over 31 percent of major Canadian firms had flex plans (Baarda, 2000), and about 22 percent of the private-sector firms in the more representative Compensation Practices Survey. Despite this recent levelling off in adoption, the overall picture has been one of dramatic growth. What have been the forces responsible for this growth?

FORCES PROMOTING FLEXIBLE BENEFITS

As was the case for stock options, the United States has been the forerunner in the use of flexible benefits. For example, by 1995, 85 percent of major U.S. firms had adopted flex plans, in contrast to only about 20 percent of Canadian major employers at that time (McKay, 1996), and by now only a small minority of major U.S. firms do not have flex plans. Four main forces appear to have promoted the growth of flexible benefits in the United States: (1) escalating benefits costs, (2) a more diverse workforce, (3) a desire to shift employee perceptions of benefits away from an entitlement perspective, and (4) major tax advantages. These factors are probably also valid in Canada, with the exception of tax advantages, which are not significant in this country. Other motives may include a fit with a high-involvement managerial strategy and a perception that employees will find flex benefits attractive, thus providing a competitive edge for employee recruitment and retention. Finally, firms that have been reluctant to implement fixed benefit plans because they are concerned about being locked into escalating costs may find flex plans more appealing.

Without doubt, the most important force driving the adoption of flex plans in the United States is escalating benefits costs, which are driven by health insurance costs. Between the mid-1960s and the mid-1990s, the cost of benefits in the United States rose from 10 percent of total compensation to 29 percent (Hackett, 1995). In Canada, where the cost of health insurance has not been as big a factor in benefits costs (due to government-funded medicare), benefits costs (as a proportion of total compensation costs) also escalated during that period, but not as much as in United States. Because of this, and the lack of tax advantages in Canada, Canadian firms have less incentive to introduce flex plans. However, this situation may change, as the cost of health benefits (especially prescription drug plans) has been increasing by about 14 to 17 percent per year for the past few years (Mozill, 2001). An example of drug costs cited by Mozill is new medication for rheumatoid arthritis, which runs at $17 000 per person per year.

So how do flex plans reduce costs? In some cases, firms introduce flex plans as a smokescreen to reduce the amount they devote to benefits. Because benefits plans are so complicated and are poorly understood, it is difficult for employees to tell whether the new flexible benefits plan is really delivering the same value of benefits as their previous plan.

The practice of introducing flex plans as a ploy to reduce benefits has started to give the entire concept a bad name. As one observer put it, compared with the earlier days of flex plans, "the difference now is that employees are discontent when they hear they are getting flex, before they even find out what they've lost" (Dorrell, 2000). In some cases, employees discover that they are unable to buy back their original coverage using the available credits, while in other cases, employees can do so initially but then find that increases in credits do not keep up with increases in benefit cost.

In some cases, employers may introduce a flexible benefit plan to give employees a choice about what to cut from the benefits package and/or the opportunity to buy back their original package with the use of employee contributions. In essence, employees are being given the chance to rebalance their total compensation package as they see fit in order to maintain as much value as they can. As long as the flex plan is not seen as the *cause* of the reduced employer contributions, the plan may be seen by employees as beneficial. Here, employees are being given flexible benefits as a tool to help them protect their economic well-being as best they can. In some cases, it may be argued that this can create a win-win situation, in which the employer cuts benefit costs while employees are able to maintain the value provided to them by the benefit system.

Other firms do not attempt to reduce their benefit costs in the short term, but do wish to prevent future escalation of these costs. Of course, as benefit costs increase, firms could simply reduce coverage, increase deductibles, or increase employee contributions without recourse to a flexible benefits plan at all. But the use of flexible benefits allows employee preferences to play a major role in how the benefits package evolves.

There is one other way in which flex plans may help to contain costs. In many benefit systems, many of the benefits are cost-shared between the employee and the employer. With the heightened understanding of the trade-offs between costs and coverage, some employees may opt to take less coverage if they have to pay a portion of it. Under cost sharing, this would of course also reduce the employer's share of the cost.

A second force that has promoted the use of flex benefits is the increasing diversity of the workforce. Most traditional benefit systems were developed in an era when the typical employee was a married man who had a spouse who was not employed outside the home and several dependent children. As recently as 1967, two-thirds of Canadian families had only one wage earner (McKay, 1996). Because of the homogeneity of this workforce, it was relatively easy to come up with a standard benefits package that would suit this "typical" employee.

But by 1992, in 61 percent of married couples (McKay, 1996), both spouses were employed—in some cases by the same employer. Since many benefit plans also cover family members, there may be unnecessary duplication of benefits coverage. In this case, it might be efficient for one spouse to drop the duplicate coverage and use the benefit credits that are freed up to increase other benefits, add new benefits, or even take cash. At CUC Cable in Scarborough, Ontario, benefit costs dropped by more than one-quarter after a flex plan was implemented, largely because it allowed for better coordination of benefits between spouses (Charles, 1995).

As the workforce has become more diverse, there has been increased demand for additional types of benefits, such as child care or eldercare, to supplement the traditional benefits. Flexible benefits are seen as one way of dealing with this diversity without raising the costs of the benefits package to the employer. The company simply makes the new benefit available, and employees who want the benefit simply redeploy their benefits credits from other benefits less valuable to them until they come up with the combination that best suits their personal needs. As their needs and circumstances change, they can realign their benefits accordingly. Essentially, this allows an employee to maximize the value of the benefit system for any given level of benefits expenditure by the employer. Flexible plans can help to arrange the benefits package in the most tax-advantageous way, as Mary Smith, in Box 7.3, has discovered.

A third force promoting flexible benefits is the desire of many employers to change the concept of employee benefits as an entitlement—something provided as a condition of employment—to the idea that benefits are really a type of pay that must be earned rather than simply granted. Flexible benefit systems can certainly help to encourage employees to understand the cost and value of the benefits being provided.

Another force is the change in managerial strategies, as discussed in Chapter 2. As human relations organizations move toward the high-involvement model or the classical model, their attitudes toward benefits tend to change. Flexible benefits are attractive to both high-involvement and classical organizations, although for opposite reasons. For high-involvement organizations, flexible benefits fit with the partnership concept that underlies this managerial strategy, as well as with the belief that employees are responsible individuals who are capable of choosing their benefits more wisely than the firm could do for them. It is simply one more way of increasing employee

BOX 7.3 Mary Smith Gets Her Revenge on the Tax Collector

One of your employees, Mary Smith, is annoyed that the tax collector has recently decided to declare the parking spot provided by her company as a taxable benefit. But using your company's flexible benefits plan, she has found a way to get even.

Currently, the company pays $360 per year for the premiums on Mary's $100 000 life insurance policy. At the same time, Mary has increased her dental package to the maximum level, which requires an annual contribution from her of $360. This current arrangement has two tax implications. Mary's contribution to the dental plan is not tax-deductible, so she must earn about $720 to pay for this benefit (assuming a 50 percent incremental tax bracket), since the tax collector will take about half these earnings before she can pay the company for the upgraded dental coverage. Mary will also have to pay tax on the employer's

contribution to the life insurance, which will cost her about $180 per year. Thus, the overall cost to her of these two benefits is about $900.

But Mary has a better idea. What if she pays for the life insurance herself and directs the company to allocate the $360 it saves from this to pay for the upgraded dental plan? Let's look at the tax consequences now: The money she pays for the life insurance is still not deductible, so she must use after-tax income. This means the pre-tax cost of the life insurance is $720, exactly the same as the dental upgrade would cost. But—and it is a big "but"—employer contributions to the dental plan are not taxable as income to Mary. So simply reversing the way in which the payments are made saves Mary about $180 per year in income taxes, without increasing company costs in any way.

involvement and self-control in the workplace. In contrast, classical organizations may simply see flexible benefits as an opportunity to cut benefits costs, although, as will be discussed shortly, flexible benefit plans may actually be less successful in classical organizations than in other types of organizations.

Some firms that do not currently have a benefits package may find flexible benefits appealing. These employers may have stayed away from fixed benefit plans to avoid getting enmeshed in a program where costs may get out of hand. However, a flex plan can be seen as a type of defined contribution plan, in which the employer commits to making a specified, limited sum of money available for benefits, so there is less exposure for the employer if certain benefits escalate in cost.

Firms with flex plans may enjoy a competitive advantage in terms of employee recruitment and retention. First, prospective employees may find the idea of choosing their benefits quite appealing. Second, if the flex plan is designed and communicated properly, firms with these plans should be able to deliver more value to their employees than firms without flex plans who devote the same number of dollars to employee benefits. Of course, this assumes that the flex plan is not so expensive to administer that the firm is forced to reduce the number of dollars it contributes to the plan or pay more for benefits because of loss of economies of scale and adverse selection, as will be discussed in the following section. It also assumes that flex plans are seen as attractive by employees, and not simply as code words for an inferior benefits plan, as has been discussed earlier.

Finally, there may be a type of bandwagon effect as the concept gains momentum. This effect may be based on sound reasons. For example, as knowledge accumulates about how to successfully apply the concept, it becomes easier to apply. Many benefits consultants now have expertise with the concept. In addition, computer software has been developed that makes the administration of the system far more efficient and user-friendly.

FORCES HINDERING FLEXIBLE BENEFITS

There are numerous forces hindering the implementation of flexible plans. These include the cost of implementation and administration, loss of economies of scale in the purchase of benefits, possible confusion and poor decision making among employees, lack of fit with the organizational culture, and possible resistance from employees or unions.

Clearly, there are substantial one-time implementation costs in developing the flexible plan. These involve the costs of the personnel involved in the design process, as well as the costs of consultants who are normally hired. Few firms have the in-house expertise to develop such a plan without the aid of consultants.

Administration and communication costs are also likely to be much higher. Costing out the various options, predicting employee take-up, and pricing the options fairly is a major process. Informing employees about their options, the tradeoffs involved, and simply managing the paperwork is a major task. Add to this the fact that employees may be tinkering with their benefits packages every year, and the extent of the additional administrative burden becomes clear. However, as has been discussed, the seriousness of this drawback is being reduced by the development of computerized spreadsheet packages that allow employees to calculate their various options and costs, and to submit their benefit choices. Some firms are outsourcing their benefits management to firms that specialize in so doing.

Another issue is the possible loss of economies of scale in purchasing benefits from suppliers. For example, various types of insurance are much cheaper if purchased in volume. If there is relatively low take-up on some benefits, the costs of these may be high. Further, there is the issue of adverse selection— employees with large families afflicted with many dental problems may load up on dental coverage, while those with no dental problems may forgo it entirely. Or, people in ill health may be the only ones purchasing medical coverage. These situations, of course, would drive up the costs of these benefits tremendously. To combat this problem, some firms impose mandatory minimum levels of some benefits, but this rule goes against the flexibility concept.

The problem of employee confusion is not a trivial one. For example, Sturman, Hannon, and Milkovich (1996) analyzed one firm's flex plan (which had nine benefit categories, with two to eight levels of coverage per category, and two flexible spending accounts) and discovered that employees had a choice of over *two million* benefit combinations. Critics of these plans note that this complexity could lead to employee confusion, poor benefits decisions, and decreased satisfaction with benefits.

Another possible hindrance is company culture. Human relations firms may be reluctant to move to flexible benefits for fear the system will be too complex for employees, or that employees will make unwise benefits choices that may leave them uncovered if certain unpredicted events occur. Flexible benefits may also be unsuccessful in classical organizations because these firms may not be willing to commit the resources necessary to effectively communicate their plans to employees, and employees may have little faith in the information they do receive.

Finally, especially in classical organizations, there may be high resistance from employees or their unions because of a fear that the flex plan is simply a way of tricking them into accepting reduced benefits.

EXPERIENCE WITH FLEXIBLE BENEFIT SYSTEMS

What have been the effects of flexible benefit systems? While the amount of research on this question is not large, a few studies have examined the impact of flexible benefits on employee compensation satisfaction. Two longitudinal studies of U.S. firms, looking at benefits satisfaction before and after implementation of a flexible benefit system, showed significantly higher compensation satisfaction after implementation of the flexible plan (Barber, Dunham, and Formisano, 1992; Rabin, 1994).

However, a cross-sectional study of three Canadian firms, one with a fixed benefit system, one with a modular benefit system, and one with a fully flexible system, actually showed less satisfaction with the flexible systems (Tremblay, Sire, and Pelchat, 1998). The authors explain this finding by arguing that a key determinant of benefits satisfaction is an understanding by employees of their benefits package, and this understanding is even more important for a flexible benefit system. They concluded that firms with the flexible systems had not adequately communicated the systems, causing employee discontent with the plans.

The large compensation consulting firm Hewitt Associates conducted a survey of Canadian employees who had flexible benefit plans (Hewitt Associates, 1995). The majority of employees—75 percent—reported that their firm had not reduced benefits in conjunction with the move to flexible benefits, while 25 percent reported that a reduction had taken place. Of those employees where no benefits reduction occurred, 87 percent had a favourable reaction to flexible benefits, with only 13 percent showing "mixed" reactions. Of those employees who experienced a benefits reduction, 40 percent had a favourable reaction to the flex plan, while 60 percent had a "mixed" reaction. Clearly, implementing a benefits reduction along with a flex plan has a substantial negative impact on employee perceptions of the flex plan.

Finally, an interesting study was conducted by Sturman, Hannon, and Milkovich (1996). They wanted to determine whether a computerized system to aid in benefits decision making might improve satisfaction with the benefits received in a flexible benefit system used by a major U.S. firm. They asked three randomly selected groups of employees to use either a pen and paper approach, a computerized decision support system, or a computerized expert system for conducting a simulation of the annual re-enrollment process. They found that the employees using the expert system made significantly better benefits decisions than those using the other two systems, and also experienced a significantly higher level of benefits satisfaction.

DESIGNING THE BENEFIT SYSTEM

In developing a benefit system, there are five main issues that must be dealt with. First, the role that indirect pay will play in the total compensation system needs to be defined. Can the provision of benefits contribute to the achievement of compensation objectives? If so, how? What objectives should be set for indirect pay? Second, what will be the process for designing the plan? Third, what benefit system will be used, and what specific benefits will be included? Fourth, the structural characteristics of each individual benefit need to be decided, including coverage, funding, eligibility, and flexibility. Fifth, procedures for administering, communicating, evaluating, and adapting the benefit system must be put in place.

Each of these issues will now be briefly discussed. The purpose is to provide some understanding of the kinds of issues that need to be dealt with as a part of benefit-plan design. No attempt will be made to cover all the details that need to be dealt with during this process. Without doubt, the benefit system is the most technically complex aspect of the compensation system, and an entire book would be required to deal with this area exhaustively.

ISSUE 1: DETERMINE THE ROLE OF INDIRECT PAY IN COMPENSATION STRATEGY

The first issue in establishing an indirect pay system is to identify what compensation objectives it will serve, beyond those that can be served by direct pay. Some organizations see no role for indirect pay at all. Recall Electronic Banking System from Box 2.1? This classical firm concluded that there was little to gain from offering employee benefits. For them, the cost of turnover is low, and the type of person they need is in plentiful supply. So why offer benefits?

In general, indirect pay will not be a good investment for classical firms, since it provides no task motivation. Perhaps the only circumstance in which it may be a good investment for them is when they must invest high training costs in their employees. Since a classical firm is usually not a very satisfying organization to work for, the company needs some means of retaining its investment in trained employees, and utilizing indirect pay that ties the employee to the firm may be useful in protecting this investment. Of course, it should be recognized that this commitment will likely be of a grudging, continuance type.

Thus, classical organizations will normally want to minimize the use of indirect pay, except for retaining key employees. But an irony is that many classical firms, much to their dismay, have ended up with very extensive benefit programs, as a result of the collective bargaining process. Most of these firms are probably aware that they receive very little value from these programs, and some have likely attempted to use flexible benefits as a ploy to cut costs.

If a classical organization must provide benefits, either as a result of the collective bargaining process or to match benefits of competitors, a traditional fixed benefit system would probably fit best, with employees sharing the costs of the benefits payouts (such as paying a proportion of every dental claim) to discourage frivolous use of the system. In situations where pay is tied to seniority and where employee productivity drops with age, generous pension plans may be desirable in order to encourage highly paid employees to retire.

In contrast, indirect pay is a cornerstone of the human relations managerial strategy, which is designed to show high concern for employees and to maintain high membership behaviour. As discussed earlier, the circumstances in which human relations will be a viable managerial strategy appear to be diminishing. But where human relations is still an effective managerial strategy, indirect pay will likely remain a key part of the compensation strategy, although some effort will likely be made to contain costs of benefits. While their benefit systems may include some flexible aspects, a fully flexible benefit system will not likely fit well with this approach.

High-involvement firms face a bit of a dilemma when it comes to indirect pay. In some ways indirect pay does not fit with the high-involvement concept because it does not relate to company performance. However, the key asset for any high-involvement firm is its members, so it needs to be sure that its benefit system doesn't cause employees to feel compelled to move to a firm that offers satisfactory benefits. It also needs to offer sufficient benefits that employees' lower-order needs for security are satisfied so that they can be motivated by their higher-order needs.

Since the high-involvement organization requires a high level of commitment from its employees, the benefit system also needs to recognize and facilitate this commitment. For example, various types of family-friendly benefits, such as child care, eldercare, and flexible time off, may assist employees in dealing with their family-related commitments. But aside from practical considerations, high-involvement firms do have a genuine concern for the well-being of their employees and will wish to help employees deal with any unforeseen problems that may occur.

In so doing, high-involvement organizations will favour structuring both the individual benefits and the benefit system to reinforce the partnership aspect of their strategy. Thus, a flexible benefit system, with cost sharing on the individual benefits, is a good fit. But there is also a role for some fixed benefit that encourage highly desired behaviours, such as tuition reimbursement and educational leave plans. Fitness activities may help to combat stress. Employee assistance programs will help troubled employees regain productivity. In contrast to programs in human relations firms and some classical firms, benefit programs in high-involvement companies will not be focused on continuance commitment. It is not beneficial to a high-involvement organization to "trap" people who don't fit with the organization.

One issue that has not been discussed is the possible role of indirect pay as a cost-effective substitute for direct pay. For example, at certain stages in their history, some organizations may not have the funds to offer competitive wages. But they may be able to attract employees by offering benefits that cost them very little but are highly valued by employees. For example, many airlines have been unprofitable in recent years and cannot afford high wages. But one benefit that costs them very little is to provide free air transportation to employees and their families. The cost of this is low because employees using this benefit are normally required to use only those seats that have not been sold.

Before moving on to the next set of issues, the role of, and company objectives for, indirect pay should have been defined. Examples of roles to be served might include encouraging membership, retaining senior employees, satisfying lower-order needs for economic security, adding value to the compensation package, promoting specific behaviours of strategic importance to the firm, and helping to remove possible hindrances to productivity (such as alcohol or drug abuse problems).

ISSUE 2: CHOOSE PROCESS FOR PLAN DESIGN

Once it has been decided that there is a significant role for indirect pay, and the objectives for indirect pay have been defined, the next issue is to establish a process that will produce a plan that meets these objectives. Most experts argue that employee participation in this process is highly desirable. This participation achieves three main goals. First, it provides better understanding of employee needs. If the benefit system does not address real employee needs, then it will be of little value to employees, while still costing the employer money. Second, it provides more trust and acceptance of the plan. Third, it helps communicate the plan.

Firms vary enormously in how much employee participation they provide. High-involvement firms will likely have extensive employee participation on the design team, whereas human relations and classical firms will rely more on staff specialists, management, and outside consultants. Other than through direct employee representation on the design team, input can be solicited through employee questionnaires and focus groups (Haslinger and Sheerin, 1994).

ISSUE 3: IDENTIFY THE BENEFIT SYSTEM AND BENEFITS TO BE INCLUDED

The next issue involves identifying the specific benefits that will be provided. The key considerations in evaluating each benefit include: whether it will contribute to the objectives of indirect pay, the extent to which it is valued by employees, the cost to the employer of providing the benefit, and the net value added to the compensation package by the addition of that benefit. Since firms have only a finite amount of money that they can devote to benefits, these benefits must be prioritized in order of total value to the firm.

At this point, it is important to know whether the firm is going to be using a flexible benefit system or a fixed benefit system. Obviously, a firm with a flexible system can afford to make available a broader portfolio of benefits because employees will not be able to choose all of them, given the credits provided by the employer, although they may also use their own funds to purchase valued benefits.

Issue 4: Determine the Structure of Each Benefit

For each individual benefit, there are four main structural issues to be decided: the nature of each benefit, funding, eligibility, and flexibility. These issues can be boiled down to four questions: What will the benefit provide? Who will pay for it? Who is eligible to receive it? Is it required or optional?

Coverage

A major issue with most benefits is what the benefit will cover. How much coverage is provided, how is it based, and how far does it extend? Take dental insurance, for example. Does it cover all dental expenses, only certain types of dental expenses, or all dental expenses up to a certain prescribed limit in a given period? Does it cover all the expenses of a given procedure, or does the employee need to pay a portion, say 20 percent of each bill? Is there a deductible, in which an employee must pay the first ten dollars of every claim? Do some employees receive a richer plan than others?

Is coverage restricted to the employee, or does it extend to family members? If the latter, how will family members be defined? During an era in which people live in a wide variety of relationships, defining such terms as "family member" or "spouse" may not be as straightforward as it might first appear. At what point, for example, is a common-law partner accepted as a "spouse" for the purposes of benefit coverage? What status will children of that "spouse" (but not of the employee) receive? Will they be considered dependent children of the employee or not?

Will same-sex partners be accepted as a spouse for the purposes of benefit coverage? This is a thorny issue that has possible legal ramifications. For example, many gay and lesbian groups have argued that not providing benefits coverage to same-sex partners on the same basis as opposite-sex partners contravenes human rights legislation, and there is some legal support for this position. For example, in 1996 the Ontario Human Rights Commission ordered Ontario municipalities to offer benefits to gay and lesbian couples on the same basis as married couples (*Maclean's*, 1996). In order to avoid getting entangled in legal issues, some firms have voluntarily extended coverage to same-sex couples.

Will coverage levels vary for different employees? For example, it is common for life insurance coverage to be provided as a multiple of salary. Pension contributions are also geared to salary. Other plans may be based on seniority, as in the case of Imperial Oil's savings plan, which matches 1 percent of salary the first year of employment and up to 5 percent of salary the fifth year. Will coverage continue after termination? Many firms do continue coverage of certain benefits for retirees and their immediate families.

A related issue is whether coverage will be geared to base pay only or to base pay plus performance pay. As Burns and Gherson (1996) note, many firms exclude performance pay as a basis for benefit calculations simply because they have never thought to include it. Others exclude it because it raises benefit costs. But failure to include performance pay in benefit calculations actually serves to weaken performance pay and penalizes employees with a large component of performance pay. In contrast, including performance pay in calculations of benefit entitlements provides a way of linking indirect pay to performance, thereby reinforcing performance pay and making the indirect pay system more sensitive to performance.

FUNDING

There are many possibilities for funding the benefit. It might be fully paid by the employer, by the employee, or it could be cost-shared. The basic level of the benefit could be employer-paid, and then higher levels cost-shared or employee-paid. Of course, under a flexible benefit system, the employee could have the choice of whether the benefit would be employer- or employee-paid, as in the case of Mary Smith in Box 7.3.

ELIGIBILITY

A key issue for each benefit is to define which employee groups will be eligible to receive it. Although firms typically cover all full-time employees, there is often a waiting period before new employees become eligible for all benefits.

A more complex issue is the treatment of part-time, temporary, or contract employees. In many firms, part-time employees (defined by Statistics Canada as anyone working less than 35 hours a week) are offered few or no benefits, even if they have been employees of the firm for many years. Only one province has legislation regarding benefits for part-time employees. In 1996, Saskatchewan passed legislation that all employees who work an average of at least 15 hours a week must receive the same benefits as a comparable full-time employee, although these benefits can be prorated according to hours worked. Temporary full-time employees can be excluded if they do not meet the minimum employment period for inclusion in the benefit plan, and contract employees are typically excluded. In fact, some firms use part-time, temporary, and contract workers for the express purpose of avoiding having to pay benefits.

Some firms distinguish between two categories of part-time employees. Casual part-time employees work entirely at the will of the employer when their services are required. They receive no guarantee of weekly hours, and can be terminated at will. In contrast, permanent part-time employees are considered as permanent employees of the firm, and the firm has a commitment to provide these employees with a certain minimum number of hours on a weekly basis. These employees are often included in the benefits program, although on a prorated basis. Use of permanent part-time work has developed in organizations that want to enjoy the scheduling flexibility of part-time employees but also want to encourage a permanent relationship with these employees. Permanent part-time arrangements are particularly common in industries that depend on a large number of part-time employees on a continuing basis, such as banking (e.g., for tellers) or health care (e.g., for nurses).

FLEXIBILITY

The next issue is the degree of flexibility that is allowed for each benefit. Will the benefit be mandatory or optional? If it is mandatory, will there simply be a predetermined, fixed level, or will there be minimum compulsory level, plus optional levels? If a decision has been made to have a flexible plan, will the benefit be included in the core area of coverage or in the optional area? What value of flexible credits will be offered? Can unused credits be taken as cash?

ISSUE 5: DEVELOP PROCEDURES FOR ADMINISTERING, COMMUNICATING, AND EVALUATING THE SYSTEM

Once the benefit system has been designed, a system must be put into place for administering it and communicating it to employees. The complexity of these tasks depends on the complexity and flexibility of the system that has been designed.

ADMINISTRATION OF BENEFIT SYSTEM

Ongoing administration of the benefit system can be very complex. The key administrative tasks include enrolling employees in the benefit system; updating changes to employee records and benefit packages; dealing with employees when they terminate and after they terminate; handling the tax issues associated with benefits; dealing with the fiduciary responsibilities of funds held in trust; calculating employer and employee contributions; determining the validity of benefit claims and overseeing benefit payouts; advising employees on their benefit status and answering questions; and monitoring and evaluating the program and recommending changes. One administrative issue that occurs periodically is selecting vendors for the various benefit products.

Virtually all organizations that offer benefits outsource some of this work. For some aspects, such as funds held in trust for pension plans, the law requires a separate trustee. Trust companies, banks, insurance companies, and investment firms are often used for this purpose. Most insurance firms handle the claims processing for insurance-based benefits. The degree to which the other aspects of the administrative process are outsourced varies dramatically, but as benefit systems have grown more complex, and as specialized providers of these services have emerged, use of outsourcing has been increasing (Hackett, 1995).

An advantage of outsourcing the routine benefits administration is that it frees in-house departments to focus on the strategic issues of indirect pay and on the communications aspects. However, a disadvantage of outsourcing is that firms can lose touch with employees' needs and problems. That is why evaluation should be a key in-house function, as will be discussed shortly. Most firms believe that communication should also be an in-house function.

COMMUNICATION OF BENEFIT SYSTEM

It is ironic that although indirect pay may account for as much as one-quarter of an employee's total compensation, and the company pension plan may represent the largest financial asset an employee will ever own, employee understanding of this aspect of their compensation is generally limited (Luchak and Gunderson, 2000). In one striking example, a firm conducting focus groups to improve its benefit system discovered that employees in one location didn't even know they were covered by a pension plan (Haslinger and Sheerin, 1994). It turned out that their employer had recently been acquired by another firm, and these employees mistakenly believed that their pension plan had been eliminated in the process.

If a benefit system is to shape behaviour and attitudes, then it must be understood. As discussed earlier, research shows that satisfaction with benefits increases directly in proportion with an understanding of the benefit system. There are two times when communication is especially important: when employees must make benefit decisions and when they may be eligible to receive benefits. Among the traditional methods used to communicate benefits are employee handbooks and periodic newsletters, along with an annual statement of pension coverage, which is required under law. These approaches have generally enjoyed little success, due to the arcane and legalistic language that usually prevails in these documents, combined with a lack of motivation on the part of most employees to wade through the material. However, two events may change this: the advent of benefit systems that require employees to make choices, often on an annual basis, and the development of computer-based communications technology.

EVALUATING AND ADAPTING THE BENEFIT SYSTEM

Once the system has been put into place, it needs to be evaluated on a regular basis to determine whether it is meeting the objectives set out for it, and whether it is doing so in the most cost-effective way. There are three main types of analysis. Cost analysis examines the cost of each individual benefit, and what is being received for that cost. Competitive analysis utilizes data from competitors. Employee surveys are frequently done to examine employee satisfaction with each benefit and the value to them. This issue will be dealt with in more detail in Chapter 12, in the section dealing with evaluation of the total compensation system.

SUMMARY AND IMPLICATIONS

The purpose of this chapter has been to develop an understanding of the third component of a compensation system, indirect pay. It was noted that although indirect pay is a very large and, until recently, growing component of many compensation systems, employers have often not carefully examined whether the mix between direct and indirect pay is justified. It was also noted that employers vary dramatically in the extent to which they make use of indirect pay; some possible reasons for this variation were discussed.

The advantages and disadvantages of indirect pay were discussed, and it was apparent that, properly designed, an indirect pay component in the compensation system can play a significant role in meeting compensation objectives. However, the role to be played depends on the characteristics of the firm, most notably managerial strategy. Six main categories of benefits were identified: mandatory, retirement income, health and life insurance, pay for time not worked, employee services, and miscellaneous benefits; the possible role and cost-effectiveness of each type was discussed. The trend toward flexible benefits was examined, along with their advantages and disadvantages relative to traditional fixed benefit systems. Finally, the key issues in designing a benefit system were identified.

This chapter concludes our discussion of the three compensation components. The next part of the book identifies the process through which a firm can choose among these components and structure them in such a way as to create the compensation strategy best suited to help it achieve its compensation and corporate objectives.

KEY TERMS

defined benefit plans, p. 221

defined contribution plans, p. 221

employee assistance programs (EAPs), p. 230

employee expense account, p. 234

fixed benefit system, p. 235

flexible benefit system, p. 235

health care expense account, p. 226

hybrid pension plans, p. 223

indirect pay, p. 215

mandatory benefits, p. 220

pay for time not worked, p. 227

supplemental unemployment benefits (SUBs), p. 228

EXERCISES

1. In a small group, discuss how important benefits will be to you in choosing your next job. Then, everyone should identify the three benefits that are of most importance to them. Do these vary across individuals in your group? If so, discuss why.

2. Three firms are briefly described below. For each firm, identify the role (if any) that you believe indirect pay should play in the compensation system, and the specific benefits that it would make most sense to offer. Explain why.

   • A company offers lawn maintenance and yard clean-up services in the summer and snow removal services in the winter. It employs about 600 people at peak season (in the summer) and has branches in major cities across the prairies.

   • A retail clothing chain offers personalized service and caters to upscale customers. It is located in major cities across Canada and employs approximately 600 sales staff.

   • A computer software firm develops customized software for various specialized applications for individual clients. Located near Ottawa, it employs about 1000 people.

SUGGESTED WEB SITES

Page 220: To find out more about benefits in Canada, check the Web site for the Canadian Pension and Benefits Institute <www.cpbi-icra.ca> or the Canadian site of the International Foundation of Employee Benefit Plans <www.ifebp.org/canadian.asp>

Page 220: To find out the latest requirements for mandatory benefits, check the Human Resources Development Canada, Income Security Programs Web site <www.hrdc-drhc.gc.ca/common/employr.shtml>

Page 232: For information on the federal government's "work-life balance program," click on <www.labour-travail.hrdc-drhc.gc.ca/worklife>

Page 242: To keep up-to-date on current issues in benefits management, check the Web sites of three publications: *Benefits Canada* <www.benefitscanada.com>, *Benefits and Pensions Monitor* <www.bpmmagazine.com>, and the *Canadian Human Resources Reporter* <www.hrreporter.com/home>

REFERENCES

Allen, Steven G., and Robert L. Clark, 1987. "Pensions and Firm Performance." In Morris M. Kleiner, Richard N. Block, Myron Roomkin, and Sidney W. Salsburg, eds., *Human Resources and Performance of the Firm.* Madison, WI: Industrial Relations Research Association, 195–242.

Baarda, Carolyn. 2000. *Compensation Planning Outlook 2001.* Ottawa: Conference Board of Canada.

Babcock, Wafaa, and Clare Pitcher. 2000. "Building the Perfect Plan." *Benefits Canada*, May.

Barber, A., R. Dunham, and R. Formisano. 1992. "The Impact of Flexible Benefits on Employee Satisfaction: A Field Study." *Personnel Psychology*, 45: 55–75.

Burns, John M., and Diane Gherson. 1996. "Should Variable Pay Count Towards Benefits Calculations?" *Compensation & Benefits Review*, 28(5).

Carlyle, Nathalie B. 1996. *Compensation Planning Outlook 1997.* Ottawa: Conference Board of Canada.

Charles, Julie. 1995. "Some Assembly Required." *Benefits Canada*, January: 25.

Chisholm, Patricia. 2001. "Redesigning Work." *Maclean's*, 114(10): 34–38.

Coward, Laurence E. 1991. *Mercer Handbook of Canadian Pension and Benefit Plans.* Don Mills, ON: CCH Canadian Limited.

Dorrell, Kathryn. 2000. "Passing the Buck." *Benefits Canada*, 24(5): 19.

England, Geoff, and Roderick Wood. 2001. *Employment Law in Canada.* Markham, ON: Butterworths.

Galt, Virginia. 2001. "Life and Profit on the Table in 'Family Friendly' Contracts." *The Globe and Mail*, July 16: A1.

Gerhart, Barry, and George T. Milkovich. 1992. "Employee Compensation: Research and Practice." In M.D. Dunnette and L.M. Hough, eds., *Handbook of Industrial and Organizational Psychology.* Palo Alto, CA: Consulting Psychologists Press, 484–569.

Hackett, Brian. 1995. *Transforming the Benefit Function.* New York: The Conference Board.

Haslinger, John A., and Donna Sheerin. 1994. "Employee Input: The Key to Successful Benefits Programs." *Compensation & Benefits Review*, 26(3): 61–70.

Hewitt Associates. 1995. *Survey Findings: Canadian Flexible Benefit Programs and Practices.* Toronto: Hewitt Associates.

Ho, Kwok, and Chris Robinson. 1996. *Personal Financial Planning.* Toronto: Captus Press.

Isaac, Kerry. 1995. *Compensation Planning Outlook 1996.* Ottawa: Conference Board of Canada.

Judge, Timothy A. 1993. "Validity of the Dimensions of the Pay Satisfaction Questionnaire: Evidence of Differential Prediction." *Personnel Psychology*, 46: 331–55.

Koskie, Raymond, Mark Zigler, Guy A. Jobin, and Patrick Longhurst. 1995. *Employee Benefits in Canada.* Brookfield, WI: International Foundation of Employee Benefit Plans.

KPMG. 1994. *Nineteenth Annual Survey of Employee Benefits Costs in Canada.* Toronto: KPMG.

Lawler, Edward E., Susan A. Mohrman, and Gerald E. Ledford, 1995. *Creating High Performance Organizations: Practices and Results of Employee Involvement and Total Quality Management in*

Fortune 1000 Companies. San Francisco: Jossey-Bass.

Litherland, Geoffrey J. 2000. *An Employer's Guide to Dismissal*. Aurora, ON: Aurora Professional Press.

Luchak, Andrew A., and Ian R. Gellatly. 2001. "What Kind of Commitment Does a Final Earnings Pension Plan Elicit?" *Relations industrielles/Industrial Relations*, 56(2): 387–418.

Luchak, Andrew, and Morley Gunderson. 2000. "What Do Employees Know about Their Pension Plan?" *Industrial Relations*, 39(4): 646–70.

Maclean's. 1996. "Victorious Gays." 109(38): 42.

Maclean's. 2000. "A-Ford-able Computers." February 14.

McKay, Robert J. 1996. *Canadian Handbook of Flexible Benefits*. New York: John Wiley and Sons.

Mofina, Rick. 2001. "Despite More Illness, Women Live Longer than Men." *Saskatoon Star-Phoenix*, April 27.

Mozill, Tracy U. 2001. "Benefits for Sale." *Benefits Canada*, 25(1).

Rabin, B. 1994. "Assessing Employee Benefit Satisfaction under Flexible Benefits." *Compensation and Benefits Management*, 10(3): 33–44.

Renaud, Stephane. 1998. Unions, Wages, and Total Compensation in Canada. *Relations industrielles/Industrial Relations*, 53(4): 710–29.

Scott, Sarah. 1997. "More Risk, Higher Rewards? The New Look of Company Pensions." *Maclean's*, 110(39): 46–48.

Sturman, Michael C., John M. Hannon, and George T. Milkovich. 1996. "Computerized Decision Aids for Flexible Benefits Decisions: The Effects of an Expert System and Decision Support System on Employee Intentions and Satisfaction with Benefits." *Personnel Psychology*, 49(4): 883–908.

Tremblay, Michel, Bruno Sire, and Annie Pelchat. 1998. "A Study of the Determinants and of the Impact of Flexibility on Employee Benefit Satisfaction." *Human Relations*, 51(5): 667–88.

Williams, Margaret L. 1995. "Antecedents of Employee Benefit Level Satisfaction: A Test of a Model." *Journal of Management*, 21(6): 1097–1128.

Part III

The Compensation Strategy

8

....

FORMULATING THE REWARD AND COMPENSATION STRATEGY

CHAPTER GOALS

By the end of this chapter, you should be able to:

1. Identify the four key understandings necessary for formulating an effective compensation strategy.
2. Describe the constraints that set the parameters for the compensation strategy.
3. Explain the compensation strategy formulation process and describe each step in that process.
4. Discuss the specific considerations in deciding whether to adopt a lead, lag, or match compensation-level policy.
5. Describe utility analysis and explain how it can be used.
6. Apply the compensation strategy formulation process to specific organizations.
7. Explain how to evaluate the proposed compensation strategy prior to implementation.

....

8. Discuss the special issues involved in compensating contingent workers, new employees, executives, and international employees.

Introduction

Congratulations! After slogging through the first seven chapters, you are finally in a position to start formulating the reward and compensation strategy. As you will recall from Chapter 1, the *reward strategy* is the plan for the mix of rewards, both extrinsic and intrinsic, that the organization intends to provide to its members—along with the means through which they will be provided—in order to elicit the behaviours necessary for organization success. The *compensation strategy* is one part of the reward strategy, and consists of two main aspects—the *mix* of base pay, performance pay, and indirect pay that will be utilized, and the *total amount or level* of compensation that will be provided to employees. In other words, the two key questions for compensation strategy are "how is compensation to be paid?" and "how much is to be paid?"

The Compensation Strategy Process

To answer these questions effectively is not a simple process. First, we need to define the employee behaviours necessary for organizational success, and to identify the characteristics and qualifications of people who will be able to perform these behaviours. Second, within the total organizational system that is developed to generate these behaviours, the specific role that the reward and compensation system will play needs to be defined. Third, the most appropriate mix across the three compensation components must be determined. Fourth, policies for establishing the amount of compensation that employees will receive must be formulated. Fifth, a pre-implementation evaluation of whether the proposed strategy meets our criteria for success needs to be conducted. This process is illustrated in Figure 8.1.

Four Key Understandings

To successfully carry out this process, four key understandings are essential. The first seven chapters of this book were devoted to developing three of these understandings; the fourth of these will be covered early in this chapter.

Understand Your Organizational Context
To understand what behaviours are needed, and how the reward system can best support corporate and managerial strategies, it is essential to understand the nature of the organizational context in which the reward system will be applied. Chapter 2 provided a strategic framework as a basis for this understanding.

FIGURE 8.1   THE COMPENSATION STRATEGY
              FORMULATION PROCESS

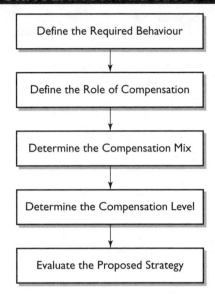

Understand Your People

To understand how behaviour can best be motivated, and the role that rewards and compensation can play in shaping behaviour, it is essential to understand the factors that drive human behaviour, and to understand the specific needs and characteristics of the people who will be performing the required behaviour. Chapter 3 provided a behavioural framework as a basis for this understanding.

Understand Your Compensation Options

To develop the compensation system that will most effectively and efficiently generate the required behaviour, it is essential to understand the compensation options that are available. Chapter 4 described the role that base pay can play in shaping behaviour, Chapters 5 and 6 described the role that different types of performance pay can play, and Chapter 7 described the possible role of indirect pay.

Understand Your Compensation Constraints

Employers cannot simply do whatever they want when they are deciding compensation. There are in fact a number of constraints that define the parameters or boundaries within which the compensation system must be designed. These constraints are of four main kinds: legal/legislated constraints, labour market constraints, product/service market constraints, and financial constraints of the organization. It is essential to understand these constraints before formulating the compensation strategy. The first part of this chapter provides a basis for this understanding.

After that, the five main steps in the process for formulating the compensation strategy will be discussed in depth, along with the issue of who should be involved in this process. A detailed example of compensation strategy formulation will reinforce your understanding of this process and its complexity. The chapter will conclude with a discussion of the special issues involved in compensating four particular groups: contingent workers, new employees, executives, and international employees.

But beware! This is a heavy agenda for one chapter, so if you are planning to tackle it in one sitting—and hope to absorb most of it—best of luck to you! Dividing it into two or three sittings would be much kinder to your grey cells!

CONSTRAINTS ON COMPENSATION

Remember the Screaming Tale Restaurant from Box 1.2? The owners of this Ontario restaurant had the wonderful idea of cutting labour costs by not paying their employees. The firm claimed it had no employees, just "volunteer workers" or "commission agents," working only for the "tips" that customers provided, thus relieving the firm of the need to pay at least minimum wages or any of the mandatory benefits. But guess what? It turned out that this arrangement was illegal, and the restaurant closed just as it was being investigated for violations of the Ontario Employment Standards Act.

As the Screaming Tale case illustrates, employers cannot simply do whatever they want in regard to compensation, even if they can find employees who will accept the compensation arrangements. In this case, the employer ran afoul of legislated constraints, specifically minimum wage laws. In addition to these, employers also face labour market constraints, product/service market constraints, and financial constraints. Each will be discussed in turn.

LEGISLATED CONSTRAINTS

In Canada, jurisdiction for labour market legislation is split between the federal government and the provinces. The federal government is empowered to pass labour legislation covering all federal employees (including those in federal Crown corporations) and workers in a number of specified industries, including transportation, communications, defence, uranium mining, and firms engaged in interprovincial or international trade. In addition to employees of the federal government and its agencies, federal labour law covers about 10 percent of private-sector employees. All other employees are covered under provincial legislation.

There are four main types of legislation that may affect compensation systems. First, every province has an Employment Standards Act, which defines minimum standards for wages, hours of work, vacation, statutory holiday and leave entitlement, termination benefits, and minimum age levels for employment. (The equivalent federal legislation is known as The Canada Labour Code.) Second, all jurisdictions have human rights acts, which prohibit discrimination among employees based on factors such as gender, race, or age. Related to this, some jurisdictions also have specific pay equity legislation, aimed at redressing past pay inequities experienced by female employees.

Third, all jurisdictions have legislation relating to unionization and collective bargaining, which affects compensation by requiring that all compensation arrangements be approved by the union, when present. This legislation also has an indirect effect on compensation, as some non-union firms will match settlements achieved at unionized competitors in order to reduce the incentive for unionization. Finally, all jurisdictions have income and corporate tax laws, which have a major influence on the type of compensation offered.

EMPLOYMENT STANDARDS LEGISLATION

Many aspects of **employment standards legislation**, such as those pertaining to paid time off, have already been discussed in conjunction with indirect pay in Chapter 7. One aspect not yet discussed is minimum wage legislation, under which each jurisdiction specifies a minimum hourly rate that must be paid. Currently, this ranges from $5.50 in Newfoundland and New Brunswick to $7.20 in Yukon. Most jurisdictions (except New Brunswick) also prescribe that when an employee works less than three hours during a shift, that person must be paid a minimum of three hours' pay.

Although minimum wage legislation applies to most workers who are at least 18 years of age (17 in Yukon), there are some exceptions. Most jurisdictions exclude domestic servants, in-home babysitters, and some types of farm labourers. Employers may also be exempted from paying minimum wages to handicapped workers, and do not have to pay minimum wages (or other mandatory benefits) to persons who are classified as contractors or agents, since they are exempted from employment standards legislation.

So a key issue is "what constitutes a contractor?" According to one labour standards expert (Braun, 1997: 17):

> *An independent contractor differs from an employee in that the contractor sets the hours of work, maintains control over work done, provides own equipment and tools, and is subject to minimal company supervision. An important additional distinction is that an independent contractor has the ability to perform work for other employers, as long as this does not compromise any existing contractual agreement.*

By this standard, "volunteer workers" at the Screaming Tale Restaurant clearly must be classified as employees, rather than as genuine commission agents, such as realtors. Moreover, although restaurant employees must declare gratuities for income tax purposes, gratuities do not count toward employee earnings to help satisfy minimum wage requirements. Thus,

employment standards legislation legislation that sets minimum standards for pay and other conditions of employment

employers must pay the minimum wage to employees, beyond any income they may receive from gratuities.

Interestingly, even with realtors, there is now some ambiguity. Historically, real estate salespeople have been considered as "agents" and therefore exempt from employment standards legislation. However, this status has been brought into question by a 1989 Ontario court case in which real estate salespeople were deemed to be employees and therefore covered by the Ontario Employment Standards Act.

So where does this leave employees who are paid only on commissions or piece rates? For example, what happens if sales personnel who are compensated only by commission—such as automobile salespeople—achieve very few or no sales in a given period? The procedure to check if minimum wage is being paid is to take the total amount earned by an employee during a workweek, and divide that by the number of hours worked. If that amount comes out to less than the minimum wage, then the employer is required to pay the difference to the employee.

Another important issue covered by employment standards legislation is overtime pay rates. Employment standards legislation normally requires higher rates of pay (normally 1.5 times normal earnings) for hours worked in excess of stipulated limits—generally eight hours per day, and 40–48 hours per week, depending on the jurisdiction. However, there are many exemptions from this part of employment standards legislation, such as professionals, supervisors, managers, students, and farm labourers, although commission salespeople and piece-rate workers are covered.

Rather than hiring new employees, many firms have been using overtime when additional production is needed. This avoids the cost of hiring new employees, and also avoids the problem of having to lay off employees if the amount of available work declines. However, employees cannot be forced to work overtime. Nor can any employee who is covered by the Employment Standards Act waive the right to receive overtime pay. Employers are not allowed to adjust the pay rates for non-overtime hours downwards to be in technical compliance with the overtime rules. However, some employers do attempt to limit application of overtime rules by classifying their employees as professional or managerial. One rule of thumb commonly used is that hourly paid employees are covered by the overtime provisions while salaried employees are not.

Another important provision that is included in employment standards or allied legislation deals with employee layoff and severance, as has been discussed in Chapter 7.

HUMAN RIGHTS LEGISLATION

Even if an employer complies with the employment standards legislation, they are still not free to pay each employee what they wish. Every jurisdiction has passed legislation that prohibits discrimination in hiring and during employ-

human rights legislation legislation that prohibits discrimination in hiring or employment on the basis of race, ethnic origin, religion, gender, marital status, or age

ment on the basis of race, ethnic origin, religion, gender, marital status, or age (within specified age ranges—normally 18 to 65 years of age). Some jurisdictions include sexual preference in this list.

To prove compliance with human rights legislation, employers must be able to demonstrate that differences of pay between employees are related only to factors such as job duties, experience, qualifications, seniority, or performance. For example, if a member of one racial group is paid significantly less than another employee with similar job duties, the employer must be able to prove that this difference is due to one or more of the factors described above.

All jurisdictions in Canada have some form of equal pay legislation aimed at dealing with the issue of wage inequality between male and female employees. This legislation prohibits employers from paying male and female employees differently if they do "identical, similar or substantially similar work." The federal legislation—The Canadian Human Rights Act—goes one step further and stipulates that male and female employees must receive equal pay for work of *equal value*, even if the work is not substantially similar.

Numerous provinces have enacted pay equity legislation specifically intended to redress gender pay inequities, although in some of these provinces (Manitoba, New Brunswick, Nova Scotia, and Prince Edward Island) the legislation applies only to governmental bodies and their agencies. Ontario, Quebec, and British Columbia have enacted pay equity legislation that applies to all employers with ten or more employees. In essence, pay equity schemes require the employer to divide the workforce into job classes designated either as male or female. (A job class is designated male or female if at least 60 or 70 percent [varying by jurisdiction] of the occupants of that job class are male or female.) After that, a gender-neutral job evaluation system is applied to each job class.

If a female-dominated job class that is evaluated equally to a male-dominated job class has lower compensation than the male class, the imbalance must be redressed. Although it is theoretically possible to redress this imbalance by reducing wages in the male-dominated classes, this is prohibited. As Box 8.1 indicates, employers have substantial limitations on how they attempt to deal with the imbalance, once it is formally identified. (Compliance with pay equity legislation will be covered in more depth in Chapter 9.)

TRADE UNION LEGISLATION

If a group of company employees is represented by a union, any changes to pay, hours of work, and working conditions are mandatory subjects of negotiation. In other words, employers cannot make changes to these matters unless these changes have been agreed to by the union representing these workers. Employers cannot make separate compensation arrangements with individual members of the bargaining unit. The practical result of this is that if a unionized firm wants to make any changes to its compensation system, it must first convince the union to accept these changes. This can be a long process and, in

trade union legislation legislation that defines the rights of parties involved in a collective bargaining relationship

In 1994, the Nova Scotia Pay Equity Commission awarded a substantial wage increase, to be phased in over a four-year period, to female crossing guards employed by the City of Dartmouth. The Commission concluded that these workers were being paid significantly less than male employees of the City who were doing work of equal value. In response, the City of Dartmouth decided to lay off all the crossing guards and contract the work from a private company that paid lower rates to crossing guards and that was not covered by the Pay Equity Commission ruling. However, the Nova Scotia Court of Appeal disallowed this course of action, on the grounds that once the award was issued, the City was prohibited from entering into contracts for reasons intended to "defeat the purpose of the Pay Equity Act" (Braun, 1997).

many cases, may rule out certain types of pay practices, such as profit sharing, that many unions have traditionally opposed.

Studies have shown that unions have a significant impact on both the structure and level of employee compensation (Renaud, 1998). In general, unionized employees are more likely to work under a seniority- rather than performance-based pay system, to receive an extensive array of employee benefits, and generally enjoy a wage premium of at least 10 percent compared with comparable non-union employees.

TAX LEGISLATION

The final way in which legislation can influence the pay system is through income and corporate tax legislation. As we have seen in Chapter 7, the tax system can serve to encourage certain types of pay approaches and discourage others. For example, tax legislation has played a significant role, over the years, in the movement away from direct pay (which is fully taxed) toward indirect pay (which often is not). However, this role may have diminished in recent years, as employee benefits have increasingly become subject to income tax. On the other hand, recent changes to tax legislation are likely to encourage use of stock options.

In passing, it should be noted that there may be income tax benefits from a change in status from "employee" to "independent contractor." As an employee, an individual has very few tax deductions that she or he can apply against employment income. But an independent contractor has many more possible deductions. For example, if employees use a portion of their home for an office, there is no tax deduction; if independent contractors do the same, there is a deduction. Employees cannot deduct the cost of getting to and from their place of employment; independent contractors can. Thus, creating "independent contractor" relationships can be attractive, at least from the tax perspective.

Labour Market Constraints

A key constraint is the nature of the labour market for the kinds of employees needed by an employer. The labour market is simply the available pool of labour from which employers may choose their employees. Labour markets are normally segmented by occupational type and geographical area. In a given geographical area, demand for a particular type of labour may be high or low, and supply of that type of labour may be high or low. For example, when demand is high but supply is low, we have a *tight* labour market, which makes it difficult to attract qualified employees, and which will likely force compensation levels up. Of course, when demand is low and supply is high, we have a *loose* labour market, making it much easier to attract employees.

Labour markets vary by region, and a major issue for firms that operate on a national level is whether to adjust compensation based on the local labour market. For example, a bank may determine pay for customer service representatives based on the market rate for these employees in Ontario, where the firm's head office is located. But in many local labour markets, such as a small town in Nova Scotia, it may well be possible to attract the necessary employees for much less than what is being offered to Ontario employees. Should the bank, therefore, pay lower rates to its Nova Scotia employees than its Ontario employees? This is one of the questions that needs to be resolved when setting compensation level policy.

As has been discussed in Chapter 4, the issue of identifying "market pay" is more complex than it sounds. It will be discussed at greater length in Chapter 10. At this point, it is enough to simply note that the labour market poses a real constraint for firms, since a compensation system that is too far below market will not attract the necessary employees, and one that is too far above market may increase costs unduly. Paying above market is particularly a problem when product/service markets are highly competitive, as will be discussed next.

labour market constraints constraints on compensation strategy flowing from the relative levels of demand and supply for particular occupational groups

Product/Service Market Constraints

A key constraint for organizations is the nature of the market for their products or services. Is demand low and supply high? If so, this results in a highly competitive business environment, and firms that pay more for their labour than competitors may be at a serious competitive disadvantage, unless they are more productive than their competitors.

These competitive constraints will be especially severe in industries that are highly labour-intensive, since labour costs constitute a higher proportion of total costs in these firms. These constraints will be still more severe if competitors are able to produce their product in labour markets where the cost of labour is much lower, or where legislated constraints, such as minimum wage laws or mandatory benefits, are less onerous. In contrast, firms in markets

product/service market constraints constraints on compensation strategy flowing from the nature of the product or service market in which the firm operates

where demand for their product is high, supply is low, and competitors are few will have much more latitude in designing their compensation systems.

Another aspect of the product/service market is its volatility. Firms that are subject to severe swings in demand for their product/service need to be able to adjust their organizational systems to deal with this fluctuation. Some firms react by using a high proportion of contingent workers, who are subject to different compensation constraints than core employees, while others react by including more variable pay in their compensation systems.

FINANCIAL CONSTRAINTS OF THE ORGANIZATION

Regardless of conditions in their labour or product/service markets, many organizations have specific financial constraints that affect the compensation system. In the private sector, this normally flows from the financial performance of the organization—firms that are unprofitable are much more limited in their compensation options than firms that are profitable. Constraints may also flow from the stage of growth that the firm is in—new firms or firms that are growing quickly often have a shortage of cash.

For public-sector organizations, financial constraints usually flow from funding limitations placed on them by those providing the funds. Many public-sector organizations, such as hospitals, postsecondary educational institutions, and the Canadian military, are faced with funding restrictions that severely limit the compensation they can offer.

Of course, rather than simply accept these constraints, organizations can and do try to change them. Public institutions can seek additional sources of funding. Some firms may attempt to escape mandatory benefits by classifying employees as independent contractors. Firms may relocate operations to areas where labour is more plentiful or where employment standards are less costly. Some firms attempt to escape union constraints by weakening the union or by contracting work to non-union enterprises.

FORMULATING THE COMPENSATION STRATEGY

Now that you understand your organization, your people, your compensation options, and your compensation constraints, you are finally in a position to formulate your compensation strategy. This section will take you through the five steps depicted in Figure 8.1, on page 257. After that, there will be a discussion of who should be involved in the process of formulating compensation strategy, and the section will conclude with a detailed example of compensation strategy formulation.

DEFINE THE REQUIRED BEHAVIOUR

The first step is to define the behaviour that your organization needs. As you will recall from Chapter 3, there are three main types of behaviour that an organization might need—membership behaviour, task behaviour, and citizenship behaviour—but the importance of these behaviours varies for different organizations. For membership behaviour, what are the costs of turnover, and is affective commitment necessary, or is continuance commitment sufficient? For task behaviour, are tasks simple or complex, do employees work under supervision, and are high performance levels required? For citizenship behaviour, how important is it for different company units and the individuals within them to cooperate, and to what extent can extra employee initiative or ideas make a difference to organizational performance?

For some firms, high levels of membership, task, or citizenship behaviour may be nice, but not worth the cost; for others, high levels of one or more of these will be essential. To understand the relative importance of the three types of behaviour, it is necessary to understand the organizational context, the most important aspect of which is the managerial strategy adopted by the organization. As has been discussed in Chapter 2, classical organizations need only minimal membership behaviour, adequate task behaviour, and no citizenship behaviour; human relations organizations need high membership behaviour, adequate task behaviour, and some citizenship behaviour; and high-involvement organizations require high levels of all three.

While every organization needs its employees to perform task behaviours, the nature of these behaviours can vary enormously. Obviously, eviscerating a chicken is different from designing a computer program, piloting an airplane, writing a newspaper editorial, or performing surgery. Tasks vary in many ways, such as their complexity, the skill required, the level of performance required, the material worked with (i.e., things or people), or the consequences of errors. Packing a chicken wing in a box of chicken legs is an error, as is removing a patient's healthy left kidney instead of a diseased right kidney (as actually happened at a Swedish hospital in 1997), but the consequences of these two errors differ dramatically.

The nature of the task behaviour that is required has implications for the type of organizational and reward systems needed to produce these behaviours. Table 8.1 lists 17 different dimensions of task behaviour. In general, the first choice in each of these dimensions (e.g., tasks that are simple, procedural, low-skilled, narrow, have low interdependence and individual output) are suited for reward systems consistent with the classical school of thought, whereas tasks characterized by the second choice in each dimension (e.g., tasks that are complex, creative, highly skilled, broad, have high interdependence and team-based output) are suited for reward systems associated with the high-involvement management strategy.

TABLE 8.1 DIMENSIONS OF TASK BEHAVIOUR

1. Are tasks simple or complex?
2. Procedural or creative?
3. Low or high skill requirements?
4. Narrow tasks or broad?
5. Low or high task interdependence?
6. Individual or team-based output?
7. Low or high cost of errors?
8. Adequate or high performance required?
9. Low or high employee risk-taking desired?
10. Low or high customer contact?
11. Low or high impact on organizational performance?
12. Low or high employee discretion over work process?
13. High or low ability for employee supervision?
14. High or low control by individual employee over output levels?
15. Individual output identifiable or not?
16. Short-term or long-term results?
17. Tasks deal with things or human beings?

Interestingly, many organizations often do not appear to understand their real behavioural needs and have recruiting systems that work at cross-purposes to these needs. For example, many a fresh university graduate has been told by recruiters that the firm is seeking creative, innovative, free-thinking employees, only to discover that what the organization really wants are people who will simply do what they are told in a reliable manner. It may be that recruiters find statements about creativity and innovation to be effective in drawing high-quality recruits, without considering the potential costs of creating disillusioned employees who are prone to quit when they discover the discrepancy between their expectations and those of their bosses (or even worse, disillusioned employees who do *not* quit).

Once the required behaviours are defined, the type of employee who is needed can be identified, including their skills, education, and other important characteristics. These are the people whom the organization must be able to attract, retain, and motivate, so it is important to understand their needs. Without understanding the needs of these employees, the organization may end up providing rewards that are not highly valued by the people being sought, a result that is both ineffective and costly.

Of course, rewards are only one part of the picture when it comes to attracting employees. Table 8.2 provides the results of a major international study that identified the factors that human resource officers believe to have a "great deal of impact" in determining which employer will be chosen by highly qualified workers (Conference Board of Canada, 1996: 8).

As can be seen, the top-ranked factor was career development/advancement opportunities, followed closely by the nature and level of direct com-

TABLE 8.2 CHARACTERISTICS THAT DEFINE AN EMPLOYER OF CHOICE*

1.	Career development/advancement opportunities	68 percent
2.	Compensation plan/level	65 percent
3.	Company reputation in community	61 percent
4.	Management/leadership style	59 percent
5.	Corporate culture	56 percent
6.	Profitability	51 percent
7.	Ethical standards	46 percent
8.	Type of industry	44 percent
9.	Benefits package	39 percent
10.	Technology	38 percent
11.	Geographic location	38 percent
12.	Training programs	34 percent

*Ranked by percentage of human resource officers believing factor to have a "great deal of impact" on the employer chosen by highly qualified employees.

Source: Conference Board of Canada, 1996: 8.

pensation. Factors such as the company's reputation in the community, its management style, corporate culture, and profitability were also cited as important by more than half of the respondents. Indirect pay (the benefits package) was ranked ninth in importance, cited by only a minority of respondents (39 percent) as an important factor.

One of the implications of these findings is that organizations with various negatives, such as a poor reputation in the community or an undesirable geographic location, will likely be forced to rely more heavily on their compensation systems to attract employees. This would be especially true for employers who do not offer advancement opportunities, either because they are not experiencing growth, or because they don't utilize a "promote from within" policy. As Table 8.2 suggests, a "promote from within" policy can be an important extrinsic reward for employees. Moreover, firms that do not have such a policy risk being seen as inequitable by their employees.

But as many firms become flatter and experience slower growth, they need to develop other types of rewards (including compensation) to make up for the loss of advancement opportunities. As discussed in earlier chapters, some firms have turned to pay-for-knowledge systems, while others have created technical ladders.

DEFINE THE ROLE OF COMPENSATION

All organizations must have some system for generating the behaviour they require. As discussed in Chapter 2, there are three main organizational systems (managerial strategies) that can be used to generate the required behaviour, and the reward system plays a different role within each system. Classical organizations tend to focus on economic needs as the main motivator of behaviour, human relations organizations tend to focus on social needs, and high-involvement organizations focus on employee needs for participation, growth, and development.

The first issue at this point is to examine to what extent intrinsic vs. extrinsic rewards will be used to motivate behaviour. An assessment needs to be made of the intrinsic rewards offered by the organization. These may be extensive or nonexistent. (Of course, where intrinsic rewards are nonexistent, it may be possible to create them through employee participation in decision making or work redesign, as was discussed in Chapter 3.) Where intrinsic rewards are not available, the compensation system will be relied on more heavily to motivate behaviour, depending on the extent to which extrinsic rewards (other than compensation) are available.

Tradeoffs are possible between compensation and other rewards. For example, some firms want to hire employees who are fully equipped with the skills and experience to perform the needed behaviours immediately on joining the firm. Other firms are willing to hire employees who possess the ability to develop the necessary skills, and then train them to perform the needed behaviours. This training may be seen by potential employees as an intrinsic reward (an opportunity for learning and growth), or an extrinsic reward (since it will likely lead to a better-paying position), or both. This will likely make it possible to attract employees for less compensation than would otherwise be necessary. In contrast, hiring fully skilled and experienced employees will require much higher compensation, although this may be offset by lower training costs and more immediate productivity.

Table 8.3 provides some examples of how the role of compensation can vary in different organizational settings. The first example, a gift shop operated by UNICEF to generate funds to help third-world children, provides no role for compensation at all. Membership and task behaviour are motivated by intrinsic rewards, including the knowledge that volunteers are helping to save young lives, and a high degree of congruence between organizational goals and personal goals, which also stimulates organizational citizenship behaviour. Clearly, this type of organization suits the high-involvement managerial strategy.

Task behaviour itself (serving customers, ringing up sales) does not necessarily contain many intrinsic rewards (although volunteers are given considerable autonomy in how they perform their roles), so the direct motivation from the task itself is moderate at best. But task behaviour is motivated by the knowledge that performing these mundane tasks is helping to accomplish the goals of the organization. Membership behaviour may also be motivated by the extrinsic social rewards (from mingling with other volunteers, for example) that may flow from belonging to this organization. Of course, the success of this reward strategy depends on the availability of people with goals and needs that are congruent with the organization, who have time to contribute, and for whom economic needs have already been met by other means.

TABLE 8.3 ROLE OF COMPENSATION AND INTRINSIC/EXTRINSIC REWARDS IN PRODUCING BEHAVIOUR FOR DIFFERENT ORGANIZATIONS

REQUIRED BEHAVIOUR	ROLE OF INTRINSIC REWARDS	ROLE OF EXTRINSIC REWARDS OTHER THAN COMPENSATION	ROLE OF COMPENSATION
UNICEF STORE (Cashiers/clerks)			
Membership behaviour	High role	Moderate role	No role
Task behaviour	Moderate role	No role	No role
Citizenship behaviour	High role	No role	No role
CHICKEN-PROCESSING PLANT (Production-line workers)			
Membership behaviour	No role	No role	High role
Task behaviour	No role	No role	No role
Citizenship behaviour	No role	No role	No role
TREE-PLANTING FIRM (Tree planters)			
Membership behaviour	Low to moderate role	Low to moderate role	High role
Task behaviour	Low to moderate role	No role	High role
Citizenship behaviour	No role	No role	No role
VACATION RESORT (Service workers)			
Membership behaviour	High role	Moderate role	Moderate role
Task behaviour	Moderate role	No role	No role
Citizenship behaviour	High role	No role	No role
HOSPITAL (Nursing staff)			
Membership behaviour	High role	Moderate role	Moderate role
Task behaviour	Moderate role	No role	No role
Citizenship behaviour	High role	No role	No role
HIGH-TECH ELECTRONICS FIRM (Design engineers)			
Membership behaviour	Moderate role	Moderate role	Moderate role
Task behaviour	High role	Moderate role	Low role
Citizenship behaviour	Moderate role	Moderate role	High role

The second example is a chicken-processing plant, similar to the one described in Box 2.4. At this organization, there are absolutely no intrinsic or extrinsic rewards for production-line workers, so the only way to motivate membership behaviour is through pay. However, because costs of turnover are so low, there is no need to offer compensation beyond the minimum level necessary to attract a sufficient stream of applicants who are able to perform the necessary task behaviours. The compensation system is not used to stimulate task behaviour; that is done directly by the technology and supervisor. Using compensation-based behaviour control (such as piece rates) is not really viable due to the interdependent nature of the work. This classical firm is not concerned about citizenship behaviour, and so it does not waste money promoting this behaviour.

The third example is a tree-planting firm, which has contracts with major forestry firms to undertake reforestation work. While there may be some intrinsic motivation for individual tree planters, who may see reforestation work as socially valuable and who may enjoy the autonomy and task identity the job provides, this alone would never motivate the necessary membership and task behaviour. Of course, tree planting is seasonal work, so it is not seen as a source of ongoing employment. Since tree planters work and live together in camps in remote areas, some may perceive some extrinsic social rewards, if camaraderie develops. On the other hand, because of the remote locations, many tree planters may experience negative social rewards due to isolation from friends and family members.

Clearly, the key motivator in this case is money. Pay can be used to both foster the necessary membership behaviour, and to direct task behaviour. Both of these can be accomplished through piece rates, where tree planters are paid according to number of trees planted. Their output is identifiable, and tasks are not interdependent. This approach fits with a classical managerial strategy.

The fourth example is a very popular vacation resort, which employs seasonal service workers. The work itself does not provide many intrinsic rewards, although there may be some satisfaction in helping guests to enjoy their stay. But there are high extrinsic rewards, because the locale in which the resort is located has many attractions, and the resort allows free use of recreational facilities when employees are not on duty. The resort also encourages friendly social relations among staff. The role of pay in attracting employees is moderate. Pay also plays a moderate role in motivating task behaviour through the tips that workers receive from guests, and small bonuses that the firm provides to employees who receive outstanding service ratings from guests. This firm practises a human relations strategy.

The fifth example is a hospital. Nursing staff receive many intrinsic rewards from the role they play in their organization, because of the work they do and the congruence between their goals and those of the organization. However, there are few extrinsic rewards and many undesirable features of the work, such as shift work. Along with intrinsic rewards, compensation is used to elicit membership behaviour. But it is not used to direct task behaviour or foster citizenship behaviour; intrinsic rewards serve this purpose. This approach fits best with a high-involvement strategy.

The sixth example is a firm that designs and manufactures high-tech electronics products. This firm practises a high-involvement strategy because the success of any new product depends on creativity, innovation, and cooperation among all parts of the organization. For design engineers, there is considerable intrinsic satisfaction to designing a successful product, and some extrinsic rewards flowing from their development of greater expertise and knowledge through the extensive training provided by the firm. The firm also provides a substantial degree of job security. The primary purpose of compensation is to motivate membership and to foster citizenship behaviour, through profit sharing and employee share ownership programs.

Once the role of compensation has been defined, organizations can develop some specific behavioural objectives for the compensation system. These flow from the analysis just completed, and may be simple or comprehensive. For example, our chicken-processing firm may be perfectly happy if the compensation system generates a minimum level of membership behaviour, and task behaviour will be shaped by other means. Our tree-planting firm goes a step further, and relies on its compensation system not only to attract employees but also to direct and control employee task behaviour.

In contrast, the electronics firm will view its compensation system as an important part of the rewards it offers to attract high-calibre employees who will remain with the firm and as a major part of its rewards strategy to engender high organizational citizenship and team-oriented behaviours. It may also use compensation to promote learning and development (through a pay-for-knowledge system or payment of tuition fees) and to promote risk-taking behaviour. But unlike the tree-planting firm, it will not depend on its compensation system to promote specific task behaviours. As has been discussed in Chapter 3, using the compensation system to promote specific task behaviours is a risky process and is suitable in only a very limited number of circumstances.

Table 8.4 provides an illustration of the behavioural objectives that each of the six organizations might set for its compensation systems, along with some indicators of goal achievement.

DETERMINE THE COMPENSATION MIX

Once the required behaviours have been identified, and the role that the compensation system will play in generating those behaviours has been defined, the next step is to identify the mix of compensation components that will elicit that behaviour in the most effective and efficient way. Figure 8.2 illustrates the choices that are available in so doing.

A number of questions must be addressed. What role will be played by base pay, performance pay, and indirect pay? And how will each component be structured? For example, will the foundation for base pay be job evaluation, market pricing, or pay for knowledge? Will performance pay be linked to individual, group, or organizational performance? Will it have a short- or long-term focus? What specific benefits or services will be included in indirect pay, which benefits will be contributory, and what degree of choice will employees have in the benefits they receive?

TABLE 8.4 SAMPLE BEHAVIOURAL OBJECTIVES FOR COMPENSATION SYSTEMS

COMPENSATION OBJECTIVE	INDICATOR
UNICEF STORE (Cashiers/clerks)	
• None (no compensation system)	• None
CHICKEN-PROCESSING PLANT (Production workers)	
• Attract job applicants able to perform basic tasks	• Flow of willing applicants exceeds terminations by 10 percent
TREE-PLANTING FIRM (Tree planters)	
• Attract applicants to staff initial needs and replace turnover	• Number of applicants exceeds requirements by 100 percent
• Maintain high retention	• Turnover during planting season less than 10 percent
• Motivate tree-planting behaviour	• Average production exceeds 200 trees per hour
VACATION RESORT (Service workers)	
• Attract applicants to staff initial needs	• Number of applicants exceeds requirements by 100 percent
• Maintain reasonable retention	• Turnover during season less than 20 percent
• Promote friendly guest service	• Customer surveys
	• Less than 2 percent of customers make complaints
HOSPITAL (Nursing staff)	
• Attract applicants to exceed turnover and maintain quality	• Number of applicants exceeds vacancies by 200 percent
• Maintain moderate to high retention	• Annual turnover less than 12 percent
HIGH-TECH ELECTRONICS (Design engineers)	
• Attract top-quality applicants well in excess of needs	• Number of applicants exceeds vacancies by 300 percent
	• 75 percent acceptance rate of job offers
• Maintain very high retention	• Turnover less than 5 percent
• Promote creativity and risk-taking	• Number of new projects proposed per engineer
	• Number of suggestions pertaining to department
• Promote high citizenship behaviour	• Employee surveys
	• Number of suggestions extending beyond department
• Promote learning and development	• Improvement in employee qualifications

FIGURE 8.2 COMPENSATION MIX CHOICES

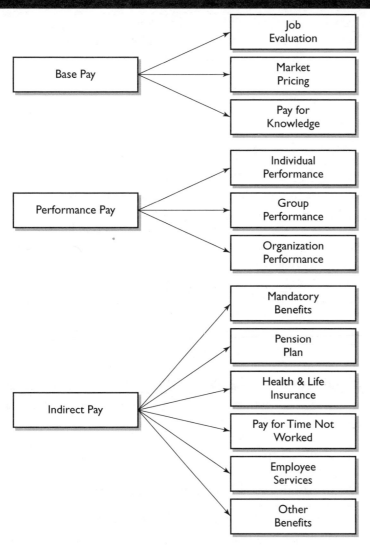

The correct answers to these questions depend on the behaviours that the firm requires, the organizational context (especially managerial strategy), the needs of the employees who are being sought, and the constraints facing the organization. Unfortunately, there is no simple formula for finding these answers, and reliance on a high degree of informed judgment at this point in the process is unavoidable. A further complication is that the mix of the main compensation components also needs to be considered in the light of the total level of compensation to be provided. For example, the greater the variable portion of the compensation, the greater the total compensation that is generally necessary to compensate employees for the uncertainty and risk in their compensation.

DETERMINE COMPENSATION LEVEL

How much compensation should be offered? Within the constraints discussed earlier, policies need to be established for determining the total amount of compensation that individuals or groups of employees will receive. In general, the question to be asked is "Will we lead, lag, or match our relevant labour market, in terms of total compensation levels?"

LAG THE MARKET

lag compensation policy
a compensation-level strategy based on paying below the average compensation level in a given labour market

Of course, the first question is, "Do we have a choice?" In some cases, the organization's financial or budgetary circumstances are such that there is no choice but to lag the market. If so, a key question is whether the organization can offer noncash rewards (perhaps including some indirect pay items) to make up for this problem. For example, the organization may sweeten its total package by offering items that cost the firm little or no cash, such as purchase discounts on company products. Or these firms may offer flexible schedules to employees, or they may provide useful training. When cash is short, provision of other extrinsic rewards, along with intrinsic rewards, becomes even more important.

It is common for small firms that are growing rapidly to have cash shortages. To entice crucial employees to join the firm, these firms frequently offer company stock, which has no current cash cost. They may also offer other types of performance pay that will be payable only when and if the company can afford to pay. To make this worthwhile in the eyes of employees, the future payout typically needs to be set quite high, in order to compensate employees for the risk of not receiving anything at all. Another potentially valuable reward this type of firm can offer is advancement opportunities, in addition to intrinsic rewards such as task variety or participation in decision making.

One consistent research finding is that smaller firms pay less than large firms. For example, a Statistics Canada study has revealed that in the manufacturing sector, small firms paid 24 percent less than the average pay in their sector (*Star-Phoenix*, 1996). This may be due to a higher unionization rate in large firms (which forces wages up in large firms), tighter cost controls in small firms, or simply a lower ability to pay in small firms. In fact, while their savings in labour costs might appear to be a competitive advantage, there is evidence that small firms pay a steep price for their compensation savings. Statistics Canada also found that productivity in small firms was 32 percent lower than industrial averages. Research also indicates that small firms have higher turnover rates and less-qualified employees than larger firms (Evans and Leighton, 1989), which helps to explain their lower productivity.

But what about firms that do have a choice in pay level? Many firms that could pay more make a conscious decision to pay below market. The motive for doing so is obvious—to save on compensation costs. But there are costs to this strategy. On average, firms that pay below market have a lower quality of applicants and higher turnover than other firms. Not surprisingly, employees also experience more reward dissatisfaction than employees at other firms.

Unless a firm has done a careful analysis of these costs, it may be that they exceed the benefits of this strategy. Firms that may find this lag strategy cost-effective are firms in which the costs of turnover are low, where the costs of recruiting are low, where labour constitutes a high percentage of total cost, and where it is possible to contain the negative consequences of reward dissatisfaction.

Other firms that may find that a below-market pay policy to be viable are those that offer other types of rewards that are highly valued by employees. If so, the firm may avoid the problems of poor-quality applicants, high turnover, and reward dissatisfaction.

LEAD THE MARKET

Why would an organization ever choose to lead the market? There are actually many possible reasons. It may need to do so if it offers poor noncompensation rewards, if there are many negative aspects associated with employment by this firm, or if the firm needs very high-quality applicants. Firms in which recruiting costs are high, turnover costs are high, and consequences of reward dissatisfaction are high may find this approach cost-effective. Firms that value employee stability, and in which employee stability is important to customer service, may favour this strategy. Firms in which labour costs are low as a proportion of total costs will find this strategy less costly than firms that are labour-intensive.

lead compensation policy a compensation-level strategy based on paying above the average compensation level in a given labour market

Firms that are seeking employees who have abilities beyond those required to do their entry-level jobs, or where heavy training investments are made, may wish to secure their workforce with high compensation. For example, firms using a pay-for-knowledge system consistently pay above market. Some firms with performance pay plans, such as profit sharing, may end up paying above the market. Many firms will gear base and indirect pay to the market and then add profit sharing, which will cause total pay to exceed the market in profitable years. As has been discussed earlier, there is evidence that employees in profit-sharing firms receive higher total compensation than employees in firms without profit sharing.

In some cases, firms do not intend to lead the market in total compensation, but they end up doing so nonetheless. This can occur if the compensation structure results in increases beyond market increases, if there is no systematic assessment of what is happening in the market, or if there is a strong union. Firms can also end up paying over market if they have a poorly designed compensation system that includes rewards that do not add value for the employee or the employer, but still cost money.

In some cases, large firms that are geographically dispersed end up leading the market in numerous parts of the country, even if they are only matching the market in other parts of the country. But from their point of view, it is simply not worth the cost of determining what a market-matching wage would be at every branch of their organization. Furthermore, inconsistent wages for similar jobs may create perceptions of inequity and make it difficult to transfer employees to the lower-wage branches.

MATCH THE MARKET

match compensation policy a compensation-level strategy based on paying at average compensation levels in a given labour market

Many firms settle on a "match the market" strategy as a way of "playing it safe." Their reasoning is that this avoids the possible disadvantages of paying below market, while still remaining cost-competitive by not offering excessively high wages. They are simply not sure whether either a lag or lead policy will pay off, so they stick to the middle. In some cases, of course, this is the optimal solution. But this cannot be confirmed without systematic analysis.

UTILITY ANALYSIS

utility analysis a method used to analyze whether a lead, lag, or match compensation-level strategy is most efficient for a given organization

In order to help managers to determine which compensation-level strategy is most appropriate, which can be a complicated process, computer-based "utility analysis" models are beginning to be developed (Klaas and McClendon, 1996). **Utility analysis** is a method intended to help analyze whether a lead, lag, or match strategy would be most efficient for a given organization. Here is how it works.

Suppose that you are the head of compensation at a credit union, and you are trying to decide on the pay-level strategy for your 400 tellers. Currently, your policy is to match the market. But would the bank be better off to switch to either a lead or a lag policy? Changing the policy would be expected to have an impact on turnover and on the quality of employees who would be hired and would remain with the bank. You have examined other banks that pay more or less than you do, and have found that firms that pay 20 percent more have a 10 percent lower turnover rate than you do, and that firms that pay 20 percent less have a 10 percent higher turnover rate. Your current turnover rate for tellers is running at 30 percent per year, so each year you have to replace 120 tellers.

You first need to calculate the costs of turnover. What is the cost of recruiting each teller, and what is the cost of training them? Let's assume that it costs approximately $1000 to replace each teller, including advertising, interviewing, and the administrative costs of putting the new employee on the payroll and taking the former employee off the payroll. Let's suppose that training costs $4000 per employee, counting out-of-pocket training costs and reduced productivity during the training period. Currently, you are paying each teller $24 000 direct pay per year, with benefits adding another $6000, for a cost per employee of $30 000 per year. The total cost for tellers per year is the cost of their compensation (400 × $30 000 = $12 000 000) plus the costs of turnover, which amounts to 120 × $5000, or $600 000, for a total of $12 600 000.

You now need to estimate the change in performance that will occur from a change in the quality of your workforce due to a lag or lead policy. If you lag the market by 20 percent, you expect that your new workforce will produce 5 percent less work and make 7 percent more errors. Considering the time needed to identify and correct the errors, you calculate that the new workforce will be 12 percent less productive. You also need to decide whether the lead pay policy would improve productivity by the same amount. Let's suppose that it does. Now, let's follow through with the analysis for the lag and the lead policy in turn.

Let's suppose we lag by 20 percent. Because productivity is 12 percent less, we will now need 448 tellers. At 33 percent turnover, we will need to replace 149 tellers per year. With the 20 percent wage reduction, it will now cost us $24 000 per employee per year in salary and benefits. So the total cost will be 448 times $24 000 ($10 752 000) plus 149 times $5000 ($745 000), which totals $11 497 000, considerably lower than our current costs.

But wait! If we have 12 percent more employees, then we need 12 percent more office space, and 12 percent more office equipment and the like. Assuming that it costs an additional $3000 per employee per year for computer equipment and support, and $1000 for office space and miscellaneous expenses, we can expect additional costs of $192 000, resulting in a total cost of $11 689 000. This is still a savings of nearly a million dollars per year.

Now, let's suppose we lead by 20 percent. Because productivity is 12 percent higher, we will now need only 352 tellers. Approximately 95 will need to be replaced each year. So our costs would be 352 times $36 000 ($12 672 000) plus 95 times $5000 ($475 000) for a total of $13 147 000. Even after allowing for reduced office space and equipment ($192 000), this is still the most expensive policy, at $12 955 000.

In reality, the actual calculations would be more complex than this. For example, introduction of the lag policy would normally apply only to new hires, and the pay of the existing employees would reduce gradually over time as no scale increases were granted. Thus, the savings in wage costs would phase in over time, along with the increases in turnover and the declines in productivity. For the lead policy, it would be necessary to raise wages of all employees immediately, so costs would rise immediately, and the turnover rate should decline immediately, but the improved quality of employees arising from this policy would only phase in over time. Computer models have been developed to do these calculations.

In this example, it does appear that adopting a lag strategy would be the most efficient, eventually generating a savings of nearly $1 000 000 per year compared with the present "match" policy. But we have not really included intangible costs, such as customer reaction to finding their favourite teller gone. Furthermore, we have not included any costs of reward dissatisfaction other than turnover. We can predict that organizational commitment would be adversely affected, but what is the cost of that? Would cooperation with management drop? Would absenteeism increase? Would attitudes toward customers deteriorate, and what might this cost in lost revenue?

What about the cost of mistakes? We have already included the time needed to discover and correct them in our productivity calculations. But what impact does a mistake have on customers and their confidence in and satisfaction with their bank? How many bank errors would you, as a customer, tolerate?

Furthermore, what if our assumptions are wrong? Is it really reasonable that employees earning direct pay of $18 000 (and knowing that most banks pay higher wages) would have a turnover rate of 33 percent, while employees earning $30 000 (and knowing that virtually no bank pays higher wages) would still have a turnover rate of 27 percent? In our hypothetical example, the 10 percent change in turnover for a 20 percent change in pay was based on research in the United States (Klaas and McClendon, 1996), since no Canadian data were available.

But what about economic conditions and unemployment? Were these figures calculated when there was a labour surplus or shortage? If there is now a labour shortage, it may be virtually impossible to recruit qualified individuals at 20 percent less than market, and selection standards might need to be lowered dramatically. Furthermore, as these employees gained experience and training, the best of them would be offered jobs at other banks. Those who couldn't get such offers would stay. How would this affect our productivity estimates? In contrast, if there is now a labour surplus, it may be that there would be virtually no turnover in the leading firms, since employees would be concerned about being able to find another comparable job.

So, what would happen if turnover changed by 20 percent, for a 20 percent change in wages? What if productivity dropped by more than 12 percent with a 20 percent drop in wages? Furthermore, perhaps the changes are not symmetrical. For example, with a 20 percent lead policy, would we be able to attract all the best employees from our competitors? We all know of instances where the best employee in a unit can do much more work than the worst, sometimes twice as much. Would it be unreasonable to expect that staffing ourselves with only top-notch employees would cause a 24 percent productivity gain? (This assumes, of course, that our selection procedures are good enough to pick out the best performers from the large pool of applicants we will have.)

Running the analysis again, changing the productivity increase for a lead policy to 24 percent results in a total cost of $10 970 000. This compares with $11 689 000 for a lag policy and $12 600 000 for a match policy. Interestingly, analysis now indicates that there are savings to be had from changing to either a lag or a lead strategy, but that the lead strategy is now optimal from a cost perspective.

As these calculations illustrate, a major advantage of utility analysis is the ability to answer "what if" questions. Normally, the analysis is run for a whole range of estimates, including worst-case and best-case projections. This also helps to identify the minimum conditions necessary for a change in policy to pay off. For example, we might determine that we need a productivity gain of at least 18 percent to move to a lead policy. We can then ask "how likely is that?"

But before making the final decision, it is important to come back to a basic point: that the pay-level strategy chosen must also support the corporate and managerial strategies being pursued and must fit the organizational context. If we are practising a high-involvement management strategy, a lag strategy may destroy at a stroke the close relationship between the organization and the employees that has been carefully nurtured. However, firms using a classical strategy may have no such concern, and have much less to lose by going to a lag strategy. The organization's competitive strategy might also be relevant—is the firm's strategy based on friendly, knowledgeable tellers, or is it based on low-cost service?

As a footnote, given the complexity and uncertainty of this whole analytical process, is it any wonder why, unless forced to change, many firms simply throw up their hands and just stick with their current policy?

HYBRID POLICIES

Aside from choosing a straight lead, lag, or match strategy, firms may choose a hybrid strategy. For example, a firm could choose to lag for entry-level positions, especially if applicants are plentiful, but lead in higher-level positions, to avoid turnover of highly trained personnel. A firm may have different policies for different compensation components—for example, to lag in base pay, to lead in performance pay, and to match in indirect pay. They may also choose to have different pay-level policies for different employee groups.

hybrid compensation policy a compensation-level strategy that varies across employee groups or compensation components

Before concluding our discussion of compensation level, it is important to again emphasize the close interrelationship between method of pay and amount of pay. To illustrate this, imagine that you are the owner of a medium-sized firm in the service sector, and you have hired two different compensation consultants to devise a compensation strategy for you. Both have come up with plans in which employees will receive $4000 per month in total compensation, on average, but there are some differences between the plans. You then submit one of these plans to an independent expert for evaluation and the other to a different expert.

One expert reports that you are very lucky you consulted her, because $4000 per month is too high a pay level! But the other expert reports that a $4000 pay level is just fine. In confusion, you submit their reports to your next-door neighbour, who happens to be compensation manager for a prominent local firm. He tells you that both independent experts are right! What is going on here?

As it turns out, one compensation plan calls for the $4000 to be distributed 67 percent to base pay and 33 percent to indirect pay. But in the second plan, the distribution is 50 percent base pay, 25 percent performance pay, and 25 percent indirect pay. On analysis, the second plan is projected to produce value for the organization in excess of $4000 per employee; but the first plan is projected to produce value of less than $4000 per employee. Thus, the *nature* of the compensation mix affects the *amount* of compensation that you can afford to pay.

EVALUATE THE PROPOSED STRATEGY

Table 1.1 in Chapter 1 listed eight goals for the effectiveness of a compensation system. At this point, before implementation, it is important to review the proposed strategy against these criteria. Three of these criteria—affordability, legality, and employee attraction—can be seen as screens through which the strategy must pass. If it can't pass all of these, the strategy is a nonstarter.

Clearly, if a compensation strategy will result in costs that are beyond the financial means of the organization, it can go no further. To determine this, it is necessary to project the cost of the system, and to compare it with what the organization can afford. However, this is often not a clear-cut process, since both the costs of the system and the funds available are often difficult to determine in advance. In many cases, the success of the compensation strategy itself will play a major role in determining whether the funds will be available to meet payroll. In a business organization, future revenues and profitability can be difficult to predict, especially for firms in turbulent environments. And although public-sector organizations may be able to predict their budgets more accurately, many of them are prone to sudden budget cuts, which have a direct impact on what they can afford.

Before the final decision is made, some estimate of the cost of the compensation system must be derived. This requires a knowledge of the number and type of employees who will be employed over the next year. To make these estimates, it is necessary to project the volume of business or service that is to be provided over the coming year. Once this has been done, the projected total compensation for each employee is then multiplied by number of employees.

In general, legality is straightforward to determine, although there can be numerous areas of ambiguity. Does your plan meet the minimum standards under the employment standards act in your jurisdiction? If piece rates or commissions are used, will they meet the standards for minimum pay and overtime under the relevant employment standards legislation? Does your plan comply with human rights legislation and pay equity legislation? If the firm is intending to use independent contractors, do they meet the necessary criteria to be so classified? If there is any uncertainty at all, many experts recommend getting an advance ruling from the appropriate government ministry.

When coupled with the other rewards the organization will offer, will the system really be able to attract employees with the necessary qualifications? There are numerous ways of testing the labour market to assess this, as will be discussed in Chapter 10.

After these basic screens are passed through, the other criteria need to be reviewed. Will the resulting behaviour contribute toward achievement of organizational goals? Is there any possibility that the system could end up promoting behaviour that is detrimental to goal achievement? Might the system promote some behaviours at the expense of other important behaviours? Does the compensation system fit with our managerial strategy and organizational structure?

Another issue is equity. Will the system be seen as equitable by those who are subject to it? Of course, it is unlikely that any system will be seen as completely equitable by all employees. But to what degree will it be seen as equitable and by how many employees? A major issue to consider here is the value of an equitable system to the organization. As has been discussed earlier, some organizations can tolerate a compensation system seen as inequitable, and others cannot. To those organizations in the latter group, equity needs to be seen as another screen through which the strategy must pass before final approval. One way of checking for this is to present the proposed plan to focus groups of employees who will be affected by it.

Finally, even if the compensation strategy meets all these criteria, one question remains: Is the proposed strategy the most efficient or cost-effective strategy for meeting all these criteria? The only way to know this is to identify all the viable alternative compensation strategies and to evaluate them against these same criteria. But given the complexity of this process, few firms will have the resources or energy to do so. This is why many of them rely on compensation consultants; however, there is no guarantee that they will come up with the optimum plan either.

Of course, once the strategy is implemented, there should be ongoing evaluation as to whether the compensation system is performing as planned, or whether adjustments need to be made. It is the rare compensation system that won't have some wrinkles to iron out. And, as discussed earlier in the book, even a strategy that was optimal when implemented can become ineffective if various circumstances change. This issue of evaluation and adaptation of ongoing compensation systems will be discussed in Chapter 12.

WHO DEVELOPS THE COMPENSATION STRATEGY?

Picture the following scenario as a method for establishing a compensation strategy: All employees of the firm attend a day-long meeting each year. Attendance is compulsory. During this meeting, the financial results of the firm are carefully studied. Then, employees vote on how much of the net profits for the year should go to shareholders, how much should go for employee bonuses, and how much should be allocated to retained earnings. The group decides on what salaries and benefits will be provided for the coming year, and whether there will be any change to the compensation strategy. Evaluation committees, elected earlier in the year, provide input on individual employee performance, and each department decides on the amount of bonus each employee will receive for the year just completed and how much of a raise each will receive for the coming year.

Sounds ridiculous, you say? How could you trust employees to make responsible decisions? Surely no firm could survive long with a system like that! Well, tell that to Windsor Factory Supply, a highly successful company in Windsor, Ontario, which uses precisely this system. But it wouldn't work for every firm, and Box 8.2 helps explain why this system works for Windsor Factory Supply.

Of course, a more conventional approach is that the CEO sits in his or her office, looks over the financial results, and simply decides what the compensation strategy will be for the coming year. This may be a viable approach for some organizations. These two contrasting examples are intended to bring us to a key issue that has not yet been addressed in this chapter: who should develop the compensation strategy?

If compensation is to serve as a strategic tool, it needs to dovetail with and support the organization's corporate and managerial strategy. For this to happen, those developing the compensation strategy must have a clear understanding of the organizational context. In fact, if an optimal compensation strategy is to be developed, all four of the key understandings discussed at the beginning of this chapter must reside within the body developing the compensation strategy.

This suggests that the body charged with developing the overall compensation strategy should be the same body that is responsible for the other strategic decisions in the organization. In many organizations, this means the chief executive officer. The key contribution that top management brings to the compensation strategy process is an understanding of the strategic context for compensation. But normally, top management cannot be expected to be experts in the other three necessary understandings, and it is the role of human resource and compensation specialists to bring this knowledge to the process.

It is also up to the compensation specialists to carry out the detailed design of the compensation system within the parameters set by the compensation strategy. These specialists may be in-house or outside consultants, but if outside consultants are used, it is crucial that the process be actively managed by the firm itself.

Another important issue is the stage at which broad employee representation is included in the process. Of course, if the organization is unionized, the

---

BOX 8.2 Employees Own Their Jobs at Windsor Factory Supply

Why does employee determination of the compensation strategy work at Windsor Factory Supply? To understand this, it is necessary to know a little more about this firm.

Windsor Factory Supply is an industrial wholesaler of a wide variety of parts associated with the automobile industry, and does about $90 million worth of business annually (up from $30 million five years ago). The firm is completely owned by its 135 employees, who completed the purchase of the firm from the original owners in 1995. The firm has no job titles and no formal hierarchy. The board of directors is elected by employee-owners each year. All employees have access to all company information, and key performance indicators come up on everyone's computer screen every morning. Employees

have a wide degree of latitude in how they do their jobs, although they must be accountable for results. The firm pays higher salaries than its competitors, but is still more profitable, due to high employee motivation and commitment.

In this high-involvement firm, employee participation in all aspects of the business, including compensation policy, is a given. Employees are committed to organizational goals, they understand the organizational context and the kind of behaviour that is required, and they certainly understand employee needs. Mix in a few employees who understand the compensation options and legal constraints facing the firm, and all the ingredients for good compensation decision making are in place.

compensation system must be acceptable to the union members. But organizations vary greatly in the degree of employee involvement that takes place prior to presentation of the proposed compensation system. In traditional classical organizations, there is usually none.

Since an understanding of employee needs, as well as acceptance by employees, is necessary if the compensation system is to achieve maximum success, many compensation experts recommend extensive employee involvement right from the early stages. But this is viable only in high-involvement organizations. There are many different stages at which employees can be involved, and it is quite rare for them to be involved in the formation of the compensation strategy.

However, it is much more common for employees to be involved in the design of the various specific elements in the compensation system. For example, it is common to have employee involvement in developing and managing employee benefits, or in designing and managing a profit-sharing plan, often through joint employee–management committees. In general, the more employee involvement in the development process, the more likely that the plan will address important employee needs, and the more likely that it will be seen as equitable.

Not all organizations will be able to engender effective employee involvement. Three critical conditions are employee commitment to organizational goals, trust between management and employees, and open and effective communication and information sharing. In general, high-involvement organizations will be able to engender the most employee involvement, classical organizations the least, and human relations organizations will fall in between.

COMPENSATION STRATEGY FORMULATION: AN EXAMPLE

All of this may sound fine in an abstract way, but it probably does not feel very real to you. Let's try to make it feel more real by putting you in the hotseat. Try to visualize the following situation.

You are president and chief executive officer of Canada Chemicals Corporation, a firm that produces industrial chemicals. While the firm is profitable, profits have been slipping in recent years, and you see some other disturbing signs. Although there could be many causes for these problems, it may be that at least part of your problem is your compensation strategy, and it may need an overhaul. But be wary: things are seldom as simple as they seem! Because formulating a new compensation strategy (and deciding whether to actually go ahead with it) is complex and requires concentration, be prepared for a whopping headache before you are done!

THE COMPANY

Canada Chemicals Corporation produces two main categories of industrial chemicals. Some of the chemicals you produce are "off-the-shelf" (OTS) products, while others are custom developed in conjunction with purchasers.

Custom-developed chemicals take much longer to sell, because their specifications have to be worked out between the purchaser and your company.

It is the job of the chemical sales engineer to interface with customers, assess their needs, and determine whether an off-the-shelf product would suit their needs. If not, the sales engineer's job is to identify the technical requirements for the product, and then develop the preliminary chemical specifications for a product that will meet these requirements. In some cases, a minor modification of an OTS product will do the trick. In others, modification of a previous custom product will work. In still other cases, the custom product needs to be developed from scratch.

This information is then sent to the chemistry department, which further refines the product formulation, examines whether there is a cheaper way of producing the product (e.g., modifying a custom product that the sales engineer wasn't aware of), verifies that it will meet customer needs, and then develops the production specifications. These specifications are then sent to the production department, which develops a cost estimate for the product, plus a preliminary estimate of how long it would take to produce the product. This goes to the vice-president of sales, who develops a price and delivery date based on these estimates and relays this to the district sales manager. All of this information then goes to the sales engineer, who prepares a detailed proposal for the customer.

Often this proposal is reviewed by the customer's chemists, who may suggest changes to the product formulation. If they do, the whole process needs to be repeated. Sometimes the customer will balk at the price or delivery date, and it is up to the sales engineer to discuss this with the district sales manager to see whether any break on price or change in delivery date can be negotiated. If the sales manager recommends a new price, the revised proposal goes back to the vice-president of sales for approval. If it is a timing problem, the sales manager takes it up with production, which can either refuse or agree to changes in the delivery date but may impose extra costs for doing so. This all then goes back to the sales engineer, who goes back to the customer.

Despite the complexity of this process, the company actually makes a much higher margin on custom products than on off-the-shelf products because there has been increasing competition in OTS products, which has caused prices to be cut to the bone. For OTS products, production costs (including labour and materials) account for 55 percent of the final selling price, resulting in a gross margin of 45 percent. For custom products, production costs amount to 35 percent, leaving a gross margin of 65 percent.

Production is complex, using an array of complex mixing and refracting equipment, much of it computer-controlled. Products are made in batches of varying sizes, ranging from as little as ten litres to 50 000 litres. A wide array of different production processes are used. Production employees require a considerable amount of skill and experience, and many of them have certificates from various technical schools.

Production employees unionized about two years ago and are paid an hourly wage, which matches the wage levels of other unionized plants but is about 10 percent higher than two non-union chemical plants that have recently opened up. The company has a modest defined benefit pension plan, and some health and life insurance, but total indirect pay is relatively modest for the industry, amounting to about 15 percent of total compensation. Tasks have been subdivided into many different jobs, and pay rates for each job are set by job evaluation. Jobs are defined narrowly and are considered boring by most production workers. Turnover among production workers is about 20 percent per year, somewhat high for the industry.

Overall, the company has about 360 employees, and total compensation runs at about $18 000 000 per annum. There are 100 sales engineers, 160 production employees, 25 chemists and lab technicians, 40 managers and supervisors, and about 15 other administrative staff. Administrative and technical staff are paid a salary that is based on job evaluation and intended to match the market. Turnover among these employees is about 15 percent per annum.

The company does about $40 000 000 of business a year, and earned a before-tax profit of about $5 000 000 last year. The company is capitalized at $30 000 000 and is listed on the Toronto Stock Exchange.

THE PROBLEMS

Although the company's financial performance was good in the past, you are concerned about several disturbing signs. Not only has total sales revenue stagnated over the past three or four years, but profits have been declining steadily (they peaked at $8 000 000 three years ago).

The reduced profits are occurring for two reasons. First, additional competitors have entered the field for OTS products, driving prices down. Second, the proportion of custom products sold has declined from about 40 percent of sales to about 25 percent over the last three years. Customers are complaining about slow service and misformulated products, and they can now go to alternative suppliers, when several years ago there were virtually no other suppliers. (When the product does not end up serving customer requirements, this is very costly for Canada Chemicals, because the entire purchase price must be refunded, and sometimes even damages must be paid. Almost always, the customer is lost.)

Sales engineers have a bachelor's degree in chemical engineering. When they join the firm, they are given a two-month intensive course on company products, how to assess customer needs, and the like. They are then assigned a territory to cover, under the supervision and guidance of a senior sales engineer in a nearby territory. Canada is divided into five regions, with a regional sales manager for each.

Currently, each sales engineer averages about $50 000 in total compensation, approximately 40 percent of which is base pay, 40 percent is commission based on volume of sales, and 20 percent is indirect pay. (Most sales engineers consider the free use of a company car as their most important benefit.) Base pay is $20 000, indirect pay amounts to $10 000, and the sales engineer receives a commission of 5 percent on gross sales (the average annual sales per sales engineer is $400 000). This system matches industry standards.

However, you perceive problems with the current sales compensation system. First, it is getting difficult to attract sales engineers, who are usually hired right from university. Last year there were only 160 applicants for the 30 vacancies, and three out of every four job offers the company made were rejected.

Many of those who refused job offers cited the compensation system as a deterrent. They indicated that while the average direct compensation of $40 000 plus car sounds okay, and while they were impressed that some sales engineers earned as much as $60 000 in direct pay (the company has about ten in this league), most were concerned about the uncertainty of their pay, given that they have high student loans to pay off. They were concerned that pay might be low in the first couple of years (while most sales engineers earned in the $40 000 to $45 000 range, average direct pay in the first two years averaged $30 000 per annum).

Second, there is a high turnover rate of new engineers, with many leaving in their first year. In fact, of the 30 you hire each year to replace vacancies, only ten survive the first year. The company also loses about ten experienced sales engineers a year. Job stress is often cited as one of the reasons for leaving.

Third, new sales engineers report that senior sales engineers show very little interest in helping them do their jobs, even though advice and tips from the senior sales engineer would be very valuable. When badgered about this problem by their district managers, the experienced sales engineers defend themselves vigorously, arguing that the only way they can make enough money is to spend all their time selling, and they have little time to help anyone else.

Fourth, most sales engineers seem to focus on the "off-the-shelf" products, even though the custom-designed products carry a much higher profit margin for the company. Sales engineers report that selling custom products is just too time-consuming and frustrating, citing lack of cooperation from the other departments. As one put it, "with friends like those (in the chemistry and production departments), who needs enemies? They don't seem to understand what it takes to sell a product, and seem to work against me more than with me. Besides, with prices dropping on the OTS products, I've got to pay most of my attention to moving these products if I want to make a living."

Fifth, there is high animosity and conflict among the chemists, the production department, and the sales engineers. Production accuses the sales engineers of always trying to cut prices on their products to stimulate sales, and the chemists of coming up with production specifications that are overly complex and do not meet customer requirements, resulting in wasted product. The chemists accuse the sales engineers of not taking the time to really find out the customer's needs, and turning in poorly defined customer requests, which often results in the wrong type of product being produced. They view the production department as being technically incompetent, fouling up the final product.

The sales engineers accuse the chemists of being too fussy in what they want, too slow to formulate the product, and prone to misformulating products. They accuse production of overpricing the product, being too slow in delivery, and producing poor-quality product. There is also high resentment among the sales engineers against top management, who are leaning on them to sell more custom products, although there is little money in it for them, and making them scapegoats for the company's drop in profitability.

FORMULATING THE NEW COMPENSATION STRATEGY

In fact, you do believe that most of the problems the firm is facing are due to poor performance of the sales engineers. You call in the VP of sales and ask him to explain this poor performance. However, he repeats the party line that the problems are not his fault. Instead, they are caused by the other departments and by the poor quality of sales engineers that the human resources department is recruiting.

You then march into the human resources department and demand to know why they are failing to do their job effectively. "If we are matching the market in total compensation, why can't we find decent sales engineers? Maybe something is wrong with our recruitment and selection procedures or with our recruiters. Maybe we even need a new head of human resources!" But, like everybody else, they claim that it is not their fault! So, you reply, if it is not their fault, whose is it? After some hesitation, they begin to reply.

You know what they are going to say: We need to pay our sales engineers more money. More money! Always more money! Don't they know our profits are going down? But they reply that there is more to it than that. It is the whole managerial system. Aha, you reply, so now it's all *my* fault!

But after calming down, you start to realize they are making sense. They talk about how the organization seemed to function fine when the environment was stable and there were few competitors. But with the increasingly competitive environment, the classical structure just doesn't seem to be performing.

The human resources manager explains: "We have a small-batch, intensive technology. We want our competitive strategy to be more like a prospector than a defender. Most of the task behaviour that we need requires creativity, high interdependence, and high skill. We require well-educated, highly skilled people, who need to collaborate across departments. We need high membership and organizational citizenship behaviour. We are a relatively small organization, so do we really need all the hierarchy and centralized decision making? Shouldn't we be moving toward a more high-involvement, flexible, collaborative managerial strategy?"

When they put it that way, you can't help but agree. So how do you get there? There are a lot of things that need to be changed, but none of that will work unless you also change your compensation system. To do that, a task force is struck, consisting of you, the head of human resources (now promoted to VP of human resources, reporting directly to you rather than to the VP of finance and administration), and the VPs of sales, chemistry, production, and finance/administration.

The task force first examines the whole array of rewards—both intrinsic and extrinsic—that the organization provides, and is depressed by what they find. At the moment, the only reward being perceived by employees is compensation, and almost nobody is satisfied with that either. Jobs are seen as boring, promotions are rare and seem mainly based on whether top management likes a person, and little training is provided. The VP of human resources suggests that in moving to a high-involvement strategy, many new intrinsic and extrinsic rewards will materialize. But it is also clear that the compensation strategy itself must also change.

After considering the options, the group decides to implement profit sharing for all employees (in order to increase employee interest in the bottom line and to create greater cohesion and cooperation within the firm) and a company stock plan to further reinforce this interest, to create a commonality of goals with the organization, and to serve as a source of retirement savings, since most employees regard the current defined benefit pension plan as inadequate.

An employee task force is then set up to help design the specific features of the profit-sharing and stock plans. The union is cautious about participating in this process, but finally agrees to allow two union officials to sit in on these meetings as "observers." However, they make it clear that this does not necessarily mean they will sign on to any plan that is developed, especially if they have to give up anything in the way of direct wages. They also make it clear that their preference would be to improve the regular defined benefit pension plan.

The proposed stock plan will allow employees to invest up to 5 percent of their total compensation in company stock, and the company will match each share one for one. If employees take full advantage of this plan, this amounts to a 5 percent increase in their total compensation. There is a minimum one-year holding period for the shares, and employees may place these shares in an RRSP. This allows them to deduct their contributions from income tax, and also serves as a vehicle for retirement savings.

The profit-sharing plan will pay out in cash every quarter, and is designed to amount to at least 5 percent of pay in a typical year. (One purpose of this plan is to provide a source of funds to invest in company stock, since many employees indicated that it would be very difficult to do so out of their current earnings.) Based on projected profits for the coming year, the rate needs to be set at 14 percent of pre-tax profits in order to amount to 5 percent of total compensation. You choke a little at this, especially when you realize that the stock plan could cost an equivalent amount, if there is full take-up, but you agree that there is no point in doing any of this if it does not make a noticeable difference to employees.

To redesign the sales compensation system, you create another task force, including you, the VPs of human resources and sales, several regional sales managers, and several sales engineers, especially several younger ones. Their first decision is to create teams of five to eight sales engineers who have the responsibility for sales in a given geographic area. Although each engineer will have her or his own territory, all are also expected to help cover the territories of other team members when they are away or need help.

Using the strategic template illustrated in Figure 8.3 as a guide to outline their options and summarize their choices, the task force formulates the following sales compensation strategy. In order to improve its ability to attract and retain top-calibre sales engineers, the company plans to lead the market in total compensation for sales engineers by 20 percent. Ten percent will be provided by implementing the new profit-sharing and stock plans.

To improve income stability, the new strategy will redistribute pay between base pay and performance pay, by increasing base pay to 50 percent of compensation (from 40 percent), and reducing performance pay to 30 percent (from 40 percent). There will also be a major redistribution within performance pay, aimed at improving teamwork. Only 10 percent will now be allocated to individual commissions, and a group commission plan that is targeted to comprise about 10 percent of compensation will be introduced. Under the group commission plan, all members of a sales team will share equally in commissions based on the total sales of that team.

To encourage more sales of custom products, commissions will now be based only half on total sales volume, and half on gross margin. The actual commission rates will be: individual commissions—0.75 percent of individual volume, 1.45 percent of individual gross margin; group commissions—0.75 percent of sales team volume, 1.45 percent of sales team gross margin. Thus, total commissions for each sales engineer will be 1.5 percent of volume and 2.9 percent of gross margin, compared with the previous 5 percent of total volume.

This is what the typical sales engineer is projected to earn under the proposed new compensation system, in comparison with the average under the current system:

	CURRENT SYSTEM	NEW SYSTEM
Base pay	$20 000	$30 000
Individual commissions	20 000	6 000
Group commissions	–	6 000
Profit sharing	–	3 000
Stock plan	–	3 000
Indirect pay	10 000	12 000
Total	$50 000	$60 000

EVALUATING THE PROPOSED COMPENSATION STRATEGY

The firm now must assess the impact of the new plan on the company. It will cost at least $1 000 000 more in sales compensation annually. Will it be worth it?

Answering that question is not easy. We have to make many assumptions, any of which could turn out to be wrong. But we have to try, and Table 8.5 illustrates an attempt to generate some projections. The first column represents the current system, as a basis for comparison, while the next two columns

FIGURE 8.3   COMPENSATION STRATEGY TEMPLATE

Job Family: *Sales Engineer*

Total Compensation Level: Match? _____   Lead? *20%*   Lag? _____

	Proportion of Total Pay
1. Base Pay	50%
a. Job evaluation	~
b. Market pricing	50%
c. Pay for knowledge	~
2. Performance Pay	30%
a. Individual performance pay	~
i. Piece rate	~
ii. Commissions	10%
iii. Merit bonuses	~
iv. Special incentives _____	~
b. Group performance pay	
i. Gain sharing	~
ii. Goal sharing	~
iii. Other group pay *Group Commissions*	10%
c. Organization performance pay	
i. Profit sharing	5%
ii. Stock plan	5%
iii. Other organization pay	~
3. Indirect Pay	20%
i. Mandatory benefits	8%
ii. Pension plan	4%
iii. Health & life insurance	3%
iv. Paid time off	~
v. Employee services	~
vi. Other benefits *Automobile*	5%

provide "best guess" projections of what might happen in years 1 and 2 under the new sales compensation plan. (Of course, we have no guarantee that the past year's results would be repeated this coming year if we don't change anything, but let's leave that issue aside for now.)

PROJECTIONS FOR YEAR 1   Our first assumption is that total sales volume in year 1 under the new system will remain constant. This will be the result of two opposing forces. It is expected that there will be more cooperation among sales engineers; more training by senior engineers; better cooperation between sales engineers, chemists, and production; a higher calibre of sales engineer hired; and lower turnover of new sales engineers, all of which

TABLE 8.5 CANADA CHEMICALS CORPORATION—PROJECTED RESULTS OF NEW SALES COMPENSATION SYSTEM

	CURRENT SYSTEM	PROPOSED SYSTEM PROJECTED RESULTS		PROPOSED SYSTEM PESSIMISTIC EXPECTATIONS	
		Year 1	Year 2	Year 1	Year 2
Sales volume	$40 000 000	$40 000 000	$42 000 000	$36 700 000	$40 000 000
Proportion of custom products	25%	33%	40%	36%	33%
Gross Margin	$20 000 000	$20 660 000	$22 260 000	$19 175 000	$20 660 000
Sales engineer compensation	$5 000 000	$6 000 000	$6 174 245	$5 792 000	$6 000 000
Sales engineer turnover	30/100	25/100	15/100	25/100	15/100
Sales training costs	$150 000	$200 000	$120 000	$200 000	$120 000
Additional training costs	–	$100 000	$100 000	$100 000	$100 000
Recruitment costs	$120 000	$100 000	$60 000	$100 000	$60 000
Gross Margin (after subtracting direct sales costs)	$14 730 000	$14 260 000	$15 805 755	$12 983 000	$14 380 000
Add production cost savings	–	$386 800	$789 600	$175 250	$386 800
Net Margin	$14 730 000	$14 6746 000	$16 595 355	$13 158 250	$14 766 800
Subtract administrative overhead	$9 730 000	$9 243 500	$9 501 345	$9 438 100	$9 243 500
Add additional production cost savings	–	$967 000	$1 381 800	$525 750	$967 000
Gross Profit before Taxes	$5 000 000	$6 369 500	$8 475 000	$4 245 900	$6 490 300
Subtract additional profit-sharing costs	–	$644 027	$854 280	$427 986	$654 222
Subtract additional stock plan costs	–	$644 027*	$644 027*	$644 027*	$644 027*
Net Profit before Taxes	$5 000 000	$5 081 446	$6 976 693	$3 173 887	$5 192 051

*Note: This assumes that all employees will purchase their full allotment of shares, which is unlikely. This also assumes that the shares contributed by the company are purchased on the market. However, if the company wished to conserve cash, it could issue treasury shares. This would, of course, dilute shareholder equity.

should work to increase sales. But against that, we expect sales engineers to devote more time to selling custom products, which is more time-consuming. Sales of senior sales engineers may drop somewhat as they spend more time helping junior sales engineers. And, as will be seen below, the new compensation system may result in the loss of some senior sales engineers, also reducing sales.

These factors will certainly reduce sales of OTS products, but by how much? We are estimating that the new system should boost the mix of custom product sold in the first year by 33 percent from $10 000 000 to $13 300 000 and that OTS product will drop to $26 700 000, resulting in no net change in sales volume.

These predictions will depend on our turnover assumptions. We are assuming that the new pay system will cut the annual turnover of first-year sales engineers from 20 engineers to 10, and of middle-level sales engineers from ten to five. But what about senior sales engineers? Under the proposed new plan, their compensation will actually drop, since their earnings are currently based mainly on high-volume, low-margin OTS products. Furthermore, part of their commissions will now be based on the average in their sales team (which is the effect of the group commissions), which will also bring down their pay. The result? Take a sales engineer currently selling $700 000 worth of OTS product and $100 000 of custom product, therefore earning direct compensation of $60 000 (i.e., 5 percent of $800 000 plus $20 000 base pay). Even if that engineer maintains these sales volumes, direct pay would drop to $57 721 under the new plan. But maintaining these sales volumes is unlikely, since senior engineers will be expected to shift more concentration to custom product, and spend more time training new sales engineers, so their income would likely drop more than this.

How will they react to this? Let's assume the worst—that we lose all ten of our top producers. This would increase turnover to 25 sales engineers in the first year of the new plan, and exert a downward push on total sales as they are replaced by new sales engineers, at least in year 1.

What about other costs? Currently, sales training costs about $5000 per new engineer, most of which is the cost of their base pay and benefits during the two-month training period. However, this cost will actually go up in year 1 under the new plan, even though we only need to train 25 engineers, rather than 30. This is because base pay and indirect pay will be higher under the new plan. We may save a little on recruiting costs, which have been running at $4000 per recruit. But in order to get the new system working, it needs to be explained to all sales engineers, and training will be needed on their new roles. Let's allocate a week to that—the cost of this will be at least $100 000, probably more.

On the positive side of the ledger, it is expected that profitability of the sales will go up, as more custom product is sold. If we reach our 33 percent increase target for custom products in year 1, and have no loss in total volume, gross margin will increase from $20 000 000 to $20 660 000. But after direct sales costs are included, gross margin would actually decrease from $14 730 000 to

$14 260 000. Thus, if all the assumptions work out the way we expect them to, the new compensation system would decrease profits by about $470 000 in year 1 compared with what they would have been with no change in the compensation system—not a very promising result.

But wait one minute! We haven't considered whether the new sales compensation might produce improvements in other areas, such as production costs. Currently, there is considerable time and effort wasted by chemists and production staff because sales engineers bring in sloppy custom orders where customer requirements have not been well assessed. In some cases, the result is unacceptable product, which is also costly.

Because of a higher calibre of sales engineer, lower turnover, and more motivation to sell custom products, you believe that better work from sales engineers can cut production costs by at least 2 percent in the first year. This would have the effect of increasing net margin to $14 646 000. That means we would almost break even in the first year of the new compensation system— not bad when you consider that most organizational changes result in an initial dip in productivity because of the costs and turmoil involved in getting the new system up and running.

As you will recall, changing the sales compensation system is not the only change being made. We are also extending profit sharing and stock ownership to everybody (assuming the union signs on). Beyond the projected cost of the new sales compensation system (which included the costs of profit sharing and stock plans), these two plans will cost an additional $1 288 054 to extend to the other 260 employees. Can we afford this?

Well, we might be able to if we assume that profit sharing and stock ownership will together reduce turnover, improve cooperation between departments, and improve productivity among the production and administrative employees (we have already included the projected impact of these plans on the sales engineers). We estimate that this should result in a 5 percent reduction in production costs, and a 5 percent reduction in administrative costs in year 1. This slightly outweighs the cost of these two programs, so the net effect of all this is virtually no change in profitability in year 1.

But what if we are being too optimistic? Can we really shift attention toward custom products, with all the extra work that entails, and lose some of our top producers, and still expect to maintain total sales volume? And what if the productivity increases and cost savings don't materialize the way we expect them to? Are we risking the company?

Let's see what would happen if we change some key assumptions to be more pessimistic. This is exactly what column 4 of Table 8.5 does. We are still assuming that the volume of custom products will increase to $13 330 000, but we are now assuming that total sales volume will drop by $3 330 000 to $36 700 000. Instead of a 2 percent drop in production costs due to better work by the sales engineers, we'll project a 1 percent reduction. Changing these two assumptions drops sales compensation to $5 792 000 (compared with $6 000 000 in the first projection) but also drops net margin to $13 158 250—a drop of over $1.5 million compared with what it would be if we carried on with the current system.

But that's not all! Let's tone down the productivity and administrative cost savings for the nonsales employees to 3 percent from 5 percent. All of this results in a reduction in projected profit from $5 000 000 under the current system to just over $3 000 000 under the proposed new system. It wouldn't put us out of business, but shareholders wouldn't be too happy. But what if no cost savings at all materialized? We would still make a profit of more than $2 000 000. So it doesn't look like we are risking the company, even if everything goes wrong, but unless you own enough shares to control the board of directors, you would likely be pounding the pavement looking for another job!

To sum up the results of all of these projections: if all goes well, we gain nothing; if all goes badly, we suffer reduced profits of nearly $3 000 000. Would you take that deal? Not likely! So far, it doesn't seem like the new compensation strategy will be worth all the trouble and turmoil it will likely cause. But we were not expecting it to pay off in the first year anyway. Changes in behaviour take some time to occur, and getting everyone up to speed on the new system won't happen overnight. Let's do some projections for a two-year period. (Luckily, you have this all loaded on a computer spreadsheet.)

Projections for Year 2   Column 3 of Table 8.5 provides projections for year 2 of the new system. It assumes that turnover of sales engineers will drop to half the original level, that sales engineers will be working together to help each other, and that working with the other departments will become significantly easier. Total sales are assumed to increase by 5 percent to $42 000 000, and 40 percent of that is assumed to be custom products. Although sales compensation now exceeds $6 million, gross margin after sales costs rises to $15 805 755. Compared with the current system, we expect more experienced and more able sales engineers to be able to provide better custom proposals and reduce production costs by 4 percent. All this results in a net margin of $16 595 355, a gain of $1.87 million from what would have happened without the new system.

For the rest of the picture, we expect administrative and overhead costs to rise by 5 percent to accommodate the higher sales volume, but then to be reduced by 7 percent as the impact of reduced turnover and more committed and cooperative employees becomes felt. For the same reasons, we expect a 7 percent drop in production costs from their pre-implementation levels. The net effect is profitability almost $2 000 000 higher than it would have been without the new system. This should make shareholders happy, as well as employees (who will also be shareholders). What's more, we will have a more flexible, cooperative company, better suited for the contextual variables it faces.

But let's be pessimistic again. Let's see what happens in year 2 under pessimistic assumptions. That's what column 5 in Table 8.5 shows. After the disastrous first year (shown in column 4), we are assuming that sales volume recovers to the original levels, but that custom work stays steady, at

$13 330 000. Assuming that performance of sales engineers reduces production costs by 2 percent, the net margin is $14 766 800—virtually identical to what it would have been with no changes in compensation. Assuming other cost savings of 5 percent, total profit for year 2 amounts to just over $5 million, similar to what it would have been without the new system. Of course, because of the nearly $2 million profit shortfall in year 1 (under the pessimistic projections), we are behind about $2 million over the two years.

MAKING THE DECISION

So do we go ahead with the new compensation system or not? If our expected projections represent reality, then of course, yes. But there are so many assumptions that could be wrong. How much confidence do we have in our "best guess" projections? What if the pessimistic estimates are closer to the truth? Why not just play it safe and stick with the current system?

Well, there is one key assumption we have not examined. For comparison purposes, we have assumed that by doing nothing, things would stay the same, including our $5 million profit. But is that really a good assumption? Consider that profitability has been dropping a million dollars a year for the last three years. Consider all the problems that are emerging. Consider the fact that application of the strategic framework (from Chapter 2) predicts that the performance decline will continue because of a mismatch between the contextual variables and the classical school of management the organization has been practising.

If this is true, then even with the pessimistic projections the new system looks good. All in all, it appears that the risks of not doing anything are greater than the risks of going ahead. If you fail to act because you are not completely sure about the consequences of your actions, then you will never act. Whatever you do, you will lose sleep, but taking decisions like this is why you are being paid the big bucks!

There are still a few things that you need to do before going ahead. One is to develop goals and indicators for evaluating your strategy, as will be discussed next. Another is to check the legality of the new plan, but there are no obvious legal problems with it. If the position of sales engineer is a primarily male job class, and if you are in a jurisdiction with pay equity laws, you may have to modify pay levels of some of your female job classes (although this wouldn't affect many employees in this particular company), since pay is going up for your male group. However, this adjustment may not be possible until the system has been in place for a year, since you don't know whether the pay of sales engineers will actually go up, or by how much.

SETTING GOALS FOR THE NEW STRATEGY

You've decided to take the plunge and go ahead. But you are still aware that this is no sure thing. We need to design a process for evaluating the success of the new compensation system once it has been implemented. To do this, we need to develop the specific goals that we hope the plan will achieve, along with performance indicators for evaluating whether these goals are being achieved. This should enable us to evaluate whether modifications to the compensation plan are needed, and to help identify what those modifications should be. Examples of possible compensation goals and performance indicators are shown in Table 8.6.

Remaining Tasks

A lot remains to be done before plan implementation. You need to identify the other factors in the managerial system that you need to change to make the compensation system work. It may also be necessary to modify the compensation strategy for other employee groups in the firm. Afterwards, the most important tasks are developing your implementation plan and creating the necessary infrastructure for operating the new compensation system and managing it on an ongoing basis. Even a sound compensation strategy can be torpedoed by poor implementation and weak ongoing management. These issues are covered in depth in Chapter 12.

Compensating Different Employee Groups

Should the compensation strategy be different for different employee groups? Traditionally, it has been. Normally, employees are categorized into several groups, and a separate compensation system is utilized for each group. These groups usually consist of hourly paid employees, clerical employees, sales employees, professional employees, managerial employees, and executives. Most firms also differentiate between permanent, full-time employees, and contingent workers—workers who are part-time or temporary. Some even have separate systems for new hires and existing employees.

Traditional hierarchical organizations (which include both classical and human relations organizations) have always based compensation on hierarchical level, on the assumption that jobs (and employees) higher in the organization are more valuable, and thus should be compensated more highly. Classical organizations typically pay their lowest-level employees based on individual performance (piece work, commissions) if they can, or else the number of hours worked. Employees higher in the hierarchy are provided with salaries and limited indirect pay. Top management is provided with base pay, indirect pay, and a large component of organizational performance pay. Their logic for providing organizational performance pay to only top management is that only they are in a position to significantly affect the success of the organization.

The compensation system in human relations firms is not much different, except that there is a greater tendency for all employees to be on salary, and indirect pay is typically more generous. Organizational performance pay is still confined to senior management.

TABLE 8.6 CANADA CHEMICALS CORPORATION— GOALS FOR NEW SALES COMPENSATION SYSTEM

GOAL	INDICATOR
Membership Behaviour	
1. Increase attraction of new sales engineers	• Increase qualified applicants from 160 to 400 • Increase offer acceptance rate from 25% to 50%
2. Increase retention of new sales engineers	• Reduce turnover of first-year engineers from 67% to 33%
3. Increase retention of other sales engineers	• Reduce turnover from 14% to 7%
Task Behaviour	
4. Increase sales of custom product	• Increase from 25% of sales to 33% in year 1 • Increase to 40% of sales in year 2
5. Maintain/increase total sales volume	• Maintain total sales volume in year 1 • Increase total sales volume by 5% in year 2
6. Improve cooperation with other sales engineers	• Sales employee surveys
7. Improve quality of custom proposals	• Reduction in rejected product due to sales errors • Reduction in hours by chemists processing proposals
Citizenship Behaviour	
8. Increase cooperation with other departments	• Surveys of other departments
9. Increase flow of suggestions for improvement	• Number of suggestions submitted
Financial Goals (Overall Compensation System)	
10. Production costs	• Reduce by 7% in year 1 • Reduce by 11% in year 2
11. Net profit	• Exceed $5 000 000 in year 1 • Exceed $7 000 000 in year 2

But there are two main trends taking place. There is a greater tendency to extend group and organizational performance pay throughout the organization. And there is a trend toward greater similarity of treatment for employees within the compensation system. Sales employees are having base pay included in their compensation plans, while other employees are having an element of performance pay added to their compensation. Stock options used to be provided only to senior management; now many firms provide them to all employees. Perks that were formerly restricted to top management are now either being offered widely or being eliminated. Some firms are moving away from hourly pay toward "all salary" systems to reduce distinctions between employee groups. In many cases, these changes are being made to create a greater sense of cohesion and unity among the workforce, particularly among firms that adopt the high-involvement model.

According to the framework developed in this book, the compensation system for various employee groups should differ if the type of required behaviour differs significantly between employee groups or if the needs of the employees in the various employee groups are significantly different. Of course, if behaviour is similar, or key elements of behaviour are similar, then the compensation system should reflect this. Aside from sales employees, who were discussed in Chapter 5, there are four main groups for whom the compensation system often differs dramatically from the compensation norm in the organization—contingent employees, new employees, executives, and international employees. Each group will now be discussed in turn.

CONTINGENT WORKERS

contingent workers
workers not employed on a permanent, full-time basis

One trend that received a lot of notice during the 1990s was the increasing use of **contingent workers**—workers not employed on a full-time, permanent basis. For example, by 1996, approximately 19 percent of Canadian employees were part-time workers, nearly a 50 percent increase since 1976 (Zeytinoglu, 1999). Other types of contingent workers—temporary full-time employees, independent contractors, and persons hired from temporary help agencies— also made up an increasing proportion of the workforce (Lebrun, 1997). Some observers even wondered whether this trend heralded the end of the full-time permanent job as the standard model of employment (Zeytinoglu, 1999).

However, the trend toward contingent workers has levelled off. For example, the proportion of part-time employees did not grow at all between 1996 and 2000 (Statistics Canada, 2001). Moreover, the average length of time that a worker is employed by the same employer, after decreasing during the 1980s and early 1990s, has returned to levels similar to what they were in the 1970s (Picot, Heisz, and Nakamura, 2000). Among the firms in the Compensation Practices Survey, 86 percent of their employees were full-time, and 94 percent were permanent employees. On average, firms outsourced about 6 percent of their labour requirements.

Nonetheless, many firms do employ a substantial number of contingent workers. Why? There are several reasons. In some cases, contingent workers are hired to handle highly skilled work for which the skills do not exist within the organization—such as designing a new computer system or planning a plant expansion—because the organization cannot afford to maintain or fully utilize them on an ongoing basis. In other cases, contingent workers are hired to assist regular employees to handle overflow work, temporary peaks in work flow that are not going to be permanent. Contingent workers are also hired as temporary replacements to handle vacations, parental leaves, and the like. The key difference from regular, permanent employees is that contingent workers are utilized only when needed and released when they are not.

However, in many cases, contingent workers are hired to do the regular work of the organization on an ongoing basis. For example, retailers may hire a few full-time cashiers, but have most of this work done by part-timers. One reason for this is that using part-timers helps to deal with a workload that may fluctuate with time of day, day of the week, and even day of the month. In many cases, these employees are not temporary at all, nor are they peripheral to the main operations of the business, but they are employed only at the will of the organization. However, some firms differentiate between casual part-time and permanent part-time employees. The latter group are not really contingent workers, since the firm makes a commitment to provide at least a certain minimal level of employment on a continuing basis.

Use of contingent workers generally frees employers from many of the legal constraints that apply to permanent employees. For example, contingent employees are typically exempt from severance pay provisions, as well as from employee benefits. Contract employees (although not part-time employees) are exempt from employment standards provisions and mandatory benefits. No cause is needed for dropping a contingent worker from the workforce, so this makes it easy to correct selection errors. Some employers, especially those from the classical school, may believe that contingent workers are easier to manage because the employer can hold the threat of dismissal over their heads.

Some firms may see contingent workers simply as a way of reducing the cost of labour, and attempt to substitute contingent workers for regular employees whenever possible. But for other firms, the motives are somewhat more complicated. These firms see their labour force as consisting of two groups of employees. One group consists of core employees, who are committed, loyal, and highly knowledgeable, with skills and training that have taken years to acquire. They are compensated accordingly.

But it is too expensive to utilize these core employees for routine, repetitive, low-skilled work, so contingent workers are utilized for this type of work. Use of contingent workers to do a portion of the organization's regular work also provides a buffer to protect core employees if product/service demand drops. Recent research in the United States showed that firms offering the most costly benefits to permanent employees used significantly more contingent workers than other employers (Houseman, 1997).

Interestingly, the Conference Board study of Canadian employers (Lebrun, 1997) found that "controlling benefits costs" and "buffering core workers against job loss" were the two *least* important reasons for using contingent workers, as each was cited by less than 15 percent of respondents. In contrast, "developing labour flexibility to meet demand fluctuations" was cited by more than 90 percent of employers, and "acquiring special expertise" was cited by about 70 percent. Nearly half cited "controlling head count," and about one-quarter saw the use of contingent workers as a way of screening candidates for future employment.

From a compensation point of view, the key issue is "how should these employees be paid?" If what they are doing is the same as permanent employees, and our current compensation system is effective, we would want to utilize the same compensation system. But if we believe that our compensation system has become too generous or expensive, particularly for some types of work, we may attempt to deal with this problem through the use of contingent workers. Of course, if the behaviour expected of contingent workers is significantly different from that of regular employees, then a different compensation system may well be justified.

Some organizations where contingent workers perform regular, important functions, such as in banking, make it a point to extend their compensation system to all employees. For example, the Royal Bank has introduced a "one employee" policy, where all employees participate in the same compensation system. But this is not the norm. In the Conference Board study, only 20 percent of respondents indicated that their firms offered the same benefits to contingent workers who worked side-by-side with regular employees, and other research has shown that contingent workers are often paid less than regular workers (Zeytinoglu, 1999).

According to equity theory, this discrepancy in pay would be expected to lead to perceptions of inequity, from which a variety of negative consequences might arise. Unfortunately, there has been little direct research evidence on this issue, although studies have found that turnover is much higher among part-time workers than full-time workers (Tilly, 1992), and satisfaction is lower (Bourhis, 1996). However, a study in the United States found no difference between the task performance of contingent and permanent office workers at a large university (Bourhis, 1996).

One factor that may influence employee reactions is whether they are doing contingent work voluntarily or involuntarily. For example, Marshall (2000) notes that the majority (73 percent) of part-time employees in Canada are engaged in part-time employment because they prefer it, or because their circumstances prevent them from accepting full-time employment. It would be expected that involuntary part-time employees will be less satisfied with part-time work, and exhibit higher turnover, than employees who prefer part-time employment. But while some studies have borne this out, such as studies of Canadian nurses (Armstrong-Stassen, Horsburgh, and Cameron, 1994) and temporary help employees (Krausz, 2000), others have not (Bourhis, 1996).

Finally, before we leave the subject of contingent work, the concept of job sharing should be clarified. To some, job sharing may appear to be a type of contingent work, since job sharers work less than a full workweek—generally half. But it is not contingent work because job sharers are considered to be permanent employees, with rights similar to those of full-time employees. Under job sharing, two individuals share one full-time job, along with the pay and benefits that attach to that job.

Employers are generally motivated to allow job sharing in order to retain valued employees who, for a variety of reasons, do not wish to work a full workweek. Not surprisingly, job sharers show greater satisfaction with their hours and pay than do casual part-time employees, according to a Statistics Canada survey (Evenson, 1997). In general, research shows that job-sharing employees are at least as committed to their employer as full-time employees, and may be more productive, because they are better able to strike a balance between their home and work lives.

NEW EMPLOYEES

One compensation practice that became popular in the early 1990s was **two-tier wage systems**, under which new employees receive lower wages than existing employees for doing exactly the same work. Of course, you could argue that seniority systems, merit pay, and pay-for-knowledge systems produce the same result.

However, the difference is that under seniority-based pay, merit pay, and pay for knowledge, new employees can eventually earn what the older employees now earn, once they acquire the same seniority, performance level, or knowledge. In contrast, the intent of many two-tier systems is that new employees will never earn as much as existing employees are earning. In this usage, a two-tier wage structure is used as a vehicle to effect a permanent reduction in compensation level that phases in as older employees terminate and new employees join the firm. Once all the existing employees are gone, there will no longer be two tiers, just one lower tier.

But if the pay level is too high, why not just cut pay levels for all employees and be done with it? Of course, some firms do just that. But for unionized employees, it is legally necessary to get them to approve these reductions, which may not be easy. Since employees who haven't yet been hired have no vote, it is often easier to sell existing employees on a two-tiered system than on across-the-board cuts.

Indeed, if existing employees believe that compensation costs must be cut in order to improve the viability of the firm, they may see a two-tier system as increasing their own job security, as well as creating employment that would not otherwise be created (Martin and Heetderks, 1990). Numerous firms also use a two-tiered approach for their non-union employees, based on the view that it would not be equitable to violate the psychological contract under which employees were hired. Their reasoning is that since new employees know what they are getting into when they join the firm, there is no violation of the psychological contract for them if they join at a lower pay level than that enjoyed by existing employees.

two-tier wage system
pay system in which new employees are subject to a different (lower) pay structure than existing employees

In some cases, it may be illegal to arbitrarily cut compensation for even non-union employees. For example, an Ontario court recently ruled in favour of a manager who, at the time of employment, was told she would be eligible for a bonus that would be paid by a specified date. When the company refused to pay the bonus, she quit her job and took the firm to court. The court ruled that the company could not arbitrarily eliminate the bonus, and ordered the firm to pay it (*Human Resources Management in Canada*, 1997).

Rather than creating a permanent pay cut, a two-tiered system can also be used to effect a temporary cut for new employees, in order to tide the firm over difficult circumstances. In fact, this approach may actually be more common than a permanent two-tier system (Martin and Heetderks, 1990). For example, a firm may now be paying a flat $20 an hour to all employees. Under a temporary two-tier plan, new employees may start at $10, and take five years to reach $20. However, this does not really constitute a full-fledged two-tier system.

Very little is known about the impact of two-tier systems on either new or existing employees, or on the relationship between the two groups. Equity theory would suggest that, once new employees learn that their pay will never match that of existing employees who are doing precisely the same work, they may find this inequitable. At Lincoln Electric (discussed in Box 5.1) existing employees strongly resisted a management push for a two-tiered system on the basis that it would be inequitable and would impede employee relationships, and the plan was rescinded.

Lower-tier employees may feel they are being treated as second-class citizens, which may hinder their relationships with management and other employees. They may try to find some other way of balancing the psychological contract, resulting in some of the negative consequences discussed in Chapter 3. Of course, offering a lower wage rate can, all things being equal, be expected to reduce the quality of the employees the firm is hiring and to increase turnover rates.

There is very little empirical evidence on the consequences of two-tier systems, but one study has been conducted by Martin and Heetderks (1990). They found that low-tier workers indeed reported significantly lower satisfaction with pay and pay fairness than high-tier workers. However, there was no difference between the two groups in absenteeism and self-reported job effort, and, even more interestingly, job satisfaction and affective commitment to the company were actually significantly lower among high-tier workers than among low-tier workers.

The explanation may be that dissatisfied high-tier employees perceived no opportunity to leave the company, since their pay was significantly higher than what they could expect from the external labour market. However, dissatisfied low-tier employees perceived little difficulty in obtaining comparable employment elsewhere, so they simply left, leaving only the satisfied low-tier employees. Thus, for high-tier employees, the pay system was apparently generating continuance commitment but not affective commitment.

As economic conditions improved during the late 1990s, two-tiered wage systems have lost popularity. They have also been subjected to challenges under human rights legislation, and some jurisdictions (notably Quebec) have amended labour standards legislation to make two-tiered wage structures illegal, although "temporary" two-tier structures are permissible (Coutu, 2000).

EXECUTIVES

Let's go from one extreme to the other. Another issue that has been attracting a lot of attention for the past few years is executive pay. This is partly because executive pay has been escalating, while the pay of rank-and-file employees has been stagnating, and partly because new disclosure laws have made executive pay more visible.

In the United States, which leads the world in executive pay, executive compensation, which averaged 43 times the pay of an average worker in 1960, had jumped to more than one hundred times by 1990 (Bok, 1993), and the total annual compensation of some chief executive officers—such as Warner Communication's CEO Steven Ross—had cracked the $100 million barrier. Following this trend, executive pay also soared in Canada, resulting in a doubling of the gap between workers and top corporate executives between 1970 and 1990 (Lohr, 1992).

Coming at a time when many employers were downsizing, and coupled with evidence that executive pay often bears little or no relation to company performance, this new-found knowledge of executive salaries caused a major hue and cry, which received extensive media coverage. To cast more light on these concerns, in 1992 the Securities and Exchange Commission in the United States toughened its already stringent requirements for disclosure of top executive salaries in publicly traded corporations, and in 1994 took this a step further, by limiting the tax deductibility (for corporate taxes) of non-performance-related executive compensation to $1 000 000 per year. In 1993, the Ontario government passed legislation modelled very closely after the 1992 U.S. legislation, which resulted in the Ontario Securities Commission establishing the first disclosure requirements ever imposed on top executive salaries in Canada.

The outcome of all this? By the beginning of the century, the average compensation of chief executive officers in publicly traded U.S. corporations reached 475 times the average pay of a factory worker (*The Economist*, 2000). This occurred during a decade when most workers had shown no real gain in their compensation. What message does this send to employees? How do you think they would react to exhortations from their CEO that "we all need to pull together" to ensure the success of "our company"?

Sure, workers may be a little disgruntled, but at least managers will stay on side. Or will they? Listen to a manager at United Technologies, which had downsized by 30 000 employees in the previous six years. A 20-year veteran of the firm, with good performance reviews, he has done slightly better than the industrial averages, with increases of about 4 percent a year for the past three years. During this period, net income of the company rose dramatically, by 28 percent in 1995 alone, a year in which shareholders received a 55 percent return on their investment.

> *I used to go to work enthusiastically. Now, I just go in to do what I have to do. I feel overloaded to the point of burnout. Most of my colleagues are actively looking for other jobs or are just resigned to doing the minimum. At the same time, the CEO is paid millions, and his salary is going up faster than anyone else's. It makes me angry and resentful. (Byrne, 1996: 100)*

In Canada, the divergence between the pay of top executives and other employees has not been as large as in the United States, and Canadian executive compensation did not rise during the 1990s to the extent enjoyed by U.S. executives. Research suggests that Canadian executives currently earn about half of what CEOs in comparable U.S. firms receive (*Report on Business*, 2000), compared with about 75 percent in the early 1990s (Magnan, St-Onge, and Thorne, 1995). Overall, the typical Canadian CEO makes about 20 times what a typical employee earns, which is similar to most European countries, although higher than in Japan (*The Economist*, 2000), where executives earn only about 11 times worker pay. According to Bok (1993), the Japanese believe that morale and teamwork within the organization will be destroyed if differences between executive pay and pay of other employees get too large.

One thing to note is that the salary levels enjoyed by U.S. and Canadian corporate executives are not enjoyed by top executives of all organizations. Take David Dodge, governor of the federal Bank of Canada, for example. Dodge has many years of experience in senior public-service positions, including five years as deputy minister of finance, and has a doctorate in economics from Princeton. The quality of his performance can make or break the Canadian economy, and can affect the livelihood of millions of Canadians and the success of tens of thousands of businesses. His current salary range: $297 800 to $349 200. At that level, he is one of the most highly paid executives in the federal government, earning more than his boss, the minister of finance ($194 640), as well as the prime minister ($262 988).

Dodge's pay may sound pretty good to the average Canadian wage earner, who received about $34 330 in 2001. But compare Dodge's compensation with that of John Cleghorn, CEO of the Royal Bank of Canada, who earned $17 400 000 in 2000 (Willis and Howlett, 2001), and it doesn't seem quite so substantial. And, to be fair, Cleghorn's compensation is not at the top of the corporate list.

So why do corporate executives make so much? A large part of the answer lies in the bonus and incentive structure of their compensation. Let's examine this by looking at the compensation of ten of Canada's highest-paid executives (*Report on Business*, 2000). Their base pay (averaging $868 000), while substantial, amounted to a very small portion of their total earnings (averaging $16 298 000). Income from exercise of stock options accounted for the biggest chunk, averaging 67 percent ($10 841 000), followed by earnings from other incentives and bonuses, which averaged 28 percent ($4 589 000).

Clearly, one reason for the surge in executive compensation in the 1990s was the buoyant stock market in the United States and Canada. Because of the thousands of stock options that executives have been granted, gains in company share prices bring them rich returns. But this does not explain the whole picture. Even excluding income from stock options, executive pay has been rising sharply for quite a few years.

What factors determine how much an executive receives? As already seen, sector makes an enormous difference, with executives in the corporate sector receiving much more than executives in the public sector. What else? Some observers argue that executive pay should be tied to the financial performance of the corporation, but research in both the United States (Gomez-Mejia and Balkin, 1992) and Canada (Magnan, St-Onge, and Thorne, 1995; Zhou, 2000) shows little or no relationship between executive compensation and company performance, when excluding stock options. Once stock options are included, there is a significant relationship between firm performance (in terms of stock market valuation) and executive compensation, although not necessarily other indicators of corporate performance (Zhou, 2000).

What other factors affect compensation of corporate executives? The most important factor is firm size, as CEOs of large firms make more than CEOs of small firms (Magnan, St-Onge, and Thorne, 1995; Zhou, 2000). Another important factor is whether the firm is management-controlled or owner-controlled. In many large firms with widely dispersed ownership, there is no single owner with the power to significantly affect management decisions. Firms where this is the case are termed management-controlled; firms where this is not the case are termed owner-controlled. In general, all other things being equal, top executives in management-controlled firms earn significantly more than top executives in owner-controlled firms (Magnan, St-Onge, and Thorne, 1995). In other words, firms in which top executives determine their own salaries set them higher than firms where top executive salaries are set by owners.

Studies in the United States suggest two other important factors (Gomez-Mejia and Balkin, 1992). Firms with fewer hierarchical levels (after controlling for size) pay their top executives less than firms with more hierarchical levels, and diversified firms pay their CEOs more than less-diversified firms. The first finding makes sense when you consider that hierarchical organizations must increase pay at each hierarchical level in order to provide an incentive for employees to try to move up the hierarchy, and the second makes sense in that more-diversified organizations are more complex to manage than less-diversified organizations.

But these factors still do not explain all of the variation in executive pay, nor all of the recent escalation. One way of examining this further is to understand the process by which executive pay gets set in large corporations. The board of directors strikes a compensation committee consisting of several directors. The committee then hires a compensation firm to provide data on how "comparable" chief executive officers are being compensated, and then uses these data as a basis for their decisions. This sounds like a rational and reasonable process.

However, the process may not always be as "rational" as it sounds. First, the compensation consultants hired are often recommended by the CEO, and it is in their best interests to keep the CEO happy, if they want to do other business with the firm. When looking for appropriate comparators, the consultants will certainly not be interested in erring on the low side. Furthermore, many boards (especially in management-controlled firms) are populated by directors recommended by top management, and these directors will not wish to incur ill will by being stingy with executive pay. One prominent observer (Crystal, 1991)—a former compensation consultant now highly critical of executive compensation practices—also points out that no board of directors wishes to believe that they have an average or below-average CEO, and that most firms attempt to pay above the market, and certainly not below the market, as Colvin (2001) has found. If the majority of firms do this, then a continually increasing "market" is inevitable.

Moreover, many corporate directors are often themselves CEOs, and can be expected to be highly sympathetic to the plight of other CEOs. Of course, high executive salaries can be used as evidence for higher compensation when it is *their* turn to be compensated as CEOs. All told, unless one is representing the owners, there is little incentive to hold executive pay down. But perhaps this will change as shareholders become more militant and as institutional investors, such as pension funds, take a more active role in corporate affairs, as the Ontario Teachers' Pension Fund has been attempting to do (Macklem, 2001).

It was noted earlier that CEO compensation does not necessarily bear any relation to company financial performance. But should it? The obvious answer would seem to be "yes," but is this really correct? One prominent commentator in this area argues that "contrary to much of what one reads in the academic and practitioner press, there is no sound theoretical basis to expect a strong relationship between executive pay and firm performance" (Gomez-Mejia, 1994: 161).

To what extent can a top executive actually influence organizational performance? In the short run, not much, especially in large organizations. In most organizations, financial performance is a function of many factors, many of which are beyond the control of the CEO, especially in the short run. But research does show an increasing impact over a longer time period (Gomez-Mejia and Balkin, 1992). This is not surprising. In general, the role of a top executive is to formulate the strategy that will best achieve organizational goals, and then create an organizational system for carrying out that strategy. Particularly in large organizations, this process may take years to pay off.

Current conditions of the firm may also be an important consideration. A CEO who takes over an organization in a tailspin may be considered a great success if he or she can slow the descent in the first year, and start to turn things around in years two and three. Does this CEO really deserve less than a CEO who takes over a prosperous firm operating in a highly favourable competitive environment?

Moreover, it may not be in the best interests of the organization or the shareholders to tie executive pay too closely to current or short-term performance. There are all kinds of things that can be done that make short-run performance look good but will ruin the firm in the longer run. For example, a CEO can cut research and development expenditures, saving money now but causing a shortage of new products when the old ones become obsolete. A CEO can cut employee compensation, causing the most-talented employees to gradually slip away. A CEO can forgo long-term investments that might be very beneficial but would take years to pay off. And a CEO so inclined can also attempt to manipulate financial results or stock performance in such a way as to obtain bonus criteria, although these actions may not reflect the true financial performance of the firm.

For these reasons, long-term incentives, rather than base pay and annual bonuses, have been forming an increasing portion of the CEO's compensation (Peck, 1996). There are three main types of longer-term incentives that are most commonly used for executive pay—stock options, restricted stock, and long-term unit/share plans. Although popular in the United States, restricted stock is less common in Canada, because it does not receive the favourable tax treatment it receives in the United States (Klein, 1996). The essence of restricted stock is that executives are granted shares of company stock, but they are not allowed to actually receive it unless certain conditions are met. Sometimes the condition is simply a holding period, say of three years, during which period the stock is forfeited if the CEO leaves the firm. In other cases, the executive will not receive the shares unless certain performance targets are reached. For example, Coca-Cola CEO Douglas Daft was granted $87.2 million in restricted shares in 2000, but will receive the full amount only if he manages to increase earnings per share by 20 percent a year between 2000 and 2005 (Lavelle, 2001a).

Stock options have been very popular, partly because they have been traditionally regarded as a virtually costless way of compensating executives. But use of stock options has increasingly come under critical scrutiny, as shareholders have come to realize that these options do have a very real cost in terms of dilution of equity (Reingold, 1997). Also, as discussed in Chapter 5, in a declining stock market, executives may be penalized despite good performance; in a rising stock market, they may reap windfall gains unrelated to their personal performance. Moreover, in recent years executives are increasingly turning to "zero cost collars"—hedges that tend to decouple performance of the company stocks from their financial returns, effectively reducing their risk (Lavelle, 2001b). Because hedges do not have to be publicly reported, other shareholders may not know that the CEO is decoupling his or her financial returns from those of the company. As Lavelle (2001b: 71) puts it: "An executive who hedges is a little bit like the captain of a ship who sees an iceberg up ahead and heads for his lifeboat without waking the sleeping passengers."

As a result of these problems, there has been some investor backlash against the use of executive stock options. For example, the Ontario Teachers' Pension Fund, the second-largest institutional investor in Canada, has been pressing for changes whereby the basis for CEO compensation is whether the firm outperforms competitors, not simply whether the stock price goes up (Macklem, 2001). In fact, this backlash against executive stock options received recent support from researchers in the United States, who found that stock options were in fact a very expensive way to motivate executives, and that restricted stock is much superior (Hall and Murphy, 2000).

As a result of the problems inherent in stock options, long-term unit/share plans (as discussed in Chapter 6) have become increasingly common, and rightly so. If structured properly, they can continually provide a longer-term perspective (three to five years) to counterbalance the short-term perspective that other types of incentives promote.

Of course, a more fundamental question can also be asked: Why should it be necessary to provide incentives to individuals who are already being compensated handsomely for doing their jobs? Is there a concern that without multi-million-dollar stock packages, executives will simply goof off? The response to this question usually focuses on attraction and retention, and not on whether executives will choose to restrict their effort in the absence of stock packages. However, even here, there is room for debate. A recent study done by researchers at the University of Texas found that a CEO's total compensation relative to others in the industry had no effect on CEO retention, suggesting that when CEOs turn over, they do so for reasons other than compensation (Hassenhuttl and Harrison, 2000).

Indirect pay can also be an important component of executive pay, especially for executives who are not in the top echelon of pay. Many executives receive a number of perks of considerable value, the most common of which include company cars, country club memberships, company plane, free travel for family members, payment of financial planning fees, and supplemental executive retirement plans. In Canada, one significant form of indirect pay for some executives (mainly those who are lured from the United States) is the equalization of personal income taxation rates with those in the United States, so these executives end up receiving the same amount of after-tax income as they would have if they were living in the United States.

One controversial item of indirect pay for executives is known as the "golden parachute." These may be structured in many ways, but the essence is that an executive who is dismissed within a certain time frame, say five years, for any reason, is guaranteed a large severance payment, usually amounting to about three to five years' pay. Sometimes there is no time limit on these payments, and they kick in whenever the CEO is dismissed.

Many observers argue that such "parachutes" take away the incentive for good performance, since the executive will do very nicely regardless of performance. Other observers argue that these "parachutes" are beneficial because they may encourage executives not to fight takeover bids that may be beneficial to shareholders but in which the CEO would lose his or her job. In addition, proponents argue that it would be difficult to lure good executives away from highly paid jobs with other firms without some financial guarantees to protect them if things do not work out for them in their new job. Opponents ask: Why would you want to hire an executive who has so little faith that an iron-clad guarantee is required?

So how should a CEO be paid? There are six decision issues:

1. the amount of performance pay relative to base pay and indirect pay;
2. the amount of short-term (annual) performance pay vs. longer-term performance pay;
3. the nature of the performance pay itself;
4. the specific type of performance indicators used as criteria for the performance pay;
5. the stringency of the performance criteria;
6. the time period to be used as the performance period for the incentive.

How do you decide on the best way to handle each of these decision areas? As with all types of compensation, the first question is, "What do we want the executive compensation system to accomplish?" There are two main aspects to this matter: a behavioural aspect and a symbolic aspect.

What executive behaviour do we want? Research has shown that executives, as is true of most people, tend to pursue actions that will maximize their compensation. It is therefore very important that the compensation system promote executive behaviour that fosters achievement of organizational goals and serves the long-term best interests of the organization. It should also be noted that the way in which the top executive is compensated will likely have a major influence on the compensation system that is implemented for other managers and employees. This compensation system will be designed to foster employee behaviour that will help the executive to achieve his or her compensation rewards. This is known as a "cascading effect." Of course, this is fine as long as these behaviours are in line with the corporate strategy the organization is pursuing.

The executive compensation system has a very important symbolic value in several ways. Because of its visibility, executive pay is seen as a signal of the kinds of behaviours the organization values. The behaviours for which top executives are rewarded will tend to be emulated by subordinates.

Executive pay also has an important equity or fairness dimension. If executive pay is structured very differently from the pay of other employees, this may cause serious motivational problems and various other negative consequences flowing from reward dissatisfaction. Recall the manager at United Technologies who had reduced his commitment to the organization because of this issue. Other employees were actively seeking other jobs or were reducing their effort to the minimum, because they believed the reward system to be inequitable when they compared their treatment and the treatment of the CEO.

The need for perceived equity will be a much bigger problem in some types of organizations than others. It will be a minimal problem in classical organizations, if the cost of turnover is low, if extra job effort and citizenship behaviour are not really needed, and if there are controls to constrain dysfunctional behaviour. It may not be a big problem in human relations organizations, if the firm has traditionally demonstrated high concern for employees and pays relatively well.

But it can be a huge problem for high-involvement organizations, where a sense of equity is essential to generating the cooperative and citizenship behaviour that is crucial for success. As Lawler (1992: 329) puts it: "High involvement management requires that senior managers ... give up some of the special perquisites and financial rewards they receive." This is because extreme divergence between executive pay and that of other employees makes a sense of commonality of interest almost impossible.

EXPATRIATE AND FOREIGN EMPLOYEES

As Canadian companies respond to globalization, an increasing number have established operations outside of Canada. Of course, employees of these foreign operations must be paid, but compensation practices that are suitable in Canada may not be appropriate in other countries, for a variety of reasons. Labour market conditions, product market conditions, and legal and cultural conditions may differ dramatically, depending on where the foreign operations are located.

Another relevant factor is whether the employees in question are foreign nationals, or expatriate Canadians sent to play a role in operating foreign subsidiaries. The compensation policy issues are very different for each of these groups, and each will be discussed separately.

For home country expatriates (those who are sent to foreign countries from the company's home country, i.e., Canada), the key issue is to create a compensation package that ensures that expatriates do not lose financially compared with their home country peers but that is still cost-effective from the company's point of view. There are four main approaches that can be used: (1) the balance sheet, (2) negotiation, (3), localization, and (4) lump sum.

balance sheet approach approach to designing expatriate compensation that attempts to provide a standard of living comparable with the home country

The most common approach has been the **balance sheet approach**. The objective of this approach is to create a compensation system that enables expatriates to maintain a standard of living comparable with what they would enjoy in their home country, regardless of the host country they are sent to.

Expatriate expenses are broken down into four main categories: (1) income taxes, (2), housing, (3) goods and services, and (4) a "reserve" or "discretionary" component. Costs of comparable income taxes, housing, and goods and services in the host country are calculated and then converted to Canadian dollars, and the "reserve" amount is added. This total amount (paid in Canadian dollars) is the base pay for the expatriate. The "reserve amount" is calculated by determining how much a comparable Canada-based employee would have left as discretionary income after deducting expenditures for income taxes, housing, and necessary goods and services. In some cases, an additional amount may be added to base pay as a "hardship allowance" to compensate expatriates who are sent to locations that have health and safety risks or other undesirable aspects.

However, there are several potential problems with this procedure. These problems include changes in the currency exchange rates in the period since conversions to Canadian dollars were calculated, as well as changes in tax rates, housing costs, or other living costs. To deal with these problems, an equalization approach can be taken. For example, for income taxes, the company can deduct the cost of Canadian income taxes from the expatriate's pay, and then simply pay the expatriate's actual income taxes in the host country, which could be more or less than the Canadian amount. This creates a tax-neutral treatment from the expatriate's point of view.

An equalization approach for housing expenses is similar. Reasonable Canadian costs are calculated, and this amount is deducted from the expatriate's income. The company then pays whatever it actually takes to provide comparable housing in the host country, either directly to the foreign landlord or by providing local currency to the employee. The same basic procedure can be followed for other living expenses. The key advantage of this approach is that expatriate employees are treated equally regardless of the host country they are sent to, and that compensation does not need to change as exchange rates or local circumstances change. Employees can also be transferred from one host country to another without changing the way they are compensated.

Besides the balance sheet approach, several other approaches have been used. *Negotiation* is a process in which the employer and employee negotiate a mutually acceptable package. However, there are numerous problems with this approach. First, the employee may not be very knowledgeable about conditions in the host country and thus may find it difficult to judge whether a package is reasonable or not. Second, there is the potential for inequity if different packages are negotiated for different employees, especially if the differences are based only on the negotiating skills of the employees. Third, because no system is used for deriving the packages, they often have no systematic procedure for changing them in response to changes in host country conditions.

Localization is the practice of paying expatriate employees the same compensation as local nationals in equivalent positions. This method fits best with assignments that are going to be long term, with companies that have extensive operations (and well-developed compensation systems) in the host country, and with host countries that have higher compensation than the home country, as is generally the case with Canadian employees assigned to the United States. Localization to home country (i.e., Canadian) rates is also often done for foreign nationals who have been assigned to the home country on other than a temporary basis.

Another approach to expatriate compensation is the *lump sum approach*. This method differs from the balance sheet approach in that the various allowance amounts (such as for housing) are paid directly in home country (i.e., Canadian) dollars to the employee, who may then decide to live in a lower standard of housing than the norm and pocket the remainder of that allowance. Problems with this approach include changes in foreign exchange or local conditions, and possible losses of some tax advantages. For example, in some countries housing allowances are not taxed as income to the employee, although salary paid directly to the employee is.

One issue common to all approaches is the extent to which a premium is paid for foreign assignments and what method of payment should be used. These premiums are paid over and above the standard expatriate compensation that is based on preserving the employee's standard of living, and they vary considerably for different countries. There is no hard and fast system for determining the amounts of these premiums, and the only method may be to assess employees' degree of aversion to each country. Of course, what may be paradise to one employee may be purgatory to another, so this is a subjective process.

The usual method for paying foreign premiums is to simply prorate them, and include them on the monthly paycheques. However, this may create a reluctance to relocate from one host country to another that pays lower premiums, or to repatriate to Canada. To deal with this problem, some firms use "mobility bonuses," in which employees are paid the premium as an up-front bonus, not on a continuing basis, thus removing disincentives for transfer.

A different variation on expatriate compensation has to do with "third-country nationals"—employees of the firm not based in the home country who are assigned to a third country. For example, suppose that a Canadian firm assigns a Spanish employee from its Spanish subsidiary to its operation in Chile. Should the employee be compensated in Spanish currency using a balance sheet approach, or should the employee be localized? While the same decision rules could be used as for Canadian expatriates, this does get very complicated, especially if the balance sheet approach is used. Another problem occurs when employees from two or more foreign countries are assigned to the same third country. For one, the balance sheet approach may be most appropriate, while for another the localization approach is best. Unless localization is used for both employees, they will have very different compensation levels, even if they perform the same work. To avoid this problem, some companies simply use the same rates as would apply to Canadian expatriates in Chile, but this may not be fair to third-country nationals from high-wage countries such as the United States. Unfortunately, there are no simple solutions.

Finally, another issue has to do with compensation of local nationals in foreign countries. Clearly, the home country compensation system could be inappropriate. But this is not to say that the most appropriate compensation strategy is to simply copy local competitors. The same understandings discussed earlier in the chapter—understanding your context, people, compensation options, and compensation constraints—need to be applied to the foreign subsidiary, along with the five steps in the compensation strategy formulation process. The resulting compensation system could well be different from that used in the home country and from that used by local competitors.

Because of the complexity of international compensation, the objective of this section has been to simply acquaint the reader with some of the key issues. An excellent source for more detailed information is Tyson (2001).

SUMMARY AND IMPLICATIONS

The purpose of this chapter was threefold: to complete the foundation of knowledge upon which an effective compensation strategy can be built; to describe the process for building that strategy; and to discuss special considerations in developing compensation strategies for four very different employee groups.

It was noted that four key understandings form the necessary foundation of knowledge for compensation strategy formulation—understanding your organization, your people, your compensation options, and your constraints. The first three of these understandings were covered in previous chapters; this chapter identified four types of constraints that set the parameters for compensation strategy—legislated, labour market, product/service market, and financial—and illustrated how an understanding of them is essential in formulating the compensation strategy.

Next, the five main steps in the formulation of the compensation strategy were described: (1) define the behaviour that the organization requires; (2) define the role the compensation system will play in eliciting that behaviour; (3) determine the best mix of compensation components; (4) determine policies for compensation level; and (5) evaluate the proposed strategy against effectiveness criteria. This was followed by a discussion of who should be involved in the compensation strategy formulation process, and a detailed example of compensation strategy formulation.

Finally, the chapter concluded with a discussion of some of the issues involved in compensating four special employee groups—contingent workers, new employees, executives, and international employees.

The remaining two parts of the book focus on how to convert the compensation strategy from a blueprint into an operational compensation system. Part IV covers the technical processes for evaluating jobs, evaluating the market, and evaluating individuals. Part V covers the processes for implementation, ongoing management, evaluation, and adaptation of the compensation system.

KEY TERMS

balance sheet approach, p. 310

contingent workers, p. 298

employment standards legislation, p. 259

human rights legislation, p. 260

hybrid compensation policy, p. 279

labour market constraints, p. 263

lag compensation policy, p. 274

lead compensation policy, p. 275

match compensation policy, p. 276

product/service market constraints, p. 263

trade union legislation, p. 261

two-tier wage system, p. 301

utility analysis, p. 276

EXERCISES

1. In your role as CEO of Canada Chemicals Corporation (described earlier in the chapter), you have just finished formulating a new compensation strategy for sales engineers. It occurs to you that in view of your movement toward high-involvement management, the firm may also need a new compensation strategy for production workers, administrative staff, and technical staff. Using a strategic compensation template similar to that used in Figure 8.3, formulate a compensation strategy for each of these employee groups.

2. You are a prominent compensation consultant, and you have been hired by the board of directors of Canada Chemicals Corporation to recommend a compensation strategy for the firm's top executives. In your report, be sure to provide the reasoning for each of your recommendations, along with the advantages and disadvantages of each recommended compensation element.

3. Canada Chemicals Corporation has decided to move to a high-involvement managerial strategy and has hired you as a consultant to that process. Aside from the compensation strategy, what other changes need to be made if this conversion is to be successful? In the process, is there any way to increase the intrinsic and extrinsic (besides compensation) rewards provided by the firm? How could this be done?

4. Susan Superfit, CEO of The Fit Stop (in the Appendix), has hired you to formulate a compensation strategy for her firm. Using the five-step process, formulate such a strategy, and summarize it using a strategic template similar to that used in Figure 8.3. Give your rationale for each element of the strategy.

5. Using the five-step process, formulate a compensation strategy for production workers at Multiproducts Corporation (in the Appendix) and summarize it using a strategic template similar to that used in Figure 8.3. Justify your recommendations.

Suggested Web Sites

Page 259: To check on current minimum wage rates in your jurisdiction and other employment standards and labour legislation, click <www.labour-travail. hrdc-drhc.gc.ca>

Page 282: Compensation strategy has become an increasingly important role for human resource professionals. To learn more about the profession, go to <www.hrpao.org>

References

Armstrong-Stassen, M., M.E. Horsburgh, and S.J. Cameron. 1994. "The Reactions of Full-Time and Part-Time Nurses to Restructuring in the Canadian Health Care System." In D.P. Moore, ed., *Academy of Management Best Paper Proceedings*. Dallas, TX: 96–100.

Bok, Derek. 1993. *The Cost of Talent*. New York: The Free Press.

Bourhis, Anne. 1996. "Attitudinal and Behavioural Reactions of Permanent and Contingent Employees." *Proceedings of the Administrative Sciences Association of Canada, Human Resources Division*, 17(9): 23–33.

Braun, Katherine. 1997. "Employment Standards Legislation in Canada." Unpublished manuscript.

Byrne, John A. 1996. "How High Can CEO Pay Go: Special Report." *Business Week*, April 22.

Colvin, Geoffrey. 2001. "The Great CEO Pay Heist." *Fortune*, June 25.

Conference Board of Canada. 1996. "The Pursuit of High Quality Workers." *HR Executive Review*, 3(4): 5–12.

Coutu, Michel. 2000. "Les clauses dites 'orphelins' et la notion de discrimination dans la Charte de droites et libertés de la personne." *Relations industrielles/Industrial Relations*, 55(2): 308–31.

Crystal, Graef S. 1991. *In Search of Excess: The Overcompensation of American Executives*. New York: W.W. Norton.

Economist, The. 2000. "Chief Executives' Pay." September 30: 110.

Evans, David S., and Linda S. Leighton. 1989. "Why Do Smaller Firms Pay Less?" *The Journal of Human Resources*, 24(2): 299–318.

Evenson, Brad. 1997. "Job Sharing Helps Balance Work, Family Life." *Star-Phoenix*, June 10: C11.

Gomez-Mejia, Luis R. 1994. "Executive Compensation: A Reassessment and a Future Research Agenda." *Research in Personnel and Human Resources Management*, 12: 161–222.

Gomez-Mejia, Luis R., and David Balkin. 1992. *Compensation, Organizational Strategy, and Firm Performance*. Cincinnati, OH: South-Western Publishing.

Hall, Brian J., and Kevin J. Murphy. 2000. *Stock Options for Undiversified Executives*. National Bureau of Economic Research.

Hassenhuttl, Maria, and J. Richard Harrison. 2000. "Exit or Loyalty: The

Effects of Compensation on CEO Turnover." Paper presented at the Academy of Management Conference, Toronto.

Houseman, Susan N. 1997. "New Institute Survey on Flexible Staffing." *Employment Research*, 4(1): 1–4.

Human Resources Management in Canada. 1997. "Unilateral Changes to Employment Contract Costs $175,700." *Report Bulletin*, 170: 6.

Klaas, Brian S., and John A. McClendon. 1996. "To Lead, Lag, or Match: Estimating the Financial Impact of Pay Level Strategies." *Personnel Psychology*, 49(1): 121–41.

Klein, Marc-Andreas. 1996. *Top Executive Compensation: United States, United Kingdom, and Canada.* New York: The Conference Board.

Krausz, Moshe. 2000. "Effects of Short- and Long-term Preference for Temporary Work upon Psychological Outcomes." *International Journal of Manpower*, 21(8): 635–47.

Lavelle, Louis. 2001a. "Executive Pay." *Business Week*, April 16: 76–80.

Lavelle, Louis. 2001b. "Undermining Pay for Performance". *Business Week*, January 15: 70–71.

Lawler, Edward E. 1992. *The Ultimate Advantage: Creating the High Involvement Organization.* San Francisco: Jossey-Bass.

Lebrun, Sharon. 1997. "Growing Contract Workforce Hindered by Lack of Rules." *Canadian HR Reporter*, May 19: 1–2.

Lohr, S. 1992. "Executive Pay Becomes a 'Hot-Button' Issue." *The Globe and Mail*, January 22: B1.

Macklem, Katherine. 2001. "Teachers' Pet Peeves." *Maclean's*, April 30: 32–33.

Magnan, Michel L., Sylvie St-Onge, and Linda Thorne. 1995. "A Comparative Analysis of the Determinants of Executive Compensation between Canadian and U.S. Firms." *Relations industrielles/Industrial Relations*, 50(2): 297–319.

Marotte, Bertrand. 1996. "CEOs Doing A-OK." *Star-Phoenix*, September 27.

Marshall, Katherine. 2000. "Part-Time by Choice." *Perspectives on Labour and Employment*, 1(2): 1.

Martin, James E., and Thomas D. Heetderks. 1990. *Two Tier Compensation Structures: Their Impacts on Unions, Employers, and Employees.* Kalamazoo, MI: W.E. Upjohn Institute.

Peck, Charles. 1996. *Executive Annual Incentive Plans.* New York: The Conference Board.

Picot, Garnett, Andrew Heisz, and Alice Nakamura. 2000. "Were 1990s Labour Markets Really Different?" *Policy Options*, July-August: 15–26.

Reingold, Jennifer. 1997. "Executive Pay: Special Report." *Business Week*, April 21.

Renaud, Stephane. 1998. "Unions, Wages, and Total Compensation in Canada." *Relations industrielles/Industrial Relations*, 53(4): 710–29.

Report on Business Magazine. 2000. "50 Best Paid Executives." July: 135–36.

Saunders, John. 1997. "Dollars and Sense." *The Globe and Mail*, April 12.

Statistics Canada. 2001. *Labour Force Survey Statistics, 1996–2000.* Ottawa: Statistics Canada.

Tilly, Chris. 1992. "Dualism in Part-time Employment." *Relations industrielles/Industrial Relations*, 31(2): 330–47.

Tyson, John, ed. 2001. *Carswell's Compensation Guide.* Toronto: Thomson Canada.

"Wages, Productivity Fall at Small Firms." 1996. *Star-Phoenix.* October 4: D9.

Willis, Andrew, and Karen Howlett. 2001. "Bankers Face Push to Reform Their Pay." *The Globe and Mail*, February 15: A1–A6.

Zeytinoglu, Isik. 1999. "Flexible Work Arrangements: An Overview of Developments in Canada." In Isik Zeytinoglu, ed., *Changing Work Relationships in Industrialized Countries*. Amsterdam: John Benjamins Publishing, 41–58.

Zhou, Xianming. 2000. "CEO Pay, Firm Size, and Corporate Performance: Evidence from Canada." *Canadian Journal of Economics*, 33(1): 213–51.

Part IV

Technical

Processes for

Compensation

9

EVALUATING JOBS

CHAPTER GOALS

By the end of this chapter, you should be able to:

1. Explain the purpose of job evaluation and describe the main steps in the job evaluation process.
2. Describe the process for job analysis and the key steps in that process.
3. Identify and briefly describe the five main methods of job evaluation.
4. Describe the steps in designing a point system of job evaluation.
5. Identify the possible pitfalls in designing a point system of job evaluation.
6. Discuss the issues involved in establishing pay grades and pay ranges.
7. Describe the key issues in managing the job evaluation process.
8. Describe the general process for conforming to pay equity legislation.

Introduction

By now, you have formulated a compensation strategy for each of your major employee groups. This is a major milestone on your road to effective compensation. But you don't yet have a compensation *system*. The purpose of the three chapters that comprise Part IV of this book is to describe the technical processes necessary to transform a compensation strategy into an operating compensation system.

Chapter 9 focuses on how to design the job evaluation process that best fits your particular organization. Chapter 10 describes how to collect and interpret relevant labour market data, to ensure that your compensation system is grounded in economic reality. Chapter 11 describes how to evaluate individual employee skills, as part of a pay-for-knowledge system, and how to evaluate individual performance, as part of a merit pay system.

Purpose of Job Evaluation

As you will recall from Chapter 4, the purpose of job evaluation is to determine the relative contribution made by each job in the organization to the success of the organization, so that each job can be remunerated accordingly. The output of job evaluation is a hierarchy of jobs, where all jobs of a similar *value* to the organization, no matter how different they may be from each other in other respects, are located at the same level on the job hierarchy. This job hierarchy provides the foundation for the development of pay grades and pay ranges.

In conducting job evaluation, key objectives are to ensure that all jobs in the organization are compensated equitably, and are *perceived* by organizational members as being compensated equitably. Effective job evaluation should also ensure that jobs are not overpaid, which is important from a cost and competitive viewpoint. The purpose of this chapter is to describe the process for accomplishing this goal.

Steps in the Job Evaluation Process

There are five main steps in the job evaluation process:

1. *Understand* the jobs to be evaluated. Accurate and reliable job information is an essential precondition for job evaluation.

2. *Decide* how many pay structures to use. Often, firms create different pay structures for different occupational groups. But for the purposes of internal equity, the fewer pay structures, the better.

3. *Select and apply* the most appropriate job evaluation method(s).

4. *Create* a pay structure with appropriate pay grades and pay ranges and procedures for moving through these ranges.

5. *Develop* procedures for evaluating and modifying the system.

This chapter starts off by describing job analysis, which is the process for collecting information about the key characteristics of jobs. Next, the different job evaluation methods that are available will be described. Particular attention will be focused on the most important of these: the point method of job evaluation. Following that, the various considerations for establishing pay grades and ranges will be discussed. Then, the process and issues involved with conducting and managing job evaluation will be outlined. The final section illustrates the necessary steps to conform with Canadian pay equity legislation, using the Ontario Pay Equity Act as a case in point.

JOB ANALYSIS

A precondition for job evaluation is accurate information about the jobs to be evaluated. The purpose of **job analysis** is to obtain this job information, which is usually summarized in the form of a job description. A **job description** is a summary of the duties, responsibilities, and reporting relationships that pertain to a particular job. Derived from the job description are the **job specifications**, which are the employee qualifications deemed necessary to successfully perform the duties involved with the job.

Beyond compensation, job descriptions can serve a wide variety of organizational purposes. These include recruitment and selection, development of training programs, provision of guidance to employees and supervisors, facilitating development of employee performance standards, and helping to ensure that all necessary organizational activities are being undertaken and that no important activities are "falling between the cracks."

NATURE OF REQUIRED INFORMATION

What information is needed for effective job evaluation? If job descriptions are accurate and up-to-date, they may provide all the necessary information for evaluating jobs. However, experience suggests that this is relatively rare, despite the fact that many organizations expend considerable effort on developing job descriptions. As one compensation practitioner (King, 1992: 4) put it:

> *More time, money, and patience are wasted on job or class descriptions than on any other aspect of personnel administration. [Yet,] in almost twenty-five years of consulting, my firm has never had a client lay claim to an up-to-date and complete set of job descriptions. [Moreover,] job descriptions never contain all the information required to evaluate jobs for compensation.*

job analysis the process of collecting information on which job descriptions are based

job description a summary of the duties, responsibilities, and reporting relationships pertaining to a particular job

job specifications the employee qualifications deemed necessary to successfully perform the job duties for a given job

So why is using job descriptions for job evaluation likely to prove so fruitless? First, some firms simply are not willing to devote the effort needed for the task of developing and updating job descriptions. But a bigger problem is that in many organizations, particularly those in more dynamic environments, job duties are changing all the time, often escaping notice by anyone in the human resources department. Moreover, as will be seen shortly, conducting job analysis effectively is an onerous task, with many obstacles to collection of valid data. In some cases, considerable effort is expended, but the resulting job descriptions omit certain pieces of information that are essential for effective job evaluation.

What should a job description contain if it is to be useful for job evaluation? Inclusion of the following elements should produce a useful job description:

1. Job title, department or location, reporting relationships, and date when job analysis was originally completed or updated.

2. A brief statement of job purpose or objectives.

3. A list of the major duties of the job, in order of priority or importance. Some indication of the proportion of time spent on each duty may be useful, although this may not be feasible for some jobs. In describing these duties, be sure to include the tools, equipment, or work aids that are utilized in performing these duties.

4. An indication of responsibilities for people, results, and organizational assets, including cash, tools, equipment, and facilities, along with the spending or budget authorities attached to the job. The consequences of error or poor performance could help illustrate this. Included here is the nature and extent of supervision given and received.

5. The mental and physical effort demanded by the job.

6. The conditions under which the work is performed, including the quality of the work environment and any hazards or dangers that may be involved in job performance.

7. A specification of the qualifications needed to perform the job, including skills, training, education, and abilities, as well as any certificates or licences required.

Figure 9.1 provides an example of a job description, along with the job specifications that apply to that job.

METHODS OF JOB ANALYSIS

If the necessary job information does not already exist, how can it be obtained? There are four main methods: observation, interviews, questionnaires, and functional job analysis. However, it should be noted that the first three can be conducted only in ongoing organizations that already have examples of the

FIGURE 9.1   EXAMPLE OF JOB DESCRIPTION

Beaver Manufacturing Corporation

Job Title: Drafter 1

Department: Engineering (Drafting Section)

Reports to: Head of Drafting

Updated: January 15, 2001

Job Purpose

This employee utilizes computer-aided design (CAD) techniques to produce and update drawings of plant facilities, based on rough sketches, diagrams, notes, and verbal instructions provided by design engineers.

Main Job Duties (listed duties are illustrative, not restrictive)

1. Prepare finished CAD drawings from sketches, diagrams, notes, and verbal instructions.
2. Search computer databases for existing information on which to base drawings.
3. Meet with engineers to clarify drawing requirements and to discuss revisions to drawings.
4. Assist with site verifications of existing facilities.
5. Share in filing of facilities records.
6. Assist other staff in locating physical records information.

Other Job Information

Works under the supervision of senior drafters, who check product before sending to engineers for final approval. Engineers provide final check on output. If undetected, errors can cause serious facilities damage. Basic keyboarding skills are required, and ability to utilize computer-assisted design equipment. Considerable concentration is required to transform input materials into finished product. Work is mainly performed in a quiet office environment. Some exterior facilities inspection required.

Job Specifications

High school graduation plus a two-year diploma in computer-assisted design from a recognized technical institute. Ability to communicate effectively in verbal and nonverbal modes.

---

jobs that need to be evaluated. Organizations that are just being created, or that are introducing new jobs, must depend on the fourth method, functional job analysis.

The job analysis process can be conducted by personnel from the human resources department or by outside consultants. In many cases, managers and supervisors may do most of the actual work, but there always needs to be some central body to ensure consistency of results.

OBSERVATION

Observation involves watching the employee as the job is performed, and noting the kinds of activities performed, with whom, utilizing what tools or equipment. The extreme version of this process is a time and motion study, as was discussed in Chapter 5. On its own, observation is mainly useful for jobs in which the activities can be easily observed, and for which the work cycle is short (i.e., all of the important activities of the job will be seen in a short period of observation). For most jobs, observation is useful only as a supplement to other methods.

INTERVIEWS

Interviews can be conducted with either a sample of employees carrying out a given job, their supervisors, or both. Interviewing only one or the other of these groups has drawbacks. Interviews with employees can lead to valid information, but the employee perspective on the importance of various job duties may be different from that of the supervisor. Moreover, if employees know that the job analysis is being conducted for the purpose of job evaluation, it is in their interest to portray the job in such a way as to maximize its value. Interviewing supervisors may produce more objective information, but supervisors may not be as aware of the realities of the job as the employee.

Therefore, in the interests of accuracy, it would seem best to interview both the supervisor and a representative sample of employees for each job being analyzed. (Of course, it may turn out that employees who were seemingly doing the same jobs are actually doing different jobs, and it is important for the job analysis to be able to pick this up so the jobs can be formally differentiated.) The main drawback to interviewing so many people is the cost of the time involved, both for the job analyst and the interviewees. Use of a structured interview format helps to reduce the time requirement, as well as providing more consistent information.

QUESTIONNAIRES

Questionnaires may vary on two dimensions. They may be open or closed, and they may be firm-specific or proprietary. An open questionnaire asks the respondent (either the supervisor or the job incumbent) a series of questions, such as the purpose and main duties of the job. A closed questionnaire asks the respondent to check off, from a list of phrases, those phrases that best describe the job. In order to cover the variety of jobs in an organization, the questionnaire must contain a wide variety of possible duties and activities. Care must be taken to ensure that the questionnaire is reliable (i.e., that two independent observers would answer it in the same way) and is valid (i.e., that the information collected accurately reflects reality.)

Because development of reliable and valid questionnaires is a complex process, many organizations use proprietary questionnaires that have been developed by outside specialists. Perhaps the best known is the Position Analysis Questionnaire (PAQ) developed more than 30 years ago by industrial psychologist Ernest J. McCormick (McPhail, Jeanneret, McCormick, and Mecham, 1991). Since this instrument is commonly used, we will describe some of its key features.

The PAQ focuses on the behaviours that make up a job and utilizes 187 items (called job elements) to describe work activities. These job elements are grouped into six dimensions:

- *Information input* describes the sources of information an employee uses on the job.
- *Mental processes* describe the types of reasoning, decision-making, planning, and information-processing activities that are utilized.
- *Work output* includes those items assessing physical activities and use of various tools in the work process.
- *Relationships with other persons* describes the extent to which the job involves working with other people as a part of its duties.
- *Job context* items examine the physical and social environment of the job.
- *Other job characteristics* cover other conditions of work not covered by the first five dimensions.

Each of the 187 elements (statements) are assessed through use of a specific response scale. The questionnaires may be completed by anyone who is knowledgeable about the job, including job analysts, supervisors, and job incumbents. Multiple incumbents may also be used. The questionnaires are then sent to PAQ Services Inc. for computer processing. From this information, job dimension scores are derived, along with assessments of the required employee aptitudes necessary to perform the job. These data are especially useful for recruitment and selection, but can also be used for job evaluation. A major advantage is that the system is standardized so that it can be used to compare a wide variety of jobs.

There are other standardized instruments. For example, the Management Position Description Questionnaire (MPDQ) focuses on task-centred characteristics of managerial jobs (Tornow and Pinto, 1976). The Executive Position Description Questionnaire (EPDQ), first created by Hemphill (1954), focuses on behaviours of senior managers. Many consulting firms have developed their own versions of standardized instruments. Some consulting firms are willing to customize their basic instruments when individual employers have special needs.

FUNCTIONAL JOB ANALYSIS

Functional job analysis (FJA) is an attempt to develop generic descriptions of jobs by using a common set of job functions. It was pioneered in the United States in the 1930s when the federal government created the *Dictionary of Occupational Titles*. A version of this system was used by the Canadian federal government in the 1970s to create the *National Occupational Classification*, which includes over 10 000 descriptions of jobs.

FJA has been refined over the years. The current system utilizes a series of task statements for each job that contain four elements: (a) who performs what, (b) to whom or what, (c) with what tools, equipment, or processes, (d) to achieve what purpose or outcome. The following is an example for the job of "Residential Counsellor" in a group home for wayward youth (adapted from Fine, Holt, and Hutchinson, 1974): "The Counsellor (a) records behaviour (b) of group home residents (c) using standardized record sheets (d) to determine the cause of undesirable behaviours." A series of statements like these is produced that, in their totality, describe the job.

These statements can then be analyzed to draw conclusions about the nature of the job, as well as the skills, effort, responsibility, and working conditions that are associated with the job. However, depending on the job, it may be difficult to draw conclusions about all of these factors, such as working conditions or responsibility. Organizations will have to modify the standard job descriptions to suit their specific circumstances and the specific responsibilities they plan to attach to each job.

IDENTIFYING JOB FAMILIES

It is often convenient, for administrative purposes (such as recruitment, selection, and training), to identify jobs that are related to one another in terms of the kind of work that is done and then to cluster them in "job families." For example, an organization may have the following job families for nonmanagerial staff: clerical (clerks, receptionists, secretaries), maintenance (plumbers, electricians, welders), technical (lab technicians, instrumentation technicians), and food services (cooks, cafeteria workers, cashiers).

However, as will be seen, evaluating job families separately for pay purposes can lead to serious inequities. Thus, unless there is a compelling need to compensate different job families in different ways—for example, with sales personnel who are on commission—job families should be grouped together as much as possible for purposes of job evaluation. Differentiation of employee groups for compensation purposes should be based on strategic or behavioural considerations, as was discussed in Chapter 8, not simply on whether the jobs are different.

PITFALLS IN JOB ANALYSIS

There are several possible pitfalls in the job analysis process. The first is to be sure to analyze the position, not the person. For example, the jobholder being interviewed may go above and beyond the call of duty, doing much more than the job calls for. On the other hand, some jobholders may perform only a portion of the intended job duties. But the analysis of the job should not be unduly influenced by either case.

Another problem is that job descriptions have been subject to gender bias. For example, Kelly (1994: 23) claims that "it has been well-documented that job analysts are particularly prone to allow gender bias to influence their analysis of jobs unless trained to do otherwise." Traditionally, different language has been applied to duties performed by men and women even though the actual duties may be virtually identical. For example, when men direct the work of employees, they "manage" these employees; when women do so, they "supervise" employees. These types of language differences must be avoided. Also, jobs traditionally held by males are often described in technical terms that sound impressive, while female jobs are often described in simpler, less impressive language, even though the importance and difficulty of the duties are similar.

Regardless of possible gender bias, technical jargon is an impediment to effective understanding of jobs, and needs to be translated into everyday language for the job description. For example, instead of something like "calibrates the FP 25 flow meter and adjusts circulant flow commensurate with these calibrations," try "performs simple tests of the measuring accuracy of water meters and adjusts the water flow accordingly."

There should be a check on job titles to make sure they are gender-neutral. Avoid oversimplifying job duties. For example, "performs general office duties" would be more informative expressed as follows: "answers incoming telephone calls from clients and redirects to the appropriate information officer," "operates word processing equipment to prepare letters and reports," "utilizes spreadsheet programs to prepare drafts of department budget," and so on. In the process, it is essential to ensure that both women's and men's jobs are described accurately, using simple, straightforward, precise, and bias-free language.

Another issue has to do with jobs that are dynamic. Job analysis, and the information it produces, is useful only as long as the job stays constant. When the job changes, this information may not only become obsolete, it may actually be misleading, causing a variety of inappropriate decisions in areas such as recruitment and selection, training, and compensation. This problem is most likely to occur in high-involvement organizations, since they tend to operate in the most dynamic environments. To avoid this problem, updating of job descriptions needs to be an ongoing process, and supervisors and workers need to be reminded to report significant changes in job duties as they occur. However, they may fail to do this, or duties may change gradually and thus may go undetected.

Job Evaluation Methods

Over time, five major methods for job evaluation have evolved: (1) ranking, (2) classification or grading, (3) factor comparison, (4) statistical/policy capturing, and (5) the point method. In addition, there are numerous proprietary systems that have been developed by compensation consulting firms, all of which use some variation of the five basic methods. For example, the Hay Plan or Profile Method, developed many years ago by Hay Associates, combines features of the factor comparison and point methods, and is intended mainly for management and executive jobs. Kelly (1994) does an excellent job describing the Hay Plan, as well as ten other proprietary plans offered by consulting firms operating in Canada. This chapter will focus on the five generic methods.

The five basic job evaluation plans can be divided into two main categories—"whole job" methods, in which human judgment is the main determinant of the job hierarchy, and methods that use quantitative factors to establish the job hierarchy. Ranking and classification/grading are in the first category, and the factor comparison, statistical/policy capturing, and point methods are in the second category. Because the point method is the most commonly used system of formal job evaluation, it will serve as the main focus of this chapter. But first, the other four methods will be briefly summarized.

RANKING/PAIRED COMPARISON

ranking method of job evaluation the relative values of different jobs are determined by knowledgeable individuals

paired comparison method of job evaluation every job is compared with every other job, providing a basis for a ranking of jobs

Simple ranking is the least complicated system for deriving an ordering of jobs. The **ranking method** involves asking a group of "judges" (e.g., managers, human resource specialists) to examine a set of job descriptions and to rank jobs according to their overall worth to the organization. The specific criteria to be used are left up to each judge, and frequently they are not formally identified. Using a group of judges is believed to cancel out individual biases in ranking.

One variant of this approach is known as the **paired comparison method**, under which each job is compared with every other job, one pair at a time. The number of times each job is ranked above another job is recorded, and this is used as the basis for ranking the jobs. While this is more systematic than simple ranking, a drawback to this approach is the very large number of comparisons that must be made if a large number of jobs are being evaluated.

Although less elaborate to establish than other systems, ranking/paired comparison methods have a number of drawbacks. First, it may be difficult to get the group of judges to agree, since different factors may have different weights in the minds of each judge. Second, this method does not establish the *relative* intervals between jobs. For example, the ninth-, tenth-, and eleventh-ranked jobs may be quite close in terms of importance, while the eighth-ranked job may be much more important than the ninth. This method would not recognize that difference.

Perhaps most important, this method provides no explicit basis for explaining why jobs are ranked as they are, leaving the results of the plan open to charges of inequity. Indeed, because of its subjectivity, the ranking/paired comparison method is not deemed an acceptable method for job evaluation for organizations in jurisdictions covered by pay equity legislation (although an adapted version may be acceptable, as will be discussed later in the chapter).

Once a hierarchy of jobs has been created, by whatever means, new jobs can be added using a method known as "slotting." Under this method, new jobs are compared with the hierarchy of existing jobs, and simply placed at the level where they seem to match the best.

CLASSIFICATION/GRADING

The **classification/grading method** operates by establishing and defining general classes of jobs (e.g., managerial, professional, clerical) and then creating a series of grade descriptions for each class. Different grades possess different levels of knowledge and skills, complexity of duties, supervision, and other key characteristics. By means of job descriptions, jobs are compared with the grade descriptions, within the appropriate class, and the pay grade that appears to match the best is selected. Jobs in the same grade within a given class will receive the same remuneration.

classification/grading method of job evaluation the use of generic grade descriptions for various classes of jobs to assign pay grades to specific jobs

Figure 9.2 provides an illustration of the type of classification guide that might be used for employees in the "nonprofessional" job class at a hypothetical electrical utility. As can be seen, there are five pay grades, each of which carries a different pay range. Let us assume that we wish to determine the appropriate salary for the job of computer operator. The job description indicates some training and skill are necessary, but tasks are simple, errors are easily detected, and operators work under direct supervision of the senior computer operator. Which grade would you place this job in?

Did you pick NP-2? This job description appears to match that grade most closely. Pay ranges (in terms of dollar values) for each pay grade are usually set through identifying the market rates for typical or "benchmark" jobs in each pay grade. Where employees are unionized, pay ranges are set through collective bargaining.

The number of job classes that are used will depend largely on the nature of the organization and the variety of jobs found. Many organizations that use this system have separate classes for managerial, professional, clerical, and blue-collar jobs. The number of pay grades usually depends on the skill range and the number of jobs to be covered in each job class. This system has been very commonly used in government.

This method has the advantage of being straightforward and inexpensive, as well as being flexible enough to encompass a large number of jobs. Since the basis for a particular job rating is spelled out, the results are easier to defend than under simple ranking. On the other hand, descriptions of pay grades must be rather general in order to encompass several types of jobs, so there still may be disagreement about exactly which grade a job should be placed in. As well, since this method considers the job as a whole, no weighting is applied to different job factors.

Depending on the nature of the grade descriptions (whether they contain the four essential factors required for pay equity) and the breadth of the job classes (the broader the better), this method of job evaluation may or may not be acceptable for pay equity purposes.

FIGURE 9.2   SAMPLE GUIDE FOR JOB CLASSIFICATION METHOD

Rocky Mountain Hydro Corporation

Job Classification Guide
(Nonprofessional Job Class)

Instructions: Match the job description with one of the following categories in order to establish the appropriate pay grade.

Pay Grade	Characteristics of Typical Job
NP-1	Works under direct supervision. Tasks are simple, repetitive, and require little initiative. When made, mistakes or errors are easily detected and are not costly. Minimal level of education and training required. Examples: janitor, file clerk, general labourer.
NP-2	Works under direct supervision. Tasks generally simple and repetitive, although some training is required. Little initiative is necessary. Although easily detected, some mistakes or errors can be costly. Examples: switchboard operator/receptionist, accounting clerk, trenching machine operator.
NP-3	Generally, but not always, works under direct supervision. Although most tasks are routine, some require use of discretion. Mistakes or errors may not be easily detected and can be costly. Minimum of high school education and/or substantial training required. May have direct customer contact. Examples: customer service representative, senior accounting clerk, control room monitor.
NP-4	Frequently does not work under direct supervision. Some tasks are complicated and require considerable education or training. Considerable use of independent judgment may be required. Consequences of error may be severe and/or costly. May use costly equipment and/or materials in executing job. May involve supervision of others. Examples: accountant, senior control room monitor, electrical repair crew member, safety inspector, executive secretary.
NP-5	Does not work under direct supervision, but has responsibility for the supervision of others. Tasks are varied and require independent judgment. Substantial education, training, or experience required. Responsible for detecting errors of subordinates. Errors by subordinates not detected by incumbent may be difficult to detect and/or extremely serious. Examples: electrical repair crew leader, senior safety inspector, shift supervisor (plant), trenching and cable crew leader.

factor comparison method of job evaluation assigns pay levels to jobs based on the extent to which they embody various job factors

FACTOR COMPARISON METHOD

Because of its complexity, the **factor comparison method** is used less frequently than the other methods. This method identifies several major factors against which all jobs in a job class can be assessed, and then rates the extent to which each factor is present in each of a large set of "key jobs" that are thought to be properly compensated at the present time. Statistical analysis (multiple regression) is then used to determine the dollar value of varying degrees of each factor, and the remaining jobs are then rated for each factor and then compensated by applying the dollar values that have been derived by the multiple regression analysis. Use of these factors distinguishes this method from the previous two methods, which are known as "whole job methods" because they attempt to compare the whole job against other "whole jobs." Both this method and the point method are similar in that they both segment jobs into factors and then evaluate these factors, rather than the "whole job."

Depending on the nature of the factors used, this method may be acceptable for use under pay equity legislation.

STATISTICAL/POLICY CAPTURING METHOD

The **statistical/policy capturing method** is perhaps the most complicated method of job evaluation. This method utilizes questionnaires to gather information about the task elements of each job to be evaluated, as well as the typical time spent on each task and the relative importance of each task. Information is also collected about the level of skill or education required for each job, and possibly data on the quantity and quality of output expected for each job. Market data for certain jobs that match well (in terms of job characteristics) with jobs in the external market are incorporated, and multiple regression analysis is used to derive a formula for the value of the different job characteristics. This formula can then be used to evaluate the jobs that do not have good market matches.

This approach can also be used in conjunction with internal data based on current pay rates to identify possible inequities within current pay structures and to rectify them. Used properly, this method is acceptable under pay equity legislation, as a recent ruling by the Ontario Pay Equity Tribunal has confirmed (*Focus on Canadian Employment and Equality Rights*, 2000).

statistical/policy capturing method of job evaluation combines use of statistical methods and job questionnaires to derive job values based on prevailing external or internal pay rates

THE POINT METHOD OF JOB EVALUATION: DESIGN ISSUES

The **point method** (sometimes known as the "point-factor" method) of job evaluation is the most widely used system of job evaluation. This method identifies key job characteristics (known as "compensable factors") that differentiate the value of various jobs, weights these factors, and then determines how much of each factor is present in a given job, by assigning a certain number of points to each job. The point totals are used to create a hierarchy of jobs. As will be discussed later in the chapter, this hierarchy of jobs is then transformed into

point method of job evaluation establishes job values by the application of points to each job based on "compensable factors"

a set of pay grades and pay ranges, based on the market rates of certain key or "benchmark" jobs.

Thus, there are four main steps in developing a point system of job evaluation:

1. Identify compensable factors.
2. Scale the factors.
3. Weight the factors.
4. Test the system.

IDENTIFY COMPENSABLE FACTORS

compensable factors
characteristics of jobs that are valued by the organization and differentiate jobs from one another

Compensable factors can be defined as "those characteristics in the work that the organization values, that help it pursue its strategy and achieve its objectives" (Milkovich and Newman, 1996: 137). A useful factor is based on the work performed, supports the strategy and values of the organization, distinguishes between jobs, and is accepted by those who are affected by the job evaluations. These factors typically include job inputs (such as education, training, or experience), job requirements (e.g., mental effort, physical effort, decision making, supervision), job outputs (e.g., accuracy of output, consequences of mistakes), and job conditions (e.g., nature of work environment, hazards that may be encountered).

The variety of factors that can be used by different organizations is practically limitless, but there are four main categories of factors that are more or less universal. These are skill, effort, responsibility, and working conditions. Under pay equity legislation, organizations are required to use these four categories in evaluating work. However, employers are allowed to utilize specific factors from each of these categories that have particular relevance to them.

For example, "skill" might be represented by the factors of "education" and "experience." "Effort" could be represented by "mental effort" and "physical effort." "Responsibility" might be represented by "number of employees under supervision" and "consequences of errors." Working conditions might be represented by "pleasantness of work environment" and "hazards to physical safety."

Table 9.1 provides a listing of some of the specific factors used by organizations, clustered according to the four basic categories. As can be seen, the four categories can encompass just about any characteristic that the organization would want to measure. It can also be seen that many factors are generic, while others may be more firm-specific. A customer-oriented firm might include "amount of customer contact" as a compensable factor, thus implying that jobs with more customer contact are more important than those with less. A firm in which innovation and development of new products and services are important might include a factor entitled "amount of innovative behaviour." A firm concerned with cost might have a factor entitled "responsibility for cost containment."

TABLE 9.1 EXAMPLES OF COMMONLY USED COMPENSABLE FACTORS

SKILL	EFFORT	RESPONSIBILITY	WORKING CONDITIONS
Ability to do detailed or routine work	Attention demanded	Accountability	Attention to details
Accuracy	Concentration needed	Accuracy	Cleaning up after others
Analytical ability	Mental demands: Complexity	Cash	Constant interruptions
Aptitude required	Mental demands: Continuity	Confidential data	Danger
Communication skills: Verbal	Mental demands: Intensity	Contact with public	Dirtiness
Communication skills: Written	Mental demands: Repetitive	Contact with customers/clients	Disagreeableness
Communication skills: Second language	Mental fatigue	Coordination	Exposure to accident hazard
Dexterity	Monotony and discomfort	Consequence of error	Exposure to health hazard
Education	Muscular strain	Dependability	Intangible conditions
Experience	Nerve strain	Determining company policy	Monotony
Initiative	Physical demands: Complexity	Effect on other operations	Out-of-town travel
Interpersonal	Physical demands: Continuity	Equipment and machinery	Physical environment/ surroundings
Knowledge	Physical demands: Intensity	Goodwill and public relations	Stress of multiple demands
Managerial techniques	Physical demands: Repetitive	Monetary responsibility	Time pressure
Manual quickness	Physical fatigue	Personnel	
Manual or motor skills	Pressure of work	Physical property	
Problem solving	Stress from dealing with difficult people	Quality	
Resourcefulness	Plant and services	Records	
Social skills	Visual application	Safety of others	
Versatility	Volume of work	Spoilage of materials	
Versatility		Supervision of others	
		Volume of work	

Source: Adapted from Pay Equity Commission (1989: 27–28). © Queen's Printer for Ontario, 1989. Reproduced with permission.

How many factors should be used? There is no simple answer to this question. There must be enough that they capture all the key aspects of work that are important to the organization, but not so many that they start to overlap or start to add very little additional value to the system. In general, the broader the group of jobs to be covered with a single job evaluation system, the greater the number of factors that will be needed. In recent years there has been a trend toward broadening the inclusiveness of job evaluation systems, in order to ensure fairness for all employee groups and also in response to pay equity legislation. For example, Ontario legislation requires single plans for each union bargaining unit, regardless of whether both blue- and white-collar jobs are included in the unit; if the organization is not unionized, the law requires that the same job evaluation system cover *all* jobs in the organization.

Overall, it is hard to see how a valid point system could operate with less than about eight factors (with at least one from each category), but systems that include more than a dozen factors may be including marginal factors.

One trend has been for some firms to purposely omit certain traditional factors. For example, many firms have had a factor "responsibility for supervision of subordinates," which is based on the number of subordinates supervised. But some firms have started to drop this factor, for several reasons. For example, an assembly-line supervisor may have 30 subordinates, but these employees are effectively supervised by the technology, while a director of a research project may have four subordinates doing highly complex work, for which constant supervision, coordination, and interaction are essential. Moreover, number of subordinates implies that managers who expand their staffs will be rewarded, while those who improve efficiency and cut back their staffs will be penalized. Many firms no longer want to send this message.

SCALE THE FACTORS

After the compensable factors have been selected, a number of "degrees" (sometimes called "levels") are established for each factor, resulting in a measurement scale for every factor. These degrees represent gradations in the extent to which a certain factor is present in a particular job being rated. For example, it may be decided that there should be five possible "degrees" or levels for the factor of "supervisory responsibility." Each degree needs to be carefully defined and arranged so that degree two always contains more of that factor than degree one, and so on. Table 9.2 provides examples of two factor definitions and their degree definitions.

How many degrees should be used? The number of degrees for a particular factor depends on the range of that factor. There is no reason for all factors in a job evaluation system to have the same number of degrees. For example, if relevant education ranges from elementary school to a university doctorate, then seven or eight degrees might be used. Where the range is from elementary school to completion of high school, only three or four degrees might be used. At the same time, "working conditions" might be assigned five degrees, and "experience" seven degrees.

**TABLE 9.2 SAMPLE COMPENSABLE FACTORS
ILLUSTRATING DEGREES**

Factor: Education

This factor deals with the level of formal education required to perform the job.

Degree 1: Elementary school (Completion of grade 6).

Degree 2: Junior high school (Completion of grade 9).

Degree 3: Completion of high school.

Degree 4: One year of postsecondary education.

Degree 5: Two years of postsecondary education.

Degree 6: University bachelor's degree.

Degree 7: University master's degree.

Degree 8: University doctorate.

Factor: Initiative and Ingenuity

This factor deals with the exercise of initiative and ingenuity in dealing with problems arising from normal work assignments. It includes the frequency, extent, and importance of ingenuity for successful job performance. It is limited by the amount of guidance/supervision that is available.

Degree 1: Work procedures and problems are standard; very little ingenuity required.

Degree 2: Work procedures and problems are mainly standard; occasional ingenuity required.

Degree 3: Work procedures and problems are often nonstandard; some ingenuity required.

Degree 4: Work procedures are mainly nonstandard; considerable ingenuity required, but considerable guidance available.

Degree 5: Work procedures are mainly nonstandard; considerable ingenuity required, little guidance available; consequences of poor choices of solution are not serious.

Degree 6: Work procedures are mainly nonstandard; high ingenuity required, little guidance available; consequences of poor choices of solution are moderate.

Degree 7: Work procedures are mainly nonstandard; high ingenuity required; little guidance; consequences of poor choices are very serious.

WEIGHT THE FACTORS

Not every compensable factor is equally important to the firm. To recognize this, each factor is weighted according to its importance relative to the others. For example, in one firm, education may be viewed as the most important factor, followed by customer contact, and then mental complexity, with physical environment considered the least important factor. If the maximum number of points that any job may receive is arbitrarily set at 1000, then education might be allocated 350 points, customer contact 300 points, mental complexity 250 points, and physical environment 100 points. These points are then distributed across the degrees that were defined in the previous step. For example, if "education" has seven degrees, then degree 1 would be assigned 50 points, degree 2 would be assigned 100 points, and so on, all the way to degree 7, which would be assigned 350 points.

Once all this has been done, a rating chart is developed, and all jobs to be covered by this pay structure are rated according to the degree of each factor found in each job. Figure 9.3 provides an example of a rating chart that has been used by a hospital in western Canada. This rating chart uses ten factors. Eight degrees have been established for the factor of education, seven for experience, and five for each of the remaining factors. The maximum total number of points available is 950, and the factor weights vary from 210 points (education) to 40 points (supervisory responsibilities).

How are factor weights derived? There are two methods—statistical analysis and expert judgment (sometimes known as the "a priori" method). Statistical analysis utilizes a sample of existing jobs that have been rated to determine the degree of each factor that they contain, and are thought to be paid correctly at the present time. The existing pay rate for each of these jobs (if desired, the market rate for each job can be used instead, if it is different from company pay rates) is also fed into the equation. Multiple regression analysis is used to determine the role that each factor plays in influencing the pay rate in this sample of jobs. These weights are then applied to all jobs covered by the job evaluation system.

There are several drawbacks to this approach. The first is that it is complex and not easily understood. The second is that it assumes that the current pay structure (or the market pay structure, if used) for the sample of benchmark or criterion jobs is ideal, and that all other jobs should be aligned with this pay structure. Of course, what this does is perpetuate existing pay practices. For this reason, the method may be unacceptable for pay equity purposes. It is certainly unacceptable if the organization is trying to change the pay structure to reflect changes in corporate strategy.

FIGURE 9.3 SAMPLE RATING CHART FOR POINT METHOD OF JOB EVALUATION

	Degree Rating								Points Allocated
	1	2	3	4	5	6	7	8	
a) Education	35	60	85	110	135	160	185	210	
b) Experience	30	50	70	90	110	130	150	–	
c) Mental Skill	25	50	75	100	125	–	–	–	
d) Mental Effort	15	30	45	60	75	–	–	–	
e) Physical Effort	20	40	60	80	100	–	–	–	
f) Accuracy	15	30	45	60	75	–	–	–	
g) Contacts	15	30	45	60	75	–	–	–	
h) Environment	10	20	30	40	50	–	–	–	
i) Hazards	10	20	30	40	50	–	–	–	
j) Supervisory Responsibilities	0	10	20	30	40	–	–	–	
TOTAL POINTS									

The other alternative ("expert judgment") is to form a panel or committee of knowledgeable individuals within the organization. These individuals must have a good understanding of the organization, its strategy, and its needs, as well as an accurate understanding of the meanings of each factor. Each individual independently derives a set of factor weightings, and these are then brought together. If there are major discrepancies, the reasons need to be identified. For example, perhaps one or more of the factor definitions is unclear, or perhaps different individuals have different understandings of the types of behaviour that the organization needs to elicit. The process is then repeated until the factor weightings of the experts converge.

TEST THE SYSTEM

Once a job evaluation system has been established, it is useful to test it to determine how closely it matches the market. This is done by applying the job evaluation system to a number of "key" or "benchmark" jobs, for each of which a market pay rate is determined. These benchmark jobs should be selected so that there is a spread across the range of job evaluation points. That is, some jobs with a low point total should be selected, some with a high point total, and some that fall in between. The normal practice is to use about 10 to 15 percent of the total number of jobs to be evaluated.

Then, each job is plotted on a graph, with job evaluation points on the horizontal axis, and pay rates on the vertical axis, as Figure 9.4 illustrates. Normally, a computer is used to calculate and plot a straight line that best "fits" the pattern of points on the graph, but it can also be drawn by hand. (When drawn by hand, the key is to minimize the average vertical distance that each point on the graph is away from the straight line.) This is known as a **market line**.

Next, the computer calculates a correlation coefficient that summarizes the extent to which the plots on the graph approach a straight line. The closer the plots are to a straight line, the closer that the correlation coefficient will be to 1. The farther the plots are from being in a straight line, the closer the correlation coefficient will be to zero.

In fact, a correlation coefficient can range from +1 to –1. Both +1 and –1 occur when all the points happen to fall in a perfectly straight line (this virtually never happens); +1 indicates a positive relationship between job evaluation points and pay rates, and –1 indicates a negative or inverse relationship between job evaluation points and pay rates. An inverse relationship would mean that pay is *lower* for jobs with *higher* job evaluation points. Needless to say, you should *never* have a minus sign in front of your coefficient!

There are at least three uses for the pay graph that has just been created. What the coefficient indicates is the "goodness of fit" between the point values established by job evaluation and the pay rates ascertained from the market. Obviously a coefficient that approaches zero is bad, because this says that there is little or no relationship between the importance of jobs as determined by job

market line relates market pay to job evaluation points for the benchmark jobs

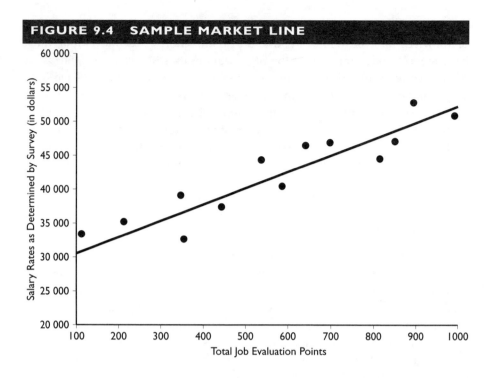

FIGURE 9.4 SAMPLE MARKET LINE

Salary Rates as Determined by Survey (in dollars) vs. *Total Job Evaluation Points*

evaluation and the value of jobs as determined by the market. If you were to stick with your job evaluation, you would find that you would be paying far more than you need to for some jobs and not enough to attract employees to others.

So the closer the coefficient is to 1 the better? Not necessarily. Some differences from the market line may well be justifiable if a job is more (or less) important to your organization than it is to the typical organization. There is no hard and fast rule about what the coefficient should be. But it certainly should be closer to 1 than to zero, and anything less than .80 needs to be carefully examined.

So how do you decide exactly what should be modified? One approach is to examine the "outlier jobs"—those that have the farthest vertical distance from the market line—to determine why they are discrepant. Have they simply been badly evaluated (their point total is incorrect, because the job evaluation system was applied poorly in this case), or are there problems with the job evaluation system itself (e.g., some factors are weighted too heavily or too lightly)? Have the wrong factors been included in the job evaluation system? There is no formula to find the right answer—it requires judgment based on studying the pattern of results. However, one temptation that needs to be avoided is to simply adjust the points of the outlier jobs so that the correlation coefficient looks better.

Aside from testing the system, another purpose that the graphing process can serve is to translate job evaluation points into actual dollar values. For example, if a strategy of matching the market has been established for the set of jobs covered by this job evaluation system, one way of determining what each job will pay is to enter the job evaluation point total for each job on the graph by drawing a vertical line up from the horizontal axis until it intersects the market line. A horizontal line is then drawn to the vertical axis, and the amount indicated is the pay rate for the job.

Of course, this would create a system of flat rates in which each job is paid one fixed sum. Although this does sometimes occur (e.g., a retail store that pays all its sales clerks $9.00 an hour), most pay systems create pay ranges for each job, as will be discussed shortly.

These graphs can also be used to estimate the payroll cost of the proposed system. For example, the rate for each job, as established by the market line, can be multiplied by the number of people holding that job, and an estimate of the total wages that would be payable under the proposed job evaluation system can be derived. (For an ongoing organization, this can then be compared with the current payroll cost.)

It can then be determined whether the organization can afford this amount. If not, either the pay rates must be reduced for at least some jobs, or the number of jobs in the higher pay grades must be reduced. For example, if the system results in most jobs receiving high point totals, perhaps the system is rating jobs too highly. Or it may not be differentiating effectively between jobs of lower and higher value.

It is also conceivable that the new plan will result in a reduction in the current payroll costs. While this may seem desirable to the employer, too large a reduction can cause perceptions of inequity among employees, which may be reflected in a higher turnover rate, particularly among the most marketable employees. Moreover, a job evaluation system that reduces the pay of current employees is not likely to be well accepted, especially the next time around. Many employees may also devote great effort to getting their jobs reevaluated.

ADVANTAGES AND DISADVANTAGES OF THE POINT SYSTEM

Advantages of the point system include its high degree of precision in measuring jobs, with its use of carefully defined factors and rating scales providing an "automatic" weighting of each factor. As a result, it is easy to apply with a high degree of consistency, removing one possible source of conflict. As well, this system provides not only an ordering of jobs but also the relative value of each. This allows jobs to be clustered in pay grades more easily.

A major disadvantage of the point system is the complexity and difficulty involved in developing such a plan. However, this problem is partly counterbalanced by the large number of "ready-made" plans offered by compensation consulting firms, although using these can be costly and there is no guarantee that the system will be the best fit possible with the organization. For firms that cannot afford these services, there are some good guidebooks available. One of the most usable guidebooks has been produced by the Ontario government (Pay Equity Commission, 1996).

Perhaps the most important drawback of the point system is that although it may appear scientific, the process of selecting relevant factors and applying particular weights is still a subjective process. There are many opportunities for flaws to enter the system, perhaps even destroying its validity, despite the massive efforts that are typically devoted to the system. The next section examines these pitfalls.

THE POINT METHOD OF JOB EVALUATION: POSSIBLE PITFALLS

In theory, the point system of job evaluation should result in a hierarchy of jobs that is both reliable and valid, and thus maximizes compensation equity for all employees. But there are a large number of possible pitfalls that may prevent this from happening. A thorough understanding of these pitfalls is the best defence against them.

There are four main categories of problems that can occur (Weiner, 1991): (1) inconsistent construct formation, (2) factor overlaps, (3) hierarchical grounding, and (4) gender bias. Each of these will now be examined, along with some additional pitfalls that fall outside these categories.

INCONSISTENT CONSTRUCT FORMATION

In a point system of job evaluation, the key is the compensable factors that are established. Each factor must be based on a separate and well-defined construct. There are three areas in which factors may not meet this test. The factor itself may be ambiguously defined, so that it is not clear to the evaluator what the factor is meant to pick up. Second, the degree or level definitions may not be consistent with the factor definition. Third, the definitions for each degree or level may not all be degrees of the same construct.

AMBIGUOUS FACTOR DEFINITIONS
Some factors may be designed in such a way that they are actually tapping numerous constructs. For example, consider the following definition of "complexity of duties" (Weiner, 1991: 124):

> **Complexity of Duties:** *This factor measures the complexity of duties involved, the degree of independent action, the extent to which the duties are circumscribed by standard practice, the exercise of judgment and the type of decisions made, the amount of resourcefulness and planning the job requires, the creative effort in devising new methods, policies, procedures or products, scientific discoveries, and original application.*

As can be seen, this example actually contains numerous factors. If they are all important, they need to be broken out into separate factors. (Of course, if some of these are not important, they should be dropped entirely.) At least four separate factors could be broken out of this factor definition: independent action/circumscribed duties, resourcefulness, planning, and creative effort.

INCONSISTENT FACTOR AND DEGREE DEFINITIONS

In some cases, the statements defining the different degrees of a given factor are actually measuring something other than the factor to which they ostensibly apply. Let's consider the following example for the factor of "analytical ability":

> **Analytical Ability:** *This factor measures the extent to which analytical ability is required to perform job duties. Analytical ability is the ability to examine information and data, to detect patterns, explanations, and causes of various phenomena, utilizing a variety of analytical tools and procedures.*
>
> *Degree 1: Little necessity for creativity in performance of job duties.*
>
> *Degree 2: New ideas and approaches to job duties occasionally needed.*
>
> *Degree 3: Frequent need to develop new approaches to job duties.*
>
> *Degree 4: Continually must use creativity in performing job duties.*

As can be seen, the degree statements actually focus on creativity and innovation in performing job duties, which is not necessarily the same as analytical ability. For example, accountants may analyze financial statements to identify potential company problems, but this does not necessarily call for creative ability. On the other hand, a graphic artist in charge of developing new company logos may need considerable creativity but does not really use analytical tools and procedures in performing this job.

INCONSISTENT DEGREE STATEMENTS

In a variation of the above problem, in some cases different degree statements are actually measuring different constructs, and only some of the statements are actually tapping the factor they are supposed to measure. Consider the following example for the factor of "supervisory responsibility":

> **Supervisory Responsibility**: *This factor deals with the extent of responsibility for managing employees and overseeing their day-to-day work.*

Degree 1: No supervisory responsibilities.

Degree 2: Responsible for supervision of one to three subordinates.

Degree 3: Responsible for supervision of four to nine subordinates.

Degree 4: Responsible for supervision of ten or more subordinates.

Degree 5: Responsible for development of all department policies.

Which one of these is not like the others? Clearly, the statement for degree 5 is tapping a different construct from the other degrees. For example, it may be possible to be responsible for development of department policy with very few or even no employees.

Factor Overlaps

One problem that frequently occurs in point systems is overlapping factors. If this does occur, then some factors are being counted twice and are thus over-weighted in the job evaluation system. In some cases, this occurs because factor titles may sound different, but their descriptions are actually very similar. For example, consider the factors of "judgment" and "freedom to act" (based on Weiner, 1991: 126):

Judgment: This factor deals with the extent to which the exercise of independent judgment is required in the performance of job duties.

Degree 1: Prescribed directions and rules limit the scope for independent judgment.

Degree 2: Standardized work routines limit the scope for independent judgment.

Degree 3: Similar procedures and methods limit the scope for independent judgment.

Freedom to Act: This factor deals with the extent to which incumbents of this job are free to act as they see fit in performing their job duties.

Degree 1: Duties are routine and specifically delineated; work is closely controlled.

Degree 2: Duties are somewhat routine and clearly delineated; work is closely controlled.

Degree 3: Characteristics of the position are such that activities and methods are clearly defined, and/or work is frequently reviewed.

As can be seen from reading the degree statements, these factors are virtually indistinguishable.

HIERARCHICAL GROUNDING

The purpose of the point method of job evaluation is to derive a hierarchy of jobs by examining the individual components ("factors") in those jobs. However, some factors in some systems "appear to confuse the outcome with the process. That is, they say if this job is at a high level in the [organization] hierarchy it should be highly rated. This is circular reasoning" (Weiner, 1991: 127). For example, take the factor of "responsibility for action":

> **Responsibility for Action**: *This factor deals with the extent to which the jobholder is expected to take independent action in addressing and solving managerial problems, and the importance of taking this action.*
>
> *Degree 1: Reports to the section supervisor.*
>
> *Degree 2: Reports to the department manager.*
>
> *Degree 3: Reports to the division manager.*
>
> *Degree 4: Reports to the vice-president.*
>
> *Degree 5: Reports to the president.*

As can be seen, the degree definitions are simply mimicking the existing organization hierarchy, assuming that the higher the job is in the organizational hierarchy, the more responsibility for action there will be. Thus, the job evaluation system is not actually deriving an independent hierarchy of jobs, which should be the result of job evaluation. Although there is a strong tendency for jobs higher in the organizational hierarchy to pay more, this example illustrates how inequity can arise. What these degree statements are really saying is that, by definition, no one who reports to a section supervisor has any responsibility to take action, when this may not be true at all for many jobs.

GENDER BIAS

Gender bias occurs when a job receives a higher or lower evaluation than it should because the job incumbents are predominantly from one gender. Weiner (1991) suggests that the ways in which gender bias can operate in job evaluation include the following:

- separate job families;
- the valuing of a factor when it is found in male jobs but not female jobs;
- confusing job content with stereotypes of inherent female attributes;
- ignoring factors found in female jobs;
- having an insufficient range of degree statements;
- biased job descriptions.

In their analysis, Kervin and Elek (2001) also note that insufficient rater training can also introduce unreliability and bias into the job evaluation process if raters fall back on unconscious stereotypes that have contributed to gender-based inequities in the past. We will now examine each of these problems.

SEPARATE JOB FAMILIES

Traditionally, each job family in an organization has been evaluated separately. However, this can defeat the purpose of job evaluation, which is to create a hierarchy of jobs within the organization. This may also cause gender bias. Even if jobs are evaluated fairly *within* job families or classes, if separate job families are used for male and female jobs, they may not be evaluated fairly *between* job classes. Box 9.1 describes how nurses were shortchanged by this practice. This is why, whenever job evaluation is used, the same system of job evaluation should cover all job families that are subject to job evaluation. Indeed, in numerous Canadian jurisdictions, this is required by law.

DIFFERENTIAL VALUATION OF FACTORS

One example of how factors can be valued differently is "visibility of dirt." Jobs carried out under dirty working conditions, such as mechanic or garbage collector, have typically been rated more highly on working conditions than jobs performed in seemingly "clean" working conditions, such as hospitals or hotels. However, working conditions in hospitals and hotels may not be as "clean" as they appear, especially from the perspective of those employees, such as nurses or maids, whose job it is to create and maintain these "clean" working conditions. Conditions may be clean when nurses or maids complete their shift, but that is because of the dirt and mess they handled during their shifts!

Another example of this type of inequity is illustrated by a municipality in the United States, where the hazards of entering people's homes (e.g., being bitten by a dog; being assaulted by a home owner) were factored into job evaluations for meter readers (who were male), but were not for public health nurses (who were female), who also had to enter people's homes as a part of their responsibilities (Weiner, 1991).

CONFUSING JOB CONTENT WITH STEREOTYPES

Certain jobs traditionally held by women are often considered to be "low-skill" jobs because the ability to do these jobs is considered "inherent to women." For example, in the U.S. Department of Labor's Directory of Occupational Titles, "dog pound attendant" was ranked higher than "child care worker."

BOX 9.1 Who Is More Valuable to a Hospital?

Who performs work that is more valuable to a hospital, nurses or painters? Intuitively, we might think nurses. But that is not what the job evaluation system at a U.S. hospital concluded, and certainly not what pay scales indicated, as painters were paid considerably more than nurses (Weiner and Gunderson, 1990).

Using the four basic categories of factors, let's take a look at these jobs more closely (Weiner and Gunderson, 1990: 62–63):

- *Skill:* To perform the job of "nurse" requires medical skills (including a licence and postsecondary training), interpersonal skills, and communication skills. To perform the job of painter requires manual dexterity and the ability to mix paint.

- *Effort:* A nurse's job requires some physical effort, such as helping to lift patients and being on your feet for extended periods of time. Painters are required to be on their feet constantly, to climb ladders, and to exercise continuous repetitive movement over the entire duration of their shift. However, painters do not need to expend much mental effort, while nurses must be

continually alert for monitoring patient health and providing correct dosages of medication.

- *Responsibility:* Nurses are responsible for the health and welfare of human beings. Painters are responsible for neatly painted walls and ceilings.

- *Working Conditions:* Working conditions for painters are often smelly, unpleasant, or dangerous, especially when working at heights, such as painting ceilings. Working conditions for nurses may also be messy, smelly, or unpleasant, as when they need to empty bedpans, clean or bathe patients, or clean up pus and vomit. Other working conditions of the "nurse" job include dealing with distraught patients, who may be in severe pain, and discovering dead patients. There is also a danger of contracting communicable diseases from patients.

This analysis suggests that a nurse's job should be evaluated more highly than a painter's job on all factors except physical effort, and therefore should be paid more. Why didn't the hospital's previous job evaluation system pick this up? Because two separate job evaluation systems were used—one for nursing staff and one for maintenance staff.

When this inequity was questioned, the response given was that dog pound attendants were more highly rated because it was more difficult to acquire the necessary skills than for child care workers (Weiner, 1991). The argument was that any skills needed to work with young children were inherent to women and therefore did not deserve to be highly rated. Of course, anybody who has actually worked with small children knows that there is considerable skill necessary to be effective, and that people (both female and male) vary greatly in these skills.

IGNORING FACTORS FOUND IN FEMALE JOBS

In a major study of job evaluation instruments, Steinberg and Haignere (1985) found that although hundreds of factors had been included in these systems, many factors relevant to jobs usually performed by females had been omitted. For example, under "effort," there were rarely factors for "involuntary interruptions" (as many secretaries must cope with) or "dealing with upset people" (as complaints clerks at department stores or nurses at hospitals must do). Indeed, Steinberg (1999) notes that the whole area of "emotional labour" has seldom been adequately incorporated into job evaluation plans. One aspect of emotional labour is dealing with people and groups who are angry, distrustful, upset, unreasonable, psychologically impaired, or under the influence of drugs or alcohol—conditions with which nurses and social workers must contend every day. Another aspect of emotional labour is the need to stay cheerful, courteous, friendly, and helpful, even in adverse circumstances, as is the case in many service-oriented jobs. Table 9.3 lists a whole range of frequently omitted factors.

TABLE 9.3   FREQUENTLY OVERLOOKED FACTORS IN FEMALE JOBS

Skill
- analytical reasoning
- communicating with upset, irate, or irrational people
- coordinating a variety of responsibilities other than "other staff or people"
- creating documents
- deciding the content and format of reports and presentations
- developing or coordinating work schedules for others
- dispensing medication to patients
- establishing and maintaining manual and automated filing systems
- handling complaints
- innovating—developing new procedures, solutions, or products
- manual dexterity required for giving injections, typing, graphic arts
- operating and maintaining different types of office equipment
- providing personal services, such as arranging vacations, and handling household accounts
- reading forms
- special body coordination or expert use of fingers and hands
- training and orienting new staff
- using a variety of computer software and database formats
- writing correspondence for others, and proofreading and editing others' work

Effort
- adjusting to rapid changes in office or plant technology
- concentrating for prolonged periods at computer terminals, lab benches, and other equipment
- frequent lifting and bending (e.g., child care work)
- frequent lifting (office supplies, retail goods, lifting or turning sick or injured adults or children)
- heavy lifting (e.g., packing goods for shipment)
- irregular and/or multiple work demands
- long periods of travel and/or isolation
- performing complex sequences of hand–eye coordination
- providing service to several people or departments, working under many simultaneous deadlines
- sitting for long periods of time at workstation (e.g., while keyboarding)

Responsibility
- acting on behalf of absent supervisors
- caring for patients, children, institutionalized people

TABLE 9.3 FREQUENTLY OVERLOOKED FACTORS IN FEMALE JOBS (continued)

- contacts with others—internal or external to the organization
- handling new or unexpected situations
- keeping public areas such as waiting rooms and offices organized
- managing petty cash
- planning, problem solving, setting objectives and goals
- preventing possible damage to equipment or people
- protecting confidentiality
- representing the workplace through communications with clients and the public
- shouldering responsibility for consequences of error in the workplace
- supervising staff
- training and orienting new employees

Working Conditions
- adjusting to a variety of working environments continuously
- cleaning offices, stores, machinery, hospital wards
- exposure to communicable diseases
- exposure to dirt from office machines and supplies
- exposure to eye strain from computer terminals
- exposure to and disposal of body fluids
- exposure to disease and stress from caring for ill people
- physical or verbal abuse from irrational clients or patients
- stress from open office noise, crowded conditions

Source: Adapted from The Ontario Pay Equity Commission document "Overlooked Factors in Female Jobs." © Queen's Printer for Ontario, 1989. Reproduced with permission.

INSUFFICIENT RANGE OF DEGREES

Once a job evaluation system has all the factors necessary to accurately assess both male and female jobs, the final concern is to ensure that there is sufficient range among the degrees to make appropriate distinctions between jobs. Weiner (1991: 130) cites the following example for "working conditions":

> *Working Conditions: This factor deals with the physical conditions under which the job is normally performed.*
>
> *Degree 1: Standard office conditions.*
>
> *Degree 2: Inside work with possible exposure to dirt, oil, noise.*
>
> *Degree 3: Some exposure to disagreeable conditions, such as fumes, cold, dust.*
>
> *Degree 4: Constant exposure to disagreeable conditions. Continuous outside work.*

This example illustrates several problems. For example, "standard office conditions" does not distinguish between spacious private offices and offices that may be crowded, noisy, hot, and full of interruptions and distractions.

Also, outside work (traditionally male) is assumed to be the most onerous. Is this always true? In some occupations, workers (e.g., gardeners, painters) are only outside during relatively pleasant conditions. Should outside work, on its own, be considered more onerous than working in a crowded, hot, noisy office, with constant interruptions?

BIASED JOB DESCRIPTIONS

Finally, even if the job evaluation system itself is fair and free of bias, one possible source of bias remains—the information on which the job evaluation is based. As was discussed earlier in the chapter, there is evidence that descriptions of jobs traditionally performed by females have been subject to bias during the job analysis process.

OTHER PITFALLS OF JOB EVALUATION

Chapter 4 has discussed the pros and cons of job evaluation systems in some depth. However, job evaluation is subject to a few other pitfalls not yet covered. As in the case of job analysis, there is often a tendency to evaluate the jobholder rather than the job itself (Weiner and Gunderson, 1990). For example, evaluators might think to themselves: "This is Joe's job. Joe really doesn't seem to work very hard any more. Therefore, his job does not deserve a high rating." Of course, Joe's performance is irrelevant in performing job evaluation; it is the importance of his job that we are evaluating, but it is easy to lose sight of this.

Another pitfall occurs when job evaluation becomes an adversarial process and a source of conflict between employees and management. And, of course, the biggest pitfall is that job evaluations may get out of date quickly, and continually updating them requires a never-ending commitment of time and effort. Yet, if they are not updated, job evaluations can become a source of inequity rather than a source of employee satisfaction. When a job does change substantially in duties, and if the revised point total for the job warrants it, prompt reclassification from one grade to the next should take place. However, even here there is an opportunity for inequity to creep in. For example, Welbourne and Trevor (2000) found in their U.S. study that more powerful departments in an organization were more likely to have their requests for reclassifications approved than were less powerful departments. Obviously, such tendencies must be avoided if the system is to be fair.

base pay structure the structure of pay grades and pay ranges, along with the criteria for movement within pay ranges, that applies to base pay

pay grade a grouping of jobs of similar value to the organization

DETERMINING PAY GRADES AND PAY RANGES

Whatever the method of job evaluation that has been used, by now a hierarchy of jobs has been created. But there is still no pay structure. A **base pay structure** normally consists of pay grades and pay ranges, along with the criteria for salary movement within the pay range. A **pay grade** is a grouping of jobs of similar value to the organization. A **pay range** provides the actual minimum and maximum pay rate, in dollar terms, for jobs in each pay grade.

pay range the minimum and maximum pay rates for jobs in a particular pay grade

ESTABLISHING PAY GRADES

There are several issues in establishing a base pay structure. The first is to decide how many pay grades to use. Narrow pay grades create a structure with many pay grades and therefore many different pay ranges. However, within each pay grade, the pay range will generally be small. Broad pay grades result in fewer pay grades, but the pay range in each grade will normally be wider to cover the wider variety of jobs included in the grade.

WHY USE PAY GRADES?

Why have pay grades at all? Why not pay each job a different rate, based on what the pay graph (Figure 9.4) indicates? There are five main reasons for clustering jobs into pay grades. First, use of grades recognizes that job evaluation is essentially a subjective process, no matter what method is used, and it makes little sense to try to make very fine distinctions between jobs. Second, pay grades make it easier to justify and explain pay rates to employees. If employees observe someone in a job that looks similar to theirs earning more money, they may perceive inequity.

Third, pay grades simplify the administration of the pay system by eliminating the need to have separate rates and pay ranges for every job. Fourth, having jobs clustered within pay grades makes it easier for employees to move across jobs in the same pay grade. Fifth, pay grades create more stability for the pay system. For example, if a job changes, but not to any great extent, there is likely no need to reevaluate, unless it is right at the boundary between two pay grades.

On the downside, pay grades do create problems with jobs on the margins of each grade. Employees with jobs on the borderline between two grades will of course push to have their jobs placed in the higher grade. However, if this is done, then the next-lower job becomes the marginal job. No one wants his or her job to be the first one *not* included in the higher grade.

HOW MANY PAY GRADES?

How many pay grades should there be? One consideration is the total range of pay of the jobs covered by the particular job evaluation system. If the jobs in the same pay structure range from $15 000 to $100 000, there is much greater scope for pay grades than one in which the jobs range from $30 000 to $60 000. Another consideration is the width of the pay ranges that will be used. If there are narrow pay ranges, or flat rates, then the only way to increase pay would be through promotion to a job in the next-higher pay grade. Therefore, it may be desirable to have many pay grades in order to provide opportunities for promotion and pay raises.

A key issue is how to establish the pay grade boundaries. In some cases they are arbitrary. For example, suppose that job evaluation points in a particular pay structure can range from 100 to 1000, and it has been decided to have nine pay grades. Dividing the possible range of points (which is 900) by 9 yields pay grades of 100 points. Thus, grade one is 100 to 200 points, grade two is 201 points to 300 points, and so on. This is known as the *equal interval* approach.

However, if the actual point totals for the various jobs are not evenly spread across the range, this could result in very few jobs in some pay grades, and possibly even the majority in one or two pay grades. This could create a problem, due to scarce opportunities for promotion into higher grades. Furthermore, the use of arbitrary boundaries may end up dividing a cluster of jobs that are really very similar. For example, take the example in the paragraph above. What if there were no jobs between 150 and 285 points, and no jobs between 320 and 400 points, but six jobs between 285 and 300 points, and six jobs between 301 and 315 points? Does it really make sense to arbitrarily divide this cluster of jobs, in which the jobs are very similar in value, and pay them differently? Therefore, another approach is to look for the natural breaks between clusters of jobs when setting up the pay grades. (This, of course, only makes sense if you are evaluating all of the organization's jobs at the same time.)

A variation of the equal interval approach is the *equal percentage* approach. Based on the notion that jobs in higher pay grades are more complex, the width of the pay grade increases by a constant percentage from the previous grade. Another variation of this is the "telescopic approach" (Thanasse, 1993), in which grade widths increase for higher-level jobs (e.g., from clerical to professional, to managerial, to executive), but not necessarily by a constant percentage.

Another approach is to look at the possibility of error in the system. For example, what would be the point difference in a job if it were consistently evaluated one degree higher or one degree lower than it should be? Assume that this would result in a 200-point difference over or under evaluation. Then 200 points could be used as the width of the pay grades, on the logic that no job would be more than one pay grade higher or lower than it should be. Theriault (1992), in fact, suggests dividing this maximum error by three, on the assumption that in reality two-thirds of the degree errors would cancel out. He gives no basis for this number, though.

In recent years, many companies have been reducing the number of pay grades in their compensation system. For example, General Electric Retailer Financial Services replaced 24 pay grades with five pay "bands" (Milkovich and Newman, 1996). This process, known as *broadbanding*, experienced some popularity in the 1990s because of the flexibility it provides. However, the fewer the pay grades, the less meaning that job evaluation results will have, as jobs with very different point totals may end up in the same band, thus receiving similar pay. Moreover, broad pay grades open the door to inconsistency across departments, and to the possibility of pay being determined by factors such as favouritism. Of course, broadbands also create a bigger distinction between the pay rate of a job that just makes it into a particular pay band, and a job that just falls short, ending up in the next-lower pay band. As these problems have become more apparent, the popularity of broadbanding has tailed off.

A thorny issue is what should be done with jobs that end up near but just below grade boundaries. Of course, one solution is to do nothing, and just leave jobs where they fall. However, this invites feelings of inequity, as well as attempts by these jobholders to get their jobs reevaluated. Some firms attempt to deal with this problem by keeping job evaluation points secret, which of course can lead to other problems, such as distrust of the job evaluation system. As mentioned previously, another method is not to use arbitrary point cutoffs, but to look for "natural breaks" in the job hierarchy. But there is no ideal solution to this problem; it is inherent in the use of pay grades.

ESTABLISHING PAY RANGES

Once the pay grades have been established, the next question to decide is the pay range for each grade, in actual dollar terms. Of course, it is possible to decide to have a pay range of "zero"—that is, to pay all jobs in a pay grade the same flat rate. But this does not allow any room to recognize differential qualifications of employees as they enter a pay grade, or to provide any raises based on seniority or performance. To provide latitude for this, most organizations do use pay ranges.

There are four main questions about pay ranges. First, how should the midpoint of the range (in dollar terms) be determined? Second, how should the range spreads be determined (i.e., the minimum and the maximum pay rates for each pay grade)? Third, should range overlaps be permitted? Fourth, how should movement through the range take place?

ESTABLISHING THE RANGE MIDPOINTS

One method to establish the midpoint of the range is to start with the graph shown in Figure 9.4, which showed how a market line was established. This market line needs to be converted to a pay policy line. For example, if the compensation strategy for the group of employees in the job evaluation system is to pay 10 percent above market, then a new line would be drawn 10 percent above the market line. This would become the pay policy line. (Of course, if the pay strategy is to match the market, then the market line simply becomes the pay policy line.)

Once the pay policy line has been drawn, the pay grades are then marked off on the graph, with a horizontal line drawn at a point where the midpoint of each line intersects the pay policy line. This is illustrated by the broken lines in Figure 9.5. For example, the midpoint of the horizontal line for pay grade 1 (which covers all jobs with point totals between zero and 200 points) intersects the pay policy line at about $32 500—which is then taken as the midpoint in the pay range for this pay grade. Similarly, the midpoint of the horizontal line for pay grade 2 (covering jobs from 201 to 400 points) intersects the pay policy line at about $36 900, so this is taken as the midpoint of the pay range for pay grade 2.

FIGURE 9.5 ILLUSTRATION OF A PAY STRUCTURE

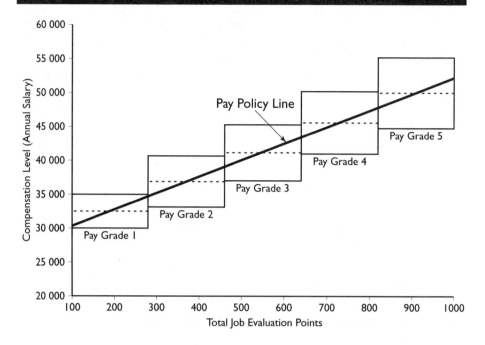

Figure 9.5 also shows the minimum and maximum for each pay grade. For example, the lower line in pay grade 1 represents the minimum for that pay grade (which is $30 000), while the upper line represents the maximum (which is $35 000). Thus, the pay range for all jobs in pay grade 1 is $30 000 to $35 000. Similarly, the pay range for all jobs in pay grade 2 would be $33 650 to $40 150. Going all the way to the highest grade in this pay structure—pay grade 5—we can see that the pay range is $44 600 to $55 600.

So let us look at this pay structure. It has five pay grades, covering 200 job evaluation points each. The minimum pay for any job is $30 000, while the maximum is $55 600. The *spread* of the pay range for pay grade 1, in dollar terms, is $5000, while in percentage terms it is about 17 percent. The percentage spread of the pay range is calculated by taking the dollar spread of the range ($5000) and dividing it by the minimum of the range ($30 000). The spread of the pay range for pay grade 5 is $11 000, or 25 percent. The midpoint of pay grade 2 is about 14 percent ($4400) higher than the midpoint for pay grade 1. (In fact, when we use equal points to delineate pay grades, and a straight pay policy line, the midpoint of each grade will always be the same dollar amount higher than the previous grade.)

Establishing the Range Spreads

In this example, the spread of the pay ranges varies from 17 to 25 percent. But how are these spreads determined? In fact, there are no hard and fast rules, but there are several considerations. The first consideration is the extent to which the organization wants to recognize differences between employees performing the same jobs, via the medium of compensation. How important is experience, and how much can performance vary across individuals in the same job? If the organization places no value on experience, and performance does not really vary across employees, the answer is simple—no spread! Instead, the midpoint becomes the flat pay rate for the job, so all jobs in pay grade 1 would pay $32 500. Remember our chicken processing plant? This is exactly what they did.

Thus, the pay range should mimic the range of performance or experience within jobs, but how do you determine this? Some consideration of the time it takes to become proficient might be a good indicator. For example, a job for which it takes four years to become fully proficient needs to have a much greater spread in pay range than a job for which it takes six months to become proficient. And even after proficiency is reached, there may still be variations in performance that the organization wants to recognize. (Of course, all of this should flow from the compensation strategy, which should already have been established before this time.)

Another consideration is the existence of promotional opportunities. If the organization is growing slowly or not at all, there may be few promotional opportunities for employees to use as a means to increase their pay. Or, it may not be desirable to promote valued employees to management jobs just to get them a pay raise. In these circumstances, a broader pay range can be used to accommodate and retain high-performing employees.

But how, exactly, do you set the pay range? One consideration is how many steps or increments you intend to have in the range. The more increments there are, the greater the spread will be. In general, the spread typically increases as jobs go up the hierarchy, because it is assumed that there is more need for experience, and more scope for performance variation, at higher levels.

Theriault (1992) states that, in practice, spreads in pay range of 10 to 25 percent are typical for production workers, 25 to 30 percent for office staff, and 30 to 50 percent for professionals. Milkovich and Newman (1996) provide slightly different numbers, indicating spreads of 10 to 25 percent for both production and office workers, 35 to 60 percent for professional and managerial jobs, while top-level management jobs may have spreads of 60 to 120 percent.

Another way to set the minimum and maximum is through reference to the labour market. Labour market data normally provide not only the midpoint or averages for each job, but also the range and quartiles. Quartiles simply indicate the pay for the lowest quarter of employees, then the second quarter, and so on. One way of setting the minimum would be to use, say, the top of the bottom quartile as the minimum, and the top of the third quartile as the maximum.

OVERLAPS BETWEEN PAY RANGES

As you can see from Figure 9.5, the pay range for each pay grade overlaps with the previous one. When there is an overlap, an employee in a lower pay grade can actually earn more than an employee in a higher pay grade. Of course, this may be seen as a threat to the integrity of the job evaluation system. So why have overlaps?

Overlaps can serve several purposes. Overlaps occur because of pay ranges. If there were very small spreads in each pay range, there would be little overlap. As the spreads increase, so does overlap. One purpose that overlap serves is to reduce the differences in pay between adjacent pay grades, thus reducing the difference in pay between jobs that fall on either side of the pay grade boundary. Overlaps also allow the pay of top performers in a lower grade to increase without having to promote to a job in a higher pay grade.

So when should overlap be a concern? One possible rule is that it should not be possible for a person in pay grade 1 to be making as much as a person in pay grade 3. That is, when overlap starts to cover two pay grades, this tends to negate the job values established by the job evaluation system, and also reduces the incentive for promotion. This can also create problems after promotion occurs. Normally, when promoted, a person will come into the next-higher job at the midpoint or lower of the pay range for that job. This allows some room for pay increases as the promoted individual gains increased experience and improves performance.

However, as can be seen from Figure 9.5, someone at the top of grade 4 being promoted to grade 5 would receive no increase at all if that person came in at the midpoint. But when employees are promoted, they normally expect some increase in pay, and rightly so. However, if they are granted a pay increase, there is little room for pay increases within the new range. Clearly, excessive overlap causes problems. One way to avoid this situation is to make sure that the top of the previous pay grade is always lower than the midpoint of the next one.

What about the differentials in midpoints between the grades (known as the **intergrade differentials**)? These may be constant, or they may increase as one goes up the scale. The purpose of having them increase, in dollar terms, is to maintain the attractiveness of promotions, in percentage terms. For example, in the pay structure illustrated in Figure 9.5, the intergrade differentials stay constant at $4400 throughout the structure. What this means is that a person who is promoted from the midpoint of pay grade 1 to the midpoint of pay grade 2 would go up 14 percent in pay, but a person being promoted from the midpoint of pay grade 4 to the midpoint of pay grade 5 would receive only a 10 percent increase.

One way to increase this percentage would be to widen the pay grades as the system goes up. One other approach would be to use an upward-curving pay line, but if the market line is actually straight, this could result in overpayment (relative to the market) at the top end of this pay structure. Of course, in some cases the pay policy line *should* be curved, depending on market conditions and pay-level strategy.

MOVEMENT THROUGH THE RANGE

Once the pay range is defined for each pay grade, criteria must be established to determine how movement within the range will occur. The three most common criteria are experience, seniority, and performance. In some cases

intergrade differentials
the differences between the midpoints of pay grades in a pay structure

these are all used. For example, a person's initial placement in the pay range may be determined by previous experience. If pay is below the midpoint of the range, it may be possible to reach the midpoint using annual seniority increases, but to pass that point requires meritorious performance. This is known as a *split pay range*, with the midpoint serving as a "control point" to prevent pay increases unless they are based on performance.

There is also the issue of how many steps or increments there should be within the pay range, and what the size of each increment should be. Theriault (1992) notes that although a pay range may have as few as three or as many as 15 steps, most have six or seven. As discussed in Chapter 5, a pay raise should constitute a "just noticeable difference (JND)," and if it doesn't reach that level, it may have little motivational or reward value.

In times of low inflation, a JND may be 4 percent. So let's look back at pay grade 1 in Figure 9.5. The minimum is $30 000 and the maximum is $35 000. A 4 percent pay raise from the minimum would be $1200. Since the range is $5000, divide it by $1200, which equals about four. Four increments would allow four raises of about 4 percent each, so this might be a reasonable number of steps for this pay grade.

Let's try another one. For pay grade 5, 4 percent of the minimum is $1784. The range is $11 000, so dividing by $1784 equals just over six. Therefore, six increments might be used for this pay grade.

Some organizations do not use fixed steps or increments at all. Instead, they view the minimum as the entry-level pay for an employee with no experience, and the midpoint as the normal pay that a typical employee would receive. Pay raises above the midpoint will take place only if performance is above average, and will reach the maximum at the discretion of the supervisor, who may vary both the timing and the amount of the raises. However, this procedure does not fit well with motivation theory, which suggests that motivation is maximized the clearer the link between future performance and future pay increases. While flexible, it also opens the door to inconsistency and favouritism.

CONDUCTING AND MANAGING THE JOB EVALUATION PROCESS

There are three main purposes for conducting a job evaluation: to control wage costs, to create an equitable pay structure, and to create perceptions of equitable pay among those covered by the system. Whether all three of these objectives are achieved depends on the processes used to conduct the job evaluations and to manage them on an ongoing basis. Five main issues need to be dealt with: (1) who conducts the job evaluations, (2) how the process should be communicated, (3) what appeals/review mechanisms are established, (4) how to apply the job evaluation results, and (5) updating job evaluations.

Who Conducts the Job Evaluations?

Most organizations create a job evaluation committee to oversee the job evaluation process, although some firms assign the task exclusively to their human resources manager, while others utilize outside consultants. When a committee is used, it typically consists of experts in job evaluation (from either inside or outside the company), a senior manager (often the head of human resources), and a representative sample of supervisors from the departments where jobs are being evaluated. In some cases, rank-and-file employees will be included.

In unionized firms, there is usually a joint union–management job evaluation committee, although some unions may prefer not to participate in the process. However, at the least, there should be continuing two-way communication with the union in order to try to prevent misunderstandings.

Employee participation in both developing the job evaluation method and conducting the job evaluation process will usually lead to greater employee satisfaction with the results. However, if this participation is attempted in a classical organization, it may not be helpful, since there is often an adversarial culture and a lack of common goals in these organizations. Employee participation will also not be very effective unless committee members receive training about job evaluation and understand the goals that are being sought in its application.

There are several necessary conditions for a committee to be successful. First, the parameters and terms of reference for the committee, including authority, must be spelled out. However, this is often left vague because top management is unsure about just how much authority they should delegate to the committee. This will be a problem for both classical and human relations firms. Second, both technical and clerical support resources need to be made available to the committee. Third, the committee needs training in job evaluation, as well as in the process for effective group functioning, including such areas as open communication and active involvement.

Communicating the Job Evaluation Process

A key issue in conducting job evaluations is communicating the process. To foster perceptions of equity, communication is essential. In general, employees need to be given an opportunity to understand the pay evaluation process that will be used and its scope and parameters, including the type of results that will likely occur. But just as important, it is essential to make known what will *not* happen. For example, job evaluation will not be used as a ploy to cut jobs or to ferret out individual employees with performance deficiencies.

A variety of methods for this process are possible. Of course, if employees sit on the job evaluation committee, they can serve as a conduit for information. Small group meetings, led by a member of the job evaluation committee, can also be useful, as well as formal written reports and policy documents. It is important that two-way communication channels be established, so employee concerns and questions can be received and addressed.

A question of concern to many employers is whether the detailed results of job evaluation should be revealed, or simply the outcome, in terms of what happens to the job and the pay grade that it is placed in. The answer depends on the nature of the organization and the purposes of the job evaluation. If the organization is a classical one and the main objective is to develop an internal pay structure that controls labour costs, management will conduct the job evaluations and not release the detailed results. This is probably best in these organizations, since the lack of trust and poor relations that often exist would likely lead to this information being misinterpreted or used in unproductive ways.

But if perceptions of compensation equity are important, as in the case of human relations and high-involvement organizations, then more open transmission of information will be desirable. Employees will not be convinced of the fairness of the process unless they understand the workings of the system.

Developing Appeal/Review Mechanisms

One key element of procedural justice is the opportunity for an individual or group to appeal decisions that they believe to be unfair. The logical body to approach first is the job evaluation committee, which can review its decisions in the light of the concerns that are expressed and any new information that may be provided by the complainant. Sometimes the problem is not necessarily due to the decision that was reached, but because the individual does not understand the process that was used to make the decision. At this point, effective communication may solve the problem. Of course, it may be that the complainant is actually correct, and the decision should be changed.

If the individual does not receive satisfaction at this level, there should be at least one other avenue to pursue. In the case of unionized employees, the typical recourse at this point is to initiate a grievance. In a non-union firm, it may be appropriate to designate a senior company official (often the head of human resources) who will review the matter and make a final determination. However, overruling the job evaluation committee is not something to be taken lightly, as this may be seen by committee members as undermining the committee, or as showing a lack of confidence in their decisions. If they are frequently overruled, committee members will grow increasingly cynical about the role played by the committee, and it may become difficult to find good members willing to serve.

Applying Job Evaluation Results

Once the evaluation process has been completed, some jobs may increase in pay and others may decrease. How to handle jobs that are out of line is an important issue to the future success and perceived fairness of job evaluation.

EMPLOYEES BELOW THE RANGE

Jobs held by employees who are currently paid below their pay ranges are known as "green-circled jobs," and incumbents of these jobs should be moved up to at least the bottom of the pay range for their jobs as soon as possible. (Indeed, if these employees are experienced and performing well, they should be moved up past the minimum, since new employees will be coming in at that level.) This would normally be the first priority with the compensation funds that are available. Since new employees will come in at the bottom of the pay range, it is not fair for experienced employees to be left below them.

EMPLOYEES ABOVE THE RANGE

A trickier problem is what to do with individuals who are being paid above the top of the pay range for their jobs. Of course, the most direct way to address this inequity would be to simply reduce their pay to the ceiling of the job's pay range. However, this approach can cause serious morale problems, since most people regard pay reduction to be unfair when it doesn't apply to everyone and when it doesn't seem necessary from an economic point of view. In this case, opposition to the entire job evaluation process could ensue.

Instead, the usual approach is to "red-circle" these individuals, and freeze their pay at their current level until salary scales catch up and the red-circled salary is now within its appropriate pay range. However, while this works quite well in times of high inflation, it doesn't work as well in times of low inflation or during periods in which pay levels are static.

Moreover, although employers may feel that they are being more than generous by red-circling, this practice can still cause serious motivational problems for the affected employees. Nobody likes to look forward to a static or declining income (when inflation is considered), and there is absolutely no financial reward for good performance during the period it takes for the pay scale to catch up, and possibly none even then, since many systems do not allow raises for employees who have reached the ceiling of their pay range.

A compromise solution that some companies adopt is to continue to grant raises based on performance, but not to adjust the pay rate for inflation. Of course, this lengthens the period of adjustment, increases compensation costs, and prolongs inequity. Other employees may start to question why they should receive less money than somebody else who is doing the same work. Therefore, a better approach might be to simply treat red-circled individuals as if they are at the top of their pay range, and therefore not eligible for merit raises (or scale increases) but still eligible for merit bonuses.

A number of other solutions may be available, depending on circumstances. For example, if the individuals are close to retirement, the problem will resolve itself as they retire. Or it may be desirable to offer early retirement, thus allowing the firm to bring in a new person at the bottom of the pay range. In other cases, it may be possible to promote the red-circled individual into a job in the next-higher pay grade, or to add job duties that would justify their current pay level. Other options could include a gradual reduction in pay for the affected individuals to allow them time to adjust to their new pay level.

UPDATING JOB EVALUATIONS

There are at least five events that can trigger a need to reevaluate jobs:

1. Whenever the job itself changes significantly. It is important to have some procedure for identifying jobs that change, because this information may not always reach those who are charged with maintaining the job evaluation system.

2. When the strategy of the organization changes, such that certain behaviours become valued more or less highly than in the past.

3. When there are signs that the job evaluation system is no longer working effectively. These signs could include a high level of appeals, or an inability to fill certain jobs with competent individuals.

4. When labour market conditions change significantly.

5. When legislative conditions require it.

As will be seen, when Ontario instituted pay equity requirements for virtually all Ontario employers in 1987, most employers had to examine both their systems and the results that they were producing.

Failure to update job evaluations is probably most likely in organizations that depended on outside consultants to develop and implement their job evaluation systems. Once the consultants leave, the tendency is to just forget about the system, especially if the consultants did not provide internal employees with the expertise to maintain the job evaluation system. As a part of any consulting contract, the organization should ensure that it provides for training of internal staff such that they have a full understanding of the system and are able to maintain it. Otherwise, provisions have to be made to retain the consultant on a continuing basis.

CONFORMING TO PAY EQUITY REQUIREMENTS

Up until now, we have described generic job evaluation procedures. Using them effectively *should* ensure gender equity. However, many Canadian jurisdictions do not want to leave this to chance, and have imposed specific procedures on employers for ensuring pay equity. In this final section, we will address the issue of how to conform with specific pay equity requirements, a subject not well understood by the general public (Forrest, 2001). Because Ontario is the largest jurisdiction, and because other provincial legislation (such as the Quebec pay equity legislation enacted in 1996 that took full force in November 2001) is patterned after its legislation, we will focus on compliance with the Ontario Pay Equity Act to illustrate the nature of the process. (The detailed process for achieving and maintaining pay equity has been described in various guidebooks put out by the Ontario Pay Equity Commission, and it is strongly recommended that Ontario employers to whom this Act applies obtain copies of the relevant guidebooks.)

The following are the main steps in the Ontario process, and each will be discussed in turn:

1. Determine what rules apply to you.
2. Identify female and male job classes.
3. Establish a body to conduct pay equity.
4. Select a gender-neutral job comparison system.
5. Collect job information.
6. Compare jobs.
7. Check for permissible differences
8. Adjust compensation.
9. Communicate the results.
10. Maintain pay equity.

DETERMINE WHAT RULES APPLY

If your organization employs fewer than ten people in Ontario (including part-time employees), Ontario pay equity legislation does not apply. It also does not apply if your organization is in the federal jurisdiction. Slightly different procedures apply to private-sector employers with ten to 99 employees, compared with larger employers. The main effect of the size differences relates to the requirement for "posting" the pay equity plan. All public-sector employers and all private-sector employers with 100 or more employees must formalize their pay equity plan in a format outlined by the Ontario Pay Equity Act and post it where all employees may have easy access to it. Smaller private-sector employers have the option of preparing and posting a plan or not posting. If they do not post it, they have an obligation to inform any employee who so requests of the process that was conducted to achieve pay equity and the results of this process.

These differences aside, the general process for pay equity is the same for all employers covered by the Act. First, the number of pay equity plans needs to be determined. If the employer is unionized, this would mean one pay equity plan for each bargaining unit in an establishment, and one for all non-union employees within the same establishment. If the firm is not unionized, there will be only one pay equity plan within a given establishment. However, a single employer may differentiate employees by geographical region and thus may have two or more "establishments" within the province. This would entitle the employer to have different pay equity plans for each establishment.

Identify Female and Male Job Classes

The second step in conducting the pay equity process is to determine whether your organization has any female job classes within each pay equity plan. A job class is a group of jobs that have similar duties, require similar qualifications, are filled by similar recruitment procedures, and have the same compensation schedule. Female job classes are those in which (1) at least 60 percent of employees holding them are women, (2) females have traditionally dominated this job class, or (3) most people commonly associate the job with female employees.

Thus, even if you have no job classes that are 60 percent female, if you have jobs that are covered under points (2) or (3), then you still have a female job class. For example, if your company has two secretaries, one of whom is male, you still must consider "secretary" a female job class. Even if your organization employs just one nurse, who happens to be male, the "nurse" job class must be considered a female job class.

If your organization has no female job classes, then there is no need to go any further in the pay equity process. But if it does, the next step is to determine if there are any male job classes in the same pay equity plan. Male job classes are defined by the same criteria noted above, except that 70 percent is the minimum proportion of male jobholders necessary to be considered a male job class. If there are no male job classes in that pay equity plan, the pay equity process does not apply, unless the firm has two or more pay equity plans, and one of those has a male job class, or unless the firm is in the public sector and is allowed to use the "proxy approach" to job comparison, as will be discussed shortly. Of course, when and if the firm creates any male job classes, pay equity would then apply.

Establish a Body for Conducting Pay Equity

If the pay equity legislation does apply, the next step is to conduct the pay equity process. If there is a bargaining agent, the Act requires that the bargaining agent be fully involved in all aspects of the pay equity process. This is usually done through a joint union–management pay equity committee. Although not required for non-union employers, it is strongly recommended that they also establish a joint employee–management pay equity committee.

Some of the benefits of such a committee were discussed along with the discussion of job evaluation committees earlier in the chapter. However, because of the nature of the pay equity process, it is probably even more important to establish such a committee. The diverse viewpoints likely to be found among committee members will help to ensure that potential pay inequities are identified. This body also serves as a communications mechanism and creates more employee confidence in the process and its results.

This committee should have a mix of employees who hold various jobs throughout the organization and should include both female and male members, if possible. Training in the pay equity process is essential for members, and it is useful to establish some ground rules for committee operation, covering issues such as confidentiality, decision-making processes, and the role of the committee and its members. More information on this subject can be found in Pay Equity Commission (1993b: 24).

SELECT A GENDER-NEUTRAL JOB COMPARISON SYSTEM

A gender-neutral job evaluation system that allows comparison of job classes on the four required factor groups—skill, effort, responsibility, and working conditions—needs to be identified and developed. The system most commonly used for pay equity is the point method. While the ranking and classification methods can be adapted to meet the requirements of the pay equity legislation, it is probably only worthwhile to do so if they are already in use by the organization and if the organization is happy with them.

To adapt the ranking system requires that each job be ranked at least four times, once for each of the four required generic job factors. These rankings are then merged to derive the job hierarchy. But unless these factors are to be of equal weight, there must be some weighting system applied to this merging process. To adapt the classification system, more general grade descriptions are prepared. Each grade description provides criteria for assessing the four required job factors.

If it relies on existing pay rates for jobs, the traditional factor comparison method is generally not suitable for pay equity purposes. It is possible to adapt it for pay equity purposes, but it is probably simpler to just abandon it and replace it with the point system. If no formal job evaluation system is currently in use, the best approach is to adopt the point method.

Once the job evaluation method has been selected, it needs to be developed to suit the needs of the organization. For example, if the point system is selected, factors that pertain to each of the four main factor groups need to selected, scaled, and weighted, as described earlier in the chapter.

COLLECT JOB INFORMATION

The next step is to gather the information on which the jobs will be evaluated. This is the process of job analysis described earlier in the chapter. A key part of this process is to avoid gender biases and the potential pitfalls in the job analysis process that have been described earlier.

COMPARE JOBS

Once the information has been collected, the job evaluation system is then applied to each job class, and a job hierarchy is developed (one for each pay equity plan). Three main methods can then be used for comparing female and male job classes: the job-to-job approach, the proportional value method, or the proxy method (only for public-sector employers).

Under the **job-to-job method**, for each female job class, a male job class "comparator" is sought. Assuming the point system has been used, point totals are compared for the various female job classes and the male job classes. This comparator class needs to be similar in that it has an equal or comparable number of points as the female job class, not that it is similar in the nature of the job. For example, the "electrician" job class might have a similar point total to the "nurse" job class, and therefore "electrician" will serve as the comparator class for the nurse job class. If there are two or more male comparator classes that are similar in point totals, the appropriate one is the lower paid. (Incidentally, neither the Pay Equity Act nor the Pay Equity Commission provide any guidance on exactly how similar the point totals have to be before the female and male job classes are considered "equal or comparable.")

Total compensation (including benefits) for the two jobs (known as the "job rates") is then compared. If the male job class (electrician) is receiving higher pay than the female job class (nurse), then pay inequity *may* exist, and, if so, would need to be corrected. (The determination of whether pay inequity does in fact exist will be discussed shortly.)

What if there is no male job class at the same level in the job hierarchy to use as a comparator? In this case, if the organization has two or more pay equity plans, the other pay plan(s) should be checked to see if an equivalent male comparator job class can be found there. If not, an attempt should be made to identify male job classes of lower value (according to job evaluation), but which are being paid more than the female job class. If there are several male job classes like this, the appropriate comparator is the one with the *highest* pay rate. But what if a suitable comparator still cannot be found?

The next course of action is to try the **proportional value method**, which was introduced in mid-1993 to deal with the problem of lack of a male comparator, which can occur in the job-to-job method. The proportional value method requires the employer to calculate what a male job class at the same point in the job hierarchy where the female job is placed would theoretically pay, based on data only from the other male job classes.

Let's use a simple example. Suppose that an organization has one female job class (let's label it "F1") and two male job classes ("M1" and "M2"). The job evaluation points for these jobs, and hourly pay rates, including benefits, are as follows:

- M2: 800 points ($24 per hour)
- F1: 600 points ($15 per hour)
- M1: 400 points ($12 an hour)

As can be seen, there is no equivalent male comparator for the female job class, so the job-to-job method cannot be used. There is a gap in the male job hierarchy at 600 points. Proportional value fills this gap by examining only classes M1 and M2 to see what a male class evaluated at 600 points would theoretically pay. This can be determined by calculating a pay line, similar to that illustrated in Figure 9.4. Job classes M1 and M2 would be plotted on the graph,

job-to-job method establishes pay equity by comparing a female job class to a male class that is comparable in terms of job evaluation criteria

proportional value method establishes pay equity where no comparator male job class exists by extrapolating a hypothetical male comparator job class based on other male job classes

a straight line would be drawn that fits these points (very simple with just two points in this example), and then 600 points would be read from the graph, which would be $18 per hour. (In fact, in this example, no complicated calculations are really necessary to show that a male job midway between 400 and 800 points would pay $18 an hour.)

What we have apparently found is pay inequity, since class F1 is in fact receiving only $15 an hour. This $3 inequity must be corrected, unless it is found to stem from what are known as "permissible differences." If the entire difference does result from permissible differences, it is not considered to be a pay inequity, and no pay adjustments are required.

What if the proportional value approach doesn't work either, because there are no male job classes (or only one)? For most organizations, this brings the pay equity process to a halt. But in what is known as the "broader public sector," the **proxy comparison method** must then be used, if the employer has a review officer's order from the Pay Equity Commission. Under this method, the employer must select another public-sector employer that has achieved pay equity and collect information on the female job classes in that "proxy" organization. This information is then subjected to job evaluation, and the proportional value method is used to calibrate the employer's female job classes. The key issue in this process is, of course, selection of the proxy employer. Further information on the proxy method can be found in Pay Equity Commission (1994).

proxy comparison method establishes pay equity in public-sector organizations where neither the job-to-job method nor the proportional value method can be used

CHECK FOR PERMISSIBLE DIFFERENCES

Pay differences are not considered pay inequities if they are due to "permissible differences." So what are these permissible differences? In the words of the Ontario Pay Equity Commission (1995: 32), **permissible differences** are allowed "where the employer is able to show that the difference is the result of the following: a formal seniority system, a temporary training or developmental assignment, a merit compensation plan, red-circling, or a temporary skills shortage." (To be eligible as a permissible difference, the "merit compensation plan" must be based on formal criteria and be communicated to all employees.)

However, it should be noted that the use of a permissible difference does not necessarily exclude a male job class from being used as a comparator. In some cases, permissible differences will account for all of the gap between the female and male job class, but in other cases they will only account for a portion of the difference. If this is the case, then the remaining portion must be addressed.

Besides those reasons cited above, there are two other allowable reasons for a difference between female and male pay. One is bargaining strength. Under the Act, after "pay equity has been achieved in an establishment, differences in compensation between a female job class and male job class are per-

permissible differences pay differences between female and male job classes not considered inequitable because they stem from certain specified allowable circumstances, such as seniority

missible if the employer is able to show that the difference is the result of differences in bargaining strength" (Pay Equity Commission, 1995: 33). But just how does an employer show that? Neither the Pay Equity Act nor the guidelines provided by the Pay Equity Commission offer any guidance on that question, although they both emphasize that the onus is on the employer to prove that an exception based on bargaining strength meets the requirements of the Act. As of 2001, no successful use of this section of the Act had ever been made.

The other allowable reason is very rarely found. Where an arbitrator or other tribunal *not* related to interest arbitration (interest arbitration is used to determine pay and benefits when the union and management reach an impasse in the bargaining process) raises the pay of a male comparator job class, the employer may select a different male comparator job class, and if one cannot be found, may use the proportional value method instead. This provision can only be used after pay equity has been achieved in the first instance, and it may serve to limit the requirement to maintain pay equity over time.

There is one other possible exception in the pay equity process. An employer (in conjunction with the bargaining agent, if any) may designate certain jobs to be "casual." Casual jobs do not fall under the purview of pay equity legislation. However, there are strict limitations on using this designation. A job *cannot* be designated casual when (Pay Equity Commission, 1995: 33):

a) *The work is performed for at least one third of the normal work period that applies to similar full-time work, or*

b) *The work is performed on a seasonal basis in the same position for the same employer, or*

c) *The work is performed on a regular and continuing basis, although for less than one third of the normal work period that applies to similar full-time work.*

Given these constraints, very few jobs can, in reality, be classified as "casual."

While pay equity must be applied to all except designated "casual" employees, it does not have to be applied to independent contractors. However, the conditions for this exclusion are stringent. For example, in a recent case, individuals who provided daycare for children in their own homes were deemed to be employees of an Ontario county (and thus subject to pay equity provisions) and not independent contractors, as the county had maintained. The providers filed their income tax as self-employed persons, held their own general liability insurance, and purchased most of their own equipment. However, because the county had a rigorous selection process for providers, often a lengthy relationship with them, and exercised control through its placement procedures, regular mandatory orientation and training sessions, regular inspection visits, and discipline and termination procedures, the Pay Equity Tribunal deemed them to be employees, not independent contractors (*Ontario Pay and Employment Equity Guide*, 2000).

ADJUST COMPENSATION

The Ontario pay equity legislation does not necessarily require employers to correct the full extent of pay inequities immediately (although the employer may well decide to do so, if it is within their financial means), as long as the employer has "posted" its pay equity plan. Essentially, this means that all employees have been provided access to the process that was conducted in determining pay equity, and have been provided with their own personal copy, if they so request. (New employers coming under the purview of the Act are expected to correct pay inequities immediately, regardless of whether they post a pay equity plan.)

If an employer has posted a pay equity plan, it must devote at least 1 percent of the previous year's payroll toward correcting pay inequities. This must then be done every year until the inequities are corrected. If the 1 percent is not sufficient to correct the inequities, the Pay Equity Act specifies how the available money will be distributed (Pay Equity Commission, 1993b: 23):

- *The [inequitable female] job class or classes with the lowest job rate in the plan must receive a greater adjustment than other [inequitable female] job classes in the same plan until pay equity is achieved.*

- *Each female job class must receive an adjustment each year until pay equity is achieved.*

- *All positions in a job class will receive the same adjustments in dollar terms.*

Finally, in case an employer may be tempted to do so, the act specifically prohibits the achievement of pay equity through the lowering of pay levels for male comparator jobs.

COMMUNICATE THE RESULTS

Once the pay equity plan has been developed, it should be communicated to employees so that they understand both the process and the results. However, the only organizations *required* to post their pay equity plans are public-sector employers and private-sector employers with at least 100 employees. In organizations that do not post their plan, employers are obligated under the Act to disclose both the process undertaken to ensure pay equity and the results of that process to any employee who so requests.

Maintain Pay Equity

Even after organizations have achieved pay equity, they are not free of their obligations under the Pay Equity Act. Employers are responsible for actively ensuring that pay equity is maintained over time. There are many changes that can occur in the employer that may have an impact on pay equity. These include the following (Pay Equity Commission, 1995: 6):

- *The restructuring of the organization*
- *Certification of a bargaining agent after a deemed-approved plan*
- *Changes in the gender of a job class*
- *New or vanishing job classes*
- *New male comparator job class for a female job class*
- *A change in the value of work performed in a job class*
- *A change in compensation system or compensation levels.*

Let us now examine each of these briefly.

Structural or Bargaining Agent Change

Various types of company restructuring may trigger a need for review of pay equity. For example, when one firm takes over or merges with another, the pay system must be reviewed for equity, looking at all jobs under the new structure. When a new bargaining agent is certified, or a bargaining agent is decertified, it will be necessary either to create another pay equity plan or to merge the previous pay equity plans.

Gender Changes

If the workforce changes such that the percentage of males and females in a particular job class changes, then this class may change from male to female, from female to male, from one of these to gender-neutral, or from gender-neutral to one of these. However, a change in the percentage of males and females does not automatically change the gender status of the job class. For example, if the percentage of secretaries who are female changes from 95 percent to 50 percent, this does not mean that the secretary job class will be reclassified as gender-neutral. In this case, "secretary" would stay a female job class because historically this has been a female job and because of the existence of a stereotype that this is a female job.

New Job Classes

Sometimes an employer creates a new job class, which then must be assessed for gender. If it turns out to be a female job class, the process described earlier kicks in, where the job-to-job or proportional value approach must be used to check for inequity. If a new male job class is created, two questions need to be asked. Should this job be used as a comparator to a female job class (if the job-to-job method is used)? Does this job affect the value for jobs established through a proportional value system?

Vanishing Job Classes

Sometimes a job class will vanish. Reasons may include technological change, company restructuring, or the sale or closure of a business or unit. If a female job class vanishes, or its gender changes, "its incumbents must be paid the full amount of their pay equity adjustments owing up until the date on which the job class disappears" (Pay Equity Commission, 1995: 21).

If a male job class vanishes, the implications depend on whether the job-to-job or proportional value method has been used. If the job-to-job method has been used, and the vanished male job class had been used as a comparator, a new comparator must be found. But if the new comparator is paid lower than the female class, compensation for the female class cannot be lowered. If the proportional value method has been used, the usual procedure is to remove that class from the male job pay line and then reassess female jobs against that. But even if it indicates a lower pay level for the female job class(es), their pay cannot be reduced from their original pay equity entitlement.

Job Value Changes

Sometimes a male or female job class will change in value, if duties or job requirements are changed. If the change is significant enough to warrant a change in its position in the job hierarchy (it is up to the employer to determine this through its gender-neutral job evaluation process), the pay level needs to be reassessed in the manner described earlier. Then, depending on whether it is a female or male job, the procedures described above will apply.

Compensation Changes

Various changes in the compensation system or compensation levels may have implications for pay equity. For example, if a male job class comparator receives a compensation increase either greater than or not received by the female job class, pay equity is threatened. Even if the female job class and its comparator receive equal percentage increases, if these apply before the female job has achieved full pay equity, this actually widens the pay gap between the male and female jobs. In both of these cases, money must be found to re-close these gaps, and this money cannot be deducted from the 1 percent minimum of annual payroll already dedicated to eliminating pay equity gaps.

Communicating Changes to Pay Equity Plan

If any of these changes occur and they have pay equity implications, it is up to the employer (or, if there is a bargaining agent, the employer and the bargaining agent) to revise the pay equity plan accordingly and repost it. The only employers not required to repost changes to their pay equity plan are those employing fewer than 100 employees and those that did not post a plan originally.

Summary and Implications

The purpose of this chapter was to start developing your understanding of the key technical processes necessary to transform the compensation strategy into an operating compensation system, beginning with the process for evaluating jobs. Not all organizations will decide to use job evaluation. But for those that do, this chapter describes how to develop a job evaluation system that will fit best with the organization, and will result in an accurate and equitable evaluation of the relative value of jobs in the organization. This chapter does not, however, discuss the pros and cons of job evaluation; it assumes that the decision to use job evaluation has already been made earlier in the compensation strategy process.

The chapter started by describing the process of job analysis, which provides the information that is the foundation for any effective job evaluation system. Various job analysis methods were described, and some possible pitfalls in the process were outlined.

Next, the chapter moved on to job evaluation methods. After brief discussion of four less commonly used methods, the focus shifted to the point system of job evaluation, the most commonly used method, and the one that generally fits best with Canadian pay equity legislation. The four main steps in developing this method (identifying compensable factors, scaling the factors, weighting the factors, testing the system) were described in depth, followed by a lengthy discussion of the possible pitfalls in using this method.

Although the point method *appears* to be objective and scientific, it is at heart subjective, and is susceptible to many problems that can compromise its reliability and validity. These pitfalls can be avoided, but only if they are first understood. The four main types of pitfalls identified were inconsistency within the factors, overlaps between factors, hierarchical grounding, and gender bias, all of which have commonly afflicted job evaluation systems (and those who were subject to these systems) in the past.

Once a hierarchy of jobs has been established by job evaluation, pay grades and pay ranges must be developed, along with the criteria for movement through the range. This is the stage where actual dollars are attached to each job, and some reference to the labour market is needed to do so.

If a job evaluation process is to be both equitable and seen to be equitable, the process for conducting and managing job evaluation is crucial. Procedures have to be worked out for who will conduct the job evaluation process, for how it will be communicated, for how procedural justice can be established, for applying the results of job evaluation, and for updating job evaluations.

Finally, many jurisdictions have specific legislation pertaining to pay equity, which mandates a specific procedure to identify jobs for which there is gender inequity in pay, and to correct any inequities that are detected. Although the legislation varies somewhat in each jurisdiction, much of it is patterned after Ontario pay equity legislation. Because of this fact, and because Ontario is the largest single jurisdiction, the process for achieving and maintaining pay equity in Ontario was selected to illustrate the process for conforming with pay equity legislation.

Before closing, let us tie the results of this chapter to those of previous chapters. In Chapter 4 it was noted that although job evaluation is consistent with classical and human relations managerial strategies, it is not philosophically or practically consistent with the high-involvement strategy, where jobs are continually evolving and changing. If job evaluation must be done because it is required under pay equity legislation, how can these high-involvement organizations cope? Do they need to continually reevaluate jobs, which will keep the pay system in a state of flux? Virtually all of the changes discussed in the section on maintaining pay equity are happening all the time in high-involvement organizations.

The answer for them would appear to be broad job definitions, which allow considerable latitude for change. What this means is that relatively few pay grades will be used, and pay ranges will be quite broad within these pay grades. They may utilize "broadbanding." But, if so, care must be taken that inequities do not emerge among individuals or among various areas of the organization, if managers have the discretion to apply pay rates as they see fit. This is why many high-involvement organizations are moving toward a pay-for-skills or competency-based pay system, the details of which will be described in Chapter 11.

In the next chapter, we move on to the process of evaluating the labour market to determine what is the "going rate" for our jobs, so that we can ground our pay system in economic reality.

KEY TERMS

base pay structure, p. 350

classification/grading method, p. 331

compensable factors, p. 334

factor comparison method, p. 332

intergrade differentials, p. 356

job analysis, p. 323

job description, p. 323

job-to-job method, p. 365

job specifications, p. 323

market line, p. 339

paired comparison method, p. 330

pay grade, p. 350

pay range, p. 351

permissible differences, p. 366

point method, p. 333

proportional value method, p. 365

proxy comparison method, p. 366

ranking method, p. 330

statistical/policy capturing method, p. 333

EXERCISES

1. Examine the job description depicted in Figure 9.1. Using the essential components for a job description outlined in the chapter, assess whether this is a good job description.

2. Examine the job descriptions that are used at Eastern Provincial University (in the Appendix). What are their strengths and weaknesses? What would you change about them?

3. Using the point system and the four basic factor groups, develop a job evaluation system for Eastern Provincial University. After that, apply it to the different jobs to derive a single hierarchy of jobs.

4. After completing Exercise 3 above, apply the procedures required under the Ontario Pay Equity Act to determine whether pay equity exists for the female job classes at Eastern Provincial University. The following hourly pay scales apply to the four job classes (as of 2000):

   - Clerk Steno I: $13.30; II: $15.19; III: $16.78 (Job class 95 percent female)
   - Draftsperson I: $15.85; II. $19.12; III: $20.78 (Job class 80 percent male)
   - Grounds Worker I: $13.33; II: $13.70; III: $14.92 (Job class 85 percent male)
   - Medical Laboratory Technologist I: $19.09; II: $21.04 (Job class 90 percent female)

SUGGESTED WEB SITES

Page 327: To check out the National Occupational Classification, click on <www.worklogic.com:81/noc/home.html>

Page 362: For information on complying with the Ontario Pay Equity Act, click on the Web site of the Ontario Pay Equity Commission <www.gov.on.ca/lab/pec>

REFERENCES

Catano, Victor M., Steven F. Cronshaw, Willi H. Wiesner, Rick D. Hackett, and Laura L. Methot. 1997. *Recruitment and Selection in Canada*. Toronto: ITP Nelson.

Elliot, Cheryl J., and Stewart D. Saxe. 1992. *Pay Equity Handbook*. Aurora, ON: Canada Law Book Inc.

Fine, Sidney A., A.M. Holt, and M.F. Hutchinson. 1974. "Functional Job Analysis: How to Standardize Task Statements." *Methods for Manpower Analysis*. Kalamazoo, MI: W.E. Upjohn Institute for Employment Research.

Focus on Canadian Employment and Equality Rights. 2000. "Policy-

Capturing Job Evaluation Methodology Considered." 5(28): 222–23.

Forrest, Anne. 2001. "Pay Equity: The State of the Debate." In Y. Reshef, C. Bernier, D. Harrisson, and T.H. Wagar, *Industrial Relations in the New Millenium: Selected Papers from the XXXVIIth Annual CIRA Conference*, 65–78.

Hemphill, J.K. 1954. "Job Descriptions for the Executive." *Harvard Business Review*, 37: 55–69.

Kelly, John G. 1994. *Pay Equity Management*. North York, ON: CCH Canadian Limited.

Kervin, John, and Marika Elek. 2001. "Where's the Bias? Sources and Types of Gender Bias in Job Evaluation." In Y. Reshef, C. Bernier, D. Harrisson, and T.H. Wagar, *Industrial Relations in the New Millenium: Selected Papers from the XXXVIIth Annual CIRA Conference*, 79–90.

King, Ian. 1992. *Compensation Administration and Equitable Pay Programs—A Practical Guide*. Don Mills, ON: CCH Canadian Limited.

McPhail, S.M., P.R. Jeanneret, E.J McCormick, and R.C. Mecham. 1991. *Position Analysis Questionnaire: Job Analysis Manual*. Palo Alto, CA: Consulting Psychologists Press.

Milkovich, George T., and Jerry M. Newman. 1996. *Compensation*. Chicago: Irwin.

Ontario Pay and Employment Equity Guide. 2000. "Home Care Providers Entitled to Pay Equity." February: 3.

Pay Equity Commission. 1989. *How to Do Pay Equity Job Comparisons*. Toronto: Ontario Pay Equity Commission.

Pay Equity Commission. 1993a. *Step by Step to Pay Equity: Using the Proportional Value Comparison Method*.

Toronto: Ontario Pay Equity Commission.

Pay Equity Commission. 1993b. *Step by Step to Pay Equity: A Guide for Small Business: Volume I: The Workbook*. Toronto: Ontario Pay Equity Commission.

Pay Equity Commission. 1994. *A Guide to the Proxy Comparison Method*. Toronto: Ontario Pay Equity Commission.

Pay Equity Commission. 1995. *Maintaining Pay Equity: Using the Job-to-Job and Proportional Value Comparison Methods*. Toronto: Ontario Pay Equity Commission.

Pay Equity Commission. 1996. *Step by Step to Pay Equity: A Guide for Small Business: Volume 2: The Job Evaluation System*. Toronto: Ontario Pay Equity Commission.

Steinberg, Ronnie J. 1999. "Emotional Labour in Job Evaluation: Redesigning Compensation Practices." *Annals of the American Academy of Political and Social Science*, 561: 143–57.

Steinberg, R., and L. Haignere. 1985. "Equitable Compensation: Methodological Criteria for Comparable Worth." Working Paper 16. Albany: Center for Women in Government, State University of New York.

Thanasse, Laura. 1993. "Banding." *Human Resources Management in Canada*, February: 40, 685–88.

Theriault, Roland. 1992. *Mercer Compensation Manual*. Boucherville, PQ: G. Morin.

Tornow, W.W., and P.R. Pinto. 1976. "The Development of a Managerial Job Taxonomy: A System for Describing, Classifying, and Evaluating Executive Positions." *Journal of Applied Psychology*, 61: 410–18.

Weiner, Nan J. 1991. "Job Evaluation Systems: A Critique." *Human Resource Management Review*, 1(2): 119–32.

Weiner, Nan J., and Morley Gunderson. 1990. *Pay Equity: Issues, Options, and Experiences.* Toronto: Butterworths.

Welbourne, Theresa, and Charlie O. Trevor. 2000. "The Roles of Departmental and Position Power in Job Evaluation." *Academy of Management Journal*, 43(4): 761–71.

10

....

EVALUATING THE MARKET

CHAPTER GOALS

By the end of this chapter, you should be able to:

1. Discuss the key factors in understanding labour markets.
2. Identify possible sources of compensation data.
3. Describe the steps in the process for conducting compensation surveys.
4. Analyze, interpret, and apply compensation survey data.

INTRODUCTION

This chapter continues our discussion of technical processes in compensation by focusing on how to evaluate the labour market. No employer can afford to ignore the market, as this could result in a compensation system set at a level that is unrealistically low or high. However, as was discussed in Chapter 4, identifying the "going market rate" for individual jobs can be a complex process, and an elusive one, since there may be no single market rate for many jobs.

After a brief orientation to the nature of labour markets, this chapter will identify sources of compensation data, including both third-party and in-house surveys. Following that, the process for conducting a compensation survey will be outlined. The chapter concludes with an illustration of the process for analyzing and interpreting compensation survey data.

UNDERSTANDING LABOUR MARKETS

Why do people get paid what they do? Surely, you say, it is based on the value or importance of the job they do. Well, consider this. The prime minister of Canada earns $262 988 per year. The lowest-paid hockey player with the Toronto Maple Leafs receives $600 000 per year. Is being a benchwarmer on a professional hockey team really a more important job than being prime minister of Canada? What's going on here?

In general, the price (wage) for a particular type of labour will depend on the demand for that labour, relative to the supply for that labour, constrained by the ability of employers to pay. In theory, whenever there is a surplus of a particular type of labour, the price for that labour will go down. In reality, wages seldom decline in ongoing firms unless the employer is experiencing financial difficulties and cutting wages is seen as a necessity. This is because wage cuts often result in a variety of negative consequences for the employer, such as increased turnover and reduced employee performance, as has been discussed in Chapter 3. However, new firms may take advantage of a labour surplus by hiring employees at a lower rate than existing employers.

In theory, faced with a labour shortage, firms in the private sector will be willing to increase the price for labour until the price matches the value (in terms of revenue generated) that the firm receives from that labour. But, in reality, how much an employer will pay for labour is a function of a variety of factors, including the employer's ability to pay. Key factors include company profitability, the importance of that labour to the operation of the organization, and the proportion of labour costs relative to total costs. For example, if labour is only a small portion of a firm's total costs, the firm can afford to pay much more for its labour than firms in which labour is a high proportion of total costs.

For public-sector organizations, such as hospitals, school boards, and government departments, the ability of employees to generate revenue is obviously not an issue. Instead, ability to pay is the key issue. If taxpayers (through their elected representatives on the school board) set the school district budget at $50 000 000, then this is what is available for all purposes, including paying teacher salaries. In Canada, public-sector employees are highly unionized, so most public-sector pay is determined through collective bargaining. If the union has the right to strike, as most do, then a key factor is how essential the service is, how willing public officials (and the general public) are to endure a strike, the available budget for pay increases, and the ability to obtain a budget increase. Higher pay levels can be granted without a budget increase, but the money must come from somewhere, usually a reduction in the number of persons who can be employed by the organization.

In general, wage compression has occurred in the public sector. Public-sector employees at the lower end of the job hierarchy usually earn more than comparable employees in the private sector, while public-sector employees at the top of the job hierarchy usually earn less than they would in the private sector (Gunderson, Hyatt, and Riddell, 2000). This is because public-sector unions are relatively powerful due to their ability to disrupt important public services. Pay equity programs, which have been in place much longer in public-sector organizations, may also play a role in this differential. But pay for top-level government officials is constrained by the visibility of their salaries and a reluctance on the part of taxpayers to pay public employees a lot more than they themselves are earning. However, there are no such constraints on private-sector employers for their top-level employees, so the public–private-sector wage gap is wide for these employees.

There are several general patterns in compensation levels. On average, unionized employees receive considerably more compensation than comparable non-union employees (Drost and Hird, 2000). Employees in large firms, on average, earn more than those in small firms; employees in Ontario and British Columbia earn more than those in other provinces; and, as Box 10.1 shows, employees in the resource sector earn more than those in the service sector.

BOX 10.1 Where Would You Choose to Work?

If you had to choose an industry based strictly on how much it pays its employees, which would you pick? The following are the average hourly earnings for different Canadian industries, as at January 2001, according to Statistics Canada:

Mining, oil, and gas	$25.11
Utilities	$24.94
Logging and forestry	20.84
Professional, scientific, technical services	19.99
Construction	21.19
Health and social services	18.74
Manufacturing	18.11
Transportation and warehousing	17.92
Finance and insurance	16.10
Public administration	15.66
Retail trade	12.94
Education and related services	12.03
Accommodation/food/beverage services	9.27

Of course, all of these seem pretty miserly when you compare them with the average pay for players in the National Hockey League, which is about $2778 an hour. (This is counting six hours of practice for every regular season game, plus game time. If you included game time only, the pay rate would be $8333 per hour.) This is nice for hockey players, but is one hour of an average hockey player's work really worth more than the combined hourly work of 148 Canadian health and social service workers? What scale would you use for judging?

---

compensating differential a higher compensation level offered by an employer because of undesirable aspects of employment at that employer

Aside from the relative scarcity of labour and its perceived value to the employer, pay is affected by what are known as **compensating differentials**. For example, many of the high-paying jobs in the resource sector are cyclical in nature, which means that workers in these industries often have to endure periods of unemployment. Their higher wage levels provide a differential that compensates them for this employment volatility. Likewise, the cost of living in Ontario and British Columbia is higher than in other provinces, and the higher wage rates help to compensate for this reality.

Other negative features that may trigger compensating differentials include poor working conditions and jobs for which the failure rate is high. For example, many people who try selling life insurance fail, but those who are successful can earn very high compensation. Another example of a negative feature that can cause a compensating differential is a poor industry reputation. This may be caused by an industry that is widely perceived as environmentally unfriendly, such as forestry, or where the product is in social disfavour, such as tobacco.

But does this theory really work? Are salaries in, say, the tobacco industry, really higher than elsewhere? Box 10.2 tries to smoke out the truth.

Defining the Relevant Labour Market

Labour markets are complex. Luckily, an employer does not need to understand the labour market as a whole, but only that segment of the market that

---

BOX 10.2 Salaries Are Really Smokin' in Tobacco!

In Chapter 3, we discussed how employees take a variety of costs and benefits into account when deciding where to seek and accept employment. We also used an example of the tobacco industry, where we suggested that many people may look with disfavour on the product, making them reluctant to accept employment in the industry, thus necessitating higher wages to get them to do so. The economic theory of compensating differentials would predict exactly the same thing. Because of the stigma attached to the industry, salaries will have to be higher in order to entice employees into the industry.

So both behavioural and economic theory agree. All other things being equal, salaries should be higher in the tobacco industry than industrial averages. But just what are the facts? Over the years, total employment in Canada's tobacco products industry (excluding growers) has been

gradually declining, from 4483 persons in 1990 to well under 4000 persons today, according to Statistics Canada. At the same time, demand for the industry's product has also been declining, from 65 billion cigarettes in 1980 to less than 50 billion today (that still amounts to about 1500 cigarettes per man, woman, and child per year).

In 1999, the average wages and salaries in the Canadian manufacturing sector were $39 304. What were they in tobacco? Try $67 201, or more than $2000 a month higher, on average! Interestingly, despite the decline in demand for tobacco employees and their product during 1990–99, wage increases in tobacco actually outpaced increases in the industrial averages during this period.

If you can stand the smoke, and think you will live long enough to enjoy your money, the tobacco industry really coughs up the dough!

---

pertains to the specific jobs that the employer needs to fill. Essentially, what an employer needs to know is what its competitors are paying their employees. There are two kinds of competitors that are relevant: competitors in the same labour market, and competitors in the same product/service market.

In some cases, firms from many industries compete for the same labour—for example, an insurance company, a chemical manufacturer, and an airline may all need accounting clerks. However, in other cases, labour is so specialized that certain jobs are found only within the same industry. For example, if you are a chemical manufacturer, and need chemical process-control engineers, you don't have to compete with the insurance company or the airline to hire them.

Labour markets and product/service markets serve as constraints to employers. If an employer is paying less than what its competitors in the labour market are paying, it will find it difficult to attract and retain good employees. If the employer is paying more than its competitors in the same product/service market, then it may have trouble offering its product or service at a competitive price.

There are two other crucial dimensions of the labour market. One is the occupational grouping. The other is the geographic scope of the market—local, regional, national, or international. But these two dimensions are interrelated, depending on how industry-specific and specialized the occupational grouping is. For example, if you are looking for a secretary, the market is usually local. Virtually every organization of any size employs one or more secretaries, so they can be found in almost all labour markets.

On the other hand, not every organization employs a chemical process engineer, and these employees may be very scarce in some local labour markets. In general, the more specialized the occupation, the wider the geographic scope of the market will be for that occupation. For example, it may be possible to hire production and office staff locally but necessary to seek technical staff across a larger region, senior managerial staff on a national basis, and specialized professional staff nationally or internationally.

Thus, before setting out to collect data, the employer needs to identify the occupational groups for which it will collect data, the geographic bounds for that group, and the industry bounds for the information. As will be discussed later on, the employer must also identify the specific compensation data it needs in order to make informed decisions.

SOURCES OF COMPENSATION DATA

Once an employer has defined the type of labour market information it needs, it needs to acquire that information. All market information is based on compensation surveys, but it is not necessary for every organization to conduct its own compensation survey. Besides collecting it yourself, there are three main "third-party" sources of compensation data: government agencies, industry groups, and compensation consulting firms. Many of these organizations have Web sites that include compensation data (see Table 10.1), although there may be a fee for accessing this information.

THIRD-PARTY SURVEYS

GOVERNMENT AGENCIES

A variety of governmental agencies survey employers to collect labour market information. At the federal level, these include Statistics Canada and Human Resources Development Canada, which maintains information on collective agreements as well as other pay information. Most provincial departments of labour also publish some data on compensation levels. Some municipal governments also publish salary surveys.

INDUSTRY GROUPS

Most industries have industry associations, many of which collect data on pay rates within their industries. Many professional associations also collect data on their own occupational groups.

TABLE 10.1   EXAMPLES OF WEB SITES WITH COMPENSATION SURVEY DATA

Government Agencies

Human Resources Development Canada	<www.on.hrdc-drhc.gc.ca/english/lmi/eaid/sources/sour11_e.html>
Statistics Canada	<www.statcan.ca>
Toronto Board of Trade	<www.bot.com>

Industry Associations

Canadian Manufacturers and Exporters Alliance	<www.cme-mec.ca>
Conference Board of Canada	<www.conferenceboard.ca>

Consulting Firms

AON Consulting	<www.aon.com>
Economic Research Institute	<www.erieri.com>
KPMG	<www.kpmg.ca>
Hewitt Associates	<was.hewitt.com/hewitt>
Watson Wyatt Worldwide	<www.watsonwyatt.com/homepage/ca>
William M. Mercer	<www.wmmercer.com/canada>

COMPENSATION CONSULTANTS

There are many firms for which collecting labour market information is a major business. These include large international firms such as AON Consulting, the Hay Group, Hewitt Associates, KPMG, Sibson and Company, Towers Perrin, William M. Mercer, and Watson Wyatt Worldwide, as well as many smaller firms that operate on a local or regional basis.

ADVANTAGES AND DISADVANTAGES OF THIRD-PARTY SURVEYS

Using compensation data acquired from third-party sources has both advantages and disadvantages. The two most obvious advantages are ease and cost. Normally, when firms are asked to participate in compensation surveys, they are promised the results, so the only cost is the cost of the time responding to the survey. Of course, it is also much easier than designing and conducting an in-house survey.

However, there are several disadvantages. Third-party surveys may not cover the desired jobs, compensation characteristics, or employers. Often, aggregate data are provided, rather than company-by-company data, so that it is not possible to separate out those employers who are the most appropriate comparators for your organization.

IN-HOUSE SURVEYS

Finally, one option is to carry out your own compensation survey. This can be done formally or informally.

INFORMAL SURVEYS

Informal approaches can range greatly, from a quick review of help wanted ads, to a question posed to a group of colleagues at an industry function, to making a few telephone calls to other firms. There are also many sources of data available on the Internet, such as <www.salaryexpert.com>. Informal surveys are usually simple and quick, but may have poor reliability and validity.

FORMAL SURVEYS

Formal surveys can be undertaken by internal staff, or they can be contracted-out to compensation firms. The main advantage of conducting an in-house survey is that the employer controls the entire process, thereby ensuring the quality and appropriateness of the data. Of course, another advantage is that the employer avoids paying the consulting fees, which can be high, depending on the amount of customization required. However, there are numerous disadvantages to conducting your own survey. If the survey is to be done by internal staff, then someone with the required expertise must be available. There may also be difficulty getting responses to the survey, since many employers are reluctant to reveal their compensation practices to their competitors, in the absence of any intermediary organization. Overall, most firms will likely find it best to contract the survey to professionals in the field.

CONDUCTING COMPENSATION SURVEYS

In conducting a compensation survey, there are four main steps: (1) identify the jobs that are to be surveyed, (2) determine the information to be collected about each job, (3) identify which employers are to be surveyed, and (4) determine the method of data collection.

IDENTIFY THE JOBS TO BE SURVEYED

Most organizations will not collect market data about every job they have, for several reasons. First, it would be very costly to do so. Second, the organization often has unique jobs for which it is hard to find matches. Third, it is not necessary. The usual rule of thumb is that surveying about 10–15 percent of jobs should be sufficient to calibrate the system. Moreover, it is not even necessary to survey these key or benchmark jobs every year. Instead, data can be obtained on what the annual increases are, and the job rates can be updated on this basis (Sibson, 1990).

key job matching
including jobs on a compensation survey that are well understood and numerous in the labour market, and asking respondents to supply compensation information for those jobs

An essential foundation for any compensation survey is an effective method of matching the jobs that the employer has to those being surveyed. The most common approach is known as **key job matching,** which involves selecting certain jobs that are well understood and numerous in the job market, and asking employers to compare their jobs with these jobs. Typically, a job title is provided, along with a brief job summary. Employers are then asked whether they have any of these jobs, and if so, to provide compensation data about them. In selecting these jobs, it is important to represent a variety of job families, and to provide examples within each family at both the entry level and the top level.

DETERMINE WHAT INFORMATION TO COLLECT

Simply collecting information about wage and salary levels will not generally provide a fair basis for comparison. Information about the base pay, the performance pay, and the indirect pay, as well as the weekly hours of work, all need to be collected for each job in the survey. In addition to the formal pay ranges for each job, it is also useful to know where most employees actually are in the pay range. This is often determined by asking how many employees are in each quartile of the pay range. Table 10.2 provides a list of some typical questions to be asked when conducting a compensation survey. Figure 10.1 provides the actual survey form used by Koenig and Associates, a Saskatoon-based human resources consulting firm.

TABLE 10.2   TYPICAL COMPENSATION SURVEY QUESTIONS

A. General Questions

1. Name of employer
2. Number of employees
3. Location of employees
4. Main products or services produced

B. Questions for Each Job

1. Do you have any employees performing the job described below?
   (The description for the specific job being surveyed appears here.)
2. How many?
3. Are the employees in this job union members?
4. What was the average base pay, performance pay, and indirect pay (estimate a dollar value for the benefits provided) received by employees in this job over the last year?
5. What is the minimum, maximum, and midpoint of the pay range for this job?
6. How many employees are in each quartile of the pay range?
7. On what basis do employees move through the pay range? (e.g., seniority, merit, training)
8. How long does it take a typical employee to move from the bottom to the top of the pay range?
9. What is the standard workweek for this job, in terms of hours?
10. Are these employees eligible for overtime? At what pay rate?

DETERMINE WHOM TO SURVEY

Determining which employers to survey is not a simple matter. In general, firms like to survey other employers that they perceive as similar to themselves, in terms of industry type, geographic location, and size. But the sample will likely vary, depending on whether the jobs being surveyed are filled by the local, regional, national, or international labour markets.

DETERMINE HOW TO COLLECT THE DATA

There are four main ways to collect the information: personal interviews, questionnaires, telephone interviews, and the Internet.

PERSONAL INTERVIEWS

In general, the personal interview is thought to provide the best quality of information. It is possible to make sure that the jobs being surveyed are actually similar to the job data being reported, and that the questions are being interpreted properly. However, this method is also very costly to utilize on any significant scale.

FIGURE 10.1 SAMPLE COMPENSATION SURVEY FORM

Salary and Benefits Survey

SALARY INFORMATION

Benchmark Job Title	YOUR Job Title	Number of Incumbents	Quality of Job Match (Please Check One)			Average Annual Base Salary	Check If Job Is Bonus Eligible	Average Bonus Paid	Minimum of Salary Range	Maximum of Salary Range
			Poor (0–60%)	Good (60–80%)	Excellent (80–100%)					

1. What are wage increases based on? _____ Cost of Living _____ Performance _____ Seniority _____ Skills/Competencies _____ Market Information
   _____ Other (please describe) _____

HOURS OF WORK AND SCHEDULING

1. What are your regular weekly business hours (e.g., 36 hours/week, 37.5 hours/week, 40 hours/week, etc.)?

2. Do you provide one or more alternative workweek schedules to your employees (e.g., 4.5 day week, one day off every other week or every third week, etc.)
   _____ Yes _____ No If yes, what is your arrangement?

3. What is the annual vacation allowance for employees? (e.g. __1__–__5__ years service earn __3__ weeks per year, etc.)
   _|_ years service earn ____ weeks per year
   _|_ years service earn ____ weeks per year

4. Do you have an allowance for paid absences due to illness and/or pressing necessity? _____Yes _____No
   If yes, what is your annual sick leave allowance? _____ How is this earned?

5. In addition to legislated statutory holidays, do you provide any other days as paid days off (e.g., Boxing Day)? _____Yes _____No If yes, how many? _____

6. Overtime is paid after _____ hours are worked in a week. At what rate is overtime paid? _____

   e. What groups of employees are eligible for overtime pay? (check as many as apply) ____ All ____ Admin ____ Technical ____ Professional ____ Management ____ Other

   f. Are employees allowed to take time off in lieu of overtime pay? ____ Yes ____ No If yes, please briefly describe policy. _____

BENEFITS

1. Please indicate (✓) which of the following benefits are provided. Detail how the cost is shared between the employer and employee (e.g., 50/50, 25/75), for each benefit listed.

2. Please indicate which of the following programs/benefits are provided. Please provide any relevant details about the design of the program in the Comments section.

BENEFIT	✓	Employer %	Employee %
Group Life Insurance			
Accidental Death & Dismemberment			
Short-Term Disability			
Long-Term Disability			
Supplementary Health Care			
Dental Plan			

BENEFIT	✓	Employer %	Employee %
Vision Care Plan			
Employee Assistance Plan			
Fitness Plan (e.g., club membership)			
Pension Plan			
Group RRSP			
Other (please list)			

Program/Benefit Offered	Available to:						Max Value	Comments/Details (please add additional pages as necessary)
	All	Admin	Technical	Professional	Mgmt	Other		
Incentive Pay Program (e.g., share ownership, commissions, etc.)								
Personal Vehicle Allowance ($x/month)								
Company Vehicle Is Personal Use Allowed?								
Payment of Professional Dues								
Payment of Association/Society Memberships								
Other Bonus Payments (e.g., Christmas bonus, etc.)								

3. Do you provide an Education/Training Allowance to employees? ____ Yes ____ No

Source: Koenig and Associates. Reprinted with permission.

Questionnaires

By far the cheapest method of data collection is the mail survey or questionnaire. However, it is also the least reliable method, since there is no control over who is filling out the survey, and no way of knowing whether it is being done correctly. It is very common for chores such as this to be delegated to the most junior member of the HR department.

Telephone Interviews

A compromise method is the telephone interview. It is much cheaper than the personal interview, yet it produces a higher quality of information than the questionnaire approach since there is an opportunity to confirm job matches and clarify survey questions. This method also provides some control over who the actual respondent is.

Internet Surveys

As the Internet has become all-pervasive, some organizations have started to use electronic means for sending out the survey and collecting responses. Internet surveys can, of course, be faster than using the mail, and can also facilitate tabulation of data. It is also easier to stay in touch with respondents during the survey process. Because Internet surveys are so new, there is no evidence whether response rates are better or worse than normal mail surveys or whether the quality of information received is any different.

Analyzing and Interpreting Survey Data

Once a wage survey has been conducted, you have raw data. You have a list of employers surveyed and what they are paying for different jobs. Hopefully, for each job, you have the minimum, maximum, and midpoints of the pay ranges, and the mean base pay, performance pay, indirect pay, and total compensation. Now what?

Analytical Procedures

mean, or simple average a measure of central tendency of a set of values derived by summing the values and dividing by the number of values

weighted mean, or weighted average a measure of central tendency of a set of values that adjusts the average based on the number of cases to which each value pertains

The first steps in analyzing the survey data involve assessing the central tendency of pay and the variation across employers. There are two main ways to assess central tendency. Using a **mean** (sometimes known as a **simple average**), the midpoints of the pay range for a given job at each company are added up and divided by the total number of companies. Of course, this weights all employers equally regardless of whether they employ one or one thousand of the employees performing the job in question. Therefore, some firms compute a **weighted mean** (sometimes known as a **weighted average**) by weighting each employer according to how many employees that employer has performing the job under consideration. A simple average or weighted average of the mean base pay, performance pay, and indirect pay for a given job across the sample of firms can also be calculated. A simple average mean pay gives an indication of pay policies used by a typical firm for a given job, while a weighted average mean pay gives a better indication of what the typical employee in a given job is earning.

One problem with a mean is that it can be distorted by extreme values. One way of avoiding extreme values when measuring central tendency is to use the **median**, which is the middle value in a ranking of pay levels, below which half of employers are paying less and above which half are paying more.

median the middle value in an ordered list of values

Dispersion of pay across employers can be assessed in several ways. One way is to look at the mean total compensation for the lowest-paying employer, and then determine what percentage more the highest-paying employer is paying. For example, if the lowest-paying employer pays its secretaries a mean total compensation of $30 000, and the highest-paying employer pays its secretaries a mean total compensation of $45 000, then the dispersion in secretarial compensation across firms is 50 percent.

Another way of examining dispersion across employers is to look at **quartiles** or **deciles**. For example, the mean total compensation levels at each firm for a given job are arranged from lowest to highest, and then the list is divided into either four groups (quartiles) or ten groups (deciles). Then, the mean total compensation within each quartile or decile is computed. This allows an assessment of what, say, the top 25 percent of firms (using quartiles) are paying, on average. Percentiles, which indicate the amount below which a certain percentage of employers would fall, can also be used. For example, if $60 000 is at the 90th percentile of total compensation levels for a given job, that means that 90 percent of firms pay less than that and 10 percent pay more. The **interquartile range** is the difference between the 25th percentile and 75th percentile values, divided by the 25th percentile value. If this is very large, it may indicate problems with the job matching, where some of the jobs in the sample are not equivalent (Tyson, 2001).

quartiles or deciles division of an ordered list of values into either four groups (quartiles) or ten groups (deciles)

interquartile range a measure of pay dispersion across employers, calcu-lated by dividing the difference between the 25th and 75th percentile values by the value of the 25th percentile

A major issue in analyzing compensation data is whether to focus on range midpoints or actual mean compensation levels. Range midpoints and pay ranges do not actually tell us what the typical employee in the job is being paid, and of course, pay ranges deal only with base pay, so a lot of the picture could be missing. Most employees may be at the top of the pay range, or the bottom. One way of assessing where employees are actually being paid in the pay range is to ask respondents to report the number of employees in each quartile of the pay range for each job.

A statistic that can be very useful in assessing the distribution of employees within their pay range is known as the **compa-ratio**. The compa-ratio is calculated by taking the mean base pay of all employees holding a particular job, and then dividing this amount by the midpoint of the pay range for that job. A compa-ratio of greater than 1.00 means that, on average, employees are being paid above the midpoint at that firm; a compa-ratio of less than 1.00 means that, on average, employees are being paid below the midpoint.

compa-ratio a measure of distribution of employees within their pay range calculated by dividing the mean base pay by the midpoint of the pay range

Besides looking at the level of compensation, analysis of survey data may also give an indication of the typical structure of compensation (or pay mix) across employers. For example, the proportion of base pay, performance pay, and indirect pay (as a percentage of total compensation) can be calculated for a given job at each firm, and these values can then be averaged (either a simple average, weighted average, or both). For example, firms in the sample may pay 70 percent of their secretaries' total compensation in base pay, 10 percent in performance pay, and 20 percent in indirect pay, on average. You can also look at the percentages for each firm to see the variation in the use of, say, performance pay, across the sample of firms.

INTERPRETING SURVEY DATA

The best way of illustrating the issues involved in interpreting survey data is to work our way through a detailed example. Table 10.3 provides an example of compensation survey results for the job of "accounting clerk."

We have surveyed ten companies, and have data regarding the number of accounting clerks that each firm employs; the minimum, maximum, and midpoints of the base pay ranges; the mean amounts of base pay, performance pay, indirect pay, and total compensation paid to accounting clerks at each firm; and the distribution of accounting clerks across the pay range in each firm by quartile.

The job summary that was used on the survey was based on the National Occupational Classification for "Accounting and Related Clerks":

> *This unit group includes clerks who calculate, prepare and process bills, invoices, accounts payable and receivable, budgets and other routine financial records according to established procedures. They are employed throughout the private and public sectors. Examples of related titles include costing clerk, ledger clerk, audit clerk, finance clerk, budget clerk, billing clerk, tax return preparer, accounts payable clerk, accounts receivable clerk, invoice clerk, deposit clerk, tax clerk, freight-rate clerk.*

INSPECTING THE DATA

So, what can we observe from Table 10.3? Base pay range midpoints range from $24 000 (Company J) to $32 000 (Company A). The average base pay range midpoint is $28 050, and the weighted average midpoint is $26 936. This suggests that firms that employ more accounting clerks have a lower pay range than firms that employ fewer of them. The median range midpoint is $28 500 (when there is an even number of cases, the median is the average of the middle two cases).

As can be seen, mean base pay is lowest at Company J ($24 600) and highest at Company A ($33 400). Interestingly, however, when total compensation is

TABLE 10.3   RESULTS OF COMPENSATION SURVEY: ACCOUNTING CLERK

Company	Total Employment	Number of Accounting Clerks Employed	Base Pay Range Minimum	Base Pay Range Midpoint	Base Pay Range Maximum	Mean Base Pay	Mean Performance Pay	Mean Indirect Pay	Mean Total Compensation	Compa-Ratio	Base Pay Quartile			
											1	2	3	4
A	700	5	$29 000	$32 000	$35 000	$33 400	$3340	$6 680	$43 420	1.04	1 (20%)	0 (-)	1 (20%)	3 (60%)
B	1700	20	28 000	31 000	34 000	33 100	4965	8 275	46 340	1.07	2 (10%)	1 (5%)	1 (5%)	16 (80%)
C	800	6	29 000	30 000	31 000	30 667	6133	9 200	46 000	1.02	1 (17%)	0 (-)	0 (-)	5 (83%)
D	2000	25	28 000	30 000	32 000	31 560	1578	12 624	45 762	1.05	2 (8%)	1 (4%)	1 (4%)	21 (84%)
E	700	9	6 000	30 000	34 000	31 333	3133	9 400	43 866	1.04	2 (22%)	1 (11%)	1 (11%)	5 (56%)
F	4000	45	25 000	27 000	29 000	27 544	1377	9 640	38 561	1.02	11 (24%)	6 (13%)	8 (18%)	20 (44%)
G	5000	65	23 500	26 500	29 500	25 923	–	7 777	33 700	0.98	20 (31%)	15 (23%)	10 (15%)	20 (31%)
H	7000	80	22 000	25 000	28 000	25 050	–	8 768	33 818	1.00	24 (30%)	18 (23%)	10 (13%)	28 (35%)
I	1000	10	21 000	25 000	29 000	25 100	–	6 275	31 375	1.00	0 (-)	7 (70%)	2 (20%)	1 (10%)
J	1000	10	21 000	24 000	27 000	24 600	3690	6 150	34 440	1.03	0 (-)	4 (40%)	4 (40%)	2 (20%)
Simple Average			$25 250	$28 050	$30 850	28 827	$2422	$8 479	$39 728					
Weighted Average			$24 165	$26 936	$29 707	27 307	$1161	$8797	$37 266					

considered, Company I pays the least ($31 375) due to poor indirect pay and no performance pay, and Company B pays the most ($46 340). There is quite a high dispersion (48 percent) between the lowest- and highest-paying firms, which may suggest that job duties of accounting clerks may be different at these firms.

Let's examine performance pay and indirect pay. As can be seen, three companies (G, H, I) don't offer any performance pay at all, and it ranges from $1377 (Company F) to $6133 (Company C) at the other firms. Indirect pay ranges from $6150 (Company J) to $12 624 (Company D). To examine the structure of the compensation mix, we have calculated (from the data in Table 10.3) the percentage of total compensation for each major pay component at each firm:

	Base Pay (%)	Performance Pay (%)	Indirect Pay (%)
Company A	77	8	15
Company B	71	11	18
Company C	67	13	20
Company D	69	3	28
Company E	71	7	21
Company F	71	4	25
Company G	77	–	23
Company H	74	–	26
Company I	80	–	20
Company J	71	11	18
Average	73	6	21

As can be seen, the companies in this sample vary considerably in their compensation mixes, in addition to their compensation levels. Base pay constitutes as much as 80 percent of total compensation, or as little as 67 percent. Performance pay ranges from as much as 13 percent of total compensation down to none, and indirect pay ranges from 28 percent down to 15 percent.

DRAWING INFERENCES FROM THE DATA

What can we make of these substantial differences in pay policies for the same job? We can infer, from its low starting pay, that Company I may be willing to accept inexperienced and/or untrained employees and then provide them with on-the-job training. With its wide pay range, the company can reward increased experience over time. Even so, total compensation is constrained by low indirect pay and zero performance pay. So how will Company I keep its accounting clerks, once they are trained?

Perhaps Company I promotes these individuals rapidly to higher jobs, such as senior accounting clerk, which may carry a considerably higher pay scale. Maybe the jobs at Company I have some intrinsic or extrinsic rewards that other firms do not offer, such as high job security. Or maybe Company I simply cannot afford to pay any more than what it pays, and simply has to put up with hiring inexperienced employees who quit to take better-paying jobs once they are trained.

What about the width of the pay ranges? It can be seen that they vary from $2000 in Company C to $8000 in Company I. The mean width of the base pay range is $5600. Beyond these facts, careful examination suggests that there may be some patterns here. For example, Company C, with a pay range of only $2000, pays a high starting base pay ($29 000). Company C also has high performance pay, which may be used to differentiate employees, since there is very little progression through the pay range.

It is possible that Company C hires only highly experienced and well-trained accounting clerks. It only employs six of them, yet expects these six to handle all the clerical accounting chores for a company of 800 employees. In comparison, Company E has nine accounting clerks for 700 employees. Of course, many factors could explain this difference in staffing, and it may not necessarily be that the accounting clerks at Company C do more work than those at Company E.

Company I (along with Company E) has the widest pay range—$8000. However, because the firm's starting pay is so low ($21 000), it is likely necessary to have a wide range if there is to be any hope of keeping good employees as they become more experienced. In contrast to Company C, Company I is likely using pay range to differentiate employees, since it has no performance pay.

This raises a question. What is the value of performance pay to employees? In our example, we have factored it into total compensation as if it is of equivalent value to base pay (dollar for dollar). However, is a dollar of performance pay really worth a dollar of base pay? Most financial experts would say no, because performance pay is uncertain. If the performance pay is based on individual performance and is allocated in a zero-sum way, there may be a strong possibility that an individual will not receive any performance pay in a given year. If the performance pay is based on company performance, such as a profit-sharing plan, there is no guarantee that the necessary threshold level will be reached next year, even if it was reached this year.

What about indirect pay? Because of the tax advantages of many types of indirect pay, some might argue that a dollar of indirect pay is worth more than a dollar of base pay. But that depends on the structure of the indirect pay, and the needs of the employee. Some employees may place very little value on benefits, because they don't use most of them. In fact, they may not even be aware of many of the benefits for which they are eligible.

In short, some firms may be spending a lot of money on benefits employees don't care about. (Of course, this is one of the problems that flexible benefits are intended to solve, by allowing employees to maximize their own cash value of benefits.) Thus, a dollar of benefits may be worth more than a dollar to some employees, and less than a dollar to others.

Let's take another angle on the data. In this survey, indirect pay averages about 21 percent of total compensation. But it is higher in larger companies than smaller companies, which is typical. For example, indirect pay averaged 26 percent of total compensation in companies with 2000 or more employees, and 19 percent in companies with less than 2000 employees. On the other hand, smaller firms used performance pay more heavily, as performance pay constituted 8 percent of total compensation in firms with less than 2000 employees, and only 2 percent in firms with 2000 or more employees. Overall, large firms paid somewhat less ($37 960) than smaller firms ($40 906). But the compensation in the larger firms was less risky, since they had higher indirect pay and lower performance pay than smaller firms.

EXAMINING PAY RANGE DISTRIBUTION

Finally, one aspect that must be considered in examining compensation data is the actual distribution of employees within their pay ranges. The last five columns in Table 10.3 present this information. As can be seen, the top-paying firms have a very different distribution across the quartiles than the lower-paying firms, with the majority of their employees in the top (fourth) quartile. This is not surprising. To illustrate, Company D has 84 percent of its accounting clerks in the top quartile. Although Company D does not pay the highest maximum base pay, it does provide some performance pay, and the best benefits (indirect pay). Why would anyone ever quit? No one does, so eventually most employees end up in the top pay quartile.

In contrast, Companies F to J have only a minority of their employees in the top bracket. This suggests higher turnover. For example, let's look at Company H, where just 35 percent of their clerks are in the top bracket. As can be seen, 30 percent are in the bottom quartile. One can infer that this firm has high turnover and is continually hiring new clerks. As they gain experience, they are likely able to get jobs with better-paying firms, so they quit. It can be seen that there is a sharp drop between quartiles 1 and 2, and between quartiles 2 and 3.

Companies I and J apparently cannot find acceptable employees at the low end of their pay ranges, and are probably bringing new clerks in at the second quartile. So the bottom end of their pay ranges is really irrelevant. Because of low indirect pay at Company I, there is nothing to retain their employees as they gain experience, so they appear to quit at their first opportunity.

Inspection of the compa-ratios also gives an indication of actual base pay relative to the pay range midpoints, and shows that most firms are currently paying their employees in the top half of the pay range, with the exception of companies G, H, and I, which are paying slightly below or at the midpoints.

APPLYING SURVEY DATA

As can be seen from this example, interpreting survey data is a complex process. But once interpreted, how do you apply it? If you are using a job evaluation system, the survey data from key (benchmark) jobs will be used to develop a market line, and the job evaluation system will be calibrated against that, as was described in the previous chapter. If you are using a pay-for-knowledge system, the process for using survey data to calibrate the system will be discussed in the next chapter.

If you are using market pricing, the market rates are simply applied to your jobs, after adjusting for compensation mix strategy and compensation level strategy. It is not necessary to survey each job every year; if one-fifth of the jobs are done each year, the others can be updated based on estimates of annual increases. In this way, every job is market tested every five years. Of course, this may be done more frequently for a particular job, if there are indications that the pay level is inappropriate. Such indications would include difficulty in recruiting or excessively high turnover.

But before applying the data, there is still one more step. Since compensation surveys are dealing with historical data, they are always somewhat out of date. Furthermore, the pay system is being planned to apply to the coming year, so there needs to be some consideration for the amount the market will increase by in the coming year. The survey data need to be adjusted to take both of these into account, before using it, a process known as **aging the data**.

aging the data the process of adjusting compensation data to bring it up-to-date with the time period in which the new compensation will take effect

There can be some thorny issues in the application of market data. For example, what happens when the pay rate indicated by job evaluation differs from that indicated by market data? Although there is not much research evidence on that question, Weber and Rynes (1991) found that market data tended to outweigh job evaluation data in an experimental study of U.S. compensation managers. Thus, managers were inclined to abandon internal equity if it conflicted with market data. This inclination is one of the reasons why advocates argue that pay equity legislation is essential, since this inclination tends to replicate market practices even if they are not equitable.

LIMITATIONS OF COMPENSATION SURVEYS

Compensation surveys are subject to numerous limitations. First, they may vary dramatically in quality of job matches and methodology. Second, they may omit important information. For example, adequately quantifying performance pay and indirect pay is not a simple process in most firms, and some elements may simply be omitted in reporting by some firms. Third, unless they are available for individual employers, they do not tell us anything about compensation strategies practised by other firms. Fourth, compensation data may not fit all of the jobs that an organization has, especially if these jobs are organized differently from the norm.

Compensation surveys were developed when compensation systems were much simpler than they are today. The extensive use of indirect pay and performance pay has complicated data gathering enormously. For example, the value of stock options is very difficult to price, as is the case with long-term incentives. Some firms may provide important benefits that are difficult to price out in monetary terms, such as the value of purchase discounts or the use of company recreational facilities. To make matters worse, some firms include some of these items when reporting indirect pay, while others do not. And surveys simply cannot capture the entire range of rewards—both extrinsic and intrinsic—offered by organizations.

Another issue is that there may well be bias in the sample of firms that respond to compensation surveys. Traditional firms with simple pay systems will find it much easier to reply to compensation surveys than nontraditional firms that have nonstandard jobs and complex pay systems. Thus, compensation surveys may misrepresent actual pay trends.

Finally, compensation surveys reflect (or attempt to reflect) the value placed on jobs by the labour market, but this does not always mean that the market values jobs fairly. As has been discussed in previous chapters, the market may underprice certain jobs for a variety of reasons. This occurrence puts employers in a quandary. If they wish to be fair, they may need to pay certain jobs (such as those traditionally held by women) more than the market would dictate. However, this puts them at a disadvantage relative to their competitors, if their competitors do not adjust their pay rates at the same time. For this reason, many critics of market compensation have little faith in voluntary measures to correct historic inequities, and argue that pay equity legislation is essential to create a level playing field for all employers.

SUMMARY AND IMPLICATIONS

The purpose of this chapter has been to explain how to evaluate the going "market rate" for a given set of jobs. After a brief discussion of forces affecting "market rate," various sources of compensation data were identified, including third-party surveys and in-house surveys. Next, the four main steps in the process for conducting a compensation survey were described. The chapter concluded with a discussion of how to analyze, interpret, and apply compensation survey data.

The next chapter completes our discussion of the technical processes in compensation by describing the processes for evaluating individual performance and for evaluating individual skills and competencies.

KEY TERMS

aging the data, p. 395

compa-ratio, p. 389

compensating differential, p. 380

decile, p. 389

interquartile range, p. 389

key job matching, p. 384

mean, or simple average, p. 388

median, p. 389

quartile, p. 389

weighted mean, or weighted average, p. 388

EXERCISES

1. Table 10.4 provides data from a compensation survey for the job of industrial engineer, collected from the same employers as the compensation survey for accounting clerks discussed earlier in the chapter. Assume you are managing a high-involvement firm that employs about 800 people, and that you employ ten industrial engineers. Develop a compensation structure for this job, indicating the amount of base pay the job will provide (including the pay ranges) and the amount and type of performance pay and indirect pay. Assume the survey data are eight months out of date, and your new compensation structure will take effect in four months, and apply to the following twelve-month period.

    The following job summary was used in the survey, which was based on the National Occupational Classification for "Industrial and Manufacturing Engineers":

    > *Industrial and Manufacturing Engineers conduct studies and develop and supervise programs to achieve efficient industrial production and efficient utilization of industrial human resources, machinery, and materials. Industrial and Manufacturing Engineers are employed in consulting firms, manufacturing and processing companies, and in government, financial, health care and other institutions. Example titles include cost engineer, computer integrated manufacturing engineer, fire prevention engineer, plant engineer, work measurement engineers, methods engineer, industrial engineer, manufacturing engineer, quality control engineer, safety engineer, production engineer, time-study engineer.*

2. After completing Exercise 1, develop a compensation structure for the same firm, but assuming it utilizes the human relations managerial strategy. Then do the same for the classical managerial strategy. How do these three compensation structures differ?

3. In a large group, survey the hourly pay levels for all those who are currently employed or were recently employed in common jobs such as sales clerk, cashier, or fast-food worker. If there are differences in pay within the same job type, discuss why these may exist.

TABLE 10.4 RESULTS OF COMPENSATION SURVEY: INDUSTRIAL ENGINEER

Company	Total Employment	Number of Industrial Engineers Employed	Base Pay Range Minimum	Base Pay Range Midpoint	Base Pay Range Maximum	Mean Base Pay	Mean Performance Pay	Mean Indirect Pay	Mean Total Compensation	Base Pay Quartile			
										1	2	3	4
A	700	2	$50 000	$55 000	$60 000	$56 000	$6 720	$11 200	$73 920	1	–	–	1
B	1700	5	48 000	52 000	56 000	54 000	9 720	13 500	77 220	1	–	1	3
C	800	1	54 000	60 000	66 000	66 000	13 200	19 800	99 000	–	–	–	1
D	2000	12	44 000	50 000	56 000	54 666	5 467	21 866	81 999	–	1	2	9
E	700	4	50 000	58 000	66 000	62 250	9 338	18 675	90 263	–	1	–	3
F	4000	17	45 000	51 000	57 000	52 205	5 221	18 272	75 698	5	2	1	9
G	5000	21	43 000	48 000	53 000	48 095	–	14 429	65 524	8	3	2	8
H	7000	40	42 000	50 000	58 000	50 100	5 010	17 535	72 645	12	6	3	18
I	1000	4	46 000	54 000	60 000	55 250	–	13 813	69 063	1	–	1	2
J	1000	3	47 000	52 000	57 000	54 667	8 200	13 667	76 534	–	1	–	2
Simple Average			$46 900	$53 000	$58 900	$55 323	$6 288	$16 276	$78 187				
Weighted Average			$43 991	$50 541	$57 018	$51 738	$4 513	$17 046	$73 298				

SUGGESTED WEB SITE

Page 378: To learn more about the salaries of NHL hockey players, click on
<www.nhlpa.com>

REFERENCES

Drost, Helmar, and H. Richard Hird.
2000. *An Introduction to the Canadian
Labour Market*. Toronto: Nelson
Thomson Learning.

Gunderson, Morley, Douglas Hyatt, and
Craig Riddell. 2000. *Pay Differences
between the Government and Private
Sectors: Labour Force Survey and Census
Estimates*. Discussion Paper No.
W/10. Ottawa: Canadian Policy
Research Networks.

Sibson, Robert E. 1990. *Compensation*.
New York: American Management
Association.

Tyson, David E. 2001. *Carswell's
Compensation Guide*. Toronto, ON:
Thomson Publishing.

Weber, Carolyn L., and Sara L. Rynes.
1991. "Effects of Compensation
Strategy on Job Pay Decisions."
Academy of Management Journal, 34(1):
86–109.

11

EVALUATING INDIVIDUALS

CHAPTER GOALS

By the end of this chapter, you should be able to:

1. Identify and explain the four main reasons for conducting performance appraisals.

2. Explain why many performance appraisal systems fail to accurately measure employee performance.

3. Identify and describe the different methods for appraising performance, along with their strengths and weaknesses.

4. Identify the possible sources of performance appraisals, and discuss the circumstances under which each would be appropriate.

5. Describe and discuss possible ways of linking pay to performance appraisals.

6. Describe the key questions to be considered in deciding whether to apply merit pay to specific employee groups.

7. Identify the key design issues in developing an effective merit system.

8. Distinguish between skill-based and competency-based pay-for-knowledge systems.

9. Identify and describe the key issues in developing a skill-based pay system.

10. Identify and describe the key issues in developing a competency-based pay system.

INTRODUCTION

Your organization has decided to utilize merit pay to reward employees who display superior performance. But how do you identify these employees in a fair and systematic way? Or perhaps your organization has decided to use skill-based pay to reward employees who have developed a superior breadth and depth of knowledge and skills. But how do you judge, in a fair and systematic way, which employees have developed these superior skill levels? And, for both types of pay systems, how can you fairly relate these judgments to actual pay decisions?

performance appraisal
the process of assessing the performance level of individual employees

The success of merit- and skill-based pay systems hinges on finding the right answers to these questions, and the purpose of this chapter is to help find those answers. The first part of the chapter will deal with the process for evaluating the level of performance displayed by individual employees (known as **performance appraisal**), and the ways in which the resulting appraisals can be linked to financial rewards. The second part of the chapter will deal with the process of evaluating individual skills, knowledge, and competencies, and the ways in which the resulting evaluations can be linked to financial rewards.

EVALUATING INDIVIDUAL PERFORMANCE

"I'd rather kick bricks with my bare feet than do appraisals!" Apparently, performance appraisal is not a favourite task for this manager at Digital Equipment Corporation (quoted in Kane and Kane, 1993: 378). Many managers feel the same way. But what about their employers?

It turns out that many employers are no happier about their performance appraisal systems than are managers. For example, Pratt and Whitney, the giant manufacturer of jet engines, was dissatisfied with its performance appraisal system and made extensive changes to it. The following year, still not happy with the system, the firm made more changes. The year after that, the firm abandoned it altogether, replacing it with a completely different system (Kane and Kane, 1993). Surveys have shown a continual state of flux in performance appraisal systems, as companies search for an appraisal system they are satisfied with (Bohl, 1996).

However, the results of all this activity do not seem to have been very fruitful. At the beginning of the twenty-first century, about 90 percent of

Canadian human resource managers who were surveyed said that their company's performance appraisal system needed to be modified or abolished, while even more—95 percent—of Canadian employees surveyed said the same thing (*Human Resources Management in Canada*, 2000). Yet, despite the disappointing history of performance appraisal, 89 percent of Canadian firms continued to use performance appraisals in 2000, covering 84 percent of their nonmanagerial employees and 92 percent of their managerial employees, according to the Compensation Practices Survey.

Two things seem evident from these facts. First, many companies can't seem to find a performance appraisal system that they are happy with. Second, despite their lack of success, they keep on trying to make performance appraisal work. Putting these two facts together suggests that while performance appraisal is highly valued as a concept, translating that concept into an effective practice is very difficult to do.

Indeed, some observers contend that translating the concept of performance appraisal into an effective practice that does more good than harm is virtually impossible. Based on their experience as consultants, Coens and Jenkins (2000) argue that performance appraisal is a fundamentally flawed concept and cannot be made to work effectively. However, while agreeing that performance appraisal often does more harm than good, other commentators (e.g., Lawler, 2000) argue that performance appraisal can be made to work effectively if applied in the right way and in the right circumstances. This second viewpoint will be adopted in this chapter.

After discussing the purposes and problems of performance appraisals, this section of the chapter will discuss specific appraisal methods and tools that can be used, along with the questions of who should be involved in the appraisal process, how appraisals should be linked to the pay system, and how an effective merit pay system can be designed.

WHY DO PERFORMANCE APPRAISALS?

If performance appraisals are so difficult to do effectively, why do them at all? Organizations conduct performance appraisals for a wide variety of reasons, but these reasons tend to fall into four main categories—administrative, developmental, supervisory, and symbolic.

Administrative reasons include identifying individuals who are not performing to required standards and for whom dismissal may be necessary; identifying individuals who should be considered for promotion or merit increases; and monitoring overall quality of performance in the firm. A well-documented set of performance appraisals can also be helpful in dealing with legal issues surrounding employee dismissal and subsequent unjust-dismissal lawsuits. The key aspect here is to measure individual performance accurately and consistently.

Developmental reasons include helping employees to better understand employer expectations and the key performance dimensions of their jobs;

assisting employees to understand strengths and weaknesses in their performance; and helping employees understand how to improve their performance. The key aspect of a developmental appraisal is provision of useful feedback—an essential part of any learning process—that can help individuals change their behaviours in productive ways. This feedback is valuable to employees even if their performance does not need improvement, since most employees want to know how their performance is being regarded by their supervisor and the organization.

Supervisory reasons include the notion that the process of conducting performance appraisals improves supervisory performance by helping supervisors to think systematically about employee performance and by encouraging communication with employees.

Symbolic reasons centre around creating the perception that management cares about good employee performance. Conducting a performance appraisal process demonstrates this concern to employees (as long, of course, as employees believe that performance is what the appraisal system truly measures).

PROBLEMS WITH PERFORMANCE APPRAISAL

However, for a variety of reasons, performance appraisals are not always an accurate reflection of employee performance. If merit pay is to serve as a motivator for effective performance, two elements are needed: (1) a system for generating reliable and valid measures of employee performance and (2) a system for linking these measures to pay increases so that significant financial rewards are seen as contingent on effective employee performance.

reliability when a measuring instrument produces the same measurement value each time the same object or construct is measured

validity when a measuring instrument actually measures what it is intended to measure

If an appraisal method has **reliability**, two different raters, judging independently, will come up with similar ratings of a given individual. If a method has **validity**, then the individuals identified by performance appraisal as the most effective employees are, in fact, the best performers.

Over the years, an enormous amount of effort has been expended, by both academics and practitioners, attempting to develop reliable and valid measures of employee performance. But despite this effort, performance appraisal frequently fails to achieve its aims. Part of the problem stems from the multiple objectives of most appraisal systems, and some experts have even argued that there should be two completely separate performance appraisal processes—one for developmental purposes and one for administrative purposes. This makes a lot of sense in some ways, since not all firms will wish to utilize merit pay, but they may still wish to evaluate individual performance to provide feedback about opportunities for performance improvement.

But for this feedback to be effective, it must be accepted by the employee as valid, it must identify specific behaviours that need to change (behaviours that are under the control of the employee), and it must take place within an environment where the feedback giver is seen as a trusted coach. However, when money is tied to appraisals, the appraiser is more likely to be seen as a feared judge than a trusted coach.

One advantage of tying pay to appraisals is that this increases the probability that appraisals will be taken seriously by all involved parties. However, when appraisals are used for pay purposes, in addition to developmental purposes, the focus of the appraisal process may change toward a judging role, in which appraisers must justify and defend their decisions about the granting or denial of merit pay. As a result, rather than engaging in a candid discussion of their shortcomings, appraisees will focus on attempting to portray their performance as favourably as possible ("given the circumstances, my performance was actually pretty good"), and attempting to defend themselves when the appraiser does not award high performance ratings ("my performance may have been lower than expected, but it wasn't my fault").

Furthermore, as will be seen, the appraisal systems that are most accurate in assessing performance level may not be the best vehicles for the generation of feedback that is useful to the appraisee. But if merit pay is denied, employees will expect to be told why, and what they can do to correct the situation. Therefore, most organizations do attempt to include a developmental (feedback) element with their administrative appraisals, even though this may make it more difficult to effectively achieve either purpose.

Why is it that appraisal systems may not produce accurate evaluations of performance? There are two main sets of reasons. One set derives from the appraisal systems themselves, which may not allow appraisers to make accurate assessments of employee performance, no matter how hard they try and how much they may want to. The second set of reasons, perhaps even more important, is that accurate measurement of performance may not in fact be the main objective of the appraiser. This latter insight has emerged only after many years of blaming performance appraisal problems on the appraisal systems themselves, so let's start by considering why appraisers may not want to produce appraisals that accurately mirror performance.

Intentional Inaccuracies in Appraisals

There is a considerable body of evidence that when supervisors start the performance appraisal process, they often have certain desired outcomes in mind, or certain consequences they are concerned about (Longenecker, Sims, and Gioia, 1987). For example: "Do I want Sally Jones to get a raise?" "Do I want Mike Wilson to be promoted?" "Do I want Greg Smith to quit?" "What impact will a low performance rating have on Jane Watson?" "Will a high or low appraisal be most likely to improve John Brown's performance?"

Supervisors may see performance appraisal as a tool to help them achieve their desired outcomes, or they may see it as a fruitless or even potentially damaging exercise. But either way, they are likely to keep the broader work context in mind when conducting appraisals, as this quote from one manager illustrates (Longenecker, Sims, and Gioia, 1987: 185):

As a manager, I will use the review process to do what is best for my people and the division. ... I've used it to get my people better raises in lean years, to kick a [person] in the pants if [he or she] really needed it, to pick up a [person] when he [or she] was down or even to tell him [or her] that he [or she] was no longer welcome here. It is a tool that the manager should use to help [her/him] do what it takes to get the job done ... Accurately describing an employee's performance is not really as important as generating ratings that keep things cooking.

Another manager illustrates concern for the possible interpersonal consequences of low performance ratings (Longenecker, Sims, and Gioia, 1987: 183):

There is really no getting around the fact that whenever I evaluate one of my people, I stop and think about the impact—the ramifications of my decisions on my relationship with the [person] and [his or her] future here. I'd be stupid not to ... in the end I've got to live with [him or her], and I'm not going to rate a [person] without thinking about the fall-out. There are a lot of games played in the rating process, and whether we admit it or not we are all guilty of playing them.

A very common practice in performance appraisal is for supervisors to inflate ratings, known as the "leniency" problem. This can take place for reasons that, to the supervisor, are consistent with or supportive of organizational goals, or it can take place for other reasons. For example, supervisors may inflate ratings if they lack confidence in the appraisal instrument or process. They may believe that the appraisal does not measure the right things (it is not valid), or that they have had insufficient opportunity to observe employee performance, or that they do not have the expertise to adequately appraise performance. In all of these cases, it would be difficult to defend poor ratings, so the problem is avoided by simply giving high ratings.

Supervisors may have a variety of other motives for giving high ratings to everyone. They may be concerned about relationships between themselves and their subordinates if they do not give high ratings. They may also be concerned about relationships among employees, as employees who receive low ratings may resent those with high ratings. Some supervisors may believe that it reflects badly on themselves if their subordinates do not appear to be performing well. Some may believe that other supervisors are giving high ratings, and that they must also do so to maintain a level playing field, and to acquire their department's "fair share" of the available merit money and promotional opportunities. Or, supervisors may simply not want to put the necessary effort into producing accurate ratings, and believe high ratings will forestall complaints about inaccuracy.

Supervisors may have specific motives for inflating the ratings of particular employees. For example, they may believe that accurate ratings would have a damaging effect on a particular subordinate's motivation and performance. They may want to improve an employee's eligibility for merit raises or promotions, perhaps on the grounds that the employee has been unfairly treated in the past. They may want to protect normally good performers whose performance is suffering because of personal problems. They may want to reward employees who show great effort, even though results are poor, or who have other valued attributes that are not measured by the appraisal instrument. On a less noble plane, supervisors may wish to get rid of poor performers by promoting them out of the department. Or, they may simply want to reward their friends.

Longenecker and Ludwig (1995) also found that managers sometimes (but much less often) *deflate* ratings. For example, they may want to "scare" better performance out of an employee who they believe could do much more or who is in danger of being fired. They may wish to punish a difficult or rebellious employee. They may want to encourage a problem employee to quit, or to create a strong case to justify a planned firing. They may be following a company edict to achieve a certain distribution in ratings, and this may require deflating the ratings of some employees. Finally, they may simply be biased against some individuals.

UNINTENTIONAL INACCURACIES IN APPRAISALS

Aside from intentional manipulations of performance appraisals, there can be numerous problems in the system itself that threaten the accuracy of appraisals. The most fundamental requirements for an accurate appraisal include an adequate opportunity to observe employee performance, along with the ability to draw valid conclusions about performance from these observations. In some cases, especially where a supervisor has many subordinates or where the supervisor and subordinates work separately, supervisors may have a very limited sample of behaviour on which to base their appraisals. In other cases, particularly with highly skilled or professional workers, the supervisor may lack the expertise to accurately gauge the quality of an employee's work.

There are also numerous perceptual errors to which humans are prone that may affect appraisal accuracy. These include central tendency, halo error, recency effect, contrast effect, similarity effect, and leniency/harshness, each of which may affect raters to a different extent. **Central tendency** occurs when appraisers tend to rate all employees as "average" in almost everything. Less commonly, some raters have the opposite tendency, and rate all individuals as either extremely good or extremely bad, with nobody in the middle. The **halo error** occurs when one characteristic for a given individual is judged to be either very good or very bad, which then causes the rater to rate all characteristics of that individual as either good or bad.

The **recency effect** refers to a tendency for appraisers to put excessive weight on recent behaviour, with earlier employee behaviour having faded

central tendency rating error occurs when appraisers rate all employees as "average" in everything

halo error occurs when appraisers rate an individual either high or low on all characteristics because one characteristic is either high or low

recency effect the tendency of appraisers to overweight recent events when appraising employee performance

contrast effect the tendency for a set of performance appraisals to be influenced upward by the presence of a very low performer, or downward by the presence of a very high performer

similarity effect the tendency of appraisers to inflate the appraisals of appraisees they see as similar to themselves

leniency effect the tendency of many appraisers to provide unduly high performance appraisals

harshness effect the tendency of some appraisers to provide unduly low performance appraisals

from memory. The **contrast effect** occurs when there is one employee who is either exceedingly good or exceedingly bad, which causes the appraiser to rate other employees either worse, or better, respectively, than they really deserve. The **similarity effect** describes a tendency for appraisers to rate individuals who are similar to themselves more highly than those who are not. Finally, some evaluators tend to be inherently more lenient and rate all subordinates highly (the **leniency effect**), while others may be inherently harsh (the **harshness effect**), rating all subordinates poorly.

These perceptual errors and inconsistencies across raters can be magnified by poor rating instruments, which provide insufficient definition of the characteristics being evaluated and of the scales used to rate these characteristics. As will be discussed shortly, some rating instruments are better than others at controlling these errors. But despite the huge amount of effort devoted by academics and practitioners over the past 50 years in attempting to develop valid appraisal processes, research indicates that rater bias still has about twice the weight in determining performance ratings as does actual ratee performance (Scullen, Mount, and Goff, 2000).

Finally, a fundamental problem that often occurs is that performance appraisal is attempted when the circumstances are simply not appropriate. For example, when work is highly interdependent, it may be virtually impossible to separate out individual behaviour, and it makes no sense to attempt to do so. And in some jobs, there is simply not much scope for individual performance to vary. Remember our chicken plant workers in Box 2.4? It makes no sense to waste time attempting individual appraisals when so little performance variation is possible.

METHODS AND INSTRUMENTS FOR APPRAISAL

In a continuing attempt to develop appraisal systems that produce accurate evaluations of performance, a variety of instruments and methods have been developed over the years. As each instrument has, in turn, been found to be unable to produce fully satisfactory results, new instruments have been developed. But despite all this effort, there is no widespread consensus that any of the existing instruments provides a fully satisfactory solution to the appraisal problem.

However, depending on the setting and the objectives being sought, some methods are more appropriate than others. This section will discuss the relative merits of each instrument, in roughly the order in which they were created. The following methods will be covered:

- ranking and forced distribution
- narrative/essay
- graphic rating scale
- critical incident
- performance checklist

- forced choice
- mixed standard scales
- behaviourally anchored rating scales
- behavioural observation scales
- performance distribution assessment
- objectives- and results-based systems
- field review
- combination approaches

RANKING AND FORCED DISTRIBUTION

Perhaps the simplest method of performance appraisal is to just rank the performance of all individuals engaged in similar jobs, from most effective to least effective. This method has the advantage that it does not require the development of complicated forms and procedures. Furthermore, most supervisors will generally have little difficulty in picking out their best and worst performers. This approach eliminates the problems of central tendency and leniency/harshness. It fits well with a system in which management decrees that only the top, say, 10 percent, of employees will receive merit pay.

However, this system has many drawbacks. It is a highly subjective procedure, does not allow for comparisons across departments, and provides very little useful feedback to the individual being rated. It is subject to numerous perceptual errors, such as recency, halo, contrast, similarity, and bias, as well as inconsistency in application across supervisors, since the bases for evaluating performance are usually not made explicit. The system also implies that the distances between the ranks are the same, when in fact there may be large gaps between, say, the third- and fourth-best performer.

It is also a win-lose system—the only way a person can improve his or her ranking is to displace someone else. This may create conflict and lack of cooperation among employees. It is also highly unfair across departments, because it does not recognize that some departments may be loaded with high performers, while other departments have very few.

Doing the ranking may be a difficult process. Although it may be easy to pick out the best and worst performers, it may be very difficult to rank the large middle group. Should, for example, an employee be ranked tenth or eleventh out of 20 employees? It may also be very difficult to justify these fine differences to ratees, and doesn't really matter anyway.

One method developed to facilitate the ranking process is the **paired comparison** method. Each individual is compared with every other individual, one at a time. The number of times each individual is judged the superior of the pair determines the rank of that employee. However, although this does simplify the process, it should be noted that the number of comparisons that must be made increases geometrically with the number of employees being ranked.

paired comparison method determines the rank order of all employees in a unit by comparing each employee with each of the other employees in the unit

The paired comparison method can also be used to rank employees on individual traits, with the individual rankings then summed. In doing so, individual traits could first be weighted in importance in order to arrive at an overall performance rating. This can provide some feedback to appraisees on strong and weak areas. However, unless these traits are well defined, and unless there has been ample opportunity to observe the extent to which these traits are in evidence for each employee, adding rankings of each trait may simply make the system more cumbersome and no more accurate.

A variation of the ranking method is the **forced distribution** method. Here, the rater is presented with a number of categories, and is required to place a certain percentage of the appraisees into each category. For example, Merck and Company, the large pharmaceuticals firm, requires supervisors to place 5 percent of employees in the top category ("exceptional"); 15 percent in the next category ("with distinction"); 70 percent in the middle ("high Merck standard"); 8 percent in the next lowest ("room for improvement"); and 2 percent in the lowest category ("not acceptable") (Kane and Kane, 1993). The company began using the system after they found that their previous rating scale was not discriminating between performance levels (almost everyone was rated at the highest level). For the same reason, IBM adopted a similar approach in 1992, requiring each supervisor to put 10 percent of employees into the highest category and 10 percent into the lowest category.

Despite a resurgence in popularity of forced distribution, it should be noted that this method still has almost all the deficiencies and problems of the ranking method, except that it is not necessary to generate a specific rank for each employee. This is a major advantage, and can simplify the appraisal process greatly. Nonetheless, this method does not fit well with either human relations or high-involvement firms.

Narrative/Essay

Another simple approach is for the appraiser to simply write out some comments summarizing the appraisee's performance. But while this approach may be useful for providing feedback to employees, it is not useful for pay purposes. It is prone to all the perceptual errors discussed earlier, and does not provide a uniform basis for making comparisons across employees and departments. Each supervisor may focus on different things, some of which may not be valid indicators of performance. However, this method may be useful in conjunction with ranking or rating scales, or for providing developmental feedback.

Graphic Rating Scale

The **graphic rating scale** has in the past been one of the most widely used performance appraisal methods and likely remains the single most popular rating method, mainly because of its simplicity. First, a number of traits or characteristics judged relevant to job performance are selected. They typically include such characteristics as quantity and quality of work performed, initiative, responsibility, and cooperation with others. Employees are rated by their

forced distribution a performance appraisal method that stipulates the distribution of employees across the performance categories

graphic rating scale an appraisal method in which appraisers use a numerical scale to rate employees on a series of characteristics

immediate superior on the extent to which they possess each characteristic. In many cases, raters are required to make written comments in support of their ratings. These narrative comments are especially useful for feedback purposes, and for justifying the ratings to the ratee.

Figure 11.1 shows a graphic rating scale that has been used by a police force in a western Canadian city. There are seven traits that are each rated in terms of six levels of performance. Although in this instance raters are required to depend on their own judgment to define both the traits being rated and the performance level, some appraisal forms also include a brief description of the traits and definitions of the performance levels. Some rating scales also weight the traits differentially.

The graphic rating scale has numerous deficiencies. First, in many cases the traits or characteristics are defined very vaguely, or even not at all, as in Figure 11.1. As a result, different supervisors may define and measure these traits in different ways. Some characteristics are very difficult for a supervisor to directly observe. Furthermore, some of the traits selected for appraisal may simply rest on someone's opinion of what is related to job performance. The performance levels are usually defined in general terms, such as "excellent," "good," "satisfactory," or "unsatisfactory," and appraisers may differ significantly in their standards for each of these rating levels. Often, this method does not provide useful feedback about behaviour to ratees.

The graphic rating scale is vulnerable to virtually all of the perceptual errors in the rating process discussed earlier, especially leniency. Although some of these problems can be reduced by rater training and careful definition of rated characteristics and response scales, this method is generally considered to be one of the least reliable or valid approaches to performance evaluation. Indeed, many supervisors required to use this method are reluctant to put much effort into it or reliance on it because of doubts about its validity.

But many organizations utilize this method because of its ease, low cost, and "face" validity. That is, it looks, on the face of it, like it should be a valid system. Since it is an absolute system (rather than a relative system, as in the case of ranking), it does avoid certain problems of ranking systems, such as the inability to make comparisons across departments. In some cases, it may be better than no system at all, especially if it is not used for pay purposes. Use of multiple raters may also improve the utility of this method.

CRITICAL INCIDENT

The **critical incident method** requires the recording of both effective and ineffective incidents of behaviour for each employee on an ongoing basis throughout the review period. The objective is to build up a database of specific employee behaviours, which the rater can then use to infer performance levels and to provide specific examples of good and bad behaviours to the employee. At the end of the review period, these incidents are classified into various performance dimensions and a rating is subjectively determined for each dimension.

critical incident method appraisals are based on analysis of recorded critical incidents of employee behaviour

FIGURE 11.1 EXAMPLE OF GRAPHIC RATING SCALE

Name _____
Rank and Number _____
Date of Appointment _____
Promoted to Present Rank _____

Type of Duty _____
Rating Period: From _____
To _____
Date of Rating _____

Critical Standards of Performance	Inferior Performance	Acceptable Performance			Superior Performance	
	Below Standard 1	Meets Minimum Standard 2	Meets Standard 3	Exceeds Standard 4	Greatly Exceeds Standard 5	Outstanding 6
1. Work Performance	☐	☐	☐	☐	☐	☐
2. Dependability	☐	☐	☐	☐	☐	☐
3. Initiative	☐	☐	☐	☐	☐	☐
4. Relationships	☐	☐	☐	☐	☐	☐
5. Appearance	☐	☐	☐	☐	☐	☐
6. Written communications	☐	☐	☐	☐	☐	☐
7. Verbal communications	☐	☐	☐	☐	☐	☐

Rater's Signature

1. _____ Rank _____
2. _____ Rank _____
3. _____ Rank _____
4. _____ Rank _____
5. _____ Rank _____

Reviewing Officer's Signature _____
Rank _____

Advantages to this approach include elimination of the recency effect, as well as the provision of concrete feedback to the employee both to explain the rating received and to allow an opportunity for the individual to see exactly what types of behaviour need to be changed.

However, there can be several problems. First, although supervisors should diligently record critical incidents as they occur throughout the review period, this is frequently neglected until just before the review. Second, bias may still occur because a supervisor may consciously or unconsciously record only positive or negative incidents for certain employees. Third, employees may resent the supervisor for keeping what may appear to be a "little black book" on them. To avoid this pitfall, the supervisor must deal with these incidents (especially if they are negative) as they occur, rather than simply recording them. Finally, it is a difficult and highly subjective process to convert the data (the recorded incidents) into an overall rating for making salary decisions.

PERFORMANCE CHECKLIST

Under the **performance checklist**, the rater simply describes employee behaviour by checking off, from a list of descriptive statements (both positive and negative), those that describe the typical behaviour of the employee. Scoring may be a simple counting of the numbers of statements checked or a summation of their weights. The weights reflect the relative importance of the behaviours in the performance of the job in question. The numerical total of the "checked" weights provides an easy mode for linking performance to pay. An illustration of a weighted checklist is shown in Figure 11.2.

performance checklist appraisal method based on checking off statements that apply to employee behaviour

FIGURE 11.2   EXAMPLE OF PERFORMANCE CHECKLIST

Employee name and number:_____

Rater's name:_____

Department:_____ Date:_____

Directions: Place a check mark next to each statement that accurately describes the ratee's behaviour.

		Weight[a]
1. Generally finishes the jobs on time	_____	+ 2.5
2. Sometimes refuses to cooperate with other employees	_____	− 2.0
3. Carries out tasks without close supervision	_____	+ 2.0
4. Has good attendance record	_____	+ 2.0
5. Often makes useful suggestions	_____	+ 1.5
6. Makes frequent serious errors in work	_____	− 3.0
.		
.		
.		
40. Always treats customers courteously	_____	+ 3.0

[a]Note: These weights are provided for illustration purposes only and would not normally appear on the rater's copy of the form.

Essentially, the purpose of this method is to systematize the critical incident approach and to establish a method for which there is some confidence about reliability and validity. It also has numerous advantages over the graphic rating scale. For example, rather than asking the appraiser to rate vaguely defined traits, with ambiguity both in the trait definitions and in the response scale, it simply asks the rater to describe behaviour by checking either "yes" or "no." The behaviours that have been selected have been tested for validity, and the system improves reliability by reducing rater discretion. Since the weightings of the various items are not revealed to the rater, this makes it somewhat more difficult to intentionally bias the ratings.

But a number of problems and drawbacks remain. The first is complexity—different forms need to be developed for different groups of jobs. Moreover, the checklist needs to be revised whenever the jobs undergo changes. Another problem is that since the supervisors do not know the weights, they may experience frustration, since they are not sure whether they are giving highly favourable ratings to employees. This method is also not very useful for feedback purposes. Despite all the work in developing the ratings, it is still prone to bias if the supervisor tends to recall only negative or positive behaviours of a particular employee, and it is still susceptible to leniency/harshness, halo, and recency errors.

FORCED CHOICE

In order to overcome many of the problems of the earlier methods, particularly the graphic rating scale, a number of newer methods have been developed. The **forced choice method** seeks to overcome common rating errors by presenting the rater with pairs of descriptive statements. The rater is forced to select one statement in each pair as most descriptive of the individual being rated. The statements in each pair appear equally desirable (or undesirable), but only one of them discriminates good performers from poor performers. Examples of two pairs of statements are below:

Pair A: 1. Can be relied upon to complete assignments on time.

2. Is at ease in any situation.

Pair B: 1. Frequently does not communicate sufficiently with subordinates.

2. The quality of work produced is not always high.

Raters are not told which items discriminate performance, and scoring of the questionnaire is done by the human resources department.

If constructed properly, the forced choice method is probably the most reliable and valid method for measuring individual performance. It eliminates most rating errors and is very difficult to intentionally bias. Because an "objective score" is obtained for employees, it can be readily used to allocate merit pay and can be used to compare employees across departments.

Ironically, this method is also one of the least-used methods. This is partly due to its high complexity, in terms of development, and partly due to low

forced choice method an appraisal method that forces raters to select the one statement that best describes employee behaviour from pairs of statements

acceptance from raters (and ratees). In many instances, neither, or both, of the statements in the pair will apply, yet the rater is forced to select one. Raters do not like being kept in the dark about whether they are giving high or low ratings to an individual, and this system takes away their discretion to use the performance appraisal system in a "flexible" (some might say "biased") way.

Raters may be reluctant to defend their ratings, knowing that they cannot meaningfully explain the basis for the performance scores with their subordinates, and cannot provide specific feedback on how to improve the performance scores. It may also be difficult to convince employees of the validity of these scores because the system is so complicated.

Mixed Standard Scales

Mixed standard scales attempt to improve on the graphic rating scale by providing a list of items that illustrate good and bad examples of different behaviours. As Figure 11.3 illustrates, the rater is then asked to indicate whether the appraisee generally performs better than, equal to, or worse than each of these items.

Because these scales give specific behaviours that the appraiser is asked to react to, and the rater is not asked to rate their extent (but simply whether performance is above, below, or equal to the statement), they are likely more reliable than the graphic rating scale. On the other hand, they are more difficult to develop, because the pool of items may need to vary for different jobs. To have full confidence in these items, they should be validated against actual performance in some way (which implies that you already have an accurate way of measuring performance).

mixed standard scales an appraisal method that asks appraiser to indicate whether appraisee performs better than, equal to, or worse than specific examples of behaviour

Behaviourally Anchored Rating Scales

Behaviourally anchored rating scales (BARS) are an attempt to improve on the graphic rating scale by providing specific descriptions of behaviours for each point on the rating scale for each job dimension.

The evidence on whether use of BARS results in an appreciable improvement in the reliability and validity of ratings is mixed, although it would seem that they should provide better guidance to raters in defining degrees of effectiveness. BARS have the advantage of yielding a total score for purposes of pay decisions and an evaluation in specific behavioural terms that is useful in providing meaningful feedback for developmental purposes. The major disadvantage is that different scales need to be developed for each job class (often for each job) in the organization, which can be both expensive and time-consuming. Another problem is that supervisors may disagree with the ordering on the scale, or there might be two items that could be checked for a given scale.

behaviourally anchored rating scales (BARS) appraisal method that provides specific descriptors for each point on the rating scale

Behavioural Observation Scales

Behavioural observation scales (BOS) were developed as an improvement to the BARS (Latham and Wexley, 1994). This method involves developing

behavioural observation scales (BOS) appraisal method under which appraisers rate the frequency of occurrence of different employee behaviours

FIGURE 11.3 EXAMPLE OF A MIXED STANDARD SCALE

DIRECTIONS: Please indicate whether the individual's performance is above (+), equal to (0), or lower (–) than each of the following standards.

1. _____ Employee uses good judgment when addressing problems and provides workable alternatives; however, at times does not take actions to prevent problems. (*medium* PROBLEM SOLVING)

2. _____ Employee lacks supervisory skills; frequently handles employees poorly and is at times argumentative. (*low* LEADERSHIP)

3. _____ Employee is extremely cooperative; can be expected to take the lead in developing cooperation among employees; completes job tasks with a positive attitude. (*high* COOPERATION)

4. _____ Employee has effective supervision skills; encourages productivity, quality, and employee development. (*medium* LEADERSHIP)

5. _____ Employee normally displays an argumentative or defensive attitude toward fellow employees and job assignments. (*low* COOPERATION)

6. _____ Employee is generally agreeable but becomes argumentative at times when given job assignments; cooperates with other employees as expected. (*medium* COOPERATION)

7. _____ Employee is not good at solving problems; uses poor judgment and does not anticipate potential difficulties. (*low* PROBLEM SOLVING)

8. _____ Employee anticipates potential problems and provides creative, proactive alternative solutions; has good attention to follow-up. (*high* PROBLEM SOLVING)

9. _____ Employee displays skilled direction; effectively coordinates unit activities; is generally a dynamic leader and motivates employees to high performance. (*high* LEADERSHIP)

Source: Reprinted with permission from Monica Belcourt, Arthur Sherman, George Bohlander, and Scott Snell, *Managing Human Resources*, 3rd ed. Toronto: Nelson Thomson Learning, 2002): 310.

behavioural statements that reflect examples of positive behaviour for each job, and then rating each employee (on a "1" to "5" scale—representing "almost never" to "almost always") on the frequency with which each behaviour occurs. Overall ratings are developed by summing the individual scores. Figure 11.4 illustrates some sample items in a BOS.

Proponents argue that this method preserves the advantages of behaviourally anchored rating scales, in terms of specifically identifying the behaviour that will be rated, while eliminating some of their disadvantages. The major advantage of BOS over BARS is that once an item is selected, there is no need to develop detailed definitions for each scale point. Furthermore, by using frequency of behaviour as the rating scale, this ensures that it is not possible to select two or more responses, as is possible for BARS.

Of course, this method also has its drawbacks. For example, frequency of a given behaviour can be hard to judge, because most supervisors have only a limited number of observations on which to base this judgment. Furthermore, some research indicates that raters will generalize from a global evaluation of the individual, rather than first determining frequencies for each item (Murphy and Cleveland, 1995). In fact, these researchers conclude that BOS may actually be more subjective than other scales, such as BARS.

PERFORMANCE DISTRIBUTION ASSESSMENT

Performance distribution assessment (PDA) is a more sophisticated version of the BOS approach. This is the only rating method that incorporates a formal process to correct appraisals so as to hold ratees accountable only for the level

performance distribution assessment appraisal method that adjusts appraisal scores for the feasibility of performance levels for each employee

---

FIGURE 11.4 SAMPLE ITEMS FROM BEHAVIOURAL OBSERVATION SCALES

INSTRUCTIONS: Please consider the Sales Representative's behaviour on the job in the past rating period. Read each statement carefully, then circle the number that indicates the extent to which the employee has demonstrated this *effective* or *ineffective* behaviour.

For each behaviour observed, use the following scale:

5 represents almost always	95–100% of the time
4 represents frequently	85–94% of the time
3 represents sometimes	75–84% of the time
2 represents seldom	65–74% of the time
1 represents almost never	0–64% of the time

Sales Productivity	Almost Never				Almost Always
1. Reviews individual productivity results with manager	1	2	3	4	5
2. Suggests to peers ways of building sales	1	2	3	4	5
3. Formulates specific objectives for each contact	1	2	3	4	5
4. Focuses on product rather than customer problem	1	2	3	4	5
5. Keeps account plans updated	1	2	3	4	5
6. Keeps customer waiting for service	1	2	3	4	5
7. Anticipates and prepares for customer concerns	1	2	3	4	5
8. Follows up on customer leads	1	2	3	4	5

Source: Reprinted with permission from Monica Belcourt, Arthur Sherman, George Bohlander, and Scott Snell, *Managing Human Resources*, 3rd ed. (Toronto: Nelson Thomson Learning, 2002): 315.

of performance that is feasible and under their control. The PDA response scale rates the frequency of desired behaviours relative to the feasible levels of performance (Bernardin and Beatty, 1984). It also rates the frequency of undesirable results or outcomes relative to the extent to which these can be realistically expected. It requires complex scoring, but does result in measures of the relative effectiveness of performance, the consistency of performance, and the frequency with which especially positive or negative outcomes are observed. However, PDA may suffer from drawbacks similar to those for BOS.

OBJECTIVES-/RESULTS-BASED SYSTEMS

An approach that first gained prominence more than three decades ago involves the establishment of goals and objectives for each employee, usually on a joint basis, and the measurement of actual performance against these objectives. This approach is known as **management by objectives (MBO)** or sometimes "management by results." MBO is regarded by many as a highly effective approach to employee motivation because of two key elements: participation by the subordinate in setting the goals, and frequent feedback on goal accomplishment. Research has consistently shown that setting goals (and providing feedback on progress) increases employee performance. To be effective, goals must be significant yet realistic, and there must be a means of measuring the extent to which they are accomplished. According to the Compensation Practices Survey, 76 percent of Canadian organizations use performance appraisals based on goal setting for their managers, and 52 percent for nonmanagers.

Although the motivational advantages of MBO systems can be significant, there are some difficulties in using them for determining pay levels. A major difficulty is that not all significant goals can be easily measured in a concrete way. Goals that cannot be measured are often neglected. Another problem is that different employees will set different goal levels. Should an individual who sets high goals but falls slightly short be penalized, while an individual who achieves low goals is rewarded? The following example illustrates this problem (Latham and Wexley, 1994: 51):

> *A high-level manager in the start-up operations of a paper products company set stringent goals to "shoot for" regarding start-up costs. Due to the inefficiencies of outside contractors, the targets were not attained. The manager was severely penalized at Christmas bonus time and again the following February at his annual performance review. He vowed that he would not repeat the same mistake.*

Latham and Wexley (1994) go on to note that the lesson that this manager (and his subordinates) learned from this experience was to set specific, relatively easy goals. The manager subsequently became a senior vice-president in his organization.

---

management by objectives (MBO) an approach to management that involves setting employee goals and providing feedback on goal accomplishment

Although most practitioners and academics agreed that management by objectives was a good concept, its usage waned in the 1980s as the practical problems in making MBO work became more apparent. This decline in popularity was hastened by the emergence of the total quality management (TQM) movement in the 1980s, which eschewed the use of numerical goals, believing them to be counterproductive. However, in recent years the concept of MBO has been resurrected under a new name—**performance management**—as part of the continuing quest to find a performance appraisal system that really works (Weiss, 2000).

Under performance management, goals for individuals and groups are set, measures for goal achievement are developed, feedback on progress is provided, managerial encouragement and support are offered, and rewards are provided for success (Tyson, 2001). When applied at the team level, performance management is really a type of goal-sharing plan (as discussed in Chapter 6). Overall, 95 percent of large Canadian employers claim to utilize "performance management," although only 31 percent rate it as "effective" or "very effective" (Baarda, 2000). About 30 percent were lukewarm about the program, and 34 percent indicated that it "required improvement."

performance management method for improving employee performance based on goal setting, feedback, encouragement and support, and rewards for success

FIELD REVIEW

The field review method involves a short period of direct observation of the job performance of the individual being rated, frequently by an individual from outside the department who is specially trained to conduct such reviews. This method is frequently used for jobs that are not normally under direct observation by the supervisor. Typical jobs appraised by this approach might include truck drivers and airline pilots. In the retail sector, "mystery shoppers" are often used to assess work performance of sales personnel.

A major advantage of this method is that a small number of specially trained raters may be able to rate many employees, thus increasing the consistency and reliability of the appraisals. This also provides the supervisor with a "second opinion" on the employee's performance, and may reduce bias and other rating errors. Normally this method is used in conjunction with other methods and provides supervisors with additional data on which to base their appraisals. The main disadvantages relate to the cost of training and utilizing specialized individuals, and to the fact that field reviews are only appropriate in a limited number of circumstances where the behaviour can be evaluated in a short time span.

COMBINATION APPROACHES

Of course, some of these methods can be used in combination with others. For example, at financial services giant J.P. Morgan, there are three components in the appraisal process. Individuals are evaluated on certain core competencies important to the firm (as measured by behavioural observation scales), their contribution to key business success criteria, and achievement of their individual performance objectives (Latham and Latham, 2001).

Sources of Appraisals

Who should conduct the performance appraisals? In the past, the answer was obvious: the employee's immediate supervisor, often augmented with an overall review of appraisals by the next-higher level of management. But more recently, it has become recognized that there may be value in including others in the appraisal process, including peers, subordinates, and even customers, and the use of these alternate sources of appraisal information has expanded. However, despite this trend, supervisory appraisals remain the mainstay of the appraisal process, according to the Compensation Practices Survey, with 84 percent of Canadian employers using only supervisory appraisals in making merit pay decisions for nonmanagerial employees, and 65 percent using only supervisory appraisals in deciding merit pay for managers.

Appraisal by Superiors

The traditional approach involves appraisals by the immediate superior. Since, under classical management theory, supervisors are responsible for the performance of their units and of the people within their units, it appears logical to give them the responsibility for appraising the performance of their subordinates. This practice also reinforces the authority of the supervisor, something important for classical organizations.

But, as has been seen, relying on the supervisor as the sole source for performance appraisals can cause a number of problems. For example, supervisors may not have had sufficient opportunities to observe behaviour, or employees may skew behaviour when they know a supervisor is observing. Supervisors may also distort ratings, both unintentionally and intentionally, as has been discussed.

The "solution" to these problems has traditionally been for the next-higher level of management to review the appraisals prepared by their subordinate managers. But while this may have some advantages, such as demonstrating that appraisers will be held accountable for their ratings, it certainly does not solve all of the performance appraisal problems that have been discussed. Since the superior will generally have even less knowledge about specific cases than the appraiser, it is important that the superior resist the temptation to tinker with individual ratings.

Peer Appraisals

To augment the information available to the manager, information is sometimes collected from employees who work at the same level as the appraisee. Overall, about 31 percent of Canadian firms use peer appraisal to supplement supervisory appraisal when deciding merit pay of managers, and 16 percent of firms do so for nonmanagerial employees.

The rationale is that peers will usually have much more contact with their co-workers than a supervisor does, and they will likely be in a position to observe typical behaviour, rather than skewed behaviour. In addition, research has shown that rating errors are usually reduced when multiple raters are used (Scullen, Mount, and Goff, 2000).

However, when appraisals are used for pay purposes, peers may be reluctant to grade down their colleagues, and the appraisal system may informally gravitate toward a mutual admiration society, in which all can benefit if they rate each other highly. Of course, the opposite may occur if there is only a limited amount of merit pay that can be awarded, and peers may give each other low ratings in an attempt to make their own performance look better, resulting in conflict and ill will among peers.

In general, research suggests that, if anything, peers are more lenient than superiors in making their ratings. As Peiperl (2001:143) put it:

> In more than one team I studied, participants in peer appraisal routinely gave all their colleagues the highest rating on all dimensions. When I questioned this practice, the responses revealed just how perplexing and risky, both personally and professionally, evaluating peers can be.

Some employees feared that providing negative feedback would damage their relationships with their peers and possibly hinder their own careers. Others felt negative peer feedback was not in keeping with the supportive work environment in which they preferred to work.

SUBORDINATE APPRAISALS

Appraisal of managers by their subordinates is playing an increased role in the performance appraisal process. According to the Compensation Practices Survey, 25 percent of Canadian firms utilize subordinate appraisals in appraising managers, covering an average of about 50 percent of their managers in user firms. The logic is that subordinates can provide valid input on the effectiveness of a manager that may not be available from a different vantage point. For example, at Canadian professional services firm Ernst and Young, all employees are being asked to respond (anonymously) to an electronic survey asking "How well does [your manager] foster a positive work environment and help our people grow?" (Southworth, 2001). The company's belief is that only employees can tell them what the atmosphere is really like "down in the trenches."

However, supervisors often have serious concerns about subordinate appraisals. They may be concerned that subordinates do not understand the full spectrum of the job demands placed on them or the constraints they are operating under. They may also fear that employees will downgrade them if they have to make unpopular decisions.

On the other hand, employees may be reluctant to be critical of their supervisor for fear of possible repercussions. In fact, a perverse situation could arise in which supervisors with good relationships with their subordinates— whose subordinates believe that they are free to be candid in their comments—

may actually receive *less* favourable evaluations than supervisors who are perceived as vindictive tyrants, since their employees may be afraid that any criticism could lead to negative repercussions.

In fact, recent research (Scullen, Mount, and Goff, 2000) has shown that subordinate appraisals are actually much less accurate in assessing managerial performance than peer or supervisory appraisals (supervisory appraisals turned out to be the most accurate of all three, even though bias was still twice as important as performance in influencing appraisee ratings). Clearly, subordinate appraisals do not fit well with classical organizations. Nor do they fit well with human relations organizations, since nobody will want to provide any negative feedback about their well-liked supervisors. In short, subordinate appraisals can be expected to work well only in high-involvement organizations, where trust and open communication are key values.

SELF-APPRAISALS

Including a self-appraisal component in the appraisal process may have several advantages—such as encouraging employees to critically examine their own performance and facilitating communication with superiors. However, self-appraisals are of very little value for pay purposes, since they tend to be inflated. Not surprisingly, the poorest employees will tend to inflate their performance the most, as Box 11.1 shows, while some high performers may be overly self-critical.

CUSTOMER APPRAISALS

In some cases, it may be feasible to include customers in the feedback process. This is very important feedback to the organization because customer satisfaction may be a key factor in company success. At Avis Rent a Car, for example, customers can evaluate employees on a "customer care balance sheet" (Kane and Kane, 1993). Limitations of this approach are that not all employees come into contact with customers, and customers may not be able to single out the performance of individual employees.

OTHER APPRAISERS

As discussed in the section of the field review method of performance appraisal, it may be feasible to utilize professional raters for some jobs. Many firms in the service industry, including Blockbuster Video, Burger King, McDonald's, Domino's Pizza, and Taco Bell, have full-time raters (known as "mystery shoppers" when they are not identified in advance) who visit specific sites and conduct detailed appraisals that are used when evaluating the manager's performance (Kane and Kane, 1993).

360-degree feedback
an appraisal system that utilizes feedback from superiors, peers, subordinates, and possibly customers

MULTI-SOURCE SYSTEMS/360-DEGREE FEEDBACK

It is possible to use any combination of these sources. A relatively new method that combines peer and subordinate appraisals (and sometimes even customer appraisals) with supervisory appraisals is known as "360-degree feedback" (Edwards and Ewen, 1996). Due to dissatisfaction with existing appraisal sys-

One reason for employee dissatisfaction with performance appraisals (but not the only one!) is that most people tend to rate their performance as "above average" (even though this can be true for no more than half of all employees), and they don't like to be told otherwise. What heightens this problem is that not only are individuals who are performing below the norm often blissfully unaware of this fact, but they also tend to be oblivious to feedback that would help them recognize their true performance level. This is illustrated by research conducted by Kruger and Dunning (1999), who performed a series of experiments using university students as their subjects.

In one experiment, subjects were given a test of grammatical ability. Before knowing their test scores, students were asked to rate their grammatical ability and estimate their test scores. Students who performed in the bottom quartile on the test estimated that they had performed at the 61st percentile, and that their overall grammatical ability was at the 67th percentile. Their actual result: the 10th percentile. Students who had performed at the second quartile also had inflated perceptions of their grammatical ability, estimating it at the 72nd percentile, when in reality it was in the 32nd percentile. Students in the third quartile (and thus actually having better-than-average grammatical ability) estimated their performance at the 70th percentile, just a few points above their actual ability, while those who were in the top quartile actually underestimated their performance, estimating it at the 72nd percentile when it was really at the 89th percentile.

Interestingly, however, not only were the students with poor grammatical skills apparently unaware of their lack of grammatical ability, but they also failed to learn from the feedback provided. After their test scores and percentile rankings were revealed to them, they were again asked to estimate their level of grammatical ability. Despite the feedback they had received, they estimated their grammatical ability at almost precisely the same inflated level they did before receiving the feedback, somehow still believing themselves "above average"!

tems, 360-degree feedback expanded rapidly in the 1990s, although this expansion appears to have slowed as some of its shortcomings have become more apparent. Originally intended as a tool for providing developmental feedback, most users also employ this system for pay and promotion purposes (Bohl, 1996). According to the Compensation Practices Survey, about 19 percent of Canadian firms are using 360-degree feedback for appraising their managers, and 16 percent are using it for nonmanagers (of course, for nonmanagers, it is really 270-degree feedback, since they generally have no subordinates).

These systems have several key characteristics. They use standardized forms that provide numerical ratings of the ratee along numerous dimensions. Individual raters (except the superior) are assured of anonymity, so they can feel free to be candid in their ratings. Importantly, the system employs several procedures to screen out invalid data. For example, in a set of ratings for a given ratee, the extreme values (at each end of the scale) are dropped before the scores are averaged. And if a rater is more than 40 percent discrepant from other raters, that person's ratings may be eliminated entirely.

Advocates claim that 360-degree systems have numerous advantages over traditional superior-only ratings (Edwards and Ewen, 1996), such as:

1. They are fair—they have less rating inflation, and more safeguards to prevent bias.

2. They are more accurate—having numerous raters results in information from a variety of perspectives.

3. They are more credible to the recipient—ratees may believe a single rater to be wrong or biased, but could all of these raters be wrong?

4. They may be more valuable for behaviour change, since work associates are likely to be more specific about behavioural feedback.

5. They may be more motivational, since peer pressure may motivate constructive behaviour changes.

However, multi-source plans are not without their drawbacks. Of course, all of the problems with peer and subordinate ratings discussed earlier can come into play. Multi-source systems can also be complicated to set up. Forms (whether paper or electronic) have to be established that ask the right questions, and different forms may be necessary for different jobs. Employees must be willing to fill out the forms voluntarily, and it may be difficult to track those who do not submit forms because they are submitted anonymously. There need to be at least four persons in each rating group (e.g., peers or subordinates) to ensure anonymity, but this number of raters may not be available for all ratees. Rater training should be provided to all raters, but this is generally not practical given the number of potential raters in this system (i.e., virtually everybody!).

Are 360-degree systems effective? Unfortunately, there is very little evidence on this question, probably because of the newness of these systems. One early study (Bohl, 1996) indicated that 360-degree systems were somewhat more effective in fostering employee performance than other types of systems (68 percent of 360-degree users reported that their appraisal system had led to better employee performance, compared with 55 percent of users of traditional systems). In regard to administrative purposes, 65 percent of 360-degree users believed that their systems produced valid information for promotions, compared with 55 percent of users of traditional systems. However, 360-degree systems had no real advantage over traditional systems in producing valid information for merit increases, as 69 percent of 360-degree firms believed their systems produced valid information for merit raises, compared with 65 percent of other firms.

In a more recent but small-scale study, researchers concluded that "more than half" of the 360-degree systems they examined were successful (Bracken, Timmreck, Fleenor, and Summers, 2001). Although there is no research evidence on this, it seems probable that, like subordinate appraisals, 360-degree systems are more likely to be successful in high-involvement than classical or human relations organizations.

LINKING PAY TO PERFORMANCE APPRAISALS

Besides accurate measurement of performance, the other crucial aspect of merit pay is having an effective way of linking pay to performance appraisals. A variety of methods can be used to do so. The simplest way (and one of the most common) allows the supervisor to simply use the appraisal as information to be used in determining whether to award a merit increment to an employee. In other cases, employees are ranked according to point totals, and only those above a cutoff point receive merit pay.

In some instances, a forced distribution is stipulated. For example, the top quarter of employees in a department may receive, say, a 10 percent merit raise, the next quarter will receive 6 percent, the third quarter will receive 3 percent, and the bottom quarter will receive no merit increase at all. In still other cases, a supervisor is simply allocated a block of merit money, to be allocated to employees as he or she sees fit, providing the wage structure is not violated.

One approach that can be used is a **merit pay grid** (sometimes known as a *merit pay matrix*). As Table 11.1 shows, this grid has two dimensions. Across the top are employee performance ratings. Along the vertical axis are quartiles of the pay range for a particular set of employees. The numbers in each cell indicate the percentage increase that employees in that cell will receive as a merit raise. For example, an employee in the second quartile of the pay range with a "good" performance rating will receive a 5 percent merit increase.

As shown in this example, a common practice is for employees in the lower quartiles of their pay range to be given a higher percentage increase in order to bring them up to the midpoint of the range quite quickly. (Of course, increments expressed in fixed dollar amounts also amount to a higher percentage increase for employees in the lower part of the range.) It can also be seen that employees in the third and fourth quartiles receive no merit increase

merit pay grid a tool for allocating merit raises, based on the performance level of the employee and the pay range quartile in which they fall

TABLE 11.1 EXAMPLE OF A MERIT PAY GRID				
	EMPLOYEE PERFORMANCE LEVEL			
	UNSATISFACTORY	**SATISFACTORY**	**GOOD**	**EXCELLENT**
Fourth (highest) quartile	–	–	3%	5%
Third quartile	–	–	4%	6%
Second quartile	–	3%	5%	7%
First (lowest) quartile	–	4%	6%	8%

for simply doing satisfactory work, although employees in the first and second pay quartiles will receive 3 or 4 percent. The logic of this is that employees paid above the midpoint in their pay are already being rewarded for "satisfactory" work, and that a higher rating is necessary to trigger a merit raise for them.

It should be noted that individuals being paid at the top of the pay range (i.e., at the top of the fourth quartile) for their pay grade are not generally eligible for further merit raises, no matter how superior their performance. One way of dealing with possible motivational problems resulting from this situation is to make merit bonuses available for those at the top of their ranges.

A key issue is to decide how much money is to be made available for merit raises in a given year. There are two main approaches. A "bottom-up approach" does not set any arbitrary amount, but simply adds up all the increments that are granted. A major disadvantage of this is that the organization has no control over labour cost increases. Because many organizations are not comfortable with that, many firms simply set a maximum amount available for raises (the "top-down approach") and then allocate it across departments. If this approach is used, the firm should ensure that it is making available sufficient funds to allow a reasonable number of merit increases.

Some firms gear the total amount of merit money available in a given year to the achievement of certain financial goals of the organization. Box 11.2 describes a system that has been used by the Royal Bank of Canada to determine how much money is available for annual merit bonuses, and how it will be allocated across employees.

Besides the total amount available for merit raises, another key issue is how the merit money should be allocated across the different performance levels. As was discussed in Chapter 4, a raise will not have much motivational

---

BOX 11.2 Tying Bonuses to Performance Ratings at the Royal Bank

Several years ago the Royal Bank of Canada introduced a new merit bonus system—called the "quality performance incentive" or "QPI"—which it applied to virtually every employee. Under this system, the total amount of the annual bonus pool is determined by the extent to which the bank achieves certain financial objectives in each year. The specific amount received by each employee is dependent on his or her annual performance rating.

The system works like this. If the company meets financial performance goals for the next year (in terms of return on equity and revenue growth) a specific sum—say $100 million—will be placed in a bonus pool. This amount will be increased by 25 percent if three other goals are

met: revenue growth exceeds that of competitors; customer satisfaction exceeds that of competitors; and employee commitment exceeds that of competitors.

The amount each employee actually receives will depend on the employee's individual performance rating. If an employee receives less than a "satisfactory" performance rating, she will normally receive none of the bonus. If she receives a "satisfactory" rating, she will receive 100 percent of the basic bonus amount available for their salary band. If she receives higher ratings, this amount will go to 130 percent, 170 percent, or 200 percent. For an employee in the lowest salary band, a standard payout could be $750, compared with $15 350 for an employee in the highest pay band.

impact if it does not create a "just noticeable difference" in the eyes of the employee. Although this amount may vary, a common rule of thumb, supported by research, is that at least a 4 percent difference between performance levels is needed to create a perception of being differentially rewarded. This rule argues for relatively few levels of performance ratings, so that the difference in pay raises between performance levels is significant. Lawler (2000) suggests that performance ratings have at most five levels—a middle "satisfactory" level in which most employees would fall, and two levels above and two below. In fact, the most common rating structure in Canada has five levels (Baarda, 2000). If sufficient funds are not available to provide a JND in a given year, the answer may be to provide merit increases only to the very top-rated performers, rather than spreading the merit money too thinly. Of course, a danger is that this may create perceptions of inequity among those not receiving increases.

An important issue is whether persons performing at simply an adequate level should receive a merit increase. In general, the answer is no. Some firms lump all their increases together, for cost of living, experience/seniority, and merit, and in this way everyone appears to get something. But this serves to obscure the performance–merit pay relationship.

Instead, if cost of living increases are justified, or if the labour market becomes highly competitive, increases should be provided across the board to all employees by raising base pay ranges or commission rates. If the organization wishes to reward seniority, seniority increases should also be held separate from merit increases. One system that might be appropriate is to provide inflation/market increases to all employees, to provide a seniority increase to all employees who are performing at a satisfactory or higher level, and to provide merit increases to only those persons clearly performing at a higher-than-satisfactory level.

CONDITIONS FOR SUCCESS OF MERIT PAY

This section addresses two key questions. First, how do you decide which employee groups (if any) should be covered under individual merit pay? Second, how do you design the right system for each group? If merit pay is to be successful, the right system must be applied to the right group.

TO WHOM SHOULD INDIVIDUAL MERIT PAY APPLY?

Although most companies claim to use merit pay, it rarely applies to all employees. Nor should it. Applying merit pay to employee groups for whom it is unsuited is a recipe for frustration and failure.

So how do we decide to whom merit pay should apply? Asking the following questions can help guide this decision process:

1. Is individual performance variable?
2. Is performance controllable by the individual?
3. Can individual performance be separated out?

4. Can an accurate measurement system be developed?
5. Will pay actually be linked to performance appraisals?
6. Will the system serve a purpose that cannot be served some other way?
7. Will there be undesirable side effects?
8. Will the system fit with the firm's culture and strategy?

First, is performance variable? In many jobs, there is not much performance variation possible or even desirable, as in the case of many routine, lower-level jobs in traditional classical organizations. If performance is not variable, why waste time and effort attempting to measure variations?

Second, is performance controllable by the individual employee? If circumstances affecting employee performance are beyond the control of the employee, then gearing pay to individual performance makes no sense.

Third, can the performance of individuals be separated out from the performance of others with whom they work? If not, an individually based system cannot be used, although some type of team-based performance pay might work.

Fourth, can an accurate performance measurement system be developed? Do jobs change so quickly that it is virtually impossible to come up with valid, up-to-date performance measures and standards? Does the organization have the resources to develop a reliable and valid system, and train raters in its use?

Fifth, will pay actually be linked to the appraisals in a meaningful way? Is the organization prepared to set aside sufficient funds to justify the merit process, and is it prepared to actually allocate this money so as to create meaningful differences between highly meritorious employees and other employees? If not, nobody will take the process seriously.

Sixth, will merit pay serve a purpose that cannot be better served in some other way? Ultimately, there are three main purposes for merit pay: to motivate employee performance; to maintain equity by making rewards commensurate with contributions; and to raise the pay of key performers so they will not be lured away by other firms.

Can something other than individual merit pay better serve these purposes? As was noted in Chapter 3, intrinsic rewards are generally more effective than extrinsic rewards for motivating task behaviour. If intrinsic motivation already exists, then merit pay may not add much motivation, and could even detract from motivation, especially if the merit pay system is not seen as fair.

If merit pay is intended to demonstrate equity, then the system needs to be carefully monitored to ensure that it actually does so, in the eyes of the employees covered by the system. If persons perceived as undeserving receive merit increases, or if persons seen as deserving do not, a merit system may actually cause perceptions of inequity. An alternative method for recognizing employee differences is pay for knowledge.

As for retaining key employees, a wide variety of means (other than merit pay) are available to foster membership behaviour, as has been discussed in earlier chapters. If pay ranges are used, experience/seniority and/or skill levels can be used as vehicles for movement through the range, rather than merit raises.

Seventh, will there be undesirable side effects? One possible side effect occurs when employees concentrate only on elements of the job most visible in the performance appraisal process. For many organizations, organizational citizenship behaviour may be far more valuable than simple task behaviour, but most performance appraisal systems focus mainly on task behaviour. In fact, there is some evidence that appraisals that focus on specific goals and performance improvements actually seem to decrease citizenship behaviour (Findley, Giles, and Mossholder, 2000). Another side effect may be lack of cooperation or conflict among employees as they attempt to jockey for scarce merit increases, if these are strictly limited. If the funds are not strictly limited, there may be a temptation for everybody to get merit awards, thus diluting the connection between merit and reward and increasing compensation costs.

Finally, does merit pay fit the culture and strategy of the organization? In classical organizations, merit pay for rank-and-file employees is often prohibited by union contracts, since employees in these organizations are usually skeptical about the ability of the organization to fairly administer merit systems. Indeed, while merit pay would appear to fit well with the emphasis on individual accountability practised in classical organizations, for many of the reasons already discussed, it is subject to abuse in these organizations. Most classical organizations have found direct control of behaviour and job simplification to be the most effective means of controlling and motivating behaviour.

Recall Electronic Banking System Inc. from Box 2.1? This firm utilizes technology (surveillance cameras, computer monitoring) to monitor employee behaviour, so there is no need for subjective performance ratings. Indeed, many classical organizations are adopting computer monitoring of employee behaviour in preference to traditional appraisal systems.

Individual merit pay does not fit at all with human relations organizations, because supervisors are concerned about social unity within the organization. Although many human relations firms do, on the surface, utilize merit pay, the reality is that either most individuals receive high ratings or there is very little distinction in pay between those receiving higher ratings and those receiving lower ratings. However, this practice is not necessarily dysfunctional for human relations organizations. They recognize that their main control mechanism—cohesive groups and positive work norms—could easily be subverted by an individual merit pay system.

At first glance, individual merit pay might appear to fit well with high-involvement organizations because of their emphasis on performance. But a closer look reveals that most high-involvement organizations have fluid jobs, many team-based processes, a high level of interdependence between employees, and flat structures, none of which fit well with traditional performance appraisal. Ability and willingness to perform, and citizenship behaviours, are the keys to effective performance in these organizations. Motivation is provided by intrinsic sources and internalized commitment to the organization.

Under these circumstances, what could individual merit pay add to a high-involvement organization? It may actually detract by causing many of the problems discussed earlier. The last thing a high-involvement organization needs is people concerned only with their own self-aggrandizement, or who insist on keeping ideas to themselves for fear someone else might get credit for them. For high-involvement organizations, ranking or forced distribution systems are particularly destructive, because they undermine the collaborative atmosphere essential to their success. Results-oriented appraisals or 360-degree feedback might be a good fit.

As a sidelight, the foregoing discussion may help to solve the mystery of why, after so many years of effort, merit pay systems based on performance appraisal are so often unsatisfactory. As can be seen, the conditions in which individual merit pay can be applied to good effect are quite rare, and they may become increasingly rare, as concepts like flextime and flexplace become more common. But this is not to say that performance appraisal itself should necessarily be dropped. In any organization, there needs to be some system for providing feedback to individuals and groups on their performance, and if done correctly, performance appraisal may be a satisfactory means of providing this feedback. Of course, as discussed in Chapter 3, the best feedback occurs when jobs themselves are designed to provide it directly.

Interestingly, the conditions in public-sector organizations may be more amenable to merit pay than in private-sector firms, where business environments are rapidly changing, and where various alternatives, such as gain sharing or profit sharing, are available. In contrast, jobs in public-sector organizations tend to be more stable and less subject to dramatic change. One occupational group that appears to fit many of the conditions for merit pay is university professors, as Box 11.3 illustrates.

ISSUES IN DESIGNING AN EFFECTIVE MERIT SYSTEM

If the circumstances in an organization are judged to be right for an individual merit pay system, the next step is to tackle the many design issues that need to be dealt with in creating an effective system. They include the following:

1. What should be the objectives of the system?
2. What is the most appropriate measurement system?
3. How frequently should appraisals be conducted?
4. How are appraisals to be linked to pay?
5. How should feedback be provided?
6. How is procedural justice to be achieved?
7. How are raters to be trained and evaluated?
8. How is the system to be evaluated?

The first issue is to define what the merit pay/performance appraisal system is designed to accomplish. Is it intended as the major vehicle to stimulate performance, to promote reward equity, to retain valued performers, to

BOX 11.3 How Would You Grade Your Professor?

As we have seen, there are limited circumstances in which merit pay will be appropriate. However, university professors appear to meet many of the criteria. For the most part, they work independently, have control over their performance, and their accomplishments can usually be separated from those of others.

So how do you evaluate the performance of professors? In general, university professors are expected to perform in three main areas: teaching, research, and university and public service. Therefore, performance in each of these areas needs to be evaluated in some way.

The usual measure of research performance is the number of publications in high-quality academic journals. Why is this such a popular measure? Because it avoids virtually all of the problems inherent in more subjective appraisal systems. When a professor believes that he or she has made a useful contribution to the state of knowledge in a particular field, that professor prepares a paper describing the research results and submits it to a journal that specializes in that type of research. This journal then has the article reviewed by two or more experts in the field, using what is known as a double-blind process. That is, the reviewers do not know whose work they are reviewing, and the researchers do not know who is reviewing their work. Thus, problems of bias, halo, and the other major rating problems are avoided. Certainly, leniency is avoided, since most reputable journals accept for publication only a small minority of the work submitted to them—often as low as 5 to 10 percent of the submissions. One could therefore argue that if there is any problem with this system, it is harshness.

Compare this practice with the evaluation of teaching. The usual process is to utilize feedback from superiors (e.g., the department head), peers (other professors), and customers (students). But superior and peer appraisals take place for only a small sample of teaching behaviour, perhaps one class per term, and it is usual practice to inform the professor well in advance of the appraisal. This, of course, allows the faculty member to alter behaviour to impress the appraisers. On the other hand, the presence of these appraisers could make the professor nervous, and detract from performance. But in any case, colleagues (department heads are normally considered as colleagues) are usually reluctant to be too critical of another colleague. In addition, since no standardized rating form is usually used, the appraisals from peers are subject to all of the errors discussed earlier in the chapter.

Students, however, have the opportunity to attend all classes and so are in a better position to judge overall behaviour. But while they are qualified to judge things like preparation and organization of material, because they are (by definition) not experts in the subject matter, they are not well-equipped to judge the rigour and academic validity of what is being taught. In addition, some faculty attempt to influence student evaluations by combining lightweight material with easy tests and few assignments, in the hope of leading students to believe that they are learning a lot (as evidenced by their high grades), or simply to curry favour by making life as easy as possible for them.

With all of these problems, it is difficult to place a high degree of confidence in the evaluations of teaching. But evaluations of university and public-service accomplishments are even less systematic, and just as subjective. For example, what value should be placed on serving on the university budget committee, or delivering a public lecture to the Rotary Club? Given the problems of accurately measuring teaching and university/public service, is it any wonder that research performance often carries the most weight in university appraisal processes?

---

promote development/learning, or to foster other desired behaviours? Is the focus to be task behaviour, membership behaviour, or citizenship behaviour?

The second issue is to determine the most appropriate performance measurement system. The particular appraisal method or process that should be used is largely dependent on the nature of the organization and the jobs being appraised. For example, in jobs where employees do not work under close supervision, use of objectives-based and/or field review methods may be necessary. A 360-degree feedback system might also be useful.

As a general rule, ranking and forced distribution systems should not be used (since they foster a win-lose competitive environment among employees), except possibly in instances where there is little or no interdependence between employees. These methods do not fit with high-involvement or human relations organizations. Job-based systems, such as BARS, are probably not appropriate in organizations where jobs change rapidly. Ideally, whatever method is utilized, it should be systematic in approach, promote consistency across various raters, and should be validated in some fashion.

Third, how frequently should appraisals be done? From an accuracy and feedback point of view, the more frequent the better. From a practical point of view, an annual basis is usually best, since merit raises are normally awarded once a year. One system that might be effective is to have two appraisals a year, with the intermediate appraisal used for feedback and development only, and to give an indication of progress toward receiving a merit award.

Fourth, how should the appraisals be linked to pay? Various options were discussed in an earlier section. To be effective, there should be a system that provides some assurance that top-rated performance will be significantly recognized. The issue of whether and how to recognize employees at the top of their pay ranges needs to be dealt with.

Fifth, how is feedback to be provided? To be useful, appraisal results should be fully communicated to employees, with concrete feedback on what can be done to improve individual performance. As well, employees should be encouraged to identify their own strengths and weaknesses, and to communicate to the supervisor their view of the appraisal results and process. While this is usually done through appraisal interviews held at the time of each formal appraisal, it is also crucial for the supervisor to provide informal performance feedback on an ongoing basis to each subordinate.

Three key factors appear necessary for an effective appraisal interview— a high degree of supervisor familiarity with the subordinate's job and performance, a supportive approach, and genuine encouragement for subordinates to present their views and perceptions. In general, a friendly approach, stressing strengths as well as weaknesses and allowing subordinates to realize for themselves where behaviour needs improvement, is most effective. The supervisor should focus on specific behaviours that are undesirable rather than simply making a general statement, such as "you have a bad attitude." A statement like this is guaranteed to generate defensiveness and resistance by the subordinate and provides no real guidance on exactly what behaviour should be changed. The appraisee should leave the interview with a knowledge of specific, concrete steps that can be taken to improve performance.

Although it is important to use a systematic and valid appraisal method, effective performance appraisal goes far beyond the appraisal method. The key is really the quality of the relationship between the supervisor and subordinates. If a climate of trust and open communication does not exist between superior and subordinate, this will severely hamper the effectiveness of the appraisal process, no matter how good the tools. For example, a recent study showed that a positive and supportive relationship with the supervisor was just as important as the performance score itself in determining ratee satisfaction with the appraisal interview (Jawahar, 2001). Dissatisfaction with the appraisal interview led to lower job satisfaction and lower organizational commitment.

Sixth, there need to be mechanisms for ensuring procedural justice. This may entail some type of appeals system. It could also involve employee participation in the merit process. A highly developed process used by a Canadian university is illustrated in Box 11.4.

Seventh, there need to be procedures for rater training and rater accountability. Raters need to be carefully trained in how to use the system, how to make observations of employee behaviour, how to relate them to the instrument, and how to provide effective feedback. There also needs to be some system for recognizing and rewarding those supervisors who take the appraisal process seriously and do it well. Supervisors need to know that one aspect of their own evaluation is how well they conduct performance appraisal for their subordinates.

Finally, how should the merit system be evaluated? A process needs to be developed to ascertain whether the system is achieving its objectives, and whether it is causing any undesirable side effects. One aspect of the system that can be easily evaluated is rater and ratee acceptance of the system, through the use of surveys. If both raters and ratees do not accept and believe in the system, it doesn't stand a chance. However, even if the system is accepted, there are many factors that may render it ineffective or dysfunctional, as seen earlier. Employee satisfaction with the system and its results is a key check on how it is performing.

EVALUATING INDIVIDUALS IN TEAMS

One final topic in performance appraisal is the issue of performance evaluation of individuals in teams. As tasks in organizations have become more complex and interrelated, and as the business environment has come to demand more speed and customer responsiveness, numerous organizations have created various types of work teams to facilitate accomplishment of work tasks. For example, the Compensation Practices Survey showed that about 18 percent of Canadian firms use work teams or project teams for their nonmanagerial employees (covering an average of 40 percent of their employees), and 23 percent have teams for their managerial personnel (covering an average of 47 percent of their managers).

Two questions then arise: (1) should you attempt to recognize individual performance when that individual spends most or all of his or her time in a team, and if so, (2) how can this be done? There are two schools of thought on the first

BOX 11.4 Does This System Have Any Merit?

The University of Saskatchewan has a complex system for merit increases. Each fall, faculty members in each academic department vote on whether to have an elected merit pay committee or to delegate this function to the department head. Then, faculty who wish to be considered for a merit increment (raise) are asked to submit evidence substantiating their case. The department committee or head then reviews these submissions, ranks them, and chooses which to submit to the College Review Committee, an elected body of faculty chaired by the Dean of the College.

The College Review Committee reviews all submissions from the departments in the college, and ranks them. The committee then awards merit increments (usually a half-increment, but occasionally a full increment) down the list until the available funds are exhausted. The funds available for merit increases are established through negotiations between the university and the faculty union, and they are usually sufficient to provide half-increments (which range from $914 to $1122 per year, depending on rank) to approximately one-third of the faculty. There is also a special university-wide pool from which additional increments can be awarded to deserving faculty members. These funds are allocated by another elected faculty committee, the University Review Committee.

In order to ensure that teaching and university/public-service performance are not neglected because they are difficult to measure, most committees go to a special effort to make sure that some awards are made on these bases. Once the awards are official, a report is provided to all faculty listing the faculty members who have received merit awards, along with a brief explanation of the basis for each award.

If an individual does not receive a merit increase, he or she has several avenues of recourse. If the department committee or head did not recommend an increase, that faculty member may appeal to the College Review Committee. If the College Review Committee does not grant an increment, he or she may then appeal to the University Review Committee.

It should also be noted that unless faculty members are at the top of the pay range for their rank, they will receive a full increment for each additional year of service, aside from whatever cost of living increase the faculty union is able to negotiate (which is not much these days). Thus, seniority usually counts about double the value of merit, even if one is among the fortunate third who receive merit increases.

You will recognize many elements of procedural justice in this system, including openness, the election of salary committees, the opportunity to make one's own case, and the two sets of appeal processes. Interestingly, despite all of these elements of procedural justice, many faculty still feel slighted if they do not receive a merit increment, and blame the system for "unfairness."

This system illustrates the difficulty inherent in developing a merit pay system that is perceived as fair by all employees. Part of the problem may be incomplete information: the brief report on merit awards that is provided to faculty typically does not portray the full spectrum of accomplishments on which the award is based, and many faculty members not receiving an award are able to point to somebody who appears to have done less then they have but were awarded a merit increment.

So is the system worthwhile? There is no clear answer, but it does accomplish several things. It signals the behaviours that are important to the university, it attempts to provide some balance between rewards and contributions, it recognizes noteworthy accomplishments, and it serves as a mechanism for raising the pay of faculty members who might otherwise be lured to other universities.

question. One is that any attempt to single out individuals (except possibly on the basis of pay for knowledge) in a team context will likely do more harm than good. The argument here is that since teams are so interdependent in accomplishing their goals, singling out individuals is inherently unfair, since team success is a product of the efforts of all team members. Singling out some team members as more responsible than others for team success may lead to resentment against those singled out, and to a less cohesive and cooperative team. There is also the danger that some members will devote more energy to looking good on the appraisal system than to being an effective team player. This perspective suggests that team-based reward systems—such as gain sharing or goal sharing—are the best means of rewarding performance in teams.

The second school of thought argues that it is inevitable that some team members will contribute more to team success than others, and it is unfair (and possibly demotivating) to high contributors not to recognize this financially. If the right behaviours are rewarded, if individual contribution level is fairly determined, and if it is used in conjunction with group-based and organization-based performance pay, individual performance pay may play a useful role even in a team context (Zigon, 2000; Zingheim and Schuster, 2000).

Which school is correct? Unfortunately, there is no definitive evidence on this issue. However, it is clear that work teams can be highly effective without the use of individual performance pay, as examples at Toyota, Saturn Corporation, and Basell Canada have shown. Whether these teams would be even more successful with an element of individual performance pay is not clear. It is conceivable that, if done right, adding individual performance pay might help to encourage and retain high contributors, without negative repercussions for the team as a whole. However, given the risks and possible pitfalls involved with utilizing individual merit pay in a team context, it may well be that the risks outweigh the possible returns in most instances.

Nonetheless, there may be instances where identifying and rewarding individual contribution is appropriate and even necessary for team success. These instances would include teams where members do not have strong intrinsic motivation, where strong positive group norms do not exist, where group sanctions against poor contributors are ineffective, and where little member commitment to overall team or organizational goals is evident. These conditions create an opportunity for free riding, and are most likely to occur in project teams that are temporary and in which membership is part-time, although they can arise in other types of teams as well. Under these conditions, recognizing individual contribution levels may be essential, not only to discourage free riding, but to assure team members who are contributing that their rewards will be different from those of the free riders. There is nothing more demoralizing to conscientious team members than the continued presence of free riders who will benefit equally from team accomplishments. This can eventually result in a downward performance spiral as all members try to "cut their losses" by competing to see who can get away with contributing the least to the team.

One way of avoiding this unfortunate outcome could be use of an **individual/team merit grid** that recognizes individual contribution while still providing incentives for team-oriented behaviour (Tyson, 2001). Table 11.2 provides an example.

individual/team merit grid method for linking individual merit pay to both individual and team performance

TABLE 11.2 EXAMPLE OF AN INDIVIDUAL/TEAM MERIT GRID

	INDIVIDUAL MEMBER CONTRIBUTION TO TEAM			
	Unsatisfactory	Effective	High	Exceptional
Team exceeds goals	–	8%	12%	16%
Team meets goals	–	4%	6%	8%
Team fails to meet goals	–	—	—	—

As can be seen, there are three levels of team performance and four levels of individual performance (defined in terms of contribution to team success) in this example. If the team does not meet its performance goals, there is no merit pay for anyone, regardless of individual performance. The message conveyed here is that there can be no individual success without team success. However, even if the team does meet its performance goals, there will be no merit pay for individuals who did not make at least an "effective" contribution to team success. If the team meets its goals, "effective contributors" (the norm) would receive a 4 percent raise or bonus, "high contributors" would receive a 6 percent raise or bonus, and "exceptional contributors" (these will generally be quite rare) would receive 8 percent. If the team exceeds its goals, these amounts are doubled. Overall, this system creates a common goal for team members while still recognizing individual contribution levels.

Of course, the key to success for this system is to have some way of identifying individual contribution levels that is both accurate and accepted as fair by team members. A crucial aspect of doing this is to recognize the key individual behaviours that contribute to team success. Of course, effectively performing individual tasks assigned by the team is important, but other behaviours that are as important, or even more important, to the team might include training and coaching new team members, mediating conflict between team members, helping to create a positive team atmosphere, helping other team members with their tasks, and exercising initiative in moving the team toward its goals. It is hard to imagine how a supervisor-based appraisal could assess all this, and therefore peer appraisal would likely play a central role in determining individual contribution levels. Team involvement in the creation and ongoing operation of the appraisal system will greatly increase the likelihood of its acceptance.

If an appraisal system that meets acceptance by the team cannot be devised, any system based on it will likely do more harm than good. However, even if a system cannot be devised to distinguish among good performers, it is still possible that a peer appraisal system could be used to identify unsatisfactory performers, so that steps could be taken to either improve their performance, if possible, or remove them from the team. Nothing is more damaging to team morale (and, ultimately, team performance) than carrying an ineffective contributor.

EVALUATING SKILLS, KNOWLEDGE, AND COMPETENCIES

In this final section of the chapter, we shift focus from evaluating individual performance to evaluating individual skills and competencies. Let's suppose that, after considering all the pros and cons of a pay-for-knowledge system (PKS), you have decided that a PKS fits your organization. Now what? What are the key issues in designing these systems?

Before we answer this question, it should be noted that there are really two distinct types of pay-for-knowledge systems. Skill-based pay systems tend to focus at the production or service provision level, while competency-based pay focuses at the managerial or professional level. Since skill-based pay is better defined than competency-based pay, it will be discussed first.

There are five steps in the design of a skill-based pay system: (1) deciding whom to include, (2) designing the skill blocks, (3) linking these skill blocks to pay, (4) providing learning opportunities, and (5) certifying skill achievement.

To Whom Should Pay for Knowledge Apply?

As was discussed in Chapter 4, pay for knowledge fits with a high-involvement approach to management. Beyond this, the most active early adopters were continuous process operations, with products ranging from chemicals to steel to dog food. Because of their high task interdependence, high-capital intensity, and an overriding need to keep the production process running, these operations are ideal sites for PKS. But increasingly, PKS has also been applied to other types of manufacturing firms and to the service sector.

Whenever the organization needs high and diverse employee skills, and can benefit from high employee flexibility, then PKS may pay off. In their study of firms using PKS in the United States, Jenkins and his colleagues (1992) found examples of successful PKS plans in a wide range of manufacturing industries, as well as in many service industries, including financial services, computer services, utilities, health services, and retailing.

Designing Skill/Knowledge Blocks

After deciding where to implement PKS, the next step is to identify the job skills that are required for effective performance of the work system, and then to "bundle" them into appropriate skill "units" or "blocks." The various skills can typically be differentiated along two dimensions—horizontal and vertical. The horizontal dimension covers different *types* of skills, while the vertical dimension covers the *depth* of each skill.

Frequently, **skill/knowledge blocks** are set out in a grid, defined by these two dimensions. Table 11.3 provides an example of such a grid for a chemical plant. As can be seen, there are five horizontal skills and four vertical skill levels, with a total of 18 skill blocks. As employees complete each skill block,

skill/knowledge blocks
the basic component of a skill-based pay system, containing a bundle of skills or knowledge necessary to carry out a specific production or service-delivery task

TABLE 11.3 EXAMPLE OF SKILL GRID FOR CHEMICAL PLANT

	Operations	Packaging	Testing	Maintenance	Coordination/Administration
Level IV	Able to operate all production equipment for all products $1200		Able to conduct all lab, chemical, and statistical tests $1200	Able to diagnose & conduct major repairs on all plant equipment $1200	Able to do all production & team coordination $1200
Level III	Able to operate all production equipment for liquid products $1000	Able to carry out all packaging processes $1000	Able to conduct advanced testing & statistical analysis $1000	Able to diagnose & repair the most common major malfunctions $1000	Able to develop production & labour schedules $1000
Level II	Able to operate all production equipment for dry products $800	Able to package liquid products $800	Able to analyze routine samples & do advanced quality control $800	Able to deal with minor breakdowns & conduct routine maintenance $800	Able to complete basic production & labour reports $800
Level I	Able to operate basic production equipment $600	Able to package dry products $600	Able to collect routine samples & monitor product quality $600	Able to make routine adjustments to all equipment $600	

they receive an increase in pay, as indicated by the dollar values shown in each skill block. (Although employees are usually expected to complete the horizontal row of skills before moving vertically to the next-higher row of skills, there may be some circumstances where it makes sense to allow some vertical skill development before the entire row is completed.) In this illustration, a fully skilled chemical plant operator will be earning $17 000 per year more than an entry-level operator just starting out with the firm.

EXAMPLES OF SKILL BLOCKS

There are many possible ways to arrange a skill-based system. At the Basell Canada Sarnia chemical plant (described in Box 4.3), there are a total of ten "job knowledge clusters" for the basic operation of the plant. In addition, there are three specialty skills (instrumentation, electrical, and pipefitting), and all shift team members must select one. To be fully qualified in a specialty skill, team members must complete 40 training modules.

At Basell, a shift team member receives a pay increase when he or she completes one job knowledge cluster and four modules of a specialty skill. Thus, ten pay raises are possible, beyond the base pay that each employee receives on joining the company. The amounts of these raises are determined by collective bargaining. Job knowledge clusters can be completed in any order, but specialty modules normally have a specified progression. Generally, it takes six or seven years for a shift team member to reach the top rate.

In general, a system of skill blocks can range from simple to complex. A simple system was used by General Mills at a plant producing fruit drinks (Ledford and Bergel, 1991). There were four main steps in the production process, and each step became a skill block. Within each skill block, there were three levels of skill, with a raise for completion of each. Employees could start in any skill block, complete all skill levels within that block, or move to another skill block after accomplishing two levels within that block.

In contrast, a much more complex system was developed at LS Electrogalvanizing. When employees join the firm, they start as a "utility" person and receive a basic entry-level salary, which is determined by collective bargaining. They start in one of five plant areas (materials entry, process, inspection, delivery, or chem plant), moving from one to the next as they master each one. Completion of each of these five blocks adds one-fifth of the difference between the "utility" wage rate and the "process technician" wage rate (set through collective bargaining) to the employee's salary. Once they master all five, they receive the designation "process technician."

At this point, employees are then expected to choose one of two intermediate skills: process/mechanical or electronic/instrumentation. The skills within each of these intermediate skill blocks are classified as minor skills, medium skills, or major skills. For each minor skill, there is a 2 percent increase in pay, for each medium skill there is a 4 percent increase, and for each major skill there is an 8 percent increase. Once employees have completed 80 percent of their intermediate skill, they may then start work on an advanced skill in one of three areas: mechanical, chem plant, or electrical.

At Nortel, a much simpler pay-for-knowledge method was used for field service technicians (whose main duty is installation of telecommunications equipment). Skill sets were built from existing equipment installation procedure manuals, and four skill blocks were established, arranged in a hierarchy. Field service technicians move from one to the next, receiving a pay increase when each is accomplished (LeBlanc, 1991).

A somewhat different process was used to design a pay-for-knowledge system for technical support engineers at Nortel, since there was no established set of procedures from which to form the skill blocks. Instead, managers were asked to identify the key dimensions of this work. They came up with seven dimensions: hardware, software, customer database, documentation, network interface, written communication, and interpersonal interaction. For each dimension, managers then identified and ranked the specific skills needed, from simplest to most complex. These were then arranged into four vertical skill blocks, with the first block including the simplest skills for each of the seven dimensions, while the second block included somewhat more complex skills for each dimension, and so on. A pay increase was granted on completion of each skill block.

ISSUES IN DESIGNING SKILL BLOCKS

In designing skill blocks, there are numerous issues that need to be dealt with. One issue is how many to have. In their study, Jenkins and associates (1992) found that the average number of skill blocks was ten, with a huge range (from 2 to 550). How many should there be? There is no clear answer, and it probably varies from case to case, but these researchers did find that the most successful plans had a slightly greater number of skill blocks (an average of 11) than "less successful" plans (an average of nine). Generally, the more complex and diverse the array of skills in a system, the more the skill blocks.

How long should it take to master a skill block? There is no empirical evidence on this question. But Jenkins and associates found the average was 20 weeks. This finding suggests that in the average plan, it takes about four to five years to reach the top skill levels. Of course, the more complex the set of skills required, the longer it would take. At LS Electrogalvanizing, the first level, process technician, can be achieved in three to four years, but reaching the top of the system takes much longer. The general thinking on this matter seems to be that, for most pay-for-knowledge plans, an employee should be able to progress through the system in no more than six to seven years.

PRICING THE SKILL BLOCKS

high-low method
determines entry level and skill block pay amounts by pricing comparable entry-level and top-level jobs in the market and allocating the difference to the various skill blocks

How are the skill blocks priced? The *relative amount* of increase for each skill block should depend on how difficult it is and/or how long it takes to complete that skill block, and on the value of that skill block to the company. But how is the *absolute amount* of the pay determined? The most common method for determining this is the **high-low method**.

Let's use the system depicted in Table 11.3 to illustrate this method. First, the firm would determine what the market base pay rates are for an entry-level chemical plant operator and for a job that contains all of the skills in level IV. Let's suppose these rates are $40 000 and $50 833. The firm then adjusts these amounts for its pay level strategy—let's suppose it wishes to pay 10 percent above the market at entry level and 20 percent above the market at top level. If so, the entry-level pay would be $44 000, and the top-level pay would be $61 000, creating a difference of $17 000. This $17 000 would then be allocated across the skill blocks according to their relative importance or the amount of time required to master them.

Of course, this process may be complicated by the fact that it is often difficult to find market data for jobs that precisely match the entry-level and top-level skill sets used under the PKS, so finding a suitable match can be a complicated issue. Another issue is whether to lead, lag, or match the market, and whether the same policy should apply at the entry and the top levels. In general, entry-level pay will have to at least match the market in order to attract the kinds of employees with the learning abilities needed to progress through the system. Typically, as the individual progresses through the system, pay levels should begin to lead the market, as the value of the employee increases. A study by Jenkins and his associates (1992) revealed that, on average, PKS firms paid somewhat higher than the market median for entry-level personnel (at the 63rd percentile), and much higher for their top pay rates (90th percentile).

Another issue is whether all skill blocks should be priced the same. There is no inherent reason why they should be, although some firms are attracted to the simplicity of doing so. Jenkins and associates found that 40 percent of the pay-for-knowledge plans they examined priced all skill blocks the same.

One pay-related issue is whether PKS employees should also be paid on other individual bases, such as seniority or individual merit. For seniority, the answer should almost always be no, because progression by seniority is the antithesis to knowledge-based progression. In most cases, the answer for individual merit pay should also be no, since it is at odds with the team approach that is usually essential for PKS to pay off. The exception to this rule may be where each employee works separately and independently of other employees, as in the case of the Nortel field service technicians discussed earlier.

This is not to say that performance appraisal (beyond the skill certification process) should not be used, but simply that it should generally not be linked to individual raises. Performance appraisal may well be useful (even essential) for developmental purposes, to make sure that skill levels are being maintained, and to identify and correct substandard performance. Jenkins and associates found that 45 percent of PKS organizations conducted regular performance appraisals.

However, while seniority or individual merit pay does not fit well with PKS, group- and organization-based performance pay fits very well, as Armstrong (1991) has noted. Use of gain sharing or goal sharing can provide

PKS employees with a financial reward for the increased productivity they are expected to generate, and profit sharing and stock ownership can help reinforce the citizenship behaviour so critical to the success of pay-for-knowledge systems.

PROVIDING LEARNING/TRAINING OPPORTUNITIES

A key issue in the success of any pay-for-knowledge system is the provision of opportunities for employees to learn the requisite skills. Based on his experience, LeBlanc (1991) argues that this is the single most difficult issue with pay-for-knowledge plans. Since pay is tied to this skill development, employees will want training opportunities. However, this can be very expensive, both in terms of the direct training costs, but also in terms of time away from the job. This often conflicts with the productivity of the unit, and even with other reward systems.

For example, at Nortel, LeBlanc (1991) found that managers were not using the employee training funds that they had been allocated. Why? Time devoted to training reduced the efficiency measures for their departments, so those managers who encouraged the most training for their personnel received the *lowest* performance ratings! The problem was solved by revising the appraisal system so that amount of training undertaken by their subordinates became a positive managerial performance indicator.

Companies using PKS have a wide array of different training techniques to choose from. For example, at LS Electrogalvanizing, these include classroom training, interactive computer-based training, and on-the-job peer training. On-the-job training is generally the largest component in most plans, especially at the lower skill levels. But a problem that frequently arises is "bottlenecking." This occurs because some skills take longer to learn than others, and for some skills there are fewer opportunities to learn them.

For example, there may be a need for only two persons to perform the product testing function at a given time, with one of them being a skilled employee to teach the unskilled employee, and it may take six months to learn this skill. This may result in a whole queue of employees waiting to have an opportunity to learn this particular job before they can complete their current skill level. This happened at General Mills. Although it was expected that employees could reach the top rate in two to three years, the reality was four to five years, creating employee frustration (Ledford and Bergel, 1991).

Another issue is the extent to which paid time off should be provided for off-the-job training, and to which individual employees should use some of their own time for training. In general, there is some blend of the two, but if a high level of job performance and involvement is expected as part of the system, it would be unfair to consume a major portion of an employee's non-work time for training. Often, the tradeoff made is that work time is provided for training for the lower-skill levels, but at the top skill levels, where classroom training often plays a major role, work time may not be provided, although out-of-pocket costs, such as tuition fees, are almost always covered.

Certifying Skill/Knowledge Block Achievement

A key issue for any firm using PKS is to have a system for determining when an employee has mastered a particular skill block (a process known as **skill certification**) that is both valid and accepted as fair by employees. In some cases there is a minimum period of time that an employee must spend working at a particular skill before certification is granted. The purpose of this rule is to ensure proficiency in the skill and to provide enough reinforcement in that skill to make sure that it is retained.

skill certification the testing process that determines whether an individual has achieved a given skill block

Skill certification systems vary dramatically in their complexity and processes. Basell Canada has a relatively straightforward three-step process. All employees are provided with self-training materials indicating the certification requirements for each skill block. When employees believe themselves ready to be tested, they must ask a fellow employee (already certified for that skill) to confirm that they are ready for testing. If the shift team coordinator agrees, the final checkoff is done by staff experts who specialize in the certification process.

At LS Electrogalvanizing, detailed checklists for each skill block have been prepared. To be certified in one of the five basic skill blocks, an employee must work for 1200 hours in that block. At 1000 hours, a formal peer review is undertaken to gauge progress and to provide feedback on areas needing improvement. After 1200 hours, an employee may apply to be certified for that skill block. To do so, he or she must receive a positive checkoff by five other certified operators, and then by the process coordinator. Overall, it takes three to four years to complete the five skill blocks necessary to become a "process technician."

Nortel uses a different process to certify field service technicians. Peer assessment is not used, because technicians generally work alone. Instead, at regular intervals, the supervisor conducts a four-step procedure. First is a "pre-assessment meeting" with the technician, during which skill accomplishments since the previous review are discussed. Training and development needs for reaching the next skill block are also assessed. Next, the supervisor conducts a field assessment in which technicians demonstrate their proficiencies on the job. Third, the supervisor presents a report on these accomplishments to an assessment committee of experienced managers, who decide whether advancement to the next skill level is warranted. After this, the results are fed back to the technician in a "postassessment" meeting. If dissatisfied with the outcome, the technician may appeal to the assessment committee.

In contrast, at General Mills, the system is almost completely peer based. Utilizing detailed checklists, an employee is certified by her or his peer trainer. Although there is a possible concern that employees may "go easy" on each other to avoid conflict, the company does not believe this to be a problem

(Ledford and Bergel, 1991). This may be due to the safeguards in the system. First, all team members must ratify the certification. Second, employees must re-qualify whenever they rotate back into the skill again. Third, if an employee is found to be unable to perform skills for which she or he is certified, the employee *and* the certifier will forgo their next pay increase. And fourth, the plant manager has final authority for approving certifications, although he has rarely felt the need to disapprove any.

OTHER SKILL-BASED PAY ISSUES

There are two other issues important to the success of a pay-for-knowledge plan. Almost all such plans require considerable refinement after initial implementation, so it is important that they be monitored on an ongoing basis. Many firms have found that the ideal vehicle for doing this is a joint employee–management committee, as is used at LS Electrogalvanizing.

The other issue is that a variety of human resource and management practices have to fit with the pay-for-knowledge system if it is to pay off for the organization. The example at Nortel illustrates how changing one aspect of the system (adding PKS) can be hindered by failure to change other parts (the managers' performance appraisal criteria). Another example is hiring practices, where ability to perform the entry-level job, or experience in traditional plants, should not be key criteria. Instead, the key recruitment needs are for employees with the ability to master all the necessary skills, the willingness to learn, the ability to help and teach others, and the disposition to work cooperatively in a group setting. Many PKS firms give the group or team a major role in the hiring process. In general, the whole range of human resource practices characterized by the high-involvement managerial strategy need to be in place if PKS is going to realize its full potential.

COMPETENCY-BASED PAY SYSTEMS

competency-based pay
pay that is based on the knowledge, skills, and behaviours, rather than performance, of individual employees

Many firms are now attempting to apply the concept of pay for knowledge to their professional and managerial personnel through the use of **competency-based pay systems**. These can vary greatly in format. For example, a defence electronics firm has a master list of more than 30 competencies that may apply to professional and managerial staff, and each department selects those most relevant to its operations (Ledford and Heneman, 2000). Pay raises are tied to achievement of each competency. In another case, a manufacturing firm pays managers for their degree of progress in mastering four managerial competencies that are deemed to apply to all managerial jobs. In a third case, professional and managerial employees negotiate "learning contracts" with their supervisor, and pay increases are based on accomplishment of these objectives.

Overall, competency-based systems are much more problematic than skill-based systems. Virtually nothing is known about their effectiveness. This is partly due to the enormous confusion and lack of precision about just what constitutes a "competency-based system." Some systems appear to be little more than the trait-rating appraisal system under a new guise. For example, one list of possible "competencies" includes traits such as "self-confidence" and "assertiveness" as well as "flexibility" and "initiative" (Williams, 1998). Although personality traits can be assessed with established psychometric measures, these measures work better as part of the selection process than as part of an ongoing competency-based pay program.

Part of the problem in discussing competency-based systems is the wide variation in definitions of "competencies." The following definition is adopted here: "competencies are demonstrable characteristics of the person, including knowledge, skills, and behaviors, that enable performance" (Ledford and Heneman, 2000: 146). Of course, a legitimate question is "why not just pay people for their performance, rather than factors at least one step removed from performance?" One answer to this is that individual performance can be hard (or even counterproductive) to measure, and another is that identifying valid competencies can serve as the basis for an effective training and development program. When specific competencies are paid for, attention is focused on exactly what needs to be learned, and there is no doubt that this can increase the rate of skill development.

In developing any competency-based pay system, there are four main issues: (1) identifying competencies that demonstrably affect performance; (2) devising methods to measure achievement of each competency; (3) compensating each competency; and (4) providing learning opportunities. Unfortunately, many so-called "competency-based" systems fail on all four counts.

Many consulting companies sell "competency-based" systems that are simply menus of any kind of trait imaginable. Firms are expected to select "appropriate" competencies from this menu, whether or not they are valid for that employer. A more sound process is to develop a list of competencies that may distinguish high performers from other employees in a particular occupational group, test all employees in that group on the presence of these competencies, and then statistically identify the competencies that differentiate the top performers from the other employees. Of course, to do this, you must already have valid performance measures for each employee. Another potential problem with this approach is that it is only valid as long as the factors that differentiated performance in the past continue to be valid.

The second issue is measurement. It may be difficult to develop reliable and valid measures for some competencies, measures that are also accepted as fair by employees.

Third, effectively relating achievement of competencies to pay is not straightforward, because there is no generally accepted method for so doing, unlike the case of skill-based pay. If a statistical process has been used for identifying the key competencies, these data can be used to determine the relative weighting of each competency in terms of how strongly it contributes to performance. However, deciding the absolute dollar value for each competency is highly subjective, because there is no external test equivalent to the high-low method used for skill-based pay. Whether to reward achievement of competencies with raises to base pay or with one-shot bonuses is another issue. If a competency is likely to be enduring, then an increase to base pay seems in order; if not, a one-shot bonus would be appropriate. Overall, a simple way of linking competencies to pay is to simply factor achievement of competencies into the merit raise system, if one exists (Brown, 2000).

The fourth issue, providing learning opportunities, is not necessarily straightforward, because some competencies are more inherent than teachable. But, as with skill-based pay, providing opportunities to develop key competencies is essential to success of the system.

Finally, it should be noted that not all organizations need all employees to have the full range of competencies possessed by top performers. If they don't need this, the firm may end up paying for capabilities it cannot utilize, leading to employee frustration and higher costs to the employer.

Summary and Implications

This chapter completes our coverage of the key technical processes necessary to transform a compensation strategy into a compensation system. The purpose of this chapter was to examine how to develop processes for evaluating two aspects of individual employees—their performance level and their skill/knowledge level. Accurate evaluation of individual performance is essential for a successful merit pay system, while accurate evaluation of individual skills and competencies is critical to the success of a pay-for-knowledge system.

Creating a reliable and valid performance appraisal system was found to be fraught with many difficulties, and dissatisfaction with current appraisal processes was found in many firms. Part of the problem is that merit pay linked to performance appraisal is just not appropriate to many of the circumstances in which it is applied and will inevitably be unsatisfactory in these circumstances. Performance appraisal can be applied effectively only where performance has scope to vary, where employees can control their performance levels, and where individual performance can be separated out and accurately assessed. It was noted that evaluating individual performance in a team context is a particularly thorny matter, although it may be necessary in some instances.

It was also noted that there are many threats to the accuracy of performance appraisal, some of them intentional. Managers usually view performance appraisal within the context of their overall task objectives, and accuracy of performance appraisal is often secondary to the achievement of their managerial goals.

Another potential source of appraisal problems is the appraisal method, of which there are many. Although no method is perfect, some methods do have much greater reliability and validity than others, and the key is to select the method that fits best with the purpose of the appraisal system, the nature of the behaviour being evaluated, and the organizational context in which it is applied. The same is true for selection of the most appropriate individuals to actually conduct the appraisals, which may include not only superiors, but peers, subordinates, and even customers.

When pay is to be based on performance appraisal, another crucial part of the process is to develop a method for effectively linking pay to the appraisal results. Once this is decided, there are still many other issues to deal with in completing the design of the merit system, including the frequency of appraisals, feedback, mechanisms for procedural justice, procedures for rater training, and a system to evaluate the merit system itself.

The second part of the chapter discussed the process for creating effective pay-for-knowledge systems, noting a distinction between skill-based pay (which is focused at the production or service provision level) and competency-based pay (which is focused at the managerial or professional level). For skill-based pay, it was noted that the type of job or industry was less important than an organizational context in which high-involvement management is practised. The main issues in developing a successful skill-based pay system included designing the skill blocks, pricing these blocks, providing learning opportunities, certifying skill achievement, and ensuring a context that provides complementary human resource practices.

In contrast to skill-based pay, it was noted that competency-based pay is a less well-defined and less-proven concept, with little or no evidence on its effectiveness. At the moment, there are many difficulties in using it effectively for pay purposes, although numerous firms appear to be using it effectively for training and development purposes.

The path to effective compensation has been a long and arduous one, but you are nearly at your destination. Now that you know how to develop a compensation strategy and design the technical processes to transform that strategy into a compensation system, only one milestone remains. This is the effective implementation and ongoing management of the compensation system, which serves as the focus for the final chapter in this volume.

KEY TERMS

behaviourally anchored rating scales (BARS), p. 415

behavioural observation scales (BOS), p. 415

central tendency rating error, p. 407

competency-based pay, p. 444

contrast effect, p. 408

critical incident method, p. 411

forced choice method, p. 414

forced distribution, p. 410

graphic rating scale, p. 410

halo error, p. 407

harshness effect, p. 408

high-low method, p. 440

individual/team merit grid, p. 435

leniency effect, p. 408

EXERCISES

1. Henderson Printing (in the Appendix), currently has no formal perfor-mance appraisal system. The CEO, Georgette Henderson, thinks that a per-formance appraisal system might be useful, and she has hired you to assess the company and recommend whether to implement one. She also wants to know whether she should link pay to the appraisals. She expects your report to include the pros and cons of each idea, along with a detailed jus-tification for your recommendations.

2. Ms. Henderson has decided to go ahead with a performance appraisal system, and she has decided to link it to merit pay. Impressed with your earlier work for the company (see Exercise 1), she has hired you to design the performance appraisal system and a merit pay system that would be linked to it. She expects your report to be sufficiently comprehensive that it could serve as the blueprint for the implementation of these systems.

3. At the Fit Stop (in the Appendix), the CEO, Susan Superfit, has decided to implement a pay-for-knowledge system for her sales staff. Hearing of your excellent work from Georgette Henderson, she has hired your firm to design the system. She expects your report to be comprehensive and detailed, containing all the necessary steps for implementing the system, and providing justification for each aspect of your proposed system.

4. In groups of six to eight people, share your experiences with performance appraisal. Group members who have been subject to a performance appraisal system should indicate whether they believe that their perfor-mance was fairly evaluated, and, if not, why not. After that, the groups should come together and discuss the overall experience of class members with performance appraisal. How many members believe that they were fairly appraised, how many members believe that they were not fairly appraised, and what were the differences between fair and unfair appraisal systems?

Suggested Web Sites

Page 403: To see the arguments of opponents of performance appraisal, click on <www.abolishappraisals.com>

Page 436: To find some good examples of performance indicators that can be used in a team context, go to <www.zigonperf.com>

References

Armstrong, Ann. 1991. "The Design and Implementation of Skill-Based Systems." *Proceedings of the Administrative Sciences Association of Canada, Personnel and Human Resources Division*, 12(8): 21–31.

Baarda, Carolyn. 2000. *Compensation Planning Outlook 2001*. Ottawa: Conference Board of Canada.

Belcourt, Monica, Arthur W. Sherman, George W. Bohlander, and Scott A. Snell. 2002. *Managing Human Resources*, 3rd. ed. Toronto: Nelson Thomson Learning.

Bernardin, H. John, and Richard W. Beatty. 1984. *Performance Appraisal: Assessing Human Behaviour at Work*. Boston: Kent Publishing.

Bohl, Don L. 1996. "Minisurvey: 360-Degree Appraisals Yield Superior Results." *Compensation & Benefits Review*, 28(5).

Bracken, David W., Carol W. Timmreck, John W. Fleenor, and Lynn Summers. 2001. "360 Degree Feedback from Another Angle." *Human Resource Management*, 40(1): 3–20.

Brown, Duncan. 2000. "Relating Competencies to Pay." In Lance A. Berger and Dorothy R. Berger, eds., *The Compensation Handbook*. New York: McGraw-Hill, 157–71.

Coens, Tom, and Mary Jenkins. 2000. *Abolishing Performance Appraisals: Why They Backfire and What to Do Instead*. San Francisco: Berrett-Koehler Publishers.

Edwards, Mark R., and Ann J. Ewen. 1996. *360° Feedback*. New York: Amacom.

Findley, Henry M., William F. Giles, and Kevin W. Mossholder. 2000. "Performance Appraisal Process and System Facets: Relationships with Contextual Performance." *Journal of Applied Psychology*, 85(4): 634–40.

Grote, Dick. 1996. *The Complete Guide to Performance Appraisal*. New York: Amacom.

Heneman, Robert L. 1992. *Merit Pay: Linking Pay Increases to Performance Ratings*. Reading, MA: Addison-Wesley.

Human Resources Management in Canada. 2000. "Performance Appraisals Get Thumbs Down." Report Bulletin 208: 4.

Jawahar, I.M. 2001. "Antecedents and Potential Consequences of Satisfaction with Performance Appraisal Interview." *Proceedings of the Annual Conference of the Administrative Sciences Association of Canada (Human Resources Division)*, 22(9): 45–54.

Jenkins, G. Douglas, Gerald E. Ledford, Nina Gupta, and D. Harold Doty. 1992. *Skill-Based Pay: Practices, Payoffs, Pitfalls, and Prescriptions*, Scottsdale, AZ: American Compensation Association.

Kane, Jeffrey S., and Kimberly F. Kane. 1993. "Performance Appraisal." In H.J. Bernardin and J.E.A. Russell, eds., *Human Resource Management: An Experimental Approach*. New York: McGraw-Hill, 377–404.

Kruger, Justin, and David Dunning. 1999. "Unskilled and Unaware of It: Difficulties in Recognizing One's Own Incompetence Lead to Inflated Self-Assessments." *Journal of Personality and Social Psychology*, 77(6):1121–34.

Landy, F.S., and J.L. Farr. 1980. "Performance Rating." *Psychological Bulletin*, 87: 72–107.

Latham, Gary P., and Soosan D. Latham. 2001. "The Importance of Performance Management to Productivity." *HR.com eBulletin*, June 11: www.hr.com.

Latham, Gary P., and Kenneth N. Wexley. 1994. *Increasing Productivity through Performance Appraisal*. Reading, MA: Addison-Wesley.

Lawler, Edward E. 2000. *Rewarding Excellence: Pay Strategies for the New Economy*. San Francisco: Jossey-Bass.

LeBlanc, Peter V. 1991. "Skill-Based Pay Case Number 2: Northern Telecom." *Compensation and Benefits Review*, 23(2): 39–56.

Ledford, Gerald E. 1991. "Three Case Studies on Skill-Based Pay: An Overview." *Compensation and Benefits Review*, 23(2): 11–23.

Ledford, Gerald E., and Gary Bergel. 1991. "Skill-Based Pay Case Number 1: General Mills." *Compensation and Benefits Review*, 23(2): 24–38.

Ledford, Gerald E., and Robert L. Heneman. 2000. "Pay for Skills, Knowledge, and Competencies." In Lance A. Berger and Dorothy R. Berger, eds., *The Compensation Handbook*. New York: McGraw-Hill, 143–56.

Longenecker, Clinton, and Dean Ludwig. 1995. "Ethical Dilemmas in Performance Appraisal Revisited." In Jacky Holloway, Jenny Lewis, and Geoff Mallory, eds., *Performance Measurement and Evaluation*, London: Sage Publications, 66–77.

Longenecker, Clinton O., H.P. Sims, and D.A. Gioia. 1987. "Behind the Mask: The Politics of Employee Appraisal." *Academy of Management Executive*, 1: 183–93.

Murphy, Kevin R., and Jeanette N. Cleveland. 1995. *Understanding Performance Appraisal*. Thousand Oaks, CA: Sage Publications.

Peiperl, Maury A. 2001. "Getting 360° Feedback Right." *Harvard Business Review*, 79(1):142–47.

Scullen, Steven E., Michael K. Mount, and Maynard Goff. 2000. "Understanding the Latent Structure of Job Performance Ratings." *Journal of Applied Psychology*, 85(6): 956–70.

Southworth, Natalie. 2001. "Managers Crucial to Curbing Turnover." *The Globe and Mail*, May 30: M1.

Tyson, David E. 2001. *Carswell's Compensation Guide*. Toronto, ON: Thomson Publishing.

Weiss, Tracey B. 2000. "Performance Management." In Lance A. Berger and Dorothy R. Berger, eds., *The Compensation Handbook*. New York: McGraw-Hill, 429–42.

Williams, Richard S. 1998. *Performance Management*. London: International Thompson Business Press.

Zigon, Jack. 2000. "Measuring the Hard Stuff: Teams and Other Hard to Measure Work." In Lance A. Berger and Dorothy R. Berger, eds., *The Compensation Handbook*. New York: McGraw-Hill, 443–66.

Zingheim, Patricia K., and Jay R. Schuster. 2000. *Pay People Right!* San Francisco: Jossey-Bass.

Part V

Implementing, Managing, Evaluating, and Adapting the Compensation System

12

....

MANAGING THE
COMPENSATION SYSTEM

CHAPTER GOALS

By the end of this chapter, you should be able to:

1. Describe the fundamentals of compensation administration.
2. Identify the key issues in preparing to implement a compensation system.
3. Describe the necessary steps in implementing the compensation system.
4. Explain how to evaluate the effectiveness of the compensation system.
5. Identify circumstances that may necessitate changes to the compensation system.
6. Discuss the issues to be considered in adapting the compensation system.

INTRODUCTION

At last! Your final destination on the road to effective compensation is in sight. You have formulated your compensation strategy. You have designed the technical processes for converting this strategy into a compensation system. What remains is to put this system in place, along with the infrastructure necessary to operate the system. Once in place, the system needs to be evaluated to ensure that it is achieving the goals set out for it, and adapted to fit changing circumstances. The purpose of this final chapter is to deal with these issues.

The first section of this chapter will outline the fundamentals of compensation administration, including the key tasks that need to be carried out, and how they may be organized. Following that, the issues that need to be dealt with in preparing to implement a new compensation system will be identified and discussed. Without adequate preparation, the difficulties in effectively implementing a new compensation system are magnified dramatically.

Next, the main steps in the implementation process will be briefly outlined, followed by a discussion of how to evaluate the compensation system. Then, key circumstances that may create needs for change to the compensation system are briefly highlighted. The chapter concludes with a discussion of some of the issues in effectively adapting the compensation system.

COMPENSATION ADMINISTRATION

For the compensation system to work, somebody has to collect the necessary information, calculate gross earnings and deductions from earnings, prepare and distribute the paycheques, and remit the proper amounts to various governmental agencies. In firms that offer employee benefits, somebody must also keep track of who is entitled to what, and ensure that proper payouts are made. Employees need to be informed of any pay changes that affect them, and they need to have a reliable source of compensation information available to them, should they have questions or concerns. This process is called **compensation administration**.

compensation administration the process through which employee earnings are calculated and the appropriate remittances are forwarded to employees, governments, and other agencies

MECHANICS OF COMPENSATION ADMINISTRATION

There are four basic steps in compensation administration: (1) collecting the necessary information, (2) performing the calculations, (3) preparing and distributing the remittances, and (4) detecting and correcting errors and other problems.

COLLECT THE NECESSARY INFORMATION
Several types of information will be required. The compensation unit must be informed of hirings, terminations, promotions, and transfers. If pay is based on an hourly or daily rate, number of hours or days worked must be collected for each pay period. If pay is based on output produced or units sold, this information must be provided for each pay period. If merit raises or bonuses have been granted, payroll must be informed. If new jobs have been created or jobs

have been changed significantly, new pay rates must be established and applied. Where employees have options about their pay or benefits, their choices need to be ascertained.

PERFORM THE CALCULATIONS

Once all the information has been collected, gross earnings for each employee can be calculated, followed by the relevant deductions for income taxes, the Canada or Quebec Pension Plan, Employment Insurance, and contributory benefits, resulting in the net pay for each employee for that pay period. Following that, the employer's contribution to EI, CPP/QPP, health taxes, and workers' compensation needs to be calculated, as well as payments to private benefits providers, such as for life insurance.

PREPARE AND DISTRIBUTE THE REMITTANCES

Once the calculations have been done, the remittances need to be prepared and distributed to employees, governments, and benefits providers. Increasingly, with electronic funds transfer, cheques are not physically prepared, but the amounts are simply deposited directly into the bank accounts of recipients.

DETECT AND CORRECT ERRORS AND PROBLEMS

It is important for the compensation process to result in correct payments. A system for auditing the process and detecting errors needs to be built into the design of the overall compensation system.

COMPENSATION COMMUNICATION

There are two types of ongoing communication that are important. One type focuses on ensuring that all those who have a role to play in operating the compensation system understand their roles. The other type focuses on ensuring that all those who are subject to the compensation system understand it. Research has shown that employee satisfaction with their compensation is directly related to their understanding of the compensation system. For example, a recent study showed that 75 percent of employees with a "very good" understanding of their compensation system thought themselves fairly paid, compared with 33 percent of those with a "poor" understanding of the system (Tyson, 2001).

KEEPING MANAGERS INFORMED

An important aspect in compensation administration is to make sure that all those who play a role in operating the compensation system understand their role in the process. Some of these roles may seem obvious, such as reporting hours worked or employee absences, but new supervisors may not be made aware of these responsibilities. Somebody must keep track of overtime hours and report them, as well as changes in job status, including terminations and hirings. When merit pay or bonuses are used, supervisors must understand the criteria and procedures for awarding these. Of course, they must also understand the compensation system so as to be able to answer employee questions about pay accurately.

Managers and supervisors must also be made aware of less obvious pay issues. For example, they need to inform the compensation unit when job duties change significantly and the job needs to be reevaluated. They also need to be kept abreast of changes to the compensation system that affect them or their employees, and the reasons underlying these changes. And if the compensation system has been designed strategically, managers need to understand the intended linkages between the compensation system and organizational performance so that they can convey this to their employees.

KEEPING EMPLOYEES INFORMED

If compensation is going to serve its intended role in shaping employee attitudes and behaviour, it is fundamental that employees understand the compensation that applies to them, in terms of the types of compensation provided, the amount, and the procedures for determining the amount. Employees need to be informed of the compensation and benefits options available to them and may need guidance in selecting the options that are best for them. Employees may have questions about their pay and how it was calculated and must have some avenues to discuss their concerns about pay.

Certain types of information, such as an annual statement of pension contributions, need to be provided on a periodic basis. Also, if pay is based on certain performance indicators, as in the case of profit sharing or gain sharing, employees should be kept up-to-date on this information.

As employee benefit choices become more complex, and as pensions move from defined benefit plans to defined contribution plans, the need for employee communication and education has increased greatly, but most firms have been slow in responding to this need. For example, a recent study of firms using defined contribution pension plans found that most employees were lacking in the basic knowledge needed to make informed choices about the management of their pension funds (Brown, 2001a). While the extent to which employers can be held legally liable for poor pension choices by employees is unclear, it is in the best interests of the employer to make some effort to ensure that employees have the tools to make informed decisions in this very important matter. For many employees, their pension fund is their single largest financial asset.

USE OF INFORMATION TECHNOLOGY IN COMPENSATION ADMINISTRATION

Because of the large number of mechanical calculations that must be performed, payroll was one of the first functions to be computerized in most organizations. Currently, many firms have introduced integrated human resource information systems, in which compensation is just one part. (For an in-depth treatment of human resource information systems, including chapters on pay systems and benefits systems, see Rampton, Turnbull, and Doran, 1997.) Computers not only facilitate compensation administration, but can also transform certain compensation concepts—such as flexible benefit plans—from a good but impractical idea into a viable practice.

For most organizations, the question is not whether to use computers in compensation administration, but how far to extend their use. Possible uses include job documentation and evaluation, analysis of compensation survey data, communication, information collection, calculation of pay and remittances, record keeping, and compensation planning and research.

JOB DOCUMENTATION AND EVALUATION

Computers are very useful for data collection for job analysis purposes, particularly when a questionnaire approach is used (as discussed in Chapter 9). Computers can also play a role in developing factor weightings for job evaluation systems, as well as performing the routine calculations needed in the job evaluation process and computing market lines and pay policy lines (Winter, 2000).

ANALYZING LABOUR MARKET DATA

As was discussed in Chapter 10, analysis of labour market and survey data is greatly facilitated by computers. Furthermore, a considerable amount of labour market data can be downloaded directly from a variety of governmental and other sources. Systems can be developed to store job matches from various surveys and then generate various "market rates" based on a number of different variables and assumptions.

COMMUNICATION

Computers are being increasingly used to communicate compensation policies and information. For example, Telus claims to have cut human resources administrative overhead dramatically through use of an "intranet"—an internal communications network whereby employees can access compensation information via computer. Box 12.1 describes how Telus uses computers to provide the information base to facilitate compensation decision making.

INFORMATION COLLECTION

On-line computer systems can be used to capture a wide variety of compensation information. Departments can use direct entry for transactions such as new hires, terminations, and pay rate changes, as well as information such as hours worked, days absent, and the like. Appraisal and performance management systems, such as 360-degree feedback, can be greatly facilitated with the use of an on-line system for data collection, compilation, and analysis (Shetzer, 2000).

The computer can also be used to collect employee choices about aspects of pay, especially benefits choices. Not only can the computer guide employees through the process of benefits selection, it can also serve as a tool to help them make choices most consistent with their own needs. Chapter 7 provided an illustration of how computerized decision aids allowed employees to make better decisions in regard to flexible benefits.

CALCULATING PAY AND REMITTANCES

Once properly programmed, computers excel at performing routine computations, such as calculating gross and net earnings, and calculating remittances to governmental agencies. Many "off-the-shelf" computer packages are available for such purposes.

RECORD KEEPING

Accurate compensation records are essential for a wide variety of purposes. These include internal control and financial reporting, and external reporting, such as for income tax or pension purposes.

COMPENSATION PLANNING AND RESEARCH

Computers can be used to make projections of future compensation costs, utilizing a variety of assumptions, and to prepare compensation budgets (Ilsemann and Simms, 2000). They can be used to analyze current pay structures or the distribution of merit money across departments. They can also be utlized for productivity analyses of various types, or to compare absenteeism or turnover rates across departments or across employee groups. They are also helpful for conducting on-line surveys of employee attitudes.

Privacy and Legal Issues

On-line computer systems have the potential to dramatically reduce the amount of paperwork in compensation administration. However, in the past, "privacy concerns and legal restrictions on the use of electronic documents, including electronic signatures, have limited employers' ability to introduce electronic alternatives for payroll purposes" (McEwen, 2001: 16). To deal with the protection of employee privacy in the face of electronic access to employee data, in 2000 the federal government passed Bill C-6, the Personal Information Protection and Electronic Documents Act. As of January 1, 2002, this legislation requires that no "personal health information" (such as employee medical or dental claims) can be released to anybody (including third-party benefits providers) without informed employee consent. This means that Web-based benefits systems must be careful to limit access to employee records to only a few authorized persons. For example, an employee's supervisor cannot be allowed access to detailed information about the employee's health claims.

Another issue is the legality of electronic forms. For example, Ontario employment standards legislation has required that individualized employee pay statements be provided to each employee every pay period in paper format. However, with the passage of Bill 88 (the Electronic Commerce Act) by the Ontario legislature in 2000, employers are now allowed to provide electronic pay statements. However, there are still some restrictions. For example, simply making the statements available on a Web site does not comply with the law; the statements must be personally sent to each employee (i.e., through electronic mail) and the employee must be able to keep (i.e., print) a copy of the statement. While the Ontario legislation now allows electronic employee "signatures" to authorize deductions from pay, federal legislation, as of 2001, had yet to change, so paper-based forms must still be used for this authorization.

Organization of Compensation Administration

A major issue confronting employers is whether to perform all aspects of compensation administration in-house or to contract some or all of it to an outside agency, which is becoming increasingly common (Murray, 1997). In deciding whether to outsource compensation administration, organizations often distinguish between direct pay (payroll) and indirect pay (benefits). Depending on the nature and extent of employee benefits offered, benefits administration can be a very complex process, and most organizations outsource at least some aspects of their benefits administration, often to the product provider, such as an insurance company. Although processing of payroll is usually more straightforward than benefits administration, many companies also outsource this work, and there are several large companies—such as Ceridian or ADP— as well as numerous smaller companies that specialize in this type of service.

Until recently, there have been few, if any, providers able to supply the full range of compensation administration services. However, this changed in 2001, when the Canadian Imperial Bank of Commerce outsourced nearly half of its human resources department, including payroll and benefits administration, to EDS Corporation. In the process, some 200 of the bank's HR employees were moved to EDS. According to bank officials, the prime motive for the move was not to save money but to free the bank's HR department from the detailed administrative work that could be done better by a specialized service provider (Brown, 2001b).

ADVANTAGES OF OUTSOURCING

There may be several advantages to outsourcing payroll administration, benefits administration, or both. The first is cost. Outside providers will generally have economies of scale that most employers could not realize. For example, the costs of computerized benefits systems are very large, but an outside provider can spread these costs across numerous customers. Outside providers also achieve economies in terms of training, as their staff can specialize in compensation administration on a full-time basis, thus also reducing costs. For example, one major Canadian service provider quotes a price of $12 per payroll run, plus $1.25 per paycheque, for firms with fewer than 30 people, a rate that declines as the number of paycheques processed increases.

A second advantage is expertise. Outside providers may be in a position to employ specialized legal and professional experts that a single employer, especially a small or medium-sized one, simply could not afford. Third, and perhaps most important, when freed of the responsibility for day-to-day administration of the compensation system, compensation managers are able to spend more time on the strategic aspects of pay rather than on simply keeping the system running (Hackett, 1995).

However, one recent development that may change the cost dynamics of the outsourcing decision is the emergence of "application service providers" (ASPs). These firms specialize in providing access to specialized business systems software over the Internet, eliminating the need for a firm to purchase and maintain its own applications software (Dobbs, 2001). For example, by paying a monthly fee, firms can receive access to specialized payroll and benefits software, thus eliminating one reason to outsource compensation administration.

DISADVANTAGES OF OUTSOURCING

One concern about outsourcing benefits administration is that the employer may lose touch with emerging problems and issues, or even lose the capacity to understand its own benefit system. The firm may become over-reliant on advice from the service provider, who may not understand the organizational context, especially if changes to managerial strategy are taking place. Moreover, service providers may not be concerned with evaluating the mix of benefits and looking for the most efficient mix to serve the particular compensation objectives of a given employer.

Managing the relationship with the vendor can be a time-consuming and difficult process. If service contracts fail to specify all the details of who is responsible for what, within what time frame, and with what recourse if performance failures occur, then disagreements may materialize that take time and energy to resolve. For example, if paycheques are late, who covers the cost to employees of bounced cheques, late payments, and the like?

One potential drawback to outsourcing is the impact on employee morale if it is necessary to lay off employees when their functions are contracted out. This is not much of an issue for classical firms, but for human relations and high-involvement firms it is a serious consideration. Costs of severance and outplacement counselling also need to be considered. Although the Canadian Imperial Bank of Commerce avoided this problem by transferring its in-house employees to the service provider, this option will not be available to all firms.

So when should outsourcing be considered? Four factors are probably key considerations: company size; internal capabilities; complexity and dynamism of the compensation system; and the strategic importance of compensation. Research has shown that many large firms believe that they can handle payroll and benefits more efficiently in-house because they can achieve economies of scale not available to smaller firms (Harrison, 1996). Related to this, internal capabilities are another consideration. If the firm is already using a sophisticated human resources information system, and if computer systems and support are already in place, it may make little sense to separate payroll and benefits from the system by outsourcing them.

The more complex, unique, and dynamic the compensation system is, the more preferable it will be to develop the expertise for running it in-house, since an outside provider may be reluctant to devote specialized resources to an individual customer, which reduces the provider's economies of scale and drives up costs. Dynamic systems also interfere with the provider's economies of scale if frequent changes need to be made, so this will either drive up costs or cause provider resistance to system changes, thus increasing the rigidity of the compensation system.

Finally, another consideration is the strategic importance of the services. The greater the extent to which compensation is regarded as a strategic variable, the more important it is to keep in-house control of the compensation system. However, as discussed earlier, some firms believe that the strategic focus of the compensation function is enhanced when routine administrative functions are outsourced. The proper balance probably differs for each firm.

PREPARING FOR IMPLEMENTATION

Even after the compensation strategy has been established and the technical processes determined, there is still much to be done before the new compensation system can be implemented. These tasks include identifying and dealing with remaining administrative details, assigning responsibilities and planning the infrastructure, documenting the system, developing a training and communications plan, developing the compensation budget, developing an evaluation plan, and developing the implementation plan itself.

Deciding the Administrative Details

Although the compensation strategy and main technical processes may have been decided, there are typically many other administrative details that must be identified and dealt with. Most of these are very mundane, sometimes so mundane that they are forgotten altogether, only to rear their heads during implementation. For example, how often will employees be paid? Weekly, biweekly, monthly? Will cheques be distributed at work or mailed to employees' homes? Will direct deposit be available?

If performance pay is used, how will the performance criteria be measured, how often, and by whom? When will performance appraisals take place, and when will pay raises take effect? If a profit-sharing committee is established, who will serve on it and how will they be selected?

If indirect pay is used, how and by whom will each of the employee benefits be provided? Will insurance claims be submitted through the employer, or directly to the service provider? If an employee assistance program is available, which agencies are to be used? If company cars are to be provided, what will be the models and options, and will they be bought or leased? If a daycare facility is to be established at the workplace, where will it be located? Who will staff it?

Assigning Responsibilities and Planning the Infrastructure

Once all of the tasks and procedures for operating the compensation system have been identified, the specific responsibilities for performing these tasks need to be assigned, and the infrastructure to support the system needs to be planned. Who exactly is responsible for inputting employee transactions? Who develops the forms for recording these transactions and the computer systems for performing the pay calculations? Who prepares the cheques: a payroll section in the human resources department? the accounting department? an outside provider?

Documenting the Compensation System

If the compensation system is to be uniformly applied, it must be documented. Two aspects are particularly important. First, the compensation system itself. If job evaluation is to be used, manuals must be prepared describing the specific procedures to be used. If pay for knowledge is used, the procedures for assessing skill levels and competencies must be documented. Benefits must be described, along with application procedures, limits, and the like.

Second, assigned responsibilities for carrying out the various compensation processes need to be documented, spelling out which departments are responsible for which tasks. Contracts with service providers need to be negotiated and drawn up. The contract needs to describe the services to be provided, including minimum performance standards and penalties for failure to meet them, as well as the employer responsibilities. Beyond addressing foreseeable tasks, the contract also needs to be flexible enough to deal with unknown future events. Quite a challenge for any document!

DEVELOPING A TRAINING AND COMMUNICATIONS PLAN

A key issue in preparing for implementation is development of a training plan. First, key support people in the human resources department must fully understand the system and its components. They can then serve as trainers and advisers for the rest of the organization. Second, there must be sufficient training for supervisors, who will play a key role in many aspects of the system, from job description, to job evaluation, to performance appraisal, to approving salary increases. The third step is the training for all others who have a role in operating the systems, ranging from secretaries (who must submit departmental time cards) to recruiters (so that they will be able to explain the compensation system accurately to potential new employees).

In conjunction with this process, a plan should be developed for communicating the new system to all organizational members who are affected by it. As was discussed earlier, a pay system will have the desired impact on attitudes and behaviour only if it is understood (although it could have a negative impact on attitudes and behaviour if it is misunderstood). Not only should the new system be communicated, but so should the underlying rationale and need for the new system. Employees are always sensitive about pay; a lack of understanding of the motives underlying the new system may cause suspicion, mistrust, and even resistance to the new system. Preventing this suspicion and mistrust is one reason why many experts recommend employee participation in compensation system development. Another advantage of so doing is that communicating the final system will be easier, since employees have been kept informed as it was being developed.

In the development of the communications plan, the media and process for communications need to be carefully thought out, along with the timing. In some cases, the communications process starts with a presentation by the chief executive officer on the general features of the new system, the motives for introduction, and its objectives. This may be followed by small group meetings conducted by supervisors (once they have been trained in the new system) or by personnel from the human resources department. If the new system is complex, separate meetings may be planned for different aspects of the new system, with one meeting for direct pay and another for indirect pay, for example.

Informational brochures typically need to be developed for each plan aspect. A telephone "hot line" for questions or a computer Web site may be set up. In some cases videotapes are prepared for use by new employees or those who missed the informational meetings.

If individual performance pay is used, performance expectations also need to be communicated. If performance pay linked to departmental or organizational indicators or objectives is to be used, then an essential part of communications is not only to communicate what the indicators are, but to provide status reports on these indicators. Indeed, in some manufacturing plants "electronic scoreboards" provide up-to-the-minute updates on achievement of organizational goals (Belli, 1991). At Saskatoon-based Cameco Corporation, one of the world's largest producers of uranium, charts showing progress toward meeting divisional and corporate incentive goals are posted at every work unit and are updated throughout the year.

Finally, aside from information about the compensation system itself, one aspect of communications to consider is how to communicate the reasons or the motives for changing the compensation system. Any change, no matter what it is, will be accepted more readily if people understand the need for the change. Not communicating the motives for the change is guaranteed to engender suspicion and mistrust of the changes, especially when the change concerns something that is so central for all employees—their compensation.

Budgeting for Compensation

A compensation budget for the coming year is usually an essential part of the planning process for most organizations. Such a budget can also serve as a way to control compensation costs (for example, if departments need authorization to exceed their budgeted allocation) and as one benchmark against which to evaluate whether the compensation system is behaving as expected when it was formulated.

Traditionally, compensation budgeting has been done in one of two ways—either top-down or bottom-up. Under the bottom-up approach, the compensation rates are applied to specific employees, probable merit and seniority increases are factored in, turnover is factored in (turnover reduces compensation costs because new employees usually start at a lower rate than those who are retiring or quitting), and the compensation budget is based on that. Under the top-down approach to compensation budgeting, management sets a limit on the total amount of compensation available for the coming year (usually based on some upward adjustment to the previous year's compensation bill), and then the available funds are divided among departments and units, who then divide it among their employees.

The approach advocated in this book is a top-down approach for the formulation of *compensation strategy*, to ensure that the compensation strategy dovetails with other key strategic aspects of the organization, but a bottom-up approach to *compensation budgeting*. A top-down approach to budgeting, where an arbitrary amount is allocated to compensation, undermines the whole notion of strategic pay. The main advantage of top-down budgeting is simplicity, but with new computer-based human resource information systems, this advantage disappears (Ilsemann and Simms, 2000).

DEVELOPING THE EVALUATION PLAN

Prior to implementation, there needs to be some plan for evaluating the success of the compensation system, along with some system for monitoring conditions that may warrant changes to the compensation system. Evaluation criteria need to be set out, as well as procedures for collecting the evaluation information. Depending on the criteria used, it may be necessary to collect some evaluation information (such as employee attitudes) prior to implementation, to serve as a benchmark for evaluating consequences of the new system. Normally, these evaluation criteria will be based on the strategic objectives for the compensation system. Each of these two crucial issues—developing evaluation criteria and monitoring organizational circumstances—will be discussed in more depth later in the chapter.

DEVELOPING THE IMPLEMENTATION PLAN

Of course, somebody or some group needs to be given responsibility for spearheading the implementation process. Depending on the magnitude and scope of the changes, it may be appropriate to have several committees or task forces, each responsible for a given aspect of the new compensation system, operating under the supervision of an umbrella group. For example, there may be one implementation task force for base pay, another for performance pay, and a third for indirect pay. There may even be separate task forces for individual programs, such as profit sharing. If the compensation plan is different for different employee groups, there may be a separate task force for each group.

The composition of these task forces is an important matter. Normally, the umbrella group will be chaired by a senior executive, such as the head of human resources, and may even include the CEO if the changes are of sufficient magnitude. This body could conceivably be the same body that developed the new compensation system. Whether or not it includes employee representatives is a reflection of the managerial strategy pursued by the organization, and inclusion of a broad spectrum of employees would certainly be expected for high-involvement organizations, particularly on the subsidiary committees or task forces.

The timing and schedule for implementation are a crucial matter. When will the system kick in? How long will it take to carry out the various steps in the implementation process? And are there other things that need to be done first or in conjunction with the new compensation system?

For example, performance pay will be effective only if employees have control over performance. For this, decentralization of decision making may be necessary. But decentralizing decision making will be irresponsible unless employees have the information to make effective decisions and the training to interpret and utilize that information. When will this training be done? When will the information systems be revamped? All of these considerations need to be taken into account when the implementation schedule is being drawn up. Of course, the greater the number of changes, the more complex all this will be, but, if you get it right, the larger the payoff will be.

One question in regard to timing is this: If extensive changes are being made, should they be phased in? In theory, no. There is an old saying: "You can't leap a chasm in two jumps." To function effectively, all complementary parts of the organizational system need to be in place at the same time. But the reality is that it simply may not be feasible to make all the needed changes at the same time. Of course, this is exactly why many compensation changes fail to produce the intended results.

However, as long as everyone understands that all the pieces are coming, then phasing in these changes may not be a problem. For example, if jobs are changed to make them more challenging and interesting, the intrinsic motivation from this alone may be enough to keep employees motivated, at least for a while. But if employees do become more productive and contribute more to the organization, this enthusiasm will likely fade if they do not perceive that this contribution is valued by the organization sufficiently to be recognized financially. Conversely, if performance pay is introduced, changes to the job structure to allow employees more control over their own performance cannot lag too far behind.

If the organization is very large and is divided into plants or business units, it may be possible to implement the new system in one of these units, in order to assess the consequences and to identify any adjustments that need to be made.

IMPLEMENTING THE COMPENSATION SYSTEM

Compared with the preparation, actual implementation of the new compensation system is relatively straightforward. The implementation task forces need to be staffed, and the administrative infrastructure put in place and tested. Training of key actors in the system needs to be conducted, and the system must be communicated. Finally, the new system needs to be launched, and the wrinkles smoothed out.

STEP 1: ESTABLISH THE IMPLEMENTATION TASK FORCES

The first step in starting the implementation process is to appoint individuals to the implementation bodies and to provide the technical and administrative support for those bodies. Task force members need to fully understand the new compensation system as well as the key issues and steps in the implementation process.

STEP 2: PUT THE INFRASTRUCTURE IN PLACE

Next, the infrastructure must be put in place. Employees need to be hired or reassigned. Facilities need to be provided. The computer system has to be developed and tested. Additional hardware may need to be purchased. Human resources personnel must be trained in the system. The forms, brochures, and communications material should be developed. Trainers need to be selected and trained.

Any necessary preimplementation evaluation material needs to be collected. For example, it is often useful to conduct surveys of key employee attitudes before system implementation in order to have a baseline for future comparisons. This should ideally be done as early in the process as possible, since information about the new system may affect these preexisting attitudes.

STEP 3: TEST THE SYSTEM

It is crucial that the compensation system be tested before implementation. One approach is to run a simulation of how it would function. Employees would be put on the system, the data would be collected and input into the system, pay would be calculated, and so on—*before* the previous system is abandoned. This allows time for identifying flaws and bugs in the system, double-checking the accuracy of the calculations, and so on.

STEP 4: CONDUCT THE TRAINING

Once the infrastructure is in place and debugged, it is time to train all those outside the HR department who will play a role in the new system. This normally includes managers, supervisors, and other personnel who play an administrative role in the process. Training sessions have to be scheduled, trainees informed, and the training conducted.

STEP 5: COMMUNICATE THE SYSTEM

The communications program that has been developed should now be activated. But simply making sure that everyone has sat through the video from the company president and has received the plan brochures doesn't guarantee that communication has taken place. Communication does not actually occur until *understanding* passes from the sender to the receiver. It is important that there be some kind of feedback as a check on whether the key elements of the message are actually being understood. Two-way communication greatly enhances the likelihood of understanding.

Step 6: Launch and Adjust the System

After all of this preparation, the actual launch of the system may seem anticlimactic. However, it is likely that the first "cycle" of the new compensation system will be an extremely hectic one, with many unanticipated problems and issues arising. No matter how careful the preparation, some things will not work the way they were planned. A variety of adjustments will need to made just to keep the system running. Some of these will be short-term fixes, which will then be incorporated into the system on a permanent basis. For example, it may be discovered that the computer system does not correctly calculate the holiday pay of permanent part-time employees who are on medical leave. So this adjustment will be calculated by hand until the computer system is adapted accordingly.

Evaluating the Compensation System

Evaluating the effectiveness of the compensation system is no easy matter. It is no coincidence that this aspect is probably the most poorly done of any in the compensation process. This is true for two main reasons. The first is that separating out the precise impact of compensation on organizational performance, and doing so with any degree of certainty, is virtually impossible. There are just too many factors that affect overall organizational performance. The second reason is that most organizations don't even try to evaluate their compensation system, either because they don't know how, or because they consider it a futile effort.

But if the right information is collected, useful inferences about the effectiveness of the compensation system can be drawn, even if the exact role of compensation in organizational success is impossible to specify. However, this will take a considerable effort, using multiple indicators, and a slipshod attempt at evaluation may do more harm than good. It is only by using a comprehensive set of relevant indicators that useful conclusions can be drawn.

The first part of this section discusses how to assess the impact of the compensation system on various aspects of organizational performance. The remainder of the section identifies a variety of specific indicators that can be used to assess the compensation system, including organizational performance indicators, behavioural indicators, and attitudinal indicators.

Evaluating the Impact of the Compensation System

What is the best design for evaluating the compensation system? In general, whenever examining the impact of any type of organizational change, the best design is what is known as a "pre-test/post-test control group" design. What this means is that scores on important indicators are measured before and after implementation of the new system in a given organizational unit. These indicators are also measured at the same points in time in a comparable unit in which the new compensation system has not been applied. The reason for having this "control group" is to make sure that any changes that occurred in the "experimental group" were really due to the new compensation system, and not due to other changes that took place in the organization.

Of course, actually using this design in real-life organizations is very difficult. Many organizations do not have units that are comparable but independent of each other to use as control groups. And even if they do, they may not wish to exclude these groups from the new compensation system. (In fact, if the unit knows that it has been excluded from the new compensation system, this knowledge alone may actually change behaviour in the unit, diminishing its value as a control group.) Some organizations try to get around this problem by using other organizations as a type of control group, if the relevant data can be obtained from them.

Another problem with using this design is that, for the results to be valid, only the compensation system, and nothing else, should change during the evaluation period. Of course, for most organizations, the reality is that many things are changing all the time. The greater the extent of other changes, the less likely it is that any increases or decreases in performance can be attributed to the compensation system.

One issue is timing of evaluation. Normally, the logical time for the first evaluation is after one year, because one complete cycle will have been carried out. But is one year a long enough period to determine whether the desired consequences of the new compensation system will materialize? The answer depends on the magnitude of the changes being made and the types of consequences that are desired. Certain indicators, such as employee attitudes, may change fairly quickly, while other indicators, such as organizational performance, will change much more slowly. In fact, a phenomenon known as the **initial dip** often takes place; this is a tendency for performance to actually decline during the initial stages of any change, until people start to understand and become proficient in the new system. In addition, costs of changes are usually immediate, while benefits are gradual. For example, a change in compensation strategy to lead the market will increase costs immediately, but will only increase productivity gradually, as the turnover rate declines, and as the firm is able to attract a higher calibre of employee.

initial dip a tendency for performance to decline during the initial stages of any change

On the other hand, some changes—such as slashing pay rates—may bring immediate gain, but long-term pain, as the company's best performers gradually slip away. But the key point is that it may take several years to really understand the impact of major changes to the compensation system, and thus evaluation should be carried out on a continuing basis.

When examining the impact of the compensation system on organizational performance, there are three main aspects to look at: the impact on compensation costs, the impact on compensation objectives, and the impact on other organizational performance indicators.

Impact on Compensation Costs

One way of examining the impact of the new system on compensation costs is to compare actual compensation costs with budgeted costs. So you do that, and discover that actual compensation expenditures are much lower than budgeted. Great news, right? Not necessarily. It turns out that senior employees hate the new system and are quitting in droves, only to be replaced by new employees who are much less qualified—and paid much less. This may make compensation costs look good but will probably have adverse consequences in terms of training costs and employee performance, which may well outweigh the compensation savings over the longer run.

Now, let's suppose the opposite has occurred, and total compensation expenditures are considerably *higher* than budgeted. This can only be bad news, right? Maybe not. Perhaps the system is doing even better than expected in retaining experienced employees, and the turnover rate is down, resulting in fewer savings from replacing senior employees with junior employees.

Another way of looking at compensation expenditures is average earnings per employee, which standardizes for any change in the number of employees. What if average earnings per employee are way higher than projected? In fact, this may be wonderful news, if these higher earnings are primarily a result of a gain-sharing plan. Since cost savings are split between the employer and employee in a gain-sharing plan, the more employees earn from it, the greater the savings to the company.

On the other hand, higher-than-budgeted compensation expenditures could also mean a number of less pleasant things. Perhaps the job evaluation system has been overly generous in rating jobs. Perhaps supervisors are granting merit increases too readily. Perhaps the performance thresholds for individual bonus plans have been set too low. Perhaps one of the employee benefits is costing much more than expected. Of course, still another possibility is that the budgeted compensation figures were not realistic in the first place.

In medium to large organizations, it may make sense to examine compensation expenditures on a unit-by-unit basis. If one or two departments stand out from the others, this may warrant investigation. Perhaps these discrepancies are justified, but this may also indicate inconsistency in the application of the new system. Other ways to assess compensation costs are to compare them with compensation expenditures in previous years, or with those of competitors.

But it should be emphasized again that unless the goal of the new system was to reduce compensation costs, compensation costs alone do not portray the whole picture. What is important is what the organization is receiving in return for its investment in compensation. So any evaluation that starts and ends with compensation costs may be worse than useless. Instead, the total impact of the system, including the impact on compensation objectives, must be assessed.

Impact on Compensation Objectives

During the formulation of the compensation strategy, objectives for the compensation system were set out. In the preimplementation phase specific indicators were identified, and procedures were set up to collect the necessary data. At this point, progress in meeting these objectives can be assessed. If they have been achieved only partially, this certainly triggers a need for careful examination of the compensation system to determine whether progress in meeting these objectives is sufficient to justify continuation of the new system, whether it should be modified, or whether it should be replaced. Of course, the objectives themselves should also be reexamined to determine whether they are realistic.

IMPACT ON OTHER INDICATORS

Let's suppose that our compensation objectives have been fully achieved. We should pat ourselves on the back, right? Not necessarily. We still need to examine whether there have been any unintended negative consequences. The following examples illustrate actual cases where compensation objectives were achieved but the net impact of the new compensation system on company performance was actually negative (Roberts, 1994).

A retailer wanted store managers to improve their sales margins by introducing higher-value products, so the firm paid a bonus to managers based on the margin level obtained. Margins did increase to the desired levels. However, at the same time, overall sales volumes and market share dropped. Closer examination revealed that most store managers had raised their margins simply by increasing prices, rather than by introducing new products.

A consumer electronics firm wished to reduce production costs of new products more rapidly after their introduction. (Whenever a new product is introduced, it is usual for production costs to decrease over time.) The firm instituted bonuses to managers based on how quickly after product launch cost reductions were achieved. The objective was achieved: reduction in production costs occurred much more rapidly after the bonus system was put in place. However, it was eventually discovered that managers achieved this cost reduction by delaying product launch until they could work out ways of reducing production costs that could be quickly implemented after product launch. This process slowed the introduction of new products and translated into losses in sales and market share.

ORGANIZATIONAL PERFORMANCE INDICATORS

The following are some examples of the indicators that can be used in measuring the impact of the compensation system on the organization as a whole.

COMPENSATION COST INDICATORS

There are two main indicators of compensation costs: compensation cost ratios and average earnings per employee. **Compensation cost ratios** are determined by taking total compensation costs as a percentage of total costs, or as a percentage of revenues. **Average employee earnings** takes total compensation and divides it by the number of full-time equivalent employees it covers. These two measures are not synonymous and tell us different things.

compensation cost ratio the ratio of total compensation costs to total costs or to revenues

average employee earnings total compensation divided by the number of full-time equivalent employees

For example, it is possible for average employee earnings to go up but for compensation cost ratio to go down. It is also possible for average employee earnings to go down but compensation cost ratio to go up. Finally, it is also possible for both average earnings and compensation cost ratio to go up and for profits to go up at the same time. How can this be?

Average employee earnings takes the perspective of the individual employee. If it goes up, then the typical employee is earning more money; if it goes down, the typical employee is earning less money. Compensation cost ratio takes the total of all compensation paid to all employees. It may increase for one of three reasons: if average employee earnings increase, if total number of employees increases, or if total costs or revenues decrease. Thus, it is possible for average earnings to increase but compensation cost ratio to decrease, if fewer employees are required to perform the work of the organization.

Compensation cost ratio may also increase, even without any increase in total compensation or average earnings, if total costs or revenues go down. If the increase in compensation cost ratio is due to lower noncompensation costs, then the increase in compensation cost ratio is not necessarily bad news at all. However, if the increase in compensation cost ratio is due to declining revenues, this is bad news. Conversely, a decrease in compensation cost ratio is not good news if it is due to increases in noncompensation costs, but is good news if it is due to increases in revenues. In the latter case, the decreased compensation cost ratio is a sign of greater productivity.

Thus, what happens to earnings and total compensation costs is just part of the picture. Also important is what happens to employee performance and productivity. Employee performance may be instrumental in reducing noncompensation costs or in increasing revenue. Higher average earnings may increase the retention rate, thus reducing recruiting and training costs.

Financial Indicators

A variety of specific financial indicators that assess overall organizational performance can also be used. These can include profitability, return on equity, revenue growth, and total costs. Gross margins and sales margins can be computed. These can be analyzed by examining them for changes over time, or by comparing them with industrial averages or those of competitors.

Other Indicators

Other types of organizational performance indicators can be used, depending on the nature of the organization. In business organizations, market share is often considered a key indicator. Some firms may consider the number of new product introductions a key indicator; steel mills may use tons of product shipped; airlines may use average percentage of seats filled; hospitals may use average death rate in surgery; universities may use number of awards won by faculty or number of research dollars generated.

BEHAVIOURAL INDICATORS

A variety of indicators can be used to assess employee behaviour. As has been discussed throughout this book, there are three kinds of behaviours that organizations may want their compensation system to foster: membership, task, and citizenship.

MEMBERSHIP BEHAVIOUR

Three key aspects of membership behaviour are attraction, retention, and attendance. Various indicators can measure how effective the organization is at attracting new members. One indicator is simply the number of qualified applicants that job postings are attracting. Another is the percentage of offers made to potential new employees that are refused.

The main indicator of retention is employee turnover. However, some types of turnover are more serious than others. For example, is turnover spread across employees performing at different performance levels, or is it mainly high-performing employees who are quitting? Is turnover concentrated in certain departments or units? Reasons for turnover are also important. Some people quit because their spouse has been transferred to another province, and some people quit because they have received a better offer from another employer. It is important to know which of these is the reason for the turnover. Many organizations use exit interviews in an attempt to ascertain why employees are quitting the organization.

Another indicator of membership behaviour is absenteeism. Absenteeism can be measured in a variety of ways. One method is to simply tally up all the days missed by employees for any reason and divide by the number of employees. However, it should be noted that some absenteeism is unavoidable, due to reasons such as illness. Therefore, many experts argue that involuntary absenteeism should be excluded from the calculations. But while it might be theoretically correct to do this, actually doing so may be quite difficult. An alternative is to add up the number of occurrences and divide by the number of employees, thus yielding a statistic that is less likely to be skewed by long absences due to serious illnesses.

TASK BEHAVIOUR

Employee performance has at least two dimensions: quantity and quality of work produced. The productivity level of employees in different organizations can be measured in a variety of ways. For example, units produced or number of clients served can be divided by the number of employees, and compared over time or with competitors. Another measure is revenue divided by number of employees. Quality of performance can be measured by indicators such as customer feedback, number of errors made, or scrap losses.

CITIZENSHIP BEHAVIOUR

Citizenship behaviour is the most difficult of the three key behaviours to measure in a quantitative way. One indicator might be the number of useful employee suggestions that are submitted. Indicators such as "shrinkage"—employee theft—would be expected to decline if citizenship increased. Other departments or customers can be surveyed to determine the degree of cooperativeness and citizenship practised by members of a given department. Feedback from customers about employees who go above and beyond the call of duty can be gathered.

ATTITUDINAL INDICATORS

Because attitudes condition behaviour, assessment of employee attitudes can play a major role in the evaluation process. For the purposes of compensation, there are two main sets of attitudes that are important: job attitudes and compensation attitudes.

JOB ATTITUDES

Throughout the book, three key job attitudes have been discussed: employee job satisfaction, work motivation, and organizational identification. Over the years, numerous survey scales that measure these attitudes have been developed. Many firms conduct employee attitude surveys on an annual basis to assess the level of these attitudes. According to the Compensation Practices Survey, about half (48 percent) of Canadian firms conduct regular employee attitude surveys.

COMPENSATION ATTITUDES

Employee attitudes toward the compensation system can also be surveyed. Several types of attitudes are important. One of these is satisfaction with the total amount of compensation being received (distributive justice). Another is satisfaction with the process by which compensation is determined (procedural justice). Both of these reflect the perceived fairness or equity of the system, as was discussed in Chapter 3.

It is also possible to examine attitudes for individual components of compensation. For example, are employees satisfied with the amount and fairness of merit pay or the profit-sharing system? Many organizations have a section on their internal compensation surveys dealing with employee benefits. Which benefits are employees most satisfied with? Least satisfied? Is the amount of the benefit satisfactory? Are benefits fairly allocated? Would employees prefer that certain benefits that are not being offered replace other benefits that are being offered?

Another important aspect to examine is employee understanding of the compensation system. Misunderstandings can cause dissatisfaction and complaints about the system. Perhaps even more important, a system that is misunderstood will not have the desired effect on employee attitudes and behaviour, even if it is designed properly. Thus, a company may add a new benefit, expecting this to improve employee compensation satisfaction and therefore employee retention, but if it is poorly communicated, employees may not even be aware of the new benefit.

Aside from the use of surveys, compensation attitudes can also be inferred from certain behaviours. The number of employee calls to the compensation office may provide an index of understanding. The number of complaints and grievances that pertain to compensation can be tallied and examined. If there is a formal appeals process for compensation, the number of appeals initiated and the number granted can also be examined.

MONITORING CHANGING CIRCUMSTANCES

"Compensation systems don't suddenly break, instead they gradually become obsolete" (Britton and Ellis, 1994: 44). In some cases, this obsolescence is so gradual that nobody notices that the compensation system is no longer adding value to the organization. In order to prevent this and ensure that the compensation system continues to add maximum value to the organization, it is necessary to be alert to changing circumstances that may signal a need for change to the system. These changing circumstances may be either external or internal to the organization.

CHANGES IN EXTERNAL CIRCUMSTANCES

External circumstances that may trigger a need for changes in the compensation system include legislative and tax changes, labour market changes, changes in competitive conditions, and socioeconomic changes.

LEGISLATIVE AND TAX CHANGES
As has been seen in earlier chapters, there are many pieces of provincial and federal legislation that have an impact on the compensation system, and this legislation changes quite frequently, due to revisions made by legislators or court decisions. Examples include employment standards legislation, human rights legislation, and pay equity legislation. At the beginning of each year, there are usually changes in regard to RRSP limits, Canada/Quebec Pension Plan payments, Employment Insurance payments, and income tax and/or corporate tax provisions. Any of these changes may have implications for the compensation system.

LABOUR MARKET CHANGES
As the demand and supply of particular categories of workers changes, it may become more or less difficult to attract and retain employees. The compensation system may need to change in response to this situation.

COMPETITIVE ENVIRONMENT CHANGES

Changes in the policies practised by competitors or the emergence of new competitors may have significant implications for compensation policies, either directly or indirectly. An example of a direct implication occurs when a competitor adds a very attractive new benefit to its compensation package, and it becomes difficult to attract employees without offering a similar benefit. An example of an indirect implication occurs when the entrance of new competitors forces existing firms to adopt a new managerial strategy.

SOCIOECONOMIC CHANGES

Changes in either social attitudes or general economic conditions may also trigger a need for changes to the compensation system. For example, if economic conditions become more buoyant, there may need to be a focus on other types of rewards, such as advancement opportunities or intrinsic rewards. If social attitudes toward a particular industry become less favourable, it may be necessary to boost pay levels.

Demographic changes may also be important. For example, an aging workforce will likely trigger a much greater focus on pension plans and health benefits than would occur when the workforce was younger. Foot and Venne (1990) point out that the baby boom generation (born from 1947 to 1966) has created a major blockage to career advancement in organizations, as the top end of hierarchies simply cannot accommodate so many people. This blockage will last until at least 2012, when the first of the boomers will finally start to reach retirement age.

spiral career paths
career advancement marked by a combination of sideways and vertical progression

In the meantime, they suggest, **spiral career paths** will become much more important, with most employees taking at least two sideways steps for each step up the hierarchy. This creates more pressure for reward systems that focus on competencies and pay for knowledge. Employees will also focus more on training and education opportunities as valued rewards, and organizations that offer these rewards will be much more attractive to employees than those that do not.

CHANGES IN INTERNAL CIRCUMSTANCES

Internal changes that can trigger a need to change the compensation system include changes in managerial strategy, in the workforce, in the organization's financial condition, and in the scope of the organization.

CHANGES IN MANAGERIAL STRATEGY

Whenever there is a change in the fundamental managerial strategy of the organization, there is a need for changes to the compensation strategy to support these changes. As has been discussed throughout the book, there are a number of factors that may drive changes to managerial strategy, including changes in the nature of the organization's environment, its technology, its competitive strategy, its size, and changes in its workforce. These changes themselves may also trigger a need for compensation changes.

CHANGES IN THE WORKFORCE

Changes in the nature of an organization's workforce may affect the reward and compensation system in a variety of ways. If the type of employee whom an organization hires changes over time, then the needs of these employees may be different from those of previous employees, and the compensation system may have to change to recognize that. If the workforce ages, there is likely to be more emphasis on pension plans and retirement income. If the workforce becomes younger, there may be more need for cash and for family benefits, such as a dental plan.

Another trend that has been taking place in many organizations is a greater diversity of employees, in terms of gender and ethnicity. This makes it more difficult to define a single reward system that meets everyone's needs. Of course, some compensation elements, such as a flexible benefits plan, can accommodate changes in the workforce more easily than other systems.

CHANGES IN FINANCIAL CIRCUMSTANCES

A decline in the organization's financial circumstances may trigger a need to cut costs, including compensation costs. The compensation strategy may be sound, but the organization may simply no longer have the funds to support it at its current level. In these circumstances, firms often ask for compensation concessions from their employees. As will be discussed later in the chapter, organizations have a variety of options in how to deal with this problem. Of course, firms with a greater degree of variable pay are less vulnerable to these changes than firms with less variable pay.

CHANGES IN SCOPE

One obvious circumstance in which adapting the compensation system will be required is when a merger or acquisition takes place. The two organizations will almost certainly have different compensation systems. Merging these systems can be a very complex process, and there are no hard-and-fast rules for doing so. Of course, in some cases integrating the compensation systems may not be necessary if the organizations are going to operate autonomously.

But when the units are to be integrated, a wide variety of compensation decisions will have to be made. The usual practice is to adopt the compensation system of the largest actor in the process, but there are many constraints on this process, including legal obligations. However, not merging the compensation systems where employees will be working together doing similar work is a formula for inequity and dissatisfaction as well as an ongoing administrative nightmare.

ADAPTING THE COMPENSATION SYSTEM

Your evaluation has indicated that your compensation system is not achieving the expected results, and you conclude that something needs to be done. But what? How do you identify the adaptations that will produce the desired results? Before you can do so, you need to know what exactly is going wrong with your current system. In fact, as will be discussed, the problems might not have anything to do with your compensation system at all! This final section discusses some key considerations in making adaptations to the compensation system. It also considers three specific situations that may call for adaptations: adapting to financial crises, adapting to labour shortages, and accommodating individuals.

IDENTIFYING WHAT TO ADAPT

Your compensation system does not seem to be producing the desired results. Your first reaction may be to ask yourself what changes to the compensation system should be made to correct this problem. But this should not be your first question.

Your first question should be "Why are the desired results not occurring?" There are many possibilities. Perhaps the compensation strategy is wrong. But maybe not. Perhaps the compensation strategy is correct, but the technical processes for transforming the strategy into a compensation system have been poorly designed. Or maybe both of these are fine, but the system has been poorly implemented, or maybe the necessary complementary policies have not been implemented. For example, a system for employee participation in decision making is necessary to realize the benefits of employee stock plans. Effective training programs are necessary for pay-for-knowledge systems to work. It could also simply be a problem of time. You are expecting too much, too soon.

Alternatively, maybe the problem is due to some cause completely unrelated to compensation, such as an aging plant or changes in quality of raw materials. And finally, perhaps your expectations for the compensation system were not realistic in the first place.

So how do you know which it is? This is one of those questions that shows that compensation is less a science than an art, and that there is no substitute for understanding the organization and its people. This is why comprehensive evaluation data are so important. Evaluation data should allow you to rule out certain causes and perhaps pinpoint the problem. For example, if employees do not understand the compensation system, or misperceive it, this should first be corrected.

The key point to remember here is that only when the cause of the perceived problem has been identified can the proper adaptations be identified. When adaptations are being considered, it is also important to put them in the context of the total system. Piecemeal changes to deal with specific problems may end up creating new problems, as will be seen shortly.

ADAPTING TO FINANCIAL CRISES

When a financial crisis hits an organization, compensation expenditures often look like a tempting target. The classical approach to cutting costs is either to lay off employees or to attempt to cut compensation. However, this may be shortsighted, depending on the cause of the crisis, its likely duration, and the nature of the organization. For example, if the crisis is not due to out-of-line compensation costs, or is likely to be short-term in duration, cutting compensation may not be a good solution. If the organization practises either human relations or high-involvement management, then cutting compensation is the least appropriate solution. Cutting compensation will cause problems for most organizations, but these problems will be least severe for classical organizations, since they likely do not have positive job attitudes and citizenship behaviour to protect, and the organization is geared toward making employees replaceable.

Cutting compensation may cause serious problems for human relations and high-involvement organizations, because this action may be seen as a violation of the psychological contract between employees and the firm, with all the negative consequences that may bring. However, there are at least five measures that can be taken to minimize the damage. One is to provide full information on the crisis, showing that all other possible avenues for addressing the problem have been exhausted. Another is to seek employee input on ways to deal with the crisis. In some cases, alternative solutions may be found, but even if they are not, this creates understanding of the crisis.

The third measure is to ensure that compensation cuts are fairly shared throughout the organization. The fourth is to consult with employees on how best to achieve the necessary compensation reductions. For example, some employee groups may prefer reductions in certain benefits rather than decreases in base pay, while others may want to keep their benefits and reduce base pay. Some employee groups may prefer to go on a shortened workweek rather than accept layoffs. Early retirement programs may also be considered.

The fifth measure is to try to boost nonfinancial rewards at the same time, or to make commitments to provide future rewards, when circumstances permit. For example, some firms have implemented employee stock bonus plans when cutting other compensation as one way of guaranteeing employees that they will participate in any upturn in the firm's fortunes.

Perhaps it is not necessary to actually cut compensation costs, but rather to contain them. Several possibilities are available (Sibson, 1990: 356):

- Extend the salary review period to a longer interval.
- Tighten controls to slow progress through the pay range.
- Tighten merit guidelines.
- Replace some raises with bonuses.
- Replace fixed pay with variable pay.
- Ensure that regional differences in wages are reflected in regional pay levels.
- Contain benefit costs.
- Create a two-tiered pay system for new employees coming in.

Of course, the best approach to financial crises is to avoid them, or to have a system in place that will adjust to financial problems. Financial problems are less likely to arise if a compensation system has been developed that adds maximum value to the organization, as has been discussed throughout the book. Variable pay systems may not only add value, they also add compensation flexibility. Some firms attempt to avoid having to cut compensation costs by maintaining production slightly below demand. Others keep a workforce of part-time employees or contingent employees to help protect core employees. Others have plans for sharing work. There are many possibilities.

ADAPTING TO LABOUR SHORTAGES

One problem frequently encountered is a shortage of particular types of labour. For example, in recent years Canada has experienced shortages of technical employees, particularly those involved with computer applications and software development. So how do firms attempt to cope with this problem? A common approach is the use of **technical premiums**, through which technical employees are compensated more highly than they otherwise would be.

technical premiums
compensation measures that increase the compensation of technical employees

According to a survey of Canadian firms conducted by Allen (1997), the most common approach to providing a technical premium was to place the needed employees higher in the pay range than would normally be justified. A third of the firms offering technical premiums offered one-time cash "signing bonuses." Other employers slotted these employees in a higher pay grade than would normally be justified. Some firms used the normal pay rates, but added a fixed percentage that would be carried along with these employees as they progressed through the pay range. A few firms offered special stock options to these employees.

The danger of making many of these adjustments is that the overall integrity of the compensation system can be undermined. There can also be equity concerns if one group of employees is being treated significantly differently from other groups of employees. Because of compounding, compensation costs can easily spin out of control, especially if incentives and benefits are calculated as a percentage of base pay. There is also the issue of how to deal with salaries when there is no longer a shortage of the particular skill in question.

Of course, rather than attempting to lure away each other's employees, one way for firms to deal with a skills shortage is through internal training. Although this may not be feasible for all employers, especially if quick expansion is needed, this approach has numerous benefits. It provides opportunities for training and development to current employees, shows commitment by the organization, is more likely to create employees with skills specific to employer needs, avoids skewing the compensation system, and helps to provide a solution to the labour shortage.

ACCOMMODATING INDIVIDUAL EMPLOYEES

One dilemma that every organization has to deal with occurs when an individual employee demands special treatment. For example, an employee may brandish a job offer from another organization, asking her or his current employer to "meet it or beat it." Of course, if this is happening all the time, it suggests that the compensation system needs to be reassessed. But what do you do about the individual employee? The temptation is to match the competitor's offer, even though it puts the individual outside the pay range for that job. However, the problem with this solution is that it undermines the integrity and equity of the total compensation system.

To avoid these negative consequences, it may well be preferable to let the employee go to the other job. It may be that to the other employer this individual is more valuable than he or she is to the current employer. Or the other job may not really be comparable—it includes other job duties. Or it may be that there is some other way of satisfying the employee, such as a transfer to more rewarding work, or some promotional or training opportunities. In fact, sometimes another job offer may represent a cry for recognition, or some other problem, rather than a true desire to leave the firm.

A similar dilemma occurs when recruiting new employees, if the market for these employees has jumped dramatically in a short period. If the firm responds by sweetening its offers to new employees, these employees may end up earning more than existing employees. Even if this inequity is subsequently corrected, this may shake employees' confidence in the equity of the system. It is far better to address this issue before it becomes a problem, or to address it in a comprehensive way, rather than in a piecemeal fashion.

SUMMARY AND IMPLICATIONS

The purpose of this chapter was to cover the final stretch of the road to effective compensation: the processes for implementing, managing, evaluating, and adapting the compensation system. The chapter started by outlining the fundamentals of compensation administration, including the mechanics of payroll preparation and compensation communication. The key role of information technology in this process was briefly discussed, along with the issue of whether to perform all compensation administration in-house or to outsource some or all of it.

Next, the process for implementing the compensation system was discussed. It was noted that the key to successful implementation is proper preparation. This preparation includes resolving any remaining administrative details, assigning specific roles and responsibilities, documenting the system, planning for training and communication, budgeting, developing evaluation procedures, and formulating the implementation plan. The implementation process itself consists of six steps: establishing the implementation bodies, putting the infrastructure in place, testing the system, conducting training, communicating the system, and launching and adjusting the system.

Following that, the process for evaluating the compensation system was discussed in considerable depth. It was noted that evaluation of the compensation system is often done poorly or not at all. It was emphasized that to truly understand the impact of the compensation system, a variety of indicators must be used, and that simply reviewing the system against projected costs or goal attainment can portray a misleading picture. Examples of possible organizational, behavioural, and attitudinal indicators were provided.

The chapter went on to note that compensation systems usually do not suddenly break, but gradually become ineffective. Vigilance in monitoring circumstances external and internal to the firms is necessary to prevent this occurrence. External circumstances include legislative, labour market, competitive, and socioeconomic changes. Internal circumstances include changes to managerial strategies, the workforce, financial conditions, and organization scope.

Finally, it was noted that even if the compensation system appears in need of change, the exact adaptations that need to be made are not always obvious. The key is to first understand what is going wrong with the current system, and it may turn out that what looked like a compensation problem is actually caused by something else. After that, the issues involved in adapting to financial problems, labour shortages, and individual employees were briefly discussed. It was noted that piecemeal adaptations or those made for the purposes of expediency can undermine the integrity of the entire compensation system.

With this chapter, you have now traversed the entire road map to compensation effectiveness. But that does not mean your journey is at an end. Unlike reading a book, the journey to effective compensation has no end, because compensation needs to evolve as the organization and circumstances change. In that respect, the road to effective compensation is more like an ever-changing maze than a speedy expressway. But that's what makes compensation so challenging and so much fun!

KEY TERMS

average employee earnings, p. 473

compensation administration, p. 456

compensation cost ratio, p. 473

initial dip, p. 471

spiral career paths, p. 478

technical premiums, p. 482

EXERCISES

1. In previous exercises, you may have prepared compensation strategies for The Fit Stop, or one of the other cases in the Appendix. If so, develop a detailed plan for implementing the new compensation strategy at one of these firms. If not, prepare a compensation strategy for one of these firms, design the technical processes, and develop the implementation plan.

2. Each member of the group should check with a current or previous employer (or some other employer if this is not convenient) to determine whether the organization is outsourcing some or all of its compensation administration. Is the company happy with the current system? Why or why not?

SUGGESTED WEB SITES

Page 456: To learn more about the specialized field of compensation administration, check out the Web site of the Canadian Payroll Association: <www.payroll.ca>

Page 461: To access the full text of Bill C-6, click <www.parl.gc.ca/common/Bills_House_Government.asp?Language=E&parl=36&Ses=2#C-6>

REFERENCES

Allen, Ann. 1997. "Trolling for Technical Employees: Using Technical Premiums as Bait." *Human Resources in Canada*, June: 621–25.

Belli, Claudio. 1991. "Strategic Compensation Communication." In M.L. Rock and L.A. Berger, eds., *The Compensation Handbook*. New York: McGraw-Hill, 604–16.

Britton, Paul B., and Christian M. Ellis. 1994. "Designing and Implementing Reward Systems: Finding a Better Way." *Compensation and Benefits Review*, 26(4): 39–46.

Brown, David. 2001a. "Employees Ill-Equipped to Make Pension Choices." *Canadian HR Reporter*, 14(10): 1, 12.

Brown, David. 2001b. "CIBC HR Department Halved as Non-Strategic Roles Outsourced." *Canadian HR Reporter*, 14(11): 1, 6.

Dobbs, Kevin. 2001. "Rightsourcing: Using a Mix of In-House and ASP Software." *Canadian HR Reporter*, 14(10): G5, G10.

Foot, David K., and Rosemary A. Venne. 1990. "Population, Pyramids, and

Promotional Prospects." *Canadian Public Policy*, 16(4): 387–98.

Hackett, Brian, 1995. *Transforming the Benefit Function*. New York: The Conference Board.

Harrison, Suzanne. 1996. *Outsourcing and the "New" Human Resource Management*. Kingston, ON: IRC Press.

Ilsemann, Anne C., and Mark Simms. 2000. "Using Information Technology for Salary Budgeting and Planning." In Lance A. Berger and Dorothy R. Berger, eds., *The Compensation Handbook*. New York: McGraw-Hill, 189–96.

McEwen, Alan. 2001. "Privacy Concerns, Technology, Fuel the Debate over Electronic Forms." *Dialogue*, April/May: 16–19.

Murray, Vic. 1997. "Contracting Out HR Services: Passing Fad or Here to Stay?" *Human Resources Management in Canada*, July: 637–41.

Rampton, Glenn M., Ian J. Turnbull, and J. Allen Doran. 1997. *Human Resources Management Systems*. Toronto: ITP Nelson.

Roberts, Alexander, 1994. "Integrating Strategy with Performance Measures." *Management Development Review*, 7(6): 13–15.

Shetzer, Larry. 2000. "On-Line 360-Degree Feedback Encourages Bottom-Up Decision-Making." *Canadian HR Reporter*, November 6.

Sibson, Robert E. 1990. *Compensation*. New York: American Management Association.

Tyson, David E. 2001. *Carswell's Compensation Guide*. Toronto, ON: Thomson Publishing.

Winter, Nadine. 2000. "Job Evaluation in a New Business Environment." *Canadian HR Reporter*, March 27: 17.

APPENDIX
Cases for Analysis

The following cases, which reflect a range of compensation issues and organizational types, can be used in a variety of ways. They are presented here without any questions attached to them, to allow instructors flexibility in their use. They can be used in conjunction with end-of-chapter exercises to illustrate a variety of compensation issues and to provide opportunities for applying compensation concepts. They could also be used as a basis for major term assignments, or for group projects. Some are short enough to be used as exam cases. And, of course, they can serve as a basis for lively class discussions of many important compensation issues.

Alliston Instruments

Alliston Instruments is a manufacturer of specialty medical instruments and is located in southern Ontario. The production process involves two types of processes. First, individual workers produce the components for the medical instruments, in batches of various sizes, using a variety of machine tools and equipment. Then, other workers assemble the components into finished products. Assembly is done through a sequential process, with each product passing through four to six workstations before it is complete. The quality of the products, which is crucial, depends on both the quality of the component parts that are produced and the quality of the assembly process.

It is late January 2002, and the financial statements for 2001 have just been released. They are grim. For the first time in the company's 50-year history, the firm has shown a loss. The company's chief executive officer believes a lot of this has to do with production problems. The 2001 production reports indicate that although units produced per employee showed a slight increase last year, the number of defective units produced reached an all-time high, along with a high rate of wastage in raw materials and other supplies. Although total sales (and therefore total production) are down from the previous year, total labour costs are up. As a result, costs per unit are at an all-time high.

Knowing you to be an expert in management, the CEO has asked for your help. As background for your work, the CEO briefs you on industry conditions. Until two years ago, the firm had enjoyed increasing sales for many years. It had also enjoyed increasing profits, with a record profit of over $3 million in 1998. However, in the last two years the medical instruments industry has suddenly become more competitive. High-quality medical instruments are now being produced by several Asian firms, two of which entered the Canadian market in 1999. (Previously, the main competitors in the Canadian market were U.S. and European firms, but the latter were not much of a problem because their products were very high-priced.)

Because of low labour costs, these Asian firms were able to price their products attractively, but buyers initially held back, concerned about potential quality problems. It looked as if Alliston's customers (mainly hospitals and health clinics) would stay loyal, even though they were themselves under pressure to cut costs, due to budget cuts. But in late 1999, an Asian competitor made a major sales push, slashing prices, and this cut into Alliston's 2000 sales dramatically. In mid-2000, Alliston laid off 50 employees. Although the firm had laid off employees from time to time in the past during production lulls, this was the largest layoff in company history.

In order to make up for the loss of sales, Alliston added a number of new products to its line. (Over the years, the company had tended to stick with the same set of products, although new products were being put into use in the hospitals.) While some of these products sold well, they didn't really make money, because production costs were higher due to needs for new equipment and extensive employee training. Moreover, most employees preferred to work on the old products, so it took a lot of pressure from supervisors to get them to work on the new products.

Alliston's 250 production workers have been unionized since the 1960s. In 1998, they staged a short but bitter strike. Because product demand was so high, the company did not want a long stoppage, and the union was able to win significant wage increases for 1999 and 2000 (a two-year contract was signed). Since then, union–management relations, never very good, have been quite strained. Relations between supervisors and workers are no better. Supervisors complain about lazy workers who don't care if they do a good job or not, and workers complain about overbearing supervisors who spend all their time watching and harassing employees and who allocate work unfairly.

Interestingly, the turnover rate is low at Alliston. Wages at the firm are above average, and the benefits package, which increases with seniority, is also good, comprising about 25 percent of total compensation. Comparable alternative employment opportunities in the area are quite scarce.

In an effort to increase efficiency, in late 2000 the firm persuaded the union to accept an incentive system in which employees would receive, in addition to their hourly wages, a bonus based on individual output, rather than an increase in base pay for 2001. A standard per-hour production rate for each item or assembly operation was established, based on estimated 2000 production levels. (However, because the firm had never kept detailed records, these standards were simply based on estimates of supervisors.)

If production per hour for a particular item exceeded 2000 levels, the employee would receive a fixed sum for each piece produced over that level. Of course, employees would not receive a bonus for those items that were not of satisfactory quality, and supervisors were expected to deduct these from the employee totals. However, there were no set standards for quality, and each supervisor seemed to set different standards.

There seem to be many problems with this new pay system. For example, workers complain that the production standards for some tasks are set too high, and they have no chance of earning a bonus on these items. Everybody tries to avoid these jobs, and productivity on them is poor. On the other hand, there are some jobs that everybody wants to do, because substantial bonuses can be earned, and productivity is up dramatically on these jobs. But the net effect is that overall units produced per employee have not really changed at all, while substantial sums are being paid out in bonuses.

During the past year, ten production workers retired or quit, and were not replaced, but this was made possible by the drop in sales during the year, not increased productivity. However, this reduction in the workforce was partially offset by the need to hire two additional supervisors to handle the increased needs for supervision, inspection, and administration, and one additional full-time clerical person in the payroll department just to handle the calculations for the new bonus system.

Supervisors have complained bitterly about the new system, saying it is creating additional pressure on them. They say it is causing increased conflict with employees because nobody wants the "bad" (poor-paying) jobs, and employees resent it when these jobs are assigned to them. They find that employees don't care about quality, as long as output meets minimum standards, nor about the high waste of raw materials. They have to supervise more closely to deal with these problems and try to keep quality and productivity up on the "bad" jobs.

And, to top it off, supervisors are now making less money than some of the workers, since they are not eligible for the bonus system. The fact that none of the non-union employees received any pay increase last year does not help their mood any. During the year, three experienced supervisors quit. The firm had never had more than one or two supervisors quit in a single year before.

Although the union is generally opposed to individual incentive plans, it accepted this one in return for a clause in the collective agreement ensuring job security for the current unionized workforce. Any workforce reductions occurring from the greater efficiency that had been expected will be handled through attrition. Management agreed to this because they did not expect to have to lay employees off. They expected the new bonus system to reduce unit costs of production so that it could lower prices and win back the business that had been lost.

It hasn't worked out that way. Financial data for the last four years are shown below. As can be seen, sales peaked two years ago at $31 million, but have since fallen to $24 million. Customers are complaining about both product price and quality. However, the company cannot afford to reduce prices, because unit costs are so high. It is clear to management that something needs to be done, and quickly, but exactly what it is that should be done is not so clear!

Year	Revenues	Total Employees	Labour Costs	Other Production Costs	Other Costs	Net Income
1998	$27 000 000	320	$9 000 000	$13 500 000	$1 350 000	$3 150 000
1999	$31 000 000	350	$12 000 000	$15 500 000	$1 550 000	$1 950 000
2000	$25 000 000	300	$11 000 000	$12 500 000	$1 500 000	—
2001	$24 000 000	293	$12 000 000	$13 000 000	$1 444 000	($2 444 000)

DUPLOX COPIERS, INC.

Shirley Symes, President of Duplox Copiers, has requested your consulting services. In recent years, the company's technical service representatives (TSRs) have shown declining attitudes toward their work and the company, as indicated by the firm's annual attitude surveys and by increasing turnover. There has also been a sharp increase in customer complaints about service quality and machine breakdowns.

The performance of TSRs is crucial to customer satisfaction with company products. Indeed, the Vice-President of Sales has been complaining bitterly that "poor performance of the service personnel is crippling the efforts of my salesforce." The Vice-President of Field Services (in charge of the TSRs) bitterly resents this criticism, believing that his department deserves praise, not criticism, for its productivity improvement during the past two years, with the same number of TSRs now servicing 20 percent more machines.

Duplox Copiers employs 5000 technical service representatives located at about 100 branch offices throughout North America. TSRs install new machines, provide scheduled maintenance at regular intervals, and provide emergency maintenance in case of breakdowns, malfunctions, or copy quality problems.

The North American operations of the company are divided into 15 geographical regions, each with six to eight branch offices. Western Canada is one such region. The Edmonton branch has about 40 TSRs and is responsible for the northern half of Alberta. The branch is headed by a branch manager, to whom three managers report: a branch service manager, a branch sales manager, and the office manager. The branch sales manager supervises approximately 25 sales representatives, and the office manager supervises four office and clerical staff.

The branch service manager supervises a small parts warehouse at the branch (most parts are kept at the regional warehouse in Vancouver, to reduce inventory costs), and five field service managers (FSMs), each of whom supervises eight TSRs. Because of an increasing variety and complexity of machines, each FSM and the TSRs under them specialize in a particular model and type of machine. Each FSM handles the scheduling of service and installation of all machines in his or her category (for example, one FSM and his TSRs handle all the installation and service requirements for the model 3200 series of copiers). When service calls come in from customers, they are received by one of the office clerks, who identifies the machine in question and directs the request to the FSM in charge of that type of machine.

Branch hours are from 8:30 a.m. to 5:00 p.m., and all TSRs are expected to adhere to these hours (so the company can avoid paying overtime), except in emergency situations that must be authorized by a field service manager. Since competition has been increasing, and company profitability levels have been slipping, expense budgets have been tightened in recent years, and the TSRs' jobs have been put under tighter control. The work of each TSR has become more specialized (limited to only one type of machine, in order to reduce training time), and the number of machines serviced by each TSR has grown larger.

Minimum monthly, weekly, and daily productivity levels are strictly specified for each TSR, and there are strict quotas on repair expenses and travel expenses. Prior approval from higher-ups is required for many actions even if they are within budget limitations. A TSR cannot order parts or tools needed for maintenance; all have to be ordered by the FSM, within strict dollar limits. Since there is often a delay in receiving the parts, in many cases the TSR who starts the job is not the TSR who finishes the job. Because of the large territory covered, the high level of TSR turnover, and the unpredictability of emergency calls, the customer seldom sees the same TSR twice in a row.

When a TSR needs technical advice from regional head office in Vancouver, where there are numerous technical experts who specialize in various types of machines, they are required to call their FSM, who would then call regional head office if he deemed it useful.

There is generally little TSR discretion over maintenance schedules and services; they are to be performed strictly according to schedule. However, in one area TSRs are not required to "go by the book." In theory, all installations of new equipment have to meet company standards, in terms of space, ventilation, and wiring. However, in practice, TSRs are not allowed to refuse installations that do not meet company specifications. This is because the sales representatives, sales managers, and the branch manager are mainly compensated based on volume of new installations (about 50 percent of their total compensation is based on volume of sales, 30 percent is salary, 20 percent is benefits). Sales reps are reluctant to tell customers that they should make expensive alterations to their facilities in order to install the machine, because they might lose the sale in this highly competitive business.

Sales reps don't seem to put much weight on the TSRs' argument that improper installation can cause higher repair and service costs. This frustrates many TSRs, especially since they are frequently criticized by sales staff for "shoddy service, which causes more breakdowns, and makes us look bad in the eyes of the customer."

TSRs are paid a flat monthly salary, plus overtime. Benefits constitute about 16 percent of their total compensation. Their performance is appraised once a year by the FSM, mainly based on how well they have adhered to productivity and expense standards, and merit increases are doled out by each FSM to one or two "deserving" TSRs each year. The branch service manager and the FSMs are paid on a salary plus bonus system. The bonus depends on whether TSR productivity met or exceeded standards in the past year, and whether repair and service expenses were below standard. In general, for the branch service manager and the field service managers, salary usually amounts to about 50 percent of their total compensation, the bonus about 30 percent, and benefits about 20 percent.

EASTERN PROVINCIAL UNIVERSITY

The following are the job descriptions that are used for compensation purposes at Eastern Provincial University, an institution that employs approximately 900 professors, 1500 non-academic staff, and has about 20 000 undergraduate and graduate students. Descriptions are provided for the Clerk Stenographer, Draftsperson, Grounds Worker, and Medical Laboratory Technologist job classes.

CLERK STENOGRAPHER I

KIND AND LEVEL OF WORK
Employees of this class perform a variety of clerical tasks of limited complexity that may include the taking and transcribing of shorthand dictation; the vocabulary involved is usually free of technical terms and limited to the everyday language of business. Typing assignments, whether from copy, dictation, or machine transcription, require only normal speed and accuracy. Material copied may include scientific papers, theses, and special reports using technical language from any one of the University subjects; the employee is only responsible for the accurate transcription of material already written or typed. These employees maintain courteous and cooperative working relations with students, and with faculty and other University staff for whom they provide typing, simple duplicating, telephone reception, and other services. While some positions are located away from the supervisors, preliminary detailed instructions and established procedures leave little responsibility for the exercise of initiative or the formation of independent judgments.

TYPICAL DUTIES AND RESPONSIBILITIES
1. Type correspondence, class assignments, and technical papers using special vocabulary, from copy.
2. Act as receptionist at the counter, and on the telephone, relaying calls, recording messages, and answering simple questions.

3. File, and withdraw from files, materials arranged in simple alphabetical, numerical, chronological, or geographical order.

4. Reproduce copies of materials by photocopy, or other simple duplicating methods.

5. Transcribe correspondence, and other materials containing everyday language, from dictating machines.

6. Prepare form letters by inserting appropriate material from files or other sources.

7. Check forms for completeness.

8. Post figures to budget accounts or other simple statistical and accounting records.

9. Open, sort, route, and deliver mail according to predetermined patterns.

10. In some positions, take and transcribe correspondence and other materials requiring only a good vocabulary or ordinary language.

Desirable Qualifications
Previous office experience desirable but not required. Grade 12 and completion of a standard course in word processing, spreadsheets, and shorthand. Ability to meet test standards in typing and shorthand (for those positions requiring the use of shorthand).

Clerk Stenographer II

Kind and Level of Work
Employees of this class perform a variety of moderately complex clerical tasks, which may include the taking and transcribing of shorthand dictation and which requires knowledge of a technical vocabulary. Their work is supervised by academic, administrative, or senior clerical employees. This position is distinguished from Clerk Stenographer I in that it requires more knowledge of the organization, programs, and policies of the work unit, and requires a higher degree of specialized clerical skills, or knowledge of a technical vocabulary, or carries independent responsibility for the maintenance of significant records, or some combination of these attributes. These workers maintain helpful and courteous relations with students and staff, for whom they provide information and services.

Typical Duties and Responsibilities
1. Compose and type, from general instructions, routine correspondence, bulletins, and other materials requiring knowledge of the departments they serve.

2. Type from copy or dictating machine, class assignments, tests, research papers, and other materials requiring understanding of technical vocabulary, the use of special symbol keyboards, or judgment in the selection of format.

3. Answer students' inquiries concerning class schedules, timetables, general course content, class prerequisites, and like matters requiring basic knowledge of calendars and departmental programs.

4. Train new employees by providing factual information on office routines, staff names and locations, work methods, and schedules.

5. Maintain, subject to periodic review, records of budget expenditure, class attendance, class credits, grade distribution, and other data requiring accurate posting and simple calculations of totals, percentages, and balances.

6. Compile simple statistical tables and graphs according to prescribed patterns, incorporating data flowing into or retained in their departments.

7. Organize, reorganize, and maintain filing systems based on alphabetic, numeric, or simple subject matter arrangement.

8. Act as receptionists for officials, screening telephone calls and visitors, providing answers to inquiries, making appointments, and referring callers to other officials.

9. Assist in the maintenance of counselling schedules at the time of student registration.

10. In some positions, take and transcribe shorthand dictation of correspondence, reports, research papers, and other materials containing technical language and concepts.

DESIRABLE QUALIFICATIONS
Several years of office experience, preferably in a university setting. Grade 12 and completion of a standard course in word processing, spreadsheets, and shorthand. Ability to meet test standards in typing and shorthand (for those positions requiring the use of shorthand).

CLERK STENOGRAPHER III

KIND AND LEVEL OF WORK
Employees of this class perform responsible, varied, and complex clerical tasks, which may include taking and transcribing shorthand dictation. Typically, their assignments require a broad understanding of the structure and division of responsibility, functions, and programs of the organizations they service. In most of these positions they are secretaries to heads of larger departments and take initiative in relieving them of administrative details that do not require professional judgment. Their work is subject to supervision by academic or administrative supervisors, but they carry out a series of clerical operations calling for decisions without detailed instruction or review. The work of this class is distinguished from that of Clerk Stenographer I and II by the broader knowledge requirements, the greater latitude, and the supervision of other clerk stenographers. In contacts with students, faculty and other staff, and the public at large, these employees attempt to promote public attitudes that will support the work of the units.

Typical Duties and Responsibilities

1. For their superiors, compose and type correspondence that requires good knowledge of departmental organization, functions, and policies.

2. Maintain records pertaining to students' marks, credits, and degree requirements, or supervise the maintenance of such records.

3. Maintain records on budget allotments, expenditures, commitments, and residual balances, and notify department office of over-expenditures and balances, thus providing a measure of budget control.

4. Give elementary counselling services to students by advising them of degree requirements, class schedules, class prerequisites, and (in general terms) course content, using information from the calendars or obtained from the faculty.

5. Schedule, at the time of registration, counselling interviews between students and professors, and maintain records so that any student will be referred to the same counsellor each time.

6. Attend and record proceedings of faculty meetings, or meetings between faculty and non-University groups, making shorthand notes summarizing discussions, and transcribing the reports for the review of superiors.

7. Give supervision to assistants and participate in their selection, assign their duties, train them, reallocate work to meet deadlines, and exercise disciplinary control in minor matters.

8. Screen phone and office calls of visitors, setting up interviews with superiors as necessary, answering questions where possible, and referring visitors to other sources where appropriate.

9. Type tests and examinations for members of the faculty, assuring that contents are kept confidential and that papers are properly secured.

Desirable Qualifications

Approximately five years of office experience, including several years in a university setting and preferably including experience in a supervisory capacity. Grade 12 and completion of a standard course in word processing, spreadsheets, and shorthand. Ability to meet test standards in typing and shorthand (for those positions requiring the use of shorthand).

Draftsperson I

Kind and Level of Work

Employees of this classification utilize computer-aided design drafting (CADD) techniques to carry out assignments delegated by their supervisor with direction from the project originator where appropriate. They work from rough sketches and notes, verbal instructions, and other sources of information. While their day-to-day work is subject only to general supervision, completed assignments are reviewed. Although the projects on which they work may range across a variety of engineering and architectural fields, the more complex work is allocated to more senior positions. They may communicate with professional engineers and others who initiate the work they do in order to clarify certain requirements and detail.

Typical Duties and Responsibilities

1. Interpret existing records and information for the purpose of producing required CADD information.

2. Prepare finished CADD drawings from rough sketches, notes, and instructions.

3. Share in filing and managing inventory of records information.

4. Assist Physical Plant staff, professional engineers, and consultants in locating physical records information.

5. Use and be familiar with operating various equipment including computer input/output devices, keyboards, digitizing equipment, and blueprint machine.

6. Assist in site verification of existing campus buildings and facilities.

7. Periodically assist in making site surveys with senior or surveying staff.

8. Participate in training programs relative to the CADD system.

9. Interact and communicate, in a professional manner, with Physical Plant staff, the University community, consultants, contractors, etc.

Desirable Qualifications

Previous related experience preferred. Grade 12 plus a two-year diploma in a related architectural/engineering-associated technical program. Inclusion of computer-assisted design and drafting in course work or equivalent experience required. Eligibility for membership as an Applied Science Technologist preferred.

Draftsperson II

Kind and Level of Work

Employees of this classification utilize more complex computer-aided design drafting techniques to carry out assignments delegated by their supervisor with direction from the project originator where appropriate. Their work is differentiated from that of junior positions by the complexity of their assignments, the judgment they use in completing their work, and the degree of independence with which they work. Delegated projects may range across a variety of engineering and architectural fields. They develop and maintain cooperative working relations with professionals and tradespersons in fulfilling their tasks.

Typical Duties and Responsibilities

1. Participate in production and design work of various projects as required.

2. Assist in the development, evaluation, implementation, and documentation of ongoing computer system procedures.

3. Assist in coordinating and supervising work of junior staff.

4. Complete site verification of existing campus buildings and facilities.

5. Participate in receiving training for CADD system applications, in learning and using the new and more complex portions of the system, and in supporting other staff as required.

6. Interact and communicate in a professional manner with Physical Plant staff, the University community, consultants, contractors, etc.

DESIRABLE QUALIFICATIONS
Minimum of two years' related experience in architectural and a variety of other engineering fields. An "operator" level of CADD and related computer operations is required. Grade 12 plus a two-year diploma in a related architectural/engineering associated technical program. Inclusion of CADD in course work or equivalent experience required. Eligibility for membership as an Applied Science Technologist is also required.

DRAFTSPERSON III

KIND AND LEVEL OF WORK
Employees of this classification are responsible for directing the operation of a unit producing computer-aided design drafting information and drawings, under the general supervision of the Facilities Management Design and Information Systems Manager. Their work is differentiated from that of other operational staff in the unit on the basis of the skill level involved and the responsibility to supervise others. They develop and maintain cooperative working relations with professionals and tradespersons to facilitate project completion.

TYPICAL DUTIES AND RESPONSIBILITIES
1. Supervise, allocate, assist, and participate in the work of subordinate staff.

2. Review work and ensure standards are maintained.

3. Assess incoming work, organize project priorities and flow, plan and schedule workloads as appropriate.

4. Train and support Physical Plant staff in the use of system applications for records information access.

5. Assist in the design of computer system enhancements and general strategies.

6. Participate in the more complex design work of various projects as required.

7. Interact and communicate in a professional manner with Physical Plant staff, the University community, consultants, contractors, etc.

DESIRABLE QUALIFICATIONS

A minimum of five years' experience in architectural and a variety of engineering fields including some experience in a supervisory capacity. Must have experience in CADD and related computer operations at an "operator" and "systems" level. Grade 12 plus a two-year diploma in a related architectural/engineering associated technical program. Inclusion of CADD in course work or equivalent experience required. Eligibility for membership as an Applied Science Technologist is also required.

GROUNDS WORKER I

KIND AND LEVEL OF WORK

The employees in this classification carry out routine gardening in maintaining the grass, flowers, and trees on the campus grounds. They either may be assigned an area on campus to look after or may work on a crew assigned to a task such as planting, pruning, or other related tasks. These employees are responsible to a Grounds Worker II acting as a lead hand, assistant supervisor, or a supervisor.

TYPICAL DUTIES AND RESPONSIBILITIES

1. Water lawns and flower beds in a particular area.
2. Trim lawns in areas where larger mowers cannot cut.
3. Hoe weeds in flower beds, shrubbery beds, and gravel parking lots.
4. Perform general clean-up work in an area.
5. Prune broken branches on shrubs and trees.
6. Use hand clippers to trim areas of lawn not accessible to machines, such as along buildings and ponds.
7. Assist in the planting of flowers, shrubs, trees, and grass.
8. Assist in sodding operation, which would involve removal of old grass, soil preparation, laying new sod, spreading peat moss, and the first watering.
9. Do minor maintenance of small machinery.

DESIRABLE QUALIFICATIONS

Gardening experience preferred but not required. Grade 8 education.

GROUNDS WORKER II

KIND AND LEVEL OF WORK

Employees of this class are responsible for a wide variety of gardening jobs involving many of those done by a Grounds Worker I. Generally, they are distinguished from the Grounds Worker I class in that they may be the lead person in a small group or may be a machine operator. These employees may be in charge of a specific operation such as the greenhouse, a maintenance department, or the nursery. They are usually supervised by an assistant supervisor and supervisor.

Typical Duties and Responsibilities
1. Supervise the grounds maintenance in a particular area.
2. Supervise a special work crew engaged in an activity such as sodding, planting, or pruning.
3. Supervise the work done in the greenhouse and the stocking of indoor planters.
4. Operate a mower for cutting playing fields and large areas of grass.
5. Operate a roto-tiller around trees and shrubs to kill weeds.
6. Operate a tractor or other large machine and all attachments such as front-end loader, grader blade, and backhoe.
7. Carry out maintenance on all equipment used in the department.
8. Train subordinates in all gardening operations.
9. Communicate instructions from the supervisor.

Desirable Qualifications
Several years' experience as a grounds worker. Grade 8 education.

Grounds Worker III

Kind and Level of Work
Employees of this classification collectively perform a wide variety of tasks related to the positions of ice making, machine operation, nursery management, irrigation, landscape maintenance, and tree and shrub pruning. Their work is distinguished from that of subordinate personnel by the degree of knowledge, skill, and understanding required to perform the duties, the extent of their supervisory and administrative responsibilities, or some combination of these factors. Their work is given general supervision and direction, usually by a supervisor or assistant supervisor, but these employees independently organize and supervise the work of the subordinates assigned to them.

Typical Duties and Responsibilities
The incumbent is expected to be able to perform all of the duties shown under the general listing below, and *one* of the specialties listed below that.

General
1. Supervise subordinate employees in their unit by training, allocating their work, assessing their performance, and ensuring acceptable standards.
2. Perform administrative work related to their units such as recording time, maintaining stocks of supplies, setting up work schedules, and arranging for replacements when necessary.

3. Be familiar with the operation and general maintenance of all machines and tools in their area of responsibility.

4. Act as a lead hand and be familiar with all duties of subordinates and be prepared to carry them out, including shift work, when appropriate.

5. Liaise with supervisors and subordinates on a regular basis to ensure effective communication and coordinated operation.

Nursery/Landscaping/Pruning

1. Read and interpret blueprint information.

2. Supervise the application of herbicides or fungicides, or the landscaping of a specific area.

3. Perform a full range of skilled horticulture duties in areas such as pruning, tree surgery, landscaping, greenhouse, and nursery. Incumbents are expected to direct the work of and train subordinate staff in the operation of tree-pruning equipment, such as extension ladders, cranes, and pruners, and chemical applicators, such as hand-held sprayers, boom sprayers, and fertilizer spreaders.

4. Diagnose and treat various types of lawn and tree diseases in conjunction with the Horticulture Supervisor and Assistant Supervisor using the proper application of appropriate chemicals.

5. Be familiar with all the duties required of a nursery person including all propagation practices such as grafting, budding, seeding, transplanting, hardening, stratification, etc.

Facilities

1. Oversee the operation of the skating and curling facilities in a cooperative spirit with the college of Physical Education to promote optimum facility usage and goodwill with patrons and staff.

2. Make ice in curling and skating rinks and paint markings on ice according to specifications.

3. Maintain ice surfaces with the use of appropriate equipment and tools.

4. Inspect mechanical rooms to ensure ice-making equipment is functioning correctly, and call service people as required.

5. Ensure that patrons conform to regulations governing behaviour in the rinks, and call for assistance from security personnel in case of serious problems.

6. Supervise personnel in ice maintenance and janitorial work.

7. Supervise gardening crews in the maintenance of playing fields, track and field facilities, and landscaped areas, parking lots, etc.

8. Be familiar with and supervise the operation of all gardening equipment used in the assigned area.

9. Inspect grounds and work areas regularly and take corrective action when required.

Machine Operator

1. Operate all the mowers for cutting playing fields and open areas.

2. Operate tree spade for tree transplanting.

3. Operate such equipment as large dump truck, front-end loader, bob-cat, and snow plows.

4. Operate sanding truck in winter, including mixing sand and loading.

5. Do maintenance work on all equipment, but with primary emphasis on the maintenance of power machines (which this person normally operates).

Irrigation

1. Read and interpret blueprint information.

2. Troubleshoot and repair electric and electronic components, and hydraulic controls of automated irrigation system as well as mechanical components.

3. Be responsible for opening and shutting down the irrigation system in spring and fall, including the blowing out of all lines.

4. Liaise with the supervisor and assistant supervisor for the scheduling of irrigation throughout the campus.

5. Through liaison with the foreman and supervisor, ensure optimum water use efficiency when setting irrigation run times and repeat cycles, considering factors such as soil capacities, turf usage, and sprinkler and line capacities and pressure, etc.

6. Repair and/or install lawn water service including cutting and fitting pipe (PVC and poly) and placing or replacing all types of fittings including galvanized, brass, PVC, and plastic.

Desirable Qualifications

(A) Several years of work experience, including experience in supervision, and in the specialty skill area that is pertinent. This must include considerable knowledge of horticultural identification of plant materials for the nursery position, and several years' experience with the installation and maintenance of manual and automatic irrigation systems for the irrigation position. Additionally, an aptitude in electrical and electronic applications would be of value in the irrigation position. (B) The ability to do rigorous manual labour. (C) Possession of a diploma in horticulture or a related field for the nursery and irrigation positions. (D) Completion of Grade 12. (E) Driver's licence. (F) Pesticide Applicator's Licence for those positions involved in the application of herbicides, insecticides, or fungicides.

Medical Laboratory Technologist I

Kind and Level of Work

This class comprises positions that require Medical Laboratory Technologist certification and involves positions that are generally located in the Medical,

Dental, and Veterinary Medical colleges of the University. These are full working-level Technologists and are expected to conduct a variety of routine and semi-specialized tests and analysis in their areas of specialization, such as bacteriology, immunology, parasitology, virology, histology, etc. They are engaged in the examination of predominantly biological materials such as blood, sera, tissue, urine, feces, etc., by chemical, bacteriological, or related techniques. After an initial orientation period, these employees work independently and are responsible for the accuracy of techniques and the reliability of results. Their work is subject to the general supervision of academic, technical, or administrative superiors.

TYPICAL DUTIES AND RESPONSIBILITIES

1. Perform routine and semi-specialized diagnostic analysis using manual and automated techniques.

2. Prepare and standardize reagents, solutions, media, and cultures for study requiring special techniques.

3. Operate basic scientific or technical equipment, maintain as necessary, and monitor quality-control procedures to ensure reliability of results.

4. Perform sample entry, recording, reporting, and filing of results.

5. Assist with the teaching program by preparing materials and providing demonstration or explanation of equipment and/or diagnostic techniques and procedures to students.

6. Assist students with material identification and with projects as required.

7. Assist in the orientation and instruction of new staff; may supervise student assistants, technical assistants, or first-level technicians.

8. Assist with research experiments by carrying out a variety of standardized quantitative and qualitative analyses by performing assays, routine spectroscopy and chromatography, and microbiological and other standard test procedures.

9. Prepare purchase requisitions, ordering, receiving, and storing supplies, tools, and equipment; care for materials and maintain required inventory and other records.

DESIRABLE QUALIFICATIONS

A minimum of one year of experience related to the position assignment. Completion of Grade 12 plus a related technical school diploma from a recognized technical institute. Current certification as a Registered Technologist with C.S.L.T.

MEDICAL LABORATORY TECHNOLOGIST II

KIND AND LEVEL OF WORK

This class comprises positions that require Medical Laboratory Technologist certification and involves positions that are generally located in the Medical,

Dental, and Veterinary Medical colleges of the University. Employees in positions allocated to this class are experienced Technologists who conduct complex tests and/or provide supervision and training to Technologists assisting with complex tests or performing common tests. Their work involves the analysis of predominantly biological materials and processes in support of a variety of specialized areas such as bacteriology, immunology, parasitology, virology, etc. This class is distinguished from the Medical Laboratory Technologist I by the complexity of tasks performed, judgment factors involved, responsibility for work output, and the involvement in training and supervision of junior staff. Their work is subject to general supervision and direction, usually by a member of faculty, but these employees independently organize and supervise the work of their assistants and laboratories.

TYPICAL DUTIES AND RESPONSIBILITIES

1. Perform complex and specialized diagnostic analysis using manual and automated techniques.

2. Operate and maintain a variety of complex scientific equipment ensuring accurate calibration and reliability of results.

3. Verify procedures, evaluate effectiveness of experiments, and modify or develop techniques and/or procedures as required.

4. Provide demonstration and problem-solving consultation involving complex equipment and/or diagnostic techniques and procedures to students in an undergraduate or graduate teaching environment, or on a one-to-one basis with students as required.

5. Participate in the selection and assume responsibility for the training, assigning, and reviewing of the work of subordinate staff or less experienced staff engaged in semi-skilled or skilled work; supervise students in the use of equipment and facilities.

6. Assist individual faculty members with research projects by carrying out experiments usually involving relatively advanced techniques and procedures, and analyze and report on results.

7. Search published scientific papers for information relating to specific projects.

8. Perform administrative work related to the units such as budgeting, advising on the purchase of material and capital equipment, maintaining appropriate inventory and records, etc.

DESIRABLE QUALIFICATIONS

Several years of work experience related to the position assignment including demonstrated supervisory experience. Grade 12 and either a technical school diploma in laboratory technology with A.R.T. standing, or a university degree relating to the position assignment. Current certification as a Registered Technologist with the C.S.L.T.

THE FIT STOP

The Fit Stop Ltd. is a brand-new firm that will open its doors exactly four months from today. Their business objective is to sell all types of training, fitness, conditioning, and exercise equipment to the general public. They plan to become specialists in this equipment and to provide customers with personalized advice geared to a customer's specific training or conditioning needs (e.g., training for a particular sport, rehabilitation from injuries, strengthening of back muscles to deal with back pain, general conditioning and fitness), whether the customer is 8 or 80 years of age.

In order to provide high-quality advice, each store will employ a physiotherapist (to provide advice on how to deal with problems such as injuries or chronic back pain) and a person with a bachelor's degree in kinesiology (to provide advice on training for various sports or other physical activities). In fact, if customers wish it, a staff member will sit down with them and develop a personalized training or conditioning program that meets their own specific objectives and needs, at no cost to the customer.

The remainder of the staff in the store will consist of a manager, with a Bachelor of Commerce degree, and sales staff, who will have at least high school diplomas. Due to the long opening hours, it is expected that between 8 and 12 salespeople will be needed for each store. Because the stores are located in shopping malls, they will operate on a seven-day-a-week basis, open 9:00 to 9:00 weekdays, 9:00 to 6:00 Saturdays, and noon to 6:00 on Sundays.

Aside from personally helping customers, the roles of the physiotherapist and kinesiologist will be to train other employees in how each type of equipment can be used for various purposes. Initially, sales staff will be given general training, but as time goes by, each salesperson will be expected to learn in depth about all the different pieces of equipment, to help customers diagnose their needs accurately, and to be able to explain proper usage of the equipment. Because of the high training required, all employees will be full-time.

The founder of the business is Susan Superfit, who has undergraduate degrees in kinesiology and commerce from the University of Saskatchewan. While at university she participated in numerous sports (and suffered numerous injuries due to her all-out style of play). She came up with the idea for this business while laid up with one of these injuries. While there were businesses that sold fitness and conditioning equipment, she often found that the people selling them had very limited knowledge of the various types of equipment, and often gave poor advice on what to buy and how to use it.

She has secured funding from private investors and from Working Ventures, a large, Canadian labour-sponsored investment fund. In order to get volume discounts on the equipment she will be purchasing and to beat competitors into the market, she wants to start off quite large, with stores in major cities in Ontario and the four western provinces, before expanding to Quebec and the Atlantic provinces. She knows that this is a risky strategy, and that cost control will be essential to keep the business going long enough to become well known and develop a stable clientele. She does not expect the business to make a profit for at least one, or maybe even two, years.

Her main competitors will be sporting goods mega-stores, and department and discount stores, each of which sells some of the same equipment. Some of these outlets will be able to price their equipment lower than The Fit Stop will be able to, but none will have the range of equipment that The Fit Stop will have, and none provide the personalized service that The Fit Stop will.

Susan believes that the key to her business success will be highly motivated and knowledgeable employees who have a strong concern for their customers and the ability to work as a team with the other employees to provide the best possible customer service. Since no two customers are exactly alike, employees will have to be innovative in developing solutions that fit their needs. It will also be crucial to keep up with the latest fitness and training trends, as knowledge about fitness is continually increasing, along with different types of specialized equipment. A key aspect of company strategy is to be the most up-to-date and advanced supplier of new products and techniques.

Although Susan has given a lot of thought to her business, one thing she hasn't really given much thought to is how to compensate her employees. Since she doesn't really know much about compensation, she tends to feel that the safest thing would be to just do what her competitors are doing.

HENDERSON PRINTING

Henderson Printing is a small to medium-sized manufacturer of account books, ledgers, and various types of record books used in business. Located in Halifax, the company has annual sales of about $10 million, mostly in the Atlantic provinces.

The owner, George Henderson, is a firm believer in making a high-quality product that will stand up to many years of use. He uses only high-grade paper, cover stock, and binding materials. Of course, this has led to high production costs and high prices. He also believes in a high level of customer service, and is willing to make the products to customers' specifications whenever they so request. However, having to reset the equipment for relatively short production runs of customized products takes considerable extra time and, of course, also drives up costs.

The firm employs about 80 people, most of whom work in production. The firm has a few supervisors to oversee production, but their responsibilities are not clearly spelled out, so they often contradict each other. There is no system for scheduling production; in fact, there are few systems of any kind. Whenever there is a problem, everyone knows that they have to go to George if you expect a definite answer.

The company also has several salespeople who travel throughout the Atlantic region, mostly relatives of George or his wife. The company has one bookkeeper to keep records and issue the paycheques, and several office employees to handle routine administrative chores. The firm has no specialists in accounting, marketing, human resources, or production; George handles these areas himself, although he has no real training and little interest in any of them except production. He focuses most of his attention on ensuring product quality and on dealing with the countless problems that everyone brings to him every day. He has often been heard to exclaim, in his usual good-natured way, "Why am I the only one who can make decisions around this place?" as he dealt with each of these problems.

When George was growing up, both his parents (his father was a printer and his mother was a seamstress in a garment factory) had to work hard in order to scratch out a living for their family. In those days, employers who showed little consideration for their employees were the norm, and George resolved that things would be different if he ever became an employer. Today, George tries hard to be a benevolent employer. Although he feels the organization cannot afford any formal employee benefits, he will often keep a sick worker on payroll for a considerable time, especially if he knows the worker has a family to support. George is well liked by most employees, who have shown little interest in unionization during the few approaches made by union organizers.

George has no formal system for pay, and tends to make all pay decisions on the spur of the moment, so almost everybody has a different pay rate. He has never gotten around to giving annual raises, so any employee who wants a raise has to approach him. He gives raises to most people who approach him, but the amount depends on his mood at the time and how well he knows the employee. For example, if the firm has just lost a major customer, raises are lower, and if the firm has just booked a large order, they are higher. They are also higher if he knows the employee has a family to support, or if the employee's spouse has been laid off, or if the employee has added a new member to the family.

George believes that a good employer should recognize the contributions made by employees during the year. So every Christmas, if profits allow, he gives a "merit bonus" to employees, which he says are based on their contribution to the firm. One day in early December, he sits down with his employee list, in alphabetical order, and pencils in an amount next to each name.

Everybody gets something, but the amounts vary greatly. If he can associate a face with the name (which is difficult sometimes, because new employees seem to turn over a lot), he tends to give larger bonuses, and if he can remember something such as a cheerful attitude, the bonuses are higher still. But if he remembers anyone complaining about the employee for some reason or another (he usually can't recall the exact reasons), the employee gets a smaller bonus. Not surprisingly, longer-term employees tend to receive much higher bonuses than new employees. He has noticed this tendency, but assumes that if an employee has been with the firm longer, that person must be more productive, so this is fair. He personally distributes the bonus cheques on the last working day before Christmas.

Since he has just turned 60, George is planning to retire in the next year or two, and turn the business over to his daughter, Georgette Henderson, who is just finishing her commerce degree at Dalhousie University. Ironically, it was on the day of his 60th birthday that his bookkeeper approached to inform him that there wasn't enough money in the bank account to meet payroll.

MULTI-PRODUCTS CORPORATION

It is early February. Late last year, the firm you work for, Multi-Products Corporation, acquired the rights to a new type of golf club, invented by a retired machinist who had been a lifelong golfer until his untimely demise (it turns out that golfing during a lightning storm is not such a great idea). The machinist had only produced a few sets of the clubs, but their superiority over existing clubs was so pronounced that word of his invention had spread far and wide. Fortunately for him (for his estate actually), he had patented the design of these clubs, so nobody could copy them.

Multi-Products Corporation has numerous divisions, each producing different products in the sporting goods field. They have never produced golf equipment of any kind, and plan to set up a separate division to produce and distribute the new clubs. You found out yesterday that you have been selected to head the division. Corporate management will provide you with all the financial resources you need to get the division going, and will also help you staff the division with experienced managers from the parent corporation. Because of their confidence in you, they have given you complete freedom to organize and operate the division as you see fit, as long as you attain the financial goals that have been set for the division.

Your first task is to design the organization structure. But before doing so, you recognize that you need to understand some key aspects about the organization and its context. Market research suggests that the demand for your product will be strong and stable. This demand will not be very price-sensitive, since golfers who want your product will generally be willing to pay what it takes to get it. Therefore, it will be relatively easy for you to secure distributors. In fact, one distributor is willing to agree to a four-year sales contract for your equipment, with a fixed volume and a fixed price. This distributor is confident enough to make this offer because they believe that nobody else will be able to manufacture a similar club, due to the patent protection.

The production side of things also looks straightforward. Your production process includes readily available materials, and there are many possible suppliers. You expect to be able to negotiate long-term contracts with suppliers at a fixed price. Acquiring the production equipment will also be straightforward, since the equipment is readily available in the marketplace.

The basic production technology, which will involve a sequential, step-by-step manufacturing process, has been in use for many years and has been refined to a high degree of efficiency. Since you know the likely volume of demand for your product, it is easy to decide on the optimum plant size, which will involve about 600 workers. The type of semi-skilled worker that you need is readily available, and unemployment is quite high in your region, so acquiring employees does not look to be very difficult. Employees in this industry are usually unionized, but the main union in the industry has not been highly militant in recent years, so labour disruptions don't seem likely.

Another possible factor that might affect your operations is government regulations. However, as long as your clubs meet CSA (Canadian Standards Association) standards, the government is unlikely to get involved with your product. Similarly, except for some groups opposed to the expansion of golf courses in ecologically sensitive areas (such as national parks), consumer and environmental groups are not likely to pose any concern.

Future technological change is another possible issue, but it does not appear to be of great concern. You will start out with the most up-to-date production equipment, which has not changed much in recent years. The product itself (golf clubs) is not likely to be replaced by anything radically different. The pace of technological change for golf clubs is quite slow, and some of the most popular clubs have been virtually unchanged in 30 years.

Plastco Packaging

Plastco Packaging Ltd. is a medium-sized manufacturer of plastic bags located on the west coast. These bags are used in the retail sector, for purposes ranging from groceries to clothing and other goods. These bags are made from a variety of types of plastic and in a variety of sizes, depending on the intended purpose. The bags usually have the retailer's name printed on them.

There are three main phases in the bag manufacturing process: (1) producing the plastic sheeting (produced as rolls of tubing); (2) printing the retailer's name on the tubing; and (3) passing the rolls of tubing through bag-making machines that cut and seal the tubing into bag lengths.

This analysis focuses on the third step of the production process, the bag-making department. The department has 12 bag-making machines. Each machine operates semi-automatically, but has to be manually loaded, set for the type of bag to be produced, started, monitored, and adjusted. The machines need frequent servicing to replace the cutting knives, to adjust slipping belts, or to lubricate the many moving parts. These functions and major repairs, when necessary, are carried out by mechanics from the maintenance department, a separate department reporting to the plant manager. The mechanics report machinery problems and future replacement and servicing needs to the maintenance supervisor, who reports significant problems to the plant manager. The plant manager then conveys any implications for production of bags to the bag-making supervisor.

There are six bag-making machine operators—each operator tends two machines. There are also six inspectors/packers, who inspect bags for quality as they come off each machine and pack them into boxes. Defective bags are thrown into waste bins based on the type of plastic. They are then melted down and remanufactured. Whenever an inspector/packer discovers poor-quality output, she must notify the operator to correct the problem. If the inspector/packer deems waste to be excessive, she is expected to report the operator to the production supervisor.

In addition, there are four utility workers who handle miscellaneous tasks, such as delivering rolls of plastic tubing and hauling boxes of finished bags to the shipping department. Traditionally, operators and utility workers have always been male, while inspectors/packers have always been female.

When a new operator is needed, the production supervisor selects one of the utility workers, who is then assigned to an experienced operator for on-the-job training. It takes up to six months before a new operator is able to consistently produce an acceptable-quality product without supervision, since the machines are "finicky" to operate. The length of time needed to do bag changeovers also declines as the new operator gains experience.

The plant is unionized, and pay is based on an hourly wage. Operators receive approximately $20 per hour, utility workers $15 per hour, and inspectors/packers $10 per hour. Overall, benefits constitute about 20 percent of total compensation, and increase with seniority.

In the view of the production supervisor, there are a number of problems at present. First is the high turnover among the inspectors/packers, as high as 100 percent a year. Turnover among the utility workers is about a third of that, and lower than that among operators, who quit or retire at the rate of about one a year. Second, while the department usually meets the minimum production levels, the production supervisor believes that productivity could be much higher.

He also believes there to be a high level of waste. However, whenever he questions an operator about this, the operator either blames maintenance for doing a poor job servicing the machines or the inspectors/packers for being unnecessarily fussy. It is also difficult to pinpoint specific operators for performing poor-quality work, since inspectors/packers seldom report an operator to the production supervisor. When one does so, the operators usually accuse the woman of incompetence. All in all, there are very poor interpersonal relationships among the operators, mechanics, and inspectors/packers. Few members of the department appear to enjoy being at work.

Another problem is that customers are complaining about inconsistent quality in the products they receive. Sometimes the bags are of very high quality and sometimes many bags are defective. These complaints are a concern to the plant manager since a new competitor has recently opened up nearby and is aggressively competing for business. This competitor seems to be producing a product with fewer defects for a lower price.

INDEX

Absenteeism, 68–69, 160–64
Administration, compensation. *See* Compensation administration
ADP, 461
Affective commitment, 82–84, 219
Agency theory, 96, 179
Aging compensation data, 395
Altamira Financial Services, 3
American Steel and Wire, 122
Analyzer corporate strategy, 37, 41
AON Consulting, 382–83
Application service providers, 462
Appraisals, performance. *See* Performance appraisal
Attendance incentives, 160–64
Attitudes, employee
  compensation, 82–83, 476–77
  job attitudes, 67–71, 476
Attitudinal indicators, 476–77
Attribution theory, 93–96

Bands, of pay grades. *See* Broadbanding
Bank of Canada, 304
Balance sheet approach, 310–11
Base pay, 5, 116–36, 350–57
Bausch and Lomb, 63–64, 65, 153
B.C. Rogers Processors, 18–19, 41–42, 69
Behavioural indicators, 475–76
Behaviourally anchored rating scales (BARS), 415–17
Behavioural observation scales (BOS), 415–17
Behaviour modification theory, 91–92
Behaviours, employee
  citizenship, 67–71, 97–99, 265, 268–72, 297, 476
  membership, 67–71, 80–84, 108, 265, 268–72, 475
  task, 67–71, 84–96, 265, 268–72, 475
Benchmark jobs, 122, 339
Benefits and Pensions Monitor, 250
Benefits Canada Magazine, 250
Benefits, employee. *See* Employee benefits
Big Sky Farms, 217
Blockbuster Video, 422

Bonuses
  competitive, 184–85
  merit, 157–58
  team-based, 184–85
Bottom-up approach to budgeting, 466–67
British Columbia Employee Investment Act, 197
Broadbanding, 125–26, 352–53
Budgeting, compensation, 466–67
Burger King, 422

Cafeteria benefits. *See* Flexible benefit systems
Cameco Corporation, 466
CAMI, 73–74, 107
Canada Pension Plan, 220
Canadian Auto Workers Union, 74, 189
Canadian Cancer Society, 23
Canadian Human Resources Reporter, 13, 250
Canadian Human Rights Act, 261
Canadian Imperial Bank of Commerce, 461–62
Canadian Manufacturers and Exporters Alliance, 382
Canadian National Exhibition, 62
Canadian National Railways, 63, 65
Canadian Payroll Association, 485
Canadian Pensions and Benefits Institute, 250
Canadian Tire, 3, 88
Cardinal River Coals, 52
Cash (current distribution) profit-sharing plans, 186, 191
Central tendency error, 407
Central tendency of pay, 388–89
CEOs. *See* Chief executive officers
Ceridian, 461
Chief executive officers, 190–91, 198, 200–201, 203–4, 303–10
Chrysler, 234
Citizenship behaviour, 67–71, 97–99, 265, 268–72, 297, 476
Classical managerial strategy, 24–27, 45–52, 71, 105–6, 122–23, 131, 242–44

Salience of needs, 89–90, 99–100
Satisfaction, employee
  with benefits, 248
  with job, 67–71, 81–84
  with pay, 75–76, 82–83, 218, 476–77
Saturn Corporation, 51, 435
Scanlon plan, 175–76
Screaming Tale Restaurant, 6–7, 13, 117, 258, 259
Sears, 3, 47–48, 50–51, 63, 65
Securities and Exchange Commission, 303
Self-appraisals, 422
Semco, 133
Semi-flexible benefits systems, 235
Seniority pay increases, 135–36, 356–57
Services, employee. *See* Employee benefits
Severance pay, 229
Share appreciation rights (SARs), 196
Shell Canada, 128–29
Shirking behaviour, 180
Sibson and Company, 383
Similarity effect, 408
Skill-based pay. *See* Pay for knowledge plans
Skill certification, 443–44
Skill/knowledge blocks, 437–42
Skills, as a compensable factor. *See* Compensable factors
Skill variety, 87
Special groups, compensation of
  contingent workers, 298–301
  executives, 198, 303–10
  expatriate employees, 310–13
  new employees, 301–3
  sales staff, 148–54
Special purpose incentives, 160–65
Spiral career paths, 478
Spruce Falls Pulp and Paper, 198
Starbucks, 3
Statistics Canada, 13, 120, 301, 382
Stock options, 195–96, 305, 307–8
Stock plans, 194–203
Straight piece rate, 145
Strategic template
  for compensation strategy, 290
  for managerial strategy, 41
Strategy. *See* Compensation strategy; Corporate strategy; Managerial strategies; Reward strategy, definition of
Structural variables
  communication, 21–22, 25–35
  control, 21–22, 25–35
  coordination, 21–22, 25–35

  decision making and leadership, 21–22, 25–35
  job design, 21–22, 25–35
  reward, 21–22, 25–35
Structure, organizational. *See* Organizational structure, definition of
Subordinate appraisals, 421–22
Suggestion systems, 164–65
Supplemental unemployment benefits (SUBs), 228
Surveys
  attitude, 476–77
  compensation/market, 384–96
  Internet, 388

Taco Bell, 422
Targeted incentives, 160–65
Task behaviour, 67–71, 84–96, 265, 268–72, 475
Task environment, 23, 40–41, 44
Task identity, 87
Task significance, 87
Tax legislation, 224–27, 229, 239, 262
Taylor, Frederick Winslow, 133, 145
Team-based merit pay, 185
Technical ladder, 160
Technical premiums, 482
Technology, 38–39, 40–41
Telus Corporation, 200, 235, 459–60
Templates
  compensation strategy, 290
  managerial strategy, 41
Third party surveys, 382–83
Thompson's typology, 38, 41
360-degree systems, 422–24
Tobacco industry, 380
Top-down approach to budgeting, 466–67
Toronto Board of Trade, 382
Toronto Maple Leafs, 378
Toronto Stock Exchange, 199
Towers Perrin, 383
Toyota Motors, 70–71, 107, 435
Trade union legislation, 261–62
Trade unions. *See* Unions
Turnover, 82–84, 108, 135, 151
Two-factor theory of motivation, 86–87
Two-tier wage system, 301–3

UNICEF, 6, 96, 97, 268–69, 272
Unions, 27, 46, 50–51, 78, 130, 131, 181, 189, 215, 261–62
  impact on compensation, 46, 181, 215, 261–62
  legislation, 261–62